Peter FitzSimons AM is Australia's bestselling non-fiction writer, and for over 35 years has also been a journalist and columnist with the *Sydney Morning Herald* and the *Sun-Herald*.

He is the author of a number of highly successful books, including *Burke and Wills*, *Monash's Masterpiece*, *Breaker Morant*, *Kokoda*, *Ned Kelly* and *Gallipoli*, as well as biographies of such notable Australians as Sir Douglas Mawson, Nancy Wake and Nick Farr-Jones. His passion is to tell Australian stories, our own stories: of great men and women, of stirring events in our history.

Peter grew up on a farm north of Sydney, went to boarding school in Sydney and attended Sydney University. An ex-Wallaby, he also lived for several years in rural France and Italy, playing rugby for regional clubs. He and his wife Lisa Wilkinson AM – journalist, magazine editor and television presenter – have three children; they live in Sydney.

Also by Peter FitzSimons
and published by Hachette Australia

Kokoda
Burke and Wills
Monash's Masterpiece
Mutiny on the Bounty
The Catalpa Rescue
James Cook
Breaker Morant
The Incredible Life of Hubert Wilkins
The Opera House

PETER FITZSIMONS

THE BATTLE OF LONG TAN

hachette AUSTRALIA

First published in Australia and New Zealand in 2022
by Hachette Australia
(an imprint of Hachette Australia Pty Limited)
Gadigal Country, Level 17, 207 Kent Street, Sydney, NSW 2000
www.hachette.com.au

This edition published in 2024

Hachette Australia acknowledges and pays our respects to the past, present and future Traditional Owners and Custodians of Country throughout Australia and recognises the continuation of cultural, spiritual and educational practices of Aboriginal and Torres Strait Islander peoples. Our head office is located on the lands of the Gadigal people of the Eora Nation.

A catalogue record for this book is available from the National Library of Australia

ISBN: 978 0 7336 4662 1 (paperback)

Cover design by Luke Causby/Blue Cork
Cover photographs courtesy of the Australian War Memorial: front cover, top, AWM P02354.004, (l to r) Lt Adrian Roberts, 2nd Lt Dennis Rainer and 2nd Lt Geoff Kendall; bottom, AWM EKN/69/0075/VN, c. 18 August 1969, soldiers of 6RAR/NZ alighting from an Iroquois helicopter in preparation to set up a memorial cross at the site of the Battle of Long Tan; back cover, AWM FOR/66/0673/VN, Lt Dave Sabben inspecting his damaged Armalite rifle after the Battle of Long Tan.
Maps © Dave Sabben
Author photo courtesy of Peter Morris/Sydney Heads
Typeset in 11.1/14.7 pt Sabon LT Pro by Bookhouse, Sydney
Printed and bound in Australia by McPherson's Printing Group

The paper this book is printed on is certified against the Forest Stewardship Council® Standards. McPherson's Printing Group holds FSC® chain of custody certification SA-COC-005379. FSC® promotes environmentally responsible, socially beneficial and economically viable management of the world's forests.

To the men of 6RAR Delta Company, those who fell, and those who made it home to Australia. Lest we forget.

CONTENTS

List of maps viii
Introduction and acknowledgements xi
Dramatis personae xv
Prologue xvii

One The apocalypse beckons 1
Two Home on the rifle range 19
Three 6RAR complete 50
Four Delta dawn 76
Five Good morning, Vietnam! 102
Six Fire, fire, burning bright 131
Seven Trouble in the wind 151
Eight Cometh the hour 188
Nine Rocked 213
Ten Fight and flight 237
Eleven Shells in hell 265
Twelve Floating targets 302
Thirteen Delta Company's last stand 326
Fourteen There goes the cavalry 356
Fifteen Dawn's harvest 381

Epilogue 401
Appendix Lest we forget 428
Endnotes 431
Bibliography 445
Index 451

LIST OF MAPS

Vietnam and surrounding regions, 1966 xviii
Phuoc Tuy province, South Vietnam 72
1ATF's Nui Dat base, Phuoc Tuy province, showing 'Line Alpha' 120
17 August bombardment, showing VC base plate sites, target areas and withdrawal tracks 177
D Company formations at first contact with small NVA patrol, 1540 hrs, 18 August 1966 210
11 Platoon location and first enemy enveloping moves, 1600–1630 hrs, 18 August 1966 231
11 Platoon positioning 238
10 Platoon returns; 12 Platoon moves south then east, 1700–1800 hrs, 18 August 1966 271
D Company disposition in the final stages of the battle, 1830–1900 hrs, 18 August 1966 319
Route taken by the APC & A/6RAR Reinforcement Column, 18 August 1966 331

When the prison doors are opened, the real dragon will fly out.

Ho Chi Minh

You have a row of dominos set up; you knock over the first one, and what will happen to the last one is that it will go over very quickly.

President Dwight D. Eisenhower, 1954

We are not about to send American boys nine or ten thousand miles away from home to do what Asian boys ought to be doing for themselves.

President Lyndon B. Johnson, two weeks before the 1964 election that he would win in a landslide

Humiliation for America could come in one of two ways – either by outright defeat, which is unlikely, or by her becoming interminably bogged down in the awful morass of this war, as France was for ten years.[1]

Arthur Calwell, Leader of the Opposition, 1965

INTRODUCTION AND ACKNOWLEDGEMENTS

This book has been a long time coming. Having written many books on other iconic Australian battles and campaigns – Breaker Morant and the Boer War, Gallipoli, Fromelles & Pozières, Villers-Bretonneux, Kokoda and Tobruk among them – a frequent question I've been asked along the way is, 'When are you going to do Long Tan?'

The short answer was, 'When I feel I can do it justice, and have lined up the right people to talk to . . .' and this is the result.

When first examining the contours of the battle and then diving into the first material that my researchers came back with, the best of all possible things happened: I was immediately hooked. Robert Graves once famously said, 'A remarkable thing about Shakespeare is that he is really very good in spite of all the people who say he is very good . . .' and I feel the same about the Battle of Long Tan.

As a story it has got everything on its own, but I also found putting the whole battle in historical context a fascinating exercise. Beyond just the battle itself, I wanted to understand why Australia was there in the first place, who took the key decisions, and what were the dynamics that caused the whole conflagration to take place. I was, allow me to say, flabbergasted with the answers.

That was what got us into Vietnam?

It was all built on . . . just . . . *that*?

Who knew?

Not me. But it was enthralling to explore.

True, in this particular saga getting accurate accounts of what was going on with the enemy proved problematic – even all these years on, the matter is sensitive with the Vietnamese – but in many ways that was very much the Australian experience at the time. They knew 'Charlie' was out there. But who he was, how many of his mates were there with him, how those mates were armed and when they were going to strike next was mostly a dark mystery. There were no interactions between both sides, like those I had found so moving in such battles as Gallipoli, the Western Front, Tobruk and so forth.

A rare boon in this book, as opposed to other military books I've done, is to have so many people available who were there, who could tell me in person *exactly* what happened and give me the fine detail I cherish, instead of having to rely only on trawling through diaries, letters, contemporary newspaper accounts and the like – though, of course, my researchers and I did that too! For the purpose of the storytelling I will put the names of those veterans of Long Tan at the end so as not to reveal in these opening pages which of the characters you are about to meet lived or died.

My dear friend, Gordon Alexander, a Vietnam vet who was at the Battle of Coral, was also a great help throughout on all fronts, but particularly artillery. Steve Conroy, himself a career Army Reserve officer and graduate of Canungra, was wonderfully helpful with providing the detail on the training regime of the conscripts. Adrian Younger provided valuable input on the Armoured Personnel Carriers. Cary Frankel flew Phantom jets for the US Air Force in Vietnam and was very generous in providing some of the fine detail I most love for my section covering Phantoms.

My warm thanks also to Dr Peter Williams, the Canberra military historian who has worked with me on six books now. Not surprisingly he proved to be an expert on Vietnam, had great contacts and happily placed them all at the service of this book. Thanks, too, to Peter Finlay for expertise on matters of military aviation and to Gregory Blake for his expert advice on all things to do with the weapons of the time.

In terms of much valued help, my principal researcher for this book was the indefatigable Barb Kelly, who trawled as mightily as ever through every document she could get her digital hands on to bring precious and often previously unrevealed detail to the account. As ever she became obsessed with the story and determined to get right to the bottom of it, and was able to provide the exact material to help bring to life previously obscure and unknown episodes. As with some of my previous books it was great that her son Lachlan was able to lend valuable assistance, finding obituaries, death notices, contemporary accounts and other material that had previously escaped the rest of us. My own son Jake is a wonderful editor, and had valuable input into the final manuscript.

As to my long-time researcher and beloved cousin, Angus FitzSimons, he was as insightful as ever, constantly turning up new angles to pursue, even while finding fresh information on previous angles. I also treasure his wise counsel, as I constantly bounced ideas off him and engaged in debate on so many aspects of the book and how best to bring the whole extraordinary story to life. This book is in his great debt.

As ever, and as I always recount at the beginning of my historical writing, I have tried to bring the story part of this history alive by putting it in the present tense and constructing it in the manner of a novel, albeit with 600 footnotes, give or take, as the pinpoint pillars on which the story rests. For the sake of the storytelling, I have occasionally created a direct quote from reported speech in a journal, diary or letter, and changed pronouns and tenses to put that reported speech in the present tense. When the story required generic language – as in the words used when commanding movements in battle – I have taken the liberty of using the words habitually used in such situations, to help bring the story to life. I hope readers will excuse the mix of metric and imperial measurements in this book, but as Long Tan took place in 1966, eyewitness accounts come in both. I have used metric where possible but retained the imperial where necessary.

Always, my goal has been to determine what were the words used, based on the primary documentary evidence presented. All books used are listed in the Bibliography, but I relied particularly on the incomparable first-hand reportage of *The Battle of Long Tan: As Told by the Commanders to Bob Grandin*, a fascinating and candid book that exactly fulfils its title; Paul Ham's masterful *Vietnam: The Australian War*; David W. Cameron's evocative *The Battle of Long Tan*; and Ian McNeill's invaluable *To Long Tan*. Terry Burstall's *The Soldiers' Story*, meanwhile, was simply superb in providing what I treasure most in trying to bring history to life: raw and credible dialogue from people who were actually there at the time. Mark Dapin's *The Nashos' War* is a brilliant portrait of the Nashos' experience. Lex McAulay's *The Battle of Long Tan: The Legend of Anzac Upheld* is also a fascinating archive of prickly reportage and recent reminiscence of battle that only becomes more valuable as memories now grow smooth in the retelling.

My thanks also to my highly skilled editor Deonie Fiford, who was as judicious as ever in working out just what of the oft esoteric way I write to preserve, and what to . . . refine.

I am also grateful to my friend and publisher Matthew Kelly of Hachette, with whom I have worked many times over the last three decades, and who was enthusiastic and supportive throughout, always giving great guidance.

It was a privilege to try and bring this story to life, and I hope it will help shine a light on an extraordinary episode in Australian history.

Peter FitzSimons
Neutral Bay, Sydney
June 2022

DRAMATIS PERSONAE

Brigadier Oliver Jackson. Commanding Officer of the 1st Australian Task Force (1ATF) 1966–1972 in South Vietnam. The son of Major General Robert Jackson, he served in North Africa and Syria during World War II and was appointed the head of 1st Battalion, Royal Australian Regiment in Korea in 1956.

Lieutenant Colonel Colin Townsend. Commanding Officer of 6RAR. First served in immediate post-war Japan, then was among the first Australian troops deployed to the Korean conflict. He wrote the Standing Operating Procedures used by Australian infantry battalions in Vietnam.

Major Harry Smith. Commanding Officer of 6RAR Delta Company. Born in Hobart, he had been with the Australian Army since 1952, and served from 1955 to 1957 in Malaya, where he fought as a Commando.

Captain Charles Mollison. Commanding Officer of 6RAR Alpha Company. Born in Victoria, he served part time in the Citizen Military Forces (CMF), attaining the rank of Major, before giving up seniority to join the Regular Army as Captain, initially with 2RAR.

Lieutenant Dave Sabben. Commander of 6RAR Delta Company 12 Platoon. Born in Suva, Fiji. Worked in advertising as a layout artist in Sydney before entering the Army.

Lieutenant Gordon Sharp. Commander of 6RAR Delta Company 11 Platoon. Born in Tamworth, he became a cameraman with *The Mavis Bramston Show* in Sydney, before entering the Army as a National Serviceman.

Lieutenant Geoff Kendall. Commander of 6RAR Delta Company 10 Platoon. Born in Brisbane, he was a professional rugby league coach in western Queensland before joining the Australian Army and becoming a Regular Officer graduate of Officer Cadet School Portsea.

Sergeant Bob Buick. 6RAR Delta Company 11 Platoon. Served with 2RAR in Malaya until July 1963. He took discharge in February 1965, before re-enlisting in July the same year. After further infantry training, he was posted to 6RAR and promoted to Sergeant.

Major Jack Kirby. 6RAR Delta Company Sergeant Major. Served in Korea with the 1st Battalion, Royal Australian Regiment, and with 3RAR in Malaya. He was promoted to the rank of Warrant Officer in January 1966.

Captain Bob Keep. Intelligence officer with the 1ATF 1st Divisional Intelligence Unit.

Private Paul Large. 6RAR, Delta Company 12 Platoon. Conscripted into the Army in the first intake of the National Service Scheme birthday ballot in 1965.

Flight Lieutenant Frank Riley. Joined the RAAF in 1953, became a flight instructor and member of the display aerobatics crew the 'Meteorites'. Deployed to Vietnam in June 1966 as a member of No. 9 Squadron.

Flight Lieutenant Bob Grandin. In 1957, at the age of 17, he joined the RAAF College in Point Cook. In June 1966, he was deployed to Vietnam as a member of No. 9 Squadron.

2nd Lieutenant Adrian Roberts. A former schoolteacher, he received his commission in June 1963. Selected to serve in Malaysia, but the Army required a Lieutenant for the newly formed Armoured Personnel Carrier (APC) Squadron in Vietnam. Reasoning that Vietnam would be the shorter conflict, Roberts chose to deploy there.

Captain Morrie Stanley. The Forward Artillery Observer Officer (FO) attached to Delta Company 6RAR. A New Zealander, at the age of 19 he won a four-year scholarship to Duntroon. His military career included a stint guarding the Tower of London before he was deployed to Saigon in 1965, initially with the 173rd Airborne Brigade.

PROLOGUE

You can kill ten of my men for every one I kill of yours. But even at those odds, you will lose and I will win.[1]

Ho Chi Minh's warning to French colonialists, 1946

People should not be overawed by the power of modern weapons. It is the value of human beings that in the end will decide victory.[2]

General Vo Nguyen Giap

19 May 1941, Hang Pac Bo, North Vietnam

Is that him?

It is!

The two Vietnamese men waiting in the mouth of a cave near the Chinese border first recognise the man they have been waiting for all day by his distinctive loping manner, a man in a hurry with much to do – the fact that he is 51 and suffering from dysentery, malaria and tuberculosis notwithstanding. They would call to him now but refrain for fear of attracting attention to what this is: no less than the grand return after 30 years of effective exile of their people's prophet. As he comes closer they take him in all the more clearly, the indomitable revolutionary with the wispy beard and old eyes who has been abroad all this time learning just how to rid their country of all who would occupy it. Pham Van Dong and Vo Nguyen Giap wait quietly until the man arrives and then gently embrace his slender form. Tonight they will stay in this cave and make plans, tomorrow they will start to lay the foundations of a country.

His name?

Please. He is not one with so plebeian an existence as to go by a single name, the one his parents gave him. Rather, by design and destiny, he

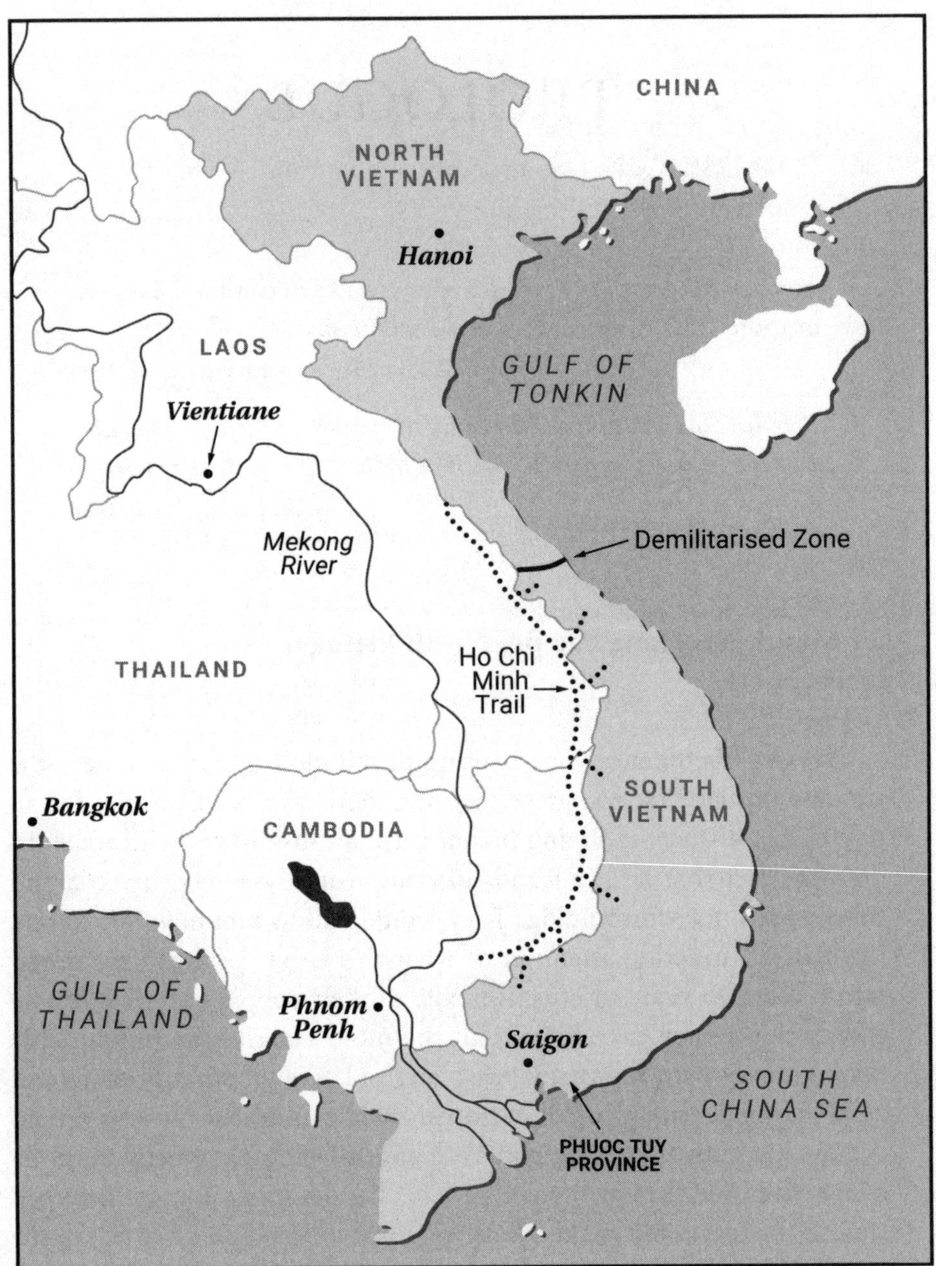

Vietnam and surrounding regions, 1966

goes by no fewer than 100 names, everything from Nguyen Sinh Cung to Nguyen Tat Thanh Nguyen Ai Quoc, to Sung Man Cho to a legion of aliases and identities he employs as needed in the life of a radical revolutionary. Born in the village of Hoang Tru and educated by his father in Confucian thought, he has travelled the world to acquire the skills that have brought him to this place, at this time, to fulfil what he sees as his destiny, the liberation of his homeland, Vietnam.

In short order he will be known as . . . Ho Chi Minh, the 'Bringer of Light', an ironic name for one who is now, for the first time, truly emerging from the mysterious darkness where he has fomented this revolution to now publicly lead it. Ho has been a student in Paris, a Bolshevik in Russia, a baker in Harlem, a wanted man in China, a professional sailor, a dishwasher in Ealing, a soldier, a poet, an assistant pastry chef at the Carlton Hotel in London, a spy and now, today, the one who intends to be the saviour of Vietnam by ridding his homeland of both the rapacious French and the merciless Japanese. A few years past, he trekked alone for five days across the mountains of China to the Communist revolutionary base in the caves of Yenan where he met with Mao Tse-Tung, now he comes to his own cave and back to his own revolution. A fellow would-be revolutionary who met with Ho in various incarnations and continents remarked that wherever they were, whether conversing with Mao or washing plates in a Soho basement, Ho had 'only one thought in his head, his country, Vietnam'.[3]

Yes, his homeland has changed in his absence, and there is now an awareness of both the need for change, and concerted violent action to achieve it, but there remains much to do to succeed, to get the country ready to be reborn. To the men he meets, Ho requests a title: not President, not General – 'Uncle'. And Uncle Ho he will be from this day on.

For Pham Van Dong, who has been trained as a revolutionary in China in 1926 by . . . Ho Chi Minh, Uncle Ho is far more than an avuncular figure. Pham Van Dong is convinced that the older man will be the founder of their new nation. Vo Nguyen Giap, a history teacher by trade, is of the same view and studies Uncle Ho the way he has previously studied the successful military strategies of the likes of Napoleon, and more particularly the way Lawrence of Arabia had been able to use a small force to inflict maximum damage on the mighty Ottoman overlords and finally destroy them. The latter is precisely the way Uncle Ho intends to take down the French who have been occupying Indochina for nearly a century.

The time is ripe for Uncle Ho and all those who follow him to make their move. The French occupiers of Vietnam are preoccupied with the newly arrived Japanese, who have come to bring an Indochina piece of empire to their ambitious and avaricious young ruler, Emperor Hirohito.

The way Uncle Ho sees it, the enemy of his enemy is a friend, and the coming chaos in the region will whet an appetite for order. He and his forces mean to be that order, and they'll see it becomes the rule of law in due time.

Uncle Ho has learnt from Mao Tse-Tung. In Vietnam his forces will start out like the grasshopper fighting the elephant. Yes, the victory seems unlikely, but they are agile, they are nimble and can live easily off the land without leaving a trace. Most importantly, right now the elephant is barely aware they exist.

That night the trio conspire in this cave, Hang Pac Bo, perched above the blue beauty of the Le Nin stream that will flow into the Bang Giang River, and their stream of words will flow into an action that will transform the land they hide in. By the flickering light of the fire, just inside the entrance of the cave, the three take a vow.

'The time has come,' Ho tells his comrades. They must form a powerful army that will bow to none and dominate all; an army of the people, filled with 'patriots of all ages and all types, peasants, workers, merchants and soldiers',[4] a force that can free them from Japan, France and whatever empire appears next to colonise or control them.

Their intent is to unleash a revolution that will liberate their land from *all* foreigners. Their Communist army born in the North must grow until it takes the South and reunites Vietnam with a notion the nation has been exiled from for a millennia: liberty. The name of the Army of the North? *Viet Nam Doc Lap Dong Minh*; the Viet Minh.

Early 1940s, Long Tan, Vietnam, prospering under the sun

Beneath the beating sun and ever-present promise of monsoonal outburst lies Long Tan, a beautiful and well-ordered village of a thousand hardy souls. The wooden homes come with terracotta-tiled roofs and covered front porches with chairs, where the villagers sit on the furniture they have made to gaze on statues of Buddha and other religious figures they have carved. Shady gardens out the back have vegetable patches, wells, fishponds, fruit trees and chickens pecking at the fertile earth alive with tropical insect bounty. On their way to and from the village school, and long into the lazy evenings, kids gambol freely on the tidy avenues of rich red soil, a little rutted from the passing bullock carts, on their way to and from the surrounding farms.

The people of the village of Long Tan, in the centre of what will soon be the famous Phuoc Tuy province, have survived for centuries – and in good decades even prospered – through quiet industriousness in peace, courage in war, and playing the long game against whatever powerful foes arrive – knowing they will win in the end.

Like their country, they have vaunted the power of the collective over the individual, resisting what can be resisted and reluctantly accommodating that which overwhelms . . . knowing that for them time is not measured by hours, days and weeks but by seasons, decades and centuries. They have seen invaders come and they have watched them go. The two sights may be centuries apart but the eyes of Long Tan will see them and know that, if not us, then our descendants will push them and all foreigners out. If we have to sacrifice our own lives to free all, our reward will be in the next life.

First the Chinese had come, and stayed for nigh on a thousand years, before Vietnam itself – which had refused to assimilate the northerners – had risen again to be free. And then the French had come in the late 1850s, storming ashore at Da Nang with 3000 French troops who immediately marched north to conquer Hue, the capital of the Nguyen Dynasty. Of course, they are just the vanguard as more troops soon arrive, followed by hungry swarms of French settlers who move across the country, establishing their own farms, mines and plantations, including the rubber plantation next to Long Tan. Yes, there had been peasants tending a lot of small plots on that very land, but as happens all over the country, the peasants are moved off their land and put to work tending larger concerns, like French-owned plantations. Those who resist are quickly taught the error of their ways by . . . being shot.

With infinite patience, the people of Long Tan have waited for the French grip on them to falter and, sure enough, it had seemed to come with the start of World War II as the Japanese had invaded Indochina just after France itself had fallen to the Nazis. Alas, alas, Japan keeps the Vichy French on as puppet rulers! And so, at least for the moment, the French rule on as compliant collaborators, until Japan finally decides to rule in its own right.

On 9 March 1945, Japan summarily announces that the rule of France is over, and from the new Empire of Vietnam, their puppet emperor, Bao Dai, will be 'ruler' once more.

That's all right. The Vietnamese people will hold.

As it happens, they needn't wait for long.

The empire lasts just six months, before two flashes to the far north-east – atomic bombs exploding on Hiroshima and Nagasaki – end in unconditional surrender by the Japanese.

And now? Who is to rule Vietnam? At last the Vietnamese themselves? Uncle Ho must move quickly, before the void is filled by yet one more power with colonial ambitions.

2 September 1945, Hanoi, an impatient declaration of independence

Hãy im lặng ngay bây giờ. Hush now. The father of this nascent nation is about to speak here in the Ba Dinh Flower Garden, before thousands of his fellow citizens. Watching closely is Ho Chi Minh's closest confederate and military commander, Vo Nguyen Giap, who just the year before had formally founded the Armed Propaganda Brigade for the Liberation of Vietnam. It had consisted of just 31 men and three women armed with flintlock rifles and an unquenchable desire for victory over foreigners – those colonisers who see Vietnam as a mine to be quarried not as a land to be lived in. Giap's small force had been a beginning, and has already grown a hundred-fold.

But be silent now with the crowd, which is pressing in close to gather every word of Ho Chi Minh ringing forth for a new generation. The Bringer of Light begins his speech with words some might find familiar: 'All men are created equal. They are endowed by their Creator with certain inalienable rights, among them are Life, Liberty, and the pursuit of Happiness.'

The crowd exults as Ho continues with his own words and lesson now: 'This immortal statement was made in the Declaration of Independence of the United States of America in 1776. In a broader sense, this means: All the peoples on the earth are equal from birth, all the peoples have a right to live, to be happy and free.

'The Declaration of the French Revolution made in 1791 on the Rights of Man and the Citizen also states: "All men are born free and with equal rights, and must always remain free and have equal rights."'

'Those are undeniable truths.

'Nevertheless, for more than 80 years, the French imperialists, abusing the standard of Liberty, Equality, and Fraternity, have violated our Fatherland and oppressed our fellow-citizens. They have acted contrary to the ideals of humanity and justice.'[5]

That, Ho Chi Minh announces, ends today, with this statement, the Declaration of Independence of the Democratic Republic of Vietnam. The Japanese have been defeated in Vietnam in no small part due to Ho Chi Minh's forces working in tandem with the Allies; the French have not returned to 'their' colony, and so this vacuum of power has been filled by the Viet Minh, the guerrilla group Ho founded and which is led by him. Vietnam will be an independent country once more, and if Ho has his way, it will be under the rule of Communism, the ideology that most notably had liberated Russia from the Tsars and is now liberating China from that capitalist running dog, Chiang Kai-Shek. Yes, there are other political forces at play in Vietnam, rivals to rule, most particularly the naïve Nationalists who want no part of Communism, but Ho Chi Minh has a plan and it does not include division or dissent.

As it happens, the French have a plan too. They take the view that while they had indeed proudly proclaimed that all men are born free, shall remain free etc., that is *not* to apply to uppity colonies struggling for freedom. Twenty-one days after Ho Chi Minh has made his proclamation, the Democratic Republic of Vietnam is attacked by France, with General Charles de Gaulle sending 80,000 troops to regain the colony it had lost to Japan, the colony which has now had the impudence to try to free itself. De Gaulle is determined that France will not be a spent Empire, and Vietnam will illustrate his desire to set the clock back to 1939.

For the moment, Ho Chi Minh cedes the ground to the French, knowing that his own forces are not yet strong enough to resist either them or China's forces under Chiang Kai-Shek, who also has designs on occupying Vietnam. Ho Chi Minh much prefers European occupiers, for the moment. Famously, he rounds on those who criticise his decision: 'You fools! Don't you realise what it means if the Chinese remain? Don't you remember your history? The last time the Chinese came they stayed a thousand years. The French are foreigners. They are weak. Colonialism is dying. The white man is finished in Asia. But if the Chinese stay now they will never go. As for me I prefer to sniff French shit for five years than eat Chinese shit for the rest of my life.'[6]

And so the French return to nominal power, only to find themselves the perpetual target of Ho Chi Minh's guerrillas who launch ambushes with galling frequency and steadfast stealth, all devoted to weakening the French grip on Vietnam. Yes, the French retain control of the cities, more or less, but the Viet Minh roam in the mountains, jungles and villages of the South. Try and follow them into any of their lairs, and you risk ambush and annihilation.

To keep his forces supplied with munitions, which come from Communist revolutionaries in China, Ho Chi Minh unleashes his forces – the people – through the jungles of neighbouring Laos and Cambodia, uphill, down dale, through forests, up mountains, across creeks, through swamps. It is a technique of stealthy transportation – these trails of Ho Chi Minh carry the life-blood of weaponry and ammunition his forces need – through countries that the French would have to invade to put a stop to it. As ambushes and guerrilla attacks on their forces abound, France becomes *extrêmement désespéré* to put a definitive stop to it . . .

March 1946, near the Chinese border, *carpe diem*

Ngo Dinh Diem is nothing if not pragmatic in his pursuit of power. While there is no doubt the slender 45-year-old with the piercing eyes is one of the most brilliant men in all of Vietnam, the son of no less than a Mandarin, he has still lent his abilities to prop up Vietnamese emperors and waning French empires, without having a scintilla of fondness for either. And though a Catholic in a Buddhist land, he reads Confucius every day. The most curious thing about him though is that despite being a bureaucrat *par excellence* who insists that others observe the rules and regulations of the government, his own behaviour and tastes are closer to that of a monarch.

Not that everything goes his way for all that.

Right now, for example, he is being held as a prisoner in Hanoi – surely the most elegant-looking prisoner this particular cell in the Hoa Lo prison has ever seen. His garb is immaculate, his skin is flawless, his teeth gleam like that of an expensive doll – one whose feet barely touch the ground as he sits on a chair.

Today, the very man who ordered his capture while he was on a secret trip to the North Vietnamese capital is due to meet with him. But first Ho Chi Minh – Chairman of the Provisional Government, Premier of the Democratic Republic of Vietnam – studies the intelligence report on Diem, trying to get a feel for the kind of man he is.

Born 1901. Worked in the rice fields as a child before attending a private school that was opened by his own father. Offered a scholarship to study in France; turned it down to enter the priesthood, then turned down the priesthood! Unmarried, there is no sign he has any interest in women at all, though this may be a sign of just how busy he has been in so many fields. For Diem has been a lawyer, a civil servant, an activist and even a Provincial Governor at the extraordinarily young age of 25 – something completely unheard of in a country where familial connection rather than merit dictate such an ascension, and even then usually only for those over 50.

Initially he had worked for the French in the Ministry of Interior, only to resign when they rejected his proposed reforms, at which point he started a nationalist movement to free his country from Empire. In 1945, with Japan's collapse, Diem had moved quickly, travelling from Saigon and heading to Hue with the intent of making an intriguing suggestion to Emperor Bao Dai. Why not become a *real* ruler?

As it happened, Viet Minh agents had arrested Diem mid journey, bound him up and taken him to this remote, tiny village near the Chinese border. Just one bit of news from the outside world gets through to him in the next six months of captivity: his brother Khoi and Khoi's son had both been shot by the Viet Minh as counter-revolutionaries. Devastated, the only thing Diem knows for sure is that the man who is ultimately responsible is the man he is about to meet: Ho Chi Minh.

Diem stands, a cigarette almost falling from his lips, as his captor enters his latest prison, a makeshift barrack room of the Viet Minh. Ho Chi Minh is alone and stands silently, waiting for Diem to speak.

'What do you want of me?'[7] Diem asks finally.

'I want of you what you've always wanted with me,' Ho Chi Minh replies in reasonable fashion, 'your co-operation gaining independence. We seek the same thing. We should work together.'[8]

Work *together*?

'You're a criminal who has burned and destroyed the country and you have held me prisoner.'[9]

'I apologise for that unfortunate incident,' Ho Chi Minh replies, almost as if he is serious. And yet Diem has no doubt that Ho Chi Minh is serious; that he dwells in a world where the ends always justify the means and that if people die violently or are imprisoned because of Communist theories then that is unfortunate but no more than that.

'When people who have been oppressed revolt, mistakes are inevitable, and tragedies occur,' Ho Chi Minh lectures Diem with chilling calm. 'But always, I believe that the welfare of the people outweighs such errors. You have grievances against us but let's forget them.'[10]

Grievances? Let's start with actual grief.

'You want me to forget that your followers killed my brother?'[11] Diem retorts angrily.

'I knew nothing of it,' Ho says with the calm of one saying no, he has not seen a lost dog. 'I had nothing to do with your brother's death. I deplore such excesses as much as you do.'[12]

Diem shakes his head, but still Ho continues.

'How could I have done such a thing when I gave the order to have you brought here? Not only that but I brought you here to take a position of high importance in our government.'[13]

Can he be *serious*? Diem spits out his reply with steady contempt.

'My brother and his son are only two of the hundreds who have died – and hundreds more who have been betrayed. How can you *dare* invite me to work with you?'

'Your mind is focused on the past,' answers Ho. 'Think of the future – education, improved standards of living for the people.'

Says the man who killed his brother, his nephew, and now they have no life or future thanks to Ho Chi Minh's cruel policies?

'You speak a language without conscience,' Diem spits back. 'I work for the good of the nation, but I cannot be influenced by pressure. I'm a *free* man. I shall *always* be a free man.'

Diem steps towards Ho now.

'Look me in the face. Am I a man who fears oppression or death?'

Clearly not. For no such man would dare raise his voice to Ho Chi Minh, let alone take a step forward and challenge him.

And yet, whatever else Uncle Ho might think, he respects strength and steel. He responds softly, so much so that Diem has to lean in to hear it. Words he was not expecting. 'You're a free man.'[14]

And with that Ho nods to the guards who open the door. Diem is free to go. Scarcely believing it can be true, he walks out onto the streets of Hanoi, and heads back to Saigon and his rendezvous with destiny: to rally and lead the people of South Vietnam.

March 1954, Dien Bien Phu, *très bien*, Viet Minh

Vo Nguyen Giap's army has grown from a notion to a nation. Yes, the infernal French try to contain it with brutal executions but the Viet Minh is like a hydra, with the death of each village soldier radicalising a dozen more. It is the product of a remarkable man and a relentless mind.

When a schoolboy at the *Lycée Nationale* at Hanoi, Giap had once sat enthralled listening to the Vietnamese nationalist Phan Boi Chau talk of how the war of ideas could be made into *revolution*, and had gone on to read smuggled pamphlets from a very different nationalist, Ho Chi Minh. He had become so inspired he'd joined a demonstration against the French which had resulted in his arrest – the only 14-year-old boy at the school with a police record – and it all led to him being here now.

Instead of studying history, he is making it, and is now leading an army no less than 270,000 strong.

While Uncle Ho had grown the movement as a whole, 'General Giap' as he had styled himself, despite having never received military training – had led the army with such skill they had become a real threat to the French from 1949 when Chairman Mao had taken over as the leader of China and delivered serious artillery and munitions to his Communist brothers of Vietnam. (He has given the same help to Communist insurgencies in Indonesia, Burma and Malaya. And the fact that the Soviet Union now officially recognises the alternative government of Ho Chi Minh, even as the Americans recognise the government of the French puppet Emperor Bao Dai, means that Vietnam is becoming *the* testing ground for what will become known as the 'Cold War' – a struggle for supremacy between the major powers, fought by proxy.)

And now, eight years into the war the French decide on a bold move. Most of the supplies on these damn trails of Ho Chi Minh – a plague of paths with the singular purpose of supplying the hidden enemy – move through a remote and narrow valley containing the settlement of Dien Bien Phu near the Laotian border. So why not set up a garrison there with a string of seven forts from where they can send out patrols and definitively block the supply line? Ideally, the Viet Minh will be forced to break from cover and try to overwhelm them, which is precisely what the French commander General Henri Navarre wants. Get them in the open field, to fight like men in conventional warfare! Superior French firepower, including from the air, will wipe them out.

C'est ca! If it all works as planned, Dien Bien Phu will be nothing less than 'a carefully designed killing ground where they could destroy the enemy as he at last came out to fight them'.[15]

The main French fear is that the enemy will avoid the fight.

Ah, but if only they could have known . . .

For no sooner are the French installed in their garrison and attendant forts than General Giap – who will become known in the West as 'the Red Napoleon' for his staggering military skill – gives his orders.

Soon, all along the Ho Chi Minh trail, hundreds of thousands of Vietnamese men, women and children start carrying armaments, ammunition, disassembled pieces of guns and associated *materiel* – most particularly including 105-millimetre and 120-millimetre guns and ammunition provided by China, together with Soviet 37-millimetre anti-aircraft guns – all with one aim: the humiliation of the French.

The sun and the moon rise and fall on this tide of committed cadres, hauling the *materiel* on their backs, on heavily loaded bicycles, as well as with the most faithful transport mode in Asia: carts drawn by buffalos. These Vietnamese men, women and children are not Communists, fighting for ideology. They are nationalists. They want the French gone, and they know that with their massive combined efforts they can deliver defeat to the invaders.

The trails are so long and so steep that Giap jokes that it takes 21 kilograms of rice to give the porters enough strength to push one kilogram of rice to the front line! To pull off a chain of supply is not impossible, just incredibly improbable and this is exactly what Giap relies on: the French will not conceive of what they are doing because it is ridiculous. Just as his hero Lawrence of Arabia stunned the Turks by attacking the impregnable Aqaba from an uncrossable desert while all guns were trained on the sea, Giap will surround the French with a sea of men.

When completed, all of the artillery of the 'People's Army of Viet Nam' is so well dug in that only their muzzles are exposed to counter-fire from the French as well as aerial bombardment. And now come the Viet Minh troops themselves.

Cao Xuan Nghia is one typical infantryman travelling for 45 days just to meet his unit here on the hills over Dien Bien Phu. The closer he gets, the more companions from his unit he meets, all of them converging from distant parts: 'We had to cross mountains and jungles, marching at night and sleeping by day.'[16] After nine years in the Viet Minh, Cao Xuan Nghia has become used to living and fighting by stealth. What he is not used to is seeing so many men joined in the open; commandos combined and co-ordinated; thousands of trails, men and miles leading to five divisions of Giap's Viet Minh army – 50,000 combat soldiers and 15,000 logistics personnel – assembled, with supplies, in one of the most remote parts of Vietnam.

By early March, all is in position with the Viet Minh secreted on the heights of what General Giap will describe as a geographical 'rice bowl' while some 16,000 French soldiers are in their main fortress and seven outposts on the valley floor.

Courtesy of the Vietnamese servants the French have seconded to do their menial domestic duties, the Viet Minh know *exactly* where both the French artillery and their ammunition dumps are situated, and have trained their guns accordingly – while also reserving some fire for the French airstrip to ensure that its runway is destroyed. This will mean that the invaders can only be resupplied by air, which will be a problem in itself as the Red Napoleon also has hundreds of anti-aircraft guns equally well dug in, all with secure supplies of ammunition.

At precisely five o'clock on the sultry afternoon of 13 March 1954, it begins.

As one, the big guns of two Viet Minh batteries of 105-millimetre and another two batteries of 120-millimetre mortars fire, their shells and mortars crashing into the north-eastern French outpost of Béatrice held by the 3rd Battalion of the 13th Foreign Legion Demi-Brigade. A direct hit is scored on the French command post, killing the outpost's commanding officer and most of the HQ staff.

The most astonishing and truly galling thing for the Gauls? This devastating attack was just *hors d'oeuvres*! For the Viet Minh attack is only warming up and becomes still more intense in coming hours as more and more French soldiers are killed. The thought dawns slowly: this is a siege! We, the French overlords, are under siege from the very people we have rapaciously ruled for nearly a hundred years!

Though the Viet Minh have the upper hills and the upper hand, they do not bring the battle on. Why? Because Giap does not want a quick victory, he wants a slow spectacle; a Goliath pecked by pebbles until all the world will watch in fascination. The Viet Minh have the French tiger in a cage and will take their time to kill it, first ensuring its total isolation.

Yes, the French artillery does its best to destroy the Viet Minh batteries with their counter-fire but the batteries have been too well dug in.

Desperate, the French launch sorties and patrols in the hope of revealing the true strength of their enemies. The results are devastating. For the first time they realise just how massive the forces encircling them are.

But what was that line about the man who kept reading that smoking caused cancer so . . . he gave up reading?

Well, from Hanoi, General René Cogny – one-time hero of World War II, now French Commander of the *Forces Terrestres du Nord* – directs his commander at Dien Bien Phu, Colonel Christian de Castries, to . . . make no more such sorties. In other words; attack is off *la table*. It will be a siege. Hold your nerve, *mon brave*. We are but the tip of an imperial spear; France will send supplies and forces soon.

It's just not clear yet how they will do that.

For, in a manner that would do Lawrence of Arabia proud, Giap has chosen his battlefield with great thought. Landing planes on the Dien Bien Phu airstrip is tough at the best of times, so swirling are the winds, so narrow the approaches, let alone when under heavy ack-ack fire and when trying to dodge recently blown shell-holes.

The worst thing of all for the French?

The Viet Minh are not content with artillery alone but are soon sending whole waves of Viet Minh soldiers of the 312th Division from the heights to attack them.

Mon Dieu! No sooner is one wave cut down than the next wave appears. The French shell them, wiping out whole chunks of a wave at a time. But the survivors go to ground and join the next wave as it comes through. These are not just brave soldiers, they are possessed!

And yet, the siege has only just begun, as no fewer than 40,000 'guerrillas' continue to assault the French positions over coming weeks, registering victory after victory as the outposts of Gabrielle and Anne-Marie also fall. The demoralised Gauls continue to fall back, shocked at how well organised the enemy is, how brave the soldiers are, and how *unrelenting*.

It is a display of military might, of planning, tactics, manpower and logistics that the French did not think their enemy possessed; a checkmate being constructed by pawns alone, an impossibility that the nobles of France cannot conceive of but now must experience before the astonished world.

The Viet Minh are supposed to be a vanishing army, guerrillas who flit in and out of fitful fray. But now they stand steady for all to see, and the French begin to feel like the British in the Zulu wars: uniformed, stiff, still and hopelessly waiting for a sea of foes to drown them with sheer numbers.

Before the eyes of its former Allies of World War II – all of whom decline to send help – the French twist slowly in the tropical breeze, the once mighty Indochina overlords in a slow agony of destruction, with no way out. They are left to fight their own battle; a battle that is a cautionary tale unfolding and unending day after day.

For their part, the Viet Minh continue their feverish attacks, pausing only momentarily when, out of a clear blue sky one day, a case of French champagne drops on them by parachute. The explanation? They have no clue. Back to work! More guns, more munitions, more men, all of them being put into place.

The crisis for the French is duly reported in Australian newspapers. In an irony that cannot help but be noted, the French are appealing for allies to join in a new Asian war while they are attending peace talks in Geneva to end an old Asian war; the Korean conflict is being concluded by diplomats and statesmen. It is while attending the peace talks that President Eisenhower lays out his new 'Domino' theory. Australian newspaper readers learn how this child's game is now a very serious metaphor:

'The President devoted most of his press conference to explaining why the loss of Indochina would be incalculable to the free world. Some 450,000,000 people in Asia had already come under Communist dominance, and President Eisenhower cited what he called the "falling domino" principle.

'He mentioned the importance of Burma, Thailand and Indonesia, and said the Communist conquest in this area would threaten the defensive chain of which Japan, Formosa and the Philippines were a part. Australia and New Zealand would also be threatened, Mr Eisenhower said. The loss of Indochina could be the beginning of a process of disintegration that would have most profound effects on the whole free world.'[17]

The battle at Dien Bien Phu goes on, and the French grow weaker each day as the Viet Minh tighten their tiger noose.

The US at least lend a logistical hand by providing air support for dropping supplies. Major General Chester McCarty of the 315th Air Division gives tactical advice but is amazed to see the French attitude to 'supplies'. For example, when, at the height of the battle Colonel de Castries had been promoted to *Brigadier* General de Castries, his first order had been to have champagne and ice delivered by parachute. Alas, the report soon came in that although the ice landed, the champagne had not, and could the Americans do something?

No.

The fact that the Viet Minh will be drinking room-temperature champagne strikes Chester McCarty as perhaps the smallest victory ever recorded but symbolic of the curiously, ludicrously antiquated French customs of war.

7 May 1954, Dien Bien Phu, mind the Giap

At last, all is in readiness. There are fewer than 12,000 exhausted French troops left in the major garrison, running low on ammunition, while General Giap has amassed no fewer than 25,000 Viet Minh to execute the *coup de grâce*.

By now three of the French outposts of the Dien Bien Phu valley have been captured and the Viet Minh continue to advance in relentless waves on the others.

The fighting is now hand to hand and though the French fight with great courage, the fact is there are 10 sets of Viet Minh hands to every set of French hands, and there is simply no overcoming that incontrovertible calculus of catastrophe.

And now General de Castries is back on the radio, his voice breaking as he speaks to his old comrade General Cogny: 'I'm blowing up the installations. The ammunition dumps are already exploding. *Au revoir*.'

'Well, then,' General Cogny replies calmly, '*au revoir, mon vieux*.'[18]

The radio is almost silent, only a fading, sputtering static remains until it manages a final, strangled cry – the last gasp of the original operator.

'The enemy has overrun us. We are blowing up everything. Goodbye to our families. *Vive la France!*'[19]

(*Finis.*)

Ho Chi Minh, of course, orders that the French humiliation is recorded on film so that the entire world will be able to see the 12,000 French prisoners – count 'em, twelve *thousand* – meekly submitting to his forces.

For just as Waterloo came to symbolise the fall of the Emperor Napoleon, so too will Dien Bien Phu become a synonym for the fall of the French Empire. It is a humiliation so unexpected and so complete; a mighty Western power mightily defeated by a foe previously thought too insignificant to merit serious notice. Yet the Viet Minh have routed the French not in a chaotic day, but in careful months, a vice tightened into victory, deliberate, decisive and definitive.

True, it is something that the French had never been so reduced as to raise the white flag of surrender, and had fought to the very end, but now, late on this day of 7 May 1954, it is the red flag of the Viet Minh that flutters over the former French command bunker in the tropical twilight. It doesn't matter that, at the conclusion of the battle, the 8000 Viet Minh dead dwarf the French fatalities by a factor of five. All that counts is that the once mighty Gauls have suffered a public defeat at the hands of a ragtag army of guerrillas. It is exactly as Ho Chi Minh has proclaimed: they can lose 10 soldiers for every one the enemy loses and still win.

The timing of the Viet Minh feat and French defeat is exquisite for the Viet Minh and excruciating for the French, as it is the very next morning that nine delegations including from France, China, the USA, the UK, the Soviet Union, the Viet Minh and the State of Vietnam are meeting in Geneva to discuss the fate of Indochina.

After 12 weeks, a treaty is agreed; *oui*, the French will leave. They will be replaced by Ho Chi Minh ruling a Communist regime in North Vietnam, while the puppet Prime Minister Ngo Dinh Diem will rule a nominally democratic regime in the South, with the puppet Vietnamese Emperor Bao Dai – currently living in Paris – as Head of State. Under this peace deal, Vietnam will be temporarily split either side of the 17th Parallel. Those believing in Communism will congregate in the North. Those who believe in anything from capitalism to Catholicism to anything *but* Communism, head to the South.

But never fear: North and South Vietnam shall be reunited after a free election is held in a year; a nation finally allowed to self-determine.

(As it turns out Diem proves to be more than a dab hand at running elections, as witness his garnering no less than 98.2 per cent of the vote against Emperor Bao Dai for the position of Head of State! Certainly there are troubling reports of Diem's thugs using swinging clubs and pepper spray to scare off Bao Dai supporters but – the Devil you know, and can control – he remains the American choice.) When Diem goes on to declare that the national election involving the North will not take place, as they cannot in his words be 'absolutely free',[20] it is clear he means free of opposition.

Once installed as President, Diem wastes no time in attacking any Communist agents in the South. There are plenty of these to be sure, but Diem allows suspicion, rather than certainty, to be the basis for death. Peasant farmers with an eye to the main chance are happy to denounce their neighbours as 'sympathisers' with their land confiscated and handed over to the informer as a reward. At the trials, for those lucky enough to be given them, defendants do not have counsel and are tortured while giving evidence, to ensure the evidence is as the court would desire it. Prisoners are 'interrogated' in front of watching American journalists, so laissez faire is the Diem regime's attitude to the rule of law. While reporting for *Time Magazine* the legendary journalist Stanley Karnow is even told he may watch a VC prisoner being 'interrogated'. With note-book in hand, Karnow watches expectantly as a reedy teenage youth in black cotton 'pyjamas' is led into the square of a village in the Mekong Delta. And what are the soldiers with him doing now?

Good God, no?

Are they really . . . ?

They are. As the boy sits passively, the soldiers are attaching wires to his fingers, and now flick a switch, which sees the lad's face shudder and judder, before an officer with a shockingly calm face asks him some questions. Receiving no answer, the officer ensures the switch is flicked again, which sees a repeat. No answer. The electricity is increased and the questions continue, slowly, smoothly. We have all day.

Karnow faces the journalist's dilemma when faced with outrage. Is he an observer, or a participant? Is he here merely as an observer to the outside world or, as a fellow human, is it his sacred duty to protest and use his journalistic clout to get them to stop this atrocity and . . .

And now, at last, the prisoner surrenders a short phrase and the power is cut. *What did the boy say?* The officer smiles and refuses to translate it. Karnow watches as the scorched and shaking youth is led away.

What happened to him? 'He may have been released. He may have been executed.'[21]

It clearly doesn't matter much to the officer.

It is clear to Ho Chi Minh and Blind Freddy that there will be no peaceful reunification process with the South; there will be no progress whatsoever. Korea stands as a model of what Diem wants and expects: a land divided, North and South, permanently split, each with a foreign sponsor to prop it up 'independently'. The remnants of the Viet Minh in the South are destroyed and in 1957 Diem visits the United States to be saluted as Asia's 'miracle man'[22] by President Eisenhower. (Privately, Ike acknowledges the truth: in a head-to-head election, America's man Diem would be lucky to garner 20 per cent of the vote.)

Ho Chi Minh knows that Diem, with strong American support, can only be removed by force and so – with the patience that is his hallmark – gives the orders. In training camps across North Vietnam, those Communist cadres from South Vietnam who have fled North from the attacks of the Diem regime begin to be trained in the violent art of guerrilla warfare, in preparation for being sent back into South Vietnam.

In the meantime, Uncle Ho is far from avuncular in his approach to those north of the 17th Parallel, as his government launches a program of land redistribution which sees all successful farmers with more than two acres of land framed as 'enemies of the people' who must hand over their land to poorer peasants or die – often doing both. No fewer than 15,000 of them die, with at least 100,000 being thrown into prison or deported.

•

In Australia, the saga of Dien Bien Phu and its aftermath has been watched with a certain shocked amazement. Once again, as had happened in Singapore in 1942, the white man has been humiliated, brought to his very knees by the Asian man. And there is no sign of it ending any time soon.

It is the Minister for External Affairs, Richard Casey, who puts it most starkly. 'With the black cloud of Communist China hanging to the north,' he says, 'we must make sure that our children do not end up pulling rickshaws with hammer and sickle signs on the side.'[23]

But at least, even in the absence of other Europeans in Asia, the scourge of Communism might be contained?

The Queensland paper the *Daily Mercury* spells out the situation.

'Tragic as it is, Dien Bien Phu is not the end in Indochina. The real strategic prize remains. The rich rice bowl of the Red River delta is still Vietnam property, and the object towards which all Viet Minh energies will now be directed, with the vigour and the morale of the victor, and in a race against the monsoons. The Viet Minh success here will pose a problem of far greater magnitude than Dien Bien Phu for the Pacific nations and their Western allies. As the diseased carry their scourge with them the Viet Minh, in their victory, would complete the submission of Indochina to the cancer of Asian Communism, and pave the way for the rich offerings of the Malay Peninsula – and beyond.'[24]

•

The government of Ngo Dinh Diem does not pretend to be anything other than what it is: effectively a puppet government, supported by Western powers, starting with the Americans. At least Ho Chi Minh and his government in the North have genuinely fought their way to power by kicking out the French and Japanese. And while they accept arms and munitions from the Soviets and Chinese, there is no sense of them answering to their diktats.

The last façade of the 'peace' engendered by the Geneva agreement is ripped away in 1959 when Ho gives new orders: mass assassination of all traitors who have co-operated with Diem's regime, starting with local mayors, head men of hamlets and the higher ranks of Diem's military.

In the Mekong Delta in the South, particularly, waves of bloody violence are soon unleashed. One night in the small settlement of Thanh My Tay, the villagers are suddenly woken in the wee hours by armed men, who oblige everyone to assemble in the village square.

The names of four young men are read out, and they are required to step forward, whereupon they are not only accused of crimes against the people by co-operating with the Diem regime, but also tried, convicted and beheaded. Their heads are nailed to a nearby bridge.

Let this be a warning to all: this is the deserved fate for all who stand against Uncle Ho.

No fewer than 1200 such 'traitors' are killed in the first year. The result? Diem appoints more military men to these bureaucratic positions, which in turn results in 4000 of these men being killed in a year. The local bureaucrats of the South now live in fortified homes, surrounded by troops (and soon with US 'advisers' to aid them).

And so this war that is not a war begins; a target wave of assassination that becomes an open state of war denied by both sides. Ho Chi Minh orders regiments in the North Vietnamese Army across the southern border, even as boats move down the coast and drop off thousands more newly trained operatives on South Vietnamese shores in the moonlight. The war is to be fought in earnest now, until there is no North or South left to fight it.

1 June 1961, Versailles, courted French

Of course the dashing young President John F. Kennedy is celebrated wherever he goes. But this is a little different. For the first time since becoming President he must play . . . second fiddle to . . . his wife! Yes, on his first official visit to France, it is clear that while the French are happy to see him, they are completely besotted by Jacqueline Kennedy. Entranced by her glamour, delighted by her fluent French, it is for good reason that Jack Kennedy will drolly remark, bemused and proud, 'I am the man who accompanied Jacqueline Kennedy to Paris'.[25]

France's foremost military hero, the former Prime Minister and current President, Charles de Gaulle, joins the legion of French singing Jackie's praises – but on this grand evening, he wishes to speak privately to *Monsieur le President* Kennedy about Indochina. *Oui*, he knows that the American leader has vowed to help the Diem regime fight off North Vietnamese incursions. But de Gaulle has, to his regret, starred in this same movie himself and it did not end well. *Donc, ecoutez, s'il vous plait, Monsieur le President*:

'For you, intervention in [Vietnam] will be an entanglement without end . . . The ideology that you invoke will not change anything. Even more, the masses will confuse it with your will to exert power. This is why the more you commit yourself there against Communism, the more the Communists will appear to be champions of national independence, the more they will receive help and first of all, that which comes from desperation.'[26]

Kennedy listens, rapt, as the great man speaks with the weariness of age, the age he has lived through; with the weight of history, the history he has helped steer and too often suffered through. And here in the halls of Versailles, his words have a particular resonance. How many times have warnings here gone unheeded as the circle and cycle of years repeats and retreats?

De Gaulle continues, his finger stabbing each syllable into being. A lecture? *Mais, non!*

It is a warning, worn into his face, and you must listen!

'We French have experienced this . . . I predict to you that you will, step by step, become sucked into a bottomless military and political quagmire despite the losses and expenditure that you may squander.'[27]

President Kennedy nods in firm agreement. The New Frontier has no intention of repeating the folly of Old Empires. *Les hommes* rejoin the ladies; the evening and the world moves on.

Just six weeks later, however, there is another old military man – and that rarest of figures, one who has actually led a victorious war effort in Asia – who also wants to have a word with President Kennedy in the Oval Office.

It is none other than General Douglas MacArthur, most recently the supreme commander of the Korean conflict and before that a commander of the World War II Pacific forces, where Kennedy himself had served with distinction as a PT boat commander. With such a résumé, when General MacArthur makes his grand entrance into the very office he once thought he would occupy as President himself, Kennedy expects a barrage of can-do bravado from the old war dog. And yet, once the legend removes the famous corn-cob pipe from his mouth MacArthur begins where he wants Kennedy to end: *do not send troops to Vietnam.*

'There is no end to Asian manpower,' MacArthur warns. 'Even if you pour a million American infantry soldiers into that continent, you would still find yourself outnumbered on every side.'[28]

Again, President Kennedy assures an old man he has no intention of sending troops to Vietnam, and true to his word, by May 1961, President Kennedy sends military 'advisers' instead – military men who will nominally take no active part in actual fighting, and advise only. They will, nevertheless, reserve the right to defend themselves and the South Vietnamese troops they are advising from any enemy attack. It is a frankly farcical situation; a fig leaf that allows John F. Kennedy to say that they are not at war; but the Jesuitical distinction will be lost on the enemy being shot by advisory bullets or strafed from an advisory chopper.

Australia watches with alarm, as the traditional 'Yellow peril' and 'Red menace' combine into one multicoloured nightmare.

For after the shock of losing China in 1949, now *Vietnam* is in danger of turning fully Communist, unless the Americans can lead an action to stop them?

It is deeply troubling.

Fighting fascism in faraway Europe in World War II had been one thing. And even fighting the Communist North Koreans in the previous decade had been in the Northern Hemisphere. But this is different. This looks like naked Communist aggression right on Australia's own doorstep.

And it is all happening while Australia has no more than three regular infantry battalions – less than 3000 men in all, under arms – one of which is already committed in Malaysia, supporting Britain in fighting Communists. In World War I, with half the population, Australia had boasted 60 infantry battalions.

In such extreme circumstances, the words of former Prime Minister John Curtin's dictum on 27 December 1941, just after the Japanese bombing of Pearl Harbor, resonate like a slow drumbeat marching as to war. When it comes to military alliances to keep our country secure, 'Australia looks to America . . .'[29]

And that means if the Americans now require support, the Australian Government of Robert Menzies feels it has no choice but to support them, in whatever manner the Americans see fit.

One way or another for Menzies, the 'strange malignant demon'[30] of Communism, must be defeated.

June 1962, Vietnam, rose-coloured eye of the beholder

The Commanding Officer of the Australian Army Training Team Vietnam (AATTV), Colonel Ted Serong – who is to lead the Australian advisers in Vietnam and is now conducting reconnaissance for this impending task – is a no-nonsense lifelong military man from Melbourne with a unique mind, a steely will and a rare résumé. A staunch Catholic who had been at school with Australia's most famous and relentless anti-Communist B. A. Santamaria, Serong had served Australia with distinction in World War II fighting against the Japanese in the Pacific, before returning to Australia to take over as the Head of the Jungle Warfare Training Centre at Canungra, and then leading Australia's counter-insurgency campaign in Burma.

On this day Serong is in Vietnam and focused on another military man who is unlike him in every way. A very loud American, General Paul D. Harkins, the highest ranking American military man in Vietnam, is doing what he does best: telling reporters just how wonderfully well President Diem and South Vietnam are doing in the face of North Vietnamese aggression, and all because of American assistance! The reporters, exhausted from listening to such endless . . . to use the technical term . . . bullshit, listen with glazed eyes.

In truth, General Harkins would not know of the situation for instead of getting out among the nitty-gritty and the blood 'n' guts of the front lines he stays happily ensconced in Saigon, where he is often seen strolling the streets in an immaculate uniform and smiling; mostly due to the fact that he has been devouring carefully crafted memos worded to ensure his perpetual optimism. Not for nothing have a couple of reporters composed a special song in his honour, to be sung late at night in a bar with fellow scribes, to the tune of 'Jesus Loves Me, This I Know':

We are winning, this I know, General Harkins tells me so
In the mountains, things are rough,
In the Delta, mighty tough
But the V.C. will soon go, General Harkins tells me so![31]

But Serong is clear: God help South Vietnam if they think military leaders of the likes of General Harkins will do anything but steer them merrily into defeat whilst proclaiming victory.

Serong's own duty is clear: to write a clear-eyed report on the situation in Vietnam for the Australian Government. Just the facts, ma'am. The paper sits in the typewriter as he smashes the keys into coherence:

General Situation . . .

Well, that is a perfect title and succinct summation of the problem. The General is the situation that needs to be changed. Either he is lying or his staff is lying to him and he's too stupid to see it. Serong lays out with simple clarity the illusion he was promised and the reality he sees:

> Worse than I had been led to believe, and worsening. VC plan is steadily developing. Govt. plan is developing – on paper! In fact?
>
> Strategic policy is passive and reactionary. Not active. No unified control. General Harkins has not grasped the nature of his task. Let's hope he does soon, for all our sakes.

The truth is that the VC are growing ever stronger, gathering ever more peasants into their force and shrinking the real territory under Diem's control by the day. If Australians become part of a war led by a General like Harkins, there is no way around it, we will be part of a long, slow defeat. The most tragic irony of the lot is that while the US is here acting as 'advisers' the truth is they have little clue of fighting against guerrillas in the jungle and they have no interest in taking advice from people like Serong who have *actually* fought guerrilla wars in this region and succeeded.

But if they won't listen, the least that Serong can insist on is that whatever Australian soldiers are committed to this must fight in the Australian way. In Serong's words 'conventional soldiers think of the jungle as being full of lurking enemies. Under our system, we will do the lurking.'[32]

Serong insists that Australia cannot be a mere component of the expensive, noisy, costly-in-lives American war machine in Vietnam. They must fight their own war, if it comes to that.

•

Listen closely. Aboard the big Qantas charter jet, 30 men who are highly trained in destruction are obliged to lean forward as the stewardess gives a safety demonstration. *In case of emergency . . .*

Funny she should say that. For that's what these 30 'advisers' of the AATTV are doing now – answering an emergency call from Vietnam, put out by the Americans. The US need help to put steel in the South Vietnamese military spine, train their officers up, and give them the tools they need to stave off Communist forces.

Lifting off from Kingsford Smith Airport, the gleam of the bright wintry Sydney morning bounces through each window on the eastern side as this charter flight of 29 July 1962 starts to gain altitude. Up the front, his head buried in a newspaper that has no news of their departure, is Colonel Ted Serong, determined to bring Australian tactics to

South Vietnam – deep probe patrols and intel to correct the advice they just got from General Harkins.

Serong is relishing another opportunity to match wits with a wily enemy – just the way he likes them – and make proper soldiers in the field. The AATTV are a unit made to be dispersed; they will join briefly with their US counterparts before being broken up into smaller groups, and spread among the South Vietnamese Army and various spots all over the country, teaching modern techniques of jungle warfare and the lessons they have gleaned from fighting in Malaya, particularly. All of the Australian advisers have been formally told not to take part in combat missions, but to simply observe and advise unless actually fired upon themselves – though all understand that the line is so blurry not even Coke-bottle glasses smeared with Vaseline would do it justice. There are US troops in South Vietnam. Now there will be Australian troops in South Vietnam. And we are here to win a war.

Other key allies? Not many . . .

Despite being pressed, the French prefer, refer and defer to the advice already given by Charles de Gaulle to President Kennedy – 'You will, step by step, become sucked into a bottomless military and political quagmire' – and decline to send any advisers of their own. Great Britain feels the same. Already deeply immersed in fighting the Indonesians in Malaya and Borneo, the Brits have no stomach to add another Indochina war 'emergency' to the books, and will leave Vietnam as a US problem. Britain's Labour PM, Harold Wilson, will be resolutely against it, though is shrewd enough not to criticise American involvement. When asked why he is not more forthright, he famously replies: 'Because we can't kick our creditor in the balls!'[33]

•

Voices in the night.

Late into every evening, usually at the village *dinh lang*, meeting house, the elders and the young bucks gather.

For each settlement in South Vietnam is facing the same agonising choice: are we with Diem or the Viet Minh? And what are the consequences of each decision? If we choose Diem will the Viet Minh leave us alone? And the reverse? What is our best chance of stability?

It's obvious that the Viet Minh can now reach into the South at will, their forays co-ordinated by the 'National Liberation Front', the

NLF, a shadowy political body entirely devoted to bringing down the Southern puppets by having revolutionaries strike constantly and with extreme violence.

The raging civil war, for it is now no less than that, goes on.

No choice is final, each village knows that whatever decision they take will likely bring violent consequences, either at the hands of Ho Chi Minh's Southern Army – the Viet Cong – or Saigon's South Vietnamese Army. Inevitably some villages are divided in their opinion, which means they become a bit of both, with the South Vietnamese Army patrolling and controlling by day, while the VC arrive by night, using some houses as safe harbours and supply depots. Other villages which give themselves over to the Viet Cong entirely become a veritable warren of tunnels, and underground rooms, secretly secreting supplies and weapons.

2 January 1963, Ap Bac, guerrillas in the midst

American 'advisers' have so advised the South Vietnamese Army that, courtesy of US Intelligence, they have detected radio transmissions in the tiny hamlet of Ap Tan Thoi, just 60 kilometres south-west of Saigon.

Meaning?

The VC are there, and you have to go and get 'em, before they get away!

The terrible surprise, however, is that that the radio transmissions are simply a lure.

The VC lie in wait at nearby Ap Bac, waiting for targets in the sky. David is taking on Goliath today and the results are extraordinary.

The key is to get close.

Like they are now.

Awaiting their moment, the VC guerrillas secreted close to the killing field, who have held their fire to this point, allow the US choppers to come into range and now fire furiously. A chopper comes down, cartwheeling to catastrophe. And another and another, while the other choppers desperately try to escape the ambush. Too late for some. In the end no fewer than five American choppers are downed, a catastrophe and a humiliation larger than the USA has faced to this point in Vietnam.

Like the French, like the Japanese, they had seriously underestimated the power of this enemy. They might be Gulliver but the Lilliputians are armed, dangerous and *everywhere*.

Never again will chopper pilots feel at ease in Vietnam; their flying machine is a puzzle that has been solved and now they are a permanent target.

From now on, choppers will descend and rise with incredible speed from battlefields in Vietnam, to linger any longer in the sky is to tempt destruction; the roar of helicopter blades now signals a prize in the offing for the North Vietnamese.

Today, the VC vanish from Ap Bac and Ap Tan Thoi after the battle is won, because that was the object of the temporary occupation in the first place. They have no interest in holding ground for the sake of it. It is *you* they want. They want to destroy you. After you are defeated, and humiliated before your own people, you will leave Vietnam, and all the land will be theirs.

•

In reality Thich Quang Duc has had no home to call his own since the first years of the century. At the age of just seven he had left his mother and father to be a Buddhist disciple. In the course of his life since he has had a part in building no fewer than 31 temples – *not* for the glory of Buddha, for that is not the Buddhist way, but to honour his teachings and to further *the* way. In the entire life of this quiet holy man that way has never been under such attack as now, and all because of the actions of the American puppet, President Diem. Buddhists have been forcibly converted to Diem's Catholicism, just as the only way for an officer in Diem's army to survive has been, if he is not already, to become a Catholic. Catholic lands are untaxed, Buddhist land is seized for the state. South Vietnam itself had become officially dedicated to the Virgin Mary in 1959, despite the fact that 90 per cent of the country is Buddhist.

The Buddhists protest as do the students – collectively out on the streets for an entire month – but the world is very nearly as indifferent as Diem himself, which is saying something. And yet Thich Quang Duc has come up with a plan to get their attention, and has the word spread to journalists in Saigon: something very newsworthy is to happen today, 11 June 1963, directly outside the Cambodian Embassy in Saigon and you need to bring cameras.

Most of them don't care. After all, who bothers about another protest? We've already covered them and American readers are indifferent about another solemn march, or yet another barrage of prayers. And what is even going to take place outside the Cambodian Embassy? The mystery just adds a further level of obscurity that Americans won't bother to wade through.

In the end, there is just one eager young American journalist with the *New York Times*, David Halberstam – relatively new to his Vietnam posting – who feels obliged to attend.

And so Halberstam on this hot-dog day afternoon waits, notepad dutifully in hand, as a procession of 300 or so Buddhist monks and nuns carrying placards, and chanting, heaves into view. So far, so dull. He has seen it all before, and could have written this story from memory without leaving the office. Another journalist, Malcolm Browne, from the AP, is barely stifling a yawn while dutifully readying his camera to capture the stock shot.

But what now?

Unusually, a car is slowly coming to the front of the march, an old, clapped-out Austin Westminster sedan. It stops and out steps one very calm, barely blinking old monk, while with him are two other monks who are clearly agitated. And now, after one of the upset monks gets a cushion from the car and places it upon the ground in front of the embassy, the first monk sits down and assumes the lotus position, with each foot placed on the opposing thigh, the hands down and open.

The third monk opens the boot of the car and takes out . . . a five gallon can of petrol.

Halberstam and Browne exchange looks. This doesn't look good. Browne brings his camera to bear, and focuses.

And now the first monk starts an unearthly chant, even as the third monk drenches him in petrol. Halberstam is frozen in horror.

He's not going to . . .

Surely to *God* he's not going to *actually* . . .

Oh yes, he is.

Within seconds Quang Duc reaches into his robes, takes out a box of matches and, with no hesitation, strikes it. In an instant, he is engulfed in flames, a live pyre burning there on the pavement as the stench of a melting man fills the air. A flash.

Malcolm Browne's camera has just taken a shot that will haunt the annals of history ever after.

Despite it all, the old monk sits completely still, completely calm as the flames envelop him. History is littered with the ashes of Catholic martyrs who were burned by Protestants, and died screaming at the stake. But that is not his way, and it is not *the* way.

And as it happens there is no way for even the fire trucks to get to him to put him out, as young monks calmly lie down on the road in front of their wheels.

Quang Duc is martyred by his own hand, uninterrupted, and accepts the fate that he has created in silence. Behind him a monk chants, in English, into a microphone, so the world may hear: 'A Buddhist priest burns himself to death. A Buddhist priest becomes a martyr.'[34]

Halberstam is profoundly shocked, it will be only an hour later that he will write the words that convey just how horrific and other-worldly the whole experience is:

'Flames were coming from a human being; his body was slowly withering and shrivelling up, his head blackening and charring. In the air was the smell of burning human flesh; human beings burn surprisingly quickly.'[35]

Through his self-sacrifice, Quang Duc has lit a fire of horror for the world. What is happening in Vietnam? What is America allowing to happen in Vietnam? Every Buddhist hopes to achieve enlightenment, a concept hard to even explain to Westerners. Awakening; that is enlightenment. You were asleep, now you have woken.

Quang Duc has taught his final lesson. The West is enlightened to suffering. Vietnam is not just an anonymous place; it is a vivid nightmare. It is here, now. *Wake up.*

The whole shocking episode highlights the sense that this is a conflict like no other that the West has been involved in, that these *people* are like no other.

All is strange, surreal, like nothing people of the West have ever experienced. It is one of several events which convinces Kennedy that the warnings of both President de Gaulle and General MacArthur have been proven correct – it would be a mistake to commit American forces too heavily in Vietnam – and he is determined to find a way that the USA can withdraw with honour.

Privately, though, Kennedy is already confident he will have US forces leave Vietnam within two years; regardless of the state of the war. His sceptical aide O'Donnell puts the riddle to his boss: 'How can you manage a military withdrawal without losing American prestige in Southeast Asia?'

'Easy,' replies the grinning President. 'Put a government in there that will ask us to leave!'[36]

They just need to get rid of the one they've got.

•

As coups against corrupt despots go, this one starts off in the traditional manner. The threatened leader and his closest lieutenants and lackeys fill their pockets with as many riches as they can. They appeal for help from all those forces still loyal to them. They race for the exits.

On this occasion, after slipping away from the Gia Long Palace, President Diem and his brother Nhu re-emerge at the nearby Cha Tam Catholic Church where they hope to find sanctuary. Alas, word of their flight has reached those leading the coup, and they are soon confronted by coup leaders backed by armed soldiers bearing handcuffs – which are quickly fastened around their wrists. In short order, the two brothers are in the back of an Armoured Personnel Carrier being driven back to Tan Son Nhat, the Joint General Staff Headquarters, in the tight company of two of the coup leaders, Major Nghia and Captain Nguyen van Nhung, who are under orders to deliver the fallen President and his brother safely, so they can be put on trial for their crimes.

But now, as the wagon slows to a halt at a train crossing, Captain Nhung springs forward and stabs Nhu with a bayonet! Not five times, nor even ten. He does not want to grievously wound him. He wants to kill him, and then wreck the corpse. Captain Nhung stabs President Diem's brother no less than 20 times. President Diem shouts at the first thrusts, trying to stop the attack, but he will keep. For once Captain Nhung is done, he draws his pistol, points it at the corrupt dictator's head, and pulls the trigger.

Under the circumstances it is not surprising that Major Nghia decides the time is not right to give Captain Nhung an earnest lecture on following the chain of command. Rather, it is time for them to work out an explanation for what has happened: why they will be delivering two dead bodies, one of them with 20 stab wounds and one bullet-hole.

The image of the murdered President Diem, the key American ally in Asia, is flashed around the world. President Kennedy is aghast to see such an uncivilised assassination. Diem had been a bad man, and the Americans had wanted to be rid of him, but not like this. Assassinations are so barbaric in this day and age, but it is apparently an Asian specialty.

Kennedy's Vice President, the blustery Texan, Lyndon Baines Johnson feels the same and reads the headlines in the papers with disgust. What outrages him even more, however, is that once again he has been left out of the loop and no-one in the rest of the Kennedy Administration had bothered to inform him that a coup was about to take place. To see Diem, a man LBJ had sat with and been photographed with as Kennedy's emissary, gunned down 'like a dog', with a wink and nod from the Administration that he is nominally a part of, is sickening.

The *Canberra Times* – cognisant of the fact that Australia still has 30 'advisers' in the country, to go with the 16,000 US military 'advisers' helping prop up the Diem regime – gives Australian readers the news of Diem's death but adds a strange twist, proffering a rather unlikely official cause of death . . .

'. . . The picture of Diem showed him lying beside a personnel carrier with a soldier leaning over him. His body was bullet-riddled. He seemed to have been shot in the head. Nhu's body bore bruises as though he had been beaten. He was stabbed to death, informed sources said. The official explanation of the men's deaths was that they had committed suicide . . .'[37]

•

Less than three weeks later a former marine by the name of Lee Harvey Oswald stands at a window on the sixth floor of the building where he currently works, the Texas Book Depository. As all of his fellow employees have gone downstairs to wave at President John F. Kennedy and his wife, Jackie – the Camelot couple who are due to drive by in their open-topped four-door Lincoln Continental – Oswald is alone.

And here are the Kennedys now! As the car enters Dealey Plaza, Oswald aims his Mannlicher-Carcano rifle and . . . pulls the trigger three times.

The first shot misses. The second shot hits just to the left of the base of President Kennedy's neck, passes through his body and into Texan Governor John Connally. The third shot blows the President's skull open. Oswald hides the rifle under some empty carboard boxes and walks downstairs into the depository lunchroom drinking a can of Coke. A Dallas Police officer, Marrion Baker, holding his gun in a firing position, is running towards him, with another man, Oswald's supervisor, Roy Truly. Truly tells Baker that Oswald works here and they both run past, upstairs to where the shots have been fired by some crazed assassin. Oswald looks a little startled, having had a gun pointed at him and all. Another employee, a clerk, Mrs Reid, steps forward and tells him the news. 'The President has been shot!'[38]

Desperate for a place to hide, Oswald decides to watch a movie in The Texas Theatre. No matter that he doesn't have enough money on him, he can see that the box office cashier – one Judith Postal – is distracted by a magazine she is reading. He sneaks past without paying and sits with the other 24 people in the session, feeling relatively safe for the first time in 30 minutes. But he has been seen. A shoe store employee next door, Mr Brewer, had noticed him sneaking in, and liking Judith, alerts her.

Did that guy who just went in pay?

'No, by Golly, he didn't!' Judith Postal replies.

She calls the police! You can't break the law like that in Dallas!

What does the man look like?

Miss Postal is not sure, but Mr Brewer is: a weedy, nervous-looking guy with dark hair . . .

Lee Harvey Oswald is arrested while watching *War is Hell*, a movie about US soldiers fighting a battle against impossible odds in an Asian land war, the Korean War.

•

At 2.38 pm Dallas time, with the blood-splattered bride of his predecessor standing next to him on Air Force One, Lyndon Johnson takes the Presidential oath and command of the US military. South Vietnam will have three different administrations in his first three months as President, and three more before his first year is done. It is rolling chaos, and Johnson is furious to find himself stuck with the mess created by his now sanctified predecessor. Still, Vietnam is a problem for policy wonks, it is not a country or a problem that the average American or Australian ever thinks of, at least not for long.

•

In Newcastle, a troubled young labourer by the name of Peter Kocan – more anonymous than a wrong number – is fascinated by both of the assassinations and more particularly the attention it gives their assassins. All day and late into the night he keeps thinking what it would be like to have that level of fame.

•

Out in far western Queensland, a likely sort of bloke by the name of Geoff Kendall, a former half-back for the Wynnum Manly rugby league team in the Brisbane comp, has just come off a tough season as captain–coach of the Tara league team in south-western Queensland on 12 pounds a week and is now making ends meet, just, flogging televisions in his elder brother's electronics shop, when he happens upon an advertisement in the local paper.

Would you like to be an officer in Australia's Army?[39]

As Kendall reads the details of the ad and gazes at the accompanying photo of a dashing officer, he forms the distinct impression that 'all one had to do was spend a year at a sort of holiday resort called Portsea, with sport, a hectic social life and eventual graduation as a dashing Lieutenant'.[40]

Well, it doesn't take too long to think about it. Yes, he bloody well would like to have a go at that! Whatever else, it has to be more interesting than selling TVs on weekdays and trying to knock over rampaging jackaroos on Saturday afternoons. So he writes away, and is soon given his chance. After filling out some aptitude tests he is asked to appear before a Brisbane selection board for an in-depth interview to see if they think he has what it takes to be an officer. On his way down the ol' Moonie Highway he is trying to pick up some music on the local radio station, but all he can catch for now is the news. He notes something about a curiously named general in Vietnam called 'Big Minh' who has just taken over the military after a coup.

Sure. Drive on. Toowoomba up ahead. And Brissie a couple of hours after that.

'And what,' the selection panel asks him the next day, 'do you think about the current state of affairs in Vietnam?'

Well, I am concerned about the tactics and policies of Big Minh, I presume you gentlemen are familiar . . .

His listeners beam. Clearly, they are looking at officer material.

Well, they certainly are when it comes to hoodwinking brass.

'Luckily, they didn't ask me to show them on a map where Vietnam was. I wouldn't have had a clue!'[41]

A week later Geoff gets the news in the mail. He is going to be trained up to be an Australian Army Officer, at the Officer Cadet School at Portsea in Victoria. Visions come of making a whole bunch of new mates in Victoria, learning stuff, playing football, and graduating in a year as a spiffing brand-new Lieutenant of the Australian Army!

2 March 1964, The Oval Office, pressed to decide

When President Lyndon Baines Johnson is upset, he has a tendency to yell louder than his ordinary conversation, which already threatens to deafen. He glowers and towers his massive frame over friend and foe alike, either will do to exorcise his displeasure. On this afternoon he is more than usually upset. It's about this gung-ho hawk journalist for *The Washington Post*, name Joe Alsop, who has been *seriously* proposing in his column that the United States should be at war with Vietnam!

Sarcastically – another LBJ specialty – he tells National Security Advisor McGeorge Bundy to ask Alsop to outline just what his 'program' is and if, maybe, he would like to start another Korean War?

'What is your own internal thinking on this, Mr President?' Bundy asks frankly. 'That we've just got to stick on this middle course as long as there's any possible hope . . . ?'

(Bundy doesn't know it but every word of their conversation is being recorded, courtesy of a practice started by President John F. Kennedy, on the grounds the transcripts would be useful for a future memoir while also enabling him to deal with those turncoats who shifted their positions in public from what they had already agreed in private.)

'There may be another coup,' Johnson says, 'but I don't know what we can do if there is . . . What alternatives do we have then? We're not going to send our troops in there are we?'[42]

Of course not! That would be unthinkable. It is obvious to both men that Alsop is mad and sending a mass of troops into an Asian quagmire, so far from home, so difficult to supply, against an implacable foe, would be madness.

Everything that President Johnson has learned about the situation, and everything that has happened since, has confirmed the wisdom of General de Gaulle's previous warning to President Kennedy. Vietnam would be an unwinnable war.

And yet, ere three months have passed, the *New York Times* breaks the news.

'The White House announced today that Gen. Paul D. Harkins, military assistance commander in South Vietnam, would return to the United States within 10 days. Lieut. Gen. William C. Westmoreland, the deputy commander, will take over full responsibility immediately. President Johnson plans to promote him to full general. General Harkins' recall to Washington, prior to retirement, and his succession by General Westmoreland were not surprising but appear to have been ordered at least a few weeks earlier than contemplated.'[43]

One way or another, LBJ has had enough of negative press reports and wants action on the ground, and reports of victorious American battles to fill the airwaves. 'Westy', as he is known to all, is hopefully the man to deliver precisely that.

CHAPTER ONE

THE APOCALYPSE BECKONS

He cried in a whisper at some image, at some vision – he cried out twice, a cry that was no more than a breath – 'The horror! The horror!'

Joseph Conrad, *Heart of Darkness*

4 August 1964, The Gulf of Tonkin: 'Riders on the Storm'

It is, yes, a dark and stormy night.

And the darkness comes not just from the lack of light, nor even the forces at play, but in the confusion that abounds all around. The physical storm is all too real, but there is now a lot more at play than mere thunder, lightning and howling winds.

Among other things Captain George Stephen Morrison, the commander of the entire US fleet in the Gulf of Tonkin, off the coast of North Vietnam, misses his son Jim, a film student at UCLA with rough ambitions to write lyrics and maybe one day front a rock band. Jim Morrison just needs some of the right doors to open for him.

An extraordinary radio message reaches Captain Morrison now, that the USS *Turner Joy*, a US destroyer, has had *20 torpedoes* fired at it! There have been recent small 'advisory' skirmishes and warning shots fired from both the Americans and North Vietnamese sides but this is another level; this is an act of war if true. At 7.40 am Washington time on 4 August 1964, Secretary of Defense Robert McNamara receives the news, and a meeting of the Joint Chiefs is hastily held. Admiral Grant Sharp in Honolulu confirms the reports and at 11.06 am McNamara calls President Johnson, entirely unaware that Johnson records all incoming calls to his office.

'Mr President,' McNamara says, 'we just had word by telephone from Admiral Sharp that the destroyer is under torpedo attack.'[1]

Johnson replies with something between a groan and a sigh, before asking the obvious question.

LBJ: 'Now where are these torpedoes coming from?'

McNamara: 'We don't know . . .'[2]

Well, find out, Admiral Sharp. Admiral Sharp calls Captain Morrison.

A 'flash' message is sent in reply to Honolulu and Washington arriving at 1.27 pm Washington time: 'Review of action makes many reported contacts in torpedoes fired appeared doubtful. Freak weather effects on radar and overeager sonarman may have accounted for many reports.'[3]

In short, quite possibly a false alarm.

McNamara needs to know if it's real or not and calls Admiral Sharp in Honolulu at 4.08 pm.

McNamara: 'What's the latest information we have on the action?'[4]

Sharp: 'The latest we have, sir, indicates a little doubt on just exactly what went on . . .'

McNamara shakes his head as he hears Sharp talk of 'freak radar echoes' and jumpy sonar operators, which is to say 'young fellows . . . apt to say any noise is a torpedo, so that, undoubtedly, there were not as many torpedoes . . .'[5] It might even have been dolphins.

The Secretary of Defense cuts to the chase.

McNamara: 'There isn't any possibility that there was *no* attack, is there?'

A pause.

Sharp: 'Yes, I would say that there is a slight possibility.'[6]

A slight possibility! They are about to start a *war*, Admiral, a retaliatory strike of US forces is planned.

McNamara: 'We obviously don't want to do it before we are damned sure what happened.'[7]

At 5.23 pm Admiral Sharp calls with the latest and the last word: 'No doubt now exists that an attack on the destroyers had been carried out.'[8]

Thank God for that.

Just two days later, the 'Gulf of Tonkin Resolution' is passed by the US Congress – 88–2 in the Senate, 416–0 in the House – authorising President Lyndon Johnson to 'take all necessary measures to repel any armed attack against the forces of the United States and to prevent further aggression'[9] by North Vietnam's Communist government.

Only two Senators had spoken against it, with one of them, Senator Wayne Morse, a Democrat from Oregon, putting it in the starkest of terms.

'I believe this resolution to be a historic mistake. I believe that within the next century, future generations will look with dismay and great disappointment upon a Congress which is now about to make such a historic mistake.'

The warning is lost in the fury and fuss of the moment, with both the political and media class clear swept away with the need to now *act* on the Resolution.

No, it is not an official declaration of war, but it does give the President the authority to combat the Communist threat in Vietnam, without seeking further leave from Congress.

As the New York correspondent of the *Canberra Times* makes clear to Australian readers on 11 August 1964, the move is nothing if not popular with American voters as the US leader visits Syracuse University in upstate New York in the days after the Resolution is passed:

'Tall and grave in a dark pin-striped suit, President Johnson moved slowly along the fence holding back a big crowd, at the airport shaking eagerly-thrust-out hands. As he did so a voice shouted: "Give 'em hell, Lyndon!" The voice, ringing out in the brisk morning air, and the 100,000 cheering people lining the route of his motorcade into the city, confirmed what has since become apparent: that Americans were solidly behind him in his determination to show resoluteness in the face of Communist attack . . .

'The President told a crowd of 20,000 that the US was not a country divided during the presidential campaign. His words were met with long applause. Instinctively, the US had closed ranks. It had taken North Vietnamese torpedo boats in the Gulf of Tonkin to do it, but it had been done.

'As matters stand, the US has been attacked where it is strongest – at sea. The Seventh Fleet is the mightiest single unit of sea-power in the world, it will stay in South-East Asian waters, come what may. But on land, the US is in more difficulty. US military personnel in South Vietnam are officially only "advisers," not organised fighting units. There are 16,000 of them, soon to be boosted to 21,000. Against 40,000 well-trained guerrillas and Ho Chi Minh's army, it is not much.'[10]

And the gap in numbers will have to be made up, both from the USA, and allies. In the meantime, however, Lyndon Baines Johnson has the wind in his sails as never before, what with the 1964 presidential election looming. So far he has been running on a corpse, promising to fulfil the promises of the slain JFK. But now he has a platform and a war of his own, Vietnam.

Johnson eschews Kennedy's ambivalence about Vietnam. LBJ is his own man, his own President, and he is certain. We're going in, and we're going in hard. Kennedy had forged his reputation with his unwavering steeliness during the Cuban Missile Crisis.

Well, this will be Johnson's moment.

When President Johnson's popularity surges by 10 points in the wake of the Gulf of Tonkin Resolution, there is no more talk of dolphins.

10 November 1964, Canberra, Ming the merciless

Luckily, the US has a loyal ally like Australia, an ANZUS partner, with an enthusiastic Prime Minister by the name of Sir Robert Menzies to provide manpower.

Addressing the Federal Parliament on this day, the Australian Prime Minister has some good news, and some bad news for the nation.

To the good news first.

'Global war – that is, unrestricted conflict between the major world powers – has receded in probability because of the deterrent effect of nuclear weapons, and we continue to believe that it is unlikely except as a result of miscalculation.'

Against that?

'[But] armed conflicts short of general war could develop at any time in areas of tension throughout the world. Communist powers will continue to press their aims through all the varied Cold War techniques of subversion and insurgency . . .

'In particular, in South Vietnam the continued instability of government has made the task of resistance more difficult and to some extent frustrates the massive efforts of the United States and our own necessarily small contributions.'[11]

Australia, after all, is in the direct path of the dominos that shall fall, as Sir Robert will explain in a later speech: 'The takeover of South Vietnam would be a direct military threat to Australia and all the countries of South-East Asia. It must be seen as part of a thrust by Communist China between the Indian and Pacific oceans . . .'[12]

'After an examination of all the factors, and in full consultation with our military advisers, we have reached the conclusion that the Regular Army should be built up as rapidly as possible from the present 22,750 to an effective strength of 33,000 men, which means a total force of 37,500 . . .

'It seems clear, on our military advice and our own carefully formed judgment, that we cannot expect by voluntary means to achieve a build up in the Army's strength of the order we require and to the timing which is necessary . . . The Government has therefore decided that there is no alternative to the introduction of selective compulsory national service.'[13]

Indonesia has a regular and guerrilla army that already absorbs the fighting forces we have at the ready for foreign service. Vietnam will require a new force, and an old method to get them if necessary.

Sir Robert continues.

'Both the Government and the nation would urge that as high a percentage as possible of those in our armed services should be those who, of their own choice, and in the spirit of a great national tradition, have joined one or other of those Services.'

And now the Honourable Member for Hindmarsh, Clyde Cameron, of the ALP interjects rather pointedly. 'I know one who dodged it in 1914!'

In World War I, Sir Robert had been the only one of three eligible Menzies brothers who had not served.

Sir Robert replies: 'You do not. You must not repeat other people's lies.'

Cameron, backs off, just a little: 'Well, 1915 . . .'[14]

Along with almost every paper and journal of note, *The Bulletin* backs Australian troops being sent to fight in Vietnam as: 'it has been plain to the whole world in South Vietnam is Australia's front line and the South Vietnamese have been fighting and dying for what are Australia's interests as much as their own'.[15] Of course, there will always be those who say the US should withdraw from Vietnam but any such retreat 'has been impossible; for America it will be a colossal set back in the world, for Australia it would be close to suicide'.[16]

8 March 1965, Da Nang, and the thunder rolls

Send in the Marines?

Yes. And this event is *precisely* what General Douglas MacArthur and *Generale* Charles de Gaulle had warned against. For on this day, at the very spot the French had come ashore at Da Nang 107 years ago, American troops make their landing – the vanguard of a massive force that President Lyndon Johnson is sending to South Vietnam.

The job of these 2000 Marines of the 9th Marine Expeditionary Brigade will be to secure the nearby air base to make sure it is in shape to receive the planeloads of men and *materiel* which will soon be on their way.

Of course, under the circumstances, the South Vietnamese authorities have ensured that the whole thing will look like anything *but* an invasion – women and children are there to greet them on the beach offering flowers, and a sign says 'Welcome, Gallant Marines' – but no matter what you call it, the effect is the same. American troops are now arriving, *en masse*, to stop the domino of South Vietnam falling.

In the meantime, Operation Rolling Thunder has now begun, a relentless American bombing campaign intended to drive the North staggering back to Hanoi. Targets in the North – ammunition dumps, barracks, radar sites – are destroyed in LBJ's attempt to cripple the North Vietnamese Army (NVA) and force Ho Chi Minh to the negotiation table.

To a visiting Australian officer, Colonel Oliver Jackson, such an occurrence seems unlikely. Touring around South Vietnam, trying to get a feel for the situation, he is distinctly underwhelmed.

'I saw almost every important government post,' he will recount. 'I certainly saw every place where Australians were deployed. The impression I gained, a very real impression, was the war was lost from a military point of view. Wherever I went there were Vietnamese Army forces on hilltops, behind barbed wire. They very rarely went outside that wire. If they did go outside to relieve one post by another they were frequently ambushed in strength by the VC – and it was nothing for a whole battalion or more of South Vietnamese troops to be butchered. There was very little in the way of offensive action from anywhere in the Vietnamese Army; the Viet Cong were thoroughly on top from a military point of view. I would have said that it was just a matter of weeks or months before the war was militarily lost in Vietnam – it was as bad as that in my opinion, and a lot of people agreed with me.'[17]

10 March 1965, Melbourne, birthdate with destiny

It's called the first 'National Service birthday ballot', the day when the birthdates of those about to be conscripted is to be decided. A fortunate few of us specially selected gentlemen of the press have been allowed to enter into the boardroom of the Department of Labour and National Service in Melbourne where we first see the Federal Member for Corangamite, Mr Dan Mackinnon, MHR, himself a World War II veteran, standing beside a barrel with a lid on the side, placed horizontally on two pivots either end that allow it to spin. Inside are a whole mess of wooden marbles, each marked with a number from 1 to 181, and each representing a date between 1 January and 30 June 1945.

After the barrel is turned, we are allowed to see Mr Mackinnon reach in and pull out the first marble, which is carefully put into a basket, but now we are ushered from the room.

Oh, and just in case anyone is wondering if the ballot is going to be fair, don't you worry about that, sunshine: 'The barrel used in the ballot was one which has been used for more than 50 years to draw horses for Tattersalls' sweeps on important Cup meetings.'[18]

If it's good enough for Phar Lap, it's good enough for you, mate.

The politician will, we know, go on to pick out 95 more marbles, each corresponding to the specific birthdates of 4200 20-year-old men around the country. Those young men will soon have registered letters sent to them, informing them they are in the one-in-twelve section of men their age required for National Service for the next two years of their lives – subject to their health and qualifications for deferment.

Of course, they could always just print their names in the paper, but this might lead to embarrassment, as Mr Mackinnon explains by proffering the example of a hypothetical famous footballer: 'If this man happens to be a conscientious objector, or did not pass the required medical or aptitude tests, there would be a certain odium. People would want to know why he had not been called up.'[19] So a discreet letter will be sent.

The first half will enter the training camp at Puckapunyal in Victoria, and Kapooka near Wagga Wagga, in late June. After Mum and Dad see the passing-out parade at Puckapunyal and Kapooka, the second intake will go in mid-September, replacing them.

Still not old enough to vote, these 20-year-olds will be trained up to be ready to kill. Outside the building, two young men and a young woman parade up and down the footpath, wearing sandwich boards proclaiming WE DON'T WANT TO KILL, DON'T BALLOT OUR LIVES and NO WAR.[20]

(They are clearly oddballs, and only mentioned in the press by way of novelty. Students will protest about *anything* these days, the army will make a man of them. Well, the male students anyway . . . As to the cowardly so-called 'conscientious objectors', well, don't get us started. Not to worry about it. We of the press barely mention them.)

29 April 1965, Parliament House, Canberra, the call is coming from inside the House . . .

When it comes to co-operating with the US President Johnson, Prime Minister Menzies is generous to a fault. When LBJ asks for some more Australian advisers, Mr Menzies offers him a battalion.

True, there is the problem that the South Vietnamese Government hasn't actually *asked* for an Australian battalion to arrive on their shores but Sir Robert is able to rise to the occasion. Via diplomatic channels he asks them if they would mind asking Australia to come, and a plea dutifully comes . . . at least sort of. It is not quite from the South Vietnamese Government, but certainly from South Vietnam – even if the cable is sent from the Australian Embassy in Saigon. No matter, Australia accepts its own invitation. It is all just a bit of political theatre, before the theatre of war is entered.

In his entire time as Prime Minister, across two stints, the only announcement that Sir Robert Menzies has made of more import than this one was the Declaration of War, back at the beginning of World War II in 1939.

And this speech comes with clear echoes of that . . .

'The Australian Government,' he begins in his stentorian tones, 'is now in receipt of a request from the Government of South Vietnam for further military assistance. We have decided – and this has been after close consultation with the Government of the United States – to provide an infantry battalion for service in South Vietnam. In case there is any misunderstanding, I think I should say, Sir, that we decided in principle some time ago – weeks and weeks ago – that we would be willing to do this if we received the necessary request from the Government of South Vietnam and the necessary collaboration with the United States. This is not to be regarded as something that has suddenly arisen out of more recent events . . .'

Aware of the stirring in the House, particularly from the Opposition benches where there is dismay, and even disgust at the Prime Minister's words, he goes on.

'Assessing all this, it is our judgment that the decision to commit a battalion in South Vietnam represents the most useful additional contribution which we can make to the defence of the region at this time.'[21]

•

There is one radical rag that is against the move – *The Australian*, that creation of young Rupert Murdoch, whose father, Keith, had been such a mover and shaker as a journalist and the man most responsible for sounding the alarm to get the Diggers evacuated out of Gallipoli before winter had set in. Sensible Australians will shake their heads as they read this one voice in the wilderness.

'The Menzies government has made a reckless decision on Vietnam which this nation may live to regret,' the paper thunders. 'It has decided to send Australian soldiers into a savage revolutionary war in which the Americans are grievously involved – so that America may shelve a tiny part of her embarrassment . . . It could be that historians will recall this day with tears.'[22]

They say that Rupert Murdoch feels so passionately on the subject, he wrote it himself.

And he is not the only one who feels so strongly against it.

1 May 1965, Sydney Domain, mayday, mayday, mayday

Like most of the May Day rallies all over the country, bringing the workers together, this one in Sydney is the biggest seen in 30 years. What has brought them out is the news of Australia getting involved in the burgeoning conflict in Vietnam.

After assembling in Hay Street, Chinatown, the parade of 21 bands, 26 floats and thousands of workers, led by drum majorettes and marching girls, snakes down George Street, right on Market Street – their placards rising just above the mob, 'STOP THE WAR!' 'END CONSCRIPTION!' 'AUSSIE BLOOD FOR YANK DOLLARS'[23] – and follows the contours of Hyde Park until it gets to St Mary's Cathedral, where it makes its way to the vast flat green expanse of the Domain, so people can listen to the speeches. The key speaker is the Federal President of the Sheet Metal Workers' Union, Mr T. Wright, and he makes no bones about it, shouting into a loud-hailer that sending the 1st Battalion, Royal Australian Regiment (1RAR) to South Vietnam will be forever regarded as 'an everlasting disgrace to Australia'.[24] Not only is South Vietnam not democratic, he insists, but it has been run by a series of military-fascist dictatorships since 1954, all of them propped by the so-called exemplar of liberty and democracy, America.

'The US,' he thunders, 'is using Hitler tactics – the Big Lie – to continue its policies in South Vietnam.'[25]

He finishes by calling for three cheers for 'the people of Vietnam's fight for peace'.[26]

Three hip-hips roll over the Domain, each one followed by a hooray and each one louder than the last.

The cheers are so strong they are heard on Macquarie Street and as far away as Pitt Street.

4 May 1965, House of Representatives, Canberra, Calwell calls well

Arthur Calwell, Leader of the Opposition, is about to give a speech that will ensure he will never become Prime Minister of Australia, nothing less than a political suicide note. Yes, there has been outrage over the government's decision to send troops to Vietnam – the May Day marches around the country boasting protests were only a part of it – and yet there is equally no doubt that a majority of Australians are on Menzies' side of the argument. That much can be seen by Letters to the Editor, the word on the street and the sudden surge in patriotic fervour.

But can he, as Opposition Leader, support something which he is certain will be a disaster for his country and, beyond everything else, is just wrong?

He cannot. And he must say so, rising now in Parliament to give Labor's response. He is an old man now, close to 70, a veteran of bruising politics for nigh on half a century and it all shows in his craggy face, the timbre of his rusty corrugated-iron voice.

'On behalf of all my colleagues of Her Majesty's Opposition,' he says, 'I say that we *oppose* the Government's decision to send 800 men to fight in Vietnam. We oppose it firmly and completely . . .

'We do not think it is a wise decision. We do not think it is a timely decision. We do not think it is a right decision. We do not think it will help the fight against Communism . . . We do not believe it will promote the welfare of the people of Vietnam . . .'

Parliament stirs, aware of the significance of this speech, an absolute rebuttal of the government's position at a time when it has full support. Does Calwell have a political death wish? No, but he is saying things that must be said. Through his thick glasses, he stares down the few hecklers on the government benches, and keeps going, an old torpedo in an ill-fitting suit aimed straight at the Menzies Government.

'Our men will be fighting the largely indigenous Viet Cong in their own home territory. They will be fighting in the midst of a largely indifferent, if not resentful, and frightened population. Our present policy will, if not changed, surely and inexorably lead to American humiliation in Asia . . .

'To exhaust our resources in the bottomless pit of jungle warfare, in a war in which we have not even defined our purpose honestly, or explained what we would accept as victory, is the very height of folly and the very depths of despair.

'Humiliation for America could come in one of two ways – either by outright defeat, which is unlikely, or by her becoming interminably bogged down in the awful morass of this war, as France was for ten years. That situation would in turn lead to one of two things – withdrawal through despair, or all-out war, through despair . . .'

How bad could things get? That is the very question he seeks to pose now, to draw the parliament and the people's attention to the horror before them all.

'How long will it be,' he says, his voice rasping with emotion, his right index finger stabbing the air, 'before we are drawing upon our conscript youth to service these growing and endless requirements?'[27]

Oh, the horror! Conscripted men sent to fight a war by force of the law? It is *unthinkable*.

The Bulletin, as ever, couldn't disagree more.

'The decision to send the First Royal Australian Regiment to Vietnam has been welcomed throughout Australia,' it editorialises, 'although enthusiasm will be tempered by a heavy heart since Australian casualties in that dirty war are inevitable. But it has been plain to the whole world that South Vietnam is Australia's front line and that the South Vietnamese have been fighting and dying for what are Australia's interests as much as their own.'[28]

•

Just one month after Menzies tells a surprised Australia it is joining a war, HMAS *Sydney* sets sail in the dead of night for Vietnam. On board are troops from 1RAR, all of them Regular Army, of course. True, it is a bit odd to be leaving their home port at such an ungodly hour – 0100 hours – as the lights of Sydney fall behind and they swing to the north, but that's the Army for you. Or maybe it's the Royal Australian Navy. All they care is, they are on their way!

6 June 1965, Enoggera Barracks, Brisbane, fall in

It is an exceedingly odd thing to create an entirely new battalion, remarkable for its bloodless, bureaucratic nature – all sealed orders, endless signed forms and tedious triplicate.

But such is the way of this day, as the 6th Royal Australian Regiment is formed at Enoggera Barracks, under the command of Lieutenant Colonel Colin Maurice Townsend, a lifelong soldier from Duntroon by way of Ingham, whose nickname of 'Mousey' is a reflection of his physical stature and mild manner. (Though he had been a fine soldier himself, and no mistake, particularly shining as a Platoon Commander in Korea, including a notable action in the Battle of Apple Orchard on 22 October 1950, where he had led his men on a raid to rescue a besieged American parachute battalion.)

With him he has several experienced officers like Officer Commanding Administration Company 6RAR, Major Owen O'Brien . . . and Major Harry Smith commanding D Company, and a veteran Regimental Sergeant Major in George Chinn.

The nucleus of 6RAR's soldiers comes by transferring half the Regular Army soldiers from the 2nd Battalion, Royal Australian Regiment, some 300 in all. Their task for the moment – placed in Bravo and Charlie Companies – will be to continue some training while also preparing for the arrival of another 300 or so men after the current harvest of newly recruited National Service conscripts have completed their Basic Training and 6RAR can get its fair share. That will include, perhaps, some of the Nashos that might prove worthy of being officers in these new companies.

Late June 1965, Sydney, lights, cameraman, action!

Still others head off to the intake, with great reluctance. Not so far away in Sydney, young Gordon Sharp is more than a little underwhelmed when his number comes up. Enlisting for National Service on 30 June 1965 had not remotely been a part of his plans. At 21 he is currently holding down a dream job as a television cameraman on the smash hit *Mavis Bramston Show* in Sydney, and has plans to one day perhaps move into production or even acting himself. Yes, the government has legislated that all permanent employees who are conscripted must be able to resume their positions on return, but he'll still miss out on all the fun of *The Mavis Bramston Show* and two whole years of TV experience.

But short of being – what's that phrase again? – a 'conscientious objector', he has no choice. Look, given his proximity to a certain level of renown, courtesy of the hugely popular show he is working on, it is no surprise the press takes interest in him and he is honest enough to tell them he is opposed to the whole *concept* of conscription.

His mate, John O'Halloran, is not remotely surprised that Sharpie stays with it anyway, and makes no effort to get out.

'It was not within Gordon's makeup to disobey the law,' he will recount. 'In an analogy from his favourite pastime, playing poker, he would have felt obliged to play with the cards he had been dealt.'[29]

O'Halloran and Sharp go way back. They have known each other since their first day at primary school and been with each other all through their time at secondary school, Christian Brothers College in Tamworth. Their parents had become great friends and had even been married on the same day.

John's grandfather had been something of a war hero in World War I, while his father had shirked World War II and done little since. Given the two examples before him, John had decided to do his bit and is so insistent that he will do National Service he even declines his doctor's offer to get him out of it because of a recent foot injury. No, he is going, and that is that.

Very well then, the two old mates will join National Service on the same day, the difference being that to say goodbye to his loving parents, Eric and Roma, Gordon Sharp must head off to Puckapunyal, while his mate O'Halloran will do his Basic Training at Kapooka.

O'Halloran and several other mates leave from Tamworth railway station on the evening of 30 June 1965, headed for Sydney, where Army officials meet them on the platform at Central Station and herd them towards the train that awaits to take them to Wagga Wagga, where buses await to drop them at Kapooka.

And so it goes, all over the country, as the notice is received, decisions are taken . . .

What about you, Paul Large?

Up Coolah way – a tiny town between Dubbo and The Black Stump, with a population of no more than 1000 wringing wet – Paul Large, a young man with five sisters, a settled life with his girlfriend, Noeline, and old black mongrel dog, Monty, and lots of mates with whom he delights in catching craydabs in the creek most weekends, or going out eeling over the range, to have feasts washed down by gallons of beer, does *not* want to go. Why would he? What could be better than this life? When they're not fishing, he and his mates go hunting rabbits and roos in the hills behind Coolah and Bundella, and he knows he is maybe the best shot south of The Black Stump, and certainly west of Woop Woop. Right now he is working at the Mudgee General Post Office, but soon he wants to be a shearer.

His mates agree, and encourage him to look at ways of getting out of it. Feigning a medical condition is one obvious way, while you could also play the 'conscientious objector' card where you say it's against your religion or your conscience or something to fight. Some of his mates are quite rabid about it. Tell 'em to get fucked!

In the end Paul insists. He is not going to cop out. He will do his duty, he will go.

Doug Salveron, of Coorparoo on the edge of Brisbane, a quietly spoken young chap who has *no* interest in joining the Army, also reluctantly decides he must do his duty, whatever that may be.

It is the same with Kenny Gant, a butcher's apprentice at Brissie's famous Edwards & Lambs. One day he comes home and simply says, 'Mum, that's it.'

'What's what?' she replies.

'I'm going away.'

'You're not.'

'Yeah,' Kenny replies. 'We're going, got me number called up.'

Lots of people tell him ways he could get out of it, but Kenny – known as 'Bing' to everyone for his singing ability that could rival Bing Crosby – won't hear of it.

'Mum,' he says, 'I'm not a coward. I wasn't brought up a coward. I'll go along with them.'[30]

Jack Jewry, of Saint Marys in Sydney, who has just married his 19-year-old sweetheart, Susanne – with whom he has been going steady since he was 14 and she was just 13 – is deeply upset at being called up, but after deep reflection and long talks with Susanne, decides to go. It is only two years, darling.

Down in Port Lincoln in South Australia, Errol Noack takes a similar view. This fine-looking and strapping six-footer only just started working with his father as a fisherman four months earlier and doesn't want to leave. But what can he do? As he tells his pastor, Father Fischer: 'I don't want to go to war but I must obey the call to duty. I will go and do my best.'[31]

The key obstacle all must overcome is their medical.

Before designated medicos around the country, they must leave their dignity by the door, bow to authority, drop their shorts and be poked, prodded and pulled for the next 20 minutes or so, even as they answer questions. The idea is to screen out all conscripts who are suffering anything from a heart condition to hernias, diarrhoea to diabetes, hay fever to homosexuality.

1 July 1965, Kapooka, tag, you're it

Phil Norris can barely believe it. They've only just started going out. Everything is happening so fast! When he first had the nerve to ask his young sweetheart Maryanne Matthews out he was a postman in Granville; now he is the one being delivered up to the army, express post.

And of course they had known this day was coming, the day Phil was to leave for National Service training, but it has just rushed upon them so quickly. And someone with the stripes of a Sergeant on his upper sleeve is shouting at all the similarly lost young men milling about.

'You will pick up your bags in your left hand and also your coats in your left hand, leaving your right hand free . . . on command you will march straight ahead . . . on the right there is a platoon area . . . you will not go there . . . that is not your area . . . you will march on to the second area.'[32]

'If you have a red tag, you are going to Puckapunyal. If you have a yellow tag you are going to Kapooka. Move!'[33]

Phil, with a red tag, is off to Puckapunyal and has time for one last lingering look at the weeping Maryanne, before he is . . . gone. Right next to him is Jack Jewry, saying goodbye to his pregnant 19-year-old wife, Susanne. Jack, too, is off to Puckapunyal and, holding his weeping wife closely, promises to write as soon as he gets there.

Similar scenes are taking place all over the country. Up in Queensland, the new recruits gather at the Kelvin Grove Training Area, where Greyhound buses are on standby to take them to the RAAF's Amberley Air Base.

In Western Australia, once vetted at their local recruiting depot, they are assigned an economy-class rail journey across the continent, *bound for glory*, *bound for freedom*, bound for Puckapunyal.

In Tasmania, they too are destined for Puckapunyal.

About half of those in the first intake of Nashos march in to Kapooka just as an intake of Regular Army recruits – who have been there for 10 weeks of boot camp, transformed from gormless civilians to the makings of military might – march out, soon to be posted to their different battalions. No matter that the blokes marching out are broadly of the same age, it feels like men and boys passing in opposite directions on a bridge.

The Australian Regular Army soldiers begin by looking hard, knowing that they are looking at their past – *did we really look like these blokes, lambs to the slaughter, such a short time ago?* – and finish with a malicious glee. For they know better than anyone what awaits the new boys, their future; a little present that will begin opening presently and change them forever.

Dr Forbes, the Minister for the Army, is optimistic about the attitude of these conscripts. Yes, there has been publicity given to anti-war student types and the Labor Party oppose as usual – they oppose everything – but Dr Forbes tells the *Canberra Times* that, 'I would be surprised to find any opposition to recruitment in the ranks of the trainees'.[34]

Really? Yes. Taking another swipe at certain unnamed leaders of the Labor Party – though bigger than a bread-box and rhymes with fall well – the Liberal Minister explains further: 'As a whole, the younger people have a more realistic and down-to-earth approach to the situation than some of their elders.'[35] The *Canberra Times* notes that six down-to-earth youths have failed to report to training in Sydney; they are so down to earth they apparently have gone to ground. An official helpfully informs reporters that 'As yet we are not treating them as defaulters.'[36]

They are just tardy with intent.

1 July 1965, Victoria Barracks, Sydney, compulsive service

Of course, not all young people are against conscription, not even those who are conscripted.

That young fellow there, for example, who has just turned up at the gates of the Army's Victoria Barracks on Sydney's Oxford Street. He is just 21 years old, a restless graphic artist from Sydney by way of Fiji and British Honduras and Trinity Grammar, but David Sabben had been so disappointed when, despite his number coming up, he had *not* been taken in the first intake that he has decided to insist. As he tells the guard on the gate, he wants to join now, and start training immediately!

You *what*?

I'm here. I want to join the army right now, to volunteer for National Service, and start training immediately. Yes, I did a medical and had to admit I broke a bone in my hand playing rugby against Knox Grammar School, but I hope that won't count me out? I want to join now! I got a letter saying they wouldn't take me in this intake, but would consider me for the September intake. I want to go *now*.

Well you can't. You must come back in September like it says on your letter.

But I insist. I want to start my National Service NOW.

It takes a bit to sort out but, more or less to stop this well-spoken, well-educated young man pestering them incessantly, the authorities relent. It is arranged for him to be sent to the 1st Recruit Training Battalion (1RTB) at Kapooka, just outside of Wagga Wagga, and he is on the train south just a little over eight hours after his Call-Up Notice had been issued. There had been so little time to pack he has really just brought his essentials: a change of underwear, his razor, toothbrush and of course his Bible.

For he is certain he is answering God's call. From a family that lived with the Holy Bible, the idea of men as warriors doing their duty is in his very bones. After all, who does not know the Lord's instruction in the Book of Numbers, Chapter 1, Verses 2 & 3: 'Take ye the sum of all the congregation of the children of Israel, after their families, by the house of their fathers, with the number of their names, every male by their polls. From 20 years old and upward, all that are able to go forth to war in Israel: thou and Aaron shall number them by their armies.'

Look, if you can't see it, Dave certainly can.

'My logic,' he will recount, 'is that if God loves me as much as He loved Israel, then I should do as He told Israel to do.'[37]

Like Kokoda, Tobruk, El Alamein, Gallipoli and the Western Front – young men are happy to do their bit, and even test themselves against whatever Indonesia's bellicose leader General Sukarno and his men can throw at them. Or maybe, they might be sent to Malaysia, where the Malayan Communist Party was raising trouble. There is even an outside chance they might wind up in Vietnam, where the Americans had landed a year before, and there had even been some Australians training the locals.

•

Opposition Leader Arthur Calwell is one who is slow to anger and generally not a man for whom attacks come naturally. But this *latest* pronouncement from Sir Robert Menzies on a trip to London is outrageous.

At a black-tie gathering at The Australian Club of London, the Prime Minister has stated plainly, 'We are at war . . . make no mistake about it. There is a war going on in South Vietnam.'[38]

Really?

Well, shouldn't the PM share that information with the Australian public?

'Although two months have elapsed since the Australian commitment of troops to Vietnam,' the gnarled leader of the ALP rasps to the press, 'the public has waited in vain for some statement of purpose or objectives in this war. And if Australia is at war, with whom . . . ? Our troops are committed to fight and die in this struggle against the Viet Cong, but the Prime Minister has derided the idea of entering into any talks with the Viet Cong or giving recognition of the fact that the National Liberation Front, which is their political organisation, even exists . . .

'Are we at war with North Vietnam? If so, why was war not declared before now or why is it still not declared? If we are at war, at what time and on what day did Australia declare war, who declared it and against whom was it declared?

'Are we at war with China? If so, why are we selling hundreds of millions of pounds of strategic materials to China each year, and all the time trying to promote more trade? . . .

'Above all, if we are at war, why have neither the Parliament nor the people been told clearly and why we are at war, what are the objectives of the war, and what sacrifices are expected of the nation as well as our conscripted youth?'[39]

In sum, this is *hopeless*. Australia appears to have drifted into an undeclared war, putting it squarely in the middle of a civil war in which the only certainty is that there will be no winners and many deaths.

CHAPTER TWO

HOME ON THE RIFLE RANGE

Around 90 per cent of the diggers in my platoon were conscripts from the first intake. At that stage if you asked me the difference between a Nasho and a regular soldier I would have said the Nasho was a fair bit smarter. Many of the regulars had joined the army because they were poorly educated and found it difficult to get employment elsewhere.[1]

Lieutenant John O'Halloran, 6RAR

Victorious warriors win first and then go to war, while defeated warriors go to war first and then seek to win.

Sun Tzu, *The Art of War*

It's silly talking about how many years we will have to spend in the jungles of Vietnam when we could pave the whole country and put parking stripes on it and still be home by Christmas.

Governor Ronald Reagan, quoted in *The Fresno Bee*, 10 October 1965

Mid-1965, Kapooka, gnashing the Nashos

Christ Almighty, what is this going to be like?

The National Service recruits don't have to wait long to find out. The very second their buses lurch to a halt inside the gates of the Kapooka Army Recruit Training Centre, they meet their friendly Sergeants:

'RIGHT. GET OFF THIS FUCKING BUS OR YOU'LL DO PUSH-UPS UNTIL THIS PLACE IS BELOW SEA LEVEL.'[2]

For some reason we cannot yet fathom, the red-faced man currently screaming at us appears very cross? Even though we haven't done anything yet that he can possibly be cross about?

But yes, he is carpet-biting mad, and *also* as mad as a cut snake, and will remain so until we leave. We Nashos are going to have to get used to hearing abuse as standard fare in our every interaction with these men, an abuse that starts – *right fucking now!* – with being addressed as 'Girls'.

FORM UP IN THREE RANKS, GIRLS![3]

For variation, there are other epithets.

'Get over there you dickhead, not there you stupid arsehole. What are you a fuckwit or something? Answer me you penis-with-ears . . . or I'll come down on you so fucking hard you won't get up for a month . . . What's your name, you dopey prick?'[4]

Phil Norris, Sir, and I am a postie from Granville.

THAT IS YOUR PAST LIFE, AND BARELY EXISTS ANYMORE! YOU ARE IN THE ARMY NOW, AND WE ARE GOING TO MAKE SOLDIERS OF YOU!

An early part of their training is to have the chain of command practically tattooed on their foreheads.

'At the top of the pile there's the General.'[5]

Got it.

'Then there's the Brigadier, the Full Colonel, Lieutenant Colonel, Major, Captain, Full Lieutenant, Second Lieutenant, Warrant Officers 1 and 2.'

Right.

'Staff Sergeant, Sergeants, Corporal, Lance Corporal and Private.'

Okay.

'Then there are rats and mice, blowflies and cockroaches. Then there are YOU FUCKING COCKROACHES.'[6]

Got that, Girls?

Yes, Sergeant.

Who?

Yes, SERGEANT!

'What are ya . . . ?'

'SHIT, SERGEANT.'[7]

(It is not *always* this way. Some Sergeants and officers have already been counselled not to needlessly abuse the fresh conscripts with unnecessarily rough language, which will see some being told in training such things as: 'Cons, get your arms up or you'll be sexually intercoursed!'[8])

First up they are each given a regimental number, a uniform, ill-fitting boots and a short back and sides haircut, meaning that within hours of their arrival the previously disparate group from diverse backgrounds starts to *look* the same, right down to the 'giggle hat', the green floppy specimen they're given to top everything off, the one that makes everybody who wears it look equally ridiculous.

Oh, and don't forget your webbing.

Our what?

Your webbing. It is like a vest with a heavy belt, with many pouches and hooks, in which, and from which, they can hang and secrete military paraphernalia from rations to ammunition to grenades to material for first aid. They may not be soldiers yet, but they can at least start to look like soldiers!

The challenge will be to get them to fight like soldiers, in cohesive unison, with the skills and fitness required to be a powerful fighting force capable of withstanding whatever the enemy throws at them.

For now they must settle in, in groups of a dozen or so, to some World War II vintage 'Nissen huts' – rather like half of a large and rusty corrugated-iron tank put on its side with doors added either end – which seem specifically designed to keep them cold, wet and uncomfortable at all times they are in there.

Not for nothing does Kapooka mean 'place of winds', the only surprise being that it isn't 'place of *cold* winds'.

John Robbins is one young Nasho – a one-time Queensland jackaroo – who is coming to the conclusion that 'army intelligence' just might be a contradiction in terms. Like now, his first night at Kapooka, as he receives his first pair of Army boots, tied together. But as he tells the 'NCO' – which is apparently a 'Non Commissioned Officer', as if that explains anything at all – there is a problem.

'I've got a pair of boots here, one is right and one is wrong. I have got a size ten and a size eight.'

The Sergeant considers the statement, then replies: 'What do you want, them both the same?'

'Well, it would help a bit, wouldn't it?' answers Robbins, a little bemused.

'You're a bit of a smart bastard, aren't you?'

'Well,' says Robbins with a grin, 'if you think I am that good, why don't you put me down for the intelligence corps?'

The NCO puts him down for an immediate bollocking instead, and Robbins will be clumping his way through weeks of ill-fitting boots before things are sorted. Welcome to the army, Nasho. We don't like smart bastards here.[9]

Every morning from now starts at 0530 hours – not '5.30' or 'half-past five', but 0530 hours, so get it right! – when they have an hour to shower, dress, make their bunks so well you can bounce coins off them, polish their boots so they shine like the sun, clean their rifles, before being on mess parade at 0630 hours.

And now the real fun starts . . .

And lefffft!

And leftttt!

And left, right, lefffft!

Marching, of course, is the least of it. As part of their Basic Training they must also reach a high level of fitness and strength which can only be accomplished through relentless training – no-one will leave here who can't run a mile in under six minutes. They must learn how to assemble, load and fire military weapons, as well as disassembling them, cleaning them, maintaining them, and doing it all at pace. And now do it with blindfolds on, because you are going to have to be able to do this in the dark, to clear a jam. Get through this obstacle course! Climb this rock face! And now we want you to change from full battle-order kit into sandshoes and running shorts in no more than two minutes. Quick lunch. Back into battle-order kit in three minutes, and now we will complete a nine kilometre march in under an hour. And maintain the base! Nothing has changed from the oldest army training dictum of the lot: 'If it moves, salute it; if it doesn't move, pick it up; and if you can't pick it up, paint it.'[10]

Work as part of a team, as we practise section movement and fire!

Sorry, what, you dickheads?

You don't know what a 'section' is? It is the basic building block of the army: ten soldiers, usually composed of four riflemen, two scouts who take the forward positions on patrol, a machine-gunner and his 'number 2', all commanded by a Corporal and his second-in-command, the Lance Corporal.

And from there it goes broadly in threes. Three sections form the heart of a platoon commanded by a Lieutenant, with his second-in-command usually being a grizzled Sergeant, not forgetting a radio operator and a medic to make Platoon HQ complete.

Three rifle platoons of about 34 men each form the heart of a company. Four companies form the heart of a battalion, and most of you blokes will likely wind up in either the 5th or the 6th Battalion of the Royal Australian Regiment, which are being formed up as we speak.

You have to learn it all, and quickly!

The idea, of course, is to give them the very basic knowledge and skills of being an Australian soldier – together with the requisite fitness and toughness – and from now on their days will be filled with endless lectures and drills. It means they must start early, and finish late.

Each day before dawn, the wintry fog that Wagga Wagga specialises in drifts in to each Nissen hut, usually through broken windowpanes, wraps itself around each sleeping recruit and makes sure that they are freezing right down to the very marrow of their bones. If this is the 'fog of war' that they have heard about, let the record show they *hate* it, and all the more so when a bawling Sergeant gets them up and out of bed and soon standing to attention before making sure the bed is properly made.

Everything is now regulated on the 24-hour clock – in which the day is measured from midnight to midnight, divided into 24 hours. Breakfast is at 0630 hours, while training starts at 0730 hours, and on particularly full days, they will go till 1900 hours.

A further curiosity for the recruits is that, as a holdover from spending so long on France's Western Front in the Great War, the Australian Army uses the metric system of measurement for everything from the range of its rifles and artillery, to its machinery and transportation and things like fitness assessments. If you want to take your place in this man's army, for example, you have to pass the Basic Fitness Assessment which consists of 50 sit-ups done to a cadence of around two seconds per repetition, seven 'heaves' (chin-ups) without faltering, add to that running five kilometres in 25 minutes or less. No, they are not expected to beat that time in the first two days, but they are required to do it not long after they put their kits down so their instructors can know from the start just how much work remains to be done to turn them into actual *soldiers*.

Abuse is a constant.

'Get a fucken move on!'

'You're running out of time, slackarse. This is a piece of piss. A fucken girl could do it faster than you!'

'Get the lead out!'[11]

Most of them struggle, though there is one notable exception. His name is Bob Buick and he has already done all this before, having trained at Kapooka when he first joined the Australian Regular Army as an 18-year-old in 1959 before going on to serve with 2RAR in Malaya. Earlier this very year he had been discharged, before thinking better of it, and now here he is, joining up again, going through precisely the same training.

The things that the other much younger and wet-behind-the-ears recruits are struggling to learn, Buick can do without blinking or thinking. As he was later to state, 'I'd been in the army for six years. I was a qualified Sergeant when I got back in again so I knew the ropes and I didn't do anything at Kapooka.'[12]

For the rest of them it is hard yakka and no mistake.

With just 10 weeks to work with, there is much that has to be done, as fitness is only the beginning. Over this next intense period they will also have to get up to speed on everything from 'Drill & ceremonial'; weapons handling; developing proficiency in all aspects of operating and effectively firing a L1A1 7.62 millimetre Self-Loading Rifle; field craft, which includes navigating cross-country, finding shelter in the bush and living off the land; combat first aid and hand signals.

The last is particularly important as they learn how, as a section of 10 or so men, they can move through the bush in the most effective manner, following the hand signals of their commander. Speed up: *Clenched fist, up and down motion from elbow.* Slow down: *Flat, open hand, up and down motion from elbow.* Enemy ahead: *Thumbs down.* Obstacle ahead: *Arms crossed.*

The signals are also used for communicating with each other, as they become ever more silently cohesive as a lethal, fully functioning unit.

Forward scouts are out the front, looking for the enemy, booby traps and obstacles. Machine-gunners are next, then riflemen, signallers and last but definitely not least, the rear scout (also known as 'Tail End Charlie' – or more affectionately, 'Arse End Arnold'). Each section also has a Section Commander (usually a Corporal), and a Section 2IC (usually a Lance Corporal). The soldiers come to understand: they are not just individuals. They are part of a strong but malleable structure uniquely designed, from probing to attack to defence in a split second, and each man must learn not only his own role but also the roles of those around him so that each person can build their own response on the known foundations of the actions of others. Changes to the structure can be ordered by the leader through the use of just a couple of fingers if necessary – a tap on the head, followed by two fingers to the bicep is an order for the Corporal, with the two stripes on his arm, to come forward.

They need to go through drill after drill so that at first contact with the enemy, or first sighting, they will react instantaneously through trained instinct.

Most instructive are the firing drills, which not only tend to separate the men from the boys, but more importantly the hard country boys from the soft city slickers.

With the exception of those city boys who have been to elite private schools with a cadets program – men like Dave Sabben – most of them are so hopeless it is clear they couldn't hit a barn door with a wet mop, let alone put a bullet in a small circle at a distance of a hundred metres.

But the real country boys, like Paul Large, who could fire a gun at about the same time they could ride a bike and certainly by the time they could ride a horse, are outstanding. Back at Coolah – where he was one of the 'free-range ferals' with his mates Mick, Grimmy and Bogan, always rambling around the country hunting rabbits, kangaroos and whatever else came up – Paul could shoot a rollie out of a sparrow's mouth at 100 metres on a windy day. And now they want him to shoot a still target in perfect conditions?

The perpetually smiling 'Largey' as he is universally known can barely stand to wait his turn, is bursting to 'show 'em how', and so he does, achieving the perfect score. 10/10!

The others are impressed.

But not the laughing Largey.

What else was he going to get?

Next time, give him a hard one.

Now, unbeknownst to most of the soldiers, even while they are going through many of the early drills some of them are being closely observed to see which of them might be officer material. If so, they are in line to be picked for the Officer Training Course, a program up on the outskirts of Sydney designed to take simple soldiers and turn them into highly trained leaders of men. It will go for only 22 weeks, just under half the time of the officer courses in the Regular Army.

And there will be no need for you to learn the finer points of comportment at formal dinners – passing port to the left, and toasting the Queen – as formal dinners are not in your future.

What they want is to produce officers who are outstanding at one thing only: commanding a platoon capable of excelling in counter-revolutionary jungle warfare in a South-East Asian environment. As Australia is moving rapidly from three battalions to nine battalions with its defence expansion, there is an enormous dearth of experienced officers to go round, and while there will be a lot of promotions across the board, with most experienced ranks moving up, the only way to get enough Lieutenants in position to take command of the freshly created platoons in the new Royal Australian Regiments is to put the best of the Nashos through an officer course.

But how to sort who is capable, *and* willing?

A fortnight into their training course, the National Service recruits are, as they have learnt to be, 'standing to attention', with their clenched fists by their sides, as they stare straight ahead, when the bellicose 'Company Sergeant Major' – (not sure what that is, but it has authority, with no heart and a big mouth, and always seems pissed off) – makes an announcement.

'Everyone who has got the Leaving Certificate, *and* would like to be considered for officer training, step forward.'

It is one of those moments.

Some blokes are not interested, on principle.

Paul Large, though a natural leader and popular with his peers, is, like many Australian soldiers, of the view that the most telling feature about officers is that they have tickets on themselves. The officer course is not for him. He is one of the boys.

No matter. There are plenty of others to choose from.

One who is interested is the Tamworth man, John O'Halloran.

'The thought of becoming an officer appealed to me even though it hadn't crossed my mind until then,' he will recount. 'The pay was higher, going immediately to a Corporal's wage, and the thought of them turning a larrikin like me into an officer and maybe a gentleman tickled my fancy.'[13]

For his part, Dave Sabben is also interested, feeling that, 'If I was going to give two years of my life to the army, I might as well get as much out of it as I can, and have them teach me things I don't know.'[14]

One way or another, the courses of entire lives change in a split second, it is just that it is not yet apparent.

All up, several hundred applicants have stepped forward – one in ten of the common herd – and are soon separated from the mob, where it is explained they will be going through a few days of tests to see if the reckoning is they have what it takes. Those who are picked will depart for Sydney almost immediately, where a further winnowing will take place as they sort the chaff from the wheat.

All of the prospective candidates are put together in groups of eight and put through several days of task exercises – physical problem-solving requiring teamwork, with no nominated leader – while they are closely observed by assessment officers holding clipboards and a grudge.

For their first task they are told by a barking Sergeant Major: 'The sandpit is a river. Here are some ropes and poles. Get that barrel across the river without touching the sand. You're being timed. Go.'[15]

In this way the natural leaders should emerge, those capable of coming up with the right solution, convincing the others that their plan is better than the alternatives, and then actually succeeding in pulling it off. Who resists? Who is just tagging along with no notable opinions one way or another?

Now, put two bricks in your backpack and let's see if you can cover eight kilometres in under an hour. We don't expect you to be the fittest of all your soldiers, but you certainly have to be on the top shelf.

Within two days, at least half of the candidates have been sent back to the ranks, while the rest are put through more tests.

For now we want you to change uniforms before the next exercise while we put you on the clock – and assess how you get on with fellow candidates when put under pressure like this, stumbling over each other in your haste.

Who becomes easily flustered, and starts to make mistakes under pressure? How do they get on with their peers when the tide is not going their way and the wind is against them? When that happens, do they know how to change course to achieve a better result? How long does it take?

Time, gentlemen, please!

Now, let's see if you can get through some of the physical tests we are giving the usual soldiers, but let's see if you can do the same thing with a couple more bricks in your backpacks. We want only the finest physical specimens to be officers, the ones who will always naturally be in the rough lead, no matter their level of exhaustion.

Candidates must face interviews with an array of officers who measure the cut of their jib by determining how clearly the young men communicate, what kind of views they have on the politics of the day and their general knowledge.

'What do you think about the French defeat at Dien Bien Phu? Were the French right to be there? Why were the Americans helping them?'

What do they know?

Can they think on their feet?

Is there *any* sign of sympathy for Communism?

All right, five minutes from now, we want you to speak for exactly that long on, say, what the price of tea in China might be next year.

Can they cope with pressure? Can they communicate clearly, and *sound* like a leader?

And now talk to your peers about your life, the things you've done, the things you've seen.

Are these blokes open books?

Or are they hiding something?

Now look at this map showing rivers, hills and open field. Just say you had to set up a base somewhere in the territory that this map covers, where would you build it, and why?

Who among them seems to have an innate sense of military strategy?

Who can easily justify the decision they have made?

Day by day those who don't make the grade are winnowed out, and sent back to the ranks.

Now come to the Officers' Mess, for drinks with us and our wives.

Who flirts with our wives?

Who drinks too much wine?

We want officers *and* gentlemen, and any ungentlemanly behaviour will see a large black line drawn through your name.

And now sit down for a chat with individual officers on what you think about leadership, before talking to all the officers together. Are you engaging? Do you have the confidence necessary to *lead* men into battle?

Oh yes, and a written exam to test your general knowledge, before other tests on Maths and English. After all, we need to determine your aptitude to do things like give precise co-ordinates from a map to guide artillery support, so a grasp of mathematical principles is important.

And do you have sufficient grammar, spelling and expression to write totally clear orders to subordinates that are legible and impossible to misinterpret?

From the first, one of the standouts is Dave Sabben whose education shines through in all the written tests which he tops or near tops. Down in Puckapunyal – where precisely the same threshing out program is taking place – Gordon Sharp similarly has a calm about him under pressure, and an ability to perform *in extremis*, that the assessors cannot ignore.

Yes, but can they lead?

At the conclusion of every stage, candidates are removed without explanation – a tap on the shoulder and a finger pointing them back to the common herd of soldiers. It is gruelling for those who remain, and Dave Sabben will long recall the words of one of the grizzled NCOs involved.

'Don't think this assessment's jus f'yer selection, wetback. If yer in, yer next six munths is gunna make yer think this wuz a picnic.'[16]

Onwards.

The final step is social drinks to determine if you can hold your liquor like a gentleman, and don't have any unfortunate habits like stubbing your smokes out on the carpet.

On the third morning, the names of the men who have made it through are announced. Among them is indeed Dave Sabben, who has sailed through with remarkable ease while so many others have struggled.

Another is Gordon Sharp.

Yes, the Tamworth man had spoken out against the whole concept of conscription in the first place, but it is not held against him at the Puckapunyal officer training. All that counts is that he clearly has talent in the realms of leading men, is respected by his fellow soldiers, and with the right training really could be an outstanding officer.

At Kapooka, both Sabben and O'Halloran, with other successful candidates, are whisked away with barely time to say goodbye to the other Nasho soldiers they had come in with, just over a fortnight ago.

As they leave in buses for Wagga Wagga airport, the other blokes are out on the parade ground, practising marching: *and left, and left, leffft, leffft, left, right left . . .*

Not for O'Halloran and Sabben now, the endless drills of Basic Training. They are two of just 120 soldiers – out of the hundreds who had volunteered – to be given the chance to become an officer, to be able to lead men into battle.

The Douglas DC-4 plane that awaits them on the tarmac is soon flying them in roaring fashion to Sydney, where buses take them to their new home: Scheyville Officer Training Unit just outside of Windsor, and conveniently situated right on the edge of Scheyville National Park, which comes complete with precisely the kind of natural terrain to break the weak and harden the tough.

Here at Scheyville, as soon as they get off the buses to stand to rigid attention on the parade ground, it is explained to them they will be busy as never before for the next 22 weeks, seeing if they have what it takes to be a National Service junior officer.

There is simply no time for the usual course with you National Service blokes. For one thing, you have only signed up for two years. For another, the way the situation is looking in Asia – with all of Borneo, Malaysia, Indonesia and lately, Vietnam, causing trouble – we will need officers sooner, rather than later.

So we have just a little over five months to turn you into men capable of commanding an infantry platoon of 30 soldiers 'to engage in Counter-Revolutionary Warfare (CRW) in a South East Asia environment'.[17]

You will learn all about contact drills, field craft, map-reading, field signals, calling in artillery – just like it says on the can, everything you need to know to survive in a counter-revolutionary war against guerrillas.

One of the first things you must grasp is the importance of communication, including radio net procedures – how each platoon, company and battalion has its own frequency, just like the artillery, the RAAF, the Armoured Personnel Carriers and so forth – and it is through using coded language on those nets that you can give orders, take orders and receive information, without the enemy having any clue what you are doing.

'Sunray' is the Commander of any unit.

'Shelldrake' is the Artillery.

A 'Sitrep' is a situation report, for the current situation of any unit.

A 'Locstat' is a location statement, usually a series of numbers to give your grid reference on a map.

'Ironsides' refer to Armoured Personnel Carriers and tanks.

'Foxhounds' are infantry.

And so on . . .

Now, don't think because you have left the grunts behind at Kapooka you will be escaping their Basic Training. Oh no, you have to do that, *too*. Your Officer Training is on top of that. We have you for the next 150 days, less just four days off, and in that time you will be in training for an average of 18 hours a day – most of the physical stuff during the daylight hours, most of the lectures in the evenings. Among other things you will be taught how to expertly maintain, aim and fire any number of weaponry, and, when all else fails, the finer points of unarmed combat so you can completely disable even much bigger and stronger enemy soldiers.

A lot to get through?

Yes. You will have to *run* between lessons and no fewer than a third of you will fail and be returned to Kapooka, Puckapunyal or Singleton to rejoin your Recruit Training Battalion, if early in the course, or direct to a unit if later in the course. The job now is not only to confirm if you are indeed officer material but, if so, to make you into a First Class one!

At least now that they are prospective 'officers and gentlemen' the days of Nissen huts are long behind them and each of them has his own room – and an Officers' Mess to dine in, together with an impressive formal uniform all in white and one in blue – but just like the Nissen hut it matters little because there is so little time spent inside it.

After John O'Halloran puts his duffel bag in the room assigned to him and makes the bed in the regulation manner – with the sheets so tight with hospital corners that you could bounce a coin off it – he is as delighted as he is stunned to see a familiar face from Tamworth.

Gordon Sharp!

'What in the fuck are you doing here?' the younger of the old schoolmates gurgles happily, clapping him on the back.

The answer is: the same as you, Johnno. Looks like more fun than being a grunt soldier, the pay will be better if we get through it, and there is a certain cachet in being an officer if we make it. Besides, the chicks will love it!

But there is little time to chat as they already must race to their first review on the parade ground. Each day begins with an 0530 hours Reveille – that bloody bugle! a *quick* breakfast and then start working as sections in tight pods of six, with a grizzled guidance officer watching their every move and occasionally barking . . .

What's this, Sabben, a *fly* in your room?

You are charged with keeping a pet.

A dead fly?

You are charged with killing a pet.

We told you to keep your rooms spotlessly clean, and we mean it. Pay attention to *detail*, in this and all things. Getting the detail right can turn a battle. And if you don't think this is a fair charge, fine. Let's see how you cope with unfairness, the same way you must learn to cope with everything else.

Cope!

Putting the fitness, the knowledge, the attention to detail and the ability to cope all together, they go on field exercises in the wild country around the Hawkesbury River, and more major exercises in the Pokolbin State Forest, bush-bashing in different formations, practising both how to react to an ambush, and how to set up an ambush of your own.

The whole while, they are being assessed – and once again those who don't make the grade get a quiet tap on the shoulder and the bum's rush back to Kapooka or Puckapunyal. There is no fanfare. It is nothing for the others to come back from a brutal day to find the room next to them empty, and their mate gone.

Onwards.

Dave Sabben, his superiors note, is outstanding from the first, most particularly in all things academic. He not only tops most subjects, but in map-reading he scores an extraordinary 100 per cent.

Which is as well, because map-reading is a key skill. To be able to glance at the straight lines and swirling squiggles on a page and instantly conjure hills, valleys, rivers and ravines is to be able to navigate precisely, understand where likely threats will be coming from, and most importantly be able to work out exactly where you are, where the enemy is, and how to bring artillery shells crashing down on his noggin.

Sabben fits easily into the army; yes it has ridiculous discipline, ludicrous rules and a light sprinkling of daily bastardisation, but to someone who attended Trinity Grammar School as a boarder, it feels a little like home. And when it comes to studies, unlike school, there is a real point to every exercise. This is not arcane algebra, and memorising French conjugations. It is learning skills that may very well be the difference between life and death, not just for you, but for the men you are entrusted to lead. So *concentrate*. As to all the pressure and provocation that they must deal with every day in officer training, Sabben's simple solution works for him: 'Suppress the ego, maintain the output.'[18] Well put, and faithfully followed by this young man who is finding somewhere he fits in the world.

For the most part their instructors – veterans from World War II and such campaigns as Korea, Borneo and Malaya – are harsh but fair, notwithstanding that some of them have clear resentment at these young blokes taking a short-cut to being officers, even though it is their very job to facilitate it. Everyone is in uncharted waters, even them.

'They were very difficult to teach indeed as they were bloody smart,' one instructor would recall. 'It was fast-paced learning as we crammed four years' training into six months.'[19]

Beyond the formal instruction, the cadet officers also learn values; bits of advice from their veteran instructors that will remain with them – or at least with those with whom their message resonates.

'Do *not* fraternise with your diggers,' Warrant Officer Bill Lapthorne, a Korean veteran, tells his cadets. 'If you come under fire you want them to carry out your orders and it has to be an instantaneous reaction. You don't want them thinking why should I follow orders from him because he is just one of us. He is even a bigger drunk than I am.'[20]

When you're in the jungle, stay off the tracks! It doesn't matter how much longer it takes, the tracks make it too easy for the enemy to set you up with booby traps and ambushes. Bush-bash. Move slowly. Only put your foot down on virgin bush.

Your best friend in the jungle is the wildlife. You mustn't disturb it; the sounds of nature are a sign that all is well. As long as you can hear it, you know Charlie isn't nearby. And as long as they can hear it, they know YOU aren't nearby. If it goes silent, even for a second, shits are trumps.

And when you're under fire, don't worry about the sound of bullets whizzing past your ears. That's proof you're still breathing. Never forget: 'You never hear the round that hits you.'

More formally, there are lectures on *The Principles of Leadership*.

1. Know yourself and seek self-improvement.
2. Be proficient.
3. Seek and accept responsibility.
4. Lead by example.
5. Provide direction and keep your team informed.

6. Know and care for your people.
7. Develop the potential of your people.
8. Make sound and timely decisions.
9. Build the team and challenge their abilities.
10. Communicate effectively.[21]

Truly? It feels more like we're learning how to open a new branch of IBM, rather than lead a platoon in battle.

Seriously.

'Know and care for your people'? Are they auditioning to be benevolent monarchs, or kill people? Is this about learning how to be a more vicious fighting force, or getting a touch of Norman Vincent Peale, *How to Win Friends And Influence Soldiers*. Still the officer candidates soak it all up dutifully, making notes and learning what they can to fight a 'modern' war.

•

The wheels of the bus are going round and round as the Nashos head back to Kapooka from an exercise when a singalong starts, featuring every old faithful from 'Return to Sender' to 'A Pub With No Beer' all trotted out and sung in various competing but cheerful keys. But now something remarkable occurs . . . as the oldest and most beloved of all old chestnuts breaks out:

O Danny boy, the pipes, the pipes are calling
From glen to glen and down the mountainside

The remarkable bit? How the other voices fall away in awe, as the tones of one singer are so strong, so pure, it would be indecent to try to complement them, let alone compete:

The summer's gone and all the roses falling
'Tis you, 'tis you must go and I must bide

Who is it? It's Private Kenny 'Bing' Gant, and he sings alone now; and bloody hell, he *could* give Der Bingle a run for his money; his beautiful baritone soaring effortlessly close to tenor and sweeping back down beautifully at the fall of the line.

But come ye baaaack when summer's in the meadow
Or all the valley's hushed and white with snow

I'll be here in sunshine or in shadow
O Danny boy, O Danny boy, I love you so

It is something unexpected and beautiful, Kenny's voice bringing a lump to the throat of every man in the rattling bus that bumps and . . . stops. Even the driver wants to hear Kenny sing clearly. Go on, son:

O Danny boy, the stream flows cool and slowly
And pipes still call and echo 'cross the glen
Your broken mother sighs and feels so lowly
For you have not returned to smile again.

Kenny stops and all applaud. He grins and gives a mock bow to true cheers as the beaming bus driver starts up and they head off once more.

Back at Kapooka and Puckapunyal the training of the soldiers themselves also proceeds apace . . . at some pace in fact, as they get ever fitter and tougher, and more adept with their weaponry. By now their SLR rifles feel like extensions of their arms.

Every man is also now expert in using a weapon that few will actually use, if all goes well, the Owen sub-machine gun. It was beloved by Diggers of World War II for the fact that – despite having a killing range of not much more than the length of a cricket pitch – it is so reliable! Even well into the last stretch of the campaign against the Japanese on the Kokoda Track, the ol' Owen could be counted on to burst forth when you pulled the trigger – the only thing is it gives such a kick when you pull the trigger that you have to *lean into it*, and brace!

Speaking of bracing, each morning they do just that as the day begins with a Sergeant with a voice like a foghorn – it only has one volume, LOUD, and can rattle windows – rousing them out of their bunks for a quick breakfast in 'the mess hall' before the soldiers' days are filled with instruction.

Over the coming weeks they learn how you clean and fire mortars. They come to understand how to set up a defensive perimeter when in the bush, with your guns to the fore and positioned. They are given expert instruction on how you could penetrate such a perimeter when *you* were attacking; how you set up an ambush; how to react when ambushed – GET OUT OF THE KILL ZONE!

Determine the source of the attack! Bring fire to bear! What are they firing at you with? A machine gun? It is probably at least a section of

10 men. Two machine guns? More likely a platoon, of 30 men. How are they positioned? How can you best outflank them? How can you use the lie of the land to help you and deny them?

The key is to make your *collective* reaction instantaneous, and make sure that once the enemy launch their ambush, you attack them. Merely 'getting down' automatically means you are in the very kill zone they have planned for you, and you will more than likely be killed in the cross-fire. No, you must all fight your way out of the kill zone, by practising these drills over and over again until your nose bleeds.

More or less the same applies when you come under artillery and mortar fire. Yes, take shelter on the instant, but the key is to *move*! Work out where they are firing from, and then get there as quickly as you can. They will be weighed down by their weaponry, so you should be able to move faster than them. And even if they are gone, look for the 'base plate', the tell-tale signs of where the mortar was fired from. True, it's usually not a plate at all, and more likely a shallow pit, or a cluster of rocks. But once you've worked out their pattern of past fire, you're a fair chance of not only predicting their future but making sure you have one.

In mid-August, a journalist from the *Canberra Times* visits Kapooka, observes the conscripts closely as they practise rifle drills, talks to their officer instructors and is able to report to his readers: 'Even to the unpractised eye it is obvious that five weeks has been sufficient time for the Army to lay the groundwork for the production of Australia's fighting reserves. Certainly, drill lacks polish, ranks need closing up, dress needs a little more attention, weapon handling is still in its infancy stages, recruits could be fitter, but one must consider that in the eyes of the Army these men five weeks ago were the rawest material available.'

They are getting there!

'"Give us another five weeks and we'll have these fellows looking like soldiers," said one old campaigner at Kapooka.

'The Army is genuinely pleased with the results of the first five weeks of National Service training at Kapooka, but, as one officer said: "It's like teaching a baby to walk".'[22]

'Cept few babies are shouted at to 'Get going!' the way these soldiers are. Nevertheless, that, too, is part of the Army's plan. The fact that all the soldiers are suffering the same at the hands of their brute instructors helps bind them together, as deep bonds are formed and they learn to trust each other when under stress.

Ten weeks in, their Basic Training is complete, and they must separate and specialise. Each one of them must fill in a form to list their preferences of where they wish to go now – to have another three months of being transformed into an infantryman, engineer or signaller, or to master the medical corps, the art of artillery or the delights of transport, catering, dental etc. The system is simple and elegant – the men are formed together in Basic, slotted and allotted a speciality and then will be reassembled in January.

Now, under normal circumstances, after completing Basic Training these newly minted soldiers allotted to infantry would head to Corps Training at the Infantry Centre at Ingleburn Army Camp just southwest of Sydney, but there is no time for that now – it is decided to put them straight into their battalions, to train side by side with members of the Australian Regular Army, most of them going to either the 5th or 6th Battalion of the Royal Australian Regiment, the former based at Holsworthy Barracks in Sydney and the latter at Enoggera Barracks in Brisbane, comprising the two newly established infantry battalions.

Phil Norris, the Granville postie, is among the most thrilled of all as he really has been sent to his top pick, heading off to the School of Artillery at Sydney's North Head, where he is due to undergo a course to turn him into Gunner Norris, if you please.

No, he doesn't have a particular thing for the big guns, but what counts is that his course is in Sydney, which will mean more of a chance to see his girlfriend Maryanne.

•

By this time, very strong friendships have formed between many of the soldiers and, while for most of them the battalion to which they are assigned is little more than a number, what does matter is whether or not they have been assigned to the same battalion as their best mate. Private Paul Large is one who is particularly pleased that his mate Private Dave Beahan from up Armidale way has been posted with him to 6RAR. And they've *both* been placed in 12 Platoon of D Company, under the command of a bloke by the name of Major Harry Smith.

Frank Alcorta, a relatively recent immigrant from Spain's Basque country who had settled in Queensland after a long stint living in the

Amazon, is pleased to be posted to 6RAR's A Company with his mate Ronnie Brett. John Robbins is now best mates with John Heslewood, a bank teller from Brissie and they wind up in 6RAR's Delta Company together, which proves to be made up primarily of Nashos, a prime reason that Regular Army men will be sceptical of them as a fighting unit.

•

At Scheyville, the sun beats down, the beat goes on and the bastard instructors won't let up.

Fie, the drums of war.

Again and again, their instructors try to replicate battle conditions.

You're in command of the platoon. Your platoon is in arrowhead formation and the lead section comes under fire and goes to ground.

What do you do?

'Move my left-hand section around the enemy flank?'

No, I'm asking the questions, you give statements. Give orders with authority, doubt is contagious.

'Move my left-hand section around the enemy flank!'

Better. They've just been pinned down by mortar fire. What do you do *now*?

Quick, you must react!

Who do you move forward? What precise command do you give?

How do you reconfigure your platoon?

Now, your three sections are moving forward in extended formation to the east, when suddenly your extreme left section comes under heavy attack from their left flank. How do you support them?

Correct! You move your extreme right section up to make an 'L' shape, so your right-hand section can fire across the other two sections and bring direct fire to bear on the enemy.

What precise orders do you give?

Quick!

Some react well.

Some freeze. The latter get the tap, and are gone by sundown.

Again and again, the officer candidates are taught about 'appreciations' – how to understand the environment they are operating in, the resources they have, the known resources of the enemy, the best way they can configure their own resources so as to minimise damage to themselves, and maximise damage to the enemy. Your ability to assess and react must become innate, and doing an 'appreciation' under these subheadings will order your thinking, as you proceed on an endless loop.

1. *Aim.* What am I here to do? *What's changed since I last thought about this?*
2. *Friendlies.* What resources do I have? *What's changed since I last thought about this?*
3. *Enemy.* What resources does the enemy have? *What's changed since I last thought about this?*
4. *Time & space.* Ground, weather, time of day, etc. *What's changed since I last thought about this?*
5. *Administration.* Food, water, sleep, ammo, casualties . . . *What's changed since I last thought about this?*

One of the keys, they learn, is to react to changed situations. You must *constantly* be assessing, appreciating and reacting!

'From a commander's point of view,' Sabben will note, 'when you're in the field, on patrols, the changing appreciation is always in your mind, and it's always when you finished at number five question, you go back to number one, and you're always rotating around. Having an appreciation of the situation is the key.'[23]

Mid-September 1965, Enoggera, Delta dawn

Major Harry Smith has been impatient.

Worse than being all dressed up with no place to go is to be in charge of a regiment with just a few officers and only half a battalion's worth of Army regulars. But on this great day, the first of the Nashos arrive, those men who have completed their Basic Infantry Training, and must now be trained up to the next level so they may boast an entirely different range of skills.

Most important for them will be learning how to work as part of a 10-man section, under the command of a Sergeant and Corporal, before, in a few weeks, the sections can learn how to interact as part of a 30-man platoon. Thereafter the platoons can learn how to work together as part of a company before the final step – having the companies work together as part of the whole 850-strong battalion, 6RAR!

And so, for the likes of Paul Large, Dave Beahan and all their new-found mates, it begins. In the bushland near Enoggera they learn how to move silently as an infantry section in whatever action or formation their instructor designates by hand signals. A hand swinging from the rear to the front, means to move forward. A fist moving up and down means move faster – palm down moving up and down means move more slowly. Raising both arms parallel to the ground, on the other hand, doesn't mean you want to take off and are only awaiting the go-ahead from the control tower, it indicates it is time to transform into extended line formation.

And so it goes, as they soon learn to converse by hand signals without even really needing to think about it.

Thumb down means enemy sighted or suspected ahead. And if it is enemy they contact, they learn contact drills – 'fire and movement', whereby while the section's machine-gun group puts down covering fire to keep the enemies' head down, the section's rifle group rapidly advances to a flank, before putting down their own fire to return the favour and committing to an assault through the enemy.

Meanwhile a clenched hand with extended forefinger moving in circular motion means that what the officer requires is for his soldiers to form the classic 'harbour' formation, with machine-gunners and riflemen to the right and left in the likely direction of the known enemy, and the riflemen behind, all protecting the Platoon HQ in the middle, which continues to control them all. (Those selected as machine-gunners are inevitably big brutes of men. They have to be, as the weight alone of hauling the machine gun and ammo is near enough to an extra 30 kilograms, *beyond* that carried by the other soldiers.)[24]

At night, the 'harbour' concept also applies as they set up camp in a defensive position, whereby defensive firepower is to the fore, sentries are on duty, and if the dark of night is interrupted by the flash of a muzzle, everyone knows where everyone else is, and how they should react.

In each building block of the battalion, starting with the sections, the most important thing to protect is the 'brain' of the body, the commanders of each unit – be they Corporals of Sections, Lieutenants of Platoons, Captains of Companies, or whatever – the ones who must be relied on to give the orders that will best protect the whole and allow them to most effectively strike.

As sections they practise patrolling and tracking, refine their skills of navigation and reading maps. There is instruction on firing machine guns, operating radios and dressing wounds, even for those who are not specialist machine-gunners, signallers or medics – for it is important that each man in the section is multi-skilled enough that the section can still operate even when there are casualties.

Taking them through the drills again and again are the Corporals, watched over by the Sergeants, nearly all of them grizzled veterans of campaigns like Korea, Malaya and Borneo.

And of course, in Delta Company, watching the lot of them is Major Smith who, like so many officers in this newly expanded army, is himself newly promoted and eager to prove himself worthy of the higher rank. As energetic as he is demanding – which is saying something – he is assiduous in ensuring that everything is proceeding *exactly* the way he wants it to. Most promisingly, a month after their arrival, his soldiers are no longer strangers to each other and there is a certain common purpose, a sense of *belonging*, in no small part due to the fact that with their short back and sides, common uniform, uniform suffering, and insufferable schedule, living cheek by jowl by towel under the same roof, a certain fraternity has already grown up between them.

The only way to get through this is together, as mates, and already blokes that had never met each other a month ago are inseparable.

Big Paul Large from Coolah is always in the company of Dave Beahan from Armidale; you never see Kenny Gant that Jim Richmond is not right over his shoulder, and a whole group of blokes are forming up around the larrikin personality known as Shorty Brown, always laughing and joking no matter how long the march, how gruelling the exercise. The other Shorty, Shorty Thomas, is always thick as thieves with his best mate, Doug Salveron.

It is early days, but there is already a growing sense that we are no longer a group of disparate and desperate Nashos, so much as proud members of what is often referred to as Delta Company, just as A, B and C companies are often known as Alpha, Bravo and Charlie Companies.

True, Delta Company is still not complete, as two platoons still lack Lieutenants but once those Lieutenants have finished their training at Scheyville, those final two pieces of the puzzle he is building will be dispatched to them.

•

Look, to some people Sydney's North Head seems an odd place to have an Artillery School. It is so scenic, so close to suburbia, so removed from the stark reality of a conflict where artillery would prove necessary . . .

But it actually does make sense. For one thing, both heads of Sydney Harbour had long held defensive infrastructure as Sydney had sought to defend itself from nearly the first days of the colony being established – and the Artillery School had been established on that land. For another, the open space at the top of Manly Hill means that there is room for both a large barracks to house all the soldiers and an artillery range. And finally, there is even scope for the raw artillery crews to practise their skills on targets.

All up, bit by bit, those Nashos like Phil Norris who have completed their Basic Training are now getting specialised training at North Head. From dawn till dusk, they learn their trade: the art and science of firing the 105 millimetre L5 howitzer, designed in Italy and capable of sending a 13 kilogram shell as far as 10 kilometres with an accuracy that, in the hands of experts – which is what you blokes will soon be! – can land within metres of a designated spot, and throw out fatal shell fragments as far as 125 metres from the point of impact. Following the Gunners Course, they will join their unit, the 103rd Battery of the 1st Field Regiment of the Royal Regiment of Australian Artillery, at Holsworthy Barracks, in western Sydney – for further training together as a fully manned battery.

The key is the capacity of the seven-man artillery crew to 'set' the gun accurately, and for every man-jack of you to fulfil your role without error and – if necessary – keep going for hours on end. Remember, it only takes one error, and only a small error at that, and instead of the shell landing on the enemy, it might land on your mates! So, get this right . . .

Each gun crew is led by the Gun Sergeant. The number 2 is the Layer who is responsible for adjusting the sight, traversing the gun on its horizontal axis to the precise specifications given by the Battery Command Post (BCP). Number 3 sets the gun to the precise elevation; opens and closes the breech and pulls the lanyard to fire the gun. Another three in the crew unpack the ammunition, set the fuses, deliver the readied ammunition and load the gun. The 2IC, a Bombardier, carefully ensures the proper preparation of the ammunition where one small error can spell disaster at the 'other end'.

Now, each battery has six guns and when you are all firing at once, you will be receiving directions from the Gun Position Officer (GPO) over what is known as the Tannoy speaker system.

It is for the GPO to determine the powder charge to use – how many bags of cordite to be left in the cartridge case – which affects the distance the round will travel.

Usually, the first call will be 'Adjusting round' to fire one ranging shot so that the Forward Observer (FO), situated close enough to the target that he can observe where it lands, can start to 'walk in' the next shots, offering directions – *'Drop five zero . . . Left five zero . . .'* – so that the shell-fire gets ever more accurate.

When all is in readiness, the GPO orders the Battery to . . . 'Fire!', which will see all six guns in the Battery fire in unison, while announcing to the FO, 'SHOT!' to signal that the round is in flight.

When the FO is satisfied that the shells are right on target, the order is to 'Fire For Effect', so many rounds which he might 'Repeat' until the end of the mission.

They learn the vernacular.

When an infantry unit is in actual contact with the enemy it is called a 'Contact Fire Mission', meaning it is given priority over all other missions. When all available batteries are needed to support one unit, it is time for a 'Regimental Fire Mission'. When shells are landing within 150 metres of your own men, the call is 'Danger Close', which means that extra care must be taken in all settings of the gun – so that even a small error won't kill your own people. With Danger Close, a precisely calibrated instrument called a clinometer is used for the elevation setting to ensure even more accuracy.

Occasionally, when going flat out, 19 to the dozen, they can fire as many as 10 rounds a minute! The crews become a blur as the number 4 puts the shell in the breech, the Layer pulls the lanyard, opens the breech. Then 4, using an asbestos glove, tosses the spent cartridge case out of the way to the rear. Again and again and again!

But be *careful.* No matter how fast you are firing, remember that it takes just one error and your own men can die.

Gunner Phil Norris learns with the best of them, and is popular with his mates – the key difference being that, on their rare days off, while his mates head down the hill to try their luck with the young women of Manly, Phil races straight home to see Maryanne.

•

Those freshly trained Regulars that the National Service recruits had seen marching out when they had first arrived at Kapooka?

Many of them had wound up with 1RAR, which had seen them serve as the third battalion of the American 173rd Airborne. For the last few months they have been working with the Yanks in Bien Hoa province, leaving the Americans astonished at how differently the 'Ossies' do things.

Whereas the Yanks use the locals as servants, the Australians will not allow the locals within a bull's roar of their base which – get this! – they surround with rolls of barbed wire and machine-gun pits! Even more amazing, the Australians regularly don camouflage and go out on silent patrols.

The Australians in turn have been shocked to watch the Yanks saunter out on patrol with transistor radios playing louder than the colours of the insignia on their uniforms. Some of them are actually smoking cigars! And look at the way the Americans fight with massive hardware and firepower, shooting on suspicion and asking questions later – all while hoping to be home by Christmas!

The Australians had reeled, horrified by the Yanks' level of casualties: their own, the enemy's, civilians. Among the many appalling practices they engage in is frequently dropping an Ace of Spades on enemy corpses. The Yanks claim it as part of 'psychological warfare'. The Australians find it distasteful and stupid.

For their part the Yanks find the Australians' approach of carefully seeking out the VC lurking in the bush rather than just destroying every bit of bush they see with napalm before churning it up with a mechanised brigade firing in every direction, as something between gun-shy and . . . quaint. For the life of them, the Australians find the American practice in the jungle, of making as much noise as possible in the *hope* of attracting the enemy to come out and fight, completely ludicrous.

After high-level discussion, it is decided that it is better that they each fight their own patch – with the only remaining problem being to decide what patch will best suit the Australians.

•

Back at Scheyville, after two solid months of unending training, lectures and exams, the officer candidates are granted a weekend's leave. Those who are Sydney-based, like Dave Sabben, are able to go home. Those who come from further afield must make their own arrangements. Some, like Gordon Sharp, John O'Halloran, Laurie Muller and a few of their Tamworth and New England mates and others, camp out at the Long Reef Surf Lifesaving Club on Sydney's Northern Beaches. Inevitably they gravitate to the most iconic beer garden in the area, the Newport Arms Hotel – a place beloved by surfies, rugby players and even the odd bikie.

And who are these wankers walking in?

'Ave a look at 'em!

Their short back and sides, their regulation 'look' – *Army* wankers! Nashos, too stupid to get out of the call-up.

'Some of the local surf boat crewmen and rugby players,' John O'Halloran will recount, 'got a bit annoyed we were drinking at their pub. They were . . . known as The Newport Nasties and wore board shorts and rugby tops.'[25]

The Scheyville Nashos aren't fussed what the Newport Nasties think and ignore them right up until the moment that two of the bigger Nasties pick out O'Halloran and Laurie Muller to pour beer over their heads – the clearest Australian pub signal of the lot for . . . let's have a brawl!

The most played song on the jukebox right now is the Beatles' hit, 'We Can Work It Out', but this is not a case in point . . .

For within seconds, it is *on*.

Both O'Halloran and Muller come up swinging and – fit, strong and now well-trained in unarmed combat as never before – *connecting*. But the Nasties are numerous, and not backing off.

As tables and chairs are turned over, and beer jugs and glasses go flying, the officer candidates of Scheyville are nothing if not relentless. After eight weeks of training for war, this is their first genuine battle, and they don't miss.

'Our unarmed combat instructors would have been proud because we got the better of them,' O'Halloran will recount. 'The big bouncer took our side and after some time kicked the other mob out of their own pub using substandard dress as his excuse.'[26]

Now, where were we?

'We settled in for some more drinking. This was the teamwork we had been trained for.'[27]

Scheyville Nashos 1, Newport Nasties 0.

•

Back at Scheyville by 8 pm on the Sunday evening, they are once again into the training by dawn the next day, and push on, getting harder, stronger, more skilled and better prepared for whatever the future might throw at them.

A case in point is Gordon Sharp, who on an exercise getting over and through an obstacle course while carrying a rifle with full kit, throws himself on one of the high scramble nets but loses his grip and falls to the ground some three metres below – knocking himself out and breaking both wrists. The only upside is it allows his mates to practise some of their new-found skills as battlefield medics, and apply makeshift splints before rousing him and getting him to some real doctors at Concord Hospital, who put both arms in plaster before Gordon Sharp heads back on a very quick trip home to Tamworth.

'There's your way out,' his cousin Don tells him with glee, 'if you don't want to go on.'

'No,' Gordon replies evenly, 'I'm staying in and doing my time.'[28]

He is back at Scheyville within days, in time for the Army to give them a demonstration of this new American weapon the Australian Army is going to shortly be issued with, the special light-weight and enormously powerful Armalite AR-16, made substantially from plastic and fibreglass, and perfect for killing when the enemy is as far away as 300 metres. Its 30-round magazine can turn fully automatic with the flick of a small lever. But wait till you see someone pull the trigger, you blokes just watch and see.

The officer candidates line up to the side of two 44-gallon drums filled with water, as an instructor steps forth with the standard SLR 7.62 millimetre and a new Armalite.

First up, he aims the Self-Loading Rifle – that ingenious device that uses the gas energy of the last cartridge fired to force the bolt back into the firing position – squarely in the middle of the left-hand drum.

'Fire!'

Two thin streams of water come out of the entry and exit bullet-holes.

Now he takes up the new Armalite, and takes aim.

'Fire!'

The entry bullet-hole is the same as the first shot, a thin stream.

But the exit hole? It is inches wide, and the water gushes out, a wet torrent from a gaping hole.

For the first time they also learn about tracer bullets, which come complete with a small amount of phosphorus tucked into the bullet's base, which ignites to flare some 50 metres from the muzzle. Having one in five of your bullets as a tracer allows you to aim with almost laser-like precision as you can see where it's going, without alerting the enemy to exactly where you are. And if you place a tracer as your second-last bullet in an otherwise normal magazine, it gives you warning of when you are about to run out.

With just two weeks to go before graduation in mid-December, if they make it, there is time for one more exercise: some endurance training in the Pokolbin State Forest near the Singleton Army Base, 220 kilometres north of Scheyville.

They are hauled up there sitting on planks in the back of Army trucks.

And where are their barracks?

No, you blokes don't understand. There are no barracks for you. You will be on field exercises the entire time.

One way or another, however, Gordon Sharp is there on graduation day in the third week of December as, in their dress uniforms, eyes right, they march past the saluting dais.

Both John O'Halloran's and Gordon Sharp's parents are there – 'Digger' and Grace O'Halloran and Eric and Roma Sharp, sitting side by side in the stands, proud as punch – and it is testament to Gordon's commitment that he had to let his uniform out, to cope with the plaster casts that are still on both his arms. He hasn't changed his mind about the virtues of National Service: he is still not for it. But once started on a thing, he'll be buggered if he is going to cop out. In the presentations, O'Halloran graduates 28th in the class, Sharp is 50th in the graduating class of 76, and 22nd is Dave Sabben.

That night there is a ball, and these new officers and gentlemen celebrate with their girlfriends – some of whom are local lasses from Windsor – and are able to dance the night away.

It feels like the night of their lives.

They are young. They have graduated. They are at the height of their powers. And they are getting closer to seeing some *real* action. The lucky ones, they feel, will be assigned to an infantry battalion, and ideally one that will soon be on its way to Vietnam, because the mail is getting stronger that when 1RAR comes back after their tough year is completed – they've already had a couple of dozen killed and well over 100 wounded – there might be as many as two battalions sent to replace them.

The following morning, their placement is on the bulletin board. Dave Sabben's eyes rove restlessly.

There!

D. Sabben. 6RAR. Officer Commanding, 12 Platoon, Delta Company.

Goodness! He is really going to be in charge of a platoon of 30 men?

Four other graduates will be joining him at what other battalions are referring to as the 'Baby Battalion' – because of its new formation – 6RAR, including those two best mates, John O'Halloran and Gordon Sharp.

Gordon is to command D Company's 11 Platoon, while Johnny will command B Company's 5 Platoon.

16 December 1965, Castlemaine, press to play

Opposition Leader Arthur Calwell has had enough.

For months now, rumours have swirled about the Menzies Government preparing to send National Service soldiers to Vietnam. And for the last week he has specifically pressed the government for information on what their plans are – all for no result.

And so on this afternoon, addressing this ALP rally at Castlemaine in Victoria, he does not mince words.

'The people of Australia wait, appalled and bewildered, another announcement of further commitment of our meagre military forces to Vietnam. We know this is going to happen, not because the Government has told us so, but because the Press have told us; because American Congressmen have told us and because any intelligent reading of the terrible events in that unhappy country and the policy of our Government in relation to those events informs us that this will happen.'[29]

Not only that, but the Menzies Government, he says, is so committed to sending so many more Australian troops to Vietnam, they are fully expecting 20,000 casualties over the next five years!

Sir Robert Menzies is not long in making reply from Canberra.

'If we were to receive a request from the Government of South Vietnam we would have to consider it then on its merits,' the Prime Minister insists.[30]

Following up in subsequent days, Sir Robert won't let the Calwell accusation go: 'This is an absurd suggestion. Mr Calwell has let his imagination run away with him. It is quite a ridiculous claim for which there is absolutely no foundation.'[31]

Sir Robert insists his government has received no requests for more troops from either South Vietnam or America.

'The Government has made no decision of any kind and can accept no responsibility for such rumours as exist. Whenever we decide anything in any of these fields, we announce it ourselves.'[32]

CHAPTER THREE

6RAR COMPLETE

The difference between how the services 'secure a building'. Army: Clear the building and put up defensive fortifications. Navy: Turn out the lights and lock the doors.

RAAF: Take out a 10 year lease with an option to buy.

Old saying in Australian Army

I know we oughtn't to be [in Vietnam], but I can't get out. I just can't be the architect of surrender . . .[1]

President Lyndon Baines Johnson, in the Oval Office, 1 February 1966

10 January 1966, Enoggera Barracks, if the shoe fits

On this warm evening, on the parade ground at Enoggera, the newly anointed *Lieutenant* Dave Sabben, if you please, salutes the 6RAR adjutant – *reporting for duty, Suh!* – immaculate in his conception as a freshly ironed and entirely buttoned-down young officer: a single pip on each shoulder, kitted and outfitted to perfection. With him is Lieutenant Gordon Sharp, also newly elevated and also a little nervous, nearly as well ironed if not quite as buttoned down.

They are directed to their new Lord and Saviour, the Officer Commanding Delta Company – one of the four rifle companies of the 6RAR battalion, the others being Alpha, Bravo and Charlie Companies – and are very shortly offering him a sharp salute before standing to attention.

Major Harry Smith returns their salute with a gimlet eye. So *young*, these National Service Lieutenants. Will they really be up to the task of leading a platoon of 30 men in a battle?

Time will tell, but his hard eyes say he is not at all sure.

Known to one and all as 'Harry the Ratcatcher', Major Smith is regarded as one of the toughest bastards in the army; one who never misses a trick, never loses a fight fair or foul, never loses the thrill of the drill and never stops never stopping. He is a human dynamo of improvement and correction, who drives his men further (much further), harder (bloody hard) and longer (looooooonger) to be the best. Why? Because he is Harry the Ratcatcher, that's why. Every new recruit asks where the nickname came from and every old hand can answer it, Sonny Jim.

See, over a decade earlier in Malaya after, at last, catching some of his soldiers playing a craps game that he had forbidden them to indulge in, ol' Harry – technically only 32, he was probably *born* old – had leapt into their tent to shout gleefully, 'Got you, you Rats!'[2]

And from that day thereafter, he had remained 'Harry the Ratcatcher', for the name told you everything you needed to know. Harry is the stickler's stickler; he can spot a transgression at 200 yards and yell it into submission at 100.

For he doesn't miss much and these new arrivals are a case in point. For yes, while Sabben is immaculate, just one glance tells Major Smith that this graduate of Trinity Grammar is a damn sight *too* immaculate. This jumped-up wanker is wearing handmade Italian shoes! They don't squeak as he walks. Despite their obvious newness he's not hobbling the way he *should* be with Army dress regulation shoes. Yes, they are so black and so well cleaned, so polished you could see your face reflected in them even *after* you ate your breakfast off them, which means to the untutored eye they really do look like regulation Army shoes. But that's the point.

The eye of Harry the Ratcatcher is tutored. He's been in this man's army for 11 years, and he is more than happy to give 'Lieutenant' Sabben – the quotation marks around Lieutenant perfectly matching the curl of his lips – some of his insights into the virtues of dressing like an *actual* Army officer if you really want to *be* an Army officer. The exact words would peel paint and are lost, but the gist has an emotional force that leave an imprint on the young man's soul and are preserved:

> 'HANDMADE ITALIAN SHOES ARE NOT REPRESENTED IN THE ARMY SUPPLY SYSTEM. FURTHER, WHEN THE ARMY SEES THE ERROR OF ITS WAYS AND BEGINS TO SUPPLY THEM, THEN, AND ONLY THEN, WILL YOU BE ENTITLED TO WEAR THEM. BUT NOT BEFORE!'[3]

Sabben takes the sabre, and the point remains: Harry the Ratcatcher is 'a stickler for detail and insanely committed to standards'.[4]

True, in the case of uniforms, Major Smith does make an exception for himself and insists on wearing a green commando beret instead of the regulation British peaked cap, which draws the ire of Smith's commander, Lieutenant Colonel 'Mousey' Townsend, the Commanding Officer of 6RAR. But for Smith, giving uptight and upright Townsend the shits is just a bonus. They do not get on, and Smith doesn't care.

But he does care about junior officers turning up in Italian boots, and you will GET THEM CHANGED IMMEDIATELY, SABBEN. And yet, as the younger man will also soon learn when it comes to Harry the Ratcatcher, his standards are not standard standards. He is after exceptional standards. Close enough is not good enough, it is not even *close* to good enough; he wants his officers and men to be precise, to be outstanding, to be *the best* in all of 6RAR and he will get that or have your guts for garters, what will I have?

My guts for garters, Major Smith.

•

Today is the day that newly minted Lieutenants Dave Sabben, Gordon Sharp and John O'Halloran must meet for the first time the men they are to command; the day when the officers are put together with their respective platoons. Right now they are standing on the edge of the parade ground at Enoggera Barracks, lightly sweating – but not just because of the heat of the Queensland morning sun.

The fellow they'd only met the previous evening, Lieutenant Geoff Kendall – the Regular Army commander of 10 Platoon, with far more experience in such matters – is delighted by their nervousness, and can't resist adding to it, as the sound of marching men gets nearer.

'Here's your moment of truth, fellas . . .' Kendall whispers in *sotto voce* theatricality. 'They're gonna laugh their heads off . . . Bet you blow yer first salute . . .'[5]

Kendall, a former rugby league player from Western Queensland, is a tower of strength! No wonder they sweat.

After all, since arriving at Enoggera late the evening before, following Christmas leave, the new Lieutenants are about to take over the command of their platoons, with the capacity to punish any or all of 30 soldiers if they don't salute them properly. They are meant to lead them into battle, guide them, inspire them, all when not one of them has ever even heard a shot fired in anger, let alone had one fired at them?

And on this hot and humid morning, on this parade ground without shade, here they come! It is a little like the opening stanzas of A. E. Housman's poem, 'On the Idle Hill of Summer':

On the idle hill of summer,
Sleepy with the flow of streams,
Far I hear the steady drummer
Drumming like a noise in dreams.

Far and near and low and louder
On the roads of earth go by,
Dear to friends and food for powder,
Soldiers marching, all to die ...

With practised ease, and in military cadence, the three platoons of Delta march on the parade ground, each heading to their designated spot, until ...

'Company ... HALT!' 6RAR Delta Company Sergeant Major Jack Kirby barks.

As one, Delta Company come to a halt with their right feet stamping down in unison as they stand to attention facing the front, their rifles now down by their right side. Every part of them, and not just their boots and brass, shines. Their trousers have creases, their shirts are crisp, their hair is shorn tight and they are shaved as smooth as a baby's bottom.

'Right ... face!'

As one, and with another synchronised right foot stamp, they turn to face the front.

And now CSM Kirby advises the figure at the front, with a sharp salute which is returned in kind: 'Your parade, Sir.'

Kirby does a sharp about-face and with eyes forward, and high staccato strides, he marches to the rear.

The heavy silence is broken by Major Harry Smith, his back ramrod straight, his voice precise, informing the men that today is the day they meet their new officers to make Delta Company complete.

And now, Major Smith gives the next order: 'March on, the officers!'[6]

Eyes forward, backs straight, boots flicked rhythmically forward with every stride, the three Lieutenants of 6RAR Delta Company march on to the parade ground, coming to a halt before their respective platoons, where they in turn exchange salutes with the Sergeants they have met the night before, at which point command of each platoon is formally handed over to each Lieutenant.

And hush now as the bloke with the steely eyes up the front, Major Smith, sets out the training schedule for the week ahead.

'Today we will be embarking on a 20 kilometre march, with full kit, starting at 0830 hours.

'Tomorrow we will split in platoons, with 10 Platoon doing the obstacle course, 11 Platoon doing a navigation exercise and . . .'

And so forth.

And he wants to make one thing clear now that the platoons are fully together for the first time.

'Anyone who fails to live up to my expectations will be moved on,' he says. 'Everything you do must be done right. Not 90 per cent right; 100 per cent right, with *maximum* effort. If that's not the way you want to do things, get out now.'[7]

His new Lieutenants survey him warily. They have heard a little about Smith but are about to learn a whole lot more.

A hard man himself, who has seen hard action in the Malayan Emergency – when they had fought Communist guerrillas in the Malay jungle – he knows what is required in warfare and is intent from the beginning in forming a unit that will be up to it. What Harry the Ratcatcher wants today, and every day hereafter, is for his now completed Delta Company to throw themselves into training, to be integrated, skilled, the best they can be! And that starts with training . . . this morning.

'Delta COMPANY . . . dismissed!'

But not all of Delta Company, for as Company Sergeant Major Jack Kirby quickly makes clear, the Major wants to hold his first O Group – short for 'Orders Group' – meeting of the officers and senior NCOs.

It doesn't take long. Just enough for Smith to set out his expectations for each platoon, and the standards he wants each one to reach in the week ahead, as each officer takes notes. Fall out and be back here at 0830 hours for the route march.

For the likes of Lieutenants Sabben, Sharp and O'Halloran, this first exposure to their new platoons is a little . . . difficult.

After all, here they are, still in their early 20s and in command of platoons that boast grizzled Sergeants, Corporals and a few actual soldiers who are veterans of Malaya and Borneo.

Among the most experienced of all is Company Sergeant Major Jack Kirby from Sydney – essentially, Delta Company's disciplinarian, father confessor and wise head – a big bear of a man with fists like slabs of ham, who could roar like a wounded bull when aggrieved and laugh like a kookaburra when amused. He is Smith's right-hand man when it comes to enforcing discipline, and making sure orders are followed. George Orwell had once written of men exactly like him, 'People sleep peaceably in their beds at night only because rough men stand ready to do violence on their behalf,'[8] though with Kirby the roughness is on the outside only.

Truly, the man is naturally cheerful, his jowly features – that would put a British bulldog to shame – nearly always smiling, even when yelling at his soldiers in his trademark sarcasm disguised as formal manners . . . like a butler turning the air blue while passing you the sodding port, pissant. A veteran of both the Korean War *and* the Malayan Emergency, he is a soldier's soldier, vastly experienced with years of active service under his very large belt, which only just manages to hold him in.

A singularly good man, Kirby has a way about him which acknowledges two things: he knows 20 times more about the army than these young pup Lieutenants do – whatever their training and superior rank – *but* he will keep his remarks in check so that their authority is preserved via a carefully calibrated *pas-de-deux*.

'Mr Sabben, sir,' he says with a smile, not long after they meet, 'with great respect, sir, get a haircut, sir.'

A pause.

'Before the weekend, sir . . .'[9]

Thank you, CSM Kirby, I was about to do precisely that.

Kirby's best mate is Lieutenant Dave Sabben's offsider at 12 Platoon, Sergeant Paddy Todd, who was born in Ireland but has been with the Australian Army for a decade-and-a-half, serving in the occupation of Japan, the Korean War and the Malayan Emergency, *twice*.

And 22-year-old Sabben is meant to tell this grizzled soldier in his mid-30s what to do and how to do it? They both know it is absurd, even if Todd – already old enough and wise enough to be a father-figure to the troops – is gracious enough not to say so, and Sabben is smart enough not to give him orders in the first place.

'If you're smart,' Dave Sabben will later note, 'you acknowledge that the Sergeant is really in charge of the platoon and you let him have his way, and he hints to you what he wants done and you do it without actually him giving you orders. They were prepared to put up with this guy wet-behind-the-ears but the wet-behind-the-ears guy had to sort of know his place. If he cut up a bit rough they'd put him in his place and you sort of accepted that, yes, he's gonna salute you but you should beat him to the salute if you're smart.'[10]

And the thing that the fresh Lieutenants have going for them with their Sergeants is that it is in the Sergeants' own interests to nurture their Lieutenants into good officers, because their own lives might well depend on it! Todd is one who manages to be entirely protective of his Lieutenant, without ever being remotely obsequious. He is his own man, while still being intent that Sabben is fully supported.

For his part, 10 Platoon's Lieutenant Geoff Kendall, the Army Regular, soon has installed as his NCO the newly promoted Sergeant Bob Buick. Of them all, it is Buick who appears to struggle most with keeping up the veneer, the forced façade, of deferring to fresh Lieutenants who don't know their arse from their elbow, but he appears to do his best.

Buick also finds a problem the other way – dealing with these new Nasho soldiers. Turn this mob into a fighting force? Can it even be done? He will do his best, in his oft brusque manner.

As to the Lieutenants, though they are unlikely, yet, to take on any of the NCOs, it is another matter with the common soldiers under their command.

As a matter of fact, passing Lieutenant Geoff Kendall now is one of the new recruits, drifting along like the lost lout he is, with no clue that his whole world has changed. In his world he doesn't even quite know what an officer is, let alone how to recognise one by the insignia on the epaulettes that Kendall is wearing.

The lad ambles past Kendall just the way he'd pass by an insignificant stranger on a city street.

Kendall lets him go for another five steps before roaring in a manner to wake the dead, the dead-beats and the dead-*stupid*: 'DON'T YOU SALUTE OFFICERS?'

Jumping in fright like a wombat stung by a wasp, the recruit turns, mimics what he thinks a salute looks like from the few he has seen in the movies and says, 'Oh, Jesus, sorry, mate!'[11]

It is all Kendall can do not to laugh, and he softens. After all, getting any Australian to treat any authority with elaborate respect is like training a dog to stand on its hind legs – it can be done, but it is just against nature.

What's your name, soldier? Well, he's not really a soldier and his name is Phil Duncan. Phil is pleased to meet you, sir.

Geoff Kendall has come a long way from the day he had first driven down the Moonie Highway, as the 21-year-old captain–coach of the Tara rugby league side, hoping to be selected for the Officer Training Course at Portsea. He is two years in the army, a regular, a Second Lieutenant determined to be second to none. Just the sort of young officer that Harry the Ratcatcher is demanding.

Many of the grizzled instructors at Enoggera share the attitude that being asked to get mere conscripts up to speed is like entering a race with an FJ Holden that has a buggered carburettor.

I mean, we're *what* . . . ?

We're having to cope with an influx of Nashos, and train them up – a bunch of blokes who are only here in the first place because they're unlucky losers. It is *not* our idea of what this man's army should be, and as they say in the classics, fuck this for a game of soldiers!

20 January 1966, Canberra, meet the new boss, same as the old boss

After serving no less than 18 years, 5 months and 12 days as Prime Minister, Sir Robert Menzies suddenly announces his resignation on this day.

He has had enough, and will be gone by the morrow.

And the new bloke?

No matter that, like Robert Menzies himself, he had been one of the few of his generation who had not gone to war – he'd pulled out after five weeks of Basic Training at Puckapunyal in 1940, from a unit that went on to see action at Tobruk and New Guinea – Prime Minister Holt is keen on the Vietnam War from the first.

'With great determination and resolution we can carry through the prime task to check Communist aggression in [Vietnam],'[12] he will affirm only shortly after becoming Prime Minister and his broad approach will famously be boiled down to just five words: 'All the way with LBJ.'[13]

And yet while the departure of Sir Robert makes front-page news around the country and leads every news bulletin, there is a certain group who is all but entirely unaware of it. They are the newly minted

Lieutenants of 6RAR who have barely had time to put their kit down before they are whisked away for the weekend to Levers Plateau, some 110 kilometres to the south-west, which boasts some of the roughest terrain in all of Australia. They are quickly engaged conducting platoon level training, contact drills in country with thick vegetation heavily laced with swamps, gullies and cliffs.

For the Lieutenants of Delta Company, Major Smith is still at their shoulder, observing, taking notes and occasionally bursting out when dissatisfied.

No! The hand signal for 'machine gun ahead' is a clenched fist – the signal for 'enemy soldiers sighted' is a down-turned thumb.

Fucking well get it right – LIVES depend on it!

Still far from convinced that mere conscripts can actually be turned into good officers in the short time they had, what he really wants now is to observe them up close, to assess just what he has inherited, and work out what needs to be done to bring them up to speed. He rates and berates, he judges the bludgers, he surveys and praises, he leaves none of them in any doubt just where they sit in his regard on the basis of a singularly intense 48 hours.

Never, EVER, salute a superior officer while out on patrol! Not even the *hint* of one! It is the surest way for the enemy to know which is the best head to put a bullet in. It is as unimaginable as wearing pips while within sight of the enemy. Just as your platoon must blend with the bushes, you must blend in with them!

And stop giving verbal orders when hand signals will do! Silence is not only golden, it is your only hope of survival!

Who is smoking? *For fuck's sake!* Cigarette smoke can be detected 100 yards downwind!

And so it goes for two days and nights as the new Lieutenants get a feel for their Major, just as he gets a feel for them, before they all head back to Enoggera to commence training proper with their platoons.

As it happens, Delta Company's completion, with all parts now put together as a cohesive whole, comes at an enormously significant moment. For only days after the roster is complete, Colonel Townsend places all of 6RAR on a semi-war footing.

Nothing is yet certain, except for the fact they can't escape: 5RAR and 6RAR will head to Vietnam sometime in late May. Their training must now take on a renewed urgency, as they go from dawn to dusk six days a week – apart from Tuesdays and Thursdays when . . . it would continue until 2130 hours.

At Enoggera, as with all the exercises they undertake in the bush near and far, no-one pushes his men harder than Harry Smith of Delta Company.

As the likes of Sabben and Sharp soon discover, Smith has a particular way about him, even beyond his dislike of Italian boots – and it is all because of his background. Having been taken into National Service himself in the 1950s, he had liked it so much he had joined the Regular Army from there, and served in the Malayan Emergency, where he had been in the front line of the Commandos – those elite and multi-skilled soldiers who, in groups of 10 or so are trained to move silently behind enemy lines before wreaking havoc.

It was an experience that had marked him and guides him now. For no matter whether Delta Company serves in Indonesia, Malaya or Vietnam, there is no doubt that they will be fighting in jungles against an elusive enemy just like he had faced in the Malayan Emergency. As a matter of fact he had just completed Special Forces training with 2 Commando Company in Melbourne when he had got the posting to 6RAR as Delta Company Commander.

So why not train D Company like that, to Commando standard? The Melbourne Commandos had not even been made up of Regular Army recruits, they were 'civilians in uniform'; D Company is 50 per cent Nasho, so they should be able to go twice as hard!

True, this is a much higher standard in terms of fitness, skills and malleability than the standard expected of other infantry companies, but so what?

He is the Commanding Officer of Delta Company and with that comes a certain amount of autonomy. The Army demands a minimum standard be achieved, but there is nothing limiting the maximum standard, so why not take it much, much higher?

The best fighting force in the jungle is a section of eight to ten superbly fit and multi-skilled men, each with a specific role, but each one capable of taking over the role of the man next to him if necessary, so that – just like the SAS – the unit as a whole can still function and be a fighting force come what may. In the months that remain, Smith is determined that

Delta Company will be as highly trained, as toughened and as fit as they possibly can be, and if that means starting earlier, working harder, and finishing later than Alpha, Bravo and Charlie Companies, then so be it.

Don't like it? Great. You are not the kind of man we are looking for, so it's best we part company now rather than later. Shape up (*literally*) or ship out (*right bloody now!*).

No matter what Colonel Townsend asks of 6RAR as a whole, Smith asks more of his men of Delta Company. When Colonel Townsend demands that by the end of the week, each platoon must be able to march eight kilometres in 85 minutes carrying full kit, Smith insists his men do it in 70 minutes. By next week he wants it down to 65 minutes.

Oddly, for a Company Commander, Smith does all the activities himself.

'Townsend,' Smith will note, 'did not take kindly to my "modus operandi" of training my company along commando lines with eight-kilometre runs each morning. I was accused of elevating my company above the standards required for an infantry battalion.'[14]

Townsend demands his soldiers carry 15 kilogram packs on long training marches; Smith makes sure they all weigh in at 20 kilograms. When a Townsend mandated activity requires sandshoes, Smith orders them to wear their Army boots and gaiters. (And NO Italian boots, did he mention?)

Oddly, the man who struggles most in these physically gruelling exercises is the one who complains least: their slightly roly-poly Sergeant Major, Jack Kirby. Kirby outweighs Major Smith himself by at least 30 kilograms, and most of the rest of the company by 25 kilograms – which is why he struggles in tasks of endurance. Nevertheless, they are always completed and what he lacks in speed over long distances he more than makes up for in sheer physical strength, capable of carrying an M60 machine gun with ease or, if it comes to it, a wounded man over his shoulder.

There is, true, a little grumbling from some of the Regular Army soldiers – particularly the vets – who know that ol' Harry is pushing them far more than the standard, but these men of the National Service just assume *they're in the Army now*, and get on with it, becoming fitter, stronger and tougher with every week.

•

On the one hand, Delta Company being so conspicuously more intense in approach than the other companies might be regarded as Delta lifting the whole battalion.

Or, it could be viewed as problematic because while armies thrive on uniformity, a mass of mavericks are more trouble than they are worth, particularly when they become aware of just how much better they are than the other companies and their marching gait seems to take on a certain strut.

For his part, Colonel Colin Townsend tends to the latter view, the fire of his ire focused on Delta generally and Major Harry Smith specifically – he who is the most maverick of the lot.

'He and I often seemed to be in conflict,' Smith will recall, 'which was probably a combination of two factors. I was far more outspoken than most of the other company commanders and refused to be what was known as a "yes man". Also, I could make quick common sense decisions and get on with the job, rather than sit around and procrastinate, which may have given him the impression that I was at risk of making hasty decisions.'[15]

One way or another, however, Townsend's antipathy to Smith makes no difference to the latter's approach or the activities of his charges.

As the weeks pass, Delta Company comes to be regarded as the fittest and fastest, the best trained, the most lethal, and the most cohesive in the battalion. Well, at least that's the way they see themselves.

And whatever that thing is which binds disparate men together into the one unit to which they are all proud to belong, the Delta men have it – in the field and on their rare forays to the pubs, they have each other's backs, with no 'hang you, Jack' apparent.

As for the tension between Colonel Townsend and Major Smith, for the most part the soldiers themselves know nothing of it – with the only manifestation being that on exercises it is Delta Company that generally seem to be assigned the hardest of tasks, the unit that has to go furthest, fastest and well beyond the sun going down.

Too bad. If Townsend hadn't given them the roughest end of the pineapple Major Smith would have anyway, just on principle. For Smith, Townsend's approach is no problem at all. He *wants* his men under extra pressure, and to be given the dirtiest of tasks. Pressure creates diamonds, rough and ready ones at that. Just a little bit of polish, and they will cut the enemy to pieces.

1 February 1966, The Oval Office, not all the way with LBJ

In the very seat of American power, President Lyndon Johnson is struggling with still more bad news coming out of Vietnam. He had never wanted to commit so many troops, it had just . . . turned out that way. Right now there are 190,000 US troops in Vietnam, compared to 25,000 a year earlier. And it had never occurred to him that the USA, with all of its soldiers and collective firepower, would be on anything other than the winning side, but every update seems worse.

On this day he is talking to leading Democrat Senator Eugene McCarthy in the Oval Office and despite the President's slow Texas drawl he is quick to get to the point.

'What they really think,' he says, referring to the doves of their own party, the anti-war Democrats who torment him daily, 'is we oughtn't to be there and we ought to get out. Well, I know we oughtn't to be there, but I can't get out. I just can't be the architect of surrender . . . But they, they don't have the pressure that will bring them to the table as of yet. We don't know whether they ever will . . . I'm willing to do damn near anything . . . I'm willing to do nearly anything a human can do, if I can do it with any honor at all. But, uh . . . uh . . . they started with me on Diem, you remember.'

'Yeah,' says McCarthy.

'That he was corrupt and he ought to be killed,' President Johnson continues. 'So we killed him. We all got together and got a goddam bunch of thugs and we went in and assassinated him . . . Now, we've really had no political stability since then.'[16]

The whole thing is a complete disaster.

And truly, President Johnson would like to get all the troops out of Vietnam as quickly as possible. But in the absence of being able to – for the South Vietnamese Government would immediately collapse – he feels there is no other way forward than to commit *more* troops to it, in the hope that a greater commitment might destroy the enemy to the point that the USA can finally disengage.

From where he sits in the Oval Office that seems highly unlikely, but he can see no other way. And if that means more soldiers will die, that is unfortunate, but that is simply what happens in war.

•

All four companies of 6RAR are to undergo an 'exercise' in the hinterland of Rockhampton. It is a classic 'hurry up and wait' affair; all ready to be awoken and moved like chess pieces for imaginary squabbles and battles; one hour notice is all you will get to up the digs you have just dug and move on to dig in somewhere else. All of the companies are scattered on different points of the map, and must converge on an 'enemy camp', attacking from different angles. Guess who has far and away the longest trek, through the most difficult terrain, covering 40 kilometres in two days? Of course, it's Colonel Townsend's least favourite officer, Major Harry Smith, together with his strutting peacocks. Perhaps this might knock a little of the stuffing out of Delta!

'Commandos', are you? Let's see.

No problem. Major Smith is certain that Delta will eventually strike; just not in the way that Townsend might think. They have a starting point: where they are standing now; and an end point: where the enemy is going to be. So? So, they are going to bush-bash this thing, cutting across ridges and hills at a cracking pace; saving themselves, in theory, many miles and a lot of sweat. As they do this, Harry will call in false locations, so nobody outside Delta will be the wiser as to their position. Now, if Harry is wrong, and they get trapped on some uncrossable ridge instead of weaving around it, there will be hell to pay with Townsend. But what the hell, let's do it!

Delta sets a furious pace, delighting in the deception. The sweat and the heat will not defeat their glee in this Commando commandeering of the 'exercise'. When Townsend calls in new co-ordinates for them to reach and 'attack', deliberately impossibly far away, Harry the Ratcatcher cheerfully replies that Delta will do their best to get there, sir. And they just might too, because Harry keeps calling in false locations on the impossibly long route Townsend has set them, as they relentlessly advance on their new goal, crashing and thrashing their way through the bush and scrub.

Oh what a beautiful morning, oh what a beautiful day, oh what a beautiful thing it will be to see Harry publicly brought down a peg or two and it is with some glee that Colonel Townsend leans in to the lack of progress of Delta. So much for Smith's bloody Commando training, his commander is teaching him a lesson about what follows pride: a fall. Oh yes, Harry, you've always carried on about going above and beyond and turned up your long nose at those slackers happy to reach just a *standard* standard.

No, he could hardly punish the bloody man for training to excess; it would be like handing out a charge because his boots are too shiny; but you can prove a point. It's true that Harry Smith's voice always seems surprisingly and disappointingly cool and calm as he calls through with another woeful set of co-ordinates, despite the disaster Delta is facing, but Townsend is at least content to have brought him back to the pack. The only question is should he tell Smith when they slink in, 'I told you so,' or perhaps, 'I hope we have all learnt a valuable lesson'. Actually a combination of both for this Come to Jesus moment for Harry Bloody Smith and . . .

And, Colonel? Delta are here!

Jesus Christ! They made it in less than two days! How the bloody hell did those bastards pull it off? No men could make that territory in that time! No, they couldn't; but this is a battle simulation and Harry the Ratcatcher has outwitted his enemy, Colonel Townsend. Nobody owns up to the trick, but Townsend can tell by the grins on Delta faces that someone has pulled a fastie and it is very likely bloody Smith again.

Next time, can we have a hard one?

Infuriated, Colonel Townsend has just the thing.

Delta's next task is to march 16 kilometres through shocking country and put in three separate platoon attacks on three separate targets.

Fine!

This time, like the boxer Muhammad Ali, who claims to be so fast he can switch the light off and be in bed before it gets dark, Major Smith has his soldiers cover the distance in such quick time that they get to their targets a good eight hours before it is considered possible. It means they manage to 'attack' and overwhelm the enemy while they are still digging in, camouflaging themselves . . . and, in one case, brewing a billy of tea!

No matter. Smith's view is that all is fair in love, war, and war exercises and he is proud and completely unapologetic that Delta Company continues to stay within the parameters of such exercises and outsmarts all comers. It is exactly the approach he wants his men to take in real battles and this is enormously valuable preparation. And yet, proving their collegiality, they now join up with Bravo Company for a successful final advance and co-ordinated assault.

All up, they have trekked more than 56 kilometres in just three days, while carrying full kits and always moving in their designated formations.

Done, yet?

No!

There remains one last exercise, which is to 'clear the peninsula' to the east in rough competition with other companies. Delta makes the competition a lot rougher actually, with some typical sleight of hand and bending of rules. The night before the mock assault, Dave Sabben takes a three-man patrol to the 'enemy' camp, gets in under the wire, maps the camp from the inside, then gets out! The next day Major Smith delights in bringing an intelligence report to Colonel Townsend with full details of the enemy camp, up to and including where their dunnies are positioned! *How the bloody hell?* Townsend throws a fit when he realises those Delta buggers somehow had men inside the camp. Very well, they will be given the longest and most difficult route to this camp. No matter, again all the previous work they have put into their fitness and toughness pays off. They reach the 'enemy camp' first.

The whole thing feeds into Colonel Townsend's eternal suspicion of Harry's ambition and rigour.

Perish the thought, sir. It is the very nature of the Army to want things done by the book – and Smith is the exemplar of that desire with his own men. But the problem comes when you want to write a better book.

In Smith's book, Townsend is something of an Army Lifer stick-in-the-mud, almost bureaucratic in his approach and still fighting old wars in tired ways. Smith's vision of leadership is much more vigorous and, ideally, inspirational.

And he can already see the results with Delta Company!

For it is in the achievement of the Delta training triumph over Townsend (involving, yes, a bit of jiggery, a pinch of pokery and a few liberties with 'accurate' co-ordinates) that they begin to feel like more than just a company and in fact start to feel like *the* company. As they lope through the bush towards the 'enemy', someone switches on a transistor radio and a Rockhampton station blares out Nancy Sinatra's latest hit 'These Boots Are Made for Walkin'', a moment of perfect timing:

These boots are made for walkin'
And that's just what they'll do
One of these days these boots are gonna . . .
Walk all over you!

As that wonderful bass riff washes out over them they begin to chant along with it. Want to screw with Delta Company? Good luck, because they'll *dum dum dum dum dum dum* walk all over you, mate, as they all start to chant the words.

Harry the Ratcatcher loves it, and Dave Sabben is duly designated as the Andy Warhol of Delta – he is the officer Harry commissions to come up with a logo: it must use boots, the initial D and Delta's colour: red. A number of drafts later and it's done: a Greek Delta, comprised of a terrific triangle of red and a pair of golden boots. Outlandish? Yes. Unnecessary? Certainly. Typical? Definitely. It's Delta and if you don't like it, guess what? They'll *dum dum dum dum* walk all over you.

•

Harry Smith encourages both that sense of separatism, and the pride in being a cut above. They will be doing things *his* way, and they will NOT be making the mistakes of other units. And let us embrace our difference!

Smith has now decided that, 'If we are going to be different, we might as well *look* different,' and from now on everyone in Delta Company will wear these camouflage floppy bush hats that he has had the Quartermaster buy out of the Delta Company budget.

Again, the derision from the other companies is palpable, and sometimes noisy.

'Get a load of 'em. Harry's heroes, in their floppy hats!'

'Here come the "floppy hats" again!'[17]

Delta doesn't care.

In truth, after these months together, Delta Company even has, like all of the nascent companies bound for Vietnam, something perilously close to their own language, or at least their own slang, as this tightly bound group of men inevitably embrace a shorthand-speak completely lost to the outside world.

To be 'warrie' is to be 'warrior like', and there is little higher commendation than to be referred to as 'a warrie bastard'. Delta Company no longer has lunch, or dinner, they have 'a fang', on meals that have been put together by men who used to be known as 'cooks', but are now 'ration assassins', 'bait layers', or even 'tucker-fuckers' and frequently sleep out at night under 'hoochies', all-purpose bits of green plastic that can be fashioned, after a fashion, into a half-arsed tent. Sleeping rough like that is something that the 'Shiny-arses', the Army clerks on administrative duty, will never have to do. And those lucky Army blokes who get to stay relatively safe inside the wire, working as cooks, Quartermaster staff, mechanics, plumbers, signallers, maintenance, laundry, admin and all the rest? They are 'Pogos' as in 'Posted on Garrison Operations', also known as 'blanket folders', 'base bludgers' and half-a-dozen other pejoratives. And yet that doesn't even scratch the surface of the acronyms that roll off their tongue now, without blinking. They'd learnt RSM and CSM early on through pain of death, just like they'd learnt CO for Commanding Officer. But now they come to understand that the FDL is the Forward Defence Line, as in the perimeter where their sentries must go; that the artillery has an FOO for Forward Observation Officer who has to call the fire in, and that a TAOR is a Tactical Area of Responsibility that they will be responsible for, making sure – upon pain of death, for them and their mates – it is clear of the enemy.

So, if you warrie bastards can finish your fang fast, leave the clean-up to the Pogos and take care of your TAOR ASAP, that would please your RSM and his CO as your CO needs you to stand duty on the FDL. Not happy? FU.

•

The reaction to Delta's all-round uppitiness gets ever stronger among their brethren of 6RAR.

They *what?* Delta Company have got a company song, a logo, and their own bloody uniform now? What kind of wankers are Delta Company? So far up themselves they could tickle their own tonsils with the tops of their heads.

The other companies are not impressed, and laugh openly at them.

Perhaps the least impressed, beyond Colonel Townsend, is Alpha Company's Captain Charles Mollison, a Victorian blue-blood who had come through the Citizen Military Forces and was already notable among his troops for his connections with such rising political luminaries as Andrew Peacock, who had just replaced Sir Robert Menzies in the seat of Kooyong.

'I took my lead from Colonel Townsend,' this officer with a rather bureaucratic bent would later note rather acidly, 'and set about training my company to be the "quiet achiever" – the company that could do everything asked of it with the minimum of fuss.'[18]

Delta Company doesn't care.

We are Delta Company.

We really *are* different.

And the most important thing is that we do *not* make the mistakes of other units.

Like on this night, when Smith and the Company Sergeant Major Jack Kirby gather Delta Company officers and Sergeants together, and play for them footage of some film that has just arrived from Vietnam, where they see their Australian compatriots, 1RAR, in an operational environment with the Yanks.

For reasons that will very shortly be known, Harry looks like *thunder* as the black and white images flicker on the screen.

Once done, Harry goes through it again, stopping it on specific frames.

Look at these blokes.

LOOK at these blokes!

They've got their shirts unbuttoned, their dog-tags showing, and their sleeves rolled up. We won't be doing it like that! All dog-tags will be taped together with black electrical tape to prevent them either clinking or reflecting sunlight to alert the enemy of your presence.

And look at the way these bastards have got bandoliers of ammo strapped cross-ways across their chest!

For Harry, with his deep experience in jungle warfare in Malaya, this was like a training film of what *not* to do.

When you are in the jungle, your skin needs as much protection as possible from mosquitos, leeches and overhanging branches. Your shirts are buttoned up, your sleeves are rolled down. Oh, and all of you wear your black plastic Army-issue 'Mickey Mouse' watches – not some monstrous US chrome timepiece dangling from your wrist! Don't make it easy for the snipers.

And now, look closely at their helmets. Some of the Americans have actually got fucking radios wired in, so they can listen to music while on patrol. We will not be doing that. We will not even be wearing helmets in the first place, or even slouch hats. We will be wearing camouflage bush hats to allow us to be *of* the jungle, and not just in it.

Okay, keep rolling.

Look now at their wild spray of machine-gun and automatic fire! War is not a Western, gentlemen, and you are not John Bloody Wayne. George Washington commanded his men to wait until they saw the whites of the enemies' eyes before they fired, modern American soldiers just seem to wait until daylight. This is not our way, not today, not ever. We will learn 'fire control', the art – and it is an art – of making sure your ammunition goes as far as possible and that every bullet counts. You do *not* pull the trigger unless you have a certain and worthy target in your sights. I don't care if you have set up base in the centre of an ammunition factory, you conserve and preserve; if you spray you'll pay. Got it? We are *not* going to do this the American way. We are going to do it our way.

From now on, all day every day, you will charge any of your soldiers who have buttons undone, sleeves rolled up, or dog-tags that aren't held down firmly with electrical tape, are we clear?

We are clear.

Watch them as they head into the jungle, with slings over their weapons which are pointing one way, while their eyes are pointing the other way. Wrong! Wrong! Wrong!

No slings. You *hold* your weapon when you are on patrol. And wherever your eyes are scanning, *that* is where the muzzle of the weapon must be pointing.

Major Smith makes it absolutely clear to his Lieutenants and NCOs: this is on you. This is a matter of life or death. From now on, if I see any of your men not obeying these diktats, it is not just them who will be answering to me. You will be. Get it right. Your shout.

And so they do, shout by shout, yell by yell, until just a raised eyebrow from Harry, *or* one of his Lieutenants, is enough to make any soldier go through his mental checklist at frightening, lightning speed of what transgression might have been made, until none are made. What used to be a pedantic checklist becomes writ large in their very *soul*, to the point that getting it right becomes as natural as breathing.

Within Delta it is 12 Platoon under Lieutenant Dave Sabben which begins to emerge as the hardest working of the lot. Though still feeling his way in terms of military protocols and tactics, a constant with Sabben is the virtues of hard work, the rewards of embracing the biblical admonition 'to go the extra mile', and he pushes his men accordingly.

He has no more interest in his men reaching the 50 per cent pass mark in any exercise than he had in getting 50 per cent in exams back at Scheyville. After all, once you remove those who failed that puts you at the very bottom of those who got through. And don't talk to him about 75 per cent. That still makes you average. Be your best! Push harder!

Helping to lift his confidence in making such demands, Sabben has Sergeant Paddy Todd, the gentle but vastly experienced Irishman, at his shoulder offering usually unspoken guidance. With an infinitesimally raised eyebrow from Paddy, Sabben knows he might be taking a wrong turn. But when Paddy steps forward and says to the soldiers, 'Listen to the boss!'[19] he goes still harder.

Occasionally Sabben will take him aside to ask whether, as Lieutenant, he had got something right, and would always receive the stock reply: 'It's all right, Skipper. I'll tell you when you get it wrong.'[20]

Lieutenant Gordon Sharp takes a similar approach to Sergeant Neil Rankin, a quietly spoken Regular Army soldier from Wollongong, who, though only 24, evinces a paternal care for his soldiers and is accorded great respect, in part because of his status as a veteran of Malaya.

Bit by bit, the nervousness of the new Lieutenants starts to disappear, their confidence to rise.

When Lieutenant Dave Sabben hand-signals to the platoon, as they move from open country into close bush, 'Change from extended line to arrowhead formation, 7 Section to lead,'[21] he *means* exactly that, and wants to see it done promptly and silently.

(I think? Quick look to Sergeant Todd, who gives an all but imperceptible nod of approval.)

'Go!'

•

As it happens, Major Smith is not the only one to have come to the conclusion that the Australian soldiers need to forge an entirely different path from the Americans. Last August, Brigadier Ken Mackay had journeyed to Saigon to talk with the American supremo General William Westmoreland about the Australian soldiers running their own race.

After moving beyond mere sentry duty at Bien Hoa, the Australians had already proved themselves good soldiers and effective in the jungle but had also chafed under the American command.

The Australians want a geographically distinct part of South Vietnam where the VC are active but not overwhelming, where the Americans have little presence and the Australian effort will be valuable, an area that is not bordering Cambodia, Laos or the demilitarised zone. And ideally it should come complete with a port and secure airstrips so that there is no issue of supply for the Australian forces.

For both Brigadier Mackay and Chief of the General Staff, General Wilton, there is just one province that answers these needs in full. It is the one that used to be named Baria, but has recently been renamed Phuoc Tuy – which translates to 'prosperous and peaceful' in Vietnamese. ('Owned by the VC' might have been a better translation right now, but that is the very issue at hand.)

'Just put a ring around Phuoc Tuy province,'[22] Brigadier Mackay had told his American counterpart General William DePuy. 'If we're going to come in with a force, *this* is the place.'[23]

Bemused, DePuy had sealed the deal. 'Okay, we'll put a thumb mark on it for you.'[24]

Sold!

The Americans remain puzzled. Why can't the Australians take them up on their own kind offer – simply building a base next to one of their own? That way they could be flown out to fight in more remote areas. But the Australians had simply said, what's that word again, 'Nah'. They're happy to be a good ally, but they'll be buggered if they want to live in a kennel built next door to the Big Dog. That is decidedly *not* the Australian way. They much prefer to fight or fall on their own ground; their own way.

Phuoc Tuy is an important province for many reasons, not least that it boasts the port of Vung Tau, where so much war *materiel* arrives to be transported along Route 15 to Saigon, just 96 kilometres away. Yes, Saigon already has its own port on the Sai Gon River but when, as so often happens, the VC attack the shipping going up that aquatic thoroughfare, then Phuoc Tuy becomes crucial to the war effort. The totally enemy-dominated Route 15 must remain open and if the Australians can suppress the VC in the area who are keeping it shut down, they will have rendered the war effort a great service.

No more than a fortnight after Major Smith had shown the men of 6RAR Delta Company the errors of the American way, the Cabinet of

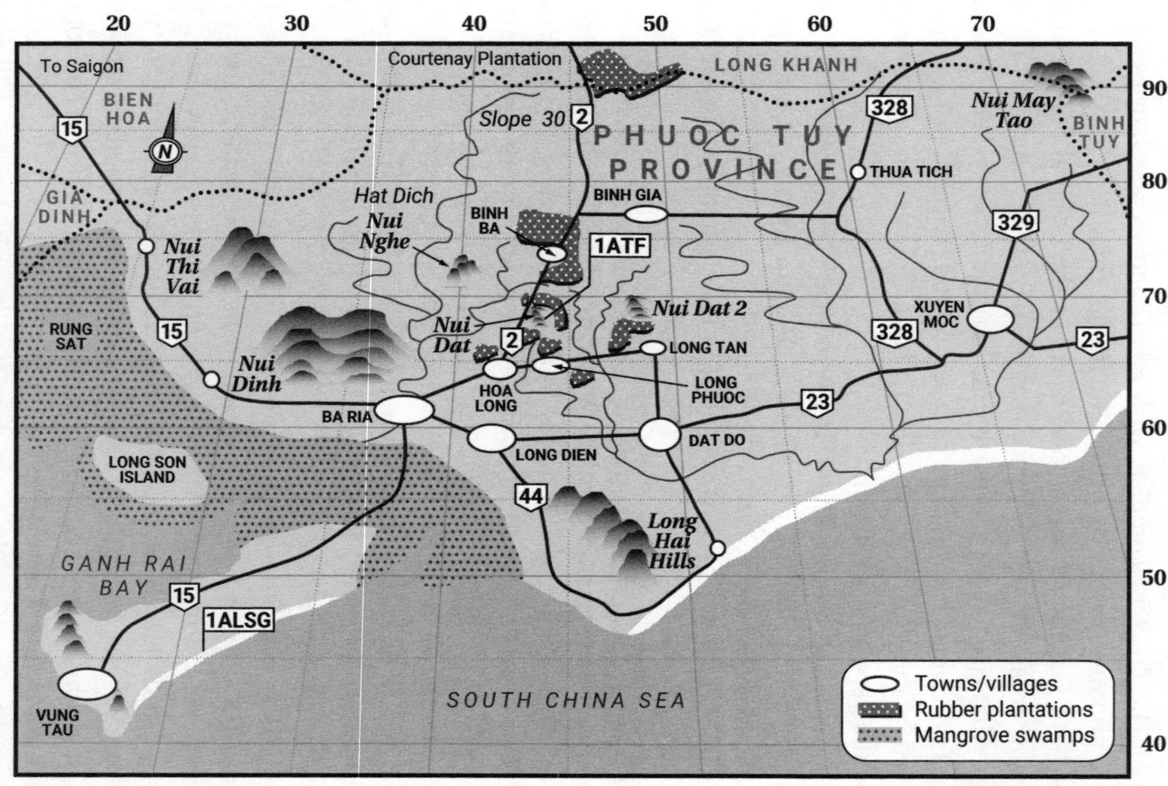

Phuoc Tuy province, South Vietnam

the Holt Government meets in Canberra on 2 March 1966 and deliberates on the proposal put forward by Defence Minister Allen Fairhall on ways the Australian force will be structured. It will be called the 1st Australian Task Force and be composed of two battalions (5RAR and 6RAR), a field regiment of artillery together with an elite SAS squadron, ancillary combat and logistics support units, like the 1st Armoured Personnel Carrier Squadron, an Intelligence unit and Signal unit, together with eight RAAF Iroquois helicopters. The newly promoted Brigadier Oliver Jackson, who only a year earlier had been convinced that the war was already lost, is assigned to command, a role he is used to with Australian Army Force Vietnam (AAFV), and in turn his past position is now filled by Major General Ken Mackay; well, almost. Mackay now heads the AFV, that is the Australian Force Vietnam. The acronyms grow shorter as the forces grow bigger; the Royal Australian Navy and the Royal Australian Air Force are now under Mackay's control in Vietnam.

The Cabinet approves the plan, and in short order General Wilton is on his way to Saigon once more to liaise with the Americans and sign a 'Military Working Agreement' with General William C. Westmoreland. Whether it does work remains to seen . . .

•

Ready?

Ready.

With only the smallest hesitation on the evening of this third day of March 1966, the three youths strike their Redhead matches, and bring them closer to their National Service registration certificates as the 200-strong crowd roars its approval. This protest by the Youth Campaign Against Conscription had first gathered at Central Station in Sydney to let the third intake of conscripts heading to Kapooka know that they had support, that they could jump off the train now! Alas, the Army had foiled them by having the train depart earlier, so now they have gone over the road to Belmore Park to burn, baby, burn their papers!

Wayne Haylen, Barry Robinson and Greg Barker – all students, all mates, and the first two co-founders of the YCAC – are resolute. The whole idea of being forced to conscript to go to an outrageous war in Vietnam is an angry anathema to them. Their papers are suddenly aflame, the crowd roars even more and they hold them right to the point that their fingers will burn if they don't let go. It is done. They *won't* be conscripted, let the law do what it will. And yes, the papers – when they run the photos given to them by no less than the NSW Police's Special Branch of intelligence operatives – will focus on Haylen as he is the son of a well-known former Labor MP, and Opposition Leader Arthur Calwell's godson, but the young law student doesn't care. Conscription is an outrage!

8 March 1966, Parliament House, Canberra, Holt swept away

Just like President Kennedy some years earlier, Prime Minister Harold Holt is getting mixed reports on how the war effort fares in Vietnam but for this occasion, in the Federal Parliament, as the political journalists scribble, he chooses to go with the most upbeat account he has, and ignore the calls and muttered insults from Arthur Calwell's Opposition.

Order. *Order!*

'The information we and the Americans have,' Prime Minister Holt proudly announces, in his first speech in Parliament as the nation's leader, 'is that the tide of war is turning in our favour. Progress is being made in rescuing new areas, in clearing them of Viet Cong and in preparing them for orderly civil government . . .

'This is no civil war. It is the principal present manifestation of the expansionist activities of Communist China. These activities are channelled through, and directed from, Hanoi. All the countries in South East Asia are facing the threat of Communist China's expansion in one form or another . . .'

Which brings him to the thrust of what he must say today.

'The Government has for some time been made aware of the desire of the Government of South Vietnam that we increase the size of the Australian force there. There has been a very large build-up in strength of the United States forces. It is evident that the allies must put forward an increased effort if military successes are to be achieved and then followed effectively by the tasks of reconstruction. Honourable members will be aware that there are at present serving in Vietnam more than 1500 Australian Service personnel comprising the Army training team, the 1RAR battalion group, and associated headquarters and Royal Australian Air Force personnel.

'At the request of the Government of South Vietnam, the Government has decided that the battalion will be replaced by a self-contained Australian task force under Australian command embracing all personnel serving there and enlarging our contribution to a total of some 4500 men – in effect, a trebling of the current strength of our military forces there . . .

'The Australian task force which we will be sending to Vietnam in the middle of the year will contain two Army battalions, the 5th and 6th Battalions, Royal Australian Regiment. And there will be a self-contained Logistics Support Group (1ALSG) based at Vung Tau.

'I am sure that honourable members will, in the light of what I have already said, appreciate the necessity for the Government's decisions. They are decisions of great responsibility and we have not taken them lightly. Australia cannot stand aside from the struggle to resist the aggressive thrust of Communism in Asia and to ensure conditions in which stability can be achieved. Our own national security demands this course. Do honourable members opposite, who are interjecting, deny that?'

Arthur Calwell can bear it no longer, and cries out: 'Yes. I deny it flatly.'

But Harold Holt does not waver.

'If they do,' Prime Minister Holt continues, 'let them stand and be counted when the time comes. We cannot be isolationist or neutralist, placed as we are geographically and occupying, as we do, with limited national strength, this vast continent. We cannot leave it solely to our allies – and their national servicemen – to defend in the region the rights of countries to their independence and the peaceful pursuit of their national way of life. I am confident that a majority of this Parliament and of this country will warmly support this increase in the Australian contribution.'[25]

That support will not include the paper of the national capital, at least not in the full-blooded sense, as the following day the *Canberra Times* makes no bones about it:

'WE ARE AT WAR: The Vietnam decision overshadows all in Mr Holt's speech. It is dramatic. Sir Robert Menzies said last year, "We are at war". The statement was premature. Our actions did not prove it. But we are, beyond all question and argument, at war now . . . And while the search for peace will go on, the Prime Minister sees a long period of fighting as the prospect we have to face. Every Australian must feel a pang at this decision. The casualty lists will reflect our fears . . .'[26]

CHAPTER FOUR

DELTA DAWN

When our soldiers are again threatened, as they are today, we will be asked for more money and for more men. We will not be able to refuse. And millions upon millions, fresh troops on top of fresh troops will lead to our exhaustion. Gentlemen, we must block this route.[1]

Georges Clemenceau, addressing the French Parliament, March 1885

9 March 1966, Shoalwater Bay, Queensland, Mouse that roared

At eight o'clock in the morning of this 9 March, the order goes out: *all* of 6RAR, even those in the sick bay, are to form up on the sports field, the only place large enough to accommodate them for a full battalion parade.

No exceptions.

Colonel Townsend will address you.

Lined up by company, standing at ease and gazing straight ahead, they are all present and accounted for, *Suh!*, when at 0800 hours on the dot, Colonel Townsend climbs the small bank on one side of the field, allowing many of them to get a close-up look at their Commanding Officer for the first time. For starters, it ain't hard to see why they call him 'Mousey'. A diminutive figure with a voice to match, he does not come across as the bloke who would have stormed the cliffs of Gallipoli back in the day, and more likely as the one who did a great job of booking the boats to get them to the beaches. A career Army officer, there is no doubt he is competent, it's just that he is a little bit . . . mousey.

But today Mousey has called them together to announce the news. The rumours are confirmed. It is all locked down.

In sum . . .

'The battalion is going to Vietnam,' Mousey says. 'If you don't want to go, step over there on the lawn.'[2]

After no more than 20 seconds, there is a light stirring in the ranks. And now, over on the left, a man steps out, and heads to the lawn. And now another from over on the right. And now a couple more. Little by little, the first few drops become a trickle which becomes a stronger trickle, and one or two more late-goers and now it stops.

Over on the lawn, nigh on a dozen 6RAR soldiers stand collected. Under the watch of the Administration Company Commander of 6RAR, Major Owen O'Brien, they can be re-assigned to home duties, or discharged, it is not yet determined. Their spots can be taken by 'reos', reinforcements, who want to go to Vietnam, which means, ideally, they can be counted on not to go to water when the bullets start to fly.

Now, one more thing.

For there is only one man in all of 6RAR with any experience in fighting in Vietnam and it is the Regimental Sergeant Major, George Chinn, a man with an actual chin like a clenched fist and a forceful personality to match; a man, in the words of Lieutenant Dave Sabben, who, like all officers, was 'to be respected, admired and avoided'.[3]

A Warrant Officer Class 1, Chinn had first been kicked out of the Australian Army during World War II for lying about his age in his eagerness to serve, but had gone on to serve with the Air Training Corps before seeing action in both the Korean War and Malaya. It was as an experienced veteran, thus, that he had headed to Vietnam with the Australian Army Training Team Vietnam in 1964, where with US forces he had covered himself in glory. On one occasion, *in extremis*, he had stopped observing and started fighting, leading his group of South Vietnamese soldiers to victory over the VC – for which he was awarded the Distinguished Conduct Medal. He is a battle veteran, described by the men as a '3F man – firm, fair and friendly'.[4]

Not that he is particularly friendly at this very moment. For he has something to say that needs to be said.

Chinn tells both the officers and soldiers of 6RAR, and he says it with the authority of one who has returned from Vietnam less than a year ago:

'The Viet Cong are fair dinkum fighters, and make no mistake, *very* good soldiers. They are well trained, seriously well experienced and they don't know how to back off. Soon, you are going to meet them and fight against them. We are going to have to train harder than ever to make sure we are ready for them. You think you're doing well, and in some ways you are, but you can do better and you *must* do better, because your lives and the lives of your mates might depend on it.'[5]

They're masters of camouflage, able to strike from close up when you least expect it, before instantly disappearing. Generally, they 'shoot and scoot', avoiding pitched battles unless they outnumber you. Some of them are seriously well trained soldiers from the North Vietnamese Army. Others are young guerrillas trained up from their regions, and they are known as the Viet Cong – or as the Americans call them, 'Charlie'.

But Chinn returns again and again to his key point.

'Do *not* believe all the talk about how "the little yellow man", can't fight,' he says firmly. 'These blokes are great fighters. They are not doing it part-time. They are fighting for their lives, and they're backed up by solid North Vietnamese Army regular soldiers who are not only better trained than you are, they are vastly more experienced than you because they've been fighting the French for decades. And they're better equipped than you are and know how to live off the land better than you do. And there are hundreds of thousands of them!'[6]

The intake of air and subsequent gasp of 6RAR is just audible. It is *the* moment when, for most of them, they realise that the contours of the task before them look more like a mountain than merely a good-sized hill. Whatever else, exactly as Townsend and Chinn have intended, the talk gives them renewed focus, as things now move out of the realm of training for training's sake and into the realms of the real. First up: the enemy are not wearing a nice green uniform like you lot; the typical uniform of the enemy is black pyjamas. No, not pyjamas to sleep in, black pyjamas to hunt and kill in. Look for the black and watch your back. Pay close attention now, you bastards, 'cos this is really important – the VC are masters, among other things, at setting up booby traps to gut you a dozen different ways.

The nascent Diggers lean in close, as their instructors give them the good oil on just what might be awaiting them.

Now when it comes to booby traps, the Viet Cong are innovators. How can they kill thee? Let me count the ways . . .

Firstly, there are punji sticks, sharp bamboo stakes covered with piss and shit. The VC put them at the bottom of pits, pointing up, and cover the pit with bamboo under a little earth. You'll be walking along, fall in, and if they don't kill you, they'll infect you, maim you and slow your platoon down.

Snake pits are a little different. They tie the snakes around the grates at the entrances to tunnels. Remove the grate and . . . you might find a snake tied to it, and the snake won't be in a good mood. They also like to hide snakes in backpacks, so if you find an abandoned pack, check to see if it's moving before you put your hand into it.

Tripwires are as you imagine. You trip on a wire, and it pulls the pins of two grenades with short fuses hidden in two tin cans tied on either side of the path. They explode at head height, inches away from their targets. Or they might get you with a bamboo whip, an ancient booby trap. They get a bunch of sharp spikes of bamboo, attach them to a long piece of bamboo, which they stretch as far as it will go, with a catch attached to the wire, and wait for the enemy to step on the wire – at which point the bamboo whips into your chest or your face, and you are now a bloody mess.

Watching your step in Vietnam is not a metaphor, it's the only way to survive.

You get the drift. The VC have thought of 20 ways to kill and maim you, before you have even had your morning fart.

True, this is as far from Christmas as it gets, but still not a Digger stirs, as they silently contemplate what they are being told here. Fuck. *Seriously?* The Vietnamese set booby traps like this? It hardly seems like cricket, and certainly nothing like any warfare they have heard of. (Sure, we Australians will have use of the American Claymore mines – easily secreted, and capable of removing both of a man's legs with exploding steel balls – but that somehow seems a much more decent way to kill an enemy.) But again, their instructors go on, so there is little time to reflect on it.

For you must understand, the danger you will be facing is not just booby traps; there are treasure troves of weapons left in pits – some dug deep enough for a man to stand in, others are '1/2 man', made for snatched sleep and a quick cache where guns and ammunition can be concealed for months at a time. If you wait for them to be revealed by the North Vietnamese, it could well be the last thing you see; so watch for freshly dug ground. If it looks abandoned, that is your clue that it hides something other than men: food or weapons, both waiting to feed your enemy. 'Search and Destroy' is a command that applies to stores more than soldiers; cut off these buried outposts and you will starve your enemy of concealment, forcing him to fight in the orderly open and abandon the helpful maze of the jungle.

Look there is more, lots actually, but just focus on these for a start. Any soldier who is led through this list never walks carefree in the jungle again; you are permanently paranoid, which is precisely the way you should be in Vietnam.

The most dangerous thing of all in these villages, of course, will be secreted Viet Cong soldiers who might suddenly ambush you. So that's why we want you to move through Snap Shooting Range, to practise looking for danger.

Safety catches off, and move through in formation, the point man – the one at the front – taking it slowly and scanning left, right and straight ahead for the tiniest sign of the enemy while the men behind look to the flanks.

Everyone must strain to spot the enemy before he spots you, judge his distance and direction and get your shot off accurately, *without* accidentally shooting an innocent female villager who just happens to be in the wrong place at the wrong time.

There!

One moment they are moving through the mock village, and the next the plywood cut-out image of a VC soldier pops up as a spring is released. And another one on the right, and three more on the left!

Take them DOWN!

Using live ammunition for the first time outside of a rifle range, making everyone a little nervous, the men of Delta Company are trained to instantly put two rounds of their rifles into each target – ideally in the torso – or if they have an automatic weapon, up to five rounds. Remember, the most common failing of soldiers is to shoot high when they are tense as the gun bucks up – so aim around the legs, and it will sort. Again and again and again they practise.

And look out for tunnels! Entire networks have been dug between houses and even villages, capable of both secreting guerrilla armies and allowing them to move about undetected. This is not like any enemy that Diggers have ever faced before. And just because you chase Charlie into one hut and surround him, doesn't mean he can't pop up behind you and mow you all down. Stay on guard, you bastards, and always look behind you!

No doubt about it, it is sobering instruction.

On the other hand, there is barely a man among them who doubts but they will have the VC's number.

We are Australians, we will knock these bastards over.

•

They don't call her Little Pattie for nothing. She will make five feet tall if she puts on high heels . . . *and* jumps. The former student from Sydney Girls High has been a national pop star since she was 14 when her surf craze smash hit 'He's My Blonde Headed, Stompie Wompie, Real Gone Surfer Boy' delighted teenagers and drove parents across Australia nuts as it played from every transistor radio in the land. The only thing that had kept it from being No. 1 on the Top 40 had been some novelty act from Liverpool, performed by blokes with weird haircuts, 'I Want to Hold Your Hand'. Not a bad song, true, but you couldn't stomp to it, like you could with Little Pattie's.

On this afternoon, Little Pattie has just got back to her family home at Mascot, when the phone rings and is picked up by her mother. Of course the young one leans in to listen. Phones don't ring often, and it is usually something important.

'I . . . I don't know,' her mother is saying. 'I'll have to ask her father. He's not home yet.'

. . .

'Where's that you say? Borneo? Vietnam?'

. . .

'All right, thank you. Yes, I will talk to him. Please call back in maybe a few days . . .'

(*Click.*)

'What was that about, Mum?'

'It was a man from the Department of Defence,' her mother replies uncertainly. 'He wants you to go on a tour entertaining the troops. It includes going to Vietnam.'

'Oh yeah?' says Pattie 'We've got soldiers over there, haven't we?'

'Yes,' says her mother, not overly impressed with her daughter's grasp of current events.

'And what would I do?' asks Pattie.

'Sing!' replies her mother.

Vietnam. Overseas! thinks Pattie. *An overseas trip!*

The young woman is immediately intrigued. Though she's sung all over Australia she's never been overseas, and it sounds exciting. But of course both she and her mother, and the government for that matter, will have to convince her father.

As it happens, Mr Amphlett is a little bit better informed about Vietnam than both his wife and daughter and, to use the technical term, 'goes bananas'.

Joe Amphlett is resolutely against the Vietnam War, and particularly against Australia being involved in any way whatsoever.

As a matter of fact, father's Final Word, delivered from on high and on lounge chair, does not take long: 'No, you're not going.'

And yet the conversation continues regardless. The nice man from the Department keeps ringing, almost *insisting* that Little Pattie must go, as her duty to Australia. To the Diggers. To the war effort.

Mrs Amphlett gives daily updates to her unimpressed husband.

'They'll be sleeping all right.' Hmmm.

'Playing in Borneo as well!' Yup.

'She'll be getting three square meals a day.' So do prisoners.

'They are going for free!' Yes, a free trip overseas! Well, technically the government will be paying them but at $1 a day it's nothing to get excited about, and the only duty free shopping you'll be doing will be window shopping, but it's an honour to be asked.

Look, Joe, there's no question of her being in danger. They haven't even mentioned war zones. And they'll be playing in beautiful Saigon, entertaining Aussie and Yank troops getting a break from their duties.

'Pattie?' *Yes, Dad?* 'You're not going.'

In response to Mr Amphlett's continued opposition his wife counters with her knockout argument: 'I think, Joe, we can trust this man. After all, he is from the government!'[7]

Mr Amphlett teeters but the man who ends up getting him over the line is Col Joye; because Australia's favourite singer – our own answer to Elvis – and the Joy Boys have been invited too and they are *definitely* going. Mr Amphlett knows Col is part big brother to Pattie, part dad when they tour and all gentleman, all of the time. And the Joy Boys are the same. They look after his girl. They have toured with Little Pattie all over the country, and looked after her like a silk-worm, every step, and stomp, of the way. No louts, touts, roughs or toughs get within ten feet of Pattie when they are around. They'll perform together. Mr Amphlett revises his Final Word: All right, if Col is going with you, you can go, Patricia.

She is thrilled.

Vietnam! *Overseas!*

•

As Vietnam is covered with tropical jungle the key now is to give the soldiers of 6RAR as much experience as possible in like conditions, and happily Queensland has many hot, steamy, rough places with thick vegetation that, if it is not always jungle, would at least get you 60 cents on the dollar for the same. In the first exercise they head off to Spring Mountain Forest, some 50 kilometres south-west of Brisbane, where they endlessly practise how to move through the bush in offensive and defensive formations, depending on what is required and the hand signals of their commanding officer. It is just a beginning as – unwashed, for they need to smell just like animals do – they learn how to make camp and spend the night without leaving a trace of their presence; how to both set up ambushes and not be victims of the same; how to use camouflage and spot the enemy's; what to do upon contact; how to dress wounds, practise basic bushcraft and . . . even now they are just scratching the surface. And speaking of scratches, understand this. Standard Operating Procedure is to 'eat, shave and shit' in that order. (In New Guinea in World War II, they had suffered more medical casualties than battle casualties, and more from dysentery than malaria. The Army had thereafter determined that shaving first thing after stand to in the morning meant at least washed faces, particularly around the mouth and nose, and would cut down infections.)

In the final week of February they head to Tin Can Bay, about 60 kilometres north-east of Gympie, to fire with live ammunition in the bush for the first time even as they engage in platoon-level exercises.

Company by company, meantime, they head for 10-day stints at Canungra Jungle Training Centre in South-Eastern Queensland just north of Lamington National Park – legendary, among other things, for the fact that it was here that many of the heroes of the victorious Kokoda Track campaign of World War II had applied their 'lessons learnt' and developed the training systems for all future soldiers bound for Vietnam.

True, with Canungra's flagpoles and immaculate gardens, its small wooden cottages, the endless waft of bird-song, the rich smell of the rainforest, it is an oddly peaceful place to be taught the finer points of killing. On the other hand, the point is made to them, one needs to kill to preserve the peace. For these new Diggers, the training begins from the moment they arrive to find they are not living in barracks but in tents perched beneath 'Scale A' Battle Ridge, which is specifically designed to resemble living conditions in Vietnam. All around them are 'obstacle courses, combat skills training areas and even replica Asian hamlets'.[8]

There are still some uniquely *Australian* features though. This, they discover one morning while hauling their weary arses though an obstacle course of ropes, ladders, more bloody ropes, under rolls of barbed wire, across the monkey bars, over the rocks, through a tunnel, through a pipe, they now cross the last hurdle, which is not a hurdle, but a ditch. And there it is: the reason the ditch is so *rank*. It is a dead and rotting kangaroo. Their stomachs heave, their nose-hairs curl, their eyes glaze over. They push on. There seems little chance of coming across half a dead Skippy in Vietnam, but if it happens they won't be able to say they were never prepared for it. And they have learnt a valuable lesson: bisected dead kangaroos give off a stench that would kill a brown dog.

The course has been put together by some of those within the Australian Army with the most experience of jungle warfare, and who have understood the terrain in Vietnam. The broad idea is to harden the soldiers under actual battle conditions, aided and abetted by the fact that the weather is already tropical – very hot, horribly humid and as wet and as unpleasant as a half-drowned cat.

The key is to both intuitively *understand* how to fight in the jungle and to be so heavily trained in it that, even when under severe pressure – being ambushed, under heavy fire, heavily outnumbered – you will *react instantly* to limit damage done and maximise your chances of overcoming the enemy.

This applies to both the way you react, and how everyone around you both reacts and interacts with each other.

So we must practise, again and again and again – until your noses bleed, and then some more – what to do when under sudden fire. And this will help you concentrate. For, gentlemen? This fire will be done with *live* rounds. We are done training with blanks, so aim carefully and when we say get low, GET LOW.

Time and again they go through the drills for jungle-fighting, continually on the clock to do them faster and better and always under the critical eyes of staff, who push them to do the drill so often, and at such speed, that it becomes second nature.

Their days begin well before the sun rises – Delta Company becomes used to completing 15-kilometre hikes in full gear carrying full kit before the sun is truly up – and usually continue for the next 18 hours. Their trainers want them to be exhausted, lacking sleep, frazzled, flustered, but *still* performing!

No water? No worries. You can fill your water-bottle from dripping rocks.

No tent? Adapt! Use these all-purpose stretches of cloth you've all been issued with, called 'hoochies', and you can string it up in a manner to give yourself some shelter.

Throughout the jungle, mock Vietnamese villages have been constructed that come complete with bamboo huts, cows and dogs, secret tunnels and caches of weaponry.

•

For the officers, particularly, there is a lot to learn about the whole situation in Vietnam, and just what the enemy can be expected to look like.

Our job is to disrupt, to take back as much of the regions as we can. And we will do it, not by conducting large operations like the Americans, but by using counter-insurgency doctrine we used in Malaya. We'll get among them in the jungle. *We* will do the lurking.

'You're going to have a big problem finding them and when you do find them, you'll have an even bigger problem engaging them because they'll run away.'[9]

As ever for Delta Company, Major Harry Smith is around, observing, urging, *lashing* those who are in need of it. Often with CSM Jack Kirby by his side, he would compare what he had with what he needed and wanted and prune or nurture accordingly. Frequently he would take notes before gathering his Lieutenants and Warrant Officers in a meeting of the O Group where he would go through it all, point by point, from what he has seen from the day.

'Lieutenant Sabben, your men are too slow in taking action after contact is called. Your left-hand section was bloody slow today, and need a kick up the arse. Pay attention to how quickly the machine-gunners can swing into action.'

'Lieutenant Kendall. I cannot tell you again that your men are showing skin. I don't care how hot it is. It will be hot in Vietnam! They must be camouflaged. *No* white skin is to show!'

And to Lieutenant Gordon Sharp, who on this day had become lost with his patrol. In such a situation, many a Major would have torn strips off him. But when the matter is obvious, when the officer in question knows he has stuffed up, there is no need. Expert in knowing when to tear down, when to build up, and when to note that work needs to be done, Major Smith simply says, relatively mildly, 'Blessed are those who travel in big circles, Gordon, for they shall be known as "big wheels".'[10]

Sharp winces, but no more than that. He will be *particularly* careful in his map-reading from now on, and there has been no need to humiliate him in front of his fellow officers.

'Harry Smith's approach,' Dave Sabben would characterise it, 'was very simple. He knew he was better than us, but he wanted us to be as good as he was. And he would tell you exactly where you were failing, what you had to do.'[11]

The new officers learn tips along the way, picked up from other veterans, often their own Sergeants. When you get leeches, the best way to get rid of them is to sprinkle on them a little of the salt you should always have with you in the jungle. Failing that, the glowing embers of a cigarette make them shrivel and drop off, though with rollies you still tend to bleed.

Also, remember this: the shell you can hear whistling, see, is *not* the one that will kill you, as you will only hear that whistling once it has gone over your head. In any case, in Vietnam you're less likely to be killed by artillery, which Charlie doesn't use much, and much more likely to go down to a medium-range launcher like mortars, or tiny grenades hurled by rocket launchers, because their troops can disassemble those launchers, carry them separately, fire and then disappear once more into the jungle.

Only rarely, the Diggers learn, will Charlie fight a pitched battle – much preferring the 'shoot and scoot' kind of attack.

But if there is a pitched battle?

Lieutenant John O'Halloran of Bravo Company keeps drilling it into his men.

'When we come under fire you blokes form a circle around me so that I can get home safely.'

'Now what happens if we come across the enemy?' O'Halloran asks gravely.

The answer comes back: 'Boss, we will form a circle around you to make sure you get home safely!' [12]

They all laugh, and continue training, into the pitch dark.

14 March 1966, Nui Dat, plantation station

Things have moved quickly for General Wilton and the whole concept of the 1st Australian Task Force.

In the helicopter, Wilton and Brigadier Oliver Jackson are now flying low over the Phuoc Tuy province and, with a tap on the shoulder from Jackson, the helicopter pilot hovers just at safe altitude above a stray enemy rifle shot, right next to a small hill that pokes above the surrounding rubber plantation. They call it Nui Dat ('Dirt Hill' in the Vietnamese language), and Jackson now points it out to Wilton.

This hill, and the surrounding plantation, is the spot that Jackson – an officious officer, even as officers go – has selected. Clearly, Wilton likes the look of it, for he nods and says back to Jackson:

'Well one day there'll be an empire down there, won't there?'

'And,' says Jackson, 'we had in other words pretty much agreed that that's where the task force should go.'[13]

It makes so much sense! In Phuoc Tuy, most of the population is concentrated in the south and south-west corner, while most of the VC are established in the bush in an arc from the north-east to the north-west. By establishing the base at Nui Dat, right in the middle of the province and between the bulk of the population and the VC, the Australians can protect the former from the latter. As to the ground selected for the base, it was perfect. All was flat for the bulk of the base, while the Nui Dat hill itself would provide the high ground for observation of the surrounding countryside.

As Wilton will explain, 'if the war went really bad and some frightful disaster was impending, we could look after ourselves'.[14]

All up?

Wilton makes the call in March 1966, saying: 'All right, we'll go to Phuoc Tuy province.'[15]

The Americans – while flabbergasted that the Australians wanted to set up in the middle of a province, far from tanks, guns, planes, ships, helicopter gunships and tens of thousands of American soldiers – agree, and the first moves are soon put in place.

And yet not everyone is convinced that Phuoc Tuy is the answer. It is well-known that when the French had been occupying the area, the Viet Minh had given them no end of trouble. But on the other hand . . . ?

On the other hand, that is just the French all over. The French had always been convinced of both their own innate superiority, and their need for creature comforts – which meant they had stayed mostly in the large towns, and rarely ventured out into regions.

We Australians will be going about things in a different way, going to where the actual action is, and taking on the VC on the ground. Apparently, Charlie has a very strong grip on the entire area, with whole towns declared for the VC – and neither the French nor the South Vietnamese Government has ever succeeded in controlling it – but we will burn that bridge when we come to it.

•

When it comes to training, Harry demands Delta's officers always be fiercely focused on the flow of battle. It is not enough to learn set tactics or enact a plan; there is no fixed map for battle, there are moving pathways that must be noted and leapt to or from.

'Appreciation' is what the young officers are told to call it. Buddha would call it being 'Present' in the moment. Don't just let the moments flow past. Pause. Stop. Appreciate the situation. Know how your men may be diminished, know if your enemy has strengthened, know how a change in the weather may give you an advantage and change tactics accordingly.

The Delta officers are trained to have an endless loop going round in their minds: Where are we? What's changed? Is there an enemy probe creeping around our flank? How do we counter it?

Don't be sure of yourself, *question* yourself, and appreciate that each action you take will bring a reaction from them. What can you do to thwart that reaction before it arises? Think! Act! There is a new way of doing things. To fight the last war, whether it be a Malayan Emergency or D-Day, is to lose the next war. Delta will be mentally and physically limber, fit for battle in both senses of that phrase.

'The level of our training, and not only mine but of everyone,' Lieutenant Dave Sabben would recall, 'was of such a good standard that when action was required we slipped into it, and certainly myself I slipped into it very easily. I was able to focus on the things that I needed to focus on. Your environment closes around you and, in my experience, nothing else matters. Particularly as an officer. This is what I need to know. I need to know where my troops are. I need to know where the enemy is. I don't need to know how scared I am. I don't need to know that I need a drink of water or something. I'm totally focused on what I need here. I've got my map. I've got my radio. I've got my weapon if I need to fire it.'[16]

Again using his commando experience as his reference point, however, the absolute key for Smith – his foundational belief in terms of training his men to be ready for Vietnam – was that the most important unit was not the company, not the platoon, but the sections. Go on field exercises as sections, march as sections, train as sections, travel as sections, and you will *fight* as sections. In Smith's vision, each section must be like a squad of commandos, a fit and highly trained band of brothers, capable of operating independently at all times out on their own, or as part of a cohesive force with other sections of their platoon, who in turn had to endlessly practise how to integrate with fellow platoons as part of Delta Company.

Again and again and again Harry Smith drills them.

They have more drills than BHP. There are obstacle-crossing drills, contact drills, harbour drills, ambush drills, drills to sharpen drills, and successive drills where you do all of the above in quick but changing succession, so that the previously awkward becomes instinctive, the unnatural no less than second nature. In between drills they learn movement formation, camouflage and concealment, ambush procedures, more field signals and silent mobility. There is so much to learn it is hard to keep track.

Not that there aren't lighter moments – at least the way the men look at it.

After one particular night's camp, Harry Smith gathers his O Group to him – his senior officers and NCOs – who, among other things, have the task of passing on and enforcing his orders from on high, and this evening all are present and accounted for: Dave Sabben will deliver Harry's ten commandments to 12 Platoon, Gordon Sharp the 11th, Geoff Kendall will pass on word to the 10th, while that great bear of a man that is Sergeant Major Jack Kirby leans in to gather every word, as Harry the Ratcatcher gives a new order to be disseminated to the men. Now hear this:

From now on, there will be neither farting, nor coughing in the mornings. (But *especially* no farting.)

The likes of Sabben, Sharp, Kendall et al. stare back at him. Is he . . . serious?

He is?

Too noisy. In the jungle, it might be the difference between life and death. From now Delta Company will be making every effort possible to be . . . silent but deadly.

•

In the growing camaraderie among the officers, the Tamworth man, Lieutenant Gordon Sharp is a standout, managing to combine two seemingly completely incompatible things.

On the one hand when they are on R & R breaks in Brisbane you can always count on Sharpie to be the life of the party.

On the other hand, he doesn't drink! Never a drop. Just doesn't like it. And in any case, his natural exuberance is such that he doesn't need grog to get him going.

'We'd go to a party and he'd be rolling around the bloody floor and honestly, you'd think he was pissed – we'd all be on the syrup,'[17] his comrade Lieutenant John O'Halloran would say. But not a bit of it. That is just Sharp!

And women – particularly the nursing sisters and airline hostesses the single officers knock around with on leave in Brisbane – seem to find him irresistible.

'He was,' according to O'Halloran, 'the biggest pantsman you've ever known.'[18]

3 April 1966, Enoggera, Alpha grade for Delta

Major Harry Smith, Lieutenant Dave Sabben and their soldiers could not be more thrilled. And 12 Platoon's Private Paul Large is just one of many of the platoon's soldiers to write a letter home bearing the glad tidings.

'... The CO of Canungra announced on Friday night that Delta Company was the best company, and 12 Platoon the best platoon, that has been through since World War II. It might not seem like much to you, but, believe me, it is an achievement that any company would be proud to have. We will have a reputation to live up to, but after working with all the blokes out there, we are all sure we can live up to it.'[19]

The best since World War II! That is two decades!

Yes, maybe he says that to all the boys who pass through, but maybe not. That grouchy bastard isn't disposed to light compliments, and was actually genuine about it. It gives Delta Company in general, and 12 Platoon in particular, a great confidence boost. Who knows what they will face in Vietnam? But, whatever it is, there is a growing sense that they are up for it, that they couldn't have trained harder, or been better prepared in the short time they had available.

Bring it on!

4 April 1966, Long Tan, destroyed to save

The first thing the people of Long Tan village in Phuoc Tuy hear on the morning of 4 April 1966 is the staccato *whump-whump-whump* of approaching helicopters, a noise they have heard pass overhead before; but now it is a noise that hovers, that gathers, multiplies and descends.

And *what's that?* The ground is vibrating. Diesel engines and rhythmic clanking are heard from the south. It is a troop of Armoured Personnel Carriers approaching, and within 10 minutes their village swarms with soldiers of the ARVN, the South Vietnamese Army.

Is a battle to begin? No, the battle for the fate of this village has already been lost; the lives and the homes of the villagers have been requisitioned and repositioned. As their countrymen of the ARVN explain, the people of Long Tan can no longer remain here.

Ý bạn là gì? What?

Đúng rồi. True!

And it is. For now from the north and north-east the villagers can see American soldiers appear, those loping giants with their casually tipped helmets and carefully pressed uniforms; their dog-tags glinting as they start their 'search and destroy' missions looking for VC soldiers. As it happens, only VC soldiers who are deaf and blind might be in danger of capture, as all the rest have surely long gone. It means the only people who could not and would not flee in an instant are now ordered to flee in precisely half an hour. Yes, that would be the weeping and incredulous farmers and their families, those who have toiled so long at Long Tan in these remnant plantations, and who must now uproot. You have 30 minutes to pack your belongings, for you are being moved.

Where to?

They will be divided up and sent to nearby villages of Dat Do, Long Dien and Hoa Long.

Why?

The villagers are not told.

Theirs not to reason why, theirs but to move or die – and there will be no compensation.

But even as the outraged villagers are being cleared out, the small hill covered in rubber trees just a few miles to their north-west, Nui Dat, is being surveyed by engineers. The engineers have been told to prepare the specifications for building a base for the Australians, a place to hold as many as 5000 of them, with an exclusion zone of four miles around it, with its perimeter known as the 'Alpha Line', a distance established so Charlie's mortars are kept out of range of the base. Inside that exclusion zone, no Vietnamese will be allowed to reside or work. From now, this will be a 'free fire zone', meaning that the locals are not allowed inside it, under pain of being arrested and/or shot. Anyone found fleeing within that zone will be presumed to be an enemy agent and definitely shot.

Onwards.

Establishing this base at Nui Dat is like building a battlefield fortress, a statement in itself: let the word go forth, the Australians are the kings of the castle, atop their hill, and if the dirty rascals of the VC lowlands think they can continue as before, they are mistaken.

Not that the Americans have it all their way as the local VC force, the D445, are able, over the next fortnight, to send enough mortars raining upon them, and launch enough ambushes, that the Americans lose 23 killed and have 160 wounded. But the job is done, as the beginnings of a base are established at Nui Dat.

•

Major Smith's intensity never wavers. He has been told by Townsend that they may be in Vietnam and operational by as early as May, meaning these men would have just 12 months of training under their belts before potentially being in situations where they are fighting for their lives.

With that short a time frame what choice does he have but to push them to their limits?

Do some of his soldiers bridle at all the extra work?

Bugger-all, and for good reason.

By now, all the faint hearts and weak minds have joined the coughers and farters in some other location and Delta is a company confident in any task.

As Harry Smith knows better than anyone, building a cohesive military unit is not unlike building a pyramid. There is a strong aspect of assemblage to it, refining every separate part before carefully integrating them with other equal parts and continuing to build until it becomes an absolutely solid hierarchical whole. In the last few months, they have taken individuals and moulded them into sections, which have then been integrated into platoons. In due course those platoons have engaged in exercises with other platoons to form the company whole, and from there the companies will learn how to engage with each other as a battalion, before finally operating as a task force.

Right now is the time for the platoons to head out into the bush, to survive, navigate, and engage in exercises that will help refine their skills and allow them to pad through the jungle like stealthy animals, giving little warning and leaving less trace.

April 1966, Hanoi, the man from uncle

Ho Chi Minh is about to speak to the world, or at least to Japanese television, on the Nihon Denpa News. Homes in the United States and Australia will not have this interview broadcast into their homes, for the obvious reasons. As an enemy of the state, as a filthy *Communist*, Ho will not be allowed to spread his poisonous propaganda on their screens. No matter, on this day, placid and calm, he is content to answer the enthusiastic questions with a combination of world-weariness and certainty that make his responses compelling.

Reporter: 'Mr. President, would you please tell us about the characteristic feature of the war in Vietnam in the recent period and its prospects?'

Ho Chi Minh: 'This characteristic feature is: The more US imperialists bring troops into South Vietnam and intensify the air raids against towns and villages of the Democratic Republic of Vietnam, the heavier are their defeats.'[20]

Would he care to elaborate? He would and will:

'During the first two months of 1966 alone, the South Vietnam army and people wiped out 32,000 enemy troops (including 16,000 Americans), neatly annihilated seven enemy battalions and 30 enemy companies (including four US battalions), shot down or destroyed over 500 planes, and destroyed about 300 military vehicles.'[21]

As for those who hope for peace talks, Ho has no interest and is firm: the North will win this war, the US will lose it. He notes that the US is practically bereft of allies, and for good reason.

'On the international front, the US so-called peace offensive has also failed. It has not been able to deceive anybody; instead, it has only increased US isolation.'

He is happy to give fair warning to any ally that does join the US. They will join President Johnson in long, lingering defeat:

'Now, President Johnson is feverishly preparing to dispatch tens of thousands of additional US troops to South Vietnam. The army of aggression from the United States and its satellites is carrying out the savage and criminal "kill all, burn all, destroy all" policy. But as the enemy grows more ferocious, the Vietnamese people become more closely united and firmly determined to defeat him. In the end, the US imperialists will inevitably be defeated. Although the Vietnamese people's Resistance War against US aggression for national salvation is to be a protracted and arduous one, its victory is left in no doubt.'[22]

Thank you, Mr President.

15 April 1966, Shoalwater Bay, no atheists in the foxhole

Positions everyone.

After nine months of solid training for most of the conscripts, after integrating into sections, then platoons, then companies, then battalions, it is time for the last act of rehearsal, the one with the big guns – artillery.

After 6RAR is flown in RAAF troop carriers up to Shoalwater Bay in North Queensland – an ideal spot, about halfway between Brisbane and Cairns – the entire battalion must take part in 'Operation Foxhole', a manoeuvre, or mock battle, against the 'Queensland Cong', *aka* a company of men from their brother regiment of 2RAR. For the first time, to get to the starting point of this exercise they are put in things called Armoured Personnel Carriers or APCs – armoured hot-boxes on wheels, with the commander in the centre and on top, operating from behind a metal shield, a .50 calibre machine gun poking out just above and to the right of the head of the driver. The APCs can transport up to 11 soldiers at a time in relative safety from ambushes, the Diggers gaining access from a large rear ramp, while there is also a large roof hatch.

In this case, once the soldiers of 6RAR are deposited in the rough hinterland of Shoalwater Bay, they must sweat profusely in the tropical heat for the next three weeks, as they try to cope with the heavy humidity and the frequent rain, manoeuvring against these elusive 'Cong', before getting to grips with the Australian Army's answer to the Big Bang theory.

On the seventh day of the exercise, they work closely with the six big guns of 101 Battery, as they fight off an attack by the wrong Cong.

The key to such 'fire support', as the platoon commanders keenly appreciate, is to have a precision fix on your map as to exactly where you are, and exactly where the enemy is. Now, no matter that the 101 Battery can neither see you nor the enemy. Ideally, by use of one of their Forward Observers who is embedded with you as you move through the countryside, you can provide the battery with such precise co-ordinates that the enemy can be blown away – or at least have their attack disrupted.

It is for the platoon commander to assess the situation, and after liaising with his Forward Observer, direct the artillery. A single 'ranging shot', well over the heads of your platoon, will give both you and the battery a precise fix and then, ideally, you can 'walk in' the artillery from there. Once the artillery is on target, they can 'fire for effect'.

No, they do not use live shells as the risk is too great for accidents, and it would only need one drop-short and you would have so many casualties that the outcry might place the whole war effort at risk, but they are able to at least give both the officers and soldiers *some* feeling of what it might be like when taking on the actual VC.

Early May 1966, Australia, hello, goodbye

Things are going in a blur.

There is now just a fortnight to go before the departure of the first 6RAR Company to go to Vietnam, set for 23 May 1966.

All our kit must be packed. All the heavy Q-store equipment has to be scrubbed down, broken into parts if large, stowed and audited. And while your sleeves are rolled up, men, hold still for a moment while we jab you with needles for your vaccinations against cholera, typhus and yellow fever.

Now, with just 10 days to go before we depart for Vietnam, all you soldiers may return home to say goodbye to friends and family, but make sure you are back by . . .

They're gone.

Kenny Gant is home within the hour, throwing his hat on the easy chair and calling out, 'The soldier's home!'[23] before bathing his mother, Beryl, in kisses and taking over the cooking of dinner from her, for his younger brothers and sisters, just as he had always done to give his frequently ill mother a break.

'Bing's home!'[24]

All is good with the world.

Paul Large goes back to Coolah, where he sees his beloved girlfriend, Noeline, and delights in telling his mates, 'The bastards can't shoot!'[25]

Ah, it is so good to have 'Largey' back, even for just a few days. On the spot, the Coolah Rugby League Club arranges to have a gathering of the boys at 'Headlock' Jenkins' old café on Black Stump Way to give a proper farewell to the promising inside centre of the Reserve Grade side of the previous year. Yes, Paul is fairly small as far as footballers go, and he'd only played a few games before being called up, but he'd done enough to earn the coveted Coolah team blazer, and it is presented with due ceremony as all the boys applaud and Noeline gets a little teary, seeing how happy it makes him, how proud he is . . . Best of all is when his revered brother-in-law, Jimmy Manning – who not only plays inside-centre for Coolah Firsts, but also plays that position in the Group 14 and Western Division rep team – comes up and shakes his hand, and tells him when he gets back from Vietnam he'll probably play Firsts, too!

That evening, after Paul drops Noeline back home, it is just like the old days. Paul and all his mates gather at the large homestead and play riotous cards into the wee hours – low stakes poker, for the fun, not the money.

'Vic and Dulce had to be the most easy-going people on God's earth to put up with us,' Lawrie Lovegrove would recall of Paul's parents, 'for I can't ever remember either of them complaining about noise or even suggesting "Shouldn't we be going home soon?".'[26]

For their part, the likes of Gordon Sharp, John O'Halloran and the rest of their local crew head home to Tamworth where they catch up with friends and family – including each other's families – as they attend a wonderfully unending round of boozy farewell lunches and dinners.

Gordon, as ever, doesn't drink at all but still sparkles. The fact that six Nashos from the New England region are heading off to Vietnam is big local news, and the *Northern Daily Leader* doesn't miss it.

For the most part they are enthusiastic, with the notable exception of Gordon.

Yes, he is now an officer, commanding 30 men, and yes, he has done well.

But still he makes no bones about it, in many conversations with friends and family. Every month in Vietnam will be another month lost in his TV career, and he is not happy about it. He'd really rather not go, as much as he feels he must go.

Meanwhile, though Major Harry Smith is married, he does not return to see his wife, feeling like he has too much work to get through.

Alpha Company's Captain Charles Mollison feels the same, but takes it a step further when his wife visits the barracks to say goodbye. 'My wife drove me to the barracks with our two young children, but I sent her home. I thought it inappropriate to have a teary wife hanging around when I had a job to do . . .'[27]

Lieutenant Geoff Kendall returns to Brisbane, to gather his new bride and spend his last few precious days with her, the first of which are wondrous. But the end must come as the hour for parting looms.

'Suddenly, it was not so much fun. I packed off my beautiful brand-new wife to live with my folks in South Australia and as she climbed the steps of the plane I felt very much alone.'[28]

Sergeant Bob Buick returns to Brisbane to see his wife, Beverley, and his daughter, Tracey: 'We had not seen each other since April and it was wonderful to be united as a family again.'[29] They reunite knowing they are about to separate, not for a training exercise but for a war.

Gunner Phil Norris gets back to Granville and, practically on the spot, marries Maryanne. As to Dave Sabben, as his own parents are away in Mauritius, he must make do with a letter from his mother affirming her belief that the Lord would keep him safe in the palm of His hand, a faith that he shares in the form of: 'God will look after me, if I look after myself.'[30]

18 May 1966, The White House, go all the way, LBJ

President Johnson is coming under heavy attack – on this occasion from Republican Congressman Melvin Laird from Wisconsin, who is armed and dangerous with devastating figures. Right now, the US has 254,000 troops serving in Vietnam! And an *additional* 90,000 men in 'support staff'. Simply incredible.

Why, this is LBJ's 'credibility gap' in action! For, with so many men on the ground, *why on earth is the President not escalating the ground war now?*

Because, Laird thunders, because of politics. With men's lives in play, he is waiting for the mid-term elections!

LBJ cannot win, abroad or at home. He should withdraw, he should advance; he is a belligerent warmonger, he is a craven coward. He is a hard-liner, he is an appeaser who would make Neville Chamberlain blush.

He is trapped and no matter which way he turns, he is heading to destruction – and American soldiers are dying by their thousands! Every week President Johnson makes a point of phoning the families of soldiers who have died; the results feeling less cathartic and more catastrophic. Waves of emotion flooding over the families as pride competes with grief as they talk of their sons and to their President. *Don't let their sacrifice be in vain, Mr President.* He will not. He cannot.

20 May 1966, onward Brisbane soldiers, marching as to war

One way or another, the whole of 6RAR is complete again by 20 May, just in time for a farewell parade on the morrow, right down Brisbane's main thoroughfare of Queen Street – a neat month to the day since 5RAR had had their own farewell parade down Sydney's George Street, just before their own departure to Vietnam.

Dressed in their jungle greens, their slouch hats adjusted to a rakish angle, their rifles with fixed bayonets slung by their sides . . . oh how proudly they march. And though they have not yet fired a shot in anger, it is clear they are already heroes. For look at the mob who have turned up this Saturday morning as 6RAR march by.

They are five deep, clapping, whistling, cheering! From on high, people have come out from their balconies and are throwing down torn-up pieces of paper that are landing on the regiment, which has become proudly referred to as 'Brisbane's own', like confetti.

And oh, the glory of it, as they march past the official podium on the steps of Brisbane Town Hall and offer sharp salutes to His Excellency the Governor of Queensland, Sir Alan Mansfield; the Minister for the Army, The Honourable Malcolm Fraser; the Queensland Premier,

Frank Nicklin, together with an assembly of brass from the highest echelons of the Australian Army, all beaming out at them. Slouch hats at attention now, lads, dazzle as we go.

Marching beside his best mate in the army, Dave Beahan, Paul Large notices a bystander grinning at him, an anonymous Australian bloke who now yells at him, 'Good onya, Dig!'[31]

That's me! A 'Digger', an heir to the tradition of those who fought so honourably and well at Gallipoli, Tobruk, El Alamein and Kokoda. Those names just roll off the tongue. Who knows whether we will make our own mark at a place yet unknown? But, whatever happens, we are now that most respected of all things in Australian life, a Digger.

As Paul will later write to his sisters and parents back in Coolah, he feels as proud as he ever has in his life.

Onwards.

As they march past the GPO, John O'Halloran also hears someone shout out, 'Give 'em hell!'[32]

They intend to, but some have a feeling the Viet Cong won't be averse to giving them at least a bit back in return.

For now, they return to Enoggera to begin the process of packing all their kit and supplies. Much of the heavier stuff – like the additional APCs, heavy crates of ammunition and drums of fuel – will head to Vietnam by ship, the HMAS *Sydney*, but 6RAR itself will be *flown* in, by chartered jet aircraft.

24 May 1966, Nui Dat, death and denial

The 5th Royal Australian Regiment is not only well ahead of their brothers at 6RAR, they are already on the ground at Nui Dat – helping to clear the surrounding area of inhabitants so they can establish a free fire zone and make the base safe from mortar attack. On 24 May, after Alpha and Bravo Companies are dropped in by helicopters, they move out in patrols clearing the area to the east and north of the base to a distance of five kilometres. Part of the clearing involves spraying a new defoliant herbicide by the name of Agent Orange on the thickest of the jungle growth to eliminate places where the VC might be able to set up mortars to attack the base while remaining completely hidden.

It is heavy, hot and thirsty work, and the Diggers find they must guzzle water as quickly as the sweat pours out of them, or risk fainting. In this particular hell on earth that is Vietnam, the sweat pouring out of you can be as dangerous as wearing a red shirt in a bull-fight: making the front and back of your green shirt so wet it becomes dark green, which can look like black if the light fades, not unlike . . . black pyjamas.

When Privates Errol Noack, Kevin Borger and John O'Callaghan are sent forward to set up a listening post, which will give warning of any enemy moves on the main body of Australians, they gratefully pause at a creek to fill up their water-bottles. Kevin Borger had lost his giggle hat earlier in the day and wraps a sweat rag around his head to protect him from the sun. Noack, the young fisherman from Port Lincoln – now known to his fellow Diggers as 'Flex', for his muscular physique – has just asked Kevin about the best way to use their water purification tablets when suddenly there is the roar of gunfire in the near-distance and bullets start spraying all around them.

'Hit the deck!'[33] O'Callaghan yells, which they all do. But for some reason – perhaps to see where the fire is coming from – Noack briefly rises, at which point a bullet comes and drills him in the stomach, taking him down, hard.

'I can't feel anything,' he croaks weakly. 'I'm dying. God help me.'[34]

At least the firing soon stops, meaning the medic from B Company can quickly get to him. And the medevac chopper also gets down quickly and rushes him to Vung Tau. And yet *still* the darkness presses, the light ebbs, the spirit flickers, and . . . only shortly after arriving at the Military Hospital at Vung Tau, Errol Noack, aged just 21, becomes the first National Serviceman to die in Vietnam – a bare 10 days after arriving in this country. Thirty-six Australian soldiers have died in this Vietnam conflict to date. But this is different. They had been professional soldiers who had chosen to be there.

Errol is the first Nasho to die, but was it even at the hands of the enemy? Or, had he been shot by his own men, who had mistaken his wet and dark uniform for the black pyjamas worn by the enemy and opened fire? The answer is clear – it is the latter – but it does not bear thinking about and will not be officially recorded as such. For the moment the claim must stand, as the Australian Task Force Commander, Brigadier Oliver Jackson insists: Errol Noack was killed by enemy fire. Prime Minister Harold Holt weeps when he hears the news.

A pall falls across 5RAR as the reality of life – and death – in a war zone, sinks in. They, too, are told it was the VC who are responsible. (But from now on, you blokes better dry your hat when you can and make sure you see *pitch* black in the uniform of the enemy before you fire.)

There will be actual contacts with the VC over the next few days, but mercifully no more deaths. The main thing is that, at least tentatively, the broad contours of Nui Dat have been secured for the Australians, meaning that 5RAR can detach from the American Brigade to come under the control of the very 'Australian Task Force Headquarters', that they now set about further securing, putting up the beginnings of a wire fence around the whole area and digging weapons pits, together with bunkers to hold machine guns.

CHAPTER FIVE

GOOD MORNING, VIETNAM!

They had this terrible thing called 'body count', which was a hideous thing and I'm glad to hear a couple of our generals said, 'We don't believe in the body count philosophy. No, we want to win the war, not just kill people.'[1]

Major Bob Hagerty, APC Squadron

We the unwilling, led by the unqualified, to kill the unfortunate, die for the ungrateful.

Popular phrase among American soldiers, often printed on Zippo lighters

Late May and early June 1966, Amberley Air Base, Queensland, heading north

Beryl Gant is one of the lucky ones, living close enough that she has been able to come to say goodbye to her boy, Kenny, off to Vietnam.

Other soldiers are filing past, forming up, and she is weeping when Kenny interrupts.

'Mum,' he says, 'hang on a minute. I've got to go and get me cigarettes. I want to have a smoke.'

'All right.'

Fifteen minutes later, though, and he has not returned.

'Where the devil is he?'[2]

Just as she says it, she and the rest of the family hear the roar of the plane engines warming up.

All the troops, including Kenny, are now on board.

And that's her Kenny all over, just wanting to avoid a fuss.

•

Always, it's the same bloody thing with Qantas. The seat aisles are so close together there's never any room for your rifle, or your cobber's.

It's midnight, we haven't even taken off yet and good luck trying to get some bloody shut-eye with an SLR from the row behind tapping against your head. So there is only one option. The luggage compartments will have to do. The men of 6RAR turn their rifles long-ways and cram them into the compartments, with their rounds of ammunition and grenades tucked neatly around them.

The engines roar, the Boeing 707 vibrates, and starts to trundle down the runway before lifting off. Manila next stop, just for some petrol, then on to Saigon, *Vietnam!*

Now, although the means and method of transport changes through the ages, the essential sentiment remains the same. Always for Australian soldiers leaving on their way to war, there comes that moment as Australia itself is receding from view and anxious eyes scan the horizon for one last glimpse . . . before the inevitable thought comes: *will I ever see my homeland again?*

Few will feel it more strongly than Paul Large who turns 21 on the day of departure, still with the hangover from his new Army mates taking him out on the town on their last night, knowing celebrations today would be out of the question.

On this night, all that is visible are the weirdly attractive twinkling lights of Brisbane out to their right before altitude and cloud mean the last of the lights . . . . . . fade . . . . . . and they are left, alone, roaring to their fate – whatever it is – at 30,000 feet and 600 miles per hour.

This is not the usual experience of Australian soldiers heading to Vietnam, as most go via the famed 'Vung Tau ferry', a voyage on the former aircraft carrier and now massive troop-ship HMAS *Sydney*, which takes a fortnight. But there is no time for that now. They are needed in Vietnam, immediately.

First stop is Manila where they are scheduled to transfer to some US Air Force troop planes that are meant to be waiting for them. In their absence, for the moment, the good news is they are allowed to get off the plane and head into the airport terminal where, within 30 seconds, they have found some bars. The obvious ensues as – in the spirit of *eat, DRINK and be merry, for tomorrow we die* – they proceed to drink the place dry.

'All the time I was thinking,' Bravo Company's Lieutenant John O'Halloran will recount, 'This is the best bloody war I have ever been to.'[3]

Of course no-one can leave the airport, and there are hot and cold Philippine Military Policemen, with real guns, watching them closely to make sure that no Australian in uniform gets the twitch for an hour of tourism. But, really, how thorough are those MPs anyways? The answer will come in a few days' time when three of the Australian soldiers report with a strain of gonorrhoea most commonly found in . . . Manila! How the hell did that happen? Lieutenant Geoff Kendall has no idea but he knows that one should 'never underestimate the ability of the Australian soldier to find booze, women or gambling'.[4]

Delta Company, above and beyond!

•

In Vietnam itself, the men of 1RAR – who the fresh troops of 5RAR and 6RAR are to replace – ready themselves to head home after 12 months of continuous service on the front lines, where they have tragically lost 18 of their number. In the weeks leading up to their departure, Private Terry Burstall – a fresh reinforcement, 'reo', from Australia – spends his first weeks in Vietnam with 1RAR at Bien Hoa, the enormous United States air base, before he is due to transfer to 6RAR when they arrive.

He is shocked at the whole experience of seeing how the Yanks operate.

It is not just the amount of drinking the Americans get through in their canteens, though that is one thing.

It's how they wake you up . . . RATATATATTATATTATTATATATA-TATATATATATAT!!!!!!

What the fuck is that? It sounds like somebody is hammering his hangover into his head. Looking out blearily from over the lines at D Company, Terry can see a bloody big boofhead Yank firing a bloody big .50 calibre machine gun from the top of a big wooden tower.

This, he is soon advised, is the equivalent of a morning 'patrol' for the Yanks. After all, why go to all the effort of getting all kitted up and actually going out into the jungle, when you can let your gun have a look for you? Every day this is the way the watchtower machine-gunner says 'Good morning!' and 'Good night!' to any VC who might be in the area. If any of the VC out there are lost, they'll be able to find their way to Bien Hoa by noise alone.

•

Finally landing in Vietnam some 16 hours after having first reached Manila, the doors open to allow the men of 6RAR to stumble, blinking, down the stairs and into the steamy heat of the sweltering tarmac on the northern corner of Tan Son Nhut International Airport, Saigon and . . .

And good Lord, get a load of it!

Everywhere they look there are planes. Little ones. Big ones. ENORMOUS ones! On the ground. In the air. Taxiing. Taking off. Landing. There are so many planes and choppers – many of them bristling with guns and rocket launchers on their undersides – in such a relatively small space that there are no niceties about one plane taking off before another one lands. All the while helicopters whir back and forth like angry black flies, fighting for what little space is left in the sky. The whole place is swarming – the only wonder being that with so many flying machines in such a small place, going in every direction, so far none of them have run into each other. I mean, look at that bloody beauty! I think it's a Phantom! No, it's *four* bloody Phantoms taking off in tandem as four more land! Those planes are the pride of the US Air Force. They don't glide through the air, they shatter it; they are supersonic jet interceptors, fighter-bombers that fire incredible sidewinder missiles with an accuracy that is literally and fatally breathtaking. Those on the ground are being fed by the raft of refuelling trucks careening around this carelessly organised chaos. What must be fresh Yankee troops are emerging in serried rows from the bowels of troop planes, including a lot of Black Americans. And over there . . . some coffins wrapped in American flags are solemnly being carried on to another plane. Nearby, soldiers with missing limbs, bloody bandages and glazed eyes are being carried on stretchers into the bowels of a big Hercules with a red cross on it. The stench of aviation fuel is overpowering, and you'd swear if someone lit a match we'd all go up with it.

They can actually *hear* the sounds of bombing and artillery fire.

Where from?

Over there!

As one they gaze to the hills in the west where they can see massive explosions followed by plumes of smoke, all where the shells of the nearby artillery are landing.

Jesus Christ!

Their expostulations, however, are swallowed by the shattering roar of two American F-100 Super Sabre jet fighters scrambling down the runway and taking off on some emergency response.

Jesus Christ.

We've only just landed and we are *already* in a WAR ZONE.

Mercifully, many of the choppers they see are actually here to take them to their destination and a third of them are soon on board and heading south. No doubt there is a fine view for the pilots but for those in the bowels of the choppers there is nothing to see but the back of the head of the bloke in front of you.

The rest of them are to be flown south-east in what is known as 'Wallaby Airlines', Caribous from the RAAF's No. 35 Squadron doing regular shuttle runs around South Vietnam.

Yes, those ones over there.

Wide-eyed they march up the ramps that have been let down at the back of the planes, into the very belly of the beast, to take their place on the canvas seats that line the sides. Before they know it the ramp is up, the engines are roaring and they have lift-off, before steeply banking – no doubt to get out of the way of the next planes to land on the runway they have just left. F-100 Super Sabre jet fighters flash by.

The ramps of the planes and hatches of the choppers open within the hour to reveal the detritus of an airstrip in a place called – can you see the sign? – 'Vung Tau'. Here, it is quieter, not just because of the lack of roaring aircraft, but because most of the men are shocked. After all the excitement of leaving Amberley, the fun of sinking piss in Manila, suddenly they are confronted by reality, as they pile into trucks and buses – the latter of which have grates instead of windows, to keep the grenades out – which take them down a dusty road to a remarkably ugly part of the world, just north of Vung Tau, filled with mangrove swamps, sand hills and scrub.

As the bus trundles along they see . . . VC!

Look, bold as brass, and just as they had been warned, there is one of the brutes wearing the black pyjamas that had been drilled into their heads as a target. This bold bastard that has the balls to just stroll . . . no, look there, make that *two* bold bastards in black pyjamas . . .

Actually?

Actually, now that we look, there is an entire field of men in black pyjamas over there adopting the disguise of farmers. Actually, they *are* farmers! (The hoes are a dead giveaway.) Laughter rings out as the realisation sets in.

'Well, excuse me, Sir?' asks one cheeky soldier. 'But every bastard I can see is wearing [black pyjamas]! Do we shoot or what?'[5]

The VC wear the same clothing as every villager, every farmer – a uniform that blends perfectly with a perfectly uniform rural society that wears . . . all together . . . black pyjamas!

The bus rolls to a stop and . . . oh. Here we are. If God was ever going to give Vietnam an enema, this is where he would insert the tube. Hold still, this won't hurt a bit.

Welcome to Back Beach!

You blokes are sleeping over there, the Lieutenant gestures to an empty patch of what looks to be a strange and rank mix of mud and sand, which for some reason has spools of barbed wire everywhere.

Where? There are no barracks?

Of course there are no barracks, and as a matter of fact there aren't even enough tents! You are in 'Nam now, and have to make do. Those of you without tents can sleep under your hoochies.

But *where*?

Over there, in the space you'll find *between* the barbed wire. (That's for your protection.)

The heat surrounds and confounds them, the humidity is like a dead weight and all are amazed at just how much they can sweat.

But, as the redoubtable Regimental Sergeant Major George Chinn DCM remarks, for a battalion that had been born on 6 June 1965, that means that 'on its first birthday it is in Vietnam in a war zone', something that has likely never happened before to any other battalion in the Australian Army, not even in World War II.[6]

It is on his orders that 1200 cans of beer have been secured, and – after a parade in the hot sun on sand scraped flat by a bulldozer, where 6RAR's Commanding Officer Lieutenant Colonel Colin Townsend does a quick inspection of the front ranks before taking the salute – they can celebrate their birthday, sucking on beer while looking out on the low scrub in this strange land.

Over their shoulders as they savour every drop, out in Vung Tau Bay, the just arrived HMAS *Sydney* continues to unload the heavy *materiel* from Australia including, on this afternoon, the M113 Armoured Personnel Carriers from 2 Troop Squadron 1, distinguishable – for those in the know – by the fact they don't yet have their gun-shields attached to protect the soldier manning the .50 calibre machine gun. A crane lifts them one by one on to the army landing ship the *Vernon Sturdee* which soon nudges to the shore, lowers its ramp and allows the APCs to be driven off.

Overhead, both American and Australian choppers – the latter from RAAF No. 9 Squadron – go back and forth to the No. 35 Squadron RAAF Air Base at Vung Tau. You can tell the difference because the American choppers mostly look like flying tanks, bristling with armour and weaponry, while the Australian ones are more to the order of flying Coke cans, baby chicks around the hulking Yankee mother-ships.

The Australians are on their way to deploying their largest number of soldiers on the ground since World War II but it will only be with heavy US air support.

Inevitably, the cameras are there to capture the almost triumphant footage of the young Australians arriving – albeit also chronicling how difficult it is to look like you're saving the day when wobbling with heavy kit on a bloody sandy beach. (General MacArthur had got it down to a fine art: insisting his footage only be of him jumping into the shallows, and walking on the hard sand, striding forward!)

The primary impression of all of them is that none of them, not even the blokes from far North Queensland, have experienced anything like the heat and humidity that greet them now.

'Pom' Rencher, like many Poms, has a natural gift for complaining, but he is telling God's truth when he says that 'Even the South China Sea was warm and sticky.'[7]

When the bloody *ocean* makes you feel hot – whoever heard of such a thing? – it is a sign that shits are trumps in this hell-hole. Delta's storeman, Tubby Campbell, even decides that the only way to make it more bearable is to sample his own stores. Half a bottle of gin later he has a solution. He is bloody well going to swim home, and part swimming, part swigging, starts to swim in the general direction of where he reckons Queensland must be. The laughter of his mates fades first in the distance and then from alarm as he actually does a bloody good job at getting out to sea. Thankfully a passing chopper comes low and angles its blades, practically blowing *him* back to shore.

In short order the sodden Tubby is with the other new arrivals in the back of a truck being shifted to a nearby bit of flat, swampy ground with mangroves nearby – your basic nightmare of heat, humidity and huge mosquitos.

The heat – did they mention? – is appalling and all of them have dark rings of sweat stemming from the armpits of their khaki uniforms. Wading through muddy swamps is one thing, looking like one is another.

At least the landscape – of swamps, open fields, plantations, bamboo thicket and steep hills covered in scrub – isn't *totally* unfamiliar as a lot of it really is remarkably similar to the terrain they had trained in, back around Canungra and around Shoalwater Bay.

Either way, they are there for only a few days before news comes through. Instead of being there for the planned two weeks of acclimatisation, their marching orders have been brought forward and they are moving to some new place called Nui Dat.

What's that?

No-one knows.

But wherever it is, and whatever it is, it can't be worse than where they are now.

Right now, all that matters is the rumour that they're going early because there has been some enemy activity up that way, and we have a good chance of seeing some action!

In the meantime the new arrivals continue to get acquainted with this extraordinary and *strange* land.

Their eyes widen at the exotic sights even as their nostrils crinkle at the penetrating smells, and they try to get their heads around the rickshaws, the streaming streets of people and animals competing for space, the peddlers hawking their wares to the unwary, the beautiful young women wrapped in colours so bright they could go to a fancy-dress party as a rainbow and win hands down!

Life here is raw, unfiltered and often . . . bloody. With staggering casualness the Vietnamese slaughter animals for food right here on the street, carve them up and hang the fresh meat from hooks, still dripping blood.

Some of those strolling about in the villages, and particularly Vung Tau, speak an all but completely incomprehensible language, which is filled with strange sounds going ninety-to-the-dozen most of the time. And that is just the Americans.

This is Vietnam.

Old men and women on rickety bikes carrying loads so large on the handle-bars they can only just peer over them. Naked children happily running about in the street. Workers with conical hats in the rice paddies – nearly all of them women – chipping away with ancient wooden hoes, briefly gaze inscrutably at them as they pass before getting back to it. Men on buffalo carts, carrying cargos unknown, reluctantly get off the road as the Australians pass.

(*Are they Viet Cong? Or on our side? How on earth could anyone know?*)

And did we mention the smells?

Some of those smells – from the filth, the excrement in the gutters, the unwashed bodies – hit you in the head like a dead fish. Other smells – the whiff of clove and cardamom and cinnamon – are a far cry from the boiled chicken and potatoes and faint suggestion of salt they were used to at home. Who even knew food could give off aromas like this?

And you can be just breathing it in, in all its glory, when the next instant you get hit in the head with the dead fish again. As to the weather it is as hot and steamy as a tiny commercial laundry for most of the day until, every day at around about 5 pm, the monsoonal rains hit with such force the streets flood, and the camp at Back Beach turns into one large sodden mess.

They had always, mostly, appreciated home, but never as much as now. What a country to fight a fucking war in!

But to work.

Now that they are on the ground in Vietnam, the key thing is to acclimatise them to the heat, the humidity, the hassles of being in a war zone – and the only way is to put the new arrivals through a series of training exercises. In their first week there, they learn about smoke grenades, whose plumes can do everything from guiding a plane to drop napalm to signalling a chopper where to pick up a wounded Digger.

With their full kit, the Diggers must practise getting on and off Huey choppers at speed – at *speed*, I said! – precisely the way they might have to be dropped in and retrieved from actual battles. You have 10 seconds to board, and five seconds to get off.

Not fast enough! Do it again!

•

Vung Tau!

Faded French mansions. Masses of Vietnamese swirling around soldiers just like them, on R & R. Food stalls. Cafés. Tropical gardens.

Bars! Nightclubs! Grog!

Boom-Boom girls.

Relieving the misery of the situation for many of the soldiers in these first couple of weeks in Vietnam, some lucky soldiers are allowed 24-hour passes to leave Back Beach and go to the town of Vung Tau itself, a former French resort town now taken back by the locals to act as *the* place for R & R for the visiting Americans and their allies like the Australians.

For many a young Australian the allure of Vung Tau is overwhelming.

Everywhere they look, drop-dead gorgeous young Vietnamese women are promising to 'love you long-time', just for a short time, for the equivalent of 2.50 US dollars for three hours.

They're everywhere!

You can get a 'steam and cream' in one of the bathhouses, which is pretty much what it sounds like; a straight root in one of the massage parlours; or nominally get your hair cut at the barber for the equivalent of one dollar, while it is four for a haircut *and* a tug, and five for a haircut, a tug and a blow-job, hold the tomato sauce and the onions.

The Brylcreem is free.

(Not for nothing will the joke run among the Diggers: 'Q: What was your worst head job like? A: Bloody magnificent.'[8])

If bars are your fancy, try the glittering Lily Bar, the Blue Angel, the Rose Bar or maybe the Phan Than Uc Dai Loi, the last three words meaning 'Australian' which had originated from the AUSTRALIA sign on the vehicles around Baria and Vung Tau: AUS *uc*; TRA *dai*; LIA, loi.

Fair dinkum, it doesn't matter if you fell out of the ugly tree and got hit by every branch on the way down – no sooner have you stepped out of the heat and light and into the darker cool than you are *swamped* by Boom-Boom girls who storm ashore all over your general person. You are outnumbered, and there is no use fighting it.

'You buy me Saigon Tea. I give number one suck fuck!'

'You Number One Boom Boom!'

'I love you bookoo.'[9]

Time for one more root before heading back to Nui Dat, but blown most of your money? No wuckers. You can always go to 'Hundred P Alley' where the woman will lean back against the wall and lift her skirt, while you have a knee-trembler for the ages. And it only costs the equivalent of ten Australian cents! The pox is for free . . .

•

Among those who enjoy their time at Vung Tau are the RAAF's chopper pilots, who get to live in a one-time French villa down on the waterfront, and no-one more than Flight Lieutenant Frank Riley, a one-time electrical fitter from Katoomba, who lives hard and fast, flies by the seat of his pants, rants about the failings of his superior officers, and could drink for Australia. A wild man like they don't like them anymore, one of his party tricks – and he needs a few, given the number of parties he attends – is to get right below the ceiling fans that constantly whir, and then jam his head right into it at the precise time and angle that his melon doesn't even bear a mark. Brings the house down, every time. More drinks for Frank! It is for good reason that the wild chopper pilot attends Mass every Saturday night, religiously, as he has a lot of confession to get through, and says, 'If I go to confession, I can do whatever I like the rest of the week.'[10]

And he does.

In terms of keeping up the morale of the RAAF No. 9 Squadron in oft difficult circumstances, there is always a current story going about Frank, some scrape he has got into, or out of, or just survived, but something the other blokes are always talking about.

Have you heard the latest? No, not the one about the fact that in his early days as a pilot of fixed-wing planes he was famous for doing loop-de-loops the wrong way round, first turning his plane upside down and *then* doing it – that is *old* news.

Well, the latest is, Frank has managed to swap a slouch hat for an American jeep!

TRUE. Frank was drinking with a Yank officer who said he'd give anything for a slouch hat, whereupon Frank said, ''ow bout one of your jeeps?' and the Yank said 'Yes!' The Yanks are so well supplied with everything a jeep wouldn't be missed, and that's why if you look through the window, even as we speak, you can see it proudly parked there: a Yank jeep!

Inevitably, in the brothels and bars, the newly arrived Australians meet and talk with some of the veteran American soldiers, mostly big strapping men from places like Idaho and Kansas, who swagger around like they own the joint, and are constantly talking of 'Charlie'. It is not just in appearance these Yanks – part of an American contingent now 300,000 strong in Vietnam – look and act like cowboys in army fatigues.

Their fighting song, which they all sing together at a moment's notice whether drunk or not, is the theme from the television show *Rawhide*.

But of course they also talk to the new arrivals about the war, and what the Australians are here to do.

'You're going *where*?' they drawl curiously in that curious twang of theirs, like someone is sitting on all their vowels, flattening them.

Well, they reckon it is to a place called Nui Dat, right in the middle of Phuoc Tuy province, the one that 5RAR is already up there building.

Jesus wept. There is a look the Americans give them.

This is serious. Charlie is strong in that area. Strong in organisation. Strongly resourced, well trained, highly disciplined and . . . thick on the ground. If this whole area was a fucking zoo – and it is – then the lion's den is right around Nui Dat. There are whole villages around there that are openly VC and don't even bother pretending to have any fealty to the South Vietnamese Government. The good thing is, you can expect some action. The 173rd Airborne Brigade to which the Australian 1RAR had been attached had done quite a few operations in that area, and it had not taken long to get acquainted with Charlie – and there had been lots of casualties on both sides.

One or two of the veteran Americans even talk to them, with haunted eyes, of the Battle of Xa Cam My, a village just north of Nui Dat where Charlie Company of the 2/16th Infantry US 1st Division had been all but wiped out – 36 killed and 71 wounded – when they had pursued what had been thought to be a small VC force into a rubber plantation, only to be hit by a fucking VC battalion!

Okay. Great. We look forward to it.

In the meantime, let's have another 'amber sandwich', beer, and you can give me some tips about which brothel to visit tomorrow, or even the best 'barber' to visit.

•

The actual Vietnam War itself is somewhere out there and no doubt about it, but there seems little danger in this sprawling sandy camp of trenches and stenches by the mangrove swamps. Not that their officers let them relax anyway. No, now that they are on the ground in Vietnam, the need for fitness – by going on shattering training runs; for posting sentries on the edge of camp; for conducting patrols all around looking for any signs of the enemy are more important than ever and Delta

Company is in it with the best of them, sweating profusely in the staggering humidity. There is the occasional pause for a sandy meal of US 'C' rations – nominally cans of meat, fruit, cake, peanut butter and so forth, but it all rather tastes the same, no matter what – before they are back at it again.

Typically, Delta's feet have barely touched the beach before Harry Smith puts them out on a series of training exercises which include overnight patrols to get familiar with the conditions – mud, vines, stinging nettles, leeches, snakes, spiders, monkeys, mites, mountain wasps and more mud – and, as ever, they do things completely different from the other companies.

When you harbour for the night, no using machetes to give yourself space. No shell-scrapes when you make camp, and no fires! It is Harry's order from the first. We do not want to advertise where we have been, leaving machete hacks to mark our path, and 100 imprints on the jungle floor where we camp. We want to blend with it, and leave nothing behind. Nor do we want the enemy to hear us, which is why Harry also bans us using the li-lo blow-up mattresses we have all been issued with, as they are too squeaky – and that could be the difference between life and death. Instead, we cut them into separated tubes of black rubber which can be used to cover the bandoliers of M60 machine-gun ammunition we carry draped cross-ways over each shoulder. That will keep them dry, mud-free *and* minimise the chance of a glint of sun coming off the silver bullets and making the enemy aware of our presence. Delta Platoon has trained like Commandos, and now we must *be* Commandos, in Vietnam.

All up, while on such patrols, and standing sentry duty on the camp perimeter, it is an extraordinary thing to put live ammunition in your weapon. Back in Australia it was really only on the rifle range you did that, and all under strictly controlled conditions. But not here. Here, it is for real.

'Here,' Terry Burstall will note, 'live ammunition was a part of everyday life. It gave me a feeling of definite power, and fear, when on my first patrol I cocked a live round up the spout of my rifle and realised it was there to kill a human being if need be, and . . .'[11]

And, shots fired!

A battle up ahead?

Emerging from a deep swamp, with their rifles held above their heads, D Company moves into assault formation, scouts forward, and approaches.

Oh.

It proves to be a South Vietnamese Army firing range where their local allies are firing at – and, it has to be said, mostly missing – a series of targets. Up close, these soldiers they are here to help are far from prepossessing. Serious soldiers have a way of carrying themselves, a confidence, a swagger, an attitude which says 'I can handle whatever the day throws at me'.

These soldiers are not like that.

Physically small, in tattered uniforms, they rather resemble kids playing at soldiers than the real thing. They're not, frankly, the kind of blokes you'd want to have at your back in a blue. Still, maybe they'll manage? Broadly, the job of the ARVN, the Army of the Republic of Vietnam, will be to suppress the VC in the villages and towns, while it is for the Americans, Australians, Kiwis et al. to suppress them in the bush.

But do you dinkum think 'Marvin the ARVN', as the Americans dismissively refer to them, can do it? Why doesn't Marvin fight like Charlie does?

The return journey through the swamp is rather maudlin because of it, as the sense grows among the Australians they are in deep here, and without much support. They get into Back Beach just before dusk, the lack of light perfectly matching their mood.

•

It's a worry all right.

For well over a fortnight now, the soldiers of 5RAR have been digging in and doing their best to establish the base at Nui Dat, but now come still more reports from Intelligence. A regiment of Viet Cong – about 1000 strong! – is pushing their way from the north-west and is only half-a-day's march away!

In all likelihood, they intend to disrupt the supply pathway routes, blowing up bridges and attacking convoys.

The fact that three 120 millimetre mortar rounds land just beyond the nascent perimeter that day, and that after reports of movement on Route 2 after dark the Australian artillery must open up in the wee hours, heightens the sense of menace from without, and vulnerability within. Ropes have been found outside the perimeter with knots in them, suggesting that Charlie is trying to get a *precise* reckoning of distances, so as to be able to drop his mortars even more accurately.

5RAR needs help, and they need it as soon as it can possibly be arranged.

Fortunately, help is at hand. The newly arrived APCs, ideal for moving soldiers through what the Yanks refer to as 'Indian Country' – territory swarming with Charlie – can take an advance guard up there immediately to set up the basics, and we'll chopper the rest in.

•

Shake a leg, you bastards.

Apparently at this Nui Dat place, which is about six minutes flying time into the interior, the blokes from 5RAR have just begun building a base, and we have to do the rest.

At least we'll be arriving in style . . .

For they call these beauties 'Chinooks', and there are eight of them! They are huge, heavily armoured and armed American Air Force choppers with dual rotors, and on the morning of 14 June the first of the soldiers of 6RAR run, bent double, across the tarmac at Vung Tau to jump aboard, to quickly be whisked away in an aerial convoy. These convoys will be going back and forth between Vung Tau and Nui Dat all day for most of the rest of the week. The paddy fields, plantations and villages of Phuoc Tuy soon form a rich mosaic below, as the men gaze once more on this strange, beautiful and dangerous land from a different angle.

Just five minutes later, the distant detail becomes clearer as they lose altitude, the ants become Vietnamese peasants, the plantations become individual trees, and what looked to be an open field surrounded by strange green blobs very quickly becomes a landing area surrounded by tents.

They are here. A lop-sided sign with scrawled white paint tells them their landing area is called . . .

Kangaroo Pad.

Again, bending double, they run from the massive wash thrown down by the rotors – which manages to throw up a strange combination of mud and dust straight into their faces and all over their uniforms – and start to get their bearings. All around are exhausted-looking soldiers of

5RAR who have been here for three weeks, all of them covered in the same red mud everyone is now standing in. This is a wet, sticky, humid, *hot* place. Away from the LZ, they are in the remains of a rubber plantation, which at least gives some protection from the sun. Still, if they thought the mud was bad when they landed, it is as nothing to what happens when the monsoonal rains hit that afternoon, as they hit *every* afternoon.

And speaking of that mud, it's time, men, to get digging your shell-scrapes so you can have some protection in the unlikely event we come under mortar attack, before putting your hoochies over them.

6RAR are the new boys providing 850 new troops. Accompanying them is the 1st Armoured Personnel Carrier unit of the Australian Army, the 4th/19th Prince of Wales's Light Horse. (Yes, they had lost the actual horses since the Great War, but retained the prestigious Light Horse nomenclature as, in any case, Light Horsepower never had the same ring of romance. Sadly, cavalry charges are a thing of the past, more's the pity.)

There is also an assortment of artillery, including Kiwi and Yank batteries – engineers, signals and sundry – all now under the iron rule of Brigadier Oliver Jackson. (He is a man not to be trifled with. If not quite 'born-to-rule', he is not one to encourage discussion among his underlings as to what he should do. For he always has the air of *knowing* what must be done, and simply pronounces from on high.

'A tall gaunt man with what one might call piercing eyes,' a contemporary underling will describe him, 'he had a commanding presence. Certainly he was one not to be trifled with – and no one did.')[12]

As to the RAAF, they have six Caribou planes based down at Vung Tau but – as ever with the RAAF – though nominally there to support the Army, they are outside the command of Jackson. All up, the Australians are currently a well-organised motley crew, trying to work out how to fit into the sweaty sprawl that meets their eyes.

Bit by bit, those few who get time to climb to the top of the Nui Dat hill to get their bearings – read the officers, and most particularly the artillery officers, for whom an understanding of the topography is everything – come to understand the basic area. Right away, given how – from the top of the hill – they have close to 360 degrees vision of much of the province, including its settlements, roads and plantations, it is clear how disruptive their presence is going to be to the Viet Cong.

We are smack-bang in the middle of the lot, and our base is central to the major thoroughfares through the province, both clandestine and open. For the first time in these parts, Charlie will have to worry about *our* patrols and ambushes!

On this day, the man making his way to the top of Nui Dat is a quietly spoken New Zealander, Captain Maurice 'Morrie' Stanley, who has arrived here with the 161st Field Battery, Royal New Zealand Artillery, and has already been assigned to 6RAR's Delta Company under the command of Major Harry Smith. As a Forward Observer, Stanley's job will be to travel with Delta Company when they go out on patrol and be ready at a moment's notice to give precise co-ordinates to his comrades at the 161st, so they can drop shells where they are most needed. A professional soldier of great standing, Stanley had completed his final two years of school at a cadet unit in Wellington before winning a four-year cadetship to train at Duntroon, and he now takes it all in, comparing the features he can see with the map he holds in his hand, the one they have all been issued with. Ideally this familiarity will allow him, once he is out there on patrol, to be able to get a certain fix just by seeing a crook in the road, a river bend, the corner of a plantation.

(More importantly still? If things go bad for them on patrol, and they are under attack, he will be able to give precise co-ordinates for where Charlie is, and if it's anywhere within the artillery's 10-kilometre range, he can bring shells raining down on the enemy's head. It is his creed, and the company's need: know where you are at all times; you may think you are in the middle of nowhere, but you are in fact in the quadrant of a grid that can save you and the entire company.) No matter that Stanley is generally beloved as one of nature's gentlemen – albeit with a strong strain of no-nonsense about him – when it comes to ruthlessly raining down hell with extreme violence upon the enemy, there is little of the gentleman about him. An artilleryman of over a decade's standing, he has commanded a battery, and worked well with 1RAR and 5RAR for six months before 6RAR's arrival.

Time to focus . . .

To the south and south-east are rice paddies that have had to be abandoned because of the exclusion zone, together with a mosaic of equally abandoned smaller rice paddies, and banana and rubber plantations, together with a little jungle. To the north and west it is basically heavy virgin scrub, with small patches here and there as farmers have attempted to carve out a living.

To the immediate east there is heavy scrub, mixed with elephant grass so high – *as high as an elephant's eye* – that it can extend two feet higher than the tallest soldier. You could hide a division of soldiers in there and no-one would know. Beyond that is what had originally been a kind of mangrove swamp now substantially drained by a stream called the Suoi Da Bang which carries the daily monsoonal rains from the whole area, and beyond that again, he can recognise, *let's see*, the rubber plantation that lies beside the abandoned village of Long Tan – where, apparently, the residents have been cleared out and re-settled beyond the exclusion zone. Beyond the plantation is a slightly smaller but more heavily wooded hill very like the one they are standing on, carefully marked on the maps as . . . Nui Dat 2.

Captain Stanley heads back down the hill, memorising his surroundings, to find that the nascent base remains a hive of activity.

For in the meantime, where will we sleep tonight?

Yes, good question.

Due to some administrative oversight, the tents have not yet arrived for us soldiers – the officers have mostly been looked after – so we will just have to make the best of it, sleeping 'neath hoochies, with blow-up mattresses for a bed.

It is, true, something of a problem, because in these parts the rain is, if not a constant, pretty bloody frequent and it is hard to stay dry and impossible not to be covered in the red mud that our feet and machinery are constantly churning up. The worst of it is digging the gun pits.

John Robbins of 11 Platoon can't remember the last time he wasn't knee-deep in mud and slush, and can't even imagine a future time when he might be dry. Every time it looks like it might drain, the next tropical downpour explodes upon them, which means you are bailing like a navvy from the navy in a leaky boat. From bitter experience John has learnt to go without undies – like everyone around here, commandos go commando if they are to avoid a rash while digging or at least delay one. Most irritating though is not the perpetually wet clothes, but the squelching boots. If you don't dry your toes you'll get tinea; but you can't take your bloody boots off when you're digging and swinging picks about. The best he can, Robbins tries to be philosophical – other soldiers must have had it tougher, surely. It's just that he can't think of

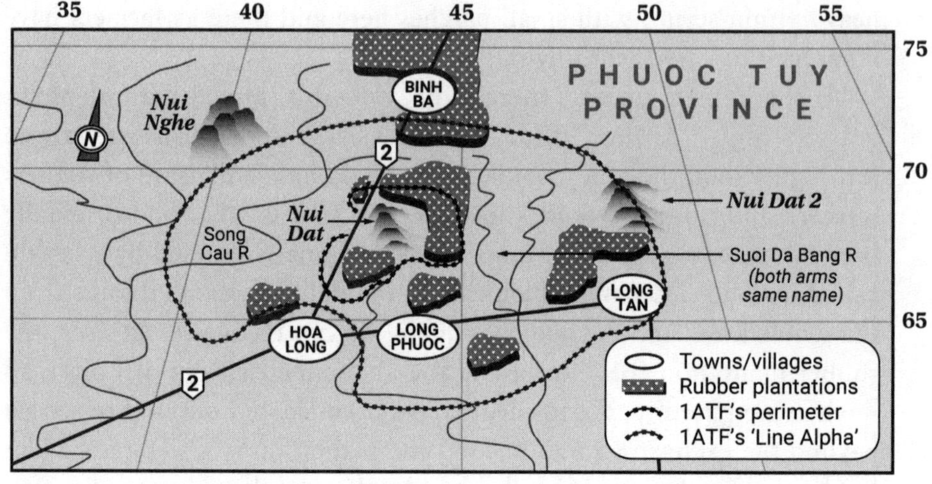

1ATF's Nui Dat base, Phuoc Tuy province, showing 'Line Alpha'

any right now. Come on, youse blokes, keep digging! And bailing. We'll finish this thing or it'll finish us.

Another problem is no kitchens have been set up yet, so we must live out of ration packs with no hot meals, but, look, you can't have everything you know?

At least we have ablution pits: long trenches, with an equally long log over them, for you to perch on in hessian 'thunder boxes' as you do your business, before throwing lime on it to stop the smell – no, really.

All such places have to have deep trenches built around them to drain the monsoonal rains and prevent everything turning into a wretched muddle of a mud-heap.

And so – as every day starts with those platoons on the perimeter being woken half an hour before sunrise to stand to in their weapons pit until half an hour after first light – the real work begins.

Their most important task is to continue the work of building a defensible perimeter extending 12 kilometres around the whole base, which in the short-term means driving in fence-posts and stringing up wire between them, while also building trenches where they could stand, protecting most of their bodies while keeping heavy fire on whoever might be attacking. What attacks them mostly is the rain, which visits every afternoon with a long vengeance and makes just enough cameo appearances in the day to make sure nothing is ever dry. In between downpours, bunkers are also built for HQs, as well as storage of equipment and ammunition.

Now with a good back-hoe they might have been able to make short work of it, but the Americans – it was a Yank who wrote *Catch-22* after all – will only release any of their precious machines when the base is secure, and as they *can't* secure it without a fence and trenches it means . . . they can't have a back-hoe.

Dig, Diggers?

They dig.

Eponymously, they scratch away at the red soil with whatever entrenching tools they can get their hands on, using their guts and gumption to get the job done.

It is hard, back-breaking work, day after day after bloody day, and the worst of it is there is neither enough of them to do it, nor never quite enough supplies to do the job properly.

Wire is in such short supply, and so desperately required, that no sooner does a Land Rover arrive with more wire than it is instantly unloaded and strung out in the next couple of hours by Diggers eager to get *some* protection in this strange and menacing world.

In the end, in those first weeks they can build no more than a rough kind of cattle fence, with a few rolls of concertina wire in front of it, while fence-posts are so few and far between they have to be spaced out as much as 20 metres apart. Even their M60 machine guns, an infantry section's main source of firepower, are so thin on the ground that there is always a struggle between those going on patrol – referred to by the Diggers as a 'walk in the weeds' – and those building the fences who should have the most machine guns, against the chance they will be attacked. Further protection against the base being overwhelmed and . . . killing them all . . . is separating the areas where each platoon is camped by whatever concertina wire they can grab so that even if the enemy takes over one area, they will have to fight to get through to the next area. And if they do breach the wire anywhere, at least the phone line to the 547 Signal Troop will alert them?

To get in and out of the perimeter, heavily camouflaged entrances are constructed – designed to be completely indistinguishable from the normal perimeter – and as an added precaution a zig-zag arrangement of concertina barbed wire rising to two metres high is arranged so that even if the enemy did force the entrance, they would soon be cut to pieces.

Still, the powers-that-be clearly have the view that there is very little risk of that. No, the only enemy out there is the local D445 Battalion, which is no more than 500 strong. They would not have the strength to attack the base in force, so the fact that we don't even have Claymore mines to place strategic minefields in front of likely points of attack is regrettable, but not regarded as any more critical than having no sandbag gun emplacements on the outer side of the pits, which in turn have no overhead cover.

'Our defences were ratshit,' Sergeant Bob Buick would recount. 'We only had a couple of strands of barbed wire up basically. Couldn't even stop a bull in heat . . . They could have attacked the base one night, killed two or three hundred Australians and we would have been . . . down the beach a week later waiting for the *Sydney* to come and take us home.'[13]

But it shouldn't come to that, because there's just not enough of the VC out there.

Yes, there had been movement heard around the perimeter on their first few nights there, as Charlie sends out probing patrols trying to determine the exact contours of their defences, and outright panic with the first report of torches being seen coming close to the outside of the wire. Mercifully, despite shots being fired in the direction of the 'torches', it is later established they aren't torches at all, but rather a tight swarm of fireflies buzzing around in the grass outside the wire.

(Torpedoes for dolphins, anyone?)

Either way, beyond the barbed wire, the principal defence against an attack on Nui Dat is sending out endless patrols in the area looking for signs of Charlie congregating – with each company given a specific area to be responsible for, so the entire area between the perimeter and the Alpha Line is covered – but there is little expectation of coming across a major force of VC.

'It was very hard work,' Corporal Laurie Drinkwater, a Taree boy now of 12 Platoon D Company, will recall, 'because you never got time to rest because you had to put up your defences, you had to dig your hole in the ground; you had to keep active on patrols out the front and making sure that no-one's creeping up on you and all that, and just everything had to be done and we hardly got any sleep at all – it was shocking.'[14]

In the face of actually having to do such patrols, to *actually* go out into enemy territory as a genuine exercise where you might get shot dead, some blokes grow, and some blokes shrink. And it is not just a matter of those who are naturally brave and those whose pupils look like blowflies in a bottle the whole time they are out.

The ones who are most admired are those who somehow master their fear and bloody well get on with it. The Coolah man, little Paul Large, is a case in point, for as a point of honour he insists on taking the most difficult position of the lot, that of forward scout, the one most susceptible to booby traps and ambushes. Behind him come the section commander with his compass and map, followed by the machine-gunner ready to lay down suppressing fire at the first sign of trouble. But it is Paul at forward scout who must painstakingly carve a path through the grass, vines and undergrowth, his eyes straining for the smallest sign of booby traps, for the tiniest disturbance in the ground he is about to put his foot on. And all this while he keeps his SLR in the other hand, ready to fire. His whole body tingles with the knowledge that at any moment a bullet with his name on it might be coming his way. But he keeps doing it!

'[He was] full of bravado,' Private Noel Grimes would recall, 'but everybody knew that a lot of it was front with him. He was always – oh yeah – he was one of these definitely "oh we'll show them". But everybody knew he wasn't sort of that brave and it used to really sort of – he was a nervous wreck really but he used to pretend he was – you know, "I'm happy".'[15]

And that is the most admirable thing of all. To be scared and not do something is understandable, but troubling in the military context. But to be scared of doing the most dangerous job of the lot, and still do it, sparing others from having to do it, is extraordinary. Large's stature and that of the other forward scouts in all the platoons grows.

•

Later on, at least there are a few breaks in the sheer gut-wrenching tedium of it all. Very occasionally companies are given two days' leave R & R to blow off steam at Vung Tau, something that really does help lift morale in the short term though there is admittedly sometimes a problem in the shorter term with dreadful cases among the soldiers of venereal disease.

Less troublesome is when, occasionally, the Diggers are invited to join the Yanks of the 2/35th Artillery Battalion to watch R-rated movies while guzzling Budweiser beer in a big tent set up for the purpose. It is a real break in the tedium and the Americans themselves enjoy showing hospitality to the 'Ossies', as they call them.

(One would mention being troubled down in Vung Tau when they had showed some Western movies to the South Vietnamese, and couldn't help but notice their guests were cheering the Indians.)

•

Soon enough the tents start to arrive – 20 foot by 20 foot marquee canvas tents – which is the good news. The bad news is they look and feel as if they might have been used by our blokes at Gallipoli, and in fact really do date from World War II! They reckon the bloody things have been used by 1RAR at Bien Hoa, but one look says they must have been used for target practice, so appalling is their condition, with more holes in them than ol' Mrs Kafoops' stockings.

This is quite a place; it's bloody wet and bloody hot, but never quite hot enough to dry the bloody wet, meaning there is actually more mud than solid ground, particularly when churned up by feet and wheels. This mud sticks to tyres and boots with equal unshakeability and you only have to walk or drive on it for a few minutes on major thoroughfares before you have a coating of three or four inches.

'The soil in our area is Red Mud,' one Digger will write home. 'RED BLOODY MUD. It drives me mad. I put on clean greens. 2 minutes later I'm wearing RED greens.'[16]

There is *no* respite.

'Man and machine waged war against the weather and the weather seemed to be winning hands down,' Private Burstall will chronicle. 'Washing facilities were non-existent but as everyone smelled the same, body odours were unnoticed . . . The rain kept coming and the mud got thicker and heavier and everyone became dirtier, more tired, and more depressed.'[17]

And yet, bit by bit, the 1ATF base at Nui Dat, a veritable tent-city, starts to emerge from their labours, both in terms of a more secure perimeter that surrounds the four square kilometres, and the areas made their own by the men: 5RAR takes the north side, 6RAR the east. And those newly arrived blokes who have just been choppered in by Chinooks with their guns hanging from the belly of the beast – and ammunition packs hanging below that – are from Australia's 103rd Field Battery. They join their comrades from the 105th Field Battery and the Kiwis'

161st Field Battery. (The Kiwis and the Australians fighting together on a foreign field is, of course, a generational renewal – a revisitation of something that had first happened at Gallipoli with the grandfathers of these young ANZACs. This, now is a proud partnership and an eerie echo in one. The Artillery and Engineers are in the southern part of the base, while – go west, young man – the rest is left for the 1st Armoured Personnel Carrier Squadron, the 103rd Signals Squadron and the elite Special Air Service Regiment SAS unit. By the end of the first month there will be nigh on 3000 personnel at Nui Dat.

For the most part, those in individual units know little of those in other units, with no time for socialising even if they wanted to, and every one of the roughly 3000 blokes on base fully occupied on their own tasks. If they have to refer to those in other units, it is more often than not derisively. The Armoured Personnel Carrier crew sometimes known as 'turret-heads'? They will drive us to where the real action is. The same goes for the artillery, otherwise known as the 'drop-shorts' or the 'nine mile snipers'. Could there be a cushier job than throwing shells into a barrel and letting it rip? It ain't *real* soldiering.

The RAAF blokes, otherwise known as the 'Brylcreem boys'? Well, you know what they say: 'The navy navigates by the stars, the army sleeps under the stars, and the RAAF stays in five stars.' Those bastards get to base themselves in Vung Tau in any case, ferrying back and forth to this base by landing either at 'Kangaroo Pad', 'Eagle Farm' or 'Tiger 5', the bases of 1ATF, 6RAR and 5RAR respectively.

As to the 'Pogos', the most common interaction they have with the 'real men' who go out beyond the wire is to serve them lunch and dinner, or maybe give them the R & R forms they must sign to go to Vung Tau. On a small path, when a Pogo comes face to face with a soldier, it is the Pogo who must give way, and everyone understands it.

And so for us front line soldiers, it is time to get to the job at hand.

For each platoon everything is done on three-day rotations. For the first day they must patrol that specific part of the area outside the wire they have been assigned to, their 'TAOR', or Tactical Area of Responsibility, looking for any sign of the enemy before setting up for ambushes of the enemy anywhere from one to three miles out. Contacts are occasional, but neither vicious nor enduring – classic shoot'n'scoot. Following up, the Australians often see the distinctive tracks oft left by the local VC guerrillas – the truncated tyre tracks known as 'Ho Chi Minh sandals', footwear made out of used tyres.

Onwards into the next day. Once returned from patrol, no sooner have they dropped their kit than they must pick up a shovel to build earthworks on the same perimeter they must defend that night – not forgetting doing endless bailing of water out of their trenches to keep the monsoonal waters at bay. The third day is a mixture of all of the above, together with kitchen duties and setting up and manning listening posts out in the scrub beyond the wire, and then the cycle begins again. Most of the soldiers are getting no more than five hours interrupted sleep a night and the whole experience is something close to a wet hell on earth.[18]

•

Piece by piece the base is built, with medical facilities, canteens, streets, tented villages, a post office, a rubbish dump, and even a dentist. If they should die, think only this of them, there is a corner of a foreign field that is pretty much Australian, right down to the meat pies they often eat, every now and then washed down by VB and Foster's beer they are occasionally allowed to drink.

It's just that few parts of Australia have heat and humidity, rain and mud like this, let alone this number of stinging insects. Still, for the brass, there are bigger and more persistent pests about than mosquitos and one of them is Captain Bob Keep. He is an Intelligence officer masquerading as a dog with a bone that won't let go. Tall and slight, with every facial feature a tight angle with no curves, he has permanently furrowed eyebrows that look like they are so lost in thought they'll never find their way back. Keep has an intensity about him that would kill a brown dog, and every time you see him he looks thinner – as if he is burning so much nervous energy it can't compete with the rations that he occasionally remembers to eat. Keep has been out here long enough to have seen it all, but now he is hearing and seeing something different; a pattern broken and a new mould being set so quietly that nobody else has noticed. Now, the fact that Keep has already been labelled as 'highly unreliable' by US Intelligence is only one reason you should listen to him. Brigadier Jackson has also taken a shine to him, so much so that amused observers nickname them Batman and Robin, although who is Batman and who is Robin? Keep can keep Jackson musing for hours on his brilliant speculations – a combination of information and deductive intuition that gets more convincing the more you listen to it.

If only Keep wasn't such an *eccentric* fellow. He does not exactly provide a textbook example of dress and demeanour, and his whirling enthusiasms while unfurling his predictions raise eyebrows. And he is not the bloke likely to be elbowing you out of the way to get to the Boom-Boom girls . . . He can appear drunk when sober, so eager is he to convince you of his latest intelligence. Too clever by half? More like too brilliant by three-quarters; a restless mind that doesn't just jump at shadows he then tries to wrestle them into submission, and is not content till everyone applauds. It is well known the VC are a hit and run force in this war, but Keep keeps persisting with his notion that they could be planning a mass attack, a Dien Bien Phu just for you.

Much of Keep's energies are devoted to trying to work out just what Charlie has out beyond the wire. Most of his time is spent reading the previous intelligence reports left by the 173rd Airborne, as well as whatever reports come in from the South Vietnamese Government's paid operatives in the area, and also the reports that come in from the many patrols going out, of the things they see and hear from the interrogations they conduct.

It makes for sobering reading, with the latest intelligence report from 1 June 1966 stating matter-of-factly that Charlie has no less than a *division* with its HQ in this very province.

> ENEMY FORCES SITUATION
> The main force controlling the area of operations is the 5th Division (Main Force) . . . This Division has two sub units namely the 274th and the 275th Regiments totalling 3850 men.
>
> 274th Regiment (Main Force) comprises 2000 well trained men . . . Apart from the normal complement of weapons . . . it is strongly suspected that it possesses 120 mm mortars. It is believed that this Regiment is moving to our area probably, 1 A.T.F., with the intention of initiating a major action.
>
> 275th Regiment located well to the N.E. has a strength of 1850 men approx . . .[19]

It is the National Liberation Front (NLF) that co-ordinates all, starting with the North Vietnamese cadres fighting in the south, the Viet Cong soldiers of the 274th and 275th, the local force D445 Provincial Mobile

Battalion. These last are 350 local soldiers, well armed with rifles, heavy machine guns (HMGs) and mortars supplied by the North, and who can act as the 'meeters, greeters and feeders'[20] for those from the tiers above. And then there are the purely local units, volunteers from a village who by day work with their families and by night often do the work of the North – setting booby traps and sniping.

Between them the NLF can put a force on the ground that more than rivals the power of South Vietnam's Government, and they are without mercy in punishing those who are seen to cede to the South. Suspect villagers are sent off to 're-education camps', where they learn how to be tortured at length.

How do you know who is who?

Essentially, the NVA wear olive green uniforms with pith helmets and are usually armed with Russian-made or Chinese-made AK-47 assault rifles, heavy machine guns, mortars and rocket-propelled grenades.

As to the local fighters, the D445 Battalion usually wear either green khaki uniforms or 'black pyjamas'. As the local guerrillas of the villages, they are particularly good at setting booby traps, sniping, watching the movements of invaders and spotting opportunities for the NLF and NVA to damage the occupiers.

Captain Bob Keep of the Intelligence Unit puts the report down with something between a heavy sigh and a whistle. His thin frame twitches, a bundle of nervous tics that illustrate each jolt of thought that courses through his relentless mind. A *division* of VC operating in the north-east of this very province? True, it is not as if it is an entire mass of men marching towards them, as the very nature of Charlie is rarely to mass but always move connected splinters, but the sheer numbers are staggering. And that part about the regiment moving to our area with the intention of initiating a major action is particularly sobering. It highlights the need for strengthening the defences as quickly as possible – no matter how exhausted the troops are – as well as constant patrolling, and . . . *I thought I told you I don't care how shattered with exhaustion they are?* – as well as intense intelligence work to keep track of them. Ever since the 1st Australian Task Force had arrived in Phuoc Tuy, tight pods of SAS commandos had been sent out on probing patrols – dropping in by choppers – to gather intel on the Communist forces. Now intelligence reports are suggesting that 3500 regular troops and an unknown number of guerrillas are in the area, they *must* get as much warning as possible if Charlie tries to launch an attack on the base. And more than ever it highlights the need to secure the exclusion zone around the base so that if he launches it will by necessity be from a distance, and not from up close.

But is anyone else listening?

For it is just one report of many, and there is no way of knowing just how solid the information is. Brigadier Jackson – a remote figure for most of 1ATF base, spied in the distance, at best, always with a bush hat on and a cigarette perpetually dangling from the corners of his mouth – makes no demonstrable reaction at all, and will later say he cannot even remember reading it. It is one thing for a report to say this base is being established in a hornet's nest, and that the hornets are gathering to swarm – and quite another to prove it.

Still, the fact that Charlie is out there and not far away is underlined – if still not headlined – by the fact that on 10 June three mortar rounds land just outside the wire establishing the perimeter. This, on a day that Intelligence was warning that an entire VC regiment was coming at Nui Dat[21] from the north-east and is just six miles away!

No-one is hurt, but . . .

But they're out there all right. That much is beyond doubt from the moment 5RAR finds trails of blood in crushed foliage. When the trails are followed they lead to six dead VC, in three groups of two, the shattered pieces of a patrol wiped out by some random artillery.

Yup, they're there. Watching us. And most likely getting ready to strike once they have worked out what our points of weakness are.

And how long can that take, after all? To the stupefaction of many, the base has been set up encompassing one of Phuoc Tuy's two north–south roads, Route 2, meaning there is a constant drip of traffic – mostly peasants with bullock carts – passing through. Of course, all of them are stopped to have their papers checked, and not once do those papers reveal 'North Vietnamese Operative, Here For the Duration'. And they are also under strict instructions not to deviate from the road, but . . . the damage is being done.

For, day after day, among those passing through the base are operatives for the VC, making careful observations. Here, in the south-western sector of the base, is the artillery compound where they can see – count 'em – 24 big guns, four batteries in all, with one of those batteries on the right-hand side of the road as you travel north. Right beside it, just

100 metres away, is the ammunition dump where all the shells are stored. Proceeding on into the rubber plantation proper, they can see through the avenues the heavily guarded 1ATF HQ, and 100 metres further is the Armoured Personnel Carrier compound, next to its workshops.

Now, let's see. Taking down the numbers on every APC they see, for they all have numbers clearly marked upon them, it is soon clear that they are relatively few. Behind them, on the lower slopes of Nui Dat hill, they can see bunkers and machine-gun posts. Is the open area in front of it mined?

That question is soon settled by having the young boys herd some buffalo over it and when none of the beasts lose legs, the answer comes back: no mines.

Of course the Australians are running intelligence operations of their own, including having choppers drop tight pods of SAS commandos behind enemy lines to observe, gather information and occasionally capture and interrogate enemy soldiers. They would also occasionally be dropped on what were known as 'killer patrols', setting up ambushes on known VC routes and hitting hard, before decamping to an agreed rendezvous point, a small clearing in the jungle where, again, it is for the choppers to instantly pluck them out. (It is hairy work for the pilots of RAAF No. 9 Squadron, but they refine their methods as they go along. The key is for one chopper to get to a safe altitude where it can clearly see the rendezvous point, and then guide the second chopper to come in fast, hard and low – to get in, get down, get them and get out all in 20 seconds.)

One of the SAS intelligence reports is particularly startling. It suggests that not long after the Australians had arrived so too had an entire *battalion* of the North Vietnamese Army – seriously well trained and superbly equipped soldiers – with the task of organising the Viet Cong and the local guerrilla units to wipe out the intruders. Concerned, Jackson informs Lieutenant General John Wilton, the Chief of the General Staff; the information is noted but not found credible. To this point NVA cadres had only been spotted in Cambodia and it does not seem possible that they could be here in Phuoc Tuy already.

CHAPTER SIX

FIRE, FIRE, BURNING BRIGHT

It became necessary to destroy the town to save it.

An unnamed US Major explains to famed AP correspondent Peter Arnett why the US had to bomb a village, 45 miles south of Saigon, out of existence during the Tet Offensive

21 June 1966, Mosman Town Hall, Sydney, a shot from the grassy verge

'Hear, hear!' *'Hear, hear!'* 'HEAR, HEAR!'

Mosman Council Chambers on Sydney's leafy North Shore might be an unlikely place for the leader of Her Majesty's Opposition, Mr Arthur Calwell, to be receiving such public commendation instead of his usual fare in these Blue Ribbon Liberal parts – condemnation – but he is speaking with passion on a subject that many of the local denizens of the 800-strong throng agree with.

Arthur Calwell wants Australia to pull out of the civil war in Vietnam. It is as simple as that. Events in those parts are tragic, but it is a civil war, and large swathes of the population want nothing more than foreigners – which, of course, includes Australians – to go home.

'Hear, hear!' *'Hear, hear!'* 'HEAR, HEAR!'

Listening up the back, his godson, young Wayne Haylen – who has recently gained more press for publicly burning his National Conscription registration papers – claps more than most. He has come with his fellow paper-burner Barry Robinson, and the last three months have been grim. Somewhere in Sydney, he suspects, there is a very cold, nude chicken, so many white feathers has he received. But at least Arthur is saying a lot of what needs to be said. He just wishes he'd go in even harder!

Alas, there is one for whom Calwell's words are anathema.

Just outside the chambers, listening to the rumbling stentorian tones of the politician, a troubled 19-year-old man from Centennial Park by the name of Peter Kocan – he who had been so impressed by the assassinations of Presidents Diem and Kennedy – is lurking. Beneath his coat he has secreted a loaded sawn-off .22 rifle.

The meeting closes at 10.30 pm, whereupon most attendees meander home. Calwell lingers, saying his goodbyes. When he emerges just before 11 pm, escorted by Senator Doug McClelland, scores of his supporters are gathered on the footpath outside, waiting to see him go. He gives them a wave, oblivious of the brooding figure lurking nearby. But once inside the car, it all happens so quickly. The 69-year-old is tired and is just settling down in the front passenger seat for the short trip back to his hotel with the window down as always, when first his godson Wayne Haylen appears, vociferously urging him to advocate for a law whereby conscripts could not serve overseas. The lad is so strong about it that the Opposition Leader first remonstrates and then angrily winds the window up in his face. Only a few seconds later Calwell becomes aware of a figure approaching the window at pace, no doubt a last well-wisher wanting to say goodbye from the grassy verge.

Suddenly there is a loud bang, like a firecracker going off, followed by the shattering of glass. Calwell's hands instinctively go up to his face, which is wet.

'I've been shot!' cries the alternative prime minister and slumps across the lap of his driver.

The driver, aghast, pulls him upright and yells, 'What's the matter?'

'I've been shot! I've been shot!'

Well, sort of. In fact, the bullet has mercifully been deflected by the window to lodge harmlessly in the lapel of his coat. Splinters of flying glass have inflicted the damage.

Meanwhile, a furtive figure is seen hurrying away from the drama. The cry goes up: 'Arthur Calwell has been assassinated!'[1] Wayne Haylen doesn't hesitate. And nor does Barry Robinson beside him. Both set out in hot pursuit down Myahgah Road, after a figure they know to be armed and dangerous. It is Haylen who reaches him first, and manages to collar the would-be assassin. There is no need to subdue him, particularly, as this strange fellow wearing the big Army boots – which Haylen is sure was the reason he'd been able to catch him – is hauled back to the police.

Arthur Calwell will quickly recover. But Australia is shocked. In the history of the Australian nation it is the first assassination attempt of a leading political figure, with the possible exception of Governor Phillip being speared in 1790.

The fallout from this Vietnam War is getting ever uglier.

22 June 1966, the clearing of Long Phuoc, Operation Enoggera

Back in the day, being part of the Australian cavalry had been a generally glorious if dangerous exercise, the heirs to the tradition of the Charge of the Light Brigade, and the Household Cavalry at Waterloo, and in the purely Australian context, one of the last great death-defying cavalry charges of history, at Beersheba, which had been thunderously done by the 4th and 12th Australian Light Horse.

These days, everything is more mechanical, and the days of cavalry charges are long gone even if their troop of Armoured Personnel Carriers, 3 Troop, 1st Armoured Personnel Carrier Squadron, proudly retains its links with their tradition as part of the 4th/19th Prince of Wales's Light Horse. Rather than death-defying charges, their role now is to transport infantry into action and support them with firepower thereafter, something which sees the Yank troops, particularly, often refer to them sneeringly as 'battle taxis'.[2]

On this steaming afternoon, as ever when out on an operation, Lieutenant Adrian Roberts is all eyes, all ears and all in – focusing with every fibre of his being on the task at hand. For this operation Lieutenant Roberts, a quietly spoken though forceful former teacher from WA turning Regular Army professional, is in charge of 27 men in all, manning 13 APCs, who are to act in support of the 600 soldiers of 6RAR as they carefully approach the village of Long Phuoc just under two miles south of the base.

This is not just another village.

It is nothing less than, as one report will have it, 'the headquarters of the National Liberation Front's provincial committee . . . it stood on a little maze of tunnels, one of which ran three kilometres to Long Tan. While it existed, it offered an enemy fortress within a few kilometres from Nui Dat. Under every home, beneath every bed or kitchen table, or behind false walls, trapdoors fell away to reveal bunkers and tunnels. The approaches to Long Phuoc had bristled with punji stakes and booby traps.'[3]

Yes, the previous month the 173rd Airborne had already done much of the truly difficult and upsetting work, forcibly resettling most of the

3000 villagers to the villages of Hoa Long, Dat Do and Long Dien, well outside the exclusion zone.

They had found the village to be 'fortified', complete with bunkers, caches of arms and ammunition. A comprehensive maze of tunnels had not only hidden hundreds of VC soldiers, but – after a pitched battle which had seen elements of Charlie's D445 Battalion and the Chau Duc District's 21 Company kill 19 American soldiers and wound 90 – allowed many of them to get away. The caches had been emptied, the bunkers and tunnels destroyed – at least those that had been found – and many VC captured or killed.

But reports had come in: there are still people there. They must be captured, killed or moved. And the village itself must now be *completely* destroyed to prevent any chance of them coming back. Yes, tough for the villagers but unavoidable: beyond everything else, their forced removal means Nui Dat will no longer be so easily within enemy mortar range. Once all the civilians are moved out, it will mean the only ones who remain will be Charlie, and patrols will be able to fire at will. Equally any activity out there can be pounded with Nui Dat artillery without fear of hitting innocents. Because from now, if you are inside the Alpha Line, you are automatically *guilty*.

For all that, the soldiers of 6RAR are wary – this is so different from the way they had trained at Canungra, starting with this time they really might get shot.

And while it is one thing to comprehensively outnumber whoever might still be in there, it is quite another to get the job done without losing any of our own. At any moment, Charlie, cornered, might fire or throw a grenade and take out as many of us as he can.

Under the circumstances Lieutenant Roberts, rumbling towards the village in his APC, has every reason to keep himself and his men on highest alert, ready for the first sign of resistance – which might be well entrenched, as this is not a village of wooden huts like so many in the area, but a prosperous one of well-constructed brick and stone houses on large plots. Like Long Tan, many people have done well out of the rubber; the fact that the French had taken most of the wealth notwithstanding.

In short order it is done.

The village is completely surrounded.

Each of the 6RAR companies is assigned a quarter of the village to cordon off, search and flush out any guerrillas that might be hiding there, and they get to work. Once a house is cleared, the first thing to look for is religious artefacts.

(It has become apparent that moving the villagers out at the point of bayonets a few months earlier had created thousands of instant VC sympathisers, spreading their rage to new villages. And the thing that had most driven them berko, even beyond losing their homes and livelihoods, had been the loss of their holy relics. 6RAR are under orders to gather them in, so they can be handed back – and under no circumstances to burn down any churches or pagodas.)

The second thing is to locate the tunnels, throw grenades into them and then destroy what remains. Torch the lot. Yup, and can you get some more fuel for my flamethrower, I'm nearly out.

From an observation post could be seen 'a grove of fruit trees, church and pagoda spires and tile roofs neat enough to make a Nasho homesick for Mosman. This was Long Phuoc . . . a village of deep, cool wells, of fishponds shaded by flowering shrubs, of verandas made for children to play around and to shade the old from the Phuoc Tuy sun. It was a village of subsistence farmers and fishermen. It was also, it turned out, a village of riflemen. It was honeycombed with tunnels. It stood among thick jungle. While it stood it would for ever be a base from which to kill Australians. This outweighed all other considerations.'[4]

Acrid smoke is soon billowing from all over the once prosperous village, which had made just one mistake – it had allowed the VC to come and set up there as a base. And now it must pay the price.

The Officer Commanding Delta Company, Major Harry Smith, watches as his men search a temple, and sure enough . . . a discovery! Hidden within a wall niche they find a beautiful brass figurine of a goddess with a metal skirt. Soldiers being what they are, the skirt is tilted up to reveal . . . a 'huge brass penis'[5]! Harry Smith is not sure precisely which religion this belongs to, but it is unlikely to be C of E.

None of their business.

It is put aside to be handed over.

For the rest, many of the soldiers transform into antique connoisseurs having a good look around each house, looking for possible souvenirs – something between purloining and looting. (Their reasoning – it is all about to be torched, so what does it matter?) One picks out a mother-of-pearl plaque, another a beautiful brass totem, still another some children's toys that might be fun for his own children back home in Australia.

The houses scoured and torched, on to the next job.

'Once we cleared each house, we burned them as level as we could,'[6] Delta Company's Lieutenant Dave Sabben will recall of his and his men's work with flamethrowers that soon see plumes of billowing smoke filling the skies. Only the holy places, the churches and pagodas are spared. To preserve religious sites is meaningful to Lieutenant Sabben, particularly.

And yes, there are soldiers who feel terrible about burning simple dwellings, but it does not last too long.

'The indignation felt by some Diggers ordered to set fire to houses quickly changed,' Lieutenant John O'Halloran will recall, 'when ammunition stored inside began to explode and sent them scurrying for cover.'[7]

And yet that is not the only ammunition going off . . .

Alpha Company Corporal Mike Martin feels a sting in his skin. Looking down he sees he has been shot, a sniper succeeding in locating Martin's forearm with a bullet. *Find the sniper!* Bullets fly in both directions and in seconds four 'enemy' are dead. Three dead men, Vietnamese, are formally classified as 'VC', though of course questions can't be asked.

And the fourth body is a story waiting to be told.

While moving through a banana grove on the edge of the village, a patrol from Geoff Kendall's 10 Platoon spy a figure dressed in black . . .

There isn't a second to check if they're pyjamas. Black is enough. They open fire and he is dead before there's time for the black to turn red.

He, right?

They approach, sure he is dead, but wary all the –

Oh God.

Jesus wept.

It is an old woman in a black *áo dài*, now lying on her back with red splotches all over her torso, the bananas she has just picked now scattered all around her. She has no weaponry, the most hostile thing about her the look of angry grief she has died with.

'Sadly,' 10 Platoon's Sergeant Bob Buick will recount, 'she died before medical assistance arrived. This was the first and only incident the company had on the operation and unfortunately it had involved shooting an unarmed local. We buried the woman with what dignity we could and marked her grave.'[8]

Nevertheless, she too is classified as 'enemy'. Jesus Christ, this war is a dirty business; nobody will escape it with clean memories. Everyone can see she is a civilian. No matter; her status is burnt in the line of fire and she is not alive to argue the point.

Kenny Gant is particularly affected. Something about this old woman reminds him of his own mother, Beryl. And now she lies here, as innocent as she is dead. It could have been his own mum.

The work of the week goes on, as house after house is destroyed. But the tunnels beneath them remain, and it is now for the engineers to do their work, destroying them. It will take days, using everything from TNT to diesel to plastic explosive, to completely blow them apart – with soldiers always standing by to kill any VC who try to escape.

Meantime, the men of 6RAR burn the rest of the village to the ground. Two hundred years of history go up in flames, the billowing smoke a warning to all villages within coo-ee: this is what happens if you accommodate the VC.

The mood among the Australian soldiers of 6RAR is grim – no-one likes doing this, as much as it has to be done – with traces of gallows humour.

Corporal Laurie Drinkwater, of 12 Platoon D Company, remarks to the soldier next to him, 'We've done the killing and the burning, when does the raping start?'[9]

He is not serious, but the flames say that the latest round of invaders are. In the end, after destroying the houses and tunnels, the captured inventory includes 43 tonnes of rice that had been cached to feed VC guerrillas, two tonnes of salt, 10 rifles, some 105 millimetre shells and 4000 punji stakes. Yes, it had been bleak to destroy the village, but it was necessary bleakness.

This is war. The villagers are offered a resettlement in the next village south, but they remain distinctly unsettled about the whole affair.

In the distance, just outside of the village, an Iroquois chopper from the RAAF No. 9 Squadron lands, and none other than Brigadier Oliver Jackson – the highest-ranking Australian officer at Nui Dat – comes striding out of it, accompanied by two aides. The Brigadier pauses only long enough to turn and tell the helicopter captain, Flight Lieutenant Bruce Lane, to 'Stay right here, until I return,'[10] and then he and his aides are off.

Lane and his co-pilot, Flight Lieutenant Bob Grandin, look at each other. They might indeed stay right here. But then again, they might not. The RAAF doesn't answer to the Australian Army, but to the protocols developed with Canberra, which established that neither the RAAF, nor its officers, are in the Army chain of command. And in any case, given that they are on active operation right now, Lane is the captain of his aircraft and it *his* call alone what the chopper does and does not do. It is only when back at base that he is answerable to his superior officer and in this chain of command, Brigadier Oliver Jackson is not featured.

Just to be on the safe side, Lane and Grandin set their chopper up so that it is 'cocked', with all switches bar one primed and ready for take-off, so that at the first sign of danger they can get away on the instant, which . . .

Which is useful, for only five minutes after Brigadier Jackson and his entourage had headed off to the village with the billowing flames, shots from the nearby line of trees suddenly ring out.

Flight Lieutenant Bruce Lane doesn't hesitate.

'Let's get out of here,' he breathes to his co-pilot, even as he flicks the fuel pump on.

The engines roar into life, the rotors whirl, and within seconds the chopper whisks away – their last vision being an outraged Brigadier Jackson and his aides charging their way from the village.

So he may rant and rave all he likes, it is not Flight Lieutenant Lane's concern.

At Long Phuoc, the destruction at the hands, and the flamethrowers, of the Australian troops, goes on.

'When we left,' Private Terry Burstall will sadly document, 'virtually nothing remained of Long Phuoc, two hundred years of Vietnamese history wiped away . . .'[11]

That evening in Hoa Long, Dat Do and Long Dien as the news spreads of what has happened to their original village, there is both wailing . . . and shouts of fury.

'Bọn Úc khốn nạn!' Those bastard Australians!

But their revenge will come, of that they are sure. Before this they have seen off the Mongols, the Chinese, the French, the Vichy French, the Japanese, the British, and even Diem's thugs. The Americans and the Australians are merely the latest invaders. Their time will come.

•

Of all the privileges of rank, blowing your stack without fear or favour but with extra lashings of fire and fury atop is up near the top and Brigadier Jackson is not missing his mark when it comes to Group

Captain Peter Raw, bellowing: What the *hell* is going on? As they drop me at Long Phuoc, I give your men *specific* orders to wait for my return, and yet they fly off at the first sound of shooting?

But here is the nub of the problem.

Certainly Brigadier Jackson has the highest rank at the 1ATF base. But Group Captain Raw, and indeed all of the RAAF, do *not* answer to him! Canberra has been crystal clear here, the RAAF resources are so crucial and so thin on the ground in Vietnam that strict protocols are to be observed as to when, where, and in what circumstances planes and choppers can be used. And under that protocol, make no mistake, even a pilot outranks a Brigadier once they are in the air – or still out on operations as was the case in this instance.

You see, Brigadier, once Flight Lieutenant Bruce Lane determined there was danger to his chopper and his crew, it was for him to take action to keep both safe. Yes, I am indeed aware there is a war on, and so is Canberra – they're insisting on the importance of keeping some working choppers to fight with. Perhaps the Brigadier might like to go in an APC next time?

Brigadier Jackson continues to fume, but there is no way around it; not upwards anyway.

•

He's one to watch, 'Largey', as he is known, always involved in scrapes, in the middle of things that become the talk of his platoon and company. Like on this day when, out on yet another bloody patrol, 12 Platoon has no sooner stopped for lunch than the man from Coolah lets out a loud yelp which is in flagrant contravention of the strictly enforced code of silence when on patrol.

Everyone goes for their guns, only to find . . .

Largey has been stung by a scorpion – a big black bastard that appears to have unleashed all of its venom into him. The medic gets some pills into him, quick smart, but within minutes he has such a fever – despite being dowsed with much of their water supplies and quite a bit of coconut milk – and his breathing is so shallow that Lieutenant Dave Sabben puts out the radio call for an urgent 'dustoff', and 15 minutes later a medevac chopper lands to whisk him away. As Paul is being stretchered towards the instant whirlwind of dust and leaves, he looks a little recovered and, smiling, quips, 'Hurrah for the Flying Doctor!'[12]

•

In the meantime, the base at Nui Dat continues to take shape day by day even as their defences get marginally stronger. Nui Dat is now divided into seven main areas held by 5RAR, 6RAR, Engineer Squadron, the Field Artillery Regiment, the Cavalry Squadron, and two central areas partly occupied by HQ 1ATF, Provost, Signal Intelligence, SAS and Maintenance units.

At its height the base will contain 5500 men and is being built to those specifications, even though there is less than half that number there now as they help to build what is no less than a military town with large units at the base boasting stores, a post office, cinema, helipads, Salvation Army tent and chapel.

For the moment, these are little less than rough structures – tent-poles and canvas, with little set up inside for the simple reason that nothing else has yet arrived – but it is a start.

The most crucial shortage however is manpower.

There are so few of them to do such a massive amount of work *and* patrolling that the men of 5RAR and 6RAR must do both!

Their life becomes one long, dull, exhausting routine. Wake, wash, eat. Dig, drain, patrol, fill sandbags, drain, dig, patrol, eat. Patrol, put up wire, dig, drain, clearing patrol, ambush patrol, eat, night pickets, wash. Sleep. Wake, wash, eat. Add the gallons of sweat pouring out of you all day and into the night. Rinse and repeat; and repeat and repeat and repeat up the Wazoo River all the way until you get to Shit Creek, and then repeat one more time for luck.

'People were just exhausted,' Dave Sabben will recall, 'people falling asleep in the pits, and we couldn't charge them because it was happening so much and there was just sheer exhaustion and coming down sick and so on . . .

'Day one you'd go out in your patrol area all day. That night you'd ambush so you'd be awake all night – no sleeping on ambush. You would then come back by lunchtime on day two, and you'd be put into the pits developing the defences so that's the second day gone. Overnight you'd defend the base which meant that you had two hours sleep on, two hours sleep off. So all the diggers would have had just a few hours sleep during that night, not slept the night before, and then into day three. Half the platoon would be on battalion jobs like setting up the Q-stores

Ho Chi Minh. The 'Bringer of Light' – the man who intended to be the saviour of Vietnam. One of the most influential Communist leaders of the 20th century, he was President of North Vietnam from 1945 to 1969. *(Wikimedia Commons)*

President Ngo Dinh Diem meeting US President Dwight D. Eisenhower in Washington, 1957. Eisenhower hailed Diem as Asia's 'miracle man' for his apparent restoration of unity in South Vietnam. *(US National Archives)*

In 1963 Buddhist monk Thich Quang Duc makes headlines in an unimaginably tragic and horrific way, protesting the South Vietnamese Government. *(Alamy)*

Dropping numbered marbles into the tumbler for the first draw in Australia's 'National Service birthday ballot', 1965. The future of many young Australian men would be determined by the conscription lottery. *(Fairfax Media)*

Protesters take to the streets to oppose conscription and Australia's involvement in the war. Protests became larger and more organised as the war continued. *(SLNSW)*

Members of 5RAR at the Jungle Training Centre, Canungra, Queensland, January 1966. Kokoda veterans developed comprehensive training systems for those headed to the jungles of Vietnam. *(AWM HAL/66/0012/NC)*

Fresh-faced troops begin their Vietnam tour of duty, arriving in Saigon on a Qantas aircraft, April 1966. *(AWM CUN/66/0357/VN)*

Aerial view of the 1ATF Nui Dat base. This photo was taken in 1971, some years after the base had been established. *(AWM EKT/71/0672/VN)*

6RAR servicemen manning a machine gun and bailing water out of a weapons pit at Nui Dat. Mud and monsoonal downpours were ever-present elements of life at the base.
(AWM CUN/66/0479/VN)

Private Paul Large takes a long refreshing drink from his water-bottle while digging in for Operation Enoggera, the first mission by 6RAR, June 1966.
(AWM CUN/66/0509/VN)

Flight Lieutenant Frank Riley at the controls of his No. 9 Squadron, RAAF Iroquois helicopter. *(AWM VN/66/0043/05)*

August 1966. Iroquois helicopters on the pad at 1ATF HQ – ready for a troop support mission. *(AWM VN/66/0043/04)*

Aerial view of the site of the Battle of Long Tan. This photo was taken in 1971, several years after the battle. *(AWM P00510.011)*

Little Pattie and Col Joye performing for troops at Nui Dat, 18 August 1966. *(AWM P05130.001)*

Captain Robert Keep arriving with the latest intelligence report during Operation Hobart, July 1966. *(AWM P01484.001)*

An artillery crew in action, pounding Viet Cong positions during an operation. *(AWM THU/67/1256/VN)*

and digging the mortar pits and so on and half the platoon would be on company level things rather than the platoon forward defences like digging all the trenches and so on. And then that afternoon, half the platoon would go out again for half the day and then you'd come back and you'd probably be defending somebody else's perimeter because at that same time companies would be out on operations and leaving their perimeter vacant so in three consecutive nights you've been awake for one night and you've had three two-hour sleeps.'[13]

And yet the Australians are not the only ones patrolling.

So too is Charlie, constantly sending out small probing patrols to determine just where the Australian defences are, how strong they are, how well armed they are, how well they fight.

Inevitably the patrols sometimes clash and there are deaths and casualties on both sides. Though the clashes from the Australian side are mostly dealing with flitting, fleeting, fleeing figures in the distance – usually firing Parthian shots. Firefights with the enemy are called 'contacts' and they are highly prized by the Australian survivors.

Action! They have seen *action*, and fired shots in anger. Whatever else happens in Vietnam, they can actually say they have been in a battle and have been blooded – without bleeding themselves, which is the best thing of all.

Those series of minor clashes, however, have given rise to a worrying view. Various SAS patrols to the east – around the nominally deserted village of Long Tan – have come across so many enemy soldiers it seems likely that there might be a large force of VC in that very area. If so, the obvious place they would be secreted is in Nui Dat 2, just to the north of Long Tan, where the hill and thick growth would help hide them.

The choppers of RAAF No. 9 Squadron drop pods of SAS soldiers into areas east of the base and they, too, are able to observe enemy movement in the area, preferably without firing every time they spot Charlie.

According to the intelligence report, there might even be *hundreds* of them!

This, mind, is only a tenth of the 3850 VC in the intelligence report back in early June, but that had always been nebulous. This feels a lot more real.

> Situation Enemy: There have been several conflicting reports on the enemy situation in the area of operations. The only certain

> fact is that there are at least ten enemy in the area. The maximum enemy likely to be encountered is estimated at 300. From various reports the main enemy camp is to the N.E. of Xa Long Tan, and the morale of the enemy seen is good, and they keep themselves, their clothing, weapons, and equipment in good order.[14]

Operation Hobart is born – a search and destroy mission to, ideally, find this enemy force and destroy them . . .

While the 5th Royal Australian Regiment remains behind to man the fort – on the morning of 24 July all four companies of 6RAR head out into the jungle on a five-day mission to search for the enemy in the area to the east and north-east of Long Tan – and to destroy them, as well as the village of Long Tan itself.

To escape the inevitable surveillance by the enemy and take them by surprise, Colonel Townsend – who remains at Nui Dat – has ordered them to leave in the wee hours, in the pitch-blackness, which proves to be no easy thing. Getting through the jungle is hard enough in daylight, let alone when closing your eyes tightly makes the night no darker, and there is much stumbling and muffled cursing as they make their way in supremely difficult fashion to a position seven kilometres north-east of 1ATF HQ, before they 'harbour' for the rest of the night.

Even with the first dull glow of dawn, however, the problems of the night are forgotten, replaced by an air of excitement, as the battle knell is nigh. Intelligence reports have it that they are up against the local Viet Cong D445 Battalion, which means – like a vibrating chainsaw that finally gets to cut into wood – they should be about to put the last 12 months of training into actual practice.

'This was to be our first big test in combat,' John O'Halloran will recall. 'It was everything we had prepared for and most of us were excited to finally be getting amongst the action.'[15]

Each company has a separate patrol route, looking for signs of the VC, with Bravo Company, under the command of Major Noel Ford, positioned to the south-west of the other three, while Delta Company to their north-east proves to be the first to find what they are all looking for – signs of the enemy.

In this case it is the heavy tracks of a company-sized unit heading south together with – courtesy of a paid informer – a carefully secreted cache of rice. With that amount of food, an enemy unit can't be far away and an ambush is set up while the other units continue their patrols. Harry Smith's Delta Company has the first major contact with five VC soldiers in black pyjamas who nevertheless make good their escape in heavy jungle to the south-east. But in the early forenoon, it is Charlie Company who finds what they are looking for. Firing on two VC soldiers at a distance of 60 metres across a clearing proves to be the equivalent of pulling the tail of a cat – for they are suddenly under major attack from a whole COMPANY of VC lined up across a hundred metres in the jungle on the other side of the clearing.

And this proves to be just the prelude!

For now the VC are firing mortars upon them and preparing to mount a charge to . . . to what?

Horns?

Not just horns, *bugles*.

Yes, there has been a rumour around that VC forces are sometimes organised by bugles and whistles – with different tunes and blasts meaning different things – but this is the first time most have heard it. (And it is impressive. This is a much better way to synchronise a mob than shouting out orders over chattering machine guns, or giving hand signals when not everyone can see you.)

A vicious firefight ensues, which sees one of Charlie Company's machine-gunners, Bill Winterford, wipe out two enemy machine-gunners before disaster strikes. Not long after Charlie Company's Commanding Officer, Major Brian McFarlane, calls in artillery from Nui Dat to lob on the heads of the VC, one shell falls short and a piece of shrapnel neatly severs Winterford's left arm. It happens at much the same time as the brave man who has moved forward to feed the belts into Winterford's machine gun, Sapper Leslie Prowse, takes a bullet to the head, which will kill him a short time later, even as a US chopper rushes him to Vung Tau.

At least the artillery fire breaks up the VC attack, but the question now is in what direction will they head?

All of Bravo Company to the south, Delta Company to the north, and Alpha Company to the east ready themselves on the chance that Charlie is heading their way.

At 2 pm, it happens.

Two sentries placed 50 metres down the most obvious line of approach see a pack of VC coming their way down the track and prematurely open fire on the leading elements, which warns those coming behind. Again a massive firefight breaks out, which kills one Australian soldier and mortally wounds another. And again, it is the artillery called in from Nui Dat which helps tip the balance towards the Australians – occasioning a telling tactic from the VC. Instead of retreating, he moves closer still, 'grasping the enemy by the belt'.[16] The idea being to get so close to the Australians, while still firing, that they wouldn't dare – couldn't dare – to drop further shells on them, as they would risk killing their own. Like a small man gripping a big man by the belt and getting so close the brute can't properly swing.

And now, with bugles blaring once more, Charlie start attacking once more, with their soldiers moving forward even as mortar shells start landing all about Bravo Company.

There are shouts, screams and the explosions of the mortar shells, but the most unnerving thing are the piercing notes coming from those BLOODY bugles!

'*Bdaaaaaa . . . Bdda-dddaaa-ddaaaaaaa-Bdaaaaaaaa!*'

On the spot, Private 'Bluey' Bartsch, a one-time truckie from north of the Tweed, shouts to Lieutenant John O'Halloran, 'Boss, those cunts have got a band out there.'[17]

The fighting is vicious, the fire furious, and when it is finally over, Bravo Company has had two men killed, and 15 wounded – one in six of them having taken a bullet or shrapnel. It is tragic, but it is war, and as ever the one emotion stronger than grief is the even more pressing need to *survive*. As they harbour for the night the formally assigned sentries are not the only ones with their eyes open, scanning the darkness for any sign of movement.

It is difficult to get any sleep in any case, as the Nui Dat artillery keeps pounding through the night, looking to drop on places where it is thought Charlie might be.

The following morning as Bravo Company scours the area, the bodies of eight dead VC soldiers are found and they are quickly buried in keeping with Vietnamese beliefs that only a quick burial can prevent the soul wandering forever in a twilight world.

And yet it is almost as if the gods of war have singled out Major Smeaton's Alpha Company for extra attention.

For the following evening on 25 July, just as Alpha is settling down for its evening rations, a shell lands among them and Major Smeaton is among the four men badly wounded. He orders that he be the last man evacuated, even though his wounds are more serious than two of the other men.

Captain Charles Mollison, the company second in command, who has been at the village of Hoa Long, is sent for; he is to take over command of Alpha Company as soon as he can. When he arrives via chopper, he is told some terrible news. The shell? The artillery that nearly killed four men including Major Smeaton? It was friendly fire.

Delta, east of Alpha, had called in artillery to deal with a small cluster of VC. The aim of artillery was way off, and now Major Smeaton has severe wounds to his back and severe doubts as to whether he will ever command A Company again.

Through all the various changes, the solid rock of 6RAR is Regimental Sergeant Major George Chinn. Private Terry Burstall will have reason to remember him well. Burstall and his mates are working their way up the eastern side of the mountain range to the west of the base, and so completely exhausted by the effort that even their own officers call a halt in the midday sun. They will have lunch from their Australian Combat Ration – as ever, lunch is biscuits with margarine, Vegemite, cheese and jam – allowing everyone bar the sentries posted all around to have some precious rest.

One of those sentries – dammit! – is Burstall himself, and he is told to keep his eyes peeled and his ears open, alert for any sign of the enemy approaching. It is not stated because it is obvious already and they all know, but the safety of the entire platoon might depend on you fulfilling your duty.

But look, after he leans up against a handy rock, one thing leads to another. Burstall has had no more than six hours of disrupted sleep in the last 72 hours and is shattered. He doesn't mean to close his eyes, but his lids are certainly getting heavier . . . heavier . . . closed . . .

He jolts, eyes wide open when a shadow falls across him, and he finds himself staring at a pair of regulation Australian Army boots.

Oh.

Christ.

His eyeline follows the boots up to the knees, the torso and finally . . . the face, of Chinn, Colonel Townsend's right-hand man on all matters to do with discipline and enforcing the authority of the officers. He is a bit of a grizzled old bastard, but not without humanity and empathy for the Diggers – he somehow always projects the sense that he, too, was once a soldier just like them, and remembers his own mistakes. Right now, he would have the authority and every right to charge Burstall with falling asleep on sentry duty, meaning the younger man would face up to 21 days' loss of pay and 21 days' field punishment, but in fact he takes Burstall by surprise.

'Keeping your eyes out, Digger?' Chinn asks with a look which says, 'We both know you were fast asleep, so even though I am going to let it pass this time, make sure you NEVER let it happen again, or I really will have your guts for garters.'

'Yes, sir,' Burstall replies simply, now as awake as he has ever been in his life.[18]

With a grin, now that he sees his message has been received, Chinn moves on to the next sentry position, to make sure all is as it should be.

Late July 1966, near Long Tan village, red mist

Another day, another patrol.

On this day of Operation Hobart, Delta Company is in the jungle to the east and north-east of the village of Long Tan, broadly divided between two main pods: 11 Platoon and 10 Platoon to the south, while 12 Platoon and Company HQ is just a few hundred metres to the north. The air is steamy, the atmosphere tense. There have been sightings of VC in this area and anything might happen.

Suddenly . . . contact!

The forward scouts of 12 Platoon have spotted three VC soldiers – likely on patrol as Charlie is wont to do in small groups – and quickly unleash their Armalites. A small firefight ensues, before the VC break contact and head straight towards 10 Platoon to the south.

Harry Smith is instantly on the radio, advising Lieutenant Geoff Kendall and his men: 'They're coming towards you.'

At first, there is nothing. The silence is punctuated only by the sway of the trees and the whisper of the wind.

And then, a stirring.

Movement in the scrub.

Charlie appears like a monsoon rain, bursting from the green with guns drawn and eyes peeled. But Kendall and the boys are hidden.

Charlie can't see them.

Hold still boys. Never mind the whites of their eyes, you wait until *my order*.

Steady.

Steady.

Steady.

Suddenly, a great PHWOOMPH breaks the hush, a grenade flying from its launcher and landing at the feet of one of the VC men. It explodes on impact, and where a man once stood, only smoke and red mist remain.

The other two scramble, disappearing like wraiths.

Kendall is appalled, and outraged.

His own *Sergeant*, behaving in such an ill-disciplined manner!

'Everything was wrong about it . . .'[19] Kendall will note.

On the spot he has strong words with Buick, who is unremittingly, unwaveringly . . . unrepentant. In his view he has got a confirmed kill for 10 Platoon, and that is really something. A couple of times he has noticed Kendall holding fire when what was needed was *aggressive* fire, for that is what counts. And why wouldn't Buick know more about the caper than him anyway, given his own vast experience?

Back in Australia, in peace-time, Smith would have had time to mull over his response. But here, in a war zone, with a growing sense that there is shit coming down the pipes, he must make his move based on what he knows of the situation and the key people involved. So, move Buick under Sharp?

'Gordon Sharp,' he will note, '[was] an unwilling conscript but with intelligence and education that pushed him into officer school . . . he tended to be more of a soldiers' friend than a good leader.'

And therein lies the problem. The friend thing. Playing cards.

'I did not agree with this because a leader needs to be fair, firm and friendly, but never over friendly.'[20]

As to Buick, yes, he can be rough around the edges, but has redeeming features.

'Bob,' Smith will muse, 'although disliked by some for his typical South African bullish attitude, what some called arrogant, was a loyal and excellent soldier.'[21]

He will give Sharp a warning about the dangers of fraternisation and, effective immediately, make a personnel swap. Kendall will get Lieutenant Gordon Sharp's Sergeant Neil Rankin, while Sergeant Buick will go to be Sharp's offsider at 11 Platoon. In fact, the whole thing suits Smith's purposes as he knows the Regular Army veteran, Buick – despite his sometime hot-headedness – to be Old School and that may be precisely what young Sharp needs, imposing *discipline*.

'Train Sharp and sort out the platoon,'[22] Smith tells him.

Both Kendall and Buick are delighted to see the back of each other.

The succeeding nights and days offer more contacts which, though not as great as on the first day, brings home that death is a fact here, not just a possibility. In all, 13 Viet Cong soldiers are confirmed as killed in Operation Hobart, with 19 wounded, while the Australians have had three killed and 19 wounded.

For those who hadn't previously understood, what is now abundantly clear is that the VC are not just a ragtag bunch of ill-trained peasants playing soldiers. In fact, they are precisely what RSM George Chinn had warned they were: well trained, well disciplined, well equipped and merciless. Sure, they mostly shoot'n'scoot, but when it comes to it, they are not only able to stand their ground, but they are confident and skilled enough to vigorously attack.

In more formal terms, the Officer Commanding 6RAR's Bravo Company, Major Noel Ford, offers a shrewd assessment of the enemy for his superiors: 'They were determined, had good battle skills and impressive firepower, the action demonstrated the fighting ability of D445 VC Battalion is clearly far superior to the opposition we confronted in previous operations in Malaya and Borneo.'[23]

As to how the Diggers themselves are going at this point, the truth is that in the heat and humidity, bonds are frayed across the board, tempers are short and getting shorter, and blow-ups between individuals, particularly between officers and the soldiers they must keep in line, are not uncommon.

In such circumstances, blessed are the peace-makers, and the perpetually benign Sergeant of 12 Platoon, Paddy Todd – whose natural state is to be casting a happy and proud paternal eye over his charges, and whose worst punishment is a figurative light cuff rather than a hard smack – is a case in point. He is worldly, he is wise, he is worth listening to.

When Private Paul Large either 'accidentally discharges', as he claims, the new Armalite he has been issued as a forward scout – or, more likely, can't resist testing the highly prized new American weapon out on a distant sparrow beyond the wire – his insistence that his weapon had been on 'safety' and simply gone off on its own accord is, not unreasonably, disbelieved. To his enormous chagrin, he is docked 14 days' pay. He is ropable, and itching for a fight – anyone will do – which is when Paddy steps in.

'What you must do, Private Large,' the army veteran with the soft Irish lilt says quietly, 'is insist on your right to a court martial, which will so bury them in paperwork as they try to prove the unprovable, they'll drop the charges.'[24] Large does exactly that, the charges are quietly dropped, and life in 'Nam goes on.

•

The tents sweat and the tempers fray. The heat seeps into your very soul the way the cold seeped into your very bones back in Kapooka, and it means the general mood is mostly smouldering – and capable of flaring up over even the smallest thing. Bob Buick barks out orders with all the warmth of Genghis Khan with a toothache. One day Buick puts Private Barry Magnussen on a charge that the relatively inexperienced privates don't regard as serious. The very next day, Buick is inspecting the men at attention in their lines when the butt of the rifle he is carrying taps Barry on the shoulder.

Knock, knock.

Who's there?

Opportunity.

'Sergeant Buick has assaulted me with his weapon!'[25] yells Magnussen. Buick turns in amusement only to see the Diggers nodding like three wise men asked if they'd seen a star in the east. 'That's right! We saw him strike Barry with his weapon!'[26]

It is patent nonsense, and everyone understands it to be so. And yet, with the allegation made, it will have to be officially reported. Unless, that is, Sergeant Buick might have a change of heart and drop that troublesome charge from the other day? It is not quite blackmail. Extortion, is a little closer to the mark. And they have him covered. Buick does indeed have a change of heart – but the whole matter remains emblematic of the tension and tiredness in the air, all mixed with madness rising. There are more than a few Diggers and officers right now – nearly three months after their deployment – who start to feel it coming on in this sweaty, petty land where the sun doesn't shine, it beats; where the rain doesn't fall, it cascades; where . . .

Oh, forget it. We've got the shits with the whole bloody thing.

•

The results of Operation Hobart have led to much worry for Brigadier Jackson and his top command. When they hear that VC sympathisers might have gone back into the village of Long Tan, 6RAR has no sooner embarked on a sweep than the message comes through: abandon the sweep. Everyone back to base immediately as we are getting more reports of a large VC presence nearby. Some of them have been spotted near that big bend in the road on the southern side of the Long Tan plantation.

It might be that Charlie is about to attack.[27]

Few things focus a man's mind like the prospect of an imminent attack and there is soon hustle in their bustle, even as that distinctive staccato thumping of approaching choppers is heard. Haste is made, with helicopters being brought in to lift the troops back to Nui Dat. It is not a task that will be completed soon, with monsoonal rain cutting visibility as swiftly as the chopper blades cut through the drenched air, as light falls and the night rises. With fuel tanks getting dangerously low, it looks as though the last men of A Company might be in for a long walk; but the pilots make the call to continue and all men are landed safely, with barely the sniff of an oily rag to spare. Meanwhile, from HQ, Brigadier Jackson sends out patrols in every direction, seeking some proof of the reports – all to no avail. Charlie might be there, but for the moment he's hiding pretty bloody effectively.

CHAPTER SEVEN

TROUBLE IN THE WIND

War is the realm of uncertainty; three quarters of the factors on which action in war is based are wrapped in a fog of greater or lesser certainty. A sensitive and discriminating judgement is called for; a skilled intelligence to scent out the truth.[1]

Prussian military analyst Carl von Clausewitz

'That's some catch, that catch-22,' [Yossarian] observed. 'It's the best there is,' Doc Daneeka agreed.[2]

Joseph Heller, *Catch-22*

Late July to early August 1966, Nui Dat, movements in mysterious ways

In a stinking hot hut not far from the Operations Centre, a dozen men are listening intently on as many frequencies, occasionally making notes. Captain Trevor Richards – a highly experienced signals intelligence operator commanding the top-secret Australian 547 Signal Troop – at last removes his head-set and makes his final key notation on this 29th day of July. It looks certain – courtesy of the round-the-clock work done by himself and his men, and the regular sweeps done by US Air Force C-47 planes devoted to getting direction-finding fixes on enemy radio transmitters – that a significant movement is taking place.

Over the last month the men in the 'Set Room', as it is known for the 10 radio sets set up on two long tables, have been able to recognise the radios of HQ 5th Viet Cong Division, 274th VC Regiment and 275th VC Regiment, all operational in Phuoc Tuy – and all confirmed by corroborating intelligence.

The signals are distinguishable because the VC use the same operators at the same times of the day, and these operators are clearly well trained – tapping out the Morse in a smooth, professional well-practised manner – exactly the way they would be done in the military.

But what is troubling is that while the signals have remained in fixed position for most of July – perhaps resting or training, or both – those transmissions from 275th VC Regiment, thought to be about 1000-men strong, are now proceeding in a straight line, like an arrow, towards the Australian base at Nui Dat! What is more, both the frequency and the length of the transmissions is going up, which is precisely what you'd expect if they have some big plans in place.

Yes, for the moment the whole thing has to be kept under wraps – it is the very nature of this operation that under no circumstances can you let the enemy know that you know – but Richards does share what he has found with the No. 2 Intelligence Officer at Nui Dat, Captain Bob Keep.

Keep is soon engrossed, and quickly thereafter, alarmed. By comparing Richards' radio reports with other intelligence reports coming in, he soon starts to form a theory.

It is indeed the 275th Viet Cong Regiment and they're not resting, they are building in strength, and this is very likely the first signs of a big, organised attack forming. Might they be combining with the local VC regiment, D445 – estimated to be about 400 strong – to launch an attack on the Australian base?

After all, how bold might Charlie grow if he could wipe out America's key ally, so newly arrived? How great a boost to their morale on the ground; how it would burn like propane in the propaganda machine. Best not to think about it.

Captain Keep asks Captain Richards to keep a close eye on it, and to come straight to him with every fresh bit of information he finds.

Other snippets of information they are getting from their operatives in the field indicate that the VC 275th Regiment is very likely getting reinforcements from North Vietnam, building up to be at full strength. As he must, Captain Keep brings the analysis to the attention of his own superior, Major John Rowe, who does not react well.

Who the hell does this upstart Richards think he is in trying to tell him, *the* head of Intelligence at this base, his business? And why are you, Captain Keep, indulging him?

Captain Keep backs down. It is not wise to take on a superior officer under most circumstances, and less so when he is aggrieved. The Intelligence officer has no desire to get into a turf war with a superior when he could never win it. Being careful not to let the door hit him on the way out, he tactfully pauses long enough to heap praise on Major Rowe's 'masterful'[3] interpretation of the information provided.

Very quietly though?

Captain Keep is no less convinced that the 1ATF base is under serious threat, and he makes a point of checking in with Richards twice a day from now on to stay on top of the whole affair. One day the report he dreads comes from Captain Richards. The radio signals are confirming the same pattern. The VC 275th Regiment – or at least its principal radio unit – *are* steadily approaching Nui Dat.

Captain Keep is in agony. He cannot think straight. The pressure, which has been inexorable, is now overwhelming. His spirit, which has been unbreakable is . . . under strain as never before.

His superior, Major John Rowe, had been so completely dismissive of the whole concept of signal tracking, the sheer folly of basing serious military action on something so subject to the ear of the beholder, that Keep dare not approach him again. And there is equally no doubt he will be furious if he finds that his troublesome underling has gone over his head.

But in the end, Keep decides he has no choice. This is not just a matter of life and death, it is a matter of potential *mass* Australian death – including his own. The stakes are so high that Captain Keep must take extreme action, and so quietly – begging your leave, Sir – approaches Brigadier Jackson direct.

Sir, I sincerely believe there *is* a real threat out there, moving towards us. Their signals are *the* signal to raise the alarm. We must take action, by which I mean, you, Sir, must take action.

It all places Brigadier Jackson in a dashed difficult position. The Australians are meant to be wresting control of Phuoc Tuy province. It is their *raison d'être* for being here in the first place. Can it possibly be that they have somehow missed the advance of the better part of an entire North Vietnamese *Division*? Whatever Keep says, it seems highly unlikely. How could the VC hide that many men? His own intelligence reports show the radio moving just a kilometre a day! Why would any advance be so incremental? How could they keep themselves fed? Why weren't there more signs of their presence?

Brigadier Jackson is not prepared to sound a general alarm. He had, after all, been similarly told such a thing in early June, had taken action, and nothing had come of it.

And yet the Brigadier's aide, Second Lieutenant David Harris, finds Keep's case compelling. Captain Keep makes sense! Harris personally puts the markers on the map and can *see* the enemy getting closer! But what to do? Harris himself is the second-most junior officer in the whole of 1ATF HQ, he has no authority to do anything. As to Jackson, Harris regards him as 'a nice old fellow who was completely worn out'.[4] A man who seems, beyond everything else, not to have any energy for much at all, let alone taking time to focus on a once distant alarm bell now getting louder. All Harris can do for the moment is to continue gently drawing Brigadier Jackson's attention to it. In the end, as a kind of compromise, Jackson agrees that Captain Keep can go and consult the Yanks at the American Headquarters II Field Force Vietnam in Bien Hoa. It does not go well.

Not only do the Americans not take the 'intelligence' the Australian provides seriously, but they cannot see a problem in the first place. The Americans *want* Charlie to break cover, to attack *en masse*, to come out and have a fair fight. So even if you are right on this – and you have presented no solid evidence, so you are probably wrong – it is something to celebrate, not be alarmed about.

But it is not as if the tracking of the radio getting closer to Nui Dat is happening in splendid isolation from other reports.

On the afternoon of 1 August one of the many paid agents the South Vietnamese police maintain in the villages makes a significant report: on this morning he has seen no fewer than 300 green-uniformed Viet Cong – yes, 300! – carrying what looked to be disassembled weaponry just to the north of Nui Dat 2. Harry Smith's Delta Company had been out on patrol in exactly the same area, so there is some chance that the sighting was in fact them, but . . . on the other hand . . .

On the other hand it seems unlikely you could get mixed up between 100 Australians travelling light and 300 uniformed VC carrying heavy weaponry. They're both bigger than a bread-box, sure, and they're both infantrymen walking cautiously in single file, but you know your own.

The most curious thing? The police's paid agent reported seeing the uniformed VC no more than 100 metres from Nui Dat 2. And yet Harry Smith's Delta blokes had been just 200 metres from Nui Dat 2. Could the two forces really criss-cross each other in such a tight noughts and crosses board without running into each other? It just doesn't make a lick of sense.

Although things being at least a little turvy-topsy is just the way things are in this crazy hot place, as it has so often been throughout history when you are occupying places near the equator. To preserve their sanity, the Poms always made a point in far-flung hell-holes of shaving and dressing for dinner and observing elaborate rituals from home – *Gentlemen, the Queen! The Queen . . .* – never mind how uncomfortable, nor how ridiculous it made them look. To let your standards slip, to dress like a local in a manner more suitable for the climate was that worst of all things: 'going native'. Generally the only thing worse than that is 'goin' troppo'.

But bloody Bob Keep seems to be going both at once, heading to hell in a handcart. These days, his uniform is a sarong, a Hawaiian shirt and, if he is feeling formal, sandals. Look, he's always been a remote bloke, with one soldier remembering him as 'quiet, not really associating with the Other Ranks in his section. I wouldn't describe him as an officer to look up to. He was standoffish and didn't impress me at all.'[5]

But, right now, they are glad to be remote from him! His breath could make a skunk faint, and his teeth run the gamut from green to brown with some black spots speckled throughout for good measure. After all, what does it matter? What does *anything* matter? Keep is a walking black cloud, a harbinger of doom that just keeps coming. Only he can see the signs, don't you understand? The news is coming from the radio and he is the only one listening. Death is coming. Keep has leapt from 'highly strung', bounced off 'wildly eccentric' and is now right on the edge of 'bat-shit bonkers'. His paranoia affects his intelligence in two ways: his analysis becomes more apocalyptic, now bookended with a despair that goes beyond depression.

His colleagues and underlings do their best to calm him. Yes, yes, Captain Keep, of course the VC are moving into a giant force to attack us. And we accept that, upon one interpretation, the radio movements you have been tracking indicate that they are now close and an attack is imminent. We should talk on it. But in the meantime, why don't you – after you've had a shower, using soap – just pop over to the medical unit and have a loooooong chat with them.

It is very hard to accept that a crazy man might be telling you the truth.

One man, at least, still believes Captain Keep. Brigadier Jackson's Aide-de-Camp, Lieutenant David Harris, has kept marking Keep's co-ordinates of the enemy's radio on the map in the 1ATF Command Post and also keeps Keeping on with the distressed Intelligence officer, talking to him regularly.

But still, Harris is so junior, can he really approach Brigadier Jackson and urge him to take action? Finally, he decides he must. His heart in his mouth, his career possibly falling away from his outstretched fingers, he summons up his courage and says what needs to be said.

'Sir,' he says. 'We're going to be attacked. I am convinced that Captain Keep is right.'

Brigadier Jackson waves a dismissive hand.

'Nonsense,' he replies. 'They wouldn't dare to attack us here.'[6]

For all that, the troubling reports just keep coming in. On 11 August another agent in the field reports an entire Viet Cong battalion followed by two separate companies on the march in the rubber plantation that lies between the destroyed village of Long Tan and Nui Dat 2.

But none of 6RAR patrols had got a whiff of them. And so, surely the observers must be mistaken? It is a self-perpetuating loop of proof; there can be no massed VC roaming this area, for we are patrolling this area, methodically, constantly. What do you trust? Glimpses from a police agent or the taut testimony of your own patrols? Still, after one VC is shot in broad daylight, right outside that part of the perimeter being defended by 6RAR's Delta and Charlie Companies, a search of his body reveals a simply undeniable and singularly troubling truth – he had been measuring distances, no doubt to work out the right range for a mortar attack! This fits with a patrol from Delta Company a few days previously having ambushed five VC carrying mortars. And a patrol led by Delta Company's Dave Sabben has found a long rope with knots in it, which is the VC method for measuring precise distances prior to mortar attacks.

The skies above the treetops are clear for the moment, but the men cannot shake the feeling that a storm is coming. Something is brewing deep in the jungle.

In the face of it all, and particularly the radio tracking, Brigadier Jackson is unsure what to do.

Even though in his long and illustrious career this is his first exposure to signal tracking, and he is unsure of its efficacy – these other reports are starting to present a compelling case for looming catastrophe. But against that . . . ?

Well, against that such reports are not unusual. Since 6RAR arrived at Nui Dat in early June there have been reports of VC sightings, and for good reason: the very reason they had come to Phuoc Tuy in the first place was because the VC are active here. It can't be too surprising that their Intelligence network is bringing in reports about them?

One thing is for certain: to spread widely these reports would be embarrassing and potentially damaging to the war effort. The Australian presence had been meant to diminish the VC presence in the area and, in some ways, broadcasting these reports would be an acknowledgement of failure.

And so, beyond his immediate staff, Brigadier Jackson tells no-one, not even such senior officers as 5RAR's Lieutenant Colonel John Warr and 6RAR's Colonel Colin Townsend.

(It does not quite fit with the tenth and most important of the Ten Principles of Leadership taught at Scheyville, *Communicate effectively*, but that's the way it is.)

Both of the battalion commanders, in any case, already have their hands full with problems of their own. One of the key issues they are facing is the sheer fatigue of their overworked soldiers, with reports piling up of sentries being found asleep while on duty, of men coming back from patrols as quivering wrecks, of even officers suffering what appear to be nervous breakdowns. The major complaint is the unrelenting nature of everything they're facing, the fact that they never get any respite! It is just day after day of endless exertion, exhaustion interspersed with bursts of extreme terror.

Reluctantly, it is decided that the only answer is to send the men back – half a company at a time – on occasional R & R breaks to Vung Tau.

•

Mail call!

Ever and always it is the most cherished time of the lot for the Australian soldiers. The chopper comes in with the mail bags, and a short time later a Corporal of each platoon pulls out the letters one by one and shouts out the name of the addressee, immediately prompting a joyous hand to be thrust skywards with a shout of 'Here!'

News from home . . .

The St George Dragons have won the last 10 straight!

Someone fired a shot at Arthur Calwell after he said we should be coming home, and there is still no news of what happened to the missing Beaumont children who simply vanished at Glenelg Beach.

Mary's pregnant!

And of course there is a letter for Lance Corporal Jack Jewry of 10 Platoon. There always is! *Every* day, his now pregnant wife Susanne writes to him and, to the delight of his mate, sprinkles the pages with her perfume. Jack takes the letter, and devours it with his usual dreamy look. He cannot *wait* to get back to her!

Inevitably, everyone's favourite, the laughing, singing Kenny Gant has also got a letter, from his mum – she *always* writes – this one seeking confirmation that he is continuing to wear the St Christopher medal she'd given him, to help give him the Lord's protection.[7]

Of course I am, Mum. Wouldn't go anywhere without it!

The Corporal keeps reading out the names until the bag is empty and the soldiers settle down to lovingly turn over the pages one by one, and on this day – among the soldiers of Delta Company's 12 Platoon gathered under the canvas of the makeshift canteen – suddenly a cry goes up.

'You beauty! She's accepted!'

Everyone looks at Private Paul Large from Coolah, and he exultantly goes on.

'She's agreed to marry me!' he says incredulously.[8]

Congratulations, mate! You bloody *beauty*. Fancy *any* sheila agreeing to marry someone like *you*, let alone one as lovely as Noeline!

There is a lot of good-natured knocking, but everyone is pleased for him. Paul has never stopped talking about his girlfriend waiting for him at home, or showing everyone a photo of her, so it really sounds like a match made in heaven.

Only a short time later Private Dave Beahan gets a tap on the shoulder, and looks up to see Paul himself, asking if he could have a word outside.

Sure, mate.

The men carried on reading their mail, as Largey gets to the point.

'Mate,' he tells him outside. 'I want you to be my best man at the wedding.'

'Don't be bloody silly, Paul,' Dave tells him. 'You've got your school friends and your mates from Coolah.'

'No, no, read this paragraph here of the letter.'

Beahan takes the proffered letter and reads the paragraph Paul is pointing to.

> *Paul, please pick an army friend for your best man, rather than a schoolfriend or a Coolah boy.*[9]

And that is that – and very typical of the bonds formed in the Army. No matter that a year ago they had never even met. When you go through what they have been through together, you end up closer than brothers.

Both soldiers are thrilled.

•

Captain Richards from the 547 Signal Troop has news for Captain Keep. After the signal of the VC 275th Regiment had advanced towards the 1ATF base at Nui Dat for about 1000 metres a day every day for the last fortnight, it now appears to have stopped, about seven kilometres away, in the area of the small hill known as Nui Dat 2, just to the north of the Long Tan rubber plantation. If he was a betting man he would say there is a large force of VC 275th Regiment positioned just to the east of that hill.

Brigadier Jackson is advised. While still refusing to believe it, what he will allow is to increase the amount of patrolling in the area where Keep thinks the VC are. He needs to be certain before taking any action, and patrolling should either confirm it or make Charlie pull his head in.

Delta Company is one of the units sent out, patrolling to the east of 1ATF base on a route that takes them through the Long Tan rubber plantation, but there is no trace of the enemy of any significance. They return to base exhausted, relieved and unsettled all at once.

Many of them have a sense that the enemy is near, and in force, it is just that they haven't found him. Perhaps Alpha Company, going out the following day under Captain Charles Mollison, will have more luck?

7 August 1966, Nui Dat, village voice

It is bitter, brutal work, but someone has to do it. On this day it is the soldiers of 5RAR who are designated to undertake Operation Holsworthy, essentially the neutralisation of nearby Binh Ba village as a threat to the Australian Task Force base. In all of Phuoc Tuy province it is this highly cosmopolitan village of 2000 people – boasting beautifully constructed plantation workers' houses, together with many French villas surrounded by sprawling lawns including manicured lawn tennis courts and gardens with exotic flowers – which is the biggest problem. It is securely held by the Viet Cong. It is only six kilometres north of Nui Dat and, beyond being a source of intelligence on Australian movements, could be used as a real staging post for any VC attack. Binh Ba is a valuable piece of land and industry, with the French enjoying the fruits and profits of its labour until the Japanese took it over in 1941. The French were back in '45, left in '54 and then local oppressors took over.

Yes, some of the residents had resisted the VC takeover, including the head man, but when he had been tortured to death, most of the resistance had faded. Many of the village's young men had been forced to join the VC militia, with those who resisted being obliged to take a 'special course to eliminate "reactionary tendencies". If they failed to show the desired amount of reformation they were taken off and never heard of again.'[10]

And so on this morning 5RAR departs the 1ATF base at Nui Dat, marching five kilometres to the north till nightfall brings the men to the jungle on the south-west of the plantation that is the life-force of the village's economy.

Captain Robert J. O'Neill is among the men of 5RAR. Last year he completed his Doctorate in Philosophy at Oxford University. This year he is in the jungle of Vietnam but there is still something of the scholar or rather the poet about him. The mundane becomes almost magical when he observes it. Most soldiers see a red road and some green trees. O'Neill? He sees a road 'plated with red mud which blended in a harmony of rich colours with the dark green of the rubber trees'.[11] That big tree there? It isn't just a large bit of wood, it is 'a graceful study in the transfer of vertical forms to horizontal planes. The trunk rose straight up out of the earth, curving over until it flowed smoothly into one of several parallel horizontal layers of foliage which made up the character of the tree.'[12]

Yes, you are right, Captain O'Neill. It's a very big tree. *Sigh*. Poetry is best kept to oneself on patrol. Prose for the Digger, thank you, Sir. But as they return, just after 6 pm, O'Neill once more cannot help note the beauty that surrounds them; the jungle presenting a panorama for any painter:

'A narrow horizontal strip of light which ran completely across our front separated the convergence of the dark cloud of rubber leaves overhead from the carpet of dark earth beneath. This light filtered through in a pale green swathe from the opposite edge of the plantation. Thousands of thin vertical black lines, the trunks of rubber trees, linked the horizontal strips of darkness and the dark silhouettes of the assembling soldiers flitted across this static pattern.'[13]

Yes, sir, it is getting dark, isn't it? *Sigh*. Onwards.

Throughout the night the platoons and sections carefully move into position surrounding the village until they have established a secure cordon. And now, at dawn, a helicopter flies over Binh Ba with a blaring loudspeaker advising the villagers not to be afraid, but, *Bbạn bị bao vây*, you are surrounded, and the Australians are about to sweep through.

And so it proves.

The bewildered villagers soon emerge from their houses to be rounded up and herded to open space, where a long period of interrogations begins using Vietnamese interpreters, as they look to capture active VC, weed out sympathisers and re-establish Binh Ba as being under the control of the South Vietnamese Government, not the VC.

In the end, the news is relatively good. While the Viet Cong had indeed been enormously active in Binh Ba, from the moment the Australians had arrived at Nui Dat their presence and activities had reduced. The guerrillas who had once been openly based in the village had gone into hiding in the jungle, while the main force battalions of the NLF had not been through since. The Viet Cong did, however, still impose their taxation, and with the plantation workers always being paid on the fifth day of each month, the tax collectors usually appeared on the seventh, which is to say, yesterday! As it happens no fewer than six armed tax collectors had entered the village the previous evening and had already begun collecting the August revenue and rice. They are quickly rounded up.

A further 70 VC sympathisers or collaborators are taken for questioning with the message firmly being established: this is no longer a VC village. And yet, while it is one thing to have nominally secured the village, it is quite another to be able to *actually* secure the village from a VC counter-attack, all while opening the roads that the VC still control.

It will be a long process, and an entire company of 5RAR, Charlie Company, must soon settle down in Binh Ba, to make daily patrols, build defences and consolidate what they have gained. All up, after the hardships of Nui Dat, it can be no bad thing to be in such a pleasant environment for a week or two, or three?

And yet the same problem presents itself as ever. The Nui Dat base can only just secure itself as is, with two battalions. Removing one 5RAR

Company from the roster of guarding the perimeter and going out on patrol places an extraordinary strain on 6RAR.

•

The Bob Keep issue will not go away, any more than the man's smell.

For as the days pass, as the sun pounds down, the rain falls, the mud multiplies and his warnings continue to be ignored – yes, *ignored*, despite his insistence on this irrefutable evidence that continues to pile up – the behaviour of the junior Intelligence officer starts to become noticeably erratic. It's not just that he appears every bit as unkempt as he is unwashed, it is the glazed and haunted look in his eyes, the faltering speech, and the *crazy* things he is saying.

Yes, as the official history will record, he keeps 'painting a picture of impending catastrophe'.[14]

His superior, Major John Rowe, is rather more pointed.

'His exaggerated sense of self-importance reached drama queen, soap opera levels.'[15]

'We'll all be rooned,' is an Australian staple in times of drought on the farm.

'We'll all be rooned,' said Hanrahan,
In accents most forlorn,
Outside the church, ere Mass began,
One frosty Sunday morn . . .

And so around the chorus ran
'It's keepin' dry, no doubt.'
'We'll all be rooned,' said Hanrahan,
'Before the year is out.'[16]

But Keep outdoes Hanrahan, much as he tries to keep it to himself when around Major Rowe, knowing it irritates him so, he just can't help himself. We'll all be rooned! We are all going to be killed, because the VC are moving our way in force!

It might be some illness, as the doctors think possible, or maybe even some kind of nervous breakdown?

'I had this tremendous feeling of responsibility,' Keep will recount for his part, 'that all these people around me were in great peril and I could do nothing about it.'[17]

Yes, that might be closer to it.

Whatever it is, it is not good and it is clear that something must break. But no-one could have foreseen that it would end like *this*?

For on this hot morning of 9 August, Group Captain Peter Raw – a former World War II bomber pilot, who for a later feat had been personally decorated by Queen Elizabeth II, and is now no less than the most senior RAAF commander on the base – asks to see Brigadier Jackson. After a bare minimum of preliminaries, this very proper officer, with creases in his pants and steel in his spine, makes a very serious charge.

He alleges that the previous night Captain Keep had made homosexual advances upon the RAAF officer with whom he had been sharing a tent.

Those advances had been strongly rebuffed but it changes nothing.

Making homosexual advances is in violation of Military Law. Group Captain Raw insists that Captain Keep be charged and face a court martial.

Good lord.

In his whole career, Brigadier Jackson has never faced a similar situation, and it has to happen *now*, when he is dealing with so many worries?

Shaken, Jackson sends for Captain Keep's immediate superior, Major John Rowe, who will report the Brigadier 'looked deeply troubled and sad',[18] as he advises him of this dreadful situation.

Major Rowe moves quickly.

He will talk to both officers.

He is sure that the key for Group Captain Raw will be for Keep to be banished from the base, and there are other ways it could be done. If he can get a doctor to co-operate, Keep can be evacuated on medical grounds, which would prevent the scandal and such an appalling stain on Keep's record. Jackson agrees. Major Rowe salutes and moves off at some pace. By sundown, it is sorted, and Captain Keep is evacuated to Vung Tau, on the medical grounds that, officially, he is suffering from malaria and encephalitis.

•

By now, even Brigadier Jackson is showing some alarm. Now is the time for boots on the ground, looking for any signs of the 275th VC Regiment somewhere in the area of Nui Dat 2.

On 13 August, as the sun is high in the sky, a 161 Recce Flight 'Possum' helicopter – assigned to provide reconnaissance, surveillance and operational support out of Vung Tau and Nui Dat – is flying over Long Tan when . . . hello, possum! Radio transmissions are detected coming from the very base of Nui Dat 2!

Major Harry Smith's Delta Company is sent out on a patrol at once to look for traces of a major enemy force in the area, but finds nothing of note. The following day, 6RAR's Alpha Company is also dispatched on a three-day patrol, searching the area east of Nui Dat and are instructed to report in at the first sign of trouble.

•

It will become legendary as part of the American GI zeitgeist: 'And yea, verily, though I walk in the shadows of the valley of death, yet do I fear no evil, for I am the meanest mother-fucker in the valley.'

The Australians prefer to stay with the more traditional protections and on this day at their Nui Dat base that means gathering around the visiting Army priest, complete with dog-collar as he asks them to bow their heads and pray for heavenly protection.

There in the front row with their heads bowed are the childhood friends from Tamworth and now Lieutenants with 6RAR, John O'Halloran and Gordon Sharp.

They have come a long way from the days of attending Mass together as young tackers, with their parents. John O'Halloran takes further comfort in knowing that, back in Tamworth, his brother Dick still goes to church every day to pray for his safe return.

For both men, in the here and now, it is comforting to feel that God is keeping an eye on them.

They sing hymns.

They listen to the young priest's sermon on the virtues of doing one's duty no matter the cost.

They finish with their eyes closed and their heads bowed as, all together, they solemnly recite:

Our Father, who art in Heaven.
Hallow'd be thy name . . .
Give us this day our daily bread,
And forgive us our trespasses . . .

16 August 1966, north-west of Nui Dat 2, Alpha dogs

Another day, another patrol. Always, another bloody patrol.

As soon as they return it is over to Captain Charles Mollison's 6RAR Alpha Company to do the honours, and the Alpha men head out on the morning of 16 August to also patrol Nui Dat 2, where some of the troubling reports seem to indicate enemy activity, as well as the ridge that lies to its north-west.

Captain Charles Mollison is Old School. He has a job to do. He has come to Vietnam to *fight*, and that is what he intends to do.

16 August 1966, Nui Dat 2, grave matters

Mollison and his men of Alpha Company are now deep in the bush surrounding Nui Dat 2. Their faces are coated in camouflage cream; green, brown and black now completely covering what would otherwise be novice pink or veteran tan. They are as silent as the tomb as their voices will barely be raised above a whisper for the next three days; hand signals are their language now. Their uniforms are a new green and red combination; jungle green splotched with Nui Dat mud. One novel item is worn though: boots with steel inserts in the soles. Not the height of comfort, but they have been designed in Australia specifically to fight the punji pit and the spikes that lie within, so only a fool would take them off while treading these paths.

The scenery varies from gentle countryside to dense bamboo; but the men who walk through it are watching the ground; their eyes flickering for the unfamiliar, a glint of steel, a twist of rope. They know any traps will be well hidden, even if a helpful VC popped up and pointed one out precisely you still wouldn't see it, but the instinct remains: watch your step. In open country, they are in arrowhead formation; in close scrub they step into a single file; the movements do not need to be signalled, each man flows into place as the conditions dictate.

The first sign of the enemy? Salt. A small stack of it stored up high on a bamboo platform; a jungle spice rack that shows the VC are near and do not expect visitors or tourists. Three hundred metres away, tracks are found. Fresh tracks. Slowly now, they move forward with dread in each tread lest a snap will frighten off the quarry. They move in threes; the first, the forward scout, looks down for booby traps, the next man looks straight ahead, the third man looks up to the trees for snipers. Nothing is stirring. The only sound is their own laboured breathing in the heat.

Until now . . . At 3.20 pm several staccato bursts of machine-gun fire ring out! It proves to be Alpha Company's 3 Platoon, who had come across a section of enemy soldiers all in military greens. After returning fire with remarkable force and accuracy, the enemy, whoever they are, and wherever they are from, scarper! Those uniforms, though, are troubling. It is almost as if, instead of the usual local guerrillas in black pyjamas, these might be highly trained members of the North Vietnamese Army! But, surely not. The NVA have shown up in provinces north of here, but there has been no sign of them yet in Phuoc Tuy.

Wherever they are from, and whatever their uniforms, of enormous significance is something they have dropped in their eagerness to get away: a large, curved object that is nothing less than a Claymore mine. Is this their only mine? Or maybe there are others already laid out, or about to be . . . ?

The breath in their lungs quickening, the forward scouts carefully move forward. One wrong step, and the best case is they will only lose a leg. Suddenly, out to the north, there is more firing. This time it proves to be 1 Platoon who has just stumbled across an enemy patrol. A quick firefight breaks out, and 1 Platoon is able to capture one badly wounded enemy soldier, *also in military greens*, who alas dies within the hour.

On high alert, the men of Alpha stay in position, with one up the spout, ready for whatever comes their way.

There!

It is Private Johnny Needs who sees him first, another Charlie in green fatigues, and a single shot brings him down. And what's this? It turns out the shot man is carrying with him a notebook. To the Australians, of course, the Asian hieroglyphics are incomprehensible, but – as they bury the officer – the Vietnamese interpreter they have with them only has to glance at it to give them the news. It is filled with notations about the positioning of mortars.

Where?

Aimed at *what?*

At *Nui Dat?*

This, the interpreter cannot tell them.

But, clearly, the whole thing might be of vital importance.

Perhaps a photo of the slain officer would be useful?

But we have buried him.

Dig him up.

In what Mollison will describe as 'a most disturbing exercise'[19] the job is done and the enemy officer snapped with a Brownie Box. In the meantime, 1 Platoon question their only live lead, a badly wounded man who appears to be an NVA soldier. The Commander of 1 Platoon, Lieutenant Trevor Gardiner, does his best to interrogate but makes no headway at all. Not only is it clear he does not speak English, but they have no Vietnamese interpreters handy. Stranger still? Despite the fact that he is obviously bleeding to death and getting weaker by the minute – his breathing getting so raspy the death rattle must be close – the soldier uses his remaining strength to insist he refuses their medical help. And now, with his dying breath, he speaks, in English after all, rasping out: 'Go easy, *Uc Dai Loi*, go easy.'[20]

It is moving, heroic and chilling, all at once. Here is a humble man who would rather die than ask for help; rather farewell this world than risk living and reveal information that might compromise his cause.

Not for the first or last time, the soldiers are reminded that these are a people who have a commitment to their cause that seems very nearly other-worldly.

Just how can they beat that?

All put together, right now the whole thing is deeply worrying. The enemy is here in some force – as yet indeterminate, but significant. It looks like they might be NVA, not mere local insurgents from the D445 Battalion, and they are possibly building for some kind of mortar attack on a target unknown – but just as a rooster need not wonder too long what the fox on yonder horizon might be after, it seems a fair bet that shits are trumps at Nui Dat sometime in the near future.

Dusk, 16 August 1966, Nui Dat 2, every which way and loose

Dusk in the jungle falls suddenly. Light gives up the uneven struggle to penetrate the canopy and calls it a day well before the rest of the more open world. Still, in the very last dregs of this day there is just enough light for Mollison and half-a-dozen of his Alpha Company soldiers to make it to the most northerly knoll of Nui Dat 2 in their ongoing search for signs of Charlie and . . .

And halt!

They can hear something!

Yes, just down there below them, *there is movement*, and they can be no further than a stone's throw away. Mollison makes the obvious hand signal. Stay silent. Safety catches off. Rifles and machine guns at the ready. Though the heavy jungle continues to deaden the sound there is no mistaking it, nor the fact that whoever they are, they're getting closer.

Mollison and his men stand, twitching, *itching* for resolution, for action, for a result, as he will recall, 'the whole of our being straining to hear, straining to see; our mud-stained uniforms blending with the scrub. Only our eyes moved – staring out from blackened faces.'[21]

The seconds pass.

The sound grows louder, the branches crash and crack ahead of them; this is a careless foe, they clearly do not realise that an enemy is listening. Mollison starts the calculus of attack in his head, his thoughts racing towards conclusions he can't make with confidence. The enemy is ahead, and his training kicks in: 'How many? What weapons do they have? Are they dug in, or do they have overhead protection?'[22]

The blood from the leeches Mollison had squashed moments earlier keeps trickling down his leg. He can hear his own breathing, surely pinpointing his position to any of the enemy in those bushes, perhaps even now tightening their fingers on the trigger and about to unleash a deadly spray of lead?

Still they belly-bump their way forward, their sweat dripping into their eyes, trying not to blink, resolutely looking for a sign of the enemy and . . . nothing. No sign of Charlie, who is a bloody genius at camouflage, and

CRASH!

The noise is as clear as crystal thrown on the floor and yet they see nothing. What the hell? He glances across at his own men, all searching for a sign. Mollison feels the hairs on the nape of his neck rise before he hears another sound.

THUMP!

Bloody hell that was right *between* us! Like he fell from the bloody . . .

THUMP! THUMP! THUMP!

. . . sky. The foe is all around them, yelling in triumph! For they are: 'Monkeys! A bloody great family of monkeys! They bounded off, chattering and screeching into the undergrowth.'[23]

This must be the 'gorilla warfare' they have heard so much about! They move on, grinning like idiots, and trying not to laugh. This is serious! The actual enemy could be near. No monkeying about . . .

•

Under the circumstances, things are tense, fuses are short, and tempers are flaring like a bonfire on cracker night back home. Blokes belting each other is not uncommon – a case in point being recorded on this day, 16 August, in a letter Paul Large sends home to his parents in Coolah.

16 August 1966.

Dear Mum and Dad,
Sorry I have not written earlier but I have been as flat as a strap for the past few weeks . . .

Paul tells them of his recent legal victory against a Corporal, escaping any punishment for hitting said Corporal without the bother of even having a court martial:

I would have won the Court Martial for the 4 blokes said that I only defended myself and the CO must have realised this as he dismissed the charge this morning (actually this Lance Corporal called me a gutless, little 'B' and I got stuck in him, so it's a good thing I have a few lying mates. I got a victory too, might add) . . .

We got the Cup back I see. Tell the boys I am very proud of them and would have loved to have been there.

We go on a 3 day op in about 5 days and then on a big one on the 30th so I will be pretty busy for the next few weeks . . .

No more news now so I will have to close.

All my love,
Paul[24]

•

This evening at Nui Dat, Delta Company man the perimeter, but there is a man from A Company out there who might have a missive that would massively interest them. Unfortunately, it is just one report among many coming into the Australian Army Intelligence Corps at Nui Dat from patrols out in the field, this one from 6RAR's Alpha Company, concerning the notebook discovered on the officer . . .

16 Aug - 1826 hours - (A Coy to 6RAR) - Documents and dress indicate regular VC. dress - some greens, some blues, generally a mixture. Documents indicate 1 KIA had been learning to fire a mortar.[25]

Back at the base, Mollison's radioed report of Alpha Company's activities for the day are duly received and filed, but there are no senior Intelligence officers present to process and analyse them to cross-reference with other reports and, in a world ideal, reveal the truth of what Charlie is up to. For not only has Captain Bob Keep not yet been replaced, but his superior officer, Major Rowe, has also just been evacuated as his various medical ailments have worsened.

It means that Mollison's report, together with all other reports of enemy activity in the area, various sightings and ongoing radio-signal reports are simply put in a file to be examined and analysed later.

2100 hours, 16 August 1966, Nui Dat, last post

Back at the Nui Dat base, as darkness falls, it feels like just another night in 'Nam. In the heat and humidity, after yet another exhausting day for men who have had too little sleep, the worst thing of all is for those who have drawn the short straw and must do a night shift in a patrol, or who are on sentry duty, or at a listening post.

Some simply can't face it.

One of them, Corporal Brian 'Doc' Mortimer, a trained medic of the Royal Australian Army Medical Corps attached to the 103rd Field Battery, can barely keep his eyes open after a long day, and is now meant to stand to by the guns for the next four hours on the sentry picket. He just can't do it.

Happily, one of the blokes who sleeps in a hoochie just down from his own, a bloke he is mates with, Gunner Phil Norris – the postie from Granville – agrees to swap shifts, even if it does take a bit of doing. Phil will do the first shift, from 10 pm to 2 am, while Brian can get the precious sleep he needs *right now*, and Phil can then head back to his tent for the wee hours.

0100 hours, 17 August 1966, Nui Dat, house of cards

Puffs of cigarette smoke, endless swigs of beer, bullshitters in every direction. Lieutenant Gordon Sharp is like a pig in mud, a frog on a lily-pad, a lizard in the spring sunshine, completely in his element. And it's your deal. Look, it could be just about any night in any Australian pub from Penrith to Perth, Darwin to Devonport, but as it happens it is just another hot and humid night in Nui Dat where the bluffing and sledging are flying as fast as the beer is being gulped down. Out there – fuck that for a game of soldiers – we are Privates and Officers. In here, we are just Australian blokes getting pissed and playing cards, a rare pleasurable interlude in otherwise grim times in this hell-hole. Yes, even if we *are* playing by candle-light with the flaps of the tent tightly closed, so that no-one breaches the strictly enforced black-out regulations. Lieutenant Sharp has never been fussed on military protocols of any description, least of all the whole hierarchy thing about officers never fraternising with soldiers. And he was upfront about it: 'This is bullshit you know,'[26] he says to Lance Corporal John Robbins. We are all Aussie blokes, no matter what stripes or pips we have on our arm. But enough, already.

Come on, you've already shuffled the tits off the Queen. *Deal*, I said!

Sharpie loves playing cards, it helps him get to know his men as much as it lets them get to know him. And on a good night, like tonight – the light of flickering home-made lanterns, a Ba Muoi Ba beer bottle with a candle dropped neatly in it and anchored with its own wax – he can win some money to add to his meagre Army pay.

Play on!

0240 hours, 17 August 1966, Nui Dat, night moves

It is weird how the crack of artillery firing less than 100 yards away can be so ho-hum.

For it is rarely something to worry about.

It will be just the Australian 1st Field Regiment of the Royal Australian Artillery doing what they do in the night – sending out the odd shell from hell onto known routes of the VC, hoping such stabs in the dark might get a lucky direct hit, or at the very least disrupt them. Whatever else, Charlie must be made aware that the Australians are here, that he no longer has this province to himself. The drop-shorts call it 'harassment and interdiction fire'.

Stranger still?

While the crack of a gun 100 yards away doesn't lift your pulse even a smidgin, the sound of a mortar being fired – PUMPH! – about three miles to the east or thereabouts suddenly makes your guts grip and your eyes rise to the skies.

Are we under attack?

Corporal Brian 'Doc' Mortimer, doing his picket for the 103rd Battery, is sure of it.

'It's a very distinct noise,' he will recount. 'It's a whistle that goes, and then *karump* . . .'[27]

Sure enough, moments later the first of the mortar shells land and – even in the pitch-blackness imposed by the enforced black-out every night, and the fact that there is only a sliver of moon – Mortimer is able to climb down into the relative safety of his gun-pit, even if it is half full of water. Impatiently, Mortimer waits for their own guns to make reply as, on the few occasions this has happened before, their own artillery had quickly been able to sort the enemy out, once they got a bead on where exactly the mortars were coming from.

Right now, Lieutenant Dave Sabben, on Delta Company perimeter guard duty at this time – for his third straight night – is one of many engaged in that very exercise. He had been staring out into the profound darkness at the jungle in this strange land, thinking of all the little things they would be doing at home in Sydney now – like sleeping for instance, rather than sitting in the middle of the bloody jungle with a gun and a yawn until dawn – when the first of the mortar round had landed. They are quickly followed by many more in quick succession, and Sabben does his duty, using his binoculars to look for the flashes in the night, so they can start to get some precise co-ordination of the location of the mortars.

For his part, like everyone, Major Harry Smith is instantly awake and scrambling, even though he had been a little more heavily asleep than most, having had a few beers not long before with some visiting Americans at the base's answer to an officers' club – a decent den of debauchery covered with canvas.

They are under attack!

Moving so fast he has his boots on the wrong feet, Harry Smith charges into the night, narrowly avoiding other officers, Sergeants and Diggers charging in different directions. Most of them are trying to get to their slit trenches or their posts – in Smith's case, to Delta Company HQ so he can issue orders, provide a command post for whatever is coming, and await further orders (and further shells) from on high.

•

There are exceptions. Lying in their tent, Private Harley Webb with two companions, Private Colin Whiston and Private Frank Topp, who have just been assigned as 'reos', reinforcements, to Delta Company, have arrived at Nui Dat after dark, and have no idea where to go to save themselves. They decide to stay exactly where they are and just hope a mortar doesn't land on them. A very few others are similarly sanguine. When one Private, Ken Tronc, comes across Sergeant Paddy Todd down by the perimeter, he asks the Army veteran what he should do. 'Go back to bed,' Todd replies. Tronc does exactly that, though he does wear his steel helmet as one concession to flying shrapnel.

Another exception is around the table where the 11 Platoon poker game is being played, under the command of Sharpie. Yes, Sergeant Bob Buick does charge in all a'fluster, and tells them all that – for fuck's sake – those explosions they can hear are from *incoming* shells, but . . .

But they just don't care.

'There was money on the table being lost and won,' Buick will recall, 'the enemy fire was landing a kilometre or more away – it was not their problem.'

Disgusted, Buick turns on his heel and leaves. He will go out, assess[28] the situation some more and come back if necessary. Beyond his naked disgust at Sharp fraternising in such outrageous fashion, his fear is that this might be a prelude to an attack on the base.

•

Across the base, bleary Diggers – most of whom had been sleeping all but starkers beneath mosquito nets in the thick humidity – continue to scramble from their tents, struggling to get their boots on as they stumble towards the pits they have so recently dug for their own protection. A lucky few clutch the tins of toffee that have recently arrived in care packages from the Salvation Army in Australia, on the reckoning this might be a long night.

MEDIC! We need a medic over here!

Urgent cries ricochet around the camp competing with the shells. It will be a tragic night, too, as the enemy has already drawn blood and perhaps a lot of it.

In the pits, the soldiers grip their weapons and peer out, with the same question as Buick. Are these mortars the prelude to a full-blown attack, and are the VC about to over-run them? Following strict routine, the lazy arcs of many flares go up from all around the perimeter before exploding against the night sky to illuminate the cleared space on the other side of the wire. The Diggers peer out, looking not for light but for darkness, the black pyjamas that are the garb of the VC. Are there hordes of men in black racing at them?

Nervous Australian eyes strain to determine the tiniest sign of movement, the shape of anything that wasn't there at dusk and bloody well shouldn't be there now.

There is nothing. Which is not to say the buggers are not there in the high grass about 200 yards away from the wire and about to launch. *But would they?* Surely it would be too dark for them, and they would risk killing each other.

Or is that exactly what they want us to think before launching a devastating surprise attack?

Private Terry Burstall sits in his pit with Shorty Brown, whispering so quietly that they can barely hear the words they speak themselves let alone the hushed words of the other. But *listen*, Shorty . . .

'Surely, they wouldn't come in this early?'

'Before first light?'

Each question is its own hopeful answer. No. But . . .

'If it was a small commando raid . . .'

Yes, if it was that, a few dozen could swoop in, wreak havoc, kill heaps of us and . . .

'Get away before first light.'[29]

Exactly. Nah, they wouldn't, would they?

But yeah, they might.

Nah, shoot and run, that's the bloody VC pattern.

But look, shelling in the wee hours is usually not their go either, so what the hell is going on . . . ?

It will be a long night. They are not just jumping at shadows, but actively searching for them, a strange occupation at night, but moving darkness is what is feared, black on black and back to back, creeping ever closer . . .

•

Under the circumstances it is no surprise that no-one hears the PLOP . . .

But it is just one of those things. No sooner has Sergeant Bob Buick left the light of the tent where the card game is being played than – with his night vision completely gone – he walks straight into a puddle, that proves to be well over a metre deep and every bit as wide. An abandoned weapons pit that had filled up. He is completely drenched, and climbs out, shaking water and spitting chips.

'This dive into the hole did not improve my temper. I was already pissed off because of the lack of interest or urgency shown by Sharp and the others. Falling into the hole topped me up, but the volcano eruption would have to wait, as I had to get a compass bearing on the enemy's firing position.'[30]

His fears are confirmed. This is an organised attack coming at them from a wide front, and there is *every* chance that the enemy is about to launch.

Racing back to the 11 Platoon Command Post Tent, Buick's volcano is rumbling more than somewhat. In a blind fury, the veteran NCO confronts his superior officer – using language that is maybe just this side of insubordination, and maybe well to the other side – where he strongly expresses his view about the insanity of continuing to play fucking *cards* while the base is under attack! It is not just that playing cards with his soldiers is conduct unbecoming of an officer like Sharp, it is that this mortar attack is probably just the warm-up act before Charlie himself takes centre stage on their perimeter, and they all must stand to, and get ready for it.

Sharp is not moved, as he continues to deal out the cards and play his hand.

'It is nothing to do with us,' Buick will recall him saying, 'it's over the other side of the task force.'[31]

Vesuvius should be so restrained.

Buick explodes – 'the pent-up volcano within me blew'[32] – telling Sharp what he needs to be told. Yes, it is beyond insubordinate, but Sharp's actions are outrageous, and in his view this is one of the very reasons that Major Smith has put him, Buick, with this platoon in the first place – to sort this bastard out! He is confident that, if it comes to it, the Major will back him, not Sharp.

Playing cards while the base is under attack? It is the most unheard of thing Buick has ever heard of, and it is enough to blow away the veneer of respect for his Platoon Commander he has been struggling to hold on to!

And so Buick takes action, charging into the tent, turning over the table they are playing on – as the cards and money flies everywhere – roaring 'Stand to!'[33]

The gamblers grab what they can and flee into the shattered night.

'I went off,' Buick will give his own account, 'like a free keg of beer at a wharfie party. Everyone, including Sharp, bolted out of the tent, stumbling in the dark to take up their positions for "stand to".'[34]

There will be a time to call Buick to account for his outrageous presumption, but with the explosions coming ever closer it really *is* urgent to get moving right now.

Very quietly?

Lieutenant John O'Halloran, Sharp's childhood friend, agrees with Sergeant Buick.

'Gordon,' he will later say, 'was a good soldier but not a particularly good officer.'[35]

Still the mortars keep landing, all the more terrifying because unlike some shells, whose whistling sound can give you a fair clue as to whether they will land close or not, with the mortars you don't so much hear a whistle as the roar of an express train approaching. First you hear the PUMPH, as the mortar is fired, then the trailing train sound begins, then it stops . . . just long enough for you to wonder if it is coming right for you – is this the last thought you will think? – then there is a WHOOSH of the train roaring suddenly into the ground and the THUD of the burst, the explosion imploding your ears in its ferocity of velocity . . . If you hear it, you are not dead, and you win – though some other poor bastards nearby might have lost their lives.

And yet it is not just the PUMPHs that concern the likes of Harry Smith, who is a veteran at determining from sound alone just what is being fired. He can also hear the distant crack of artillery, and the occasional whistling of shells. And there is certainly the distinctive sound of the VC's rocket launchers, a kind of light artillery preferred by them because it is so light just a couple of men can carry it, and it fires small shells as far as four miles.

Looking out from their pit, Terry Burstall and Shorty Brown can see that this looks to be a seriously targeted attack, as the three areas getting most attention are the Task Force Headquarters, the engineers' compound, the artillery areas, and the depot for the Armoured Personnel Carriers. They are going after the nerve centres of the whole operation, not just lobbing the mortars into the base and hoping for the best.

Not surprisingly, those with the artillery batteries are not enjoying the attention. When the first mortars had landed among them, the men of the 103rd Battery – the hardest hit of the lot – had been in their tents,

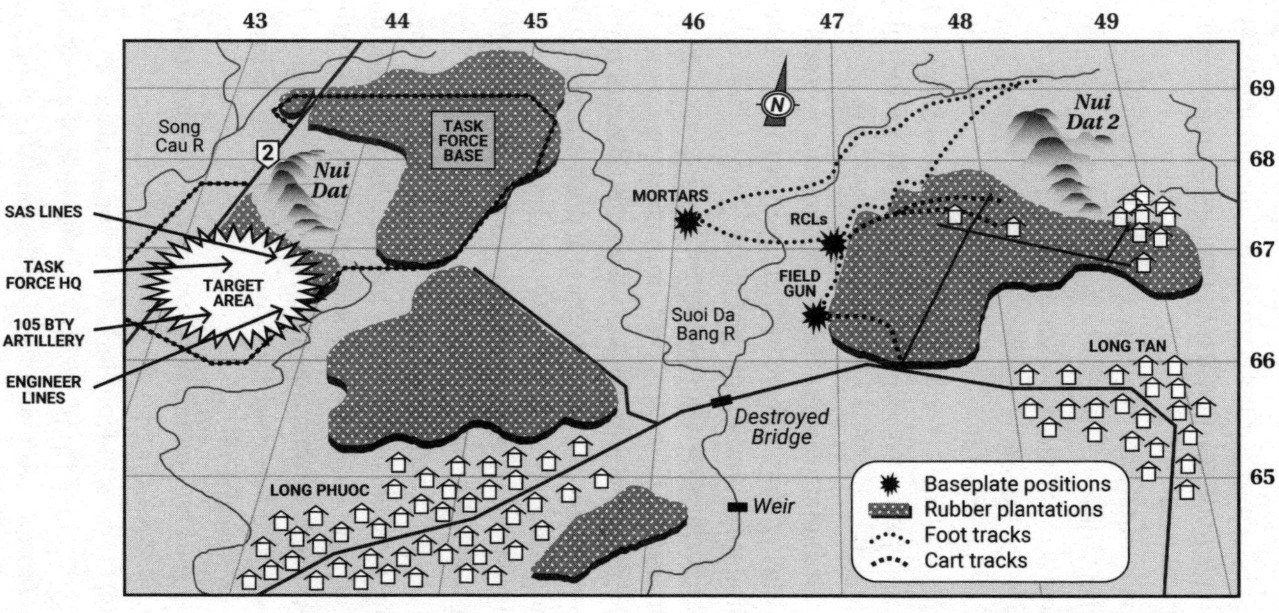

17 August bombardment, showing VC base plate sites, target areas and withdrawal tracks

no more than 10 yards from their gun. Bombardier John Burns had scrambled from his bunk to get into one of the ditches that surround their gun emplacements, and is now getting to grips. Yes, it is a muddy mess, designed to drain rainwater away from the gun position, but for the moment it will have to do, particularly as the enemy rounds continue to land all around. By getting their whole bodies below the lip of the ditch it means there would have to be a direct hit upon them to kill them . . . or bury them alive.

And yet while nearly everyone is sheltering, some, clearly, are not so lucky as the cry goes up: 'Medic!'

Christ. Someone has copped it.

Bombardier Burns risks one eye above the parapet and sees the 103rd Battery medic, Corporal Brian Mortimer, running madly to the call. But who has been wounded?

There is no way of finding out for the moment as the mortars keep landing and exploding. And now there are yet more cries for medics to come quick, as still more mortars find their mark.

But exactly where is the attack coming from?

While Lieutenant Dave Sabben has seen no flashes, he has a strong feel for the direction from the sound alone – about 80 degrees from his Command Post position – and immediately sends it down the line to Delta Company HQ, who pass it on to 6RAR HQ. From their own position further round on the perimeter, the commander of 5 Platoon in 6RAR's Bravo Company, Lieutenant John O'Halloran, does the same. Putting it together with other HQ Intelligence – like that of Alpha Company, which is actually out in the field – can give a precise angle for the direction of the flashes. The 131 Divisional Locating Battery will ideally be able to use other estimates of direction along the line to triangulate the approximate position, and allow the Fire Control Centre to co-ordinate their own artillery counter-attack.

For now, Sabben puts the phone back on its cradle, and stands to with the rest of his comrades, and indeed the entire camp.

In Command HQ, furious calculations are being made as to where precisely the attack is coming from. Written on the back of an envelope – and under these extreme circumstances, as the mortars continue to drop, it is – the enemy seem to be attacking from three separate spots. The area is situated three or four miles to the east, on the other side of the Suoi Da Bang stream in the area of the Long Tan rubber plantation, and each spot has at least two mortars, maybe more, together with recoilless rifles (RCLs) and likely some other light artillery. The co-ordinates of their location are raced to the artillery compound – which is blessedly still in action, if shaken with the pounding received – and in short order, at 2.50 am, the order given is 'Fire Mission Battery', complete with elevation and bearing of the target and the number of charges to be used. When all is ready the Gun Position Officer barks over the Tannoy speaker system: 'Five rounds, fire for effect' and for this first of many salvos to come each gun so fires.

All up, it has taken just 10 minutes from the attack beginning to getting a bead on the brutes, and sending some high explosives down their pipes for their trouble. The response is so fast and furious, going for the next 20 minutes, that the artillery boys will surely catch some of them in the open and draw blood.

The men firing are so busy, they have little time to note the arrival of Brigadier Oliver Jackson, who turns up at 103rd Battery and, after observing the smooth efficiency with which the men are operating, congratulates their Commanding Officer and heads back to Command HQ.

Look, he doesn't appear *particularly* worried, which is reassuring. Maybe a little haunted, like something is bothering him beyond the mortar attack, but he is certainly well under control.

•

Corporal Brian 'Doc' Mortimer can barely believe it. For while it had been one thing to get the phone call telling him he was needed as there were some wounded among the Gunners of the 103rd Battery, it is quite another to see just who it is. One of the mortars had landed in the branches of the trees in the tent lines among the hoochies, scattering the shrapnel, and some of it had wounded a couple of blokes. While the one with the bit of shrapnel in his rump only needed a bit of first aid, the second wounded bloke is the one that rocks him on two counts.

Firstly, his thin torch-light reveals that the man has a head wound with a bit of shrapnel poking out from the skull, which is now leaking brain fluid. And secondly . . . well, secondly, the bloke is Gunner Phil Norris, the very man he had swapped shifts with. The tragic truth, and Mortimer is aware of it from the first, is that if they had not swapped shifts, Phil would have been on duty at the gun-pits when the mortars had hit, and it would have been Mortimer himself in those hoochies.

Doc Mortimer feels sick to his stomach as he stabilises Phil Norris the best he can, and makes the call that he will need to be choppered out at first light. Phil is still talking, after a fashion, but is not making any sense.

•

Camped some two and a half miles east of Nui Dat – and thus much closer to where the firing is coming from – the men of 6RAR Alpha Company are caught between a shock, a ragged rock and a hard place. They have been out on patrol for two days, have had some contact with the enemy, other parties of whom are now pounding the Nui Dat base, and with some force!

Every PUMPH! to their east is followed some seconds later by an explosion to their west on Nui Dat.

What to do?

Is Charlie about to launch?

Should they try to move to where the firing is coming from and take them out?

No. Whichever enemy unit is firing that many mortars would not have neglected to place serious defences around it, and – in the unlikely event they were not blown apart by the shells about to descend upon the VC guns from Australian artillery at 1ATF base – approaching at night would be taking a literal stab in the dark.

Alpha's Commanding Officer, Captain Charles Mollison, at least quickly raises Battalion HQ on the Battalion net radio and talks to Captain Les Peters.

'What the hell is going on? It sounds like a regiment of mortars firing.'

'Give us a bearing quickly,' Captain Peters yells back over the sound of exploding mortars. 'They are coming down on us!'[36]

Mollison quickly obliges using his compass, giving bearings which are gratifying to Peters as they are at near right angles to the line of fire, allowing the calculations of where Charlie is firing from to be so much more accurate.

0305 hours, 17 August 1966, Nui Dat, a shot in the dark

The mortars explode, the roar rolls over the base and . . . nothing. The mortars stop and the primary sounds heard are the calls for 'Medic!' in the darkness.

As suddenly as it had started, the enemy artillery ceases, just 22 minutes after it had begun. Though the Nui Dat artillery will continue for another hour seeking retribution, or at least disruption on the aggressors, the fact that the mortars and small shells are no longer falling on them allows the Australians to get to grips, starting with getting medical attention to those who most need it. There prove to be a couple of dozen soldiers who have suffered shrapnel wounds, of whom one has had a leg neatly sheared off. Mercifully no-one has been killed, though apparently one bloke is in a bad way. Few know who it is yet.

Despite the severity of some of the wounds, still the strict black-out rules are enforced and the 1st Field Regiment doctor Captain John Taske must work by the light of a torch held by an orderly, the thin beam lighting everything from a bloody stump to neatly sliced abdominal wounds to a dangling ear. Working feverishly, he cleans, sews and bandages, trying to stabilise each patient so they can be safely choppered out to the nearest military hospital at Vung Tau.

Outside, searches are being made for more wounded or, indeed, any signs some of the enemy might be about. As the veteran Delta Company cook, Sergeant Bill O'Donnell, is strolling along, his rifle goes off accidentally – which under normal circumstances would see him lose 14 days' pay. As quick as a flash O'Donnell fires two more shots into the air and yells 'There they go!'[37]

(Now his accidental discharge has become a 'counter-attack', and he will keep his pay.)

Elsewhere, the 67 mortar craters around the base are the epicentres of circles of destruction that have all but wiped out 21 tents and done severe damage to seven army vehicles. Most significantly, the mortar rounds are indeed concentrated around the Australian artillery compound including the Fire Support Control Centre, which is the nerve centre of Nui Dat's capacity to fire co-ordinated artillery attacks on the surrounding countryside.

Clearly, this had been a very targeted attack. It had been specifically aimed at the areas which would most hurt their offensive capacity to fire artillery at a distance, their nerve centre and their main defence.

Luckily, though the mortars had come close, they hadn't really done much structural damage. In the case of the artillery this is attested to by the fact that all four batteries are not only still operational but continuing to fire heavily into the darkness now.

That firing stops just after 4 am, however, and Lieutenant Colonel Townsend, the Commanding Officer of 6RAR – under the rather strained orders of his own superior officer, Brigadier Oliver Jackson – sends for Major Noel Ford of Bravo Company and his officers.

By 5 am, just as the first flush of the rising dawn allows the shaken soldiers not on perimeter duty to more easily start cleaning up, Bravo Company under Ford has been fully briefed and is already moving to their task.

They are to immediately go out on patrol to locate the enemy firing positions, follow whatever tracks there might be wherever they may lead, and ideally capture or kill any of the enemy who might still be in the area. The positions are thought to be somewhere in the triangle formed by the abandoned villages of Long Phuoc, Long Tan, and the hill of Nui Dat 2. They are to move fast and light, as a 'fighting patrol', meaning there is no need to carry bedding or food, as they should be back in a few hours. But load up on ammunition.

Meanwhile, Alpha Company under Captain Charles Mollison will continue its patrol in the environs of Nui Dat 2, and ideally intercept some of the enemy. As to the soldiers of 5RAR, themselves out on patrol doing a 'cordon and search' of the village of Binh Ba six kilometres to the north of Nui Dat – looking for a VC HQ – they are told to continue, for the moment.

At Task Force HQ thus, all is activity and barked orders, getting things underway.

Elsewhere though – and nowhere more than in the artillery compound – things are much more grim. For the word has spread among the Gunners about who had copped it so badly last night from the artillery battery.

Brace yourself. It's Gunner Phil Norris.

Oh no!

Not Phil . . .

A popular member of the 103rd Battery, Phil the postie from Granville was always talking about his now expecting bride, 'my Maryanne', who he had married just two weeks before leaving for Vietnam! They reckon one of the mortars hit the tree branches above his tent and exploded, sending shrapnel through the tent, and Phil got a sliver in the side of his head.

It is serious as, upon close examination, they reckon Captain Taske had seen a tiny blood-tinged stream coming from the wound which indicated Phil was leaking cerebral fluid. Christ knows how serious cerebral fluid is, but it certainly doesn't sound good, and they reckon that although he was conscious, he was talking gibberish, almost like he was heavily concussed.

That chopper taking off for Vung Tau right now has got him on board.

Poor bastard.

Poor Phil.

Poor Maryanne.

•

Even before dawn the 80 men of Bravo Company, under Major Noel Ford, are on their way – well over half of them more than a little underwhelmed as they are due to go on leave the next day to Vung Tau for precious R & R, and there is a real risk they won't be back in time.

For now all they can do is move off silently into the stillness of the pre-dawn, the enveloping undergrowth and all its dark shadows. But *careful* now! Of course there are easy paths through. But if Charlie is out there, that is precisely where he has set up his ambushes and laid his booby traps. Bravo Company will not be so foolish as to give Charlie the chance, and instead will make their way through the enveloping grass, the undergrowth, the tangled roots and the endless 'wait-a-while' vines, as they call them for good reason.

At least they can all get some rest as Major Ford regularly sends forth recce parties at all angles to carefully look for the tiniest sign that the enemy has been in the area, to check whether the actual paths they regularly cross might show broken twigs, discarded items or disturbed ground, to indicate an enemy force has been through.

But there is nothing, and they are soon back at it, pushing forward, emerging into the more open country of the elephant grass where, at certain points, they can get a clear view across the Suoi Da Bang to the Long Tan rubber plantation shimmering in the hot and humid morning.

More than a few soldiers take pause.

What's in there?

Where is Charlie?

Are we walking into an ambush?

There is nothing to be done but put one foot ahead of the other.

They walk on.

•

At first light, Brigadier Jackson, accompanied by his senior officers, sets forth around the 1ATF base to inspect the aftermath, occasionally descending from the jeep, his head bowed, his eyes roving, his Aide-de-Camp hovering. The damage is bad, but not devastating.

To the eyes of Lieutenant David Harris, Brigadier Jackson's most junior Aide-de-Camp, as he would record in notes, 'the shelling had been done clearly by a main force unit although the Task Force Commander [Brigadier Jackson] seemed reluctant to accept this, stating that it was probably D445 Bn with some heavy weapon support'.[38]

I mean, look at all the craters!

To Harris, and more particularly Artillery Intelligence Officer Captain Jim Townley, they are shells from 82 millimetre mortars – a Soviet weapon only possessed by Main Force Viet Cong or the NVA; 75 millimetre recoilless rifles; and at least one 70 millimetre Japanese field gun. But Brigadier Jackson, looking exhausted, stooped, won't hear of it. Captain Townley can only just contain himself and when they pass by a particularly large crater, he stops the jeep, jumps from the vehicle and into the hole, returning triumphantly with a large mortar fin.

'Look, Sir,' he says, settling the matter, 'it is an 82 millimetre mortar.'

'Nonsense,' Brigadier Jackson replies, over-ruling a man who is an expert in the field, 'it is a 60 millimetre.'[39]

Captain Townley is profoundly shocked. He has no doubt on the matter. *Look at it!*

Lieutenant David Harris concurs, and exchanges a careful look with the Artillery Intelligence man. That careful look, however, is clearly outranked by the warning look from the Commanding Officer of 1st Field Regiment who is with them – and obviously an artillery expert to beat them all himself – Lieutenant Colonel Richmond Cubis: 'Do *not* say anything further.'[40]

Captain Townley defers, knowing his view to be beyond dispute but equally understanding you can never win an argument with a Brigadier.

And that is the end of the conversation.

0800 hours, 17 August 1966, nearing Long Tan, search and decoy

There! Hacking their way through the elephant grass towards the spot where the mortar fire had been coming from had been hard yakka and no mistake, but now is their first reward. For before them, at this spot just on the western side of the Suoi Da Bang stream, not far from the Long Tan rubber plantation, are clearly where the enemy 82 millimetre mortars had been fired from. Instead of formal base plates they have used crudely constructed beds of river rocks placed together.

Of the VC themselves, there is no immediate sign, even after Ford breaks his men up into small patrols and they sweep the area.

What now?

Colonel Townsend has the answer over the 6RAR radio net, ordering Bravo Company to march to the south, towards the deserted Long Tan village, and try to track down where the RCLs had been fired from. A hot day ensues, as they push to the south along the banks of the Suoi Da Bang stream, through jungle, abandoned rice paddies and the odd banana plantation, finding diddly on first look and, on further investigation, squat. Finding a needle in a haystack is hard, but try finding the right river rocks in a rice paddy. Yes, the artillery was fired from somewhere around here. But with the sun beating down and the risk of the enemy being secreted nearby and ready to ambush, there can be no more certainty as to what the primary source of the sweat pouring out of you is, any more than where *exactly* Charlie had fired from. Either way, keep moving.

Carefully fanning out to explore the area, they finally find other sites. It looks like there were no fewer than five 82 millimetre mortars firing on them, and right beside them are weapons pits for approximately 35 men.

Most interestingly, there are clear tracks leading away from these sites where Charlie has made his retreat, though after a couple of hours of following them they appear to fade, or at least diffuse as they disperse.

Their findings are quickly reported back to Battalion HQ at Nui Dat, who can cross-reference all the information coming in.

For, right now, Bravo Company 6RAR are one of three units in the field seeking to track down the enemy. At dawn the men of Captain Charles Mollison's Alpha Company – who had harboured up in the area north-east of Nui Dat 2 – had been moved to a position about a mile and a half north-east of Bravo while 9 Platoon of Charlie Company, which had also been out on patrol, are about 1000 yards to the south of them.

There is no sign of the enemy anywhere, though Alpha Company has reported a lot of difficulty getting their messages through because of heavy enemy jamming. Clearly, Charlie is here somewhere. They just can't see him.

17 August 1966, north end of Nui Dat, wrongward ho

A new day dawns. At 0450 hours, Mollison is instructed to continue with the patrol as planned. Military intelligence is a scarce thing indeed in Vietnam. After all his information is passed back to 1ATF HQ, at 1145 hours Captain Mollison receives a further reply that his patrol should now anticipate moving west.

To his chagrin, he receives orders from HQ 6RAR to . . . retrace their steps and set up a 'blocking position' – ready to take down the fleeing enemy, rather than pursuing him now.

'I could not believe my ears!' Mollison will recount. 'Such a move was totally at odds with our doctrine for fighting this sort of war. We had spent two months trying to come to grips with this elusive enemy and now, just when we were hot on his trail, we were being ordered to go in the opposite direction!'

Furious, Mollison insists on speaking directly to Colonel Townsend, where he forcefully puts his views.

'Sunray, this is Callsign One . . . Colonel Townsend, I am now *certain* there is a large enemy force in the vicinity of Long Tan and I want to press along our planned route.'[41]

But Colonel Townsend, seemingly under orders from Brigadier Jackson, will not budge.

With a curious mix of extant outrage and devastating dejection, Mollison orders his company back whence they came. The sense that a large enemy force is near only grows, as every time they try to get through to 6RAR HQ this afternoon, their signals are deliberately jammed only a few sentences into the conversation.

Charlie is out there all right. Listening. Probably watching. To Mollison, it feels like the pullback before the punch.

•

Shadows are falling. It has been a long, brutal day for the men of Bravo Company – bush-bashing, recce parties, wading shoulder-deep across the Suoi Da Bang stream – still in search of the enemy force that had attacked the base in the early hours of the morning. There has been no sign of the RCL launch sites, despite their extensive searching.

Major Ford gives his orders. They will make camp right here on the west bank of the Suoi Da Bang, at the point where it runs up to the western edge of the Long Tan rubber plantation.

We will set up an ambush around this track which runs north–south and man it through the night. The rest of us can sleep in harbour formation. At first light we can push on to search for the sites the rocket launchers were fired from.

As for dinner . . . there is none. A patrol from Charlie Company was meant to bring us rations, but they have been diverted. As to the lack of sleeping gear, just do your best. One night sleeping rough won't kill you.

•

After the affair of Sergeant Buick turning the table on the card game and practically ordering Lieutenant Sharp to stop fraternising with the soldiers during the mortar attack and 'Stand to!' things between the Platoon Commander of 11 Platoon and his 2IC are . . . strained.

Yes, Sharp could go to Major Smith and seek to have Buick charged with insubordination, but would Harry the Ratcatcher back Sharp or Buick? Smith is known to admire Buick's no-nonsense approach and as one who had received his nickname while destroying a card game there is surely little doubt where the older man's sympathies will lie.

For the moment, thus, Sharp will suck it up. Just don't ask him to exchange pleasantries with Buick. He will observe the military protocol, say what needs to be said, and make sure 11 Platoon is functioning, but he is not going to pretend he likes the man. Buick feels precisely the same.

18 August 1966, west of Long Tan rubber plantation, with Bravo Company

Now, this really is a 'dingo's breakfast' – no food at all.

Given the porter's party had failed to appear the previous evening, Bravo Company is left to revive on nothing on this hot morning. The only bit of good news is an order from 1ATF HQ for the 48 soldiers who are due for R & R at Vung Tau to head back immediately. Meantime the 32 men of the depleted company who remain head to the east and are soon wading across the Suoi Da Bang stream, gratefully entering the relative cool – only about 90 degrees Fahrenheit in the shade – of the Long Tan rubber plantation. At least they have been promised that a company from Nui Dat will soon be dispatched to relieve them.

CHAPTER EIGHT

COMETH THE HOUR

. . . when the blast of war blows in our ears,
Then imitate the action of the tiger;
Stiffen the sinews, summon up the blood . . .

William Shakespeare, *Henry V*

Jingle bells, rocket shells, napalm's on the way,
Oh what fun it is to call an air strike in today.
While humping through the woods,
my point man he did spy,
A group of NVA, trying to be sly.
Ho ho.
We marked them on the map, and
then before they knew,
The air was filled with screaming jets and their little lives were through.[1]

Anonymous

0800 hours, 18 August 1966, Nui Dat, news flash, Harry

You can't knock on tent flaps. And on stuff like this, in these parts, there is no ceremony to stand on. The radio signaller from HQ simply pops his head into Major Harry Smith's tent.

Lieutenant Colonel Townsend wants to see you right away, Sir. He has orders for a company patrol.

Harry Smith is not remotely surprised. He has been following events on the battalion net radio all morning, and is quite aware of what is going on.

Before leaving, Smith tells his command post duty signaller, Lance Corporal Graham Smith, to pass the word on to Delta Company: we will very likely be heading out beyond the wire. Stand to.

Heading to HQ, Smith glances to the skies.

There are rays of light, but they are few and far between, struggling to break through the roiling black clouds. It is too early in the year for a storm like this.

You asked to see me, Colonel Townsend?

Yes, Smith.

Under normal circumstances these two are not prone to exchanging pleasantries, and on this morning there are none at all. The fact that the younger man is known as 'Harry the Rat' while the older goes by the quiet sobriquet of 'Mousey' Townsend is not a fair reflection of their capacities, but certainly speaks of their approach. They are not a natural fit together, and both recognise it.

But to the situation at hand. Colonel Townsend confirms the situation.

While half of Bravo Company are on their way back, Major Ford and 31 men are still out there. They have been out for a day and a night, they're exhausted, running out of rations – they must be relieved. You and Delta Company are to do the job. Many of the men were hoping for a small delay that might allow them to see the first Col Joye and Little Pattie concert scheduled for today. (The *what*? The mortar attack? Yes, but that was no reason to cancel a concert for goodness sake!)

Colonel Townsend pauses now. Despite his sometime antipathy to the Smith approach, he respects the Tasmanian's military nous and knows that the Major is every bit as informed as he is on the situation. And so, he asks him softly, with rare collegiality . . .

'Well, what do you reckon we've got out there?'

Harry Smith pauses in turn, before saying ruminatively.

'Well, Bravo Company found what would appear to be the heavy weapons platoon base plate of D445, who fired the mortars and rockets into the task force base and who have long since gone.'[2]

In sum, Major Smith?

'Based on the facts presented, there should be a heavy weapons platoon and ammunition carriers, probably about 30 men and they've probably long gone.'[3]

Very well then.

Colonel Townsend is clear:

'Well, go and find them.'[4]

Find where they launched from, and follow the tracks that must be there.

On my way, Sir.

After Colonel Townsend reports to 1ATF HQ the forthcoming departure of 6RAR's Delta Company to join Bravo Company – all while Alpha Company is still out on patrol – Brigadier Jackson is quick to order the immediate return of 5RAR from their ongoing search for the VC HQ near Binh Ba. We need men on the ground, manning the perimeter, now. 5RAR prepares to return to base, leaving Charlie Company at the village.

•

The three freshly scrubbed and shorn Privates, looking newer than a pressed pound note, in uniforms not yet splotched with red mud, stand uncertainly in the bog just outside 6RAR Delta HQ. It's like the first nervous day of school and being a little worried about bullies – but this is the first day in an active war zone jungle, and they have to be careful not to get themselves killed. They are waiting to be told what to do and where to go by the bark of some passing member of staff and do not have to wait long.

The fellow barking at them now, they soon find out, is Major Harry Smith, the Officer Commanding Delta, and what he wants to know now is their names.

'Private Colin Whiston, Sir!'

'Private Frank Topp, Sir!'

'Private Harley Webb, Sir!'

Well, Privates, your timing is excellent. Drop your kit and get your rations. An hour from now you'll be on the other side of the wire. Welcome to the war.

Whiston and Topp are allocated to 11 Platoon, while Webb heads off to 12 Platoon. All of the soldiers they are joining and roughly being introduced to – *Gidday . . . Gidday . . . Gidday* – are well advanced in their preparations. Given that Delta had been about to go out on a three-day patrol in any case, down to the south-east of Nui Dat, it means they already have their rations, while each section rifleman has 60 rounds in three 20-round mags with spare rounds in their packs, some men carrying spare belts holding 100 rounds per belt for the M60. Just a few soldiers are designated to carry some extra rations for Bravo Company.

The main change is that the officers and NCOs must be issued with fresh maps showing the new area they are going to, with details of the Suoi Da Bang stream they must cross, the rice paddies, the two empty villages of Long Phuoc and Long Tan, the Long Tan rubber plantation and beyond that the smaller hill of Nui Dat 2.

The mood of Delta Company at the news is broad resignation. Another bloody patrol.

Everything is happening so fast the newly arrived 'reo' Private Frank Topp can barely take it all in! Frank proves to be a softly spoken bloke from Queensland, the second oldest of 11 children, born to two World War II veterans. He'd grown up on the family dairy farm at Flagstone Creek, near Helidon, gone to Downlands College in Toowoomba and had so enjoyed cadets he had *begged* his parents to allow him to sign up for the Australian Regular Army when he was just 17, just two years ago – when Vietnam was little more than the sound of distant thunder. They had resisted, insisting he was too young, but Frank wouldn't take 'Not yet' for an answer. After all, if it was good enough for you, Mum and Dad, to serve, it should be good enough for me! Finally they had relented, and he'd signed up for six glorious years!

But . . . now that he's actually here . . . actually out on his first patrol, with a *real* chance of being fired upon? Frank is, frankly, not quite so sure as he had been that this was the right thing to do.

Breathe; focus and listen. When he does, Frank is particularly interested to hear that Bravo Company is already out there and that one of his mates from training at Kapooka, Private Dave Thomas, is with them. It'll at least be a bit of fun to clap Thommo on the back from out of the blue. No more training; this is the real deal. Day one and it's begun.

0930 hours, 18 August 1966, Nui Dat Forward Defence Line, from wire to fire

There is rising tension; there is tension so thick you can cut it with a knife; and there is the sustained agony of a thousand pinpricks of pressure that are always there, announced by the extra sweat you secrete. There is the near audible thumping of your heart. There is your heavy foot-fall as you know that every step you take is pushing you towards setting off the tripwire on your psyche, which sounds alarm bells every time you must leave the relative safety of the Nui Dat base to go out 'beyond the wire'.

For young officers that tension is exacerbated by the burden of responsibility – the knowledge it is not just themselves they must keep safe. And so on this morning, all the platoon commanders gathered around Major Harry Smith for this O Group meeting – Sabben, Kendall and Sharp, together with NZ Forward Observer Captain Morrie Stanley, whose job it will be to liaise with the 161st Field Battery, Royal New Zealand Artillery, in the unlikely event that they are lucky enough to have a bit of a scrap, and Company Sergeant Major Jack Kirby – are all ears, leaning in to get the good oil on what their assignment is to be.

As is ever his way, Harry Smith gets straight to the point.

We are going outside the wire, leaving at 1100 hours. Our job is to relieve the half of B Company that is still out there, and finish the job of locating the enemy mortar positions – or at least determining if there were more than already discovered – and then chasing down Charlie and engaging him. Yes, it's probably shoot and scoot, but we shall make sure. And yes, this does mean that we will definitely be missing out on the Col Joye and Little Pattie concert, but that is just too damn bad. Our boots are made for walking, and unfortunately that's just what they'll do . . . away from the rock and towards the enemy. Or rather where the enemy was. *What a bloody waste of time.*

Just this side of military propriety, and Harry's short fuse – which means it must be *very quiet* – there is a barely perceptible but very sincere . . . collective groan. Bloody hell! Why us?

Apart from, just maybe – and very bloody likely – Colonel Townsend picking us because he's pissed off with Harry, so Delta Company has to get the rough end of the pineapple, again! Whenever and wherever there is a dirty or a pointless job, it is always the same: helter-skelter, call Delta. Harry makes his briefing brief; departure is to be prompt, speed is to be fast, single file, rendezvous with B Company ASAP.

At 1100 hours, Operation Vendetta – so called by the Ratcatcher, as they seek revenge for the mortaring of the base – will get underway. Destination: the rubber plantation, just next to the abandoned village of Long Tan to our east to meet up with Bravo Company.

Grumbling lightly, for it wouldn't do for Major Harry to hear you, each soldier heads off for a final check of their kit, making sure they have a full complement of water, rations and ammunition together with the required weaponry. And not to forget their maps, blankets, hoochies and Claymore mines, together with a sprinkling of medical kits, batteries, spare radios, smoke grenades and the like, spread among them.

Every rifle section in the company – nine in all – does a final check on their M60 machine guns, those belt-fed beauties run by a two-man team. Individual soldiers give a once-over and check ammo for their SLR 7.62 millimetre or Colt Armalite AR-15 or any one of the 10 Owen guns they are taking with them.

•

Flight Lieutenants Frank Riley and Bob Grandin don't like to show too much excitement. They are, after all, grown men not teeny-boppers but the truth of it is this is not only something to write home about, it is something they *will* write home about.

While their usual daily routine is flying their light supply chopper, an Iroquois UH-1B, back and forth between their RAAF No. 9 Squadron base at Vung Tau and the 1ATF base at Nui Dat – ferrying everything from guns to grog, medical supplies and high-level military officers too important to travel in trucks – today their cargo is different.

Pop stars!

And here they come now, walking across the tarmac, their gear carried by some goggle-eyed Diggers who can't quite believe they are this close to such celebrities, and actually *talking* to them.

Col Joye and the Joy Boys have come to Vietnam to entertain the Australian troops with three concerts at the base, this very afternoon, and they are accompanied by no less than the rising pop sensation of the day, the 17-year-old Sydney girl, Little Pattie!

'Do you think they'll talk to us?' Leading Aircraftman 'Bluey' Collins asks.

'Here's your big chance,' Bob Grandin replies as they approach.

'G'day, guys,' Col Joye – *himself!* – greets the RAAF men. 'Thanks for giving us a ride.'

'All part of the service,' Frank Riley replies lightly, before the key question occurs to the singer.

'Much danger where we're going?'

'No worries, it's been quiet for weeks.'[5]

Now, everyone strap yourselves in and put your headphones on, and we'll be on our way in less than a minute.

(All right for some. While Riley and Grandin have the fun of transporting the pop stars, on this same morning their mate, Flight Lieutenant Max Hayes, has a different task: dropping leaflets over Long Tan village, where it is thought the VC might have been lately congregating. Written in Vietnamese, the leaflets urge Charlie to bring his weapon, his heart, mind and soul over to the South Vietnamese Government's forces, in return for which he will be given land of his own!)

As the chopper takes off, the crew in the back with the performers are full of banter and chat over their head-sets, and it helps their guests relax.

For Little Pattie herself, a girl fresh out of the Sydney suburb of Mascot, it is hard to take everything in, it is all moving so fast. The tiny teen sensation is now taking in the sensations – her whole world has turned upside down to the point that, here she is, in *Vietnam*, which is, yes, an active war zone. And yes, of course the organisers had assured Little Pattie, and more particularly her doting parents, that she would be perfectly safe, but the young blonde had not been fussed either way. Her eyes are wide with general astonishment at all the extraordinary things she is seeing, not narrowed in fear that she is in any danger. And at least the feeling of safety increases somewhat once they come to land at Nui Dat and, through the now opened door, she sees over the shoulders of the several eager Diggers coming forward to help her out, a sign saying, 'Welcome to Mt Isa North'.[6]

The whole place feels like a bit of Australia transplanted to Vietnam, and she is glad to have come on this morale-building exercise for such good boys.

For such an auspicious occasion the newsreel cameras are out and capture Col Joye, the Joy Boys and Little Pattie as they climb into various trucks and APCs, ready to whisk them away to the concert venue at the new Vietnam rock arena, or paddock, Kangaroo East. Col sits up the back of the APC, right on top and leaning back like he's riding a double decker bus and decided to get some sun. He grins behind his shades and waves at the camera as they trundle past, hatless (*Rock and Roll!*), his slicked hair is impressively unaffected by the climate and a testament all on its own to the staying power of Brylcreem. The smiling, if a little nervous, Little Pattie is wearing a fetching polka dot hat. Many more soldiers than are necessary to help them mill about, grinning just to be in their presence. These people are famous! They are civilians! One of them is a gorgeous blonde! Little Pattie takes off her hat and giggles as she salutes the camera – the most attractive Australian in a five mile radius and, probably, east of Saigon.

The visitors can hear the roar of the Diggers who await them even before they get near the 'stage' – a tarpaulin roof over the back of a truck – as hundreds of Diggers start to gather just to hear them do some rehearsals and sound-checks before they embark on the first of the three concerts of the day, scheduled to start at 1 pm.

The acoustics, frankly, aren't great, but the Diggers don't care so long as a) Col Joye makes some noise and b) Little Pattie is physically present and able to be viewed from at least a 200 metre range. It is going to be one hell of a show. And even if it isn't, at least they are not out on a wretched patrol in the jungle or rubber plantations . . .

Frank Riley and Bob Grandin, meanwhile, satisfied that their work here is done – at least until it comes time to fly the singers and musicians back to Vung Tau – drift back to the Air Operations tent, which adjoins the Task Force Headquarters. They'll be able to get a coffee, have a chin-wag, and get some clue as to what their likely next operations might be.

This time they find their RAAF mates a little on the tense side of things. That serious mortar attack the night before had seriously shaken things up and there is still the live question in the air: what the hell is Charlie up to? Unused to being under attack themselves, the RAAF blokes are still telling their own 'war stories', of just where they had been when the first mortars had dropped and just how close they had come to copping it.

Riley and Grandin hear from their RAAF mate, Jeff – better known as 'Big Black' – the situation for the soldiers.

'Delta Company has been sent out on a three-day patrol. Alpha Company is returning from their two-day patrol with no major sightings of the enemy to report. They did have a couple of contacts and brought in some local females for questioning. Charlie Company patrols to the south have nothing to report. Bravo Company found the launch sites for the mortar attack, just short of the Long Tan rubber.'

'What do you reckon is going on, Black?'

'The word is that it's just a small group causing us some flak,' the navigator replies.

'No sign of a major attack?'

'Not that anyone can determine.'

'A bit of a surprise for the Task Force?'

'Yes, no-one expected it.'[7]

A little more chat and now Riley and Grandin head back down the muddy path through the rubber trees, towards Kangaroo Pad where their chopper has been left.

As they trudge, they hear the faint sound of music in the distance.

The concert!

Col Joye and the Joy Boys are dressed in the rock and roll manner of the day, while Little Pattie has what can best be described as a mini-mini-skirt. With every bob of her blonde hair, and bouncing as she sings, she presents a fetching combination and the many wolf whistles are nothing if not sincere.

Mid-morning, 18 August 1966, Long Tan plantation, looking for Charlie

It had been a busy morning for the remainder of Bravo Company, continuing the work of the previous day, looking for where Charlie had been firing the RCL and artillery from. The search begins from the north-west fringe of the Long Tan plantation.

After consultation with Major Ford, Lieutenant O'Halloran orders two of his sections to spread out and conduct 'fan patrols', essentially marching some 200 or so metres to the 12 position on an imaginary flat clock, with due north being the 12 position, before moving to the 3 position and coming back to the point of their departure – covering the shape of a large fan.

Inside the plantation, it is a different world.

Outside, things tend to be wild, hot and on the low side – with scrub stunted by the sun. Here – as they make their way through rows of smooth-trunked rubber trees – all is cooler, more ordered and towering over them, which means they can see for hundreds of metres in two directions, down their criss-crossing avenues.

But where is Charlie? Each man of Bravo Company is searching for a sign of the enemy, any sign will do.

Sergeant Harry Keen and Private David Thomas slow . . .

Something ahead.

It proves to be a small planters' hut, a place of light repose and storage for the plantation workers in better times. Carefully, their safety catches on their Armalites off, they approach the hut and glance inside . . . nothing. But near the hut is a well and by the well . . . well, well, well . . . are empty ammunition boxes, and Ho Chi Minh sandals. Even more significantly, around the well water has been slopped on the ground. Whoever was here was in a big hurry, needed a lot of water, and left not long ago. It is at that moment that Thomas and Keen notice something remarkable – silence. There is no bird-song, no breath of breeze, no movement of any tree, it is uncanny. And menacing. This is not normal. Something is up. Without a word, both Australians do precisely the same thing as if rehearsed, they slide, ever so slowly, down the trunk of a rubber tree onto the ground.

'I call it sixth sense or whatever,' Thomas will recount, hardly able to explain it himself. 'I was born and raised in the bush. One could feel that something was around, but it was not going to declare itself.'

Something dangerous? No doubt.

'I was never a superstitious person by nature,'[8] Thomas will remark.

But this is not actually superstition. It is a little closer to . . . obvious. Something is coming.

Returning to Major Ford and Lieutenant O'Halloran, Keen rather shakenly reports to his superior officer, 'Boss, there's a lot of footprints around that bloody well. There are plenty of them out there somewhere.'[9]

And there really are – though clearly just a few less than there *had* been.

For when the second patrol, under Corporal Robin 'Spike' Jones, returns, it is with interesting news.

'We have found where the RCLs were fired from,' Jones reports excitedly. 'It looks like some of our random artillery fire has hit a nearby ox cart. There are bits of bodies everywhere.'[10]

And not just that. For all around there are not only weapons pits, but body parts and dozens of shell casings, together with the clear signs of where the 75 millimetre rocket launchers had been fired from. Some felled rubber trees indicate that the enemy had likely moved the guns forward on the day before the attack and then cut those trees down in the night, so they could fire uninhibited on the 1ATF base.

Investigating himself, O'Halloran, accompanied by a small posse of soldiers, confirms Spike's report. From the scattered bits of bodies it is obvious that some of the artillery shells fired from Nui Dat over 24 hours ago had hit their mark, and maybe even had a direct hit on an ox cart being used to transport those who had been firing on Nui Dat. The fact that there are clear ox cart tracks leading away from the shattered ones – with deep imprints to indicate they bore a heavy load – gives a good indication of which direction the rest of them have gone. And the fact that they have heavily wounded among them is evidenced by the streaks of blood on the track, and some more daubed on the lower reaches of the tree trunks they were likely leaning against.

'There was an eerie feeling about the rubber plantation that I find difficult to explain,' O'Halloran will recount. 'It was almost like you could sense something was going to happen. From the signs of activity we knew there had been high numbers of enemy in the rubber and we were plagued by the question: "Where have they gone?"'[11]

And are they indeed, *gone*?

'At this stage we all had the feeling that we were under observation from the east,' Corporal Spike Jones will recount. 'We were unable to see anything ourselves, but this gut feeling persisted in all of us.'[12]

O'Halloran radios Bravo Company HQ with the news and is ordered by Major Noel Ford to wait where they are, as he will come and look for himself.

With one look the Major himself takes pause.

Around and about they count no fewer than 22 empty tubes from 75 millimetre RCL rounds. Are they still near, perhaps? Maybe about to launch an attack? Could it be that the attack on the base was just a ploy to lure a force out here, a force just like them?

1100 hours, 18 August 1966, Nui Dat, wired for sound

Farewell, Nui Dat.

Delta Company 6RAR moves out through the stifling heat of high noon approaching.

They comprise three platoons, 10, 11 and 12, and with them are the three-man Forward (Artillery) Observation party from New Zealand's 161st Battery, meaning they are 108 soldiers and officers in all – 40 of them National Servicemen – moving slowly in the oppressive humidity and heat that goes with the belting sun in the Vietnamese jungle at this time, moving in single file, which is the fastest formation.

It is no easy thing pushing through the heavy resistance of the elephant grass, let alone the jungle where a combination of heavy roots and sucking mud conspire to slow them, trip them and exhaust them. Making things even more difficult is the crippling heat and humidity.

Christ.

Push on.

Descending down the terraced abandoned rice paddies, they cross the fast-flowing Suoi Da Bang stream holding their weapons above their heads, which sucks even more energy out of them – and they are acutely aware that they are never so vulnerable as right now. One VC with a machine gun could take out every man in the water at the time, and it is with great relief the first of them get to the other side, to set up a defensive position to allow the others to cross in safety. They are exhausted – with one soldier actually wobbly on his pins from heat exhaustion – but still only halfway there. At least, once they climb the equally terraced rice paddies on the other side and get back on level ground, they can now see the rubber plantation that is their destination in detail.

•

Relying on his skill with the compass Lieutenant Dave Sabben is to lead with speed with his 12 Platoon but that's easier said than done when the scout has to use every ounce of strength he has to cut through elephant grass higher than he is. Yes, it's just grass but the green, green grass of Vietnam ain't like that of home. The grass seems to grow even as you push through, a hydroponic Hydra, that exhausts the inexhaustible and flattens the fleetest. The beat of the concert rehearsal behind them is faster than the beat of their blades; the wind carrying the sound in snatches, the music mocking them as they sweat in the sun and use their machetes to carve out the path. The lead section will change on Sabben's orders every 15 minutes to prevent outright exhaustion, the men immediately behind with their rifles at the ready, their eyes scanning back and forth over their barrel, seeking the tiniest sign in the hot landscape ahead where an attack might come from.

Where does the threat lie?

What can I hear, smell, see?

Where would I hide if I were the enemy?

After a little while the seductive songs coming from the concert rehearsal fade and the only thing that penetrates the thick scrub they are hacking their way through is the booming chords of the bass guitar.

Fie, the drums of war.

They keep going even as the heat and humidity rise further still with the midday sun, 12 Platoon still in the lead, regularly rotating the heavy hack work.

•

Both patrols, after conferring with Major Ford over the radio, return to Bravo Company HQ, where it has remained beside the firing pits, forming a harbour just on the inside edge of the rubber plantation.

•

Just after 1300 hours, Bravo Company's sentries on the western side of their harbour position – just inside the canopy of the rubber plantation, where they can benefit from the shade – stiffen. Movement, nearby!

And now they can see them, through the rubber trees, their heads above the long grass that borders the plantation.

Fortunately, it is the blokes of Delta Company, who are arriving at last after a long and exhausting slog from Nui Dat.

'Their jungle greens,' John O'Halloran will recount, 'were black with the sweat still oozing from their bodies from the forced four-kilometre march in the tropical heat.'[13]

Among them, of course, is his old mate Sharpie, and as Delta Company gratefully make their way into the relatively cool shade of the plantation, the two are soon – *hail fellow, well met* – comparing notes, as are many of the men from the two companies, who by now know each other well – and in short order Delta Company forms its own harbour neatly around the much smaller Bravo as most of them settle down to a lunch. On the menu today: combat-ration packs of tinned meat and biscuits.

Some of the officers, however, must wait as, with a small party for their protection, Major Noel Ford takes the newly arrived Major Harry Smith to inspect up close the fire points and the tracks leading from them. Ford, like all the other company commanders bar one, carries a Browning 9-millimetre pistol, which is standard issue for Majors. Smith carries something more useful.

'I was the only company commander in 6RAR who carried a useful rifle and used it,' Smith will say, 'rather than the issue 9-mm Browning pistol which could at best be uselessly thrown at the enemy.'[14]

The Majors Smith and Ford go back a long way, having even been room-mates at the Officer Cadet School in Portsea, and neither stand on ceremony as Ford quickly gets to the nub of things, as they stare down, first, at the shattered bullock cart, beside which lie the tattered and bloody rags and abandoned Ho Chi Minh sandals.

'Here's the blood,' Ford points out. 'Our counter artillery attack obviously got a few of them.'[15]

Indeed. But the enemy has left things behind? It is so unlike them. The feeling is they must have departed at all speed.

The second patrol has an even more significant find when they come upon the site from which the RCLs were fired. Scattered around are many 'shell casings, and four points for 75 mm RCLs and a gun position'.[16]

The most pertinent thing they notice is a wide track leading away from the spot where they had set up their mortars – beyond that are discovered a number of rubber trees that have been felled to allow the mortars to be fired unimpeded.

From the looks of it, their weaponry must have been hauled back and forth in bullock carts, and in this muddy domain those tracks won't be hard to follow.

The tracks of the weapons platoon seem to be heading north, towards the looming and menacing tree-covered hill in the near distance, Nui Dat 2, which overlooks the rubber plantation.

If there is an enemy force secreted anywhere around here, that is the obvious place, and it would be a risky business to approach, for fear of an ambush. But the bullock-cart tracks just head east, deeper into the rubber plantation, Ford explains.

Fair enough.

'We will proceed to the east, following the tracks, in one-up formation when we are ready to move,' says Smith.[17]

After heading back to the main group, the officers join the men for lunch, with Gordon Sharp quick to throw O'Halloran a can of baked beans to warm up, which is then ravenously consumed.

It is while so doing that O'Halloran hears some very strange kind of twanging sounds coming from the direction of the base.

'What in the hell is that?' he asks his fellow Tamworth man.

'Oh, that's the band warming up for the Col Joye and Little Pattie show later on,' Sharp replies. 'We are stuck out here now and will miss the whole bloody thing.'[18]

Elsewhere, other members of Bravo Company and Delta Company are comparing notes.

Delta Company's Forward Observer, Captain Morrie Stanley, talks to his counterpart from Bravo Company, fellow Kiwi Captain Pat Murphy.

Consulting their maps, Murphy pinpoints precisely where they are, where the mortar plates are and where the shattered cart is, with the body parts.

'He briefed me on the situation as he understood it,' Stanley will recount. 'He explained about the track system and the understanding of the next line of movement that might be followed and then we had a very comfortable lunch.'[19]

Meanwhile Delta Company's Lance Corporal John Robbins goes a little out of his way to settle down one of this morning's new reos to his own section, Private Frank Topp, and has lunch with him, trying to give him the lie of the land, get to know him a bit better, and calm the fears he is surely having while being out on his first patrol.

Lance Corporal Robbins promises to keep an eye on him. In any case, Frank, this looks to be a classic Charlie 'shoot and scoot' operation. We likely won't see any of them for dust.

And it really does seem to lift the young bloke.

As Frank is finishing lunch he sees his old friend, Private David Thomas. Thommo is already 'blooded', he is returning from a patrol with B Company and looks every inch the vintage soldier. Amused, Frank notes his transformation from juvenile trainee to jaded veteran.

'You're a warrie bastard, Thommo.'

Thommo smiles: 'If they get a hold of you out there, you will be too.'[20]

No more training, Frank, this is fair dinkum. A cloud of reality passes over Frank's face. Yes, this is fair dinkum. And, having momentarily forgotten the tension of it all with the pleasure of finding a friend, he sets his jaw to the wind once more. Back to it. You can do this, Frank. Everybody must have a first time, and this is yours. Once you're blooded, you should be fine.

It is time for Bravo and Delta Companies to part, and the Company Commanders take their leave of each other.

'Noel didn't need to say anything,' Major Harry Smith will later note, 'but I knew he was glad to be out of there even though he had seen no enemy.'[21]

Gordon Sharp and John O'Halloran shake hands.

'You can go back and listen to the music,' Gordon Sharp says grimly. 'We will stay out here and face the music.'[22]

•

Bravo Company heads off through the long grass to Nui Dat, intent on getting back in time to have a shower and then get to the concert, making sure not to go too fast and walk into an ambush, or fall victims to booby traps. The closer they get, the more they can hear the riffs of the guitars, and occasional bursts of songs as the performers move through their sound-checks.

Some from Delta Company watch them go, until the last of the bobbing heads disappear in the long grass.

Suddenly Delta really is all alone . . . but with an important job to do. Pursue the enemy.

Smith radios to Colonel Townsend back at base. 6RAR's Commanding Officer asks Major Smith which direction he thinks the enemy's *main* force has retreated on.

'Look,' Smith replies lightly, 'I'll toss a coin. "Go west, young man," but in this case I'll go east.'[23]

1500 hours, 18 August 1966, Nui Dat, Kangaroo East, where you been?

The roar goes up from the assembled masses!

It is Col Joye and the Joy Boys, for their third concert of the day.[24] And don't they go hard!

But what we want to know is: *where is Little Pattie?* The joyous but impatient soldiers keep roaring their appreciation, even while gazing for some sign of Australia's little sweetheart. Sure, Col can sing but he's wearing long pants. She must be onstage soon! In the meantime, the sun beats down, the beat goes on, and the whole thing beats the hell out of being out on fucking patrol.

•

With a secure night base in mind, Smith's thoughts turn to the jungle, east beyond the plantation – less mosquitos for one, and more deep cover to prevent the enemy sneaking up on them – his decision is made a little easier.

His O Group orders are brief.

'We leave in 10 minutes. Arrowhead formation. 10 Platoon forward – follow the cart track, 11 Platoon right-rear, 12 Platoon left rear.'[25]

The deeper Delta Company gets into the rubber plantation the thicker the cover is and they momentarily have to adjust their eyes to follow the tracks of the two clearly heavily laden bullock carts which have cut deep into the red mud on the plantation floor and appear to have been in convoy.

The danger of following up hard on the cart tracks straight into the plantation?

Major Smith's appreciation is that there is very little: Bravo Company had been all through it that morning, found no-one. It is fairly clear to all that the enemy has executed just another 'shoot and scoot' operation. It is the nature of the beast. Charlie rarely stands and fights. He hits and moves. Though there is of course some risk of ambush, for Harry Smith it makes sense to pursue them.

(He has, after all, not the slightest idea that, according to the 547 Signal Troop, the radio of a 3000-plus-strong Vietnamese division is likely positioned not 1000 metres from where he now stands, and in the rough direction that he and his men are heading.)

Besides, even if Charlie turns and fights, more fool him. In broad brushstrokes, the ratio that had been worked out in the Malayan campaign was that when pursuing an enemy force, to do so relatively safely and counter the advantage they might have in setting up an ambush, the pursuers needed to be at least three times the number of those being pursued. Fine. From the looks of the two sets of tracks the total of enemy soldiers that had fired those shots was no more than 30 or so, and D Company currently has a strength of 108 men. So – unless those 30 were part of a much bigger unit secreted nearby, of which there is no evidence – onwards.

And yet, once they are into the plantation proper, Major Smith can't help but notice it suddenly seems 'deathly quiet'.[26]

For the soldiers themselves, after the exhausting morning they have experienced, this is like entering a new world, the loose landscape giving way to a pattern of new trees as the plantation completely envelops them in its cooler and shady bosom. Old, tapped and useless trees lie fallen all around. The new trees struggle to be above two metres but they show order, planning, a future being created. It is reassuring in some odd way; you feel protected as the jungle hides Nui Dat from you on one side, bamboo protects a stream from sight on the other. So strange how this country can change with just a few steps into a new terrain; you can step from one land into another so quickly.

Soon enough, the fronds of the trees close completely over them and they are bathed in an ethereal and almost inordinately *silent* light, holy light, *glories stream from heaven afar* . . .

Wholly absorbed in the task at hand, they quietly cover the ground in this transfixing touch of twilight.

Geoff Kendall's widely dispersed 10 Platoon is followed at a distance of some 100 metres by Major Smith with Company HQ.

There is no talking, and of course no smoking.

And, mate, if you let one rip, so help me God . . .

This is just like what they have trained for – hunting down enemy insurgents – and they are all hopeful of finding the brutes.

But now, what is this?

No more than 200 yards into the plantation, as Lieutenant Geoff Kendall is the first to discover, the cart tracks split, with one lot heading to the north-east and the other continuing due east, up a small slope. More interesting still, there are more signs here of a wounded enemy, with more bloody bandages and Ho Chi Minh sandals tossed aside. Look, given that they were probably thrown away all of 36 hours ago, there is no sense that the enemy might be just up ahead, but it is nevertheless satisfying to have further proof that Charlie had copped some back for his shelling of the base, and makes everyone even more keen to follow up hard.

Yes, there are boot tracks going off in different directions, including heavy trails heading north into strong ambush territory, but once Kendall reports in over the radio, Smith is more interested in pursuing the much slower and less manoeuvrable carts which, after all, will likely contain the heavy weaponry they are after. And if Charlie has gone into Nui Dat 2, he will have deep cover and likely be heavily protected even if they do find him.

Smith's orders are crisp and see a change to reverse arrowhead formation.

'10 Platoon, you follow the left-hand tracks to the north-east. 11 Platoon, you follow the right-hand tracks going straight east.'[27]

Smith's own Delta Company HQ will push along behind both lead platoons, their rear protected by 12 Platoon 200 yards behind, its soldiers still exhausted from all their hacking of the morning to get to the lunch spot. All platoons have signallers with radios, as does Delta Company HQ, so they will be able to keep in touch that way. As they move off from the track split, the company will cover some 800 yards front by 800 yards depth. That's the plan.

With Sharp's 11 Platoon on slightly higher ground, with still more high ground to its right, both forward platoons head off – *you take the high road and I'll take the low road, and I'll get to the far side of the plantation before ye* – fanned out, with the Forward Scout in the middle 10 metres ahead of those on the far flanks.

True, under normal circumstances, given that 11 Platoon is flanked by the higher ground to its right, a small patrol would be sent out that way to make sure the high ground is clear, but Sharp decides against it. If they are to have any chance of catching these bastards, they have to get moving.

•

Anyone here from Australia?

Cheers from the crowd. Col Joye pretends to look surprised.

Anyone here from Queensland?

A smaller cheer goes up.

Okay. Don't worry, I'll speak slower.

A ROAR! The oldies are the goldies. Col and the Joy Boys thump into 'Stagger Lee'.

Rock on! The troops clap on the off beat; a bit off the off beat to be precise, but who the hell cares? As the song ends the Diggers applaud wildly, because they already sense what is coming, even if she has been held back for maximum effect, and here it is. Say it, Col Joye!

Okay, you Diggers. We now have someone just a bit prettier than us. Put your hands together for . . .

ROOOOOOOOAAAAAARRRR!

Little Pattie!

The Sydney teenybopper steps out, waving, onto the stage and grins as the troops applaud her just for being here, just for looking like that! This is a real live pop princess in Nui Dat, an actual Australian girl, with them! Little Pattie is one of ours and she is everything we could ever imagine she'd be. *ROOOAAAARRRRRR!*

Col grins, knowing it's only going to get louder after she sings.

Turning to the Joy Boys, he mouths the words they've been waiting for. *'One, two, three, four!'*

1535 hours, 18 August 1966, Long Tan plantation, when the rubber hits the road

Careful.

Sunken road up ahead. It goes directly across our present path, south-west to north-east, with a three-strand wire fence, an earth ridge and a ditch on each side. It is a rare thing in this land, a large road, spanning about 20 metres, wide enough for carts to pass each other, and about one metre deeper than the land either side of it.

Easy to cross, easier to be ambushed in.

Likely?

No.

But potentially devastating, yes, as they would all be momentarily out from the shelter of the rubber trees.

The forward scout of 11 Platoon raises his right hand high, to signal for the rest of the platoon to stop, while he reconnoitres. Now, just as they have done in their obstacle-crossing drill, they will pass over it in three separate sections, with the first section crossing to secure the other side, ensure there are no signs of any ambush, and get ready to provide covering fire should such an ambush occur.

The first two sections cross without trouble and head deeper into the rubber plantation, leaving Lieutenant Gordon Sharp and the three soldiers of Platoon HQ together with the final section to cross. They cross in arrowhead formation – standard when there is only light foliage cover and a need to disperse could occur at any moment – idly noting how the track winding back has a gentle slope which cuts off a clear view to the south, but with the upside anyone approaching from there won't be able to see them either. And with the hand signals they are using, no-one should be able to hear them. They'll be ghosts.

When it is his turn, Sergeant Bob Buick with 11 Platoon HQ – though given the strain between them, he and Lieutenant Gordon Sharp, who has crossed the road with his radio man, Signaller Vic Grice, are walking 50 metres apart – approaches the road with a small sense of disquiet. For no reason he can put his finger on, it almost feels like a scene out of a movie where *things are quiet, maybe a little* too *quiet.*

But . . . never mind. Buick is about to give the necessary hand signals: quick obstacle crossing. Private Barry 'Custard' Meller stands two metres to his left, literally suffering in silence. Custard can talk 'til the cows come home and then have a long conversation with the cows until they pretend they are asleep. But the mute Meller nods and also climbs over the small wire fence, and the two are momentarily standing together in the ditch, which is a little overgrown.

But before crossing the road, Buick also does what they had taught him all the way back in kindergarten in his native South Africa, well before military training – look left, and right, and left again to make sure it is all clear. And it is while looking right, he sees them . . .

The enemy! And no pyjamas in sight, these men are in green combat fatigues. They're about 100 metres to the south, and they're . . . strolling? Yes, they are smoking, chatting happily, and have what look to be AK-47s, either loosely cradled or hanging over their shoulders.

Looking over the road, Buick can see Lieutenant Sharp and radio operator Private Vic Grice disappearing into the rubber plantation just behind 5 Section, all of them completely oblivious of what they have just missed. The VC, in turn, arriving in the 50 metre gap between Sharp and Buick, have missed seeing them by just a few seconds.

Buick knows this is 'a one in a thousand chance and probably could never happen again,'[28] but right now he is caught. If he and Meller go across the road they will be seen, just as if they climb back over the fence. Under the circumstances, Buick has no choice, and brings his Armalite AR-15 rifle to bear, aiming for the biggest enemy soldier on the right. It is kill or be killed, and he has little time for reflection as he takes aim at the heart of a fellow human being who has not even noticed his executioner and . . . pulls the trigger.

The crack of two shots rings through the plantation, and the enemy soldier staggers back before collapsing, even as his shocked comrades scramble for cover in the long grass, pausing only to drag their stricken brother with them, heading for the cover of the trees on the eastern side of the road. They are last seen fleeing to the south-east, past the right flank of 11 Platoon's 5 Section who are only just out of sight to their north.

A little more than 200 metres to the north, through the serried ranks of rubber trees, Lieutenant Geoff Kendall hears shots to his right. *Move away from the open space, and take cover behind the trees!*

What's going on can be sorted out in a moment, this moment must be spent changing to attack formation.

Shouts ring out from all directions. What is going *on*?

Lieutenant Gordon Sharp, turning, and quickly heading back to Buick to get a briefing, also reacts the way he has been trained. Private Vic Grice, the radio operator, is soon front and centre and is handing Sharp the handset to the radio on his back. Within a minute, Sharp is through to the Delta HQ radio operator, Graham Smith, and giving a succinct 'Contact!', followed by the briefest of Sitreps: which includes the fact they have even seen the fleeing figures.

'Four this four-two. Contact. Fetch Sunray,' Sharp says, using the code-word for the Company Commander. 'Seven enemy, green uniforms. One hundred yards to our front right. Two enemy casualties. Enemy bugged out east.'[29]

What now?

Once advised, 'Sunray', in this case Major Harry Smith, does the obvious, and gives Sharp orders over the radio.

'Chase them. Keep me advised.'[30]

Prima facie, it sounds like a stray patrol from D445 Battalion – the local battalion of VC – and is nothing to worry about particularly. There are 30 soldiers in 11 Platoon, and it makes sense to send them after half-a-dozen or so enemy with at least a couple of wounded.

Far from worrying, Sharp's fellow Lieutenants, Geoff Kendall with 10 Platoon and Dave Sabben with 12 Platoon, are nothing less than jealous, in Kendall's words: 'Oh, lucky bugger.'[31]

Sharp has had contact, *real* contact! It is what they all dream of, after all their training. Real contact with the enemy, where your platoon moves in and knocks 'em over.

Dave Sabben thinks what all the officers are thinking: 'Sharpy's got the firefight. He's won the lottery.' Life isn't fair! Sharpie has wandered into quick glory. 'Probably get a Military Cross for Christmas.'[32] Jammy bastard.

Others are a little less envious. At the first sound of firing ahead everyone goes to ground, of course, lest the enemy be about to launch on them too, and Terry Burstall finds himself right beside the new reo, Private Harley Webb.

'That's a good start on your first patrol,' Burstall says to him, cheerily.[33]

In reply Webb is able to manage a strained grin. If you say so.

Clearly, Webb is not one of those relishing the opportunity to fire upon the enemy, and be fired upon in turn. Look, at least the baptism by fire

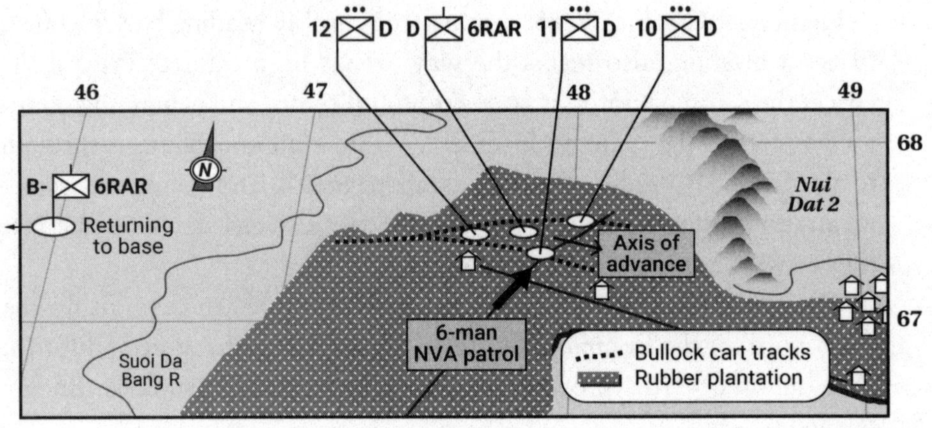

D Company formations at first contact with small NVA patrol, 1540 hrs, 18 August 1966

is out of the way, Harley. Tonight, no doubt, we'll be telling each other the story, adding details, and we'll still be telling it a decade from now!

Either way, *lucky Sharpie*. The only saving grace for those who can't wait for their own role in some story of glory starting to bloom is that they still have a chance of seeing some action themselves, as Major Smith gives orders for 10 Platoon to continue on their parallel path, while 12 Platoon and his own Company HQ will follow on behind 11 Platoon.

For 11 Platoon, there is no need to continue following the tracks in the hope of making contact. They have made *contact*, and it is time to follow up hard, to do as Harry the Ratcatcher has told them, to chase the enemy and catch them. They have been trained as Commandos, now is the time to fight like Commandos. They will follow up hard, as three sections, each capable of operating as a solo unit, or in tandem with the other units.

In a quick O Group with his Sergeant and Corporals, Sharp gives his orders.

'Battle assault formation. Extended line. 6 Section on the left, 4 Section in the centre and 5 Section on the right.'

He and Sergeant Buick place themselves centrally, for the moment ignoring the enduring bad blood from the card game. This is, after all, a different kind of poker, albeit with much higher stakes.

Once they are all in position, on Sharp's signal – with his arm swung from the rear to the front, below the waist – they now advance across a front some 300 yards wide, with 10 yards laterally between each man, and start to sweep east through the rubber plantation. As they begin, some of the men think they can see VC receding in the distance, but they can't be sure. In terms of speed, the VC have the advantage.

Each man has the butt of his rifle nestled into his shoulder, his safety catch off, his finger perched just outside the trigger guard, his antennae and pulse up, ready for anything. As they proceed, their eyes carefully scan back and forth, forward and back, looking for the smallest sign of movement – their weapons swinging back and forth in tandem – and their ears straining for the tiniest sign of danger.

But there is nothing. Well, nearly nothing, bar the bloody skid marks of someone who is badly wounded at best, and an abandoned AK-47. The latter is more than passing odd from an enemy who usually uses US origin bolt-action rifles or carbines and whose *modus operandi* is to leave behind nothing but blood. Such a sophisticated weapon suggests the North Vietnamese Army has arrived, though that would be surprising as, to this point, there have been no confirmed sightings of them this far south in South Vietnam.

The enemy's haste to leave has been extreme. And now look at the AK . . . Close examination reveals it is the Chicom type, of Chinese manufacture. It had already been odd enough that it had not been a regular carbine or old-fashioned bolt-action rifle like most of the VC have, but an AK-47 made by the Chinese? That is *serious*. And another odd thing, now that they think about it?

The enemy soldiers were not wearing the black pyjamas favoured by the irregular VC, but were dressed in khaki shirt and trousers like that of a regular *army*.

It is more than passing odd.

Still, after Sharp informs Major Smith of what they have found, the report that goes back from D Company to Task Force HQ is not unduly alarmed: 'Contact report . . . probably local – dress khaki trousers and shirts . . . Sweeping now but doubt if any casualties due to range . . . Recovered 1 AK Auto rifle 1 in 2 tracer.'[34]

Before giving chase, however, two things are done. Their Forward Observer, Captain Morrie Stanley, works out the co-ordinates of where the retreating Viet Cong were last seen heading and orders some artillery shells to come down from his battery, the New Zealand 161st Battery at Nui Dat base.

In the meantime, 10 Platoon now crosses the same road where the contact had taken place, some 200 metres north of where 11 Platoon crossed, and continues to follow the tracks – while Delta Company HQ remains some way behind the forward platoons, equidistant between the two, with 12 Platoon bringing up the rear.

There is the crack of a single shot of artillery to their west, followed by the sound of a shell going overhead, making, Dave Sabben reckons, a 'corkscrew kind of whistle',[35] noting the spinning shell had tightly packed rising and falling intonations. And finally there is the sound of the explosion of the shell landing to their south-east, in the area where Charlie was last seen heading to. It is the ranging shot, and in short order there is a series of explosions getting progressively closer as the shell-fire is 'walked in', before settling just 1000 metres or so to the east of where Buick had first seen the VC.

And now Lieutenant Gordon Sharp again gives the orders to 11 Platoon, and they move on.

The fact that a trail of blood leads away to the south-east gives a strong indication that at least one of the enemy has been badly wounded. Ideally, that might slow them down.

As the men of 11 Platoon move off, there is a real spring in their step. This is *precisely* what they have trained for: making contact with a small group of the enemy who are now fleeing. The fact that at least one of the enemy is wounded and they have dropped a weapon is a bonus. Hopefully it won't take long before they can reel them in.

CHAPTER NINE

ROCKED

The enemy is anybody who's going to get you killed, no matter which side he is on.

Joseph Heller, *Catch-22*

1542 hours, 18 August 1966, Nui Dat, what that?

Singing a torch song in steaming, streaming sunlight is as hard as Chinese calculus, but Little Pattie is giving it a red hot go, crooning her hit 'Dance Puppet Dance', backed all the way by the Joy Boys.

CRACKKK!

The New Zealand artillery are not very good at timing their timpani and Little Pattie gives a little leap and a slightly smaller yelp in surprise.

The Joy Boys jump too and the troops laugh, a reassuring sound. Nothing to worry about . . . unless you're the Viet Cong.

Besides, it is not unusual for the artillery to suddenly fire up like this: probably just a bit of HI (Harassment & Interdiction) where one of the patrols get a sniff of the enemy in a particular area and ask for a bit of curry to be sent their way. There'll be half-a-dozen shots or so to stir Charlie up, and then it will stop.

Or maybe it is a DF (Defensive Fire) task, dropping a few shells to work out the co-ordinates of a likely route of enemy attack. That way if the attack comes in the night, they can *immediately* get shells on those very co-ordinates.

For her part, Little Pattie gamely keeps singing despite the shattering noise of the firing, her brain clicking over on one track even as her voice sings her hit track.

'Gee, sounds like a bit of activity,' she thinks, while taking solace in the fact that none of the thousand soldiers in front of her dressed in green has moved.

'Well, *they* know more than me,' she reasons. 'Nobody's moving from them!'[1] So she keeps moving and bopping as the soldiers whistle even as the Kiwis *keep* firing – so it must be HI – and the men clap their encouragement. Well, when you give a concert in the theatre of war, what do you expect? Col Joye is unfamiliar with bombing, onstage or off, but he's a pro. Two shows nearly down, one more to go. Hit them with a hit, a sure-fire smash:

'Bye, Bye, Baby, Goodbye' . . . Everybody now!

CRACKKK!

Little Pattie jumps again, and they all laugh once more.

•

Out in the Long Tan plantation with Delta Company, there are one or two exceptions to the general feeling of 'Let's have at 'em!'

John Robbins has been keeping a close eye on Frank Topp.

'How you going, Frank?' he asks.

Frank grunts in reply and nods. He's fine, thanks for asking. Just trying to do his best.

Fanned out, they walk quickly, hoping to catch up with the remnants of the patrol Bob Buick fired on or perhaps the original bullock carts they had been pursuing. Such speed places them ever further ahead of 10 Platoon, who are the closest to them, with Delta HQ and 12 Platoon further to the rear again.

1559 hours, 18 August 1966, planters' hut, Charlie has left the building

Slow now.

Just up ahead of 11 Platoon's line is a small hut used by the workers in the rubber plantation. Are there voices coming from inside?

Slow!

They are almost certain of it. Is this a place where some of the enemy have taken shelter – perhaps with the casualties?

The radio report in the Commanders' Log tells the story of the 11 Platoon 'Locstat'.

'15.59 hrs – from D Coy. *Noises from a building, will clear and report in 10 minutes.*'[2]

The clearing drill for huts, houses and the like is well rehearsed and is now executed.

Weapons forward, fingers on triggers, they fan out in a semi-circle around one half of it, making sure their fields of fire don't threaten each other.

After first sneaking up to look through cracks in the wall for any sign of movement, the door is kicked in and they find . . . nobody, and not much bar some freshly strewn bloody bandages – which shows some running repairs have been done right here – and some weaponry that has been left behind.

'1602 hrs – from D Coy – Discovered 2 grenades in present loc.'[3]

Most significantly they see tracks leading from the hut, still with a heavy trail of blood. 11 Platoon's blood-lust is awoken, an ancient instinct triggered. Their enemy is in flight, likely still dragging or carrying a wounded comrade. Since the dawn of time the same dynamic applies – a strong hunter, a wounded quarry, the scent of desperate blood . . . and the pace quickens of itself.

Lieutenant Sharp again places his platoon in extended line, and they advance eastwards.

Yup. 11 Platoon, on the scent and closing fast . . .

•

Still, it's about that uniform.

No, the mind of Harry Smith is not in a whirl, for that would imply it was subject to whims and swept away in flights of fancy. Rather his thoughts are trained, shaped by years of experience, and his mind is a precise machine checking and rechecking its rolodex of manoeuvre and command as he teases another troubling thought to the surface, even as he keeps issuing orders . . . Buick had reported that the men he hit were wearing khaki uniforms, and they looked . . . fresh, and clean rather like the AK-47 that had been recovered. The thing is, that's what you might expect from Main Force soldiers; not members of the local VC . . .

Sir? Where now?

There is no time for deep reflection now. Later, much later, Harry Smith will realise that was the first harbinger. This day will be very different.

1608 hours, 18 August 1966, with 11 Platoon, pushing to the eastern edge of the plantation

Still moving confidently, eager to take over whatever straggling VC they can find, Lieutenant Gordon Sharp and 11 Platoon are placed in extended line – 6 Section on the left, 5 Section in the centre and 4 Section on the right in a line 200 metres long. By now they are nearing the eastern edge of the plantation, walking on the red earth down a very long slope in the midst of mature rubber trees six metres high with trunks as big as a strong man's thigh. Up ahead they can see the bright sunlight of a clearing, with rubber trees on the other side.

Hopes of catching up to Charlie have faded. Sergeant Buick, for one, is thinking, 'Oh well these blokes have shot through again.'

It is so disappointing.

'Where have these bastards gone? Can't we get into a decent fight?'[4]

Against that, Buick still feels that they are moving a little too fast to be safe – for one thing they have now lost all visual contact with the other platoons, who have fallen as much as 500 metres back, which is not the normal way of things. Yes, perhaps he could say so, but the atmosphere between him and Sharp has remained strained since the blow-up between them when the base was attacked, and it seems unlikely that Lieutenant Sharp would even listen to him, and there is little chance he would bow to his concerns.

Sharp pushes on, at pace. If they are ever going to catch the enemy and have a decent ding-dong they have to move faster than him. They now come to a clearing in the rubber plantation, on the other side of which is a few more young rubber trees and the creek line at the base of Nui Dat 2. The tracks they are following go straight across the clearing, but of course Sharp takes pause.

Just as with crossing the road, there is a variety of processes that can be observed when crossing open space with no cover – in this case about an acre with no rubber trees, and the gloomy light of the pre-monsoon revealing foot-high grass. One option would be to send a couple of scouts around either side of the clearing to see if the platoon will be exposed from any angle and to confirm there is no ambush set up on them anywhere. Or he could send them straight over, section by section, with the first section to secure the far side, before the others follow.

But, still eager to catch up with the enemy, Sharp quickly uses hand signals to extend their line wider still, now spread over 300 metres.

And suddenly it happens.

The bullets hit just momentarily before the sound arrives.

A machine gun is chattering!

Again and again and again, the scythe of death hacks viciously right into 11 Platoon's section on the far left.

Across the line of 11 Platoon, the training kicks in . . .

GET DOWN!

Of all the things that shock 11 Platoon, the sound is to the fore – for it is one they have never heard before.

Yes, they had been at rifle ranges and taken scattered shots.

And yes, here in Vietnam, some of them had limited contact with the VC out on patrol. But this is not scattered fire. And it is not the sounds of shots going *away* from them. It is not even distant fire coming at them where the sound of the shot rolls over you a couple of seconds after the bullet passes.

It is massed fire from up close, coming right *at them*, as men are hit, cries go up, and pieces of rubber tree start spraying down upon them.

In the wild confusion – what the FUCK is happening? – shouts abound all round.

'Where are they?'

'Over there!'

'In the trees on our left!'[5]

Christ, yes. From the base of the whole line of rubber trees on the other side of the clearing on the left, about 250 metres away, there are the weirdly attractive twinkling lights of what they *know* are muzzle flashes. And there really are *dozens* of them!

And now the first order of Lieutenant Sharp.

'Move back closer!'[6]

That's it. Regroup around Platoon HQ, the best you can. And get what shelter you can behind these rubber trees. The only small mercy is that the enemy hadn't opened up on them when they were out in the middle of the clearing.

Hearing Sharp's order, Lance Corporal John Robbins on the left-hand section of the platoon – the side that has been hardest hit – passes on the order, but even as he recognises the imperative – 'I have got to get these blokes back in, they can't be spread out like we are'[7] – he notices a couple of them are not reacting at all. Like a scalded hare, he runs over to get as close as he can . . . bullets spurting all around his ankles – when he must dive for cover behind a log.

Everything seems . . . unreal.

Like it's *happening* – but can this really be *happening?* – oh Christ, it's fucking HAPPENING!

'I didn't keep slapping my face to see if it was a bad dream,' Robbins will recall, 'but I just could not believe what was happening. We never expected anything like that, and we were the ones going to give them the touch-up, and at that stage they were giving us a mighty nice touch-up, they were in front. I couldn't believe it.'[8]

In the meantime, when the first pause in the furious fusillade comes after a couple of minutes, Sergeant Buick roars his orders, so that 4 Section on the far right will quickly reconfigure and the previous flat line of 11 Platoon becomes an 'L' shape with the far-right section as the horizontal line of the L, meaning they can fire directly in the northerly direction across the face of the badly hit 6 Section.

And yet, even as this is being put into action, withering rifle fire hits them amidships together with some rocket propelled grenade action.

That saying, that you never hear the bullet that kills you? It was surely the case with . . . Private Frank Topp. For one moment he is firing with the best of them, and the next he slumps, with a bullet through his head. The youngest soldier in 6RAR, only there by the written permission of his devoted parents, dead on his first patrol. He has been with 11 Platoon for less than 24 hours.

God help him. He was only 19.[9]

The fire upon them intensifies, as the bullets continue to throw up the mud all around them and even bring down branches of the rubber trees.

Right in the middle of Lance Corporal Robbins's section, Private Jim Richmond, a miner from Mt Isa who had thought Army work might be an easier way to make a quid and was happy to be conscripted, can barely fathom what is happening. One moment they had been pursuing a few scattered enemy – likely half-a-dozen, and surely no more than a dozen at most – and the next it feels like they are being fired on by the entire fucking Viet Cong Army!

Around and about him, blokes have sunk to the ground, several missing parts of their head, others shot through the guts. Above the endless din of the gunfire Jim can hear moans, and some screams.

Glancing around, he can see that some of his comrades are already dead.

Ideally, they could return fire straight away to give the bastards some of their own back, but any showing of your head right now and you will risk having it blown off. For the moment all they can do is keep their heads down, their bodies as close to the ground as possible, and their eyes forward looking for any sign of a rush by the enemy, something they *could* fire at – even as the bullets fly overhead. And now Jim sees something that is too good to resist. Tracer bullets coming from up in the trees over yonder!

Jim and a couple of others take careful aim and, sure enough, out of the top of the rubber trees come tumbling *three* Viet Cong. It's a start, but still the fire upon them from ground-level and tree-level is shattering, the tracers leaving their distinctive whiff of burning phosphorus as they hit.

And now here they come, the enemy soldiers themselves!

Jim Richmond can see them starting to rush towards the Australian line – jumping up, running forward, down again! Others seem to be waving their arms about and yelling for reasons unknown, though probably yelling orders, but one way or another they are – *Oh, Christ!* – getting closer.

It is those who are standing up who are of course easiest to pick off, and all of the Australians in 11 Platoon who still can take savage delight in bringing them down. But much more problematic are those of the enemy making short dashes from rubber tree to rubber tree to get close, while from another direction, others are kind of bellying their way forward like crazy snakes. Soon they'll be close enough to throw grenades!

All this, while the withering fire on the Australian soldiers forces them to keep their heads down. It is so furious that all Jim can do to protect himself is nudge his backpack forward to put in front of his noggin, in the hope that a humble can of baked beans might stop a bullet with his name on it.

And now there is shouting.

It is Shorty Thomas.

'Who is out on our left?'[10] he roars through the chatter of gunfire. Is it the enemy, or maybe our blokes coming to the rescue?

Jim roars the question further down the line, and the answer comes back: they're not ours. We can't *see* anyone, but they are firing like fuck right at us and it is getting worse!

Jim is about to pass the news on to Shorty, but before he can, Shorty calls with a strangled cry, 'I'm hit!'[11]

No matter. At least he keeps firing at the VC straight in front of them. Let the blokes on the left deal with the enemy on the left. Jim's mate Mitch crawls over to Shorty Thomas and manages to dress the wound, before crawling back. Good. Shorty is being looked after, and will pull through. Shorty's sheer *relief* is palpable. For a moment there, he thought he was a goner. But now he is going to live, he is firing back at Charlie with the best of 'em!

But Doug has gone quiet.

Jim calls out to him, for no reply, and it is Shorty who calls back with the news: 'Doug is dead.'[12]

Jim is aghast, and looks to Shorty Thomas . . . only to see Shorty himself suddenly riddled with a burst of automatic fire that near cuts him in two. At this very instant Jim sees a flicker of movement out of his left eye and turns to find a VC soldier standing over him, pointing a rifle right at his head.

If there is anything so infernally and eternally black as the black abyss of a muzzle pointed right between your eyes, Jim hasn't seen it. He accepts it in an instant. The black barrel in front of him is a promise that the end has come. He slumps, letting his head drop behind his pack – at the exact instant that the VC fires, missing Jim's head by inches.

What happened to the VC soldier is not clear but to Jim's amazement there is no second shot, and he is still alive. Likely not for long, true, but still being able to breathe is really something. But, Christ, things are grim. As one who had been haunted by a film he'd seen back at Enoggera about what the VC do to prisoners – 'torture' not quite covering it – he knows that, whatever happens, he *must* not be taken prisoner.

Not daring to stand or crawl back, or lift his head, he sneaks his hand into the pack in front and withdraws a grenade, pulling the pin, and holding the lever down. That way if the VC soldier does return to shoot him, it will relax his hold on the grenade and he can at least take the bastard with him. Throwing the grenade in the general direction of the swarming VC is out of the question as he would be just as likely to hit a rubber tree which would see the grenade bounce back. For the moment he just lies there, doggo, as the battle roars around him, and the VC surge forward. For now, the only mates at his side are dead ones.

•

What the hell is that?

The men of Bravo Company suddenly hear it from their east, from where they have just come.

Shots!

Automatic fire.

Trouble?

Quite probably.

Major Ford immediately seeks permission to turn Bravo around and go back into the Long Tan rubber plantation.

It takes some time for an answer to come back, but it is clear: permission denied.

Hold up where you are, harbour position, and await further orders.

If we can keep the artillery on the VC and get Delta more ammunition, our blokes can hopefully handle this on their own. We don't want more soldiers in the middle of it unless it should be absolutely necessary.

1610 hours, 18 August 1966, Delta Company HQ, the blink of an eye

Jesus wept.

By now it is obvious to Major Smith, who can hear the roar of fire through the trees, though he can see nothing, that 11 Platoon is under serious attack, and the most urgent thing is to get forward enough to give them covering fire to withdraw. As he, 10 Platoon and Delta Company HQ move stealthily forward, 12 Platoon under Lieutenant Dave Sabben undertakes the role of defending them all, and they move forward as one.

Not surprisingly, the radio crackles into life.

It is the strained voice of Gordon Sharp reporting in, complete with map co-ordinates of where he estimates the bulk of the enemy is situated.

'11 Platoon under heavy fire from approximately . . . 485669.'[13]

Harry Smith's finger flicks back and forth across the map, and stabs the spot.

There!

The fire is coming from the base of Nui Dat 2.

Smith is quick to give Sharp the required order to pull back, but the 21-year-old Tamworth man instantly roars back over the roar of shots that he and his men are under such heavy fire that it is impossible – for one thing, they would have to leave the wounded, and he refuses to do so.

•

And now here is Sharp again, even more strained, reporting that as well as being attacked on their left flank, from the north, there is a new attack, from right in front of them, to the east. Initially, he had thought they were being attacked by a section. But now he estimates enemy strength as at *least* platoon size, and then some.

'*Count three enemy machine guns; Enemy is my Callsign size.*'[14]

Sharp's estimation is they are facing a platoon of enemy soldiers. And yet . . . ?

Sharp and his men are taking terrible punishment. Diggers are dying. And no wonder. As one of Sharp's section heads, Private Peter Ainslie, will describe it, they are witnessing 'a million little lights', the rubber trees being shot through in front of them 'from knee height to above our heads, and a helluva noise'.[15]

Sharp's voice shrieks over the radio.

'It's bigger than I thought . . . They are attacking us!'[16]

Ahead of Sharp, the shadowy figures in the distance are now closer, and forming up into waves of soldiers firing hard as they begin to charge towards them.

The chances of stopping this many men with their own guns are . . . three-fifths of fuck-all, carry the one . . . and now, more than ever, they are going to need artillery's 'nine-mile snipers' to start dropping it right on Charlie's noggin, or they are done for.

Not just attacking, but now outflanking them to the right!

'We were,' as Sergeant Buick will recall, 'in deep shit and I'll use that in every sense.'[17]

In the absence of being able to withdraw, there is only one hope of holding Charlie off – artillery – but Sharp knows that before calling it in he needs to get his bearings, just for a bare second, or there can be no hope of deliverance. He *has* to see . . . Up! Look! *Down.*

Christ Almighty, Mother Mary, Holy Father, can this really be happening?

Not even two years ago, he'd been a happy if humble cameraman on *The Mavis Bramston Show*, safe in a studio, broadcast with a perfect signal to a laughing nation. And now? Now he is fighting for his life in Vietnam, with a couple of dozen men counting on him to lead them out of this and home to their own families. Even as bullets whistle about him, thus, Sharp barks down the line to HQ, a single broadcast.

'*Fetch Shelldrake. Target Send. Alsatian. Right two. Up three. One round.*'[18]

Translated, it means tell 'Shelldrake', NZ Forward Observer Captain Morrie Stanley, we need artillery, and here are the co-ordinates. Start with the usual ranging shot. (And then you can *pound* them, about 200 metres to the north-east of our current position, right on the southern slopes of Nui Dat 2 where most of the firing is coming from.)

Are those co-ordinates right?

It is Morrie's 161st Artillery Battery commander, Major Harry Honnor, a veteran of the Korean War, who can sense his subordinate's shock and knows that in this business you can never check co-ordinates often enough, particularly when there is stress in the air. Sharp has been directing the artillery closer ever since the first ranging shot 1000 yards out, and it is now falling on the slopes of Nui Dat 2. And yet Sharp now bursts forth with the request for a second target, the enemy *east* of him as well.

Once more, *are you sure?*

Sharp thinks so but, yes, it is worth a second look to make sure that Charlie is still where he was when the whole conflagration started. To take a second look, however, is no small thing. Up! *Look!* Down. A very slight adjustment is noted, and confirmed to his Company Commander, just before the heavens open.

As the water slams from above, latex spurts from below, the rubber trees yielding their innards with thousands of bullets streaming through. Hearing a cry to his left, Bob Buick turns to see a stunned 'Custard' Meller, looking in surprise at a patch of blood on his hand, which has come from touching his face.

'Shit! I've been shot!' Custard yells.

'Well, keep shooting!'[19] yells Buick in reply.

•

Lance Corporal Robbins, meanwhile, can't help himself.

Our Father, who art in heaven,

Hallowed be thy . . . BANG! He blasts an enemy soldier he sees coming – about 50 yards off – to hell.

Our Father who . . . JESUS! Two there!

BANG . . . BANG.

Both enemy soldiers go down.

Robbins is trying to say The Lord's Prayer while protecting what remains of 6 Section from the enemy. It is not going well, but he *is* able to keep praying, so maybe it is going well.

Deliver us from evil. Now would be good. One on the left.

BANG. Start again.

Our Father . . .

Finally, crawling along between shots, and keeping his body as close as he can to the ground, Robbins gets close enough to the left section to call out to the blokes he can see.

Which is not many.

'Where's Doug Salveron?' he yells.

The call comes back.

'Dead!'

'Where's Shorty Thomas?'

'He is killed. We saw it.'

Christ. Two best mates. Gone, just like that!

'Well . . . where's Kenny Gant?'

'Dead, too.'[20]

Jesus Christ!

Danny Boy gone, too.

Bullets are still spitting up the mud all around as Robbins crawls over to where the machine-gunner has taken a bullet through the head. He gets there at the same time as Warren Mitchell, the Nasho from Dalby in Queensland, who with great courage takes over the machine gun and brings fire to bear, while Robbins helps feed the belt through – only for brave Warren to quietly slump down beside him, dead with a shot to the head. Ever more shocked, Robbins himself now takes a bullet through the elbow and goes to ground, getting what cover he can behind a rubber tree. In the space of just 10 seconds, he has lost two dead and many more wounded.

To his right, machine-gunner Ronnie Eglinton is struggling without his No. 2, who has also been shot in the head and killed. Normally it is the No. 2 who feeds the rounds into the gun, but now the belt drags and is getting caught up in the mud, which is jamming his gun!

Without fuss Eglinton disassembles the gun, cleans it, cleans the belt the best he can, and resumes firing.

Rinse and repeat.

Along the line, the men of 11 Platoon continue to suffer withering fire, including tracer bullets, but still manage to hold the enemy off from completely storming forward and over-running them.

'That bloke's trying to kill me,' the aggrieved Allen May says at one point, most annoyed, to Bluey Moore beside him.

'Well, get the bastard first,' Bluey replies.

That makes sense. May waits his moment and as soon as Charlie pops out from behind his rubber tree May pulls the trigger of his machine gun sending tracer bullets straight at him, many of which hit.

'He stood up screaming like a banshee,' May will recount, 'and tearing at his chest and did a back flip and I reckon he died.'[21]

For his part, Lieutenant Gordon Sharp is trying to gather himself, relying on the intense training he has done.

Think, Gordon!

First the enemy had just one machine gun, then shortly after another had joined in, meaning it was likely at least 30 men. And now . . . well, now there are so many bullets flying at them that counting guns is beside the point, when the only point that counts is that the force arrayed against them is simply overwhelming.

The rain competes with the gunfire when it comes to pounding noise; the cacophonies combine as they are pelted in all directions by both.

What am I going to report? What do I know, apart from the fact that we are fucked? What the hell is out there exactly?

Sergeant Bob Buick is also working out the macabre maths; small arms obviously, machine guns, maybe with exploding rounds, because the rubber trees are being shot to pieces; the surreal sight of their white 'blood' pouring out to compete with the red mist, like a Dali nightmare come to life. And then there are the rocket propelled grenades! Some trees are just being blown apart. Think fast, act fast, or the trees won't be the only things bleeding out here.

Oh, but there is worse to come. For in short order they are not only taking heat from the left, but also from right in front, and . . . there they are! The enemy. They're not hiding either. They're simply advancing, a human tide walking through the rain. There's just so many of them, openly coming into the clearing, and moving forward in a flat line, each enemy soldier about two metres from the soldier on either side, and advancing at walking pace, firing steadily from the hip, about 100 of them in all.

Robbins looks up to see a whole *line* of VC coming their way!

'God! What's happening? This is not in the book? I haven't been told about this, there looks to be *hundreds* of them?'[22]

Whatever happened to 'shoot and scoot'? Everything they have ever bloody heard about the VC is that they are hard to find, and even harder to engage in a toe-to-toe battle. But these bastards aren't being hard to find. They have clearly found *us*, and now want to finish us off! And never, in all of their training, have they prepared for this kind of pitched battle.

Still out on the left flank, Robbins also notes a lot of the VC are getting closer, with a few of them jumping about, waving their arms and yelling out at the other soldiers – presumably to fire them up to start a wild charge straight at 11 Platoon. Still other VC are running from tree to tree and firing off shots while on the run.

Still Charlie keeps coming. And yes, the Australians are able to exact a dreadful toll on them, picking them off one by one. But so too does Charlie exact a price. Many of those who go down can still shoot, and start to snipe with deadly accuracy.

'We could not move out of this perilous situation – even leaving our dead – because the enemy small arms fire was deadly accurate,' Sergeant Buick will recount. 'Any movement drew attention to our position and drew heavy fire – it was simply asking to be killed.'[23]

•

It is a strange thing to be shot.

One second you're lining up your rifle trying to get a bead on some bastard and next . . .

Well, next thing, it's like you get this really hard punch in the guts and everything goes strange and your shirt is wet and you feel weak and . . . you sort of realise . . . you've been shot.

Still out on the left flank, in the most heavily hit section, is John Robbins with a bullet through the elbow, and the next thought is inevitable.

Am I going to die?

Maybe, but at least not just yet.

These bastards are getting ever closer, and are shooting at them from different angles. It can only be a matter of time before they are over-run, unless there is some kind of miracle.

At least the artillery continues to take a toll on the closest enemy as Sharp's strained voice keeps calling Stanley's shells ever closer: 'Drop 200 . . . drop 100 . . . drop *50* . . .'

How much closer can you cut it? It already feels close enough that the hot shrapnel risks giving them a free shave.

1615 hours, 18 August 1966, Nui Dat, trouble needs company

Down at Kangaroo Pad, Leading Aircraftman Bluey Collins and Flight Lieutenants Frank Riley and Bob Grandin have been following events closely on their radio, the atmosphere getting tense in tune with the desperation they are hearing. Finally, it is Collins who puts in to words what they are all feeling.

'They're *Australians* out there,' the crewman says, 'and they are in real trouble. Are we really going to do nothing?'[24]

Frank Riley puts the words into action.

'I am going up to the Operations Centre,' he says lightly, 'to see what's going on.'

As a crewman rather than an officer, Collins himself could have no place in such a nerve centre, and must stay behind, but Bob Grandin is also eager to find out just what is being organised, and tags along.

1616 hours, 18 August 1966, Nui Dat, New Zealand 161st Battery, sending the shells from hell

You know it makes sense. To be effective in artillery and create tightly calibrated carnage at a distance of many kilometres from you, to send hell in a shell right on the enemy and within 100 metres of your own . . . you have to be as stoic as a fence-post even when a *cyclone* of orders are constantly being yelled at you over the speaker system. Your senior officers yelling co-ordinates at you are in the thick of it. Theirs is the primary responsibility. But if you make a mistake, men die. Your own men. All of your training has concentrated on you *not* making that mistake. No matter how tired you are, how sure you are that you are on top of everything, check, check and check again. Is that exactly what he said? Does it make sense? Have you executed his instructions right down to the tiniest degree? Check again!

And now keep doing the whole thing at pace until your nose bleeds, but even when it is, check again!

The men of New Zealand 161st Battery keep firing – with every one of the seven-man crew keeping to their highly ritualised roles to send their shells five kilometres away within a margin of error of 50 metres – usually killing anyone within 30 metres of where a shell lands, and wounding anyone within 40 metres.

No. 1 is the Gun Sergeant, commander of the gun and its crew; No. 2 'lays' the gun, setting the precise direction in which it is fired by traversing the gun onto the bearing given. No. 3 is responsible for elevating or depressing the barrel to set the range, and, on order, pulling the lanyard to fire; 4, 5 and 6 don't pick up sticks, they haul the rounds from the 'ready use ammo' to the 'mating tray' – the last being where the correct number of cordite 'charge' bags are set to give it the required blast when it is fired.

And finally, No. 7 has to ensure that all is in order, all done correctly and, most particularly, that the correct number of charge bags are being used and the correct sort of shell is being fired. As a final check, the Gun Sergeant tears off the unneeded charge bags, and holds them in his hand until the round is fired. An error, of any degree, may kill a score of your own men; each double-check in place removes doubt and makes human error a phrase that remains in the manual rather than an awful reality regretted.

Once the range and direction are set, the orders from the Gun Sergeant come thick and fast.

'Load!'

'Level on ready!'

'Fire!'

Again and again and again, with some six rounds a minute roaring forth from each of the six guns in the battery when they are truly in rhythm.

No. 4 picks up the round; No. 1 sees it's the right kind of round and nods, at which point No. 4 steps forward and puts the shell into the breech before stepping back out of the line of recoil; No. 3 fires the gun and removes the shell casing; No. 5 picks up the next round and hands it to No. 4 and the whole process begins again.

1, 2, 3, 4, 5, 6, 7, blasting the enemy into heaven.

Again and again and again!

•

Still huddled as tightly to the ground as they can manage, the besieged soldiers of 11 Platoon continue to bring as much fire to bear as they can, all while the fire upon them keeps intensifying – the latter reaping a deadly harvest as Digger after Digger either yells out he's been hit or, if the bullet truly finds its mark, twitches and lies suddenly still.

Under such circumstances the sudden corkscrew whistle overhead is more than welcome. And there it is! The shell lands with a sudden flash about a quarter of the way up Nui Dat 2, hurling trees and branches in the air.

A ragged cheer goes up from the Diggers, and the fire upon them momentarily pauses.

It is the ranging shot, the single shell well beyond the Diggers themselves, which ideally will allow Lieutenant Sharp to 'walk in' the shells from there, putting them *precisely* on where most of the VC seem to be situated.

•

This is for Vietnam, for Ho Chi Minh, for our families. *The storm lets the trees show their strength*, so says Uncle Ho. The storm is here, a tempest of typhoons is here, now is the time to show your strength, men of Vietnam. We stand and we move forward, for our country.

Every few seconds another 105 millimetre shell, filled with 20 kilograms of explosive and steel lands among them, exploding into hundreds, possibly thousands of pieces of shrapnel that tear into their flesh, sever heads, arms and legs and reduce the man next to them to a bloody and screaming mass of innards that spill out over their despairing hands. And still the survivors keep coming. Not one of them turns to run away. They do their duty, do as they have been ordered, do it for Vietnam for freedom from foreigners. They keep moving forward.

•

The bullets fly, the Diggers die.

It is a fusillade of fury like they had never imagined possible, let alone experienced.

'You know what the hell is going on?' Sharp yells to his Sergeant, over the constant roar of fire.

'Shit, I don't know, mate,' Buick replies, 'the crap is coming in everywhere.'[25]

The only saving grace is that, for the moment at least, the enemy hasn't quite zoned in on them and is still firing high, most of their fusillade hitting the rubber trees two feet above their heads.

1620 hours, 18 August 1966, Nui Dat, the show must not go on

For Little Pattie, Col Joye and the Joy Boys, this is not a case of 'the show must go on'. They're happy to 'break a leg' performing here in Vietnam, they're less interested in catching a bullet.

The show must stop!

Partly because of the artillery, partly because of the rain, partly because there is some chance that the base itself will soon be under attack, it now proves impossible to continue the concert. The first Little Pattie knows about it is when she notices one of her crew just off-stage, frantically drawing his fingers across his throat – no less than an international signal for 'Cut! Call it off! Get off!'

She does exactly that. Before agreeing to her going to Vietnam, her mother had gravely assured Pattie's father that 'Pattie will be getting three square meals a day, guaranteed,' but there had been *nothing* about being in the middle of an actual battle.

Little Pattie, Col Joye and the Joy Boys are hustled away from the stage, to where – like your cleanest dirty shirt – one of the finest of the Australian Army's clapped-out Armoured Personnel Carriers awaits.

In the near distance, the great booms of big guns grow louder.

1620 hours, 18 August 1966, Nui Dat, King Cong

Second Lieutenant David Harris, Aide-de-Camp to the ATF Commander Brigadier Oliver Jackson, is listening closely on the radio in the Operations Centre, as the messages keep coming in.

Green uniforms? AK-47?

Viet Cong?

That would fit *exactly* with what Bob Keep had been telling them all through the last week before he had been sent back to Vung Tau.

If so, it means those blokes out there are likely in more trouble than they know – they might be up against as many 3000 soldiers – and Harris, despite being the second-most junior officer of 1ATF HQ, wastes no time in going to alert Brigadier Jackson, the most senior. Jackson instantly drops everything to come to the Operations Centre. If Harris is right – and increasingly alarmed messages since from Long Tan give further credence to his view – then Harry Smith and his men are going to need a lot of help.

As it happens, officially, Lieutenant Harris had finished his Tour of Duty that very morning and has no authority to do anything at all. Cognisant however of just what might be at stake here, he cannot help himself and tells Major Bob Hagerty, the Commanding Officer 1st Armoured Personnel Carrier Squadron, what he feels he needs to be told.

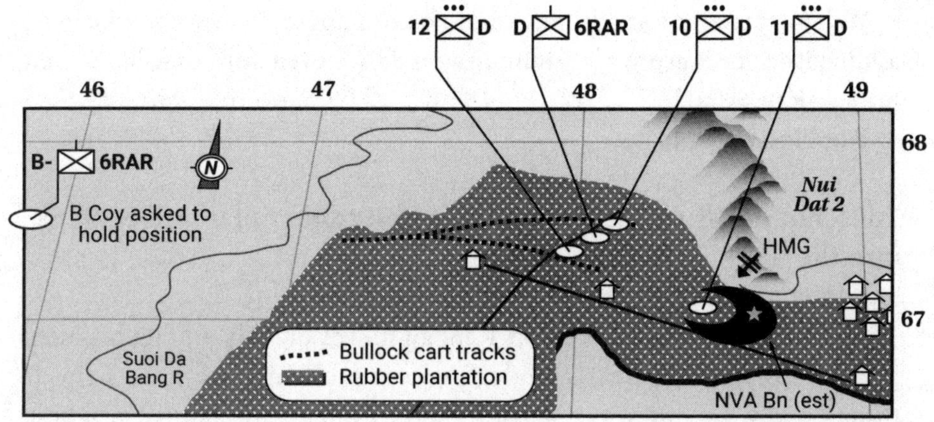

11 Platoon location and first enemy enveloping moves, 1600–1630 hrs, 18 August 1966

'Major, this is unofficial, and strictly between us . . . But I think it would be wise for you and your men to be on standby. We may need some APCs to go out to Long Tan.'[26]

•

Over on the left section of 11 Platoon, which continues to take the brunt of the fire, Lance Corporal Robbins looks out now from behind the tree at where the fire is coming from. It takes a moment to comprehend what he is seeing, but there is no doubt about it.

There are *hundreds* of enemy soldiers in the scrub yonder!

They feel like boys in short pants who have kicked an ants' nest, without any thought to how the ants might feel about it. (The short answer is, very grim.)

Robbins tries to ignore the pain in his elbow and keep firing as accurately as he can, taking precise aim with each shot and pulling the trigger, just as all the others around him are also doing – all of them acutely aware that they have limited ammunition. The way it looks, if every one of the bullets they had took out an enemy soldier there would still be hundreds of enemy left over!

Robbins keeps firing, pondering something he had never thought on before, even as the shots and cries keep going all around him.

'When you shoot at a human and he goes down, it's very unlike, say, a kangaroo, because with a human you aren't even sure that he is even hit let alone dead.'[27]

Robbins keeps firing.

1625 hours, 18 August 1966, Long Tan rubber plantation, flank into the fire

Dump your packs! Shake out! Assault formation!

10 Platoon's Lieutenant Geoff Kendall moves quickly among his men. Sharpie's platoon is clearly under major attack and will need help. If things really go our way, Sharpie might even be up against a whole platoon!

Lucky bugger, me![28] thinks Kendall.

10 Platoon will hit them from the left, Sharpie will keep up fire support and at last the one-time rugby league captain–coach will have the chance to prove himself in a *real* battle.

I'm going to lead the assault platoon! Kendall thinks. Fear is secondary to opportunity.

Yes, they could die, but as Kendall reasons, 'That's what they pay me for!'[29]

This day is going to be one to remember. Action! Actual action!

Drop your packs and move.

10 Platoon extends and bends itself towards the sound of fire. Increasing fire. And one other thing, faintly . . . the sound of bugles.

It looks like Charlie is putting the band back together.

•

Major Smith has to roar the news to Lieutenant Sharp over the sounds of guns being fired and shells landing thickly just to the front of 11 Platoon: 'We are sending help.'

Sharp roars back, his words only just making it over the sounds of the chattering machine guns, rifle fire and exploding shells: 'We are not going anywhere.'[30]

Even as 10 Platoon heads off towards the trouble, the heavens open up. They push on regardless, moving to the east, towards the foothills of Nui Dat 2, straight towards where 11 Platoon reports the fire to be coming from.

1626 hours, 18 August 1966, Delta Company HQ, mortar, mortar everywhere

What's that?

PUMPH!

PUMPH!

PUMPH!

While all are trying to close up on 11 Platoon, Harry Smith and Delta Company HQ, together with those from 10 Platoon and 12 Platoon, hear it, and turn to their east. It is the clear sound of mortars being fired. But who is the target?

They don't have to wait long to find out.

For the mortars are soon landing, just to the south of all three units. They have been spotted, and are now under attack.

Smith gives immediate orders.

Delta HQ, 10 Platoon and 12 Platoon to move 300 metres to the north, where we will hopefully be less visible to the enemy. That is the theory, anyway. Major Smith can't help noticing however that the mortars continue to land in the same place, too bloody close to them.

Smith now radios Colonel Townsend, 6RAR Commander: 'Situation report. Enemy at least my strength. My callsign is being mortared. Large force nearby. Send reinforcements.'[31]

Colonel Townsend grimaces. He can hear the strain and worry in Smith's voice, which is entirely unlike him. Things sound grim and getting grimmer. But right now he can do nothing about it and tells the Major straight: 'No-one to send. Callsign One just arriving back. Callsign Two only half strength. Callsign Three defending Forward Defence Lines.'

Translated: We are all out of reinforcements to send you. Alpha Company has just got back. Bravo Company is near you, but only half-strength, and we need Charlie Company to defend the perimeter of the base.

Smith: 'Request send Two to my location.'

Townsend: 'Wait.'[32]

And that would be a 'No', too. Brigadier Jackson wants to keep Bravo Company where they are, until it can be determined where the biggest threat lies, on Delta Company or on the 1ATF base.

For the moment, Townsend cannot send help.

Which leaves . . . Captain Morrie Stanley. After Stanley receives compass bearings from the three officers nearby, and putting it together with his own reckoning – triangulation, anyone? – Stanley is able to get an approximation for where the mortars are being fired from.

Soon thereafter, the New Zealander is able to give the Fire Support Control Centre precise co-ordinates of the enemy mortaring position, and in short order a further artillery fire mission is instigated.

Within a minute there is no more PUMPH! PUMPH! PUMPH! And yet, inevitably in this fog of war, compounded by the furious attacks, things remain confused.

Only 30 minutes ago, not only did Delta HQ know the exact position of all three of its platoons, but each platoon knew where the others were. But not now. Visual contact has been lost, even as they are changing positions. Feeling the vulnerability of this nerve centre for the whole operation, Smith gets through to Lieutenant Sabben on the radio and orders him to bring 12 Platoon forward to further the defence of the Delta Company HQ position.

•

Second Lieutenant Ian Savage has won the bet, and proudly drives Little Pattie through the throngs of his cheering mates, with the wide-eyed Sydney teenager sitting beside him on the driver's hatch. Over the cheers however, the hammering cacophony of the endless artillery blasts is a fair sign that whatever is happening out there is serious . . . and ongoing. Charlie must still be going hard if the nine-mile snipers are still shooting at him. Either way, Savage safely delivers Little Pattie and the Joy Boys to the care of the chopper crew who are ready to get them away.

Reassuringly for the young woman, most of the soldiers with the APCs are at least still relaxed enough to engage in some tomfoolery with a few even trying to 'kidnap' her, staging a bit of tug o'war, with some grabbing her legs while she squeals and the Joy Boys grab her arms from their end. It is all fun, mostly, but the Joy Boys are just a little more serious and leave no-one in any doubt – Little Pattie is coming with them.

For his part Col Joye is sitting in an APC waiting to be taken to the heliport when a Sergeant saunters over.

'Mate,' the Sarge says casually, 'will you come and talk to the people in my vehicle?'

'No, we've got to get out of here!' says Col. As in, you realise that there is actually a *war* on, yes?

The Sergeant takes his point, but he has a counter argument.

'Choppers can't take off in this rain. Just come and have a talk?'

'Oh, all right,' says Col and gets out of the APC only to find the young Sergeant is suddenly friendly frog-marching him to his covered jeep! What the *blazes* is happening?

'In here!' says Sarge, actually enacting the imperative form of address as he chucks Col in the back of the jeep, before leaping on top of him even as the jeep takes off!

The jeep has raced along a muddy field and out onto a proper road before Col is allowed to sit up and his captors introduce themselves.

'My name's Tassie Wass,' says the Sergeant. 'I'm from 5RAR. We're down the road. We didn't get to see the show. So you're *kidnapped*!'

And so he bloody is. You see, Col, fair shake of the sauce bottle. The boys need some joy. Tassie and his mates in 5RAR have only thrown their kits down from being out on patrol to find they'd missed out on seeing you and Little Pattie. And so, of course, they were hoping to rope at least you in for a private tent concert or two. Whaddya say, mate?

Yeah, it's going to be a bit of a drive so let's have a beer along the way, eh? *Here's to Col, he's true blue* . . . Col shrugs and chugs. As kidnappings go, this is a very Australian one, so it doesn't really matter. Besides, he still has his guitar with him, so what the hell? A song or two and the chopper will be there in the rain when they are back and a little merrier . . .

And sirens are now going off! And other soldiers are starting to run to various posts. Something is going on, and it doesn't look good.

Whatever it is, the pilot knows that there is no more time for fooling around and yells out, 'Hurry up! Hurry up everybody . . . !'[33]

They hurry up. Urgent hands strap belts across Little Pattie both ways into the central latch, and seemingly seconds later the chopper is hurtling skywards.

Second Lieutenant Savage, still holding his hat against the backwash from the rotors, has no sooner got back in his borrowed APC than strong orders come over the radio.

Get back here immediately. We are going out. We need you and the APC, on the double.

On the double!

•

Up, up and away.

The engines of the Iroquois chopper roar, the rotors whirl, there is a vibration, a lurch upwards and they are airborne!

Inevitably looking back to Nui Dat and the jungle beyond, Little Pattie sees a vision that will never leave her for the rest of her days. There is the dark green shroud of the jungle, and coming from it, 'thousands and thousands of orange and red lights, which was of course the rifles and machine guns . . .'[34]

Good . . . God. The horror. The absolute horror. What must the Australian boys be going through down there?

Coming here, the crew in the Huey had been laughing, there'd been lots of banter, they had joked about the show and made Pattie giggle. Now, they are silent. Pattie looks at their ashen faces, their thousand-yard stares and notices that they are not even looking at her, they're looking out to . . . the smoke. Explosions in the distance. Their machine guns are at the ready.

'I remember that instinctive . . . that feeling of – this is *very* bad; this is dangerous. This is going to be a sad night . . .'[35]

CHAPTER TEN

FIGHT AND FLIGHT

When you are flying, everything is either all right or it is not all right. If it is all right there is no need to worry. If it is not all right one of two things will happen. Either you will crash or you will not crash.

If you do not crash there is no need to worry. If you do crash one of two things is certain. Either you will be injured or you will not be injured.

If you are not injured there is no need to worry. If you are injured one of two things is certain. Either you will recover or you will not recover.

If you recover there is no need to worry. If you don't recover you can't worry.

Captain Biggleswoth, *Spitfire Parade*, by Captain W. E. Johns, 1941

1630 hours, 18 August 1966, 11 Platoon, in the moment

The fire on 11 Platoon is only intensifying, so severe it is clear there must be at least a *company* of VC shooting at them, with fire now coming at them not just from the left and front, but from the *right* as well . . .

First things first, Buick orders the right-hand section to reconfigure to deal with the threat on the right. He moves the section to a reversed 'L' position to bring fire onto the south as the enemy moved to outflank 11 Platoon from that direction.

As to the section on the left under Lance Corporal John Robbins, they must have been all but wiped out.

11 Platoon is in real strife, being attacked from three sides, with their ammo running low, and they can see the enemy less than a football field away and still moving forward.

The one hope they do have is to call in the artillery even closer, and Lieutenant Gordon Sharp momentarily lifts his head to do exactly that – wanting to be able to give HQ precise depths and directions of the enemy,

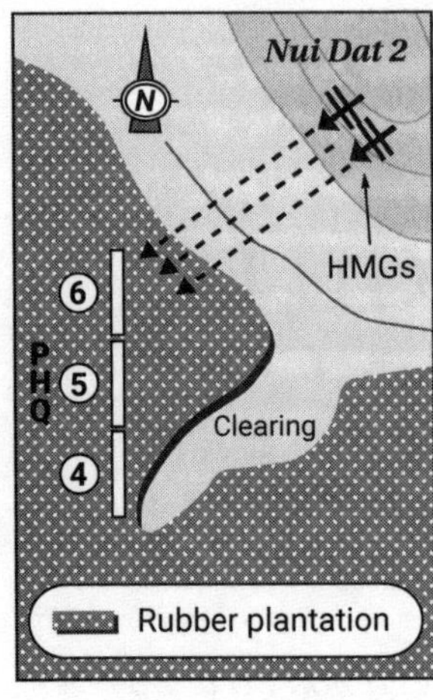

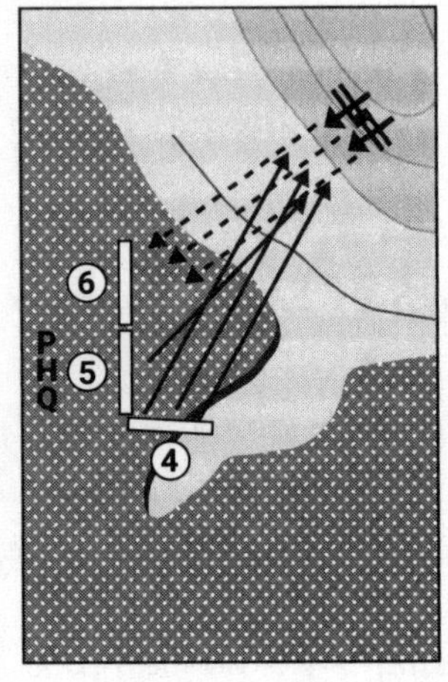

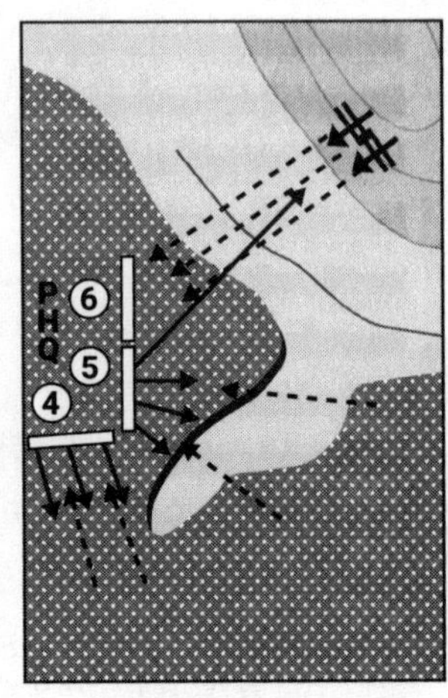

Scale: 100 yards

1608 hrs Extended line | **1612 hrs Swing 4 Sect forward** | **1630 hrs Swing 4 Sect back**

11 Platoon positioning

and advise exactly where the shells are landing – only for Sergeant Bob Buick to shout a warning, 'Keep your head down!'[1]

And maybe Sharp would do that, but this is not just his life and death, it is life and death for the whole platoon. What is clear to the Tamworth man is that they have just one chance of surviving this battle – the artillery, which must be properly directed. Right now it is landing too far away from them to be fully effective, and must be walked in based on his observations, which requires him to actually see where the shells are landing to guide them in from there.

No matter that it is a technical operation, Sharp is clearly feeling heavy emotions at the death of so many of his men as, beyond the instructions he keeps yelling down the radio – 'Left five zero . . . Drop 100' – he also utters epithets to the enemy as the shells blow them apart in flashes of fury that send geysers of mud, trees and flesh skywards.

'Mongrel bastards! Mongrel *bastards*!'[2]

The Lieutenant expresses satisfaction with his work, and ignores the danger which comes attendant with, literally, rising to the occasion, as he must keep getting up on his hands and knees to see *exactly* where the shells are landing.

Sergeant Buick is alarmed. After all, the fire is so heavy that, as he will describe it, 'If you put your hand up, you would have got three holes.'[3]

And Sharp is exposing himself to it?

It is *madness*.

'You keep on kneeling up there you're going to get bloody killed!' Buick snarls at his superior officer.

'There is not anyone up there good enough!' Sharp snaps back.

'Don't bloody give me the shits,'[4] Buick explodes.

The veneer is gone again.

Under normal circumstances an explosive argument might have broken out, but Sharp has no time. He is doing his job to save his platoon, and if that means he becomes the most obvious target there is for Charlie to take a bead on, well that's just too damn b . . .

He falls dead, with a bullet through the throat.

The bullet that kills him has removed a large chunk from his neck, while the next flurry of bullets takes out the radio antenna on the shoulders of Vic Grice.

Sergeant Bob Buick takes over. There is no time to grieve for Lieutenant Sharp, the job at hand is to make sure they don't lose any more men, and ideally can remain a fighting force capable of stopping the VC.

The shells that keep lobbing in front of them notwithstanding, 11 Platoon is now completely cut off, with only the lack of fire coming from their direct rear indicating that they are not yet completely surrounded.

Should they cut and run?

Not on your Nelly.

'The fire was so heavy that I thought if we moved, we would have no chance of getting out. Our communications were useless due to jamming by the enemy. The artillery fire missions were coming in about 50 to 75 metres to our front and were taking a lot of pressure off us, as they were landing right amongst the enemy formations. Custard [Barry] Meller and I were spotting for each other as we couldn't move at all.'[5]

For now, all they can do with their limited number – there's only a little over a dozen of them left alive, from their original contingent of 28 – is keep down and fire when you can.

Where is the rest of Delta Company?

Fuck knows.

'I kept yelling out to their soldiers all the good bullshit I could about the battalion coming and the company coming,' Buick will recall, 'but I think in my own heart I thought things were pretty useless.'[6]

And they are. Radio signaller Vic Grice is working feverishly to get the radio working again, courtesy of a spare antenna he has with him. (A good man, Vic. No fuss. Never a complaint. It wouldn't matter if the radio gets knocked out by rain, a buggered aerial or Charlie jamming the frequency with his greatest hits. Whoever or whatever is doing what, Vic can make the bloody thing work with no more than a twisted coat-hanger, a band-aid and a bit of Aussie know-how.)

•

Exhausted, starving, stinking, thirsty – all at once and twice today – the soldiers of Alpha Company could not be more pleased to at last be back in base after two days of patrolling to the north-east of Nui Dat. At least they've had a few fleeting contacts here and there, which is to say something to show for it. Right now, still in their filthy fatigues, they are readying to line up for the Choofer showers, before they intend to rip into the barbecue they have been promised.

But what now?

Alpha Company's harried-looking Officer Commanding, Captain Charles Mollison, now moves among them with new orders. Forget the showers and the barbecue. Buckle up. Get your gear together and new ammo from the Q-store.

You are on 15 minutes' notice to be ready to go out again. Delta Company is in real trouble, and the APCs are on their way. Load the extra ammo into the APCs and then get into them yourselves.

The response is a scattering of a smattering of muttered complaint, but no more than that. Delta Company is in real trouble and might need help. That is all they need to know. As to getting ready within 15 minutes though, that is a bit more problematic. Under normal circumstances it takes at least two hours to get prepared to go out on patrol with cleaned weapons, an ammo resupply and rations. Doing it in 15 minutes after they have just come in from patrol? It just can't be done.

As Alpha's Sergeant Frank Alcorta will recall, 'A beer would have been nice, but it was not to be. Many, including myself, were called to the APCs without even time to eat anything, nor did we get a briefing or explanation.'[7]

1633 hours, 18 August 1966, 10 Platoon, I see, you see, we all see VC

In the pounding rain, their safety catches off, 10 Platoon keeps moving through the strange twilight of the fading day towards where 11 Platoon is under attack, not sure of what they will find. With every step, it seems, the shocking roar of the battle they are heading to only intensifies. Clearly, 11 Platoon is in more deep shit than a Werribee duck – and the only encouraging thing is that they can't already be dead because if they were the firing would cease. We of 10 Platoon must help to get them out.

But wait!

For, after coming from a bit of a dip in the ground to a slightly higher plateau, they suddenly discern some misty figures up ahead on their right front, about 40 of them, moving forward in what looks to be assault formation.

Is this 11 Platoon?

Still not on your Nelly!

But Bob *is* your uncle.

It is bloody VC! About 40 of them!

Look at their green uniforms, the distinctive magazines of their AK-47s and their pith helmets!

Clearly, moving north to south, they must be trying to outflank 11 Platoon by first circling around them, and having just gone past the point where the 10 Platoon path would cross their own, they are not aware of the Australians' presence! Eager to maximise the damage they can do, Lieutenant Kendall gives hand signals to his men to close up on the VC as silently as possible in this teeming rain, and not to open fire until either he gives the signal, or they turn and see them. Moving stealthily but with rapidity, the men of 10 Platoon get to within just 20 yards of them, Kendall muttering to the men beside him, 'This is it. Keep going, keep going.'[8]

One of those men, Private Kev Branch, is shocked, thinking, 'Christ, he's mad! We'll be able to shake hands with 'em soon!'[9]

But now Kendall raises his right hand for the whole of 10 Platoon – stop now. And on my call . . .

'Open fire!'[10]

All the men drop to one knee, bring their rifles to their shoulders, and start firing in deafening and deadly unison. The entire right end of the Viet Cong line – those with the misfortune of being closest to the Australians – go down like wheat that has been scythed. Yes, Charlie quickly retrieves his wounded, dragging them into cover, and returns fire, but he must have lost 20 men!

Take that, you bastards!

The firefight is fast and furious.

By his own account Private Peter Doyle is trying to dig his way to China, while next to him, his mate Harry Esler is kneeling to get a better shot at the brutes and calling out in exultation: 'Fucking got one of them! Fucking got one!'

'Get down! Get down!' Doyle calls to him. 'You'll fucking get it!'

But Esler won't hear of it, and keeps firing and calling.

'Fucking got one of them!'[11]

Esler just won't be told and so Doyle does the only thing he can think of to help. Convinced that if he looks at him, it will be to see him fall into a crumpled heap of death, Doyle looks away.

And Esler keeps firing.

'Fucking got one of them!'[12]

Amazingly, Esler fucking survives!

Receiving Kendall's report over the radio, Major Smith at Delta HQ is shocked. In the space of an hour, the estimate of the enemy strength has gone from a section to a platoon to a company. But now?

Now with Kendall reporting that the enemy has a spare 40 men to send round on a flanking movement on 11 Platoon, there is no *telling* just how many they have! But, as Smith will soon report to 6RAR HQ, he has no doubt that they are at least facing a battalion.

Kendall further reports that 10 Platoon is now pinned down by withering fire, and the enemy are sounding out probing patrols on both flanks. Kendall's men are holding on but, like 11 Platoon, cannot withdraw.

•

No matter that just standing still in the jungle in Vietnam, you get a lukewarm shower at least twice a day. A hot shower is still a luxury that you must grab while you can. Lieutenant Adrian Roberts, the Commander of 3 Troop of 1 APC Squadron, has just finished having a bash with the soap and is enjoying the fleeting sensation of feeling clean and smelling sweet, as rare as that is in Nui Dat, when an out-of-breath soldier arrives in a flurry of hurry.

Major Hagerty wants to see you in his quarters, on the double, and bring your map.

The fact Roberts can now hear the roar of artillery being fired in the near distance is a fair clue that Hagerty is not seeking to discuss the weather.

Roberts, an intense and conscientious man from Western Australia, hurries. Like Hagerty himself he had known there was trouble from the moment he had first heard the artillery go off in the middle of the concert, and then noted its increasing intensity. At that rate the concert was not going to last much longer and he had given permission for his troop officer, Second Lieutenant Ian Savage, to take his own carrier to get Little Pattie and Col Joye to the chopper Landing Zone.

Rushing over to squadron headquarters, the conversation with a rather flustered Hagerty does not take long.

Major Brian Passey, the second-in-command of 6RAR, will give you any further detail you need.

Yes, Sir. Racing back to his own compound Roberts is troubled. APCs – which had been in continuous service in Vietnam since the first Australian contingent had arrived early the previous year – are far from being in good nick, and are in fact totally worn out, with dodgy engines and creaky tracks.

With a lack of supply of new parts from Australia they had been obliged to cannibalise some of their APCs to keep the others going. To make correct weight and be a complete troop of 10 APCs they will have to borrow three carriers from 2 Troop which will give him the mechanical grunt they need – even though those from 2 Troop will not have the American radios his own troop is blessed with to allow commanders to talk to the driver and them all to talk to each other. More troubling still, the borrowed APCs still lack the metal shield around their .50 calibre machine gun that Roberts had insisted be installed in his own troop.

Either way, there is no time to tarry, Harry. He needs all his blended APC Troop to gather, on the double.

•

With two platoons now in deep trouble, Delta Company needs help more than ever, starting with more manpower, and Smith is quick to again put in the request to 6RAR HQ that the Bravo Company patrol they'd had lunch with, those 32 men, be sent back to them.

While 6RAR HQ decides, Smith gets through directly to Major Noel Ford commanding the Bravo Company patrol, advising him of the request. Ford is keen to come to their aid and sends his own request to Townsend.

But once more the answer quickly comes back to both officers from Townsend.

No.

Bravo Company is to hold its position and await further orders.

Major Smith is angered.

What about, he asks Townsend, some armed Chinooks – helicopter gunships – to bring in some fresh troops, or some Phantom jets to drop napalm on Charlie? Or *both*!

The answer to the Chinooks is easy: no. Even if the RAAF's No. 9 Squadron had any Chinooks – and they don't – with no secured Landing Zone it would be entirely against regulations to risk any kind of chopper, and the men on board, by trying to land in the middle of a blazing battle. But, some canisters of napalm, delivered by a couple of Phantom jets from nearby Bien Hoa air base, to wipe out the VC with napalm across 11 Platoon's entire front, might work. Leave it with us. True, this would mean Fire Control would have to momentarily pause the artillery fire which has kept Charlie at bay so far, but it is a risk that must be taken.

In the meantime, 11 Platoon is now under attack from three points of the compass. From the north, south and east, continuous assault waves of Viet Cong are charging forth, about 50 in each line, one after the other, about two metres apart. All the Australians can do is keep firing at the first line – knocking them over like nine-pins – and hope that the Arty will continue to take out the succeeding lines.

John Heslewood is in the thick of it, advising his mate beside him.

'Mate, eight degrees down to your left, there's one in a tree.'

'Yeah, I got him.'

Once the enemy is brought down, his mate hands over the SLR.

'You have a go, it's your shot.'

'Yeah, all right.'

'You missed him.'[13]

It's always easier to be the backseat driver.

•

As the situation continues to deteriorate, Colonel Townsend's instinct is to take command of a strong relief force himself and go out to Delta Company, but he can do no such thing without the permission of 1ATF Commander Brigadier Jackson, who is responsible for the whole base.

In a quick telephone call Jackson hears the Colonel out but, at least for the moment, declines to give permission for the relief force to leave in the first place, let alone allow Townsend to accompany it.

For one thing, Jackson knows what Townsend does not.

He knows that Captain Bob Keep was right, that the signals Captain Richards had detected really were the signals of an army on the move, coming straight at them. And yet while hindsight is 20–20 vision, for the life of Brigadier Jackson he cannot see what to do right now that might display foresight. For surely the other shoe must be about to fall, and the battle at Long Tan to their east is a mere feint, drawing all of their attention and resources that way while the real attack is about to hit them from the west?

After all, it is now all but confirmed they are fighting the VC's 275th Regiment, but where exactly is the 274th Regiment?

If I send out Alpha Company to join Delta Company, and get Bravo Company to go back and join them, it means I will have the bulk of one half of my forces outside the wire, supported by *all* of my artillery. We will be defenceless ducks if a major assault really is planned.

For now, all Brigadier Jackson can do is have Townsend place his reserve forces on standby, while he monitors developments.

Townsend has no choice but to agree, although he is troubled. Something is going on, with cards being dealt from a deck that he has not even seen, but there is nothing he can do. Alpha Company can only leave when Brigadier Jackson gives his express permission, *if* he says so, and that's it.

•

The bullets are like swarms of angry bees hurtling by, with some smacking into rubber trees and drawing white blood, which trickles down the trunk.

For Geoff Kendall and his men of 10 Platoon, it is a little like the old notion of *ashes to ashes, dust to dust*, with a key difference. For starters, there ain't no dust here, just red mud. And the lower they can get into it, or move behind the trunk of a rubber tree, the less likely it is some Army chaplain will be intoning that funereal dirge over their lifeless bodies.

They're still here, still fighting, but Christ, it's going to be close.

After their successful attack on the enemy trying to outflank 11 Platoon, Kendall and his men had only been able to get another 20 yards forward before coming under heavy attack by a force to their immediate front and also to their left.

Just as is the case with 11 Platoon, there is only one hope of surviving this – artillery. With 10 Platoon signaller Private Brian Hornung right beside him, Lieutenant Kendall starts to call that artillery in, via Delta Company HQ, where Morrie Stanley is a blur of barking orders and furious note-taking as he receives urgent transmissions from Platoons 11 and 10 with precise grid references and requests for more artillery – ever more artillery – and, after processing what is possible and what is not, giving his own requests on the pattern of fire he wants from the Battery Mission.

But there will prove to be problems, none more than when Stanley is in tight conversation with Kendall, as recorded in the 6RAR Log.

Four One, Kendall: 'Drop three hundred.'

Three Four, Stanley: 'Drop three hundred. Over.'

Four One, Kendall: 'Five rounds.'

Three Four, Stanley: 'Come in. Over.'

Three Four, Stanley: 'Come in. Over.'

Three Four, Stanley: 'I do not read Four One.'

What just happened?

Lieutenant Kendall had been speaking, and he had just stopped dead.

He's not, is he?

Dead?

Come in, over.

Come in, over.

Come in, *over?*

Right beside Lieutenant Kendall, Private Hornung has suddenly slumped. A bullet has come and not only gone clean through his shoulder, but also into the radio, destroying it!

Worse still, some other men have also been hit, and they are all under such heavy fire it is impossible to evacuate them easily. Keeping his body lower than two feet – the level at which most of the bullets are coming in as the lie of the land gives them some protection – Kendall, assisted by

Sergeant Neil Rankin, manage to give Hornung and the other wounded men some first aid, and tell those who can to crawl back to Delta HQ, which should be about 300 yards to their south-west.

Oh, and one more thing . . .

'Tell the boss that the radio is gone and what does he want me to do.'[14]

They slowly head off, leaving a trail of blood in their wake.

Advancing any further under this kind of attack – and without the precise artillery support that could have been called in with a working radio – is out of the question. All Lieutenant Kendall and Sergeant Rankin can do is move their men into a defensive formation and do their best to hold on, as the furious fusillade breaks all around them and they try to press ever lower into the red mud.

'When the bullets were flying like that,' one Digger will recall, 'if I could have dug deeper with my *eyelashes* I would have. It felt like the buttons on my jacket were pushing me too high!'[15]

And yet it is not just bullets that risk killing them, as every . . .

Everyone down!

Mortars!

For the men of 10 Platoon, 100 yards to the north of the besieged men of 11 Platoon, the only warning comes with the sound of whistling, and now there are explosions all around, with shrapnel flying into mud, rubber trees and Diggers. Mercifully, the mud is able to soak up some of the mortars' rage.

But the mortars are only part of the problem, as 10 Platoon is now under even heavier attack from their front and left.

'There were guys in trees and there were guys that appeared to be quickly dug in down to our left front,' Kendall will recall, 'and there was at least one heavy machine gun firing at us from the high ground and . . .'[16]

And *still* more mortars!

As they land, Kendall looks over to Sergeant Neil Rankin who is about 20 yards away under a rubber tree, tending to one of the soldiers too gravely wounded to crawl. There is a blue flash right between Rankin's legs, and then a smouldering crater where they once were.

'There goes poor old Rankin,' Kendall thinks.

Rankin had actually been aware of the blue flash. And the next *instant* there is a kind of vortex of air above him sucking him upwards to the branches of the rubber tree – which he hits, before landing back in the blessed soft mud. He can barely believe it but, after patting himself all over to see not only that he has all his limbs, but no gaping wounds, it really seems like miracles do happen.

He is badly shaken but not physically hurt. And the badly wounded soldier?

No more wounded than before.

•

Digger coming!

The word goes out among the forward elements of Delta Company HQ. Don't shoot.

It is Private Brian Hornung, delivering the message by foot that he cannot send via radio because the radio of 10 Platoon is dead.

'It's buggered,'[17] he tells Major Smith, pale-faced through loss of blood and shock. Hornung slowed the bullet's progress as best he could, it went through his shoulder, and only then through the radio.

Even now, with blood all down the front of his shirt, Hornung unsuccessfully presses a field dressing on a shocking wound on his shoulder to try to stem the flow.

What now?

Major Smith gives his orders.

Lance Corporal Spencer, you are to take the spare radio up to 10 Platoon.

'I looked at him with horror,' Spencer will recount, 'as I didn't particularly feel like getting up and moving from where we were, as we were under fire ourselves at that time. You couldn't really get up as there was tracer coming in about two feet off the ground.'[18]

But orders are orders and he does his best.

Alas, he has gone no further than 30 yards when mortars explode all around and he is wounded. The shrapnel hits him in both his back and his legs, and he quickly loses consciousness. Other Diggers crawl out to collect him, and what is left of his shattered radio.

It is now that the reserve Delta Company HQ radio operator, Private Bill 'Yank' Akell – so-called because he was born in Boston and though he arrived in Townsville in nappies and has a broad Australian accent, once a Yank, always a Yank – speaks up.

'Sir, I have a spare radio,' he tells Delta Company Sergeant Major, Warrant Officer Jack Kirby. Kirby says just three words: 'Go, go, go!'[19]

Akell goes, pausing only to grab his trusty Owen gun and ask Kirby just where 10 Platoon is again, exactly?

And now he is gone like the wind, running through the rubber plantation, the spare radio smacking against his back, and not sure just what he will find.

When one of those things proves to be two VC soldiers who have suddenly turned at the sound of his approach, Akell is quicker than they are and brings his mighty Owen sub-machine gun to bear. True, this is not the best gun available when it comes to firing at a distance but it *is* legendary for its capacity – a little Aussie battler designed by an Aussie for the vast diversity of Australian conditions – to continue to function, no matter the mud, the dust, the rust, the rain. The mighty Owen just keeps on goin'.

The fact that the magazine is top-side means gravity is on your side and as Akell pulls the trigger of the gun, known as 'the Digger's darling', he is relieved that, once again, there is no stuff-up and the Owen gun shakes in fury as a stream of bullets burst forth and cut Charlie to ribbons.

With no time to do anything else, Akell just changes his Owen magazine and keeps running. Nothing can stop him getting this spare radio through to 10 Platoon. The lives of his mates might depend on how fast he gets there; certainly *his* life does.

•

It would not be good to look *too* stricken, but Brigadier Jackson is quietly that. Uneasy lies the head that wears the crown; and never more than when it is a crown of thorns. Delta Company are fighting for their very lives and have asked for artillery, napalm, choppers, APCs, reinforcements and relief. Getting those things to them is his responsibility and – if he fails – his fault. But it is not so simple a thing as giving the orders for those things to be sent to them.

For he has a greater responsibility too; to the nigh on 3000 Diggers at 1ATF base at Nui Dat.

What if Nui Dat is to become a Dien Bien Phu, with a VC rout *en route*? Can he really send help to Delta when they may shortly need every man, every bullet, all air support they can muster for themselves?

He keeps going over it and over it.

Is sending Delta a troop of 10 APCs filled with another company exactly what the enemy wants? Would he be putting his entire base at risk?

After all, even now, 5RAR is only just in the process of returning from its operation up Binh Ba way, and it would have to defend its part of the base's perimeter with odds and sods; while if he gives the order, 6RAR would have three of its four companies out beyond the wire, leaving just its Charlie Company to defend its own part of the perimeter. With one good attack from the NVA . . . but there's another thing . . . who is attacking Delta?

A hurried blend of VC and NVA? Are the 275th Regiment just out of sight in the jungle beyond the perimeter, waiting for the APCs to leave before attacking? Jackson has the APCs on standby, he declines to give any final authorisation until he *knows* more.

As a matter of fact, beyond contemplating things, Jackson does very little at all.

'Brigadier Jackson,' his long-time Aide-de-Camp Lieutenant David Harris will recall, 'played very little role in the actual command of the battle. The person who really controlled most of it was the Commanding Officer of 1st Field Regiment, Lieutenant Colonel Richmond Cubis. He was sitting right beside Brigadier Jackson the whole time, commanding the artillery and took most of the key decisions. He was magnificent.'[20]

•

Shouts are coming from behind, so loud they can be heard even over the roar of the battle.

'Mr Kendall! Mr Kendall!'[21]

Lieutenant Kendall turns and is stunned to see the reserve signaller from Delta HQ, 'Yank' Akell, running wildly through the rubber yelling out for him. He is holding up a radio! It is like being paged in the Plaza Hotel, except with a lot more jungle and bullets! 'Mr Kendall! Mr Kendall! Where are you?'[22] Jesus, Mary and Joseph, now it is hide and seek. Mr Kendall roars out his reply, *Yes, he is present and LYING DOWN like you should be, Yank!*

'How he got through without being hit I'll never know,' Kendall will recall, 'as anyone else that moved two feet off the ground seemed to get hit.'[23]

The mad brave bugger should get a decoration for this, thinks Kendall, but at the moment they are more concerned with not getting decorated with lead courtesy of the VC. GET DOWN!

Down Akell gets, the radio is through and the line made live.

Kendall reports back to Delta HQ, 'Pinned down on three sides and taking casualties. Cannot move forward to Callsign Four Two. Over.'

Smith reacts, 'Can you pull back to my location?'

Kendall replies smartly, 'Yes!'[24]

Get out, as quick as you can. If you can't go forward, there is no point in staying where you are. Save yourselves, get out, and come back to Delta Company HQ so we can consolidate our position here. You will have to choose your moment, when there is a lull in the fire on you, but once it comes, go hard!

1650 hours, 18 August 1966, Delta Company HQ, single spies battalion

This is not a firefight, it is an inferno. Only 30 minutes ago Major Smith had advised 6RAR HQ that Delta was under attack from, most likely, a company. But right now, it is clear that company has company, as there are so many bullets firing from so many directions that the only explanation for the furious stutter of lead that simply won't stop, chattering like a remorseless morse code with a deadly message that all can hear, is this: it's a battalion. Yes, that's right: an entire bloody battalion coming at Delta right now!

This engagement is now so big that instead of just the six guns of the 161st Royal New Zealand Battery, Smith asks for the entire 24 guns to be brought to bear. He also asks for B Company's 32 men to be sent out to them as quickly as possible. And one more thing.

Smith: 'Request urgent chopper reinforcement.'

Townsend: 'No choppers available.'[25]

Townsend will indeed consider sending B Company – it will have to be worked out – but with no secured Landing Zone it is out of the question to send them by choppers. All they can do is look at sending reinforcements out by APCs, later in the afternoon.

Smith is outraged.

'As though we were all at a ladies' tea party in downtown Toorak,' he would recount his emotions, 'Townsend instead proposed an Alpha

Company reinforcement force would come out in armoured carriers "later that afternoon"!'[26]

He puts the receiver back in its cradle, gutted.

'Until then, we were on our own,' he would recount. 'Time was against us – it would be dark in two and a half hours!'[27]

Without help it will be nearly impossible to hold on that long. The most urgent thing now is to either have 11 Platoon withdraw or, if they can't move, to get them support.

1655 hours, 18 August 1966, Nui Dat, New Zealand 161st Battery and the art of artillery

How to keep both 11 Platoon and 10 Platoon under the protection of the one artillery unit, the NZ 161st Battery, when the two platoons are 200 metres apart? There is only one way, and Major Morrie Stanley remains a blur of activity as he sends a constant stream of commands back to Fire Control, alternating its fire between the two platoons.

That this now leaves each platoon uncovered for half the time is unfortunate, but unavoidable.

Yes, 11 Platoon is continuing to fight with everything they have in them, but the truth of it – and they all recognise it – is that no matter how many of the enemy they kill through their own fire and with the artillery, the bastards just won't stop crawling out of the rubbery woodwork.

What had at first been estimated as a platoon, and then a company, is now estimated to be at *least* a battalion!

Understanding their predicament, Harry Smith is more desperate than ever to get more help to them, in the first instance with the big guns.

'I want all the guns in support – the whole regiment,' he roars down the receiver to Townsend. 'Give me all the guns they've got!'[28]

If Major Smith was a politician it would be unparliamentary language. As a military man such language is . . . not insubordination, but certainly not proper.

'Leave the guns to the gunners,' Colonel Townsend replies crisply, in a voice that reminds Smith he is talking to a superior officer. He does *not* care to converse with Smith on matters of artillery. Stanley is running that show, so keep your nose out of it.

But Smith will not be so cowed.

'I want the whole regiment *now*,' he powers back.[29]

The line goes dead, but only a short time later Captain Stanley informs Smith that they now have all four batteries, all 24 guns – including the Americans – on the job.

The American guns will not be used in close support as they are so powerful and all-encompassing, they can hardly be used as precision instruments. (That and the fact they are so novel to ANZACs that they have not yet had the time to even learn the American fire control orders.) But they will be fired in depth to harass VC formations further afield.

In short order the Australian batteries – the 103rd, 105th – and the USA Battery 2/35th with six 155 millimetre Self Propelled Guns join the furious fray, coming on incrementally, with now 12 guns, now 18 guns, and now 24 guns all unleashing hell on those trying to wipe out Delta Company. The ground shakes as never before, the sodden earth THUMPS beneath the Diggers with every shell from the US 155 millimetre guns, the air is filled with the stink of cordite, and over the sound of the explosions of the shells the Diggers can hear the screams of dying and dismembered men coming their way.

•

If the men of Australia's 103rd Field Battery are putting more vim, vigour and vengeance in to it than ever, it is because of their late mate, Gunner Phil Norris. For the word has come through.

Phil has died in the hospital in Vung Tau.

Those bastards!

Maryanne, who he was always talking about, is a widow.

So Charlie can fucking well cop this.

They rain down hell.

For Phil.

1655 hours, 18 August 1966, Long Tan plantation, Custard turns the other cheek

In the thick of the action, in the middle of the front line of 11 Platoon, Bob Buick and Private Barry 'Custard' Meller are fighting for their lives, taking turns at spotting and shooting the enemy. As the enemy is only half-a-stone's throw away – no more than 30 yards – the shooting is easy. It is to spot without being shot that is a whole lot more difficult. The fact that Lieutenant Gordon Sharp lies dead beside them is a singularly grim reminder of the dangers of having your head up for too long.

But it must be done and right now it is Meller who is popping up and down to yell targets – *Two o'clock, Charlie coming!, Twelve o'clock, three soldiers taking cover behind fallen tree!* – even as Buick, who is a strong shot, pops up himself after each tip to fire in the designated direction.

This time, however, there is a problem.

For Meller has just turned his head to the far right . . .

Three o'clock, 30 yards, one soldier is . . .

. . . a bullet hits Meller in the left cheek, and exits through his right . . .

. . . *firing from behind a tree.*

Meller *still* does not stop talking. As a matter of fact, he barely flinches.

Buick looks at him, blood is coming out of Meller's right cheek.

Does he even *know*?

On the right, group at three o'clock.

As Meller continues with the next target announced, another thought occurs to Buick. If Meller hadn't been talking, that bullet would have shot his jaw off. As it is it just passed through his cheek.

Irony? Fate? They can decide later. For now, keep going.

One o'clock! Shooter up in first branch of tree.

And now to the only bit of good news for the afternoon.

Vic Grice has got the radio working again!

Crawling to him, Buick takes the handset, and is soon reporting back to Major Smith at Delta HQ the news: 'Four Two – my Sunray killed in action.'[30]

Gordon Sharp is dead.

How strange it is to pass news of the past; a fresh death to those who hear it. Harry Smith has only a second to absorb it and to calculate how to command this new link in the chain of command. There will be time to mourn Gordon Sharp later; there will be years, decades, but for now there is no time for even cursory commiseration, just information. *Where should fire be directed to help you?* Well, as to the artillery, Sergeant Buick's primary instruction is to call for artillery to lob to their left rear, in the hope of destroying any outflanking attempt from that angle. What Buick doesn't know is that 10 Platoon is in this very position, having lost radio contact. Until contact is restored, artillery cannot rain down to a general area – a target must be precise and sighted. Delta Company HQ wait for the splutter of a live radio signal to begin death from above.

•

Major Smith hands the handset back to his signaller after talking to Buick and makes his instant assessment. Things are bad and getting worse. 11 Platoon is ever more isolated, and losing ever more men, including Lieutenant Sharp. Now, more than ever, they need help in whatever manner he can get it to them. And if they can be extricated, they will inevitably have a lot of wounded. Ammunition is to be dropped, 400 metres from Delta HQ, behind a small knoll that Major Smith has selected, thinking of making it a new defensive position. Alas, to get to such a position means moving the wounded, which is now looking nigh on impossible. Already the metrics of medicine are telling him to stay where they are.

Smith might possibly send 12 Platoon forward shortly, but for now the most important thing is for Delta Company HQ to provide a secure base for 11 Platoon to get back to. Smith has already stopped the Company HQ on a strategically advantageous bit of ground, based on years of experience and deep training in the field – *on* the field.

While still thickly within the rubber plantation, with the thick canopy overhead, this spot is on the western side of a slight slope, with most of the enemy's firepower coming from the east, giving Smith and his men a natural protection. By putting his strongest forces on the lip of the hill, with just the top part of their heads and their rifles and machine guns poking over when they want to take a shot, they would present only a very small target, while all those behind them would see most of the enemy bullets flying overhead.

Further helping them is an all but impenetrable wall of bamboo and scrub in the creek line on their left flank.

Very well then.

This is where we will make our stand.

Delta Company medic, Corporal Phil Dobson, decides to make his own stand in a small ditch some 50 yards back from the lip of the slope, and prepares for incoming wounded. A Regular Army soldier, in peacetime he is part of the Army band and has no experience in plying his trade as a medic in the middle of a battle with mass casualties, but has gritted his teeth and is determined to do his best.

True, there is something of a problem setting up in a ditch when suddenly the monsoonal rain hits heavier than ever – for it is nothing if not very wet at the bottom of the ditch – but for most of the wounded, who are already drenched, being wetter still is likely to be the least of their worries. As busy and overwhelmed as Dobson is, given that no soldiers can be spared, he personally goes to get some of the wounded – even when they are still under fire – and carries or drags them back to the ditch. He soon has so many in the ditch that moving them in the short term becomes out of the question. If Delta Company is going to make a last stand, then this looks like the spot it will take place.

1655 hours, 18 August 1966, Long Tan plantation, 11 Platoon, radio daze

It is one thing for 11 Platoon to be up Shit Creek without a paddle.

It is another to be under Shit Waterfall without an umbrella.

For that is what it feels like right now to be right in the midst of a murderous maelstrom of fire, outnumbered ten to one by Charlie, and be out of ammunition. That is not the case for all of them, true, but it certainly applies to many of those in the hottest spots who have not only fired every shot they have in the locker, but also whatever ammo they have been able to retrieve from their dead mates beside them.

For them, the only thing they can do for the war effort right now is cheer when – newly directed by Sergeant Buick, now that they have a working radio again – shells come down right among Charlie, sending him – and bits of him – sky-high in billowing bursts of flame.

True, those cheers do nothing to hurt the surviving enemy, but it makes the surviving Diggers of 11 Platoon feel better for it, and so they cheer themselves hoarse.

•

There he is!

The moment that Second Lieutenant Ian Savage returns with Lieutenant Roberts' APC after dropping the singing troupe, the Commanding Officer of 3 Troop reclaims his APC, and the whole Troop is on its way.

Roaring and clanking, the 10 APCs of 2 Troop and 3 Troop arrive in 6RAR, just before 1700 hours, whereupon Lieutenant Roberts immediately goes to 6RAR Headquarters where the officer he must see, the Operations Officer Major Brian Passey, is huddled over a map with Colonel Townsend and the New Zealand artillery commander, Major Harry Honnor. Major Passey looks up as Roberts arrives and barks his orders.

With other assignments beyond the wire, it had not been unusual to have as many as 50 pages of instructions. But not on this one. There is no time for anything other than this:

'Pick up Alpha Company, get out to Delta Company and break up the attack.'[31]

Passey's sole concession to further instruction is to put his finger down on a large circle on the map where it is thought the besieged Delta Company is to be found – right there on the eastern edge of Long Tan rubber plantation.

There is no precise grid reference.

Roberts pauses momentarily, thinking there *must* be further orders for a military operation of this nature but . . . that's it.

Get Alpha, help Delta, smash Charlie.

And that's it.

Roberts does not have to be told twice and is soon with his combined troop, clanking to a halt in the 6RAR Alpha Company lines.

Yes. But while it is one thing to have all 100 men of Alpha Company on board and ready to go, it is quite another to have the green light from Brigadier Jackson to actually *go*, and for the moment that is not forthcoming.

As a frustrated Colonel Townsend will later note, 'I obviously couldn't send A Company off until I had first cleared with the task force commander, and until that clearance was obtained . . . and the necessary arrangements had been made for the armoured personnel carriers, I couldn't really do anything.'[32]

All they can do is wait, sweating profusely in these humid hot-boxes.

1700 hours, 18 August 1966, Nui Dat, Task Force Operations Centre, living the life of Riley

Though Roberts has been satisfactorily dispatched to pick up Alpha, the scene in the Operations Centre remains tense as the radio continues to bring to them just what terrible trouble Delta Company is in, with more men being wounded and killed and now ammunition starting to run low.

Standing on the edge of proceedings with Frank Riley, Flight Lieutenant Bob Grandin will recall it as 'a lot of yelling and countermanding each other'.[33]

This is a battle being presided over by high-ranking officers with low-ranking experience. They don't know what it's like on the ground. Yes, some of them had been in the Korean War, but back then they had been the ones following the orders of the Colonels and Generals, not giving them, not taking on the colossal responsibility of command.

And even then it was unlikely the Generals back then were obliged to listen to the agony of their men right from the front lines while under attack, as is happening now, with Major Harry Smith bawling again down the line, 'I want every gun you've got!'

At one point, things become so overwhelming that the ashen-faced Brigadier Jackson removes himself from the tent with his Aide-de-Camp Lieutenant David Harris, perhaps to compose himself, before returning.

He is just in time to hear the latest from the Delta Company commander.

For Smith is now wondering where the promised Phantom jets are to drop some napalm on the enemy, and to advise the most key factor of all: *'Running short of ammo. Require drop through trees 475674.'*[34]

Which again brings up the need for choppers.

Not for reinforcements, but for ammo. After all, each rifleman had only carried three magazines from the beginning, no more than 60 bullets, and another 60 loose in, by now, small soggy cardboard boxes. And each machine gun only had 500 rounds. At the rate they have been firing, they can already see that they will soon be needing more of both with a great deal of urgency!

Brigadier Jackson looks to No. 9 RAAF Squadron's Group Captain Peter Raw.

Can we send out a couple of Iroquois?

Captain Raw blanches.

Absolutely under no circumstances!

Their Iroquois choppers are made of thin metal, with no capacity to stop a bullet, let alone a high-explosive ordnance. To send them heavily laden with ammunition out in this weather, into that maelstrom, and expect them to first find Delta Company, and second, not be blown out of the skies while hovering at treetop height, would put all on board at enormous risk of being killed.

'We cannot go into a hostile area at this stage of operation,' Group Captain Raw says in a tone that is somewhere between firm and prim. 'Such a mission would contravene Air Staff directives.'[35]

Those directives come from Canberra. There will be no Ap Bac disaster with unprotected choppers shot from the skies on their watch, and Australian choppers can only be used in battle when the forward Landing Zones are 'relatively secure'.

And that is not the case here! There is no Landing Zone at all. They are in the middle of a monsoon, and must hover at treetop level – well within rifle range of the enemy – to drop ammo onto a besieged company surrounded by the enemy at close quarters. It is nothing less than *madness*.

And even if Group Captain Raw wanted to, he would have to cable the RAAF Commander in Vietnam, Air Commodore John Dowling, who would in turn have to contact Canberra.

The mood in the room darkens. Once again – *again!* – the Australian Army and the RAAF are at loggerheads on an operational issue, with the Army taking the view that too often the RAAF goes Missing In Action, through an excess of timidity.

Canberra?

Canberra?

You think we can win a fucking war, moving swiftly, when your every move has to be first approved by *Canberra*?

'Well, I'm about to lose a company!' Jackson explodes. 'What the hell's a few more choppers and a few more pilots!'[36]

Well, Raw does not care to risk his machines or his men on such an insane venture, which would only make things worse, and will not budge. Besides everything else, Canberra has issued clear protocols from the start. RAAF choppers are to offer general support only.

Their role is *not* to be offensive, which is why right now the Brigadier's rage is precisely that.

And the Brigadier, feeling the pressure, will not change his own view: *fuck* not being offensive, this is ridiculous!

The Brigadier is ropable and upon briefly returning to the Operations Centre to gather himself – just next flap along – lets some of it out, within earshot of Sergeant Norm Austin who will long recall the explosion.

'I can't get the fucking air force to do any fucking thing!'[37]

It really is outrageous.

So, who else can get a chopper there?

There is just one possibility, and now turning to the American Air Force Air Liaison Officer, Major Dick Gerron, Jackson explores it. Only a day earlier the base had been visited by the US Chief of Air Staff and relations with the Americans are stronger than ever. Jackson now calls Gerron, to ask if the Americans could use a couple of their Hueys to drop the required ammunition.

'Dick?'

This man, an officer and a gentleman, has no hesitation.

'Well, Brigadier,' he says, 'I dare say my guys can help out.'[38]

Really?

Really. We should be able to get a couple of Hueys here in no more than 30 minutes.

All eyes turn to Group Captain Raw.

Can this Australian RAAF Captain really let the Yanks go to the aid of Australians, while they will not?

Just maybe, but Flight Lieutenant Frank Riley will be buggered if he is going to let that happen on *his* watch – for one thing 30 minutes will be far too late – and speaks up for the first time.

'Well, I'll go out there,' he says. 'I don't care if we're allowed to go or not, I'll go.'[39]

Who is this now?

The room turns to look at the Iroquois helicopter pilot, with the now goggle-eyed Bob Grandin standing beside him. (*Did Frank really just say 'I'll go out there' – by which he clearly meant 'WE will go out there' – meaning Frank is offering his and his crew's services to go and drop the ammo on Delta Company in the middle of a vicious firefight? He bloody well did!*)

Oh. It is Riley.

Can he be serious?

Yes.

When Group Captain Raw intervenes, pointing out again that Riley going would breach the protocols for sending helicopters, and in any case he was not remotely equipped for it, Riley riles up, just this side of insubordination to a superior officer.

'I don't give a damn, I'm in charge of these aeroplanes, I'm the contingent commander, I say we will go.'[40]

(Grandin blanches. He just said it! '*We* will go'!)

In the vacuum created by his words, Riley repeats his point.

'I am tactical commander of the helicopter,' he says. '*I* decide what it can and cannot do. I say we go.'[41]

(Bob Grandin winces this time: Frank's done it *again*!)

It is a delicate point.

The military protocol indeed dictates that the captain of each aircraft is the sole commander of it while it is on detachment from its base and operational – just like the captain of a ship is the sole arbiter of what is and isn't safe for his crew. And even though his chopper is on the ground right now, and he is well down the chain of command, Riley is asserting his right to do as he sees fit. Yes, he might indeed be disciplined for it afterwards, but right now if he says he is going without seeking permission, then he can indeed do exactly that.

And this gung-ho pilot – ever and always frustrated by red tape – *means* it, making the salient point for the third time.

'I am the commander of my aircraft in the field, and have the right to make tactical decisions about what I can and can't do. If I wasn't in this tent I wouldn't be asking anyone for permission.'[42]

And he is *not* asking permission now.

'I will go.'[43]

It is a neat solution.

For the likelihood, of course, is that he and his helicopter – and Flight Lieutenants Cliff Dohle and Bruce Lane, if they decide to accompany them in the other chopper – will be shot from the skies, in which case any act of discipline will be entirely beside the point. And if they are not and succeed in dropping the ammunition onto Delta Company, well, they will be bloody heroes and there will be no need to discipline them.

Brigadier Jackson looks to Riley.

'Will you really go?'[44]

'Yes.'

'*Can* he really do that?' Brigadier Jackson asks, looking at Group Captain Raw, referring to all the protocols.

Group Captain Raw recognises the truth of the situation, and also the enormous courage being displayed, the way out of the morass for all of them, while also possibly helping Delta Company.

'Are you sure, Frank?' Raw asks softly. 'This is flying into an unsafe area.'

'I would prefer to try than do nothing,' Riley responds.

'Maybe we should check with higher authority,' Raw offers uncertainly, thinking of at least consulting Wing Commander Ray Scott, the Commanding Officer of No. 9 Squadron, who is at Vung Tau.

'He will only fuck around and waste time,' Riley says firmly. 'It's *my* helicopter in this situation and *I* say we go.'

Raw falls silent. He looks up, lost in thought.

He considers all the angles, the implications, the responsibilities, the fallout if it goes wrong, which it surely will, but the obligation they all have to help Delta Company right now.

'I guess you're right,' Raw finally concedes.

'About time someone in the RAAF showed some *guts*,' Brigadier Jackson expostulates in a moment of rare public emotion, looking warmly at Riley, and not even noticing the flabbergasted Bob Grandin over the pilot's shoulder. 'Get over to Eagle Farm and load up.'[45]

Captain Raw backs down – or at least says little more.

He is not giving permission, and the flight is not officially sanctioned – as it is clearly madness to fly into the middle of a battle without any fire support of their own.

But Captain Raw is not moving to stop them.

So they have a Raw deal; the Group Captain will wash his hands and they can go out there and get dirty.

We are off to saddle up, load the helicopter with ammo, and see if the other chopper crew will accompany us on the same basis. Brigadier Jackson snaps orders for Riley to get his chopper – or choppers, if he can convince his mate – over to Eagle Farm by 1730 hours where, after more snapped orders, boxes of ammunition should be arriving within minutes.

Once outside, Bob Grandin is still reeling at how quickly everything has transpired, how they have gone from being, 'It's too risky to fly,' to 'Okay, we are doing this,' in the space of a couple of minutes.

And that is despite Grandin already trying to pull Riley into line in a hushed but heated conversation in the Operations Centre.

'How will we find them?' he'd asked Riley, *sotto voce*. 'Why won't we just be shot out of the air by a superior force? How can we land? What could we actually do that would help?'[46]

But Frank hadn't wanted to listen. Those questions were way too logical for him.

Now, Grandin needn't be so restrained.

Stopping the RAAF veteran with a paw on the shoulder, Grandin asks the question that has to be asked of his great mate, the one who is 'always looking for action',[47] which on the one hand is admirable, but in this case looks very likely to get them all *killed*.

'What the hell are you doing? This is a suicide mission. How are we going to get back?'

Riley rises to the occasion, rather like his chopper right into the teeth of a howling gale, and throws out a challenge.

'*We* probably won't,' he replies evenly. 'You don't have to come.'[48]

And meantime, Bob, while I have your complete attention?

'Shut up, stop giving me the shits.'[49]

'But there are *hordes* out there, Frank. It's impossible.'

'You don't have to come,' he responds. 'Volunteers only.'[50]

Arriving back at the Kangaroo Pad, they are met by the pilots for the second chopper, Flight Lieutenants Cliff Dohle and Bruce Lane.

Matter-of-factly, Frank tells them of the task at hand. We are going in. We are going to drop ammo to Delta Company.

'I'm with you,' Bruce Lane says to Frank immediately.

('There was no choice,' he will later characterise his decision. 'Without us, Delta Company would be lost. And with two choppers, there was double the chance that at least one of us would get through.'[51])

'Me too,' Cliff Dohle says, albeit a lot less certainly.

Et tu, Brutes? Is Bob Grandin the only sane bastard here?

It seems so. But the moment is nigh. One way or another he has to make a decision. Oddly enough, the wisp of an ancient memory comes to him on the spot.

Biggles.

Growing up with a father in the armed services, and, as a child, dreaming of becoming a pilot, he had always thrilled to the fictional story of an English pilot by the name of Major James Bigglesworth. 'Biggles', as he was known, had flown and triumphed in both World Wars and was always getting into death-defying scrapes and *always* surviving, while sending 'Jerry' and the 'damn Huns' to oblivion.

Biggles Goes To War.

Biggles Defies the Swastika.

Biggles Sorts It Out.

He had read, and devoured it all. Biggles, through his flying skill and his courage, could take on anything the world could throw at him, and young Bob had so loved all those stories it had got into his bones and even helped propel him into the RAAF in the first place. He had wanted to see action like Biggles had, wanted to triumph against the odds, like Biggles had.

And now was the moment for major action. Against all odds.

Could he really say no?

Of course he could not.

'OF COURSE I'LL COME,' the career RAAF man says finally, only just making himself heard over the crashing artillery. He waits for pauses between barrages before speaking again. 'But how are we going to pull it off?'

BOOM!

'We'll use the SAS tactics,' Riley replies. BOOM! 'We'll fly out at height, find them and then guide Cliff in.'[52] BOOM! BOOM! BOOM!

Of course. They had worked out the method in many previous exercises since arriving in Vietnam, dropping elite SAS soldiers in 'Indian Country', as the Americans call it. One chopper goes high, out of range from ground fire. The other comes in fast and low, guided in by the top chopper – *a little left, 100 metres more, a little right, drop now!* – drops them in, and gets out.

Turning to Cliff, who will be in command of the second chopper, Frank gives more instructions.

'You blokes hold back behind us. I'll locate them and then guide you in at treetop level.'[53]

Which is fine when there are only scattered forces. But they'll be flying over an intense battle!

'But we have no defences, Frank,' Grandin points out. 'What chance have we got against their weapons?'

'Stop shitting me, Bob. Let's not worry about it.'

'But I am. I don't want to die doing something stupid. We need to plan a way to get the ammunition in without too much danger to us. One hit and our helicopter will just blow up.'

'Fuckin' shut up,' Riley replies.

'This is madness, Frank,' Grandin trails off. 'It's suicidal. It will achieve nothing.'[54]

Frank Riley snarls and this part of their conversation is over.

For what else can Grandin do? Let his mate fly off alone, flying munitions that are needed for a company that will be wiped out for lack of them? It can't be done.

He *must* shut up, stop giving Frank the shits, and go.

And go he will.

CHAPTER ELEVEN

SHELLS IN HELL

Who could forget the mateship that was shown that evening given by all who served the guns in whatever capacity they served in the Regiment? I can close my eyes today and feel like it was just yesterday. The smells, sights and noise. Rain, water, mud and Aussie gunners giving their all to protect our digger mates at the hot end . . . 18 Aug '66 is still very clear in my mind. No, I don't have to blow my trumpet, but just maybe someone with the right notes will write the music to blow our trumpet one day. Until then – Remember Them.[1]

'Walshy' from North Queensland

1706 hours, 18 August 1966, Delta Company HQ, red menace

Harry Smith is calling fire from the sky: 'Will throw red smoke – will accept napalm within 100 metres. Target will be 200 metres EAST of red smoke.'[2]

At least that's where the target is right now. It is moving so fast it is hard to keep track, and the sooner that napalm gets here the better. Meantime, Delta Company must focus on the things it can control itself – starting with getting some strength in numbers.

To re-establish contact, Smith wants to bring both his own HQ, and more particularly 12 Platoon, closer to 10 Platoon and 11 Platoon. Having failed with his left hook via 10 Platoon, he now must try a right hook, by bringing 12 Platoon out of reserve, and throwing it into action.

As it happens, instead of bunching either fist, Smith simply looks Sabben's way and brings his open right hand to the top of his head and pats it twice – meaning, 'Come to me'.

Once they've arrived, Harry the Ratcatcher gives his basic orders in four words.

'Right hook. Get 11.'[3]

The only qualification is that Sabben must leave one of his three sections with HQ for defence while taking the other two forward to see if they can help relieve the pressure on 11 Platoon and extricate them.

It is a risky move from Major Smith, dispersing his company now over four spots but he feels he has no choice if 11 Platoon is going to be given any chance of being extricated.

Sabben decides how to unleash the right hook. Knowing that 10 Platoon is returning from the north-east and will likely be pursued by the enemy, it is clear they need to give them a wide berth. So he decides they will go south to the planters' hut first, to ensure they are directly west of 11 and then turn east, approaching from an unexpected angle.

1715 hours, 18 August 1966, Long Tan towards 11 Platoon, 400 yard dash

Carrying out the Ratcatcher's orders, Lieutenant Dave Sabben and 11 Platoon are soon on their way. Very quietly, however, the junior officer is distinctly underwhelmed.

Sabben will recount, 'I only had thirty men and he kept ten of them. So I actually went forward with about twenty men and I had about four hundred yards or five hundred yards to traverse between where the company headquarters unit was and where the last known position that we knew for 11 Platoon.'[4]

I mean, they're under fire from at least 100 men, and he's meant to get them out with just 20 men? With that few, even traversing 400 yards in the face of the monumental firepower the enemy has already displayed is a bloody monumental task, and no doubt about it.

Major Smith and Delta Company HQ, meanwhile, will stay where they are, with the remaining section of 12 Platoon – 9 Section – as added defence, hopeful of seeing 10 Platoon return to them soon and awaiting the ammunition on their way from on high in the sky.

When it comes to getting ammunition, one man is not waiting for the choppers. For now Morrie Stanley looks up from his co-ordinate calculations to see none other than CSM Jack Kirby hovering expectantly, almost like a waiter about to take an order.

Uh, yes, Sergeant Major?

'Excuse me, Sir, have you any spare ammunition?'

Kirby is such a surreal model of manners and procurement it really is like a P. G. Wodehouse novel, *Jeeves Visits Vietnam*. Amazed, Stanley nods and replies, 'Help yourself from my pack.'

Kirby does just that and is done in a moment.

'I am leaving you one magazine, Sir,'[5] says Kirby; for all the world sounding as though that magazine might be a copy of *National Geographic* or *The London Illustrated News* instead of bullets to kill in the battle that blazes around them. Thank you, Jeeves. Stanley nods once more and Kirby vanishes to the nearest gun that needs him.

Bloody hell, that is one polite Sergeant Major.

•

Lieutenant Kendall is choosing his moment – that rare passage of time when their enemies' fire lifts a little as they try to manoeuvre into a better position.

And . . . now!

Following Lieutenant Kendall's shouted orders, 10 Platoon uses the 'fire and movement' method they had executed so many times in training back in Enoggera, with the left-hand section giving covering fire while the right-hand section withdraws by 25 yards or so, before they go to ground and give the same protection to the left-hand section, the sequence repeated until all have retreated to the next position to be defended.

•

Proceeding carefully – well, as careful as you can be in an area where the bullets crack and the shells shock – Lieutenant Sabben leads his men of 12 Platoon to try to support the besieged 11 Platoon. Hopefully Major Smith's message to Sergeant Buick over the radio that 12 Platoon was on its way would have got through, but there is no way of knowing, as since the news had come through that Gordon Sharp had been killed and they were pinned down, little has been heard from them – likely from enemy jamming. The only thing that is known is that some of them are still alive, for Sabben and his men can hear the furious shooting coming from where 11 Platoon is situated. Sighting the hut now, they turn east and keep moving. And yet they have gone no more than 100 metres beyond the hut, when just up ahead in the heavy rain scouts suddenly see small pods of enemy soldiers, to both the north-east and south-east – clearly trying to get around behind 11 Platoon and cut off their means of retreat.

The scouts give hand signals to those behind – thumbs down, meaning enemy ahead – and Lieutenant Sabben is instantly apprised.

With one glance he can see that there are pods of enemy in front of his left-hand and right-hand sections and he comes forward accordingly. Sabben takes instant action, and with hand signals has all his men forward and down, their weapons aimed. The moment Sabben fires, all of 12 Platoon does, reaping a terrible harvest of death.

Before them, most of the pods of enemy soldiers go down . . . only to be revealed as scouting patrols of heavy masses of enemy soldiers coming behind.

Within moments it is 12 Platoon itself that is coming under heavy fire – *THUMP-THUMP-THUMP – CRACK-CRACK-CRACK* – from at least *two* heavy machine guns and the branches and trunks of the rubber trees all around them start to shatter and splatter into tatters that come down all over them, even as, like feverish wombats, they burrow still deeper, taking what shelter they can as the bullets continue to fly overhead. (It is exactly what they had been taught back at Kapooka and Puckapunyal: the natural tendency of soldiers, particularly on targets they can't see clearly, is to fire high. Well-trained soldiers compensate for this by firing a little lower.)

It now becomes beyond urgent to push forward to 11 Platoon's aid, and to keep their corridor of retreat open. As soon as the firing has died down a little, Sabben quickly leads his men forward again, only for *RAT-TAT-TAT-TAT-TAT-TAT-TAT-TAT* . . . the same thing to happen. Again, they go to ground as pieces of rubber trees fall down upon them.

'We were in a lot of shit,' Paul Large's newly nominated best man, Dave Beahan, will recall. 'We were all petrified, we were pissing our pants – not that it mattered because we were [w]ringing wet and covered in mud anyway. We were all praying, "Please don't let me get killed, God." I reckon I would have said the Hail Mary a thousand times.'[6]

Still 12 Platoon is able to maintain heavy if judicious fire of their own upon the VC who are clearly forming up to attack them.

Despite the shocking stress of the situation, Sabben falls back on the heavy training they had received at the hands of Scheyville and Harry Smith. Ever and always, his mind is going on what he will describe as an 'endless loop'.

Lance Corporal Georgie Richardson (left) and Sergeant Bob Buick give first aid to Private Jim Richmond, 12 hours after the battle. *(AWM FOR/66/0664/VN)*

A howitzer gun, one of those used in support during the battle. To make the guns lighter and more manoeuvrable, the protective shields were generally removed, as shown here. *(AWM P05396.002)*

19 August 1966. Weary Delta Company members eat a hasty rations meal before returning to the battle area. *(AWM FOR/66/0674/VN)*

Back on the battlefield after the heroic action by Delta Company. Lieutenant Dave Sabben advances cautiously through the rubber plantation, past bodies of dead VC near a Chicom 7.62 mm heavy machine gun.

(AWM FOR/66/0658/VN)

Out in the field again, soldiers from 6RAR search for fleeing VC the day after the battle. *(AWM CUN/66/0692/VN)*

Troops of 6RAR on board armoured personnel carriers of No. 1 APC Squadron wait to go back to the Nui Dat base during Operation Smithfield. *(AWM CUN/66/0695/VN)*

Some of the recovered VC weapons. *(AWM FOR/66/0667/VN)*

Task Force Commander Brigadier Oliver Jackson speaks with men of Delta Company after the battle. *(AWM FOR/66/0663/VN)*

Major Harry Smith (centre) shakes hands with Flight Lieutenant Cliff Dohle, watched by Group Captain Peter Raw. *(AWM VN/66/0043/08)*

Major Harry Smith briefs press representatives after the battle. *(AWM CUN/66/0709/VN)*

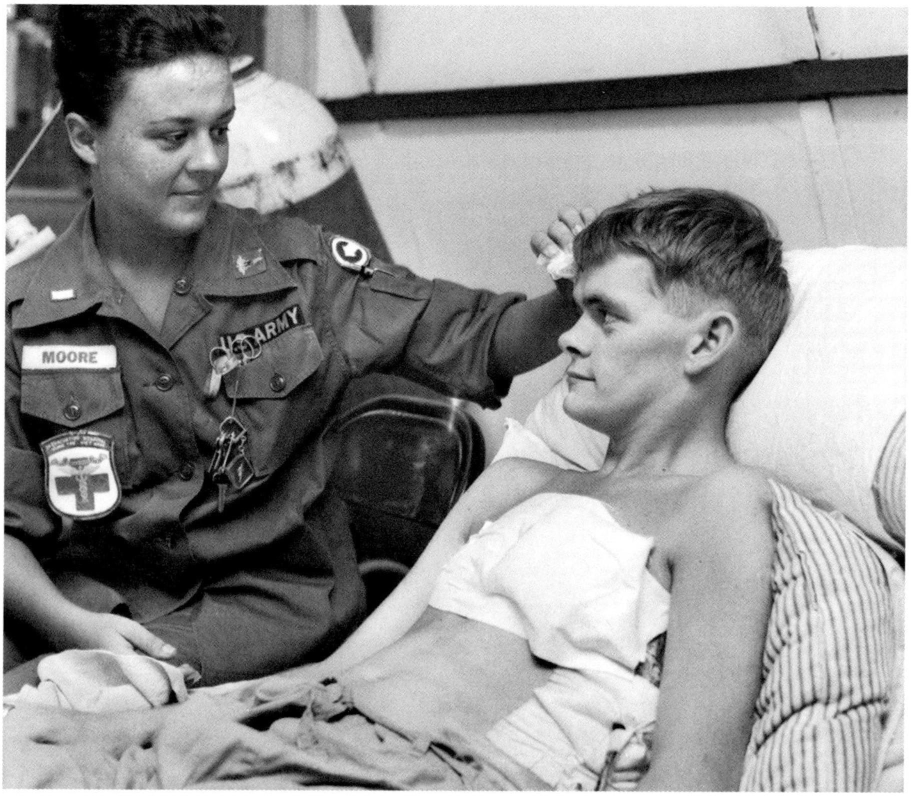

Private Jim Richmond recovers in hospital. *(AWM CUN/66/0717/VN)*

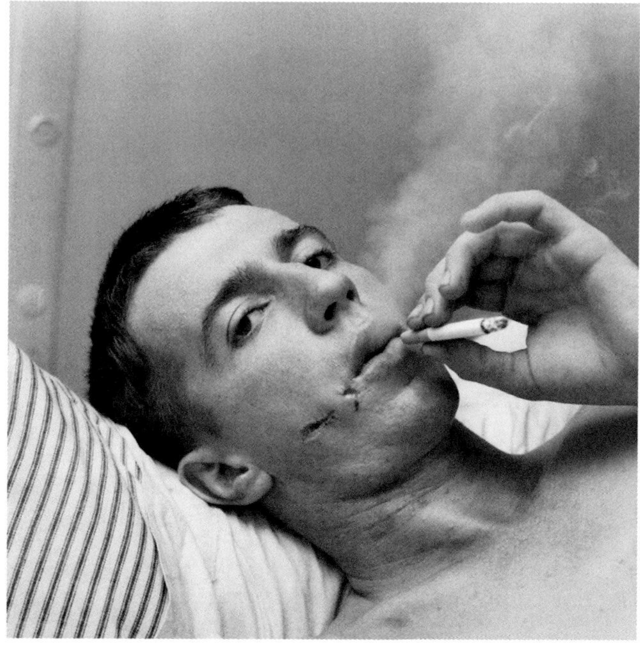

Private Barry 'Custard' Meller recovers in hospital. *(AWM CUN/66/0715A/VN)*

18 August 1969. The 'Piper's Lament' for the dead of Long Tan, played during the commemorative service held at the site of the battle. *(AWM BEL/69/0556/VN)*

'You're saying "What's changed?" "Has the enemy changed?" "Can I see more of the enemy?" "Less enemy in a different position?" "What's my current strength?" "Are all my weapons operating?" and so on. And then because it's an endless loop, when you finish considering one thing you move on to the next.'[7]

On the basis of that endless loop, and uttering orders accordingly, keeping his men in the best defensive position possible, Sabben is able to keep 12 Platoon substantially intact, despite being under such heavy fire. But for how long can that last – given that the VC are now starting to probe forward from all angles – and how long can they last with limited ammunition?

And, Christ Almighty! Now there is some movement visible *behind* them?

Who is it?

'It must be B Company coming back . . .'[8] one of the soldiers posits.

'B Company be fucked!' Neil Bextrum replies.

They are bloody VC! And without another word he starts firing on them, and it isn't long before Charlie fires back. Taking fire from three sides, 12 Platoon is now all but surrounded, while still concentrating on the task at hand, keeping the corridor between them and 11 Platoon, and from there back to Delta HQ, as open as possible. It looks like they are going to have to *fight* their way out of this!

But inevitably, it won't be without cost. For now there is a cry, and Private Kev Graham clutches his chest with two bullet-holes in him.

'Do you think you can crawl back to company headquarters?' Dave Sabben calls out to him.

'Crawl, be fucked,' Graham replies in unparliamentary language, acceptable under the circumstances. 'I can run.'[9]

With which, still clutching his chest, he is off, and – under the care of Private Graeme 'Doc' Davis – is soon stumbling from the cover of one tree to the next, angled away from where the VC are firing hardest at them from behind, and hoping for the best.

Sabben's mind races.

What to do? They have come here to relieve 11 Platoon but have not yet made contact. And yet surely Buick and his men must know they are there? They could move further forward to try to get to them, but the danger would be that the enemy would close in behind them which would leave *both* platoons cut off. *Move back?*

Out of the question. That would leave 11 Platoon completely isolated with no path of withdrawal. No, they *must* keep this corridor open, and let the blokes from 11 know exactly where they are – because the enemy certainly does, to judge from how heavy the fire now is all around.

And so, they stay put, firing on all enemy that come between them and their besieged comrades.

'We can't pull back and we can't advance,' Sabben thinks, 'so our job now is to keep the corridor open.'[10]

Each soldier has his arc of fire, responsible to shoot anything that moves within it.

But careful, you bastards!

Hold your bloody fire unless you're absolutely certain they're not our blokes.

Sabben keeps firing with the best of them, noting, in spite of himself, how extraordinary it is both to see pods of enemy wiped out by shells and to personally shoot another human being.

With the shells it is not, as he would have thought, a case of men being thrown backwards. Rather . . .

'It explodes and, in an absolute instant, there's nothing there any more except steam and smoke.'[11]

And shooting a man?

'It's just like a marionette, and you cut the strings. He just flops . . . If you hit a killing shot, through the head or the top of the chest or something, he's standing one second, and flat on his face the next second. He just slumps where he is.'

Yes, Sabben is slightly shocked at the brutality of it at first but in short order notes with surprise how little he feels.

'The novelty wears off very quickly. You're not looking at them as human beings. They're impersonal. They're enemy soldiers and you're accounting for them like they were targets.'[12]

A few of the casualties they are getting now are quite remarkable for just how casual they are. Private Terry Ryan looks down at his wrist. Hey, there's a bullet sticking in there. Somehow, it has passed through the rubber tree he had been sheltering behind and ended up in him. Sabben watches astounded as – cool as *two* cucumbers – Terry simply pulls the bullet out and hands it to him.

'Here, skip, look after this for me.'[13] *Will do*. In other circumstances, Private Ryan might be diagnosed with shock. Here, he is diagnosed as a Digger, with an overdose of courage.

They fight on.

1715 hours, 18 August 1966, 11 Platoon under siege, fireworks burning bright

Dante's hell has nothing on this.

Delta Company's 11 Platoon remains under siege, more or less exactly where they have been since they'd first been hit hard. Bullets continue to splatter all around them, including into their dead mates beside them who can no longer move. The rain pours down on them like an open tap. They are running out of ammo, and there is only one saving grace.

The shells shrieking through the sky must be giving Charlie some idea of what the seventh ring of hell might look like. Lightning flashes and the explosions of the shells themselves reveal the results of 15 kilograms of steel exploding into thousands of deadly splinters of steel, which completely decimate the enemy forces as limbs and torsos fly. If not for the artillery, 11 Platoon would be wiped out in minutes.

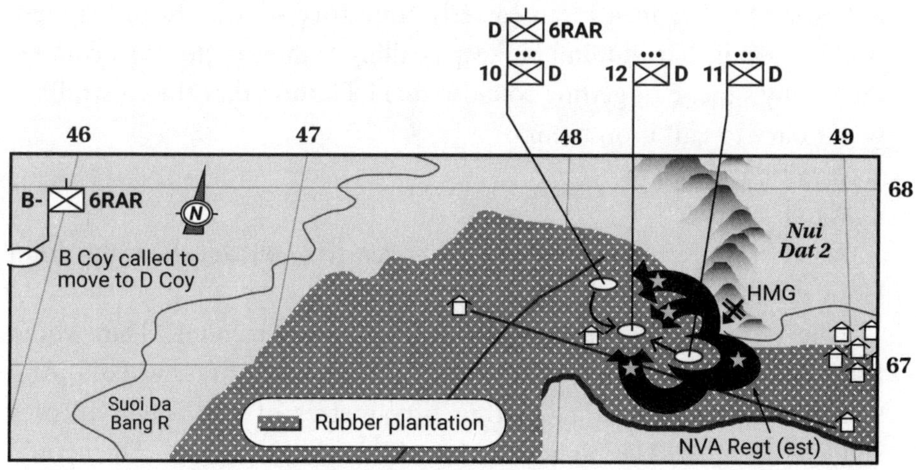

10 Platoon returns; 12 Platoon moves south then east, 1700–1800 hrs, 18 August 1966

The problem is, there are so many of the bastards – no matter how many are blown to pieces, the others just keep coming!

And now the tracer fire starts on 11 Platoon once more and, all put together, it is like a fireworks show put on for their benefit. A flash of lightning, slow trails of green tracer, regular explosions of yellow light from the exploding shells – if not for your likely imminent death, it'd fair dinkum take you back to the fun of cracker night at home. There are certainly enough penny bungers, and the tracer bullets are so thick that Bob Buick will note that they are 'like a swarm of bush flies around us'.[14]

In desperation, Sergeant Bob Buick makes another urgent call to Harry Smith. It is the same as the last; we of 11 Platoon cannot last. We're surrounded. Heavy casualties. Low ammo.

Yes, Harry is familiar with the situation.

It is the same call that Smith could make to Buick! Keep on going. We both will.

Through it all, the artillery that Buick keeps calling in – for the first time in an actual battle, but the exemplar of Smith's insistence that everyone had to be able to do multiple jobs – keeps making the difference for 11 Platoon.

Buick calculates each drop with the knowledge that the artillery fired from the west, as in this case, tends to disperse its blast, most particularly the hot shrapnel, in an easterly trajectory – away from his men. And it is with that in mind he keeps calling it in ever closer to counter the enemy's tactic of getting so close to 11 Platoon that the Australians won't dare to call it on them.

Won't dare?

Watch him.

Watching carefully from behind a fallen tree, out on the right, John Heslewood is with four mates.

'The Viet Cong were getting close to us,' he will recount. 'They would form up in groups. They didn't run, they just sort of fast walked. And sometimes they would get within fifty metres of you. Then all of a sudden out of the blue they would get hit with artillery . . . Then you'd see them withdrawing and forming up again, then they'd come again. This was happening all along our front. It wasn't just us but our artillery just kept saving us.'[15]

•

Cease fire!

In this whole conflagration, the worst thing would be to shoot your own soldiers and the men of Delta HQ have been careful not to pull the trigger on any shadowy figure unless they are sure they are VC. But these blokes coming our way aren't VC.

Look at their floppy hats!

They are *our* blokes! 10 Platoon has extricated itself from its engagement and has now made its way back. Mercifully, though they have some men wounded, they have not had any killed.

In a quick exchange, Harry Smith instructs Kendall to place his men on that part of the perimeter facing 11 Platoon's departure, and prepare to defend for their lives.

Terry Burstall pauses as he sees Brian Hornung; the bloody definition of walking wounded. Despite the rain, there is blood all over his shirt, and Brian holds his own field dressing, pressed so low on his shoulder that it is almost in his chest. Brian looks at Terry, but he doesn't see him, his eyes are blank, the thousand-yard stare at just three paces.

'There's hundreds of them out there,'[16] he says simply. Terry nods and glances at Shorty Brown and Brian Reilly. They are all thinking the same thing.

What the hell have we hit?[17]

A gusher of VC, flooding them, that's what. They watch the wounded move past them and the thought occurs; shouldn't they be moving too? Burstall climbs to a ridge and sees . . . they are the only Australians within sight!

Perhaps a gentle hint to the chain of command is required?

'We are on our own?' Private Terry Burstall says to his Corporal, a statement that is a question and a suggestion.

'If the boss wanted us to move he would have told us,' the Corporal replies. 'Keep digging in.'[18]

But Terry Burstall won't wear it, and is sure his services might be better used elsewhere. Grabbing his rifle, he runs through the rubber towards the sound of the firing and in short order comes across CSM Jack Kirby at Delta Company HQ.

Gesturing towards the small ridge where he can see other soldiers are fanned out, firing at the oncoming enemy, Terry yells, 'Do you want us up there?'[19]

Despite the dim light, it is obvious that ol' Jack has instantly turned a deep shade of purple.

'OF COURSE I WANT YOU UP HERE, YOU STUPID BASTARD,'[20] he roars back so loudly it momentarily drowns out the chatter-shatter of the machine guns. Triumphant, Terry runs back to grab the others; the Corporal is informed that yes, the boss wants us to MOVE, *you stupid bastard*, and they scramble to Kirby, who places them now on a new perimeter to defend the right flank.

They can see movement through the rubber trees, but it is distant. Jack Kirby knows what they are thinking and gives his instructions.

Don't waste ammo. If the targets are too far away to be clear, don't worry, son, they *will* come closer towards you!

Kirby rushes off in all directions, as is his wont, and they are left there watching, waiting, 'listening to the sound of the firing to our left and watching the artillery explode further to the left'. Yes, they have moved positions but: 'We were still as much in the dark about what was happening as when the first contact occurred.' When *last* contact will occur is on all their minds. What next? 'None of us in the section had any idea what the bloody hell was going on, and I suppose everybody else was in the same boat at that time.'[21]

•

Out with Bravo Company, still awaiting permission to go to Delta Company's aid, Private David Thomas is drinking from a banana leaf.

Sure, the rain is so heavy you could just open your gob and you'd half drown with water in a sec, but using the leaf somehow seems a little more civilised, and that gives comfort right now.

What the hell is going on? Bravo Company is still stalled, slap bang between Long Tan and Nui Dat. It is almost as though they've been forgotten about. At last though, the radio crackles into life. It is an order from Major Brian Passey for Bravo Company to go to Delta HQ.

Bravo's OC Major Noel Ford replies and confirms:

'Callsign Two . . . Moving to D Coy HQ at 477675.'[22]

And now an afterthought from Major Ford.

'What do you want us to do when we get there?'[23]

Major Passey replies simply: 'Kill the enemy.'[24]

Sounds like a plan . . .

1725 hours, 18 August 1966, 11 Platoon, phantoms in flight, a soldier's delight

The quarrels of Nui Dat HQ are not broadcast to the field; instead, they have only good news for Major Harry Smith. The US Air Force attack aircraft – three Phantom F-4 II jets – will be overhead in short order. Their Airborne Forward Air Controller in a light plane should hopefully be able to identify where the enemy is by red smoke grenades thrown by Delta.

Excellent!

Sergeant Buick is instructed accordingly: throw red smoke grenades to indicate your position. The Airborne Forward Controller accompanying the Phantom jets will pinpoint exactly where you are and guide them in accordingly.

Private Brian Halls retrieves the orange smoke grenades from his kit, and awaits Buick's order.

1726 hours, 18 August 1966, Long Tan plantation, Delta Company HQ, southern comfort

And now the Americans of the 2/35th Artillery join in with their own six guns, following the precise grid co-ordinates and sending their 90 pound shells, not among the shots fired by the Kiwis, but just beyond them, some 200 yards beyond 11 Platoon and ideally making those VC troops in reserve who would move forward face a gauntlet of fire.

These blasts and the flashes that come with them will hopefully serve as an additional beacon for the Phantoms.

The salvos of the American weaponry drowns out the question coming through the comms:

'Delta HQ?'

Yes, this is one and the same. The problem is, 'HQ' itself evokes order, calm, consideration and decisions carefully arrived at. Whereas the truth, right now, is that 'Delta SSC' might be closer to the mark for 'Shit Show Central' as what currently constitutes Delta Company HQ is just a few points north-by-north-west of chaos.

Smith and his staff are hanging on, still controlling this battle like cats to a curtain, barking orders, receiving reports, working out how to maximise both their defensive and offensive capacities with the resources they have, but it is a close-run thing. Even with the remnants of 10 Platoon rallying, every time they fight off one assault and think the enemy is done, it is only to find that Charlie has regrouped and is now coming at them from a different direction.

Smith's chief worry, among too many to count, is clear.

If Charlie gets a force in behind us, attacking from the west, we are done. It is the one point on the clock where we have no men in our line, which is already too thinly spread out, and they will go right through us.

And here comes the latest report.

Another attack has been spotted, forming up . . . this one on the southern side. Yes, it is a strange thing to be thankful to be attacked but, look at the bright side – it was much better to have Charlie in front of you than behind you.

•

Now, while it had been one thing for Adrian Roberts to be told to get up to A Company to pick them up, it is quite another for them to be ready – because they are not! From Alpha Company getting out of the shower to making sure they had some food in their belly to getting fresh ammunition from the Q-store is simply not something that can be done in a couple of minutes. They are rushing, yes, but they are not ready!

Roberts looks at his watch. It is just a little before 1730 hours.

His blood is boiling.

They are *still* waiting for final clearance from Brigadier Jackson before going. Of course 1ATF HQ must work out what is happening at Long Tan before committing – but how can it take *this* long? Is it not bleeding obvious to them that if they wait much longer there will be no decision to be made, as Delta will be already lost, and the only task remaining will be to retrieve their bodies?

Those around Brigadier Jackson feel the same. With each minute of deliberation, the temperature of discussion goes up. Decide, gentlemen, decisively if possible!

Lieutenant Roberts waits. And fumes.

1730 hours, 18 August 1966, in the skies above Long Tan, the smell of napalm in the evening

Steady now.

It is part of the balance of the exercise.

When managing jets and loads this powerful – Phantom F-4 II fighter bombers, each with dual turbojet engines generating 17,900 pounds of thrust, and pushing them forward at 765 miles per hour, as they prepare to drop two M47 75 pound bombs, each containing 92 gallons of the fuel gel mix known as napalm – steadiness is a must. Those bombs are so powerful, capable of incinerating everything within 2100 square metres of the point of contact, at a temperature of 1200 degrees Celsius, that even a slight miscalculation risks causing mayhem.

The three USAF pilots from the 8th Tactical Fighter Wing bring their jets into the approaches of Long Tan plantation, even as the 'Wizzos', behind each pilot – their Weapons Systems Operators, also known as GIBs, for the Guy In Back – make sure that all is ready to release the aluminium canisters, which will tumble to the jungle below and explode on impact.

Ahead of them, an Airborne Forward Air Controller in his light plane has given them the co-ordinates to put in their on-board Inertial Navigation System to guide them to the right area.

All they need is to spot coloured smoke rising from the green canopy that has been promised. In conjunction, artillery fire missions are continuing, the Phantoms' mission being to drop the napalm 200 metres to the east of 11 Platoon's position, guided by either red smoke or artillery flashes.

None of the pilots are happy. Accurately dropping napalm is a difficult exercise at the best of times. But in weather like this it is just a station or two back from 'Next To Impossible'. It is only in the urgency of this situation that the orders have been given that they must try.

The planes whine, and shudder lightly as the pilots lift the flaps, to slow their speed to 400 knots, and push their joy-sticks forward to come in at an altitude of just 400 feet. Their stomachs tighten, aware of their sudden vulnerability to fire from Charlie, who has become more sophisticated in recent times on how to draw a bead on fast-moving targets, essentially aiming just ahead of them.

Despite their relatively slow speed, villages, roads, gullies and hills all whip below like a film on fast forward, as both the pilots and their Wizzos strain for a sign of coloured smoke.

1730 hours, 18 August 1966, above Nui Dat, tie me kangaroo down, sport

It doesn't take long – but long enough for Bob Grandin to wonder if this is the second-last flight he will ever take, if he is in the last 30 minutes of his life.

With maddening insouciance, Flight Lieutenant Frank Riley expertly hops their chopper from 1ATF's Kangaroo Pad to the 6RAR pad, Eagle Farm, so it can be loaded with ammunition. They are quickly followed by Flight Lieutenants Dohle and Lane in their chopper, crewed by Corporal Harrington and Leading Aircraftman Hill.

Even as Bob Grandin continues to mutter inwardly about the insanity of it all, however, momentum for the task they have agreed to execute continues to build. Right there at Eagle Farm, the RSM George Chinn, who has just arrived, has organised a human chain of soldiers to quickly move boxes of ammunition from the Q-store to right here on the grass so the choppers can be loaded as quickly as possible – no small thing, with 1150 pounds of ammunition to get on board.

A quick discussion ensues as to just how the ammo should be presented. In the boxes, as is? Or cut the steel bands, open the boxes and put all the bullets, now loosely packed in small cardboard boxes, into magazines so they can simply be clicked in, ready to go? The decisions are quickly taken – because they must be. They will break the bands and wrap the boxes in blankets, which can be used for the wounded, but there is no time to load the bullets into magazines.

And another thing! Yes, we will use two choppers, but not evenly loaded. At Flight Lieutenant Bruce Lane's suggestion, his will take two-thirds of the weight, while Frank Riley's chopper will take a third and go high guiding them in, before coming down themselves.

So hop to, and get to the choppers!

As many willing hands set to, stacking the ammo boxes into each helicopter, Riley and Grandin don't speak about anything other than the procedures of the task ahead.

The decision has been taken.

They are going out there.

The ammo is packed in boxes, the boxes are packed in blankets. At least the ammo will feel comfortable on this flight.

And now Riley paces impatiently, even as he tunes into the battalion radio net to follow the action. Now 1730 hours, it is as clear as dog's balls that Delta is in seriously deep shit.

The worst thing of all? Even when both choppers are loaded, they *still* can't take off, as they must await final, formal approval, from Brigadier Jackson. This at least gives them time to work out one crucial thing:

Who will go with them, beyond the usual crew of two machine-gunners on both choppers who have all volunteered? For if they are engaged fighting the enemy, it will need a couple of extra blokes to push the ammunition boxes out. Immediately, George Chinn, ol' 3F himself, puts his massive hand up. He will go.

His superior, Major Owen O'Brien – 6RAR's Administration Company commander, who has come over to Eagle Farm to make sure that all is set – is not surprised, as he and George had served in the SAS together and he knows George has guts.

But, George, he insists, this is not a boy's own adventure; this is the military; our job is to organise ammunition, not to deliver it personally and bloody dangerously.

RSM George Chinn hears his old mate and superior officer out. He notes O'Brien's authority but says, firmly, he *is* going. Beyond everything else, *someone* has to do it, and can we, in good conscience, send some young soldier out on what by any measure might indeed be a suicide mission?

Well, in that case, O'Brien has something else to say, that simply has to be said.

'*Bugger* you, George, I'm coming too!'[25]

That stubborn courage is infectious!

Bob Grandin is told the news and nods.

What he thinks is: 'Beauty – two more to go up when our load of ammunition explodes with a hit from the ground.'[26]

What the hell are we doing?

But he knows the answer in his bones already. We are doing what we must if Delta is to have a chance of surviving the day.

At last the news comes over their radios.

You are good to go. Green to go.

Brigadier Jackson is making the bet of his life: both the APCs and the Iroquois are authorised to go – which will denude the 1ATF base somewhat and make it more vulnerable to an attack from the west, if that is what this is all about.

1736 hours, 18 August 1966, 11 Platoon, the thick of it

Another artillery fire mission falls upon the VC positions east of 11 Platoon.

However, the rain is so heavy, the cloud so dense, so all-encompassing, that the consequent detonation is soon obscured from above.

The gloved right hands of both Wizzos caress the red handle on the console in front of them. One firm pull, and their napalm loads will be released.

But, what now? In all the wet, all the thick green foliage below, there is also no sign of *any* smoke? They know, over the radio, that smoke canisters have been released, but that smoke has been unable to penetrate the canopy.

What to do?

Simultaneously, each artillery detonation, designed to guide the Phantoms, is soon simply fizzled out.

In their place, Mother Nature takes a stand.

Roaring thunder heralds tearing and blinding flashes of lightning which abound from all directions. Torrential rain, seemingly falling even harder, blankets the battlefield. Ahead of them, an Airborne Forward Air Controller in a light plane has given them the co-ordinates to put in their on-board Inertial Navigation System to guide them to the right area. Ideally, once the precise target is identified, he will be able to fire white phosphorus smoke rockets, known as 'Willi Pete' on or near the target to guide them in.

But the AFAC has a real problem. Looking down on the black maelstrom below, there are indeed flashes. But that is not the problem. It is that there are so *many* of them! And they are not just the flashes of artillery, but lightning! It is simply impossible to work out which flashes are lightning and which are from artillery landing.

The survivors of 11 Platoon are hoping against hope that somehow the Phantoms can pinpoint the correct position to drop their load.

They hear the roar of the Phantom jets overhead, and wait expectantly for a sudden flare of napalm just to their east, but there is nothing. Something has gone wrong.

Indeed it has.

A hurried dialogue ensues between the Airborne Forward Air Controller and the lead pilot of the first Phantom jet, with the American pilots ordered to divert and drop their bombs and napalm on the northern end of Nui Dat 2.

•

When all else fails, try ludicrous optimism.

Bob Buick yells out the only thing he can think to yell.

'Delta Company is coming to help us! APCs on their way.'[27]

The truth, which he and his men both know, is that: 'I did not have a clue what was happening 100 metres away let alone 1000 metres away.'[28]

And what is happening back at base with the APCs? Not the foggiest. But in a situation where there is no hope, faking just a tiny bit of hope, even when everyone knows it's fake, at least *feels* like a tiny ray of light in the darkness.

In the meantime, even as the bullets fly, the men continue to call to each other in the few seconds' pause that sometimes comes between fusillades.

You there, Davo . . . ?

Here!

Peter . . . ?

Here!

Each name that is called and answered gives reassurance; a battlefield roll call that moves Bob Buick deeply. Of course, there are the names that don't answer. Call them again; they must have just not heard you.

Col! You there, Col? . . . COL!

Christ. Looks like Col Whiston is gone too.

These men were just boys 11 months ago, trying to march in time (and failing) as they got off the train to Enoggera. Now they are in time and in tune as the names are yelled louder and louder. A band of brothers who refused to be drowned out by the brutal clatter of battle.

He cannot see all his men, but Buick can see the enemy. All he has to do is open his eyes. Their position?

Very, very close.

It is the now familiar VC tactic of manoeuvring so close the artillery will need a microscope to get a co-ordinate worth a damn.

Which means that if nothing changes, Delta's position is screwed; so screwed that a new edition of the Kama Sutra would have to be written just to begin to cover it. They are being fired on from three sides at once; about 200 VC are advancing that can be seen. The only thing in the Australians' favour is that the bloody rain is so thick the VC can't see just how weak they are. What now? Retreat? Too many wounded to leave; can't be done.

Advance? Well, why make your death easy? For we are going to die, every man knows that. Anyway, talking about advancing or retreating is academic, if you move at all, a hail of gunfire comes at you. Not random, concentrated. *Concentrate*, Bob! There must be a solution.

Bob Buick has it: an extreme solution if ever there was one, and he passes it on to Graham Smith, the Delta HQ signaller.

He wants the artillery shells to come down right on top of them, and gives co-ordinates for the same.

After all, there are a few men from 11 Platoon still alive out here, but they won't be alive for more than a few minutes. If they are going to die (and again 'If' is not required to start that sentence) they might as well take the enemy with them, and maybe save the rest of Delta.

Sorry, what?

As soon as the message is passed to Morrie Stanley, he assumes the obvious, that there has been some mistake, and he crawls over to his own signaller and takes the handset from him. This is Captain Stanley. Repeat what you have just said.

'We are getting over-run,' Buick says after confirming the co-ordinates. 'You had better send some shit in.'[29]

Captain Morrie Stanley has done many things in this war, but he has never brought down artillery fire on his own men, and he will not start now.

'I am not prepared to fire on your position,' he says forcefully.

Buick replies, playing his ace – of spades.

'It's simple. If you don't, we will be dead in ten minutes.'[30]

Stanley: 'Unless your troops are dug in and have overhead protection, I'm not prepared to adjust the fire.'[31]

In short, I am not going to kill you, Bob.

Yes, you bloody are!

Again Buick calls in his position and *insists* that the artillery fire on it at once.

What the hell is he thinking? Precisely this: 'These bastards are about eighty strong and at this stage of the game we are down to about twenty because of killed and wounded . . . I really don't want to have anyone killed or captured by them, we're better off to go out in a blaze of glory with a whole lot of artillery coming down and wiping everyone else out, bloody hero, you're better off to blow the shit out of everyone rather than to have anyone wounded and captured. If you are captured by the VC you are not going to survive anyway.'[32]

It's not death or glory, Morrie, it's death *and* glory. Do it!

Finally, perhaps just to shut him up, Stanley appears to concede: 'I'll drop 25.'[33]

In fact, Stanley makes no adjustment at all. But it is still falling extraordinarily close, just . . . 50 metres away from them. And it's bloody effective. Six shells fall within seconds, right in the thick of the VC.

'They shredded forty men to pieces with the first few seconds, an awesome sight.'[34]

Awesome in two senses: amazing and terrible at once. And now Bob Buick is calling for more artillery fire, a small adjustment forwards, now a touch back. No! Forward a few metres, Morrie . . . six repeats are called for and 36 more shells explode. Each one of those shells is a combination of steel and high explosives. The result? Armageddon by armament. Their position is still hopeless, but they are still alive, which is more than can be said for hundreds of the enemy. How bad is it? Bob Buick realises that he has not had a cigarette for two hours . . . and he hasn't even missed it!

The fact that 11 Platoon has managed to pull back a little means that they are now calling in shells near to their previous position, which might be problematic for any of their wounded still there, but there is nothing that can be done. They have no choice but to call in shells where the enemy is, and that is it . . .

. . . Still alive, and still holding tightly to the grenade pin, in the very position where he had first been hit, Private Jim Richmond closes his eyes. He hears what sounds like a runaway train, growing louder and closer until it's a horde of screaming banshees, an all-encompassing white noise that drowns out every other sense. And now the shell hits. Private Richmond has been smashed in the back with a 28-pound sledgehammer, the impact so hard that, even as his stomach is pounded into the mud, it bends him in two and he feels as if his head and his feet momentarily touch. The only thing he can think to do is to keep holding on to the grenade tightly. (Really, that is the best way to hold on to a grenade after you have pulled the pin and your thumb is the only thing separating you from separating.) When the dust settles, which happens faster than you would think possible thanks to the ricochet of rain, he can feel nothing from the shoulders down, but has no courage to look behind to see if, as he suspects, he has lost his legs. After all, if that is the case, he'll be dead in a minute or two anyway, so what is the difference? Better to spare himself the worry for now, but . . .

But hang on, what is that? It feels like sore legs? Maybe he still does have them? Carefully, he knocks his knees together – which is no big stretch under the circumstance – and then his ankles, and can feel them both times! Which is the good news. The bad news is that the shrapnel has opened him up like a gutted fish and every time he breathes he can feel the air sucking in and out of his chest, even as blood gurgles out of him.

So maybe he will live for the moment after all?

And yet 'moment' is the operative word here, because Jim is still holding on TO A LIVE GRENADE WITH THE PIN PULLED OUT! Back home in Brisbane such a situation would make him crap his daks. But here? In the first place that probably happened an hour or two ago anyway, he neither knows nor cares. And secondly, there is nothing like being shelled to buggery in the jungle, nearly bent into two, and torn apart by shrapnel so badly he could put his finger on his lung, all while separated from your unit and having murderous Viet Cong all around you, to give you perspective on life's little troubles. Quite frankly, the live grenade is lucky to make the top five of Things That Could Kill Jim at the moment.

That said, if he loses consciousness or falls asleep, he will be a goner on two counts – one through loss of blood, the other from letting go of the lever of the grenade and blowing himself up. So, with his free hand, you know the one not HOLDING ON TO A LIVE GRENADE, he reaches for the rubber band he keeps on his trouser legs to help keep the leeches at bay, and manages to wrap it around the lever of the grenade . . . just before passing out.

•

If 11 Platoon are still up Shit Creek, 12 Platoon are currently shooting up Shit Lake, in a barbed wire canoe. The fire on them is withering, their own ammunition is starting to run out, and the enemy is getting ever closer, now pressing in from three sides. Yes, Sabben is able to even things up a bit by continuing to call in artillery fire of an entire battery but it is obvious that, short of a miracle, they will soon be done for, overwhelmed by the relentless enemy.

And before Sabben's very eyes that miracle starts to appear!

Yes, there has been heavy rain for the better part of an hour.

But not like this.

This is not ordinary heavy rain, like being under a shower. This is so heavy it is like being under an open tap, the heaviest rain any of them have ever felt. And the wonderful thing? It is hitting the muddy water that pools all around the prone platoon with such force that it is raising, literally, a red mud-mist, which continues to rise to about a foot off the ground!

It is just enough to hide the Australians as they lie with their rifles forward, and all they have to do to take aim is lift one eye above the mist – like a crocodile's eye just above the water – line up the approaching enemy, illuminated by the flashing lightning, pull the trigger and sink back down. No, it doesn't make them quite invisible but it tips the balance their way. The VC no longer have any clear targets to fire upon – as the Australians are now covered in red mud from top to toe – while the VC are sitting ducks, their whole thighs, torsos and heads easily visible above the mist.

A miracle, sent from above.

In the famed words of drought-stricken farmers all over Australia through the ages: 'Send her down, Huey!'

Huey sends her down, the red mist protects Sabben's men, and they keep firing through it.

1740 hours, 18 August 1966, Nui Dat, New Zealand 161st Battery

In the firing pits, the men of the New Zealand 161st Battery are shattered with exhaustion, struggling to breathe and completely and utterly sodden to the marrow of their bones. When they had begun firing just before 1630 the weather had been clear and it was thought that they might be busy for 15 minutes or so until Charlie got the message.

But two things had happened. Charlie had not only pulled back, he had doubled and tripled in number and was getting stronger. The men of the artillery crews are receiving regular updates of the situation and know more than ever that their shells are the only things keeping many of the men of Delta Company alive. And no matter how exhausted they are carrying the shells forth and ramming them *once more into the breech, dear friends, once more,* they have no choice but to keep going. And the second thing is the rain had come tumbling down as never before – at the rate of *six inches an hour*! – so heavy that it suppresses the ability of the smoke from each of the guns firing at the extraordinary rate of eight shells a minute – two shells a minute more than the intense rate – to dissipate, and that smoke substantially remains within the confines of the sandbag walls that surround them. Normally, they love the smell of cordite – it has a strangely pleasing, if acrid flavour. But not now.

For the exhausted artillery crews, slipping and sliding on the hundreds of shell casings on the floor of the artillery pits, it is no longer a question of how strong is their stamina and more a question of whether or not they can stay conscious. Of course every man will go till he drops. The point is one of them has already dropped, and many more risk doing so. And it is not just the shattering exhaustion from firing the shells that is making them faint. This monsoonal downpour feels like a post-war record deluge, one that defeats and beats the little available air, all while the fumes thicken and even the strongest men among them start to . . . sw . . . aaaaay. Just how long can both the men actually manning the artillery batteries and keeping them supplied with shells keep going? Another two slump to the ground, gasping for air.

MEDIC!

At least the blokes who have fainted are odds on to wake up. The blokes at Long Tan are in for the Big Sleep unless the artillery keeps fuming. Fire away and fan as best you can; the guns are gunna go.

God help us all, this is hell on earth!

Those conscious continue, amid the pouring rain, trying not to slip over the shell casings that are littered thickly in the greasy and clinging red mud around each gun, even as they keep coughing and struggling to breathe and the shouts of the Bombardier keep going.

'LOAD!'

'CLOSE TARGET!'

'FIRE!'

Bombardier John Burns is struggling to breathe, like all of them, and keeps eyeing the diminishing pile of shells they have on the platform, the first line that had been put there, as it gets lower and lower.

'Geez,' he is thinking. 'We could have a problem here. I'm going to have to take three guys to the main dump 50 metres from the gun to get more, but if I do that we won't be able to keep up the right rate of fire.'[35]

What will they do?

How can they possibly maintain the rate of fire, and keep the blokes from Delta Company alive?

And now he sees them.

Coming out of the rubber trees towards them are a whole posse of engineers, desk jockeys, chief cooks and bottle-washers – literally the kitchen-hands – heading their way. With nary a word they roll up their sleeves and start carrying shells from the dump, through the mud, to the artillery pits. And when more arrive they form a chain, while still others set themselves to unpacking the shells and delicately screwing in the fuses to make the shells live!

In no time at all, the pile in the pits is restored and they have enough to keep going for another hour or so. But instead of going back, the men stay there, ready to leap into action again if required. (And God bless their cotton socks, some have even brought hot coffee and sandwiches – cheese and cordite, hold the pickle – for the crews!)

'No-one told them,' Burns will recount. 'They must have realised our problem and all these guys came running down to the dump to carry rounds to the guns. The bombardier in charge of the ammo was making sure they were unboxing the right kind of round. I thought this is what the Anzac spirit is all about. Doesn't matter what your job is. No-one said, "Not my job" or "I'll stay dry". It was a job that needed doing and they did it. That day it was all one army. I'll never forget seeing those guys bringing ammunition to the gun. I could not be more proud of Aussie soldiers than I was then.'[36]

The darkness continues to deepen, making the flashes from the continuing artillery all the brighter.

1740 hours, 18 August 1966, Delta Company HQ, Harry in a hurry

Major Harry Smith is beside himself with rage.

He has got the news over the radio.

Yes, in the wake of the failure of the Phantom jets to destroy the enemy with napalm, Brigadier Jackson has given approval, *in principle*, for the APCs to come to their rescue, but he had not formalised it with a written order and the APCs still can't move until he does. The point right now is that if the napalm dropped from Phantom jets is not going to save 11 Platoon, then they are more reliant than ever on the APCs, which haven't even *started* their rescue mission yet!

It is not good enough. And there is no more time for formal military language. Barking down the line, he gives it to them straight:

'If they don't hurry up and get out here then they might as well not come at all.'[37]

It is a damning verdict; and Colonel Townsend knows it will be definitive unless they do something, anything, NOW.

Taking up his own field telephone he soon has Jackson – who has retreated to his tent – on the line. A moderate man by nature, Townsend is a little less than moderate in the language used to his superior in such extreme circumstances. On the account of the Commanding Officer of Alpha Company, Captain Charles Mollison, who is at Townsend's elbow, it boils down to: 'Unless Delta Company receives immediate help, it will be over-run. The certainty of that is far worse than the possibility that the Task Force Base [will] be attacked.'[38]

There is a pause as Jackson takes in the implications of all that Townsend is telling him.

Townsend listens, thanks him, and slams the field telephone down before turning to Mollison and shouting to make himself heard above the constant cacophonous roar of artillery sending a shell a second screaming over their heads.

'Get going!'[39]

1742 hours, 18 August 1966, Nui Dat, down to the wire

Some men are slow to anger, and quick to forgive. But Captain Charles Mollison is not only not of their number, he is quite the reverse. And yet mere anger does not come close to what he is feeling right now. In this slow train comin' of APCs he is stuck in, he passed the anger station several stops ago.

Surely, under the circumstances, the lead APC he is in, that of Lieutenant Roberts, can go a lot faster?

With that in mind, he keeps pulling the leg of Roberts – and not in a good way – to yell a suggestion as insistent as it is insolent:

'Get a bloody move on!'[40]

The Troop Commander shouts back down the hatch: 'Maximum speed of 4 and a half kilometres per hour in the base area.'[41]

What? Oh yes, Lieutenant Roberts was very specific. Any faster and transport might get dangerous. That's an admin directive!

(In fact, they particularly have to slow down going past Task Force Headquarters, as there had been vociferous complaints about the noise they made, and a direct order they could have no roaring engines.)

This is a bloody war! Before Mollison has even warmed up his yelling muscles, the APCs change speed. To zero.

'WHAT THE HELL ARE WE STOPPING FOR?'[42] yells Mollison, retaining his volume despite the absence of motor competition.

Well, there is meant to be an opening in the wire here, right by the engineer's compound, and it is here somewhere. But the engineers have camouflaged it so well as a matter of security that we can't find it.

But shouldn't it have been arranged for the engineers to leave someone here on duty with the sole responsibility of making sure that the likes of us can get out, so we can help Delta, without FUCKING AROUND?

Well yes, that's a point. But we are where we are, which is here, and stopped.

BLOODY HELL!

Worst of all, the engineers are off in their mess, having dinner. All Roberts can do is to send a runner to them to come back with someone who both knows where the opening is, and can open it.

Go quick!

The 10 APCs sit there, their engines regularly snorting with frustrated impatience. The soldiers of Alpha Company who are fortunate enough to have their heads out of the hatches and in the open air, rather than baking in the hot-boxes, watch the artillery compound. The activity in the compound remains furious and now seems to include lots of blokes who aren't trained in it – every bastard there is flat-chat, but their movements are not quite as choreographed as usual?

The noise is indescribable: with all 24 guns firing six shells a minute – nearly 150 blasts every 60 seconds – happening just 50 yards away.

Even more unnerving for the soldiers of Alpha Company, who know they are heading to the very area where those shells are landing?

While they wait, the corporals are handing out extra 'shell dressings' – small cloth packs with wound dressings of gauze pads stitched on bandages, designed as first aid treatment for wounded soldiers. Whether it is thought they will be useful for their own wounds or those of Delta Company soldiers is not clear, but there will be blood.

1745 hours, 18 August 1966, Nui Dat artillery compound, not just the thunder of God

It all happens less in a split instant than a shockingly shattering one.

One second those in the artillery compound are raining down hell nineteen to the dozen upon the VC, and the next there is a blinding flash of light, a crack of doom and death – and their whole world is turned upside down. For an instant it seems like they must have taken a direct hit from a VC mortar?

But actually, no. This has come from the Lord himself – a lightning strike. The only saving grace, for the grace of God, is that it has actually struck one of the dunnies – sometimes known by the Diggers as a thunder-box, so lightning makes sense – blowing it completely apart, and not any of the guns themselves. But two men are knocked unconscious by it, and it has also wiped out the Tannoy speaker system which has been amplifying all the instructions. From now on, they will have to adapt, and those instructions will have to be shouted via a daisy chain of men.

The cooks, bottle-washers and Pogos carrying the shells barely blink. The only thing that counts is saving Delta by keeping the very artillery shells they bear pounding down on the enemy.

'Fire mission regiment!'

'Five rounds, fire for effect!'

The beat goes on.

1745 hours, 18 August 1966, Nui Dat, 1ATF base perimeter, picking the gap

It has taken a few minutes, but at last the runner returns with a disgruntled engineer he has mustered, whose own bluster and fluster does not come close to matching Lieutenant Roberts's fury. Either way, the exit point is quickly identified, even if it does take a few more minutes to remove the wire that has so cleverly camouflaged it, and . . .

And Roberts's radio suddenly bursts forth with an urgent message, coming through his head-set.

Return to 6RAR HQ. Return to 6RAR HQ. Colonel Townsend has decided he wishes to come with you, together with his senior staff.

What???

Roberts can barely believe it.

Now, Colonel Townsend wants to come? Wasn't the time to say that 30 minutes ago?

(In fact, at that time Townsend's plan had been to be dropped in by chopper after they had finished their ammunition drop, a plan abruptly shot down by the RAAF's refusal to supply choppers for ammo, let alone for a quick personal HQ relocation.)

Roberts comes to a quick decision.

'The indications were,' he will recount, 'that unless someone got out there pretty quick, they were going to go under. So I ignored the order to hold here.'[43]

Insubordination? Perhaps. But with lives on the line, Roberts feels quite justified in ignoring the order. They can court-martial him later. Right now, they *must* get to Delta Company!

It is not quite that he will *fully disobey* the order. He will just modify it a little. He will send back to 6RAR HQ two APCs – 30 Bravo and 33 Alpha, the former under the command of his 2IC, Second Lieutenant Ian Savage – while he pushes on with the other eight APCs to get to Delta Company quickly, which is all that counts. After all, quickly getting to Long Tan in the APCs is already problematic. The last thing they need now is to wait for top brass ballast.

Even as they trundle forth through the newly opened exit, the sound of their roaring engines and rattling tracks is suddenly drowned out by the thundering from choppers overhead as two Iroquois helicopters take off from Eagle Farm.

Roberts's anger does not abate.

They've lost 10 minutes with this bullshit!

That amount of time could be the difference between life and death for those poor bastards from Delta Company. As his APC races forth, the mind of Lieutenant Roberts does the same.

The key now is going to be to get to them as fast as he possibly can in the Long Tan rubber plantation. The key obstacle that lies between Nui Dat and there – apart from, possibly, a couple of regiments of Viet Cong – is the Suoi Da Bang. There had been a bridge over it, but Charlie had burnt it down not long after the establishment of the 1ATF base. It means, as Roberts knows from previous bitter experience, there is really only one relatively safe crossing in this area, the one just up from the rough dam wall which prevents you being swept downstream if anything goes wrong. The fact that is the key bullock cart crossing – with gently sloping entry and exit points – is a sure sign that they are on the right track winding back.

The fact that some of the APCs don't have a working system of 'pivot steering' – the method by which the APCs steer when afloat – is a worry, admittedly. But there are bigger, louder worries currently exploding in the distance so potentially floating un-merrily down a stream is a risk they will happily take.

Though taking the longer route, the upside of crossing there would be they would be coming to the relief of Delta Company from an unexpected direction, from the south, when Charlie would likely be expecting them to come straight from the west, from Nui Dat itself.

•

To hear one sound in the cacophony of chaos that surrounds them is difficult – albeit made easier when you know that your life may depend on it. And Major Smith can hear it now! That unnatural hum and strum of the air, blades blazing through the air, chopping. It's a Huey, coming their way! Harry Smith takes the proffered radio handset and is soon in direct contact with the pilots: a puff of smoke will signal our location. Watch for the red.

1750 hours, 18 August 1966, Alpha Company APCs, in the belly of the beast

Roberts is not the only one eager to get to Delta Company as quickly as possible.

Inside the forward-most APCs the soldiers of Alpha Company sit grim-faced and uncomfortable. For all their training – not to mention their limited experience in Vietnam so far – for most of them this is their first time inside one of these vehicles. Back in Australia there had simply been no time to integrate the APCs with the infantry to make each familiar with the other and allow each to get the best out of the other in a co-ordinated attack.

And so they now sit in their mobile hot-boxes, supremely uncomfortable, wondering what lies ahead, and – in the absence of being able to talk inside the roaring behemoths – searching for any scenery visible through the small hatch manned by the gunner.

On one APC, two soldiers, Sergeant Frank Alcorta and his best mate, Private Ronnie Brett, have been allowed to sit on top in the open air, on Alcorta's reckoning that, 'My belief was it was a lot more dangerous sitting inside a carrier, where you couldn't see what was going on and react to it, than on the top risking bullets.'[44]

In Roberts's own carrier Captain Charles Mollison is a constant and unwanted source of imprecations to go still faster – even beyond what Roberts considers to be his primary duty, which is to proceed with speed while not recklessly endangering his APCs together with the crews and soldiers they bear.

•

Cease fire!

After two solid hours of straining every muscle they have in them, the artillery crews – and all the cooks, bottle-washers and admin men who have just tasted something dangerously like soldiering – are told they can stand down for just a few minutes so that the choppers don't risk being knocked out of the sky with friendly fire.

Gratefully, many of them sink to the ground on the spot, like exhausted footballers at the end of a grand final, except on this occasion they know that with the next whistle they will have to get up and keep going.

•

The men of 12 Platoon are holding on, but by little more than a frayed thread. With attacks coming at them from an arc of 270 degrees, their principal concern, as ordered by Lieutenant Sabben, is to keep two avenues free of the enemy: the direction 11 Platoon is coming from, and the one that leads back to Delta HQ.

But just where are 11 Platoon?

And, even if 11 Platoon comes into the general area of 12 Platoon, how will they know where to find them in this monsoonal mess, where visibility is so limited?

'Drinkie!' Sabben calls out to Corporal Drinkwater. 'Throw out yellow smoke grenades towards 11 Platoon, as far as you can!'

They will burn for 40 seconds, and ideally be visible for at least a couple of minutes.

•

In the momentary lull in the artillery explosions – likely, as the enemy manoeuvres to take advantage of the pause in artillery fire to get still closer to the survivors of 11 Platoon – Sergeant Bob Buick makes his decision. As mad as it might be to try to retreat when so many of the enemy can bring so much fire to bear, what would be madder still would be to remain, which would see them *all* wiped out.

'At that time,' he will recount, '11 Platoon had no ammunition, only our shovels, machetes and hand grenades. We were getting ready for hand-to-hand fighting.'[45]

No, they have been here for all of two hours, the enemy is now pressing in from three sides and they need to get out through the only corridor left open, the one behind them, where they can hear a battle going on. That must be their comrades, D Company Diggers.

Buick, numb with exhaustion, soaked to the bone like all of them, and running out of ammunition, passes the word along the line – though it remains uncertain just how far that word will get, as there are many broken links in the chain where whole pods of Diggers have been wiped out.

Still Buick asks it to be passed on.

'When I say "go", get up and go like hell, and help anyone you can.'[46]

We will regroup about 150 yards back.

There is a brief pause, and now Buick gives the call: 'Go!'[47]

And now they're up and running as if their lives depend on it – for very good reason.

At the sight of their full-on retreat, the enemy fire from behind lifts a notch, both in volume and in aim, and some of them inevitably fall. Wounded or killed?

Buick is dimly aware that, not far from him, Vic Grice, 11 Platoon's radio operator, has gone down hard. But there is no time to check if he has tripped or been hit. The rest keep going for a good 150 yards before going down behind a clump of trees to get their bearings, regroup and try to work out where the rest of D Company is.

'What happened to Vic?' Barry Meller asks some of the blokes who had been running with him.

'He's dead,'[48] comes the answer.

With still no answer to the question of where the remainder of D Company may be, these survivors of 11 Platoon, those who have left with Buick, keep going in much the same fashion – *dash and flop, dash and flop* – in the rough direction they think their comrades must be.

In the muddy maelstrom they are running through, they know exactly what they are running away from, but just what they are running *to*, is not clear . . .

Somewhere, ahead, they hope, they will find some of their own blokes.

On the second dash it is Barry Meller himself who goes down with a bullet in the leg. In the hope of proceeding unencumbered, he throws away both his pack and his rifle, which is out of ammunition in any case, but it is hopeless. His leg is shattered, and he can't walk.

Mercifully Barry Magnussen does not take the view of every man for himself now that they have got just a little space on the enemy and stops to get Meller on his back. For them the dashes are inevitably shorter.

In the end though Magnussen is clearly so exhausted it is making them both sitting ducks – one big, double-backed waddling duck if you will – and Meller knows what he has to do.

'We aren't getting anywhere,' he says. 'Let me go. You go on ahead and I'll try to make my own way and hide if I can't make it.'[49]

Magnussen reluctantly agrees and heads off – leaving Meller hiding behind a log.

•

Meantime, as far as Lance Corporal Robbins can ascertain, out on the far left of 11 Platoon, he is the only man from the original eight soldiers in 6 Section still alive.

When he'd been shot in the elbow, he'd been incapable of firing anymore and had been aware in any case that most of his mates in this section had already been killed. Mostly he is just shocked at how fast everything had happened. They had been pursuing, they thought, just half a dozen of the enemy, but that tiny tail they had tugged on had proven to be attached to a very large and infuriated tiger that has been savaging them ever since.

'What the hell!' he keeps thinking to himself through the pain of his elbow. 'We're the aggressor, *we're* supposed to be beating *them*, and here they are coming back at us.'[50]

'I saw them set up a mortar at one stage and the artillery was coming in – the sound of that was frightening but at least we could see that it was doing some good as the mortar crew were blasted away. I could hear the sound of jets overhead and thought we'd get air support of some sort. I didn't really think that we couldn't get it because of the wet. I thought they'd find somehow to get us but they couldn't.'[51]

What he most needs right now, he knows, is to join up with the rest of 11 Platoon. The best way will be to crawl over to his right, towards the sound of the ongoing firing, which tells him they are still alive and . . .

And wait!

That's the sound of Charlie slinking through the trees, not 20 metres away! That leaves Robbins with just one hope – to play dead. At least, however, he pulls out a grenade from his pack. If they find him and kill him, he will hopefully be able to take a few with him.

In the meantime, he starts reciting the Lord's Prayer, in the hope that the Lord will steer them away from him.

Our father, who art in Heaven,
Hallowed by thy name,
Forgive us our trespasses,
As we forgive those who trespass against us . . .

In the heavy rain his piety is suddenly interrupted by a shout out to his right.

He recognises Sergeant Bob Buick's voice. He has called for their withdrawal, happening, *right now*.

The best he can, Robbins gets to his feet and runs after the scrambling mob, only to be badly hit in his right hand by a piece of shrapnel, which sees blood gushing so freely he is almost certain he must have nothing at the end of his wrist but a bloody stump but can't bring himself to look at it. Like everyone else, the only thing that counts right now is to keep running in short bursts, about 100 yards a time, until the fire all around gets too intense, at which point they go to ground behind whatever shelter they can find, and now they go again! Weighed down by his backpack, he decides to ditch it only to find that it is too hard with his wounded hand. It is at this point that Ernie Grant,[52] a nice bloke from Thurgoona, New South Wales, just 20 years old, pauses to give him a hand only for . . .

Well, only for a bullet to hit him in the head and kill him stone dead.

Aghast, stunned, there is nothing Robbins can do for him. Grant is clearly dead and that is that. All Robbins can do is gather himself and start running again. It is madness, with bullets hitting trees all around him, screams of men being hit, the constant sound of the artillery still pounding the enemy and through it all the overwhelming feeling that, come what may, he just has to keep going! Frequently he goes down. And every time he rises, so too does the volume of gunfire behind him.

Others are in the same situation.

One who is hit is Private Allen May, shot in the back and sent sprawling some 10 feet forward on his face through the mud. In shock, it takes May a moment to realise: the bullet has hit his entrenching tool. He is still all right!

What is more, he is still a chance of surviving if he can just move faster and present a less inviting target. Throwing off his backpack and water-bottles, he keeps just his rifle as he still has four rounds and if he is to go down, he wants to go down fighting. He is just getting up to go again when he hears his mate, Dougie Fabian, while running past, shout 'I'm hit!'[53]

Private May pauses, thinking, 'Shit, should I leave him?'[54]

But he just can't. He turns back, gathers him and the two dive behind a rubber tree that has just been knocked down by artillery. For the moment they are safe. Maybe they could pass the night here? It feels like they are the last two left alive.

Out to the right, Private John Heslewood and several other soldiers have been harbouring their last rounds when the shout had come. Right now, under particularly heavy fire, it is not so simple a matter as getting up and running, for getting up in the first place would likely see them immediately cut.

'We thought, will we go or not?' Heslewood will recount. 'We reckoned the fire was too heavy at that stage, so we decided to hang around for a while.'[55]

•

The figure dragging himself back through the primeval slime towards HQ (hell, towards anything) is none other than Barry Meller. His back is in agony, his gun is out of ammo and he has also been shot through the mouth.

Oh, and it's raining.

One way or another he is not in the mood for any more shit. So when he looks up and sees a VC soldier standing over him with a grenade in his hand; Meller fights with the only two things he has left, his voice and his temper: 'PISS OFF!'[56] he screams at the VC.

And piss off Charlie does, running back to the east, whence he came.

To Meller's mind, Charlie must have got a bigger shock than he had.

Meller keeps crawling to a little cover, and knows he can go no further. After his bad day at the office, this looks like it is going to be a long night.

•

With 11 Platoon's 4 Section out on the right, Private John Heslewood and his fellow soldiers are less in a spot of bother than a whole world of pain. By their reckoning, they have about three rounds left each, which is – dot three, carry seven, subtract nine – roughly 197 short of what they will likely need to survive the next hour. For it is clear that Charlie himself has no such problems, with the fire upon them so heavy it is very nearly heavier than the rain that keeps tumbling down. It hits the mud so hard the bloody stuff jumps all around into a spray, slung into your lungs as you lie low and try to breathe slow.

And the fire on them never bloody lets up! It is almost like the VC have decided to kill every damn rubber tree in coo-ee, as the Diggers continue to be relentlessly shredded with fire. Heslewood and his comrades keep waiting for it to die down, while fighting the panic that they are just waiting to die. The trees are bleeding white, the bullets are bleeding endless, there is only one sure thing to do: it is time to get the hell out of this hell on earth . . .

Those previous flitting figures in the distance are no longer flitting. These bastards are *en masse* and they are just a few trees away, clearly getting ready to wipe them out!

The decision is now upon Heslewood and his fellow soldiers, still stuck out on the right of 11 Platoon's previous position. While it had been one thing to decline to immediately follow Buick and the others, things have become grimmer.

With no more than four or five rounds left, they are either taking their chances by making a run for it or they will have no chance at all.

Everyone got it?

In the next tiny lull in the firing, Heslewood will shout 'Run!' and then we will *all* go.

Got it?

Got it.

'RUN!'[57]

And run they do, like mad things, stooped over to present a smaller target and zig-zagging between the trunks of the trees to give themselves added protection. They make it in a series of short bursts, until from behind, 'we heard the fire starting to build up just like a drum roll we'd go to ground again. We'd dive behind trees and try to get our breath back, and run again.'[58]

Proceeding for some 250 yards in that manner they inevitably become separated from each other and at one point Heslewood dives behind a tree to find a few others already there.

And now they are up and running once more, when through rain that is just starting to lose its intensity at the right time, allowing them to see further than 30 metres, they see it.

It is billowing plumes of yellow smoke.

And yes, the equally confused enemy are firing at those plumes – or at the very least they come complete with a hail of bullets whacking into the rubber trees – but that is too damn bad. Compared to where they have just come from, and the intensity of the fire there, this fire is like a bad plague of mosquitos.

And now they hear shouting!

In *English*.

'Over here!'

'Come on, you bastards!'

(*Australian* English!)

'Youse gotta keep coming!'

It *is* our blokes!

Still taking shelter behind their fallen rubber tree, Allen May and Dougie Fabian also hear all the shouting and risk a quick look when they see yellow smoke too.

That *must* be our mob!

May looks at his mate Doug and says, 'What do you reckon?'

'Well let's go,' says Fabian, 'because it's no good staying here.'[59]

He's right.

Ready?

Go!

With May supporting the wounded Fabian, the two of them break cover and head as fast as they can towards the yellow smoke.

The danger now is that they will be mistaken for Viet Cong, and they shout out accordingly.

'Don't shoot!'

'It's us!'

'Aussies coming through!'

The instant that Sabben's men of 12 Platoon have affirmed that it is the desperate Diggers of 11 Platoon running towards them from the east, they lay down heavy fire to their right and left, to make Charlie keep his bloody head down. After five or six soldiers come through – 'completely drained, stumbling like zombies, but still carrying their rifles'[60] – Sabben sees Sergeant Bob Buick himself making his way through the small gap in the line either side of which Sabben's soldiers are on their bellies firing out at the VC. Another five or six follow him fairly tightly behind.

Buick is the one Sabben has been waiting for.

'Are there any more to come?'

'No. We are all that is left.'[61]

Sabben makes an immediate radio call to Smith: 'Sunray. I have callsign Four Two. Twelve or fifteen. Treating wounded and then return ASAP.'[62]

For the survivors of 11 Platoon the sheer relief to have got out of that hell-hole is near overwhelming. No, it's not that they are safe, but they are certainly *safer* – no longer totally isolated, and not under nearly as heavy fire as they had been.

They are led back to a spot just behind the 12 Platoon front line, where they are able to get some cover behind some fallen trees where things can start to be sorted.

For John Robbins, it is a chance to get some medical attention for his arm, and the 12 Platoon medic, 'Doc' Davis – who has already been busy with five wounded soldiers in his own unit – is soon wrapping the wound in bandages. 'Can you give me some morphine?' the groaning Robbins asks.

'I haven't got any,' Davis replies, as he continues to tightly wrap the bandages to stem the bleeding . . . before the medic himself suddenly slumps.

Cue Rudyard Kipling in 'Gunga Din': '. . . *when a bullet came, and drilled the beggar clean.*'

'Get me some morphine,'[63] Davis groans, in serious pain from his own bullet wound.

'No, stuff you,' Robbins replies, 'you didn't have any for me.'[64]

The only upside is that it has clearly been a tracer bullet, which you can tell by the relative lack of bleeding, as the burning phosphorus lightly cauterises the wound as it passes through.

Continuing the war effort, Sergeant Buick goes to Paul Large from Coolah, lying down behind a rubber tree trying to clear the mud from his jammed Armalite rifle. Buick has a go and is no more successful. As the VC bullets around them start to get ever thicker and it becomes more urgent to return fire in kind, Buick at least salvages Large's ammo for his own weapon. Large retrieves the gun of a wounded soldier and carries on, as unfussed as ever – which is remarkable, given how furious the fire is upon them.

And now the worst happens!

Largey cries out.

'My smokes are wet!'[65]

While the cigarette crisis is being absorbed, Dave Sabben sets his mind once more on his 'appreciations'. Detach and assess; be clinical, run it through . . .

What's changed?

Friendly Forces: 11 Platoon survivors now at my location.

Enemy Forces: still too bloody many.

Mission: first part of mission complete.

Next move: disengage and return to DHQ.

Ahhh . . . but not so simple . . .

CHAPTER TWELVE

FLOATING TARGETS

A helicopter is 10,000 parts flying in close formation around an oil leak.

Old RAAF saying

Nudging 1800 hours, 18 August 1966, Nui Dat, Huey, Bluey and do we?

Good luck, and may God be with you. In a minute, we will stop the artillery to give you clear air.

Even as the engines start to roar and the rotors to turn, one of his crew in the back, Leading Aircraftman Dave 'Bluey' Collins, looks through the open hatch to see one of the Delta Company cooks – Corporal Cliff Marchant – still dressed in his olive-green t-shirt, and checked black-and-white pants – holding a rifle.

'What do you want?'

'I'm coming too,' Marchant says.

'What do you mean, "*I'm* coming too"?'

'They're my *mates*,' Marchant says. 'And they need help.'

'But we're not actually landing.'

'You can drop me.'

'Listen, if we took you, we'd have to let off 200 pounds of ammo. The ammo is more important right now.'[1]

Reluctantly Marchant stands down. Collins waits for the final word to go.

Now, in the highlands of New Guinea the locals even call choppers, 'Mixmaster, him come from Jesus.'

But, now, where is Jesus when you need him?

For, Jesus Christ, this is not easy!

When the radio crackles with the order relayed from the Fire Control Centre, 'The artillery is stopped. Go!' it is no simple matter.

Frank Riley and Cliff Dohle pull up on their collectives and ease forward with their cyclics – 'chopper joy-sticks' – only to find that, so heavily laden are their fragile beasts, they must be very careful not to over-pitch and lose revolutions before they achieve movement forward. Though both choppers do get into the air, only a short time after take-off in the enveloping darkness, in the howling rain storm with no signal lights, they lose sight of each other. Given that they are heading to the same place the obvious risk is that they will crash into each other.

Frank Riley might have done tougher missions, but he can't remember when. And even though their load is a lot less than the other chopper it is already clear that it will be out of the question to get up to the planned 2000 feet altitude. They will have to go in a lot lower than that. As to the other chopper, going in at treetop level is the only choice they have, because it is a flat-out miracle they have got off the ground at all.

Between them and their target, somewhere over there in the murk, lies a full-blown monsoonal storm, as dark as a rat's arsehole in a coal-mine at midnight – albeit with regular crashing flashes of thunder and lightning. Seriously, these clouds are not just dark, they are jet-black. And the lightning is not the occasional flicker, it is constant.

The whole menacing maelstrom is coming their way, and they are heading straight into it. They are buffeted by the wind and rain – and the rotors are struggling as they try to cope all at once with the weather and the load – *everything* on this machine is vibrating, including pilots and crew. There is a real danger that, with all the strain, the overworked engines will fail to hold height, at which point their only hope would be to somehow survive a crash landing. Under such circumstances, all Frank can do is gently push forward on the joy-stick between his legs and head east at a speed of no more than 20 knots. They are soon right in the intensity of the monsoonal storm, which cuts visibility all around them down to next to nothing. And yes, the windscreen wipers are going nineteen to the dozen, but even at nineteen thousand to the dozen, it would make no difference. For the problem is not the water on the Perspex – it is heavy rain beyond it, which means looking straight ahead they are flying blind.

But, as Grandin knows, even in the heaviest rain, visibility straight down is always much better, and through the windows of the canopy that lie beneath his feet, he can see features on the ground – helped by the regular flashes of lightning. This is the way to keep on track. For you see, right there is the elephant grass, the abandoned rice paddies, the Suoi Da Bang stream, the low scrub. Grandin is able to guide Frank Riley and things seem to be going well, until . . .

. . .

Christ!

. . .

'There's the bend in the road at Long Tan!' he yells to Riley over the roar of the engines. 'We're behind enemy lines. Turn back west . . . quick! QUICK!'[2]

With a kick of the tail rotor pedal and a pull on the joy-stick, their chopper rotates through 180 degrees, but have they been quick enough?

Taking off, Grandin had been merely scared. Right now he is terrified, all but certain that he is just minutes, at most, from his life ending.

Actually no. More like seconds . . .

'Did you hear that?' comes a voice from behind.

Yes. Yes, Bob Grandin did. It was a bullet whistling past, just missing the chopper's skin.

Jesus, that was close!

Just one bullet in the engine, or the rotors, or one of the many rods that come up from the engine console and control the angle of the rotors, which determines whether they go forward or back or sideways or hover or up or down, and they'd spin out of control, killing them all.

But they are away from the most obvious danger, and moving to the north, over Long Tan plantation. The besieged Delta Company is somewhere up ahead. Grandin is in radio contact, advising Delta HQ that they are close, and that they must throw out a smoke grenade.

The key is going to be to spot the smoke.

On the left side of the chopper, out of the open hatch, Bluey Collins grips his M60 machine gun on its stand, looking for the first sign of the enemy, while Leading Aircraftman George Stirling does the same out the right, the two men in the rear waiting for the moment to push the crates of ammunition out.

1802 hours, 18 August 1966, with 11 Platoon, sound of silence

For the huddled surviving troops of 11 Platoon, it is like someone has turned off a switch.

The endless roar of shells landing just in front of them stops. The guns fall silent.

1802 hours, 18 August 1966, with Delta Company HQ, chop-chop

The choppers are on their way, and should be above Delta HQ within minutes.

But where the fuck are they?

The smoke grenade had been thrown, but of the choppers, no sign!

But wait!

What is that now?

It starts as a distant drum-beat, getting ever close, and builds to that unmistakable staccato churning, loud enough to even be heard over the incessant blasts of the battle itself.

It's the sound of a chopper and it's getting close!

As the Hueys bear no lights – bar their red strobe lights on top, only visible to those in aircraft above them – and it is getting dark, the chopper is difficult to see immediately. But within a minute all eyes of Delta Company HQ not currently staring down the sights at the enemy briefly turn skywards to see through the shattered canopy of the rubber trees the unmistakable hulking silhouette of a chopper, some 200 yards to the west, and hovering high . . . *uncertainly*.

For as soon becomes apparent, those in the helicopter cannot see them!

•

Where the fuck are they?

Up in the lead chopper, the pilots and crew strain their eyes, looking for a sign of where Delta Company HQ can be found. Yes, there is clearly a battle going on, as witness the criss-crossing of tracer bullets, glimpses of the awful aftermath of artillery cratered beneath them, but to narrow their position down to the precise point they will need before dropping their load right now looks to be impossible.

Bob Grandin's heart sinks, even as he makes a conscious effort to suck himself into his armoured-plated seat so that his penis and testicles are not exposed, on the reckoning that might give them a tiny bit more protection against the bullets that are surely about to come crashing into their chopper from below once they properly descend.

He had always *known* this was going to be a dangerous mission – and had bloody well *told* Frank it would be like this! – but, fair dinkum, this is just ridiculous. They are a slow-moving target, visible to VC surely, a giant whirling bird, slow and exposed. Exposed! They make Lady Godiva look modest. They aren't tempting fate, they are *taunting* it.

For his part, Flight Lieutenant Frank Riley barely blinks. He is a picture of concentration, focusing every fibre of his being on trying to find them.

Their one hope is that, somewhere below, Delta Company HQ will see them and follow through on the promised plan, smoke grenades.

'Nine-four, throw smoke,' Grandin radios.

'Roger. Smoke thrown,' comes the crackling reply, from a Delta Company just holding on as the enemy masses to attack once more, now that the Nui Dat artillery is no longer tearing them apart.

•

And now it is those at Delta Company HQ who are confused, as the choppers have gone right over them, despite them having thrown red smoke grenades.

Lance Corporal Graham Smith, the Delta Company HQ signaller, barks into the radio: 'Smoke thrown. Over.'[3]

It is Flight Lieutenant Bob Grandin in the lead chopper who replies: 'Roger that. I see orange smoke.'[4]

Smith can't believe it, and immediately barks back.

'No! No! Wrong! Wrong!'[5]

Look for bloody *red* smoke! That is *us*!

Frank Riley wheels around again, his eyes scanning for some sign of where the besieged Delta Company is.

Harry Smith has the red smoke grenades thrown again.

•

Pushing his joy-stick over, Frank Riley is able to bank the chopper and wheel it to the south, before returning to give it another go. Barely daring to breathe, Bob Grandin is convinced that they must shortly be hit by a furious fusillade of bullets from the VC. Still, Frank brings her back in for another go, until they are approximately over the mark.

'Nine-four, throw smoke,' Grandin radios again.

'Smoke thrown.'

'I see red!'

Gold. Gold. Gold.

Flight Lieutenants Riley and Grandin see it first.

Initially it is just a wisp of red against the billowing green, but now it looks like torn crimson ribbons stretching up and over the canopy.

They head back west to guide the others to the spot.

As planned, Riley and Grandin strain for every foot of altitude they can get – about 1000 feet – so they can guide Cliffy Dohle and Bruce Lane's chopper through this downpour, calling out instructions as they go. The key is to get the second Huey in and out in a flash, even as Hughie himself sends 'er down so fast and thick the chopper blades are like giant windscreen wipers, beating a momentary clearing in the sky.

'Albatross two, come forward!' Bob Grandin calls over the radio.

And Cliffy no doubt has done exactly that, they just can't see him in the murk. Well, Bob and Frank found their way here via red smoke, so maybe a little more red might do the trick?

'Turn on your anti-collision light,' says Frank Riley.

And there it is! Down below they can now clearly see a rotating little red light coming from the top of the chopper, but invisible to the VC below! Bloody hell, Cliffy's right there!

Bring him in!

'Maintain heading.'

'A little to your right . . .'

(It is amazing how many thoughts can race through your mind in a few seconds, but one keeps revolving in Bob Grandin's head. They are carrying a huge amount of ammo, right? And they are currently circling within easy range of any VC rifle, right? So, if one well-placed bullet goes into the chopper and hits the huge amount of ammo, aren't they really a huge flying bomb? Round and round it goes: what the hell are they doing here? They have to be here or the men on the ground are as good as dead. But if one bullet from one of the enemy hits the right spot then . . . *What the hell are we doing here?*)

Frank continues giving Cliffy directions.

'Turn left . . . roll out now . . .' he intones. 'Coming up . . . overtop . . . drop now.'[6]

'Can you see it?'

'We can see it!'[7]

'Nine-four, prepare for first drop,'[8] Grandin yells into his comms.

•

Just below, Delta Company HQ is suddenly engulfed by the massive backwash of air as the chopper's rotors blow off hats and knock over the remnants of rubber trees.

Everyone stand clear!

In the moment, Frank Riley calls: 'Roll *now*!'[9] and watches as Dohle's chopper rolls on its side like a well-trained pooch, giving the chopper the sloping floor they need. In Dohle's chopper, those in the back don't have to bend their backs and heeaaavvve, as the angle and gravity does the work for them and a swift kick of a boot does the trick as the ammo boxes fall out the side, joining the rain itself in a downpour of destruction. Done! And in a moment – pulling off what the pilots refer to as a 'split arse turn', yanking the joy-stick to the right even as he kicks the pedal, to rotate the chopper 180 degrees under the rotor – Cliffy's chopper has vanished west into the rain.

Frank Riley dives from on high towards the spot Cliff just left, they roll onto their side, and crewmen 'Bluey' Collins and George Stirling, together with the two 6RAR men, George Chinn and Owen O'Brien, start furiously kicking their own boxes to get them tumbling out the open door . . . tip, kick, the ammo falls out; as if it is one motion; as though it were careful choreography not chaotic combat.

And DROP . . . And DROP . . . And DROP . . .

The boxes vanish into the canopy as the chopper – released from the terrible weight – surges upwards. Frank flicks the joy-stick to take them west to Nui Dat, even as they hear the three sweet words through the crackling radio: 'Beauty! Right on!'[10]

Riley grins and replies, 'All part of the service!'[11] It is not quite that they are home and hosed, but they are certainly wet all right. All they have to do now is get through this storm – the nearly overpowering rain from above, the fire from below and the pounding in their chests – high-tail it back to base without getting shot down, and then fill out the forms to apply to the Vatican to have it declared an official miracle.

•

Back in the iconic battle of the Kokoda Track in 1942 in New Guinea, an Australian Sergeant had survived six months of the campaign against all odds, ambushes and bayonet charges, only to be killed by a box of biscuits dropped by an American supply plane.

And on this day, CSM Jack Kirby has very nearly shared his fate, as it is a *bloody* miracle that he hasn't been killed.

A large target at the best of times, the first of the ammunition boxes tumbling from the heavens has missed him by inches.

WHUMP! WHUMP! WHUMP!

Unflappable as ever, he reaches forward and starts to unpack the box even as those near him allow themselves a second of shock. There is close, and there is *close*, and then there is *FUCKING CLOSE!*

Ol' Jack barely blinks. When good soldiers are taking bullets in the head, it would be indecent to even remark on being narrowly missed by a mere tumbling box.

Besides, Jack's safety is neither here nor there, and in this game near-misses go with the territory.

And now the choppers are gone, rattling away back to Nui Dat as many eager hands reach for the ammo boxes. The blankets can go straight to the aid post to wrap the wounded in, while we open the boxes . . .

What?

The stupid bastards have left some of the boxes wrapped in their usual steel band, which in normal circumstances requires a jemmy to open. Never mind, entrenching tools and bayonets quickly break the band, and the boxes, open.

What now?

While there are many machine-gun belts ready to go, all the rest of the SLR ammunition is in five-round clips, two clips per pocket in cloth bandoliers, as opposed to magazines, which will mean rather laborious manual loading of those magazines. Not only that, but the Australian SLRs do not host a *slick-clip* function, whereby a clip of five rounds can be easily slotted into place by merely pressing down on the top round. Instead, each clip has to be unloaded from the clip and inserted one by one into the magazine. But beggars can't be choosers; if looters want to be shooters, they have to make do!

And at least the bandoliers are easy to carry and distribute. It is Jack Kirby himself who quickly slings as many bandoliers as he can carry around his shoulders and starts to move around the perimeter, distributing them.

Those with machine guns are quickly back in action again. Those with rifles quickly take the bullets from the bandolier and shove them into their magazines, before slotting the magazines back into their weapons once more!

1805 hours, 18 August 1966, Long Tan plantation, with 12 Platoon

The rain is falling so thick and so fast that it feels like water bullets coming down vertically, the same way real bullets are coming horizontally. Dave Sabben glances around at what remains of the men he has inherited. They don't have time to be scared, they are too busy being terrified. They have so much adrenalin pumping through them that to be trapped and stationary is its own form of torture. The sounds of fire from friend and foe surround them, with those bugles, those bloody bugles, caterwauling through the cacophony. The eye of the hurricane might be calm but there is no peace in the storm of Long Tan.

In the tragic absence of Gordon Sharp, Lieutenant Sabben takes charge of both his own 12 Platoon and the survivors of 11 Platoon. The most urgent thing now is to get the wounded of both platoons – if not to safety, at least as close as they can manage – back to Delta Company HQ, where they will get better care.

Lieutenant Sabben is not sure how long they can hold on, or if it is even possible.

All around now, bullets are barking through the trees, *through* them, shattering and spattering their trunks, slipping, ripping through the plantation and blasting all into sundry. Such foliage as is left looks like a jigsaw puzzle with half the pieces missing, as if a shotgun blast has gone right through it.

Private Alan 'Blue' Parr yells to Lieutenant Sabben, 'I can see more Charlie approaching!'

'How many?'

'More than you can throw a stick at!'

'Keep firing . . .'[12]

Major Harry Smith and Captain Morrie Stanley continue to call on the Fire Control Centre for more artillery on the enemy now swarming around Sabben and his men on three sides.

Now, Lieutenant Sabben, it is *imperative* that 12 Platoon and the survivors of 11 Platoon get back to Delta Company HQ so we can make one united stand.

It is while Sabben is making his appreciation on how best to do exactly that – even as bullets continue to spurt all around – that Corporal Drinkwater asks *the* question.

'Skipper. Do you think we're going to get out of this?'

Sabben takes pause.

All of his training has steered him to look at things in sober fashion. What are the facts? Make your decisions accordingly.

So what are the facts here? They have now been under heavy attack for over two hours, and rather than the intensity falling away, it is only increasing. They have asked for reinforcements and received none. They have asked for air-strikes and got nothing. They have already lost a third of their platoon as casualties.

There is no sign of the APCs they have called for, and the longer they wait without support the more men they lose. And so he gives his answer without fear or favour, for there is no point in not being honest, the fact that his mother had promised him that God would look after him, notwithstanding.

'Look, no, I don't think so.'[13]

But, by God, they can at least fight to the last and defend to the death.

Drinkwater feels the cold grip of fear tighten around his heart.

Is he now in the last minutes of his life?

Behind them, the process of triage goes on, working out who can fight and who needs to be evacuated immediately.

Those that need first aid are given it – just enough to stop the gushing blood – and then, after swapping magazines so that the men of 11 Platoon are at least armed and dangerous once more, all are told to take up a place on the perimeter.

•

As fellow Sergeants there has always been a strong connection between Paddy Todd and Bob Buick, even though they are entirely different characters. On this occasion, one look at Buick's haunted eyes, and Todd offers him a rollie cigarette. Buick accepts gratefully and with expert ease the two manage to bend their bodies over in such a fashion that, despite the pouring rain, they can roll dry cigarettes and then suck back on them using the lip of their floppy hats to keep them dry.

It is at this very moment that – after a terrifying whistle that they just know is going to be close – a mortar round buries itself deep in the mud between Todd's feet and explodes, sending into his ankles tiny pieces of wire shrapnel. (A peculiarity of this particular enemy mortar round – a 61 millimetre – is that the explosive is wrapped in serrated wire, which upon detonation disintegrates into thousands of red hot bits of agony.) For Todd, it feels like someone has whacked him hard with a cricket bat over the back of both heels.

Another, larger, bit of shrapnel from the same mortar badly wounds the 12 Platoon medic Doc Davis, in the shoulder.

Todd waves proffered help away. He is fine, he feels.

And after all, after quickly inspecting Paddy's boots, Buick can't even find a single rip or hole in them. 'Nothing, Paddy. You're bludging, you bastard.'[14]

However, Todd's wounds are far more severe than he has realised – the blood has not yet made it through the red mud all over the boots – and it turns out that not only can he not run, he can't even walk. For, the first time he gets up, he simply falls over. Trying a second time, the same thing happens.

What to do? The obvious thing would be to get someone to help him.

But the Australian Army has a noble tradition in such matters. Back in the Kokoda Track campaign, a wounded Digger, Corporal Metson, had crawled the length of the track to get back rather than take a stretcher from mates who he felt needed it more. Following the same principle, Todd decides to do the same thing. Rather than take an able-bodied soldier away from the fluid front line, Todd sets off very quietly on his own, head down, bum up, hands and knees in the mud, leaving a trail of blood from his ankles indistinguishable from the red mud of the plantation floor. He's going to crawl to Delta HQ or die trying . . .

Behind him, Sabben is starting to get 11 Platoon organised. Yes, they are shattered with shock and exhaustion – and some of them are almost 'zombie-like' – but they can still function. And Sabben has a job for them. He has seven men Wounded In Action, who need help to get back and . . .

And hang on, where is Sergeant Paddy Todd?

Paddy is nowhere to be seen, and there is no time to find him.

Appreciation. Appreciation. Appreciation.

What is the situation. What has changed? What needs to be done now?

Paddy Todd is missing. The Sergeant the government had issued him with is nowhere to be found! He must adapt.

'Sergeant Buick,' Sabben takes action. 'You're my Acting Platoon Sergeant. I want you to get all your 11 Platoon soldiers to take my wounded soldiers back to DHQ. One man for each wounded. We don't have ammunition to give you, because we can't afford it. 200 yards. That way . . .'[15]

For the moment Sabben and his remaining 14 soldiers of 12 Platoon will stay here to protect their rear and allow them time to get back.

Buick barks orders of his own, and after personally putting the worst man hit, Doc Davis, in the care of one of his most reliable soldiers, they are sent on their way while Buick himself turns back to help Lieutenant Sabben.

1810 hours, 18 August 1966, Suoi Da Bang stream, don't pay the ferryman

Lieutenant Roberts leads his convoy on the buffalo track. As it crosses the part of the Suoi Da Bang he has chosen, he catches sight of the stream and his heart sinks. The last time he had crossed here with his APC was when he'd accompanied the Americans as they cleared out Long Phuoc, back in June, but they'd crossed *before* the monsoonal downpour of the afternoon.

Now it is a raging torrent, courtesy of the fact that on this day the monsoonal rains have fallen more heavily than in the whole time the Australians have been here. Yes, 3 Troop has trained to cross water obstacles, but only in training, and with still water. This water is *not* still, it is flowing faster than six knots, which is still not quite as many knots as each APC commander has in his stomach as he contemplates what is demanded of him. APCs 'float' in theory and in practice; but when they practised it was not with 15 heavily armed soldiers crammed on board and a hulk of ammunition. As they weigh the situation,

Major Harry Smith's voice comes crackling out a command net report: 'My Company is now concentrated but one platoon is almost completely destroyed, the other two only 75% effective and the enemy appear to be reorganising for a final assault.'[16]

Right. That's it.

'Get your troop across the bloody river!'[17] Mollison tells Roberts.

Now why didn't Roberts think of that?

Either way, in short order Roberts's APC is indeed rolling, into the river first, both to see if it is possible and to secure the other side against ambush, which has to be a big possibility as at this point the APC troop will be at its most vulnerable.

Inside, Mollison turns to his own huddled men: 'If the water starts to pour in the top hatch . . .'

Yes, sir?

'Take a deep breath.'

Excellent advice.

Oh . . .

'And don't crowd the opening.'[18]

No, sir.

They will try to float in a spacious fashion, and not crowd the single exit from their submerged death trap if it comes to that. Deeper and deeper they head into the river and . . . it *floats*! The APC floats! But only just. Mollison can see they have just millimetres of freeboard, it is so bloody close that a few more raindrops could make the difference. *Don't sweat, boys, you're only adding to the problem!*

What they don't really do – because the 'pivot steering system' in each carrier is worn out – is allow themselves to be guided in the water. Roberts's APC, in the lead, is 'swept downstream, twisting and turning in the swirling muddy water'.[19] The 'driver' has about as much control as a leaf in a gutter, but they glide and slide through the water, judder and shudder, continually bumping heavily against the dam wall as they swirl across in circles, smashing into the other side and making their way up the mud. There. Was that so hard? The other APCs will follow one at a time; if any two are in the water at the same time it will be a smash for sure. Come on now, once begun it must be done! The next APC trundles forward into the gush of water, and the rush of risk begins again.

•

Paddy Todd keeps crawling, lost in the mist, the smoke, the trees and the now enveloping darkness, and with only a rough idea of where Delta HQ lies. Could anything make his situation more miserable?

Right on cue, the intense rain returns, even more thunderously than before, rain heavier than any rain he's ever seen in his life – a life that has included a couple of tours in Borneo and Malaya. Paddy spots the hut and turns right. Now for the final stretch . . .

•

It's time.

'Sergeant,' Sabben orders Buick. 'Get these men back to DHQ . . .'[20]

But wait!

GET DOWN!

Sabben and his men suddenly see a force of about 150 soldiers – almost certainly the enemy – to their south, near the planters' hut. These soldiers are serious, all of them bristling with weaponry. VC? Yes, almost certainly, though at this distance you couldn't quite put the sheep station on it. But they're not coming for Sabben and his men, they are starting to head north down the avenue of trees towards where Delta Company HQ is situated.

They are in assault formation, and clearly about to launch an attack.

Sabben realises they will have just one opportunity to stop them, or at least do them serious damage. In the direction they are heading, in about 90 seconds they will be exposed down an oblique angle through the rubber trees about three rows away.

Sabben hisses orders at his two machine-gunners to set up on adjoining avenues, and point their machine guns straight down the line, while the rest of them position themselves in support.

'Only fire, if they are positively identified as Viet Cong,' he breathes.[21]

Even now, there is a thought that Bravo Company must be getting close, and they have to make absolutely sure that this is not them, or that the Australians don't wander into frame just as the machine-gunner, Chico Miller, pulls the trigger. This mob is not moving in any recognisable Australian patrol formation so it really is all but certain they are VC, but they cannot take chances.

Chico nods, sets up his gun and belt, and looks down the sights. Sabben stays with him as the enemy soldiers get closer, their eyes straining. And here they are!

'We recognised the curved AK-47 magazines on their rifles,' Sabben will recount, 'and the round drum magazines on their machine guns.'[22]

Of course they are VC, unless they are NVA, a battalion attached to the VC in April of . . . look, all that counts is they are *not* Australians or Yanks or Kiwis!

Still, Sabben waits just an instant longer.

As they are moving in three ranks, they let the first rank go through, and wait till the second and third ranks are fully in the frame of the Australian firepower.

Now, and only now, does Sabben give the order: 'Fire!'[23]

On the instant there is an explosive chattering, with cartridges spraying from the machine guns.

'Well,' Sabben will recount, 'you have to see the decimation that a machine gun can make at forty yards on a line of infantry soldiers. It was almost total. They almost all went down. The front rank took fright, turned around and ran through the fire of the other two machine guns. So out of that group, which was probably sixty or seventy, not many of them would have ever walked again.'[24]

The job is done. It is time to withdraw.

Sabben gives the order, and they move as quickly as they can back towards Delta Company HQ.

Behind them, one of their number remains . . .

1815 hours, 18 August 1966, Long Tan plantation, near the tapper's hut, feeling low

There is low, there is very low, there is lower than a snake's belly-button, and there is lower than shark-shit. And then there is how low Sergeant Paddy Todd gets, sucking the ground, as he finds himself caught in over-fire from his mates of 12 Platoon and presumably enemy soldiers as heavy machine-gun fire streams just inches over his head.

Lower, lower, get lower still.

He *presses* himself into the ground like a Cro-Magnon man who has not yet managed to emerge from the primeval slime. Only once it is over does he start to move again, painfully dragging himself forward through the drenching rain and sucking mud, still hopeful of getting back to the last known position of Delta Company.

1817 hours, 18 August 1966, Delta Company HQ, hanging on

Shattered with exhaustion and shock, but still – needs must – functioning well, Lieutenant Kendall is advised to expect the survivors of 11 Platoon and 12 Platoon to return to Delta HQ through 10 Platoon's perimeter, and Kendall so forewarns his men. The important thing is both to prepare for any more assaults that are coming, and to keep the passage clear so Delta Company can come completely together and make a strong and united stand – hopefully surviving long enough for the base to get help to them.

They don't have to look far to see where the danger lies.

'There were significant groups of enemy moving across the front of my left-hand section to the north,' Kendall will recall, 'and they were moving roughly in a south to north direction.'[25]

As they are well over 200 yards away, and you can only catch glimpses of them through the rubber trees when the rain clears, it is not easy knocking them over but the Australians do their best, at least making an impact on one group that stays still in an exposed spot for just long enough to be effectively fired upon. But careful now. As ammunition is getting so low, it is more important than ever to make every shot count and Kendall tells his men to only pull the trigger from now on if it is a sure shot.

And now look!

Just out of range they can see groups of the enemy, 60 or so at a time, seeming to be circling to come at their perimeter from the south. There is a strong sense of a major attack building, possibly coming at them from all sides.

'Bushy' Forsyth has one VC in his sights, bold as brass this bastard is, sauntering straight for them, with not even his rifle raised, he's . . .

Under the circumstances it is a lucky thing that the survivors of 11 Platoon aren't shot by their own men. For even as 10 Platoon ready for the attack they know is coming they can see the first soldiers of 11 Platoon heading towards them, and unbelievably shattered.

Soaked and cloaked in rain, they only become discernible as men and mates within metres; and they are so . . . few, and few of them walk alone; the wounded, with huge bloody patches over their torsos and limbs, are being supported by stronger mates.

As they get closer, Kendall can recognise individuals. Bringing up the rear is a muddy, bloody John Robbins, Ron Eglinton, John Heslewood, Allen May and Barry Magnussen, all of them with hollow eyes.

But several 11 Platoon men are missing, and one in particular.

There is little time for reflection now, though. The way things are heading, there is every chance a lot of them will be dead shortly, unless they can fight to prevent it.

And now here is Sergeant Buick coming in, with 12 Platoon's Wounded In Action group. They are in much better shape, and glad to have made it back to the rest of them. And yet they, too, are missing members.

'Where's Sharpie?' Geoff Kendall asks Buick, who is too exhausted to break the news gently.

'He's been dead for a long time,'[26] the Sergeant says as he passes.

Kendall reels, even as the walking wounded continue to stagger past him. Gordon? *Dead?*

It scarcely seems possible. The bloke had so much *life* to him! DEAD?

And where the hell is Sergeant Paddy Todd?

No-one knows.

•

Lying in the Company Aid Post with the shrapnel wounds he'd suffered trying to take the radio forward to 10 Platoon, Lance Corporal Dennis Spencer perks up a little to see the first of the survivors of 11 Platoon coming in, the bloodied John Robbins being helped in by John Heslewood. Yes, they're bloodied, but they're alive! As one who had been with 11 Platoon himself for 12 months, right up to the last two weeks when he'd been transferred to Delta Company HQ, Spencer knows these blokes well.

But hang on, Robbo, where are the rest of the blokes?

'They are dead,' Robbo replies quietly, holding his shattered elbow, as the pulsing blood keeps coming through his fingers.

Surely not! Such a truth cannot be accepted and each missing mate is asked after.

'Where's Kenny Gant?'

'Dead.'

'Where is Glenn Drabble?'

'Dead.'

'They're gone mate, that's it.'[27]

Gone. When and how are details that can be discovered later, if any dare to ask and any care to answer. But at least Ronnie Eglinton is alive!

Spencer and Eglinton are good mates, so it is a relief to see him, and Eggo has come to the aid post looking to borrow a weapon from one of the wounded blokes as he, like most of the survivors of 11 Platoon, had lost his weapon in the mad scramble to get back. Grabbing one from a Digger who looks like he is not long for this world, Eglinton heads off and Robbins gets a weapon of his own and follows him, taking up positions on the western side of the perimeter. Not long after they get there, they look out to see a large group of VC moving towards them, clearly looking to completely surround them and get between Delta Company and the base.

Robbo looks at Ronnie and says quietly, 'I think we've had it.'[28]

Ronnie looks back and silently nods.

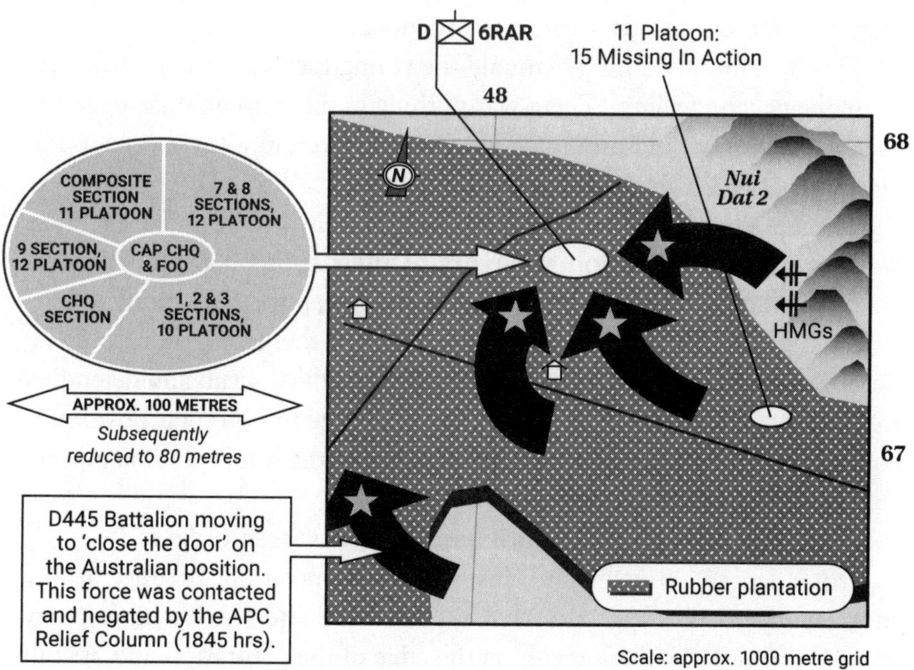

D Company disposition in the final stages of the battle, 1830–1900 hrs, 18 August 1966

As best they can, they take shots at Charlie through the haze, not knowing if their bullets are causing their enemy to die or just delay. The enemy advance continues.

Things continue grim, and getting grimmer.

For his part, 12 Platoon's Lieutenant Dave Sabben seeks out Major Harry Smith to give his quick reports – it's not bad, it's worse, there's a lot of them out there, and a lot more coming.

Major Smith, as is his wont, wastes no energy on expressing his relief that Sabben and his men have managed to get back with the survivors of 11 Platoon but simply snaps out his next orders.

'I want you to take up the perimeter from 12 o'clock to three o'clock,' he rasps. '10 Platoon will take from three o'clock until seven o'clock. We've already got people facing nine o'clock, and we'll put the survivors of 11 Platoon, facing 10 or 11, because we've seen no enemy on that part of the perimeter and will form a defensive perimeter.'[29]

Sabben, just 21 years old, nods and heads off, entrusted with the life-and-death decisions of precisely where to place his men.

For him and his men right now the most profound feeling, beyond fear, is *shock* and a certain stunned surprise.

'This isn't in the training manual,' the young Lieutenant would characterise the general feeling. 'There was nothing in the training that suggested that the enemy would attack us in *any* form even in a tiny contact and yet there's *hundreds* of the buggers out there . . .'[30]

Helping out with the placement, Sergeant Major Jack Kirby takes Buick and the 11 Platoon survivors to their spot on the north-west corner of the perimeter and tells them: 'Just keep the back door safe.'[31]

Once positioned he returns to place two of the 12 Platoon soldiers, Terry Burstall and Shorty Brown, right opposite thick scrub and defending the aid post which lies directly behind them. The fire on their position is so heavy both men crawl to nearby puddles in the hope of some protection only to find them shallow as birdbaths.

When Jack Kirby returns with ammo, he has fresh orders.

'Don't worry about behind, just keep your position, because at any moment they will twig how thin we are here and send a large party around through the thick scrub on the edge of the plantation and assault straight up the rise into your position.'[32]

And off he goes.

CHRIST ALMIGHTY.

If Burstall and Brown didn't have the wind up them before, they certainly do now as, with their eyes popping out, they stare into the scrub for the tiniest sign of movement.

Their eyes *ache* so fiercely do they stare, half-expecting an entire regiment of VC to come crawling forward. The most terrifying thing Burstall sees for the moment is 'a line of tracer slamming into the ground to my right and coming straight towards me. I put my hands over my head and I know I was gibbering something, and I could actually feel myself getting hit through the body, although I wasn't.'[33]

Sergeant Neil Rankin of 10 Platoon is experiencing much the same, as he holds the fort at three o'clock on the perimeter.

'The fire was cracking in the air over our heads, biting into the mud all round us and you'd hear the thud as bullets embedded in the rubber trees. I didn't know how it was going to end, but I knew it must end soon, one way or another, as neither side could keep up such a sustained effort for much longer. I thought either they'd over-run us because we would run out of ammo again or they'd have to withdraw because they were losing too many men; but the assaults seemed to keep coming.'[34]

To give himself strength, Rankin prays to God for help, and thinks of his cherished parents at home, realising there is very little chance he will ever see them again, that his death will break them . . . but he must at least go down fighting, and maybe, just maybe, he can come through this and get back to them.

Harley Webb, with 12 Platoon, takes a similar attitude. As one who had just arrived as a 'reo' for Delta Company that very morning, he is as terrified as he has ever been in his life, but still determined to go down fighting. Alas, as he rises just slightly, a single enemy bullet enters his right shoulder, smashes his collar bone and keeps going towards his heart . . .

Just 50 metres away at the time, Shorty Brown nudges Terry Burstall. Can you see it?

Burstall can see it.

There at the bottom of that slope is a writhing Digger, limbs flung back in terrible pain. Somebody should . . .

Terry now sees a mountain charging past him. It is of course Jack Kirby, running to the wounded man. Heroic, but mad. Kirby will be shot himself, any second.

The bullet that entered Webb's shoulder has stopped just half an inch from his heart. The 20-year-old Webb is alive, and conscious, but knows he has been badly – possibly mortally – wounded. Suddenly he is flying up to the heavens abo—

Oh.

Oh, it's not an angel picking him up, it's Delta Company's Sergeant Major carrying him 'over his shoulder like a bag of spuds'.[35]

Inspired by Kirby's staggering bravery – doing what has to be done to keep his men alive – Burstall finds himself running towards them to help, without thought of his own safety. But far from being grateful and greeted with a grin by Kirby, Terry is somewhat surprised to cop a gobful: What the BLOODY HELL do you think you're doing down here? Get the FUCK back to bloody position, you stupid bastard, and start using your bloody gun to kill the enemy instead of using what passes for your fucking brain, Burstall![36]

Well, excuse me. Then again, Sergeant Major Kirby does have a point. Burstall races back to a more sensible position and resumes firing.

Shorty Brown looks at Burstall and simply says, 'We aren't going to get out of this.'

'I know that,'[37] Burstall replies.

Pass the ammo.

It is a strange thing to be mortally certain that you have now entered the last hour of your life, that everything you have ever known is about to end. But what can they do?

They keep firing.

Still carrying the grievously wounded Harley Webb, Jack Kirby gets him back to the ditch doubling as the Company Aid Post and lays him down as gently as a baby. Not that it likely matters, particularly.

Delta Company medic Corporal Phil Dobson takes one look at him – massive hole in the shoulder, no exit wound, copious blood, shallow breathing and weak pulse – and before getting to work to try to stem the blood flow and give him some chance of living, says, 'This poor bastard's not going to make it.'[38]

He still does what he can to make him comfortable, and whatever else is quick in his response. Now Dobson is not a doctor, not even a nurse. But he has undergone weeks of training and lectures in how to give first aid and has taken the job seriously. It had been drilled into him from the first that, on the battlefield, the speed of the medics' reaction time might be the difference between life and death. If there is a heavy blood flow, get pressure on the wound. If there is the danger of infection, clean the wound as quickly as possible. If shrieking in agony, get morphine into them to calm them. If they are unconscious, pin their tongues to their bottom lips with a safety pin, so that if they have a fit they can't swallow their tongues and choke. He is busy doing all of the above on the unending stream of wounded soldiers that keep being placed in his ditch, of whom Harley Webb is just the latest, when he looks up.

Two soldiers have carried another soldier to him, one who is very badly wounded. They had found him just beyond the perimeter, and he had crawled back to them from 10 Platoon.

Dobson takes one look and blanches.

Never in his born days has he seen a wound like it. A piece of shrapnel has neatly slit this bloke from his right hip down to his ankle with such precision you'd swear it was done with a surgeon's scalpel. For the first time in his life the company medic can see a naked femur, kneecap and the curious dual bone structure of the lower legs. Trying to stay calm, Dobson cleans the wound as well as he can before tightly wrapping bandages around the entire leg. The key is to prevent him bleeding out and keeping him alive long enough that he can be evacuated to expert medical care.

He looks up again. Another soldier is being brought in. This one with a bullet through his abdomen. Put him over there.

Glancing over at Harley Webb, Dobson is surprised to see his chest all but imperceptibly rising and falling. He's alive. Just.

•

Alas, the more Paddy Todd crawls the clearer it is that he is not the only one trying to get to the D Company position, as he becomes aware that the mass of figures running past are enemy soldiers trying to get into position to launch an attack. In obvious danger himself should they stumble upon him, he takes shelter behind a fallen tree, which keeps him safe for the moment until two enemy come running right for him. With his SLR he fires two quick shots, killing both men. After a rest, he keeps crawling towards D Company, unsure how he will get through the enemy to his own people, but determined to try, while aware that his chances of getting out of this alive are slim and getting slimmer.

•

Never in the history of Nui Dat's 1ATF base has it been like this.

Now the *entire* RAAF No. 9 Squadron is gathered at Kangaroo Pad. The other six choppers had landed shortly after Frank Riley's and Cliff Dohle's choppers had returned from their successful mission against all odds – at which point the artillery had resumed – and all now await further instructions.

For the moment, there is nothing, just the continuous pounding of the artillery, leaving the pilots and their crews time to talk of the latest rumour. Charlie. He might be about to launch a surprise attack from the west. If that happens, one mortar or two into Kangaroo Pad and we would all go up in smoke, or we all might be required to become attack choppers and fire from on high. Right now, all they can do is wait. We know Delta Company have dead and wounded so at some point we will likely have to go in for a dustoff, evacuating casualties breathing and otherwise.

1825 hours, east side of the Suoi Da Bang, Major relief, APC ASAP

It has taken the APCs a good 20 minutes but now all of them are . . . safely across!

The most important thing now is to find out exactly where Delta Company is, and how they are faring – which is no easy task. Roberts's signaller, with the capacity to stay on just one frequency at any given time, must keep flicking between several nets to assess the situation, and it is only by happenstance he happens to be on the 6RAR Battalion net when the voice of Major Harry Smith comes through near and clear, if strained and drained: 'Unless we get relief quickly, we are going to be over-run!'[39]

Even with the ammunition that has been dropped by the choppers, their firing has been so heavy that they are starting to run low on that, too. If they don't get help soon, they are gone for all money.

Given that the APCs *are* the relief, it means that when a second transmission now comes through to Roberts's 3 Troop from 6RAR HQ – as the APC commander flicks back and forth between the 3 Troop net and the 6RAR Battalion net – that they *must* wait for Colonel Townsend to arrive in the delayed APCs, Lieutenant Roberts knows what he must do.

Ignore it.

'There's no use buggerising around,' he reasons.[40]

Delta Company is in real trouble. They need help.

And the APCs are meant to wait for Colonel Townsend to show up?

No.

Just . . . no.

They can court-martial me later if they have to. But this is a matter of life and death.

The flashes of artillery shells landing up ahead, followed by the low rumble of noise, are a fair clue as to which direction to head. Steer to the explosions, and the more your APC shudders with Mother Earth, the closer you are.

Looking ahead to where they can see a kind of throbbing orange glow where the shells are hitting the top of mature rubber trees and exploding in balls of fire, some of those atop the APC think it might be better inside after all – but Frank Alcorta and his mate Ronnie Brett stay put. Fuck it.

They don't want to miss out on any of the fun that awaits.

CHAPTER THIRTEEN

DELTA COMPANY'S LAST STAND

Sound trumpets! let our bloody colours wave!
And either victory, or else a grave.

William Shakespeare, *Henry VI, Part 3*

Well, I done a couple of laps around the rosary beads.[1]

Corporal Laurie Drinkwater, 12 Platoon

1820 hours, 18 August 1966, Nui Dat artillery compound, Pogo smoko

It is not exhaustion alone that is doing down the mighty artillery crews.

They can't breathe!

Every shell fired lets off toxic fumes as the cordite disperses, and under normal circumstances that smoke would be quickly dissipated in the open air. But not now. With most of the guns firing up to eight shells a minute, and the rain and lack of wind preventing dissipation, even as rain rises in hisses of steam off the smoking hot barrels, this is a fog of war that is starting to choke them. Still, they keep going, even as the artillery shells start to pile up all around the guns as – just like the toxic fumes – they are collecting more quickly than they can be dissipated. Still the Pogos go on, both carting the ammunition to the guns, and doing their best to clear the spent shells away.

All of them – gun crews, officers and Pogos – are aware just how desperate the situation is, and that right now it is only artillery that stands between Delta Company and oblivion.

1821 hours, 18 August 1966, Long Tan plantation, Delta Company HQ

Now what?

With the rain easing just a little, visibility suddenly improves to up to 300 yards, and now the Australians can see what appears to be an enormous assault line of VC soldiers forming up, and coming their way, coming at them on exactly the same line as 12 Platoon and the survivors of 11 Platoon had come in.

They're not, are they?

Going to charge?

They are! And it looks like there are *hundreds* of them. It is not just the mass of them straight in front that is alarming, it is how wide they are. Even as the Delta Company perimeter is swept by heavy machine-gun fire from the east and south-east, it is clear that the enemy intent goes far beyond firing on them. With no little urgency, Major Smith advises 1ATF HQ:

'Enemy could be reorganising to attack.'[2]

Clearly if enough of them get through, the frontal assault will quickly evolve into an assault from the flanks as well, and Delta Company would soon be completely surrounded. While the Diggers watch, mesmerised, holding their fire, the VC assault line advances at a slow walk to within 100 metres – with about eight metres between each soldier – at which point the Australians see the next horrifying thing.

It is *another* assault line right behind them, at a distance of about 60 metres!

How many of these bastards are there?

In the course of this battle the Australians' estimations of how many enemy soldiers they are up against has gone from a handful to a section, to a platoon, to a company to a battalion, if not a fucking *division*!

At least Captain Morrie Stanley, thankful for the reassuring guidance of his commanding officer, Major Harry Honnor, is doing his finest work and is now calling in heavy artillery on the reserve line, trying to make it curtains for them and putting a curtain of fire behind the first line and preventing whatever other reserves that Charlie has from coming forward.

And it is working.

'They were flattened like a pack of cards,' Geoff Kendall will chronicle, 'while the assault wave was still just a bit outside the area when we would start firing.'[3]

Another watching closely is Dave Sabben.

'Now the typical idea of artillery firing is a flash and bodies hurtling and so on, and that's what you get from the films, but reality isn't like that. There's a sudden impact where you see the whole environment just shudder, just vibrate and then everything is just steam and smoke and you don't see anything, and anything that might have been shattered has gone, and as the smoke and the steam dissipates you see the leaves just falling down or whatever else that was just falling down. Several times we saw the reserve lines simply wiped out, just simply eradicated. They're just there and then there was steam and smoke and then they weren't there . . .'[4]

As to the first assault line, they still keep getting closer and closer.

But the Diggers, as ordered, hold their fire. Yes, they could have knocked over a few of them as far away as 600 metres, and killed them as far away as 300 metres. But when the Australians are so few, and the VC so many, they must make sure that *every bullet* counts, and so they hold fire, even as the first line comes closer still.

Ninety metres, 80 metres, 70 metres, 60 metres, 50 metres and . . . FIRE!

No, the order to fire is not given, it is understood. Such is the roar of artillery shells exploding so close that no such order could have been heard in any case.

Beyond those falling over in the first line, the artillery is continuing to grimly reap a staggering toll on those in the lines behind.

The truly shocking thing though for the Diggers who manage to keep their own fire on the enemy to go with the shelling?

'We would knock them over,' Lieutenant Geoff Kendall would recount, 'and the ones that weren't hit would go to ground and lie among the dead. This was what caused most of my casualties at that stage, because those guys just lay there waiting for the next assault to come in. While they lay there they sniped at our guys as we were adjusting positions or shifting wounded around.'[5]

Those sniper shots are supported by two heavy machine guns positioned on high ground overlooking the perimeter. The flood of bullets coming the Diggers' way is designed to keep their heads down, and prevent them firing on the first assault line, but the men of the Southern Cross refuse to be bowed.

At one point when Private Rick Aldersea – a Regular Army soldier from Western Australia – tries to manoeuvre his machine gun into a better position, an enemy bullet kills him instantly, and when another soldier, Max Wales, moves forward to take over his gun, he, too, is killed.

Here and there, some enemy soldiers – with extraordinary bravery – manage to continue creeping forward, despite the heavy fire they're under. At one point, when Geoff Kendall hears a furious burst of fire being unleashed on the other side of the rubber tree to him, he looks and sees reserve signaller Yank Akell, still with his trusty Owen gun.

'Got that bastard, Sir,' Akell reports.[6]

Sure enough, just in front of the two of them, no more than three metres away is a dead VC soldier, shot straight through the top of the head.

And at least the Owen is working!

The one thing that doesn't change is the omnipresence of Company Sergeant Major Jack Kirby who keeps moving around, grabbing the wounded, handing out ammunition, and yelling encouragement, 'Keep it up!' . . . 'You're doing great!'[7]

Which they are.

And yet the incontrovertible calculus of catastrophe says that no matter how well the soldiers are doing, and how devastating the artillery fire, the enemy are so many and the soldiers so few, that the enemy forces keep on getting ever closer!

Nevertheless there are brief lulls in the fire and in one of them Dave Sabben snakes his way over to Harry Smith.

Yes, Dave?

'We're okay. No VC seen coming in from left of one o'clock.'

Harry Smith nods, pleased, and then asks Dave a leading question.

'Do you know about the Vickers machine gun?'

Of course he does. The Vickers is a water-cooled, belt-fed machine gun capable of firing l-o-n-g continuous bursts of fire without overheating, unlike the M60s! Dave Sabben had trained with them ever since the days of being a cadet!

'Yes!' he replies.

Harry smiles. 'What we could do with a couple of Vickers right now!'[8]

Thanks, Harry. Dave crawls back to his own rubber tree, thinking deeply about the sense of humour of Australian Army officers and its usefulness in battle.

1825 hours, north–south road in the Long Tan plantation, easy as APC

Here comes the cavalry!

Lieutenant Adrian Roberts and his seven remaining APCs of 2 and 3 Troop are now roaring north towards Delta Company's position – leaving a carrier to guard the dam crossing. Initially after leaving the creek they are passing rice paddies and abandoned banana plantations, but in short order the gloom of the Long Tan rubber plantation looms in the distance.

Here, right on the edge of the rubber plantation, the plants are young and the APCs can simply run over them. As the heads of the crew commanders are at least equal to their greatest height, it means each commander can get a fair view of what lies ahead to their immediate north.

No longer needing map co-ordinates they simply steer directly towards the throbbing glow of exploding shells up ahead – which must be just the other side of where D Company is situated. Roberts and his squadron now arrive at the road junction which, the map tells the Commanding Officer of the APCs, is the main road passing from west to east – which links the one-time villages of Long Phuoc and Long Tan – and the sunken road running south–north, which points like an arrow to the very heart of the fighting up ahead.

Roberts arranges his seven carriers in a 'two-up' formation, aligned on the south–north road.

While his own carrier is in the middle, just to the left of the road, he has three carriers either side, the ones on the right commanded by Sergeant Ron Richards, the ones on the left in the hands of Sergeant Blue O'Reilly, with all of Roberts, Richards and O'Reilly sitting atop their carriers with their eyes peeled, their hands on their .50 millimetre machine guns . . . and their heads above the gun-shields, making them feel a tad vulnerable.

Roberts has deliberately placed the three APCs without gun-shields with O'Reilly on the left, as the West Australian considers that is the least likely section to be attacked. All information they can glean from the radio has the enemy strength coming from their right flank as they head north, not the left.

There is about 40 metres separating each APC laterally, their whole line extending nearly 300 metres from left to right and . . .

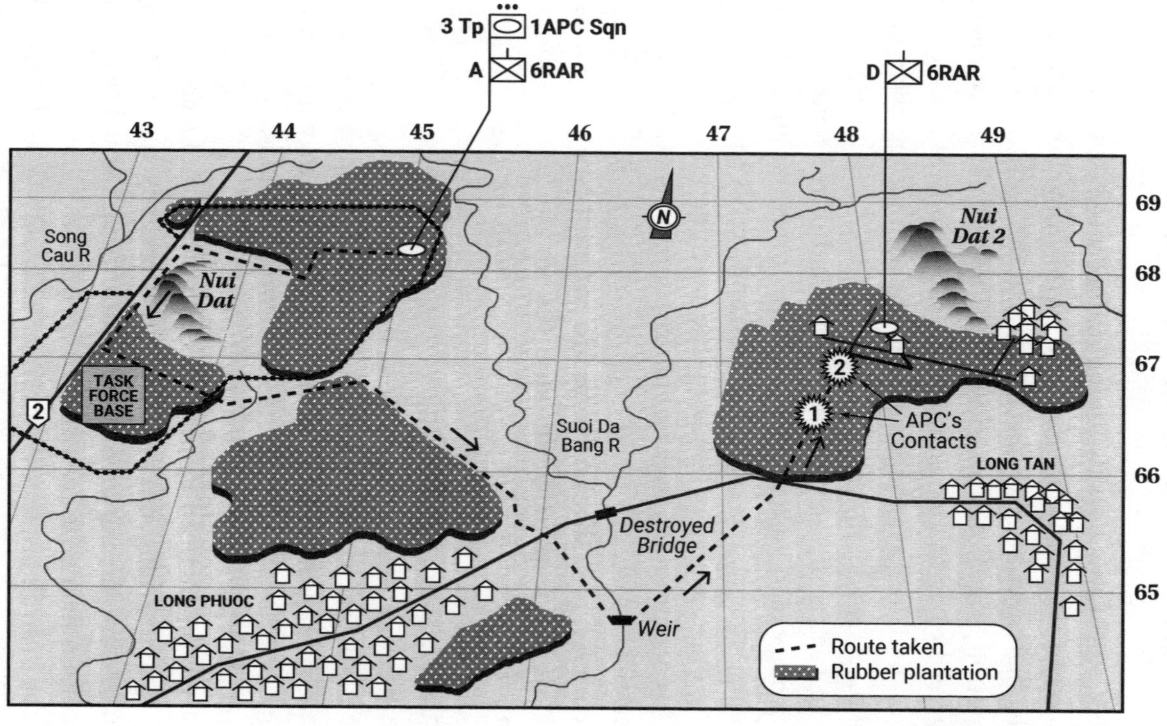

Route taken by the APC & A/6RAR Reinforcement Column, 18 August 1966

And what now?

The radio again. *Another* order to Lieutenant Roberts from Colonel Townsend, to halt until he can join them.

That is easy. As he has done the first two times, Roberts ignores the order.

'Advance . . .' Roberts gives the order, and all seven APCs move off, heading directly north, right into the heart of the Long Tan plantation. And yes, headlights would have been useful in the more sombre light of the plantation, but Roberts strictly forbids it. If there are enemy ahead, they need to be as inconspicuous as they can be, for as long as they can be – and the fact the pounding rain is muffling their noise will also help.

Roberts, in fact, is so eager to have command of the field and full vision – knowing exactly where his left and right sections are and what they are doing – that he has positioned a plank across the open hatch and is sitting on it, with his hands on the machine gun, his legs on either side, his back to the upright metal hatch, and his head above the machine-gun shield.

Sitting beneath him in the APC is his 2IC Sergeant Noel Lowes, who has right beside him Captain Mollison.

Just who is in charge, Mollison or Roberts?

Neither man has any doubt.

Roberts knows he is in command.

Mollison is certain that Roberts answers to him.

But there is no time to test it. The sound of firing to their north gives a fair clue as to how intense the action is and where they are needed most, and most of the APCs head straight towards it and . . .

And Christ Almighty, what is *that*?

Up ahead, out on the right, Roberts sees a whole stack of men wearing greens and webbing, and momentarily wonders why the Australian infantry had already dismounted when – identifying the tell-tale green pith helmets they wear – he realises.

They're not Australians, they're fucking VIET CONG, and there'd be no change from a company's worth – about a hundred of them! They are moving from east to west, in arrowhead formation like the highly trained troops they are.

'They had green hats on and their hat was basin shaped,' Roberts will note, 'and that's the way you could identify them.'[9]

Also spying them is Lieutenant Peter Dinham, the Officer Commanding Alpha Company's 2 Platoon who, though keeping his body in his APC – on the extreme right of the seven APCs – has his head out of the hatch so as to be aware at all times of the situation. Dinham shouts to Corporal Richard Gross, the commander of this APC, 32 Bravo, and Alpha Company's machine-gunner, Ron Brett: 'Open fire!'

Corporal Richard Gross, an Indigenous man said by the rest of 3 Troop to have the best eyesight of the lot of them, hesitates momentarily, concerned he may in fact be targeting Delta Company.

But now he is satisfied and yells, 'Contact. *Enemy to front!*'[10]

Ron Brett reacts with the speed of a trapdoor spider, acting on instinct more than conscious thought. Seconds later *both* guns are spitting death at the rate of 10 rounds a second.

Following 32 Bravo's lead, the other APCs in Richards' right-hand section are soon firing their own .50 calibres.

It all happens so fast. One minute the Vietnamese soldiers of the D445 Battalion are moving in a westerly direction, having been ordered to get around behind their Australian enemy and attack them from their southern flank. And the next – *right now* – they are looking up to see enormous machines charging straight at them! These machines bear no lights bar the flickering flashes coming from the machine guns they bear, each flash a bullet coming their way.

And it is now that one Australian soldier takes action that will certainly define his life – it's just a question of whether that life has seconds or decades to go. On top of the far-right carrier of the section, Lieutenant Dinham's, Sergeant Frank Alcorta – a 30-year-old recent immigrant to Australia from Spain's Basque country, an adventurer who had come to the Australian Regular Army in late 1961 as the only way he could think of to get food – can't help himself.

He jumps down, his SLR in his hands, and runs straight at the enemy he can see out to the right – away from the line of his own .50 calibre machine guns – firing from the hip.

'There was a need for immediate action,' he will recount. 'It was . . . instinctive.'[11]

Ahead of him he sees several dozen enemy soldiers.

They are 'aggressive-looking infantry wearing khaki uniforms and safari hats. I fired off my first magazine, twenty rounds, single shots and got several of them. There were a lot of bullets coming back the other way.'[12]

Once Alcorta must change magazines, of course, their vengeance will be savage, but just as he begins to rip the old magazine out, he is aware of a figure on his right making a *hell* of a noise. His mate Private Ronnie Brett has arrived with his M60 machine gun – much more lethal at longer distances – and has taken up where Alcorta left off, spraying the enemy.

And now the two Diggers are joined by the rest of the soldiers from their APC, who have been liberated upon Lieutenant Dinham's insistence to Corporal Gross that the back ramp on their machine be opened so they can get out and support their mates. The two other APCs in the right-hand section follow suit, and soon all of 2 Platoon has joined Alcorta, who is *still* leading the charge.

Not for nothing will Alcorta's OC at Alpha Company describe him as 'the bravest man I have ever met',[13] as the modern conquistador shouts to his comrades, 'Fix bayonets!'[14] before running at the enemy, as the Australians attack in extended line. It is complete carnage as the Australians, supported by the .50 calibre machine guns of the APCs, cut a swathe through the VC.

Before the Australians' very eyes, the resistance breaks and the VC start running like a herd of suddenly spooked horses, sprinting diagonally across in front of them, back towards Long Tan village.

'We estimated subsequently,' Lieutenant Dinham will say, 'that this brief action had occasioned approximately 40 casualties to the enemy.'[15]

Yes, extraordinary, but with action taking place across the line, Lieutenant Adrian Roberts is appalled at this particular action. Getting their own soldiers mixed up with the enemy in this gloom would inevitably mean two things: a delay in getting to Delta Company, and Australians firing on Australians.

'Who ordered the fucking infantry out?'[16] Roberts explodes.

There is no response, so Roberts follows up hard, uninterrupted.

'Everyone back on board. *Now!*'[17]

Now, as those soldiers are out on the ground, they are no longer actually under the command of Lieutenant Roberts. But, as it happens, Captain Mollison – who *is* in command of the men on the ground – for once is in agreement with Roberts and gives orders of his own.

Everyone back on board, immediately.

Once accomplished, and Roberts is back in full command, there is only one thing left to do, and it has the spirit of a PT Boat heading for an enemy destroyer.

RRRAMMING SPEED.

A combination of the enveloping darkness, the roar of the battle, the pounding rain and the unexpected direction from which they come – from the south – means that the APCs are able to get right amongst the enemy with little warning at all.

Accelerating on Roberts's command, the APCs start to simply plough first through the young rubber trees and now through the enemy themselves, even as the machine-gunners unleash devastating fusillades at everyone in front of them. Those inside the APCs can hear enormous thumps every time the vehicles hit someone, and often heavy bumps as the tracks squash the bodies at full speed.

'I've no idea how many casualties we caused,' Roberts will recount. 'The squashed ones were squashed and the dead ones dead. All we were interested in was getting through them. I didn't buggerise around, I just fought my way up there and didn't stop to count the men we were machine-gunning and running over.'[18]

Charlie's response speaks to his iron will.

Showing extraordinary discipline under the circumstances, even many of those in their direct path kneel down to fire, and bullets start to pepper the APCs, mercifully doing little damage.

In the meantime, Roberts's APCs continue to charge right at every soldier they see.

'We ran over them. They put up a good show, the enemy. We put up a better one. Our aim was to get to D Company so we *had* to push over the top of them.'[19]

And they are everywhere!

'Carriers were reporting these groups right along the front, so I realised there must be at least a company in front of us.'[20]

There! And there! And there!

Everywhere the commanders of the APCs look there are more of the enemy. They shoot whoever they can, and run over the rest. Thankfully, there is little time for the enemy soldiers to get organised to fight back, but through all the murderous madness the Australians are still impressed with how well trained the enemy is. They each have a bamboo loop around their ankles, and each one that goes down who still might be a chance of living is instantly dragged away by other soldiers with hooks. Yes, the VC are taking a battering, but it is amazing to see how disciplined they are. This is not a mob of poorly trained local guerrillas – these are professional military men, well trained and resourced. And yet there is no doubt just what damage they are taking.

'The infantry blokes were hanging over the side of the top hatch firing,' Sergeant O'Reilly will recount, 'and it was just bloody slaughter.'[21]

Not all of their shots hit the enemy however, and out on the right, Sergeant Richards is suddenly aware of a hole in his gun-shield that could have only come from close-quarters . . . and behind him . . .

Careful, you bloody stupid bastards!

Still, there are so many VC, and the Australians are so few by comparison, that if the VC stood their ground and swarmed them it wouldn't have been a contest and the invaders would have been massacred. But the darkness and the storm help to confuse them. The VC don't know that there are only seven APCs and no more than a company of soldiers.

The APCs continue to take heavy fire from them but mercifully, the 35 millimetre thick armour continues to protect the men of Alpha Company from any bullets.

Once through the enemy resistance, Roberts orders caution once more, concerned about going too fast and running into and – worse – *over*, Delta Company positions.

His eyes scanning back and forth, Roberts frequently orders, 'Check fire!'[22] until such times as he is absolutely positive he can see no signs of Delta Company in front of them.

1828 hours, 18 August 1966, Long Tan plantation, with 10 Platoon on the Delta Company HQ perimeter

Through the rain, the mist and the smoke, Geoff Kendall is almost sure he can see someone crawling on all fours.

Stop shooting anywhere near him!

'There's a bloke out there, and I think it's one of our blokes!'[23]

How to find out?

Well, if it is one of our blokes, he will certainly speak English.

'Take your hat off!' is all Kendall can think to shout.

Sure enough, the figure takes his hat off and waves.

'Don't shoot, don't shoot!' the crawling figure with the waving hat roars back. 'You silly bastards, it's Paddy Todd!'[24]

It *is* not just one of our blokes! It is PADDY!

In an instant, one of the soldiers from 10 Platoon, a big bear of an Indigenous man by the name of Buddy Lea, is running out, under fire, and manages to grab Todd by the collar and start to drag him towards the cover of a big log, before he can work out how to get him to Dobson's Delta Company Aid Post.

But wait!

'Hey Buddy,' Todd gasps, pointing to two looming figures off to their right. 'Have a look there.'

Buddy looks but is not worried.

'It must be our blokes from B Company coming back to us.'[25]

'You'd better have another look,' Todd gasps.

Buddy does exactly that and with a quick glance takes the point. Australian soldiers don't have pith helmets and AK-47s like those approaching do!

After first making sure that Paddy Todd has plenty of cover behind the log, Lea ducks behind a tree until they get a little closer. And . . . now! When the VC are so close he could just about throw his hat at them, he steps out from behind the tree . . . only to be immediately cut down by enemy fire. Fortunately, another Digger who has been watching dispatches the two VC, allowing Lea's 2IC in the section, Lance Corporal Jack Jewry, to rush out to Buddy and throw himself down beside him.

'How'd you rip your shirt?' he asks.

'I didn't,' Lea replies.

'Yes, you did. You've got no shirt on your back.'[26]

Looking closer, Jewry sees what has happened.

A bullet has come and not only slit the shirt from collar to tail, but also given Lea a long flesh wound.

Lance Corporal Jewry is so concerned at the rapid loss of blood and the danger it presents to Buddy he immediately gets up on his knees to better tend to the wound, only for a bullet to come and hit Jack Jewry in the head. Though she doesn't know it yet, back at St Marys in Sydney the dreams of Jack's wife Susanne of their future together have just been comprehensively dashed. And her unborn baby will grow up without a father. Jack Jewry now lies dead in the Vietnamese mud.

Both Lea and Todd are aghast, but do the only thing they can do: help each other get back to their own lines, where medic Dobson soon has them both in hand, assisted by 12 Platoon's 'Doc' Davis who, though still bleeding badly himself from his own wound, is still administering precious care.

Lieutenant Dave Sabben arrives at the aid post not long afterwards and is beyond relieved to have at last located Todd – meaning that everyone known to be alive from 12 Platoon is now accounted for.

Mercifully, Sabben is not wounded himself – just checking on one of his men who has been hit in the chest and still has a bullet in him. All up there are nearly two dozen wounded soldiers in the ditch, all in various stages of distress. Those who are only lightly wounded are being given weapons and steered to the north-western part of the perimeter, which is judged to be the least likely spot to be attacked. (Others in the Company Aid Post are loading rifle magazines from the loose-round ammunition that has been dropped from the choppers . . . all organised by, who else but Jack Kirby! The Delta HQ and Kiwi radio operators are also loading rifles when not actively on calls!)

As Sabben takes his leave, he sees Sergeant Major Jack Kirby sitting in a shell-hole with a shattered 11 Platoon Digger, Ron Eglinton.

'The 11 Platoon guy was in a pretty shocked state,' Sabben will recount, 'shivering and blank eyed. I got the machine gun I had brought back and told Kirby to get the Digger to strip and clean it and to try and get it working again. I didn't hold out much hope of getting the gun working but I thought it was necessary to get this soldier moving again as the fire was just starting to build up again and the first heavy "human wave" assault was coming in.'[27]

For now it comes again.

The perimeter of Delta Company – particularly that facing the east and south-east – now comes under concentrated machine-gun fire as a prelude to what will surely be a charge. And sure enough, they can now just see the enemy through the trees, massing about the distance of two football fields away! And now to the south, too – look there! There must be at least a hundred of them in that direction.

Harry Smith understands. Before, Delta Company had been dispersed, and the enemy had had no clue where they were, nor with what level of concentration. But not now. Now the enemy knows exactly where Delta are, and that they are few in number. So few, that just a few waves of soldiers should be guaranteed to overwhelm them.

•

After nigh on three hours waiting with rising frustration, Bravo Company finally gets the word from Colonel Townsend himself – bellowing from an APC that even now is speeding towards Long Tan – *Bravo Company to aid the besieged Diggers of Delta.*

Roger that, and the 32 men quickly set off in the enveloping darkness, their senses soon quickened by the unnerving sound of the blistering battle ahead, a cacophony that can only be created by ammunition large and small; the shells pounding and the gunfire so rapid and continuous it blurs into a single sound.

'The sound of the battle was deafening,' Lieutenant O'Halloran will recall, 'although visibility was quite good enabling us to see a fair distance.'[28]

They push hard, ignoring the usual precautions. There is no time for anything other than getting through to Delta!

1830 hours, 18 August 1966, Long Tan plantation, shady knoll, smoke gets in their eyes

If ever Harry Smith can appreciate his 'appreciation' it is now.

As one who has been making life-and-death decisions for the last three hours solid on the fly, he can take some satisfaction that he has mostly called it right. The first and most crucial decision has been where to make this stand – right here, near the top of this gentle slope that faces towards the bulk of the enemy to the east. It offers a natural protection to most of the enemy fire which flies harmlessly overhead, while also allowing those on the perimeter at the top of the slope, his strongest and freshest troops, to get clear shots at Charlie.

The bonus?

'To our advantage, [the enemy] were silhouetted in the gunfire smoke, making easy targets for my machine-gunners and riflemen.'[29]

The rest of his troops are arranged in a rough circle of 70 yards radius, so they can hold off the best they can any attempts to attack their flanks and from the rear. It is on the rear perimeter, the least likely point of attack, that he places those of his soldiers who are wounded but who can hold a rifle or machine gun.

One of those men – half-sunk in a puddle of water as it happens – is Private John Heslewood, one of the few survivors of 11 Platoon who has only just made it back and is shattered with both exhaustion and the horror of what he has experienced in the last three hours.

It is Sergeant Major Jack Kirby who first gets him into position, and now comes back with fresh ammunition for him, just as he is passing it out to all the others too.

'Don't worry about what's going on behind you,' the CSM says to him in typically kindly fashion. 'That's your field of fire out the front.'[30]

Yes, boss. Just having Jack there gives comfort and strength, just as the CSM is providing for all the other blokes who are struggling, most particularly the more severely wounded who have been gathered at the aid post near the centre of the circle – where D Company medic Corporal Phil Dobson is still working wonders keeping the grievously wounded alive. Jack is constantly going back and forth to them, checking on them, jollying them up a bit, getting them water, and doing everything he can to help.

One of those Jack is tending to in that manner is another survivor from 11 Platoon, John Robbins, who watches dazedly as the CSM keeps moving from the wounded to the perimeter of the Australian soldiers, keeping up spirits and handing out the ammunition.

'I thought he was terrific the way he got around and organised things and kept blokes' spirits up. How he never got hit himself I'll never know. The size he was, it's a miracle.'[31]

Not that he's silly about it, of course.

Now that some of the VC have pushed so close to the perimeter that some heavy fire is starting to come their way, Jack yells for everyone to 'Get down!' before throwing himself physically on top of Robbins to protect him.

'I'll get you out of here, mate, don't worry,' Kirby breathes, as the bullets fly just overhead.

'I hope you can,' Robbin gurgles in reply, 'but I won't need the VC to kill me because you'll bloody well kill me yourself if you don't get off me.'[32]

Big bastard that he is.

1832 hours, 18 August 1966, Delta Company HQ, Danger Close

They have just one chance to survive this.

'Drop the guns by 50!' Major Smith instructs Morrie Stanley.

The Kiwi looks at him.

Drop the guns by 50?

Have shells landing as close as 30 metres away?

But Smith is serious.

'Drop the guns by 50!'

This is not quite as insane as Bob Buick asking for shells to be aimed suicidally right on their noggins, but it's close. Artillery is not a scalpel, it's a big blunt instrument guaranteed to make a big and wide impact wherever it hits. To have it landing within 30 metres is to take a risk that would see even a short price bookie in a Sydney back-street say, 'Mate, are you dinkum on that? Did I hear you right?'

Morrie Stanley does as asked, providing grid co-ordinates that are no more than a stone's throw from them.

His signaller, Lance Bombardier Willie Walker, lying right beside him in the red mud – Walker with his radio, Stanley with his map – sends the orders through to Fire Control Centre.

Three Four Walker: 'Drop five zero, Danger Close, Fire for effect.'

Did he say 'Danger close'?

He did!

Three Arty HQ: 'Negative, unsafe, Over.'[33]

It causes consternation.

'We knew of the procedure,' Major Peter Tedder, Commander of the 105th Field Battery, will recall, 'but we had never used it.'[34]

We repeat.

'Negative, unsafe, Over.'[35]

Unsafe?

Unsafe?

Geez, do ya think?

Looking out at the human waves about to fall upon them, Major Smith has to concede they might have a point. It has been a little 'unsafe' around here of late.

On the other hand . . . who the fuck do these people think they are? They are in the safety of Nui Dat, looking at grid maps and presuming to tell those of us on the front lines, right in the teeth of this Cyclone Charlie, what *they* think is unsafe.

Harry Smith has had enough.

Grabbing the transmitter from Walker, he barks into it: 'Give us the fucking guns where we want them or you will lose the bloody lot of us.'[36]

There is a long pause . . . . and now the answer comes back.

Three Arty HQ: 'Acknowledge, Drop five zero, Danger Close, Fire for effect.'

Satisfied, Smith turns his attention back to the task at hand: saving as many of his men as possible.

'It was,' Harry Smith would recount, 'a competition between the enemy trying to get to us, the artillery keeping pace with the enemy, and us trying to shoot the ones that the artillery missed.'[37]

The shelling is now so close that, as well as blasts of heat and toxic vapour, Delta Company is now also being sprayed with 'hot shrapnel'. More disconcerting still, however, is they are also being showered with stray bits of Vietnamese bodies that have been blown to bits, together with parts of some of their weaponry.

1835 hours, 18 August 1966, Delta Company HQ, wave after wave after wave

And here they come again!

To this point most of the attacks on the members of Delta Company have been from figures in the distance, or pods of half-a-dozen working together to give each other cover as they move forward.

But this is not like that.

For now that the enemy is certain they have all of the enemy in just the one place, no effort is being spared and the Australians can see nothing less than a human *wave* of Charlie forming up and readying themselves for a full-blown assault, just 150 yards away. And look now, there is another one forming up about 100 yards behind them! And is that *another* one coming forward just behind the second? There appears to be somewhere between 60 and 100 in every wave.

Captain Morrie Stanley wastes no time, and quickly calls in an artillery strike on the second wave.

Bugles!

Bdaaaaaa . . . Bdda-dddaaa-ddaaaaaaa-Bdaaaaaaaa!

The weirdest thing in this whole world of weird? In some ways it is like watching yourself attack. Yes, this is all madness, but Dave Sabben for one can recognise that the method in the madness of the enemy's choreographing as they shape to launch is the same as the Australians had been trained to use.

'The formations were the same, the spacings, the rate of movement – it was all so familiar from our own training.'[38]

Given that the main thrust of the attacks are coming from the east, south-east and south – right on the area where 10 Platoon and 12 Platoon are positioned – both Sabben and Kendall are able to observe closely just how the VC attack comes in, and the extraordinary courage and discipline displayed by the enemy soldiers. And yes, they keep firing on the Australians as they come, but so well positioned is the perimeter, just below the edge of the knoll that Smith has settled on, that most of the VC fire goes right over the Australians' heads.

Better still?

'The VC,' as Harry Smith will note, 'were silhouetted against the smoke, mist, rain and cordite and our riflemen and machine-gunners mowed them down. It was like shooting ducks.'[39]

And yet *still* they come!

These blokes are professionals and . . . likely more professional than we are.

Shoot and run? Oh no. *Bdaaaaaa . . . Bdda-dddaaa-ddaaaaaaa-Bdaaaaaaaa!*

The Scots, most famously the Black Watch, would march into battle to the sound of bagpipes. Charlie has his bugles.

And here they come. The bugle blows and they move; they move steadily even though they know the artillery is coming . . .

FsssssssssBAAAAAAAAMMM!

The shells blast holes in the enemy, as individuals and as a whole. You can see the circles of death and destruction conjured amongst them . . . but they keep going. The ones who are not dead advance and . . . *Bdaaaaaa . . . Bdda-dddaaa-ddaaaaaaa-Bdaaaaaaaa!* The bugle blows once more and a new tide of men appear, filling in the sickening sea of their fallen fellows and they keep coming.

The VC are falling faster than the rain. But not all fall. And they keep coming.

Again and again and again. The bugles and the artillery, a circle of sound that repeats with no retreat.

Bdaaaaaa . . . Bdda-dddaaa-ddaaaaaaa-Bdaaaaaaaa!

To the amusement of Corporal Brian Reilly, an Australian voice calls out a brilliant lateral solution amid the din: 'All we've gotta do is hit the fuckin' bugler!'[40]

The Australians call out mock directions to the shells – gallows humour being executed by a company of men still in the shadow of death, the battle raging before them; their lives in the balance as they heckle: 'Over there', 'Here they come again . . .'

'Roll up, roll up, a penny a pull.'[41]

Calls of 'Pass the ammo' are ringing out all around, even as the acrid smell of cordite from the exploding shells that are getting ever closer gets ever stronger.

Yes, it is mostly terrifying despite the humour.

And yet, as Harry Smith will recall, personally, 'I was too bloody busy to be frightened. Everything I did was an automatic reaction, your mind just tells you what to do. I was giving orders to my platoon, talking on the radio, I didn't have five minutes to sit down and be scared.'[42]

The most shocking thing is the sheer *intensity* of the attack. What is clear is that, one way or another, the VC cannot long endure sending so many men forward. Either the Australians will be quickly overwhelmed, or Charlie must inevitably run out of machine-gun fodder.

But can Delta Company hold out?

Under the sheer weight of the swarming 'suppressive fire' coming from the enemy what they mostly must do is hug the ground. The bullets seem to have tailormade measurements of just how wide the Delta men are; the enemy's green tracers shooting past at barely a metre off the ground. You can trace the Aussies from above with tape from a crime scene, they are flat out like lizards drinking; sinking in the mud as they wait for a break in fire or an increase in artillery.

Bdaaaaaa . . . Bdda-dddaaa-BAAAAAAAMMM!

•

Stand back!

At the rate that the 1st Field Regiment has been firing, they risk running out of shells if this goes for much longer, and their call to the Americans at Vung Tau has been answered.

For now, the massive Chinook – two counter-rotating rotors, powered by two turboshaft engines mounted on each side of the helicopter's rear pylon – roars into the clear space just by the artillery compound and brings its rear wheels to the ground. With extraordinary skill, the American pilot – in order not to present a stationary target to any VC sniper who might be in the area – stays on those back wheels as the rotor pushes it along and the chopper crew push pallet after pallet of shells out the open hatch . . . before it roars off again. An instant later the Pogos swoop, and the fresh shells are being carried towards the compound once more.

•

This is no longer just hot shrapnel it is *really* hot shrapnel and it is whizzing just over their heads, cutting patterns into the rubber trees and spraying the Australians with sap.

Momentarily it seems like the shells really are going to land right on top of them, whereupon Stanley cries 'Stop! Stop! Stop!'[43] but it is only a brief pause. The Fire Controller, fellow Kiwi Major Harry Honnor, is able to assure him that they have the situation in hand and the shelling resumes – which is fortunate as the waves of VC coming at them are ever more intense.

(Bless Harry Honnor, by the way. One of the unsung heroes, he serves as the key link between Stanley and the artillery batteries, and his calm professionalism, despite the extremity of the situation, sets the tone.)

•

Bdaaaaaa . . . Bdda-dddaaa-ddaaaaaaa-Bdaaaaaaaa!

And still they come. Private Bill Doolan of 10 Platoon can't quite believe what he is seeing; hundreds of *Bdaaaaaa . . . Bdda-dddaaa-ddaaaaaaa-Bdaaaaaaaa!*

FsssssssssBAAAAAAAAMMM! . . . tens of VC heading calmly towards them. *Bdaaaaaa . . . Bdda-dddaaa-ddaaaaaaa-Bdaaaaaaaa!* And still they come, hundreds more, like water joining a wave, seeping forward, advancing at zombie-like pace. It is like a battle in slow motion; you have time to take your time while firing; the lack of haste as the bullets and artillery lay waste to the advance is more chilling than any roaring rush could be. *Some of us will die, but enough of us will live to kill you.* Well, *Bdaaaaaa . . . Bdda-dddaaa-ddaaaaaaa-Bdaaaaaaaa!* FsssssssssBAAAAAAAAMMM! . . . we'll see.

The wave of VC flows forward and Bill's bloody rifle, an SLR 7.62, with a perfect lack of timing, is misfiring. The loudest noise his rifle is producing are the oaths he yells at it. *Fuck this!* The nearest machine gun will do, its owner is wounded and gladly hands it over. Well now we're getting some . . . now the BLOODY MACHINE GUN WON'T WORK. In fury, Bill Doolan starts beating it against the nearest rubber tree; he cocks, coaxes and curses the damn thing. Apart from throwing the machine at the VC, there is little Bill can do with it: 'the bastard of a thing wouldn't work'.[44] Oh well, better a rifle that works sometimes than a machine gun permanently on strike.

And still they come. Bill can see that his bullets are making some VC fall, but when they fall, they simply lie among their own dead and keep firing. In the midst of all the carnage, the most staggering thing is how Company Sergeant Major Jack Kirby keeps running around – yes, upright, and somehow still alive – yelling encouragement to the men: 'You're doing great, fellows!'[45]

Really?

Really!

'Keep it up, fellows!'[46]

It isn't just his words. It is his *spirit*. We aren't dead yet! Keep it up! Doing great! And now watch as Jack has no sooner seen two VC in the distance setting up a rocket launcher, than he jumps up and shoots both of them dead!

Doing great, Sir, keep it up!

Bdaaaaaa . . . Bdda-dddaaa-ddaaaaaaa-Bdaaaaaaaa!

FsssssssssBAAAAAAAAMMM!

A positive attitude is one thing, but let's not get delusional. They are still so far up Shit Creek that it is now an entire shit ocean, the rain continues to piss down and everywhere you look . . . still they come. Jesus Christ. Bill Doolan thinks what every man thinks: 'Well this is it, we're all gone here.'[47]

It's only a matter of time now before the VC reach them. *Do you have bayonets?* a voice yells. No, Bill doesn't. He's got a machete though, will that do? The blade is placed next to him, at the ready, for what is coming. Still they come.

To some, like Ron Eglinton, the whole thing seems unworldly.

'All this destruction was going on,' he will recount, 'trees just being blown to bits and shredded branches coming down and every time we'd get up and try to move as a group someone would open up on us.'

The brutes are so close now they can see them, many of them silhouetted in eerie fashion by the endless flashes of artillery behind them!

'A lot of them had camouflage on, their pith helmets and branches on their backpacks, foliage all over them. But they were totally fearless. Even with this tremendous amount of artillery coming in and all of us, they just kept coming and coming.'[48]

•

Corporal Laurie Drinkwater is the most misnamed man in the Australian Army, so his fellows reckon. He'll drink anything except. Well, he could do with a drink now.

Where is the attack coming from?

No, where *isn't* it coming from?

These bastards are everywhere!

The fire and the VC fade in and out of the trees, you can barely see them because of the bloody rain. You can of course – *Bdaaaaaa . . . Bdda-dddaaa-ddaaaaaaa-Bdaaaaaaaa!* – hear them. There is a silver lining to this dark cloud, and dark thunderstorm; the VC can't see just how perilous the Australian position is. If it weren't raining, they would be drowned by the VC in a few minutes. As it is, the enemy is far more cautious than they need be; but this just means that the men of Delta will die more slowly than they might.

FssssssssssBAAAAAAAAMMM!

The artillery are bloody precise, but still they have precisely bugger all chance of making it through the day unless the cavalry arrive now. Or 10 minutes ago.

We're not going to get out of this one.

Laurie shoulders his rifle and . . . sees Paul Large, just a few yards from him, has his head down. PAUL! *PAUL!* The call is unanswered. His mate Noel Grimes also sees Paul drop his head, and has a strong feeling about what has just occurred.

At last, all his bravado has run out, and he's just 'chucked it in . . . it had gotten too much for him and he had just chucked it in'.[49]

Paul! Come on! Keep fighting!

Mate, we fucking NEED YOU!

Laurie Drinkwater throws a couple of small rocks Large's way, hoping they will hit his window of consciousness and show that he is still breathing. *Curse me, Paul, yell at me for pelting you, please.* Private Neil Bextrum crawls to Paul now, reaches out and . . . looks at Laurie first. They both know what he is going to say.

'Paul's dead!'[50]

A bullet has hit him right between the eyes, likely killing him instantly. You never hear the round that kills you, and Paul surely never heard this one.

'You don't believe that it's happening,' Large's Platoon Commander, Dave Sabben, will recall of having witnessed the actual shot that killed the man from Coolah. 'You can see a soldier lying there and there's a flinch and they go slack and that's how most soldiers [die]. It's not a hysterical flinging of the arms in the air and a double somersault backwards; it's not like that at all . . . In that split second of witnessing that, you have an image in your head. "That guy, he will never hold his kids on his lap. He'll never have a Sunday lunch with Mum and Dad again." You just sense the loss.'[51]

But the mates closest to him haven't given up.

'Can you get him back to the aid post?'[52] asks Laurie, to Neil's surprise. Such courtesies of battle seem strange in their situation, but it is heartening to harken to the normal. He nods, and Neil and Noel Grimes drag their dead comrade – despite clearly having a bullet through the head – through the mud towards the aid post.

Once they are gone, the ubiquitous Jack Kirby leaps in beside Laurie with a question.

'Do you know that bloke over there?' he asks, pointing at a soldier moving slowly towards them in the distance. Laurie looks.

'No,' says Laurie.

'Well shoot him!' replies Kirby. 'Shoot anyone you don't know.'[53]

And with that the Big Bear is away again, and Laurie Drinkwater is firing again; shooting at any man he doesn't know. There are hundreds to choose from.

And still they come . . . even as the last of the daylight ebbs to near nothing.

11 Platoon's Allen May will never forget it.

'It was eerie. They weren't running and diving behind trees like you'd expect them to. They were just walking towards us, like zombies, and every one you knocked down there were two to take his place. It was like shooting ducks in a bloody shooting gallery. I would have killed at least 40 blokes that day. I know, myself, I would have killed at least 40 Viet Cong.'[54]

The image of one enemy soldier will stay with him for the rest of his days.

Charlie is calmly walking towards May, firing from the hip and – almost as if in slow motion – the Australian can *see* the bullets coming his way.

May fires a burst of tracer in return right at him, which knocks him backwards in a flip . . . only for him to land on his feet, screaming and scratching at his chest, 'like as if he was trying to put the fire out'.[55]

The horror. Oh, the horror.

Another burst mercifully finishes him.

Ron Eglinton is equally engaged. He keeps firing and the enemy – those not already being blown apart by the shells – keep falling over. And yet *still* they keep coming!

It is all so intense he seems to have an out of body experience.

'At one stage I sort of got up above it. I just seemed to levitate.

'And I remember looking down through the trees and seeing myself there and thinking, "You're in strife", but feeling no terror.'[56]

For his part, Captain Morrie Stanley never misses a beat or a blast and simply keeps calling in the shells closer, ever closer, before he is right on the enemy front line, at which point he 'walks' it along, back and forth, wreaking a trail of destruction that is a rough parallel to their own Delta Company front line on the eastern side.

And yet *still* they keep coming!

Dave Sabben and Laurie Drinkwater look at each other.

In a war of yore it would be time for everyone to 'fix bayonets', to at least go down fighting when they run out of ammunition and are inevitably over-run.

These days bayonets are no more than an optional extra, but many of them at least take a firm grip of machetes, while others prepare to use their rifles as clubs. The VC are not known to take prisoners, so there would be no point in surrendering even if they wanted to. And they don't want to.

The one advantage they have is the enveloping darkness. In just 15 minutes' time, beneath the canopy of the rubber trees it will be so pitch black the VC would risk shooting each other. Hence this all-out attack now. If the VC don't over-run them in the next 15 minutes, the enemy will have to break off the engagement.

1840 hours, 18 August 1966, Long Tan plantation, dazed and confused

The engines roar, the twilight deepens, they continue to push forward, now among mature rubber trees that can't be knocked over; Roberts more desperate than ever to get to Delta before they are overwhelmed and . . .

And wait!

Up ahead, there are many in greens, several pods of a dozen men or so, this time moving from west to east.

Ours, or theirs?

Roberts only has to take one look at their garb and he realises.

That's Charlie all right!

And this time – despite the fact this group of enemy had clearly been moving up behind D Company – they have obviously been forewarned by the APCs' first encounter with the enemy, for they are much more ready for the Australians and have set up defences.

BOOOOM!

What now?

An explosion out to Roberts's right, across the sunken road, attracts his attention . . . and instantly alarms him. For the explosion has come from the round of an anti-tank gun that has hit the rubber tree right next to the APC set up as an ambulance, 39 Mike, and brings the tree trunk down.

And there is the VC crew, setting up to put another round in their 57 millimetre recoilless anti-tank rifle – a smaller calibre weapon, easier to carry but still powerful enough to take out armoured vehicles.

While one VC is down on one knee, another is behind him, steadying the weapon on the first VC's shoulder as he stares down the sights and clearly readies to pull the trigger!

Instantly taking action, it is Corporal John Carter himself, a Regular Army soldier from Benalla, who first instructs his driver, Trooper Paul McNamara, to stop the APC, before firing his .50 calibre machine gun at them, only for it to jam up. No problem. On Carter's call, McNamara throws him his Owen gun, at which point Carter stands boldly on the roof of the APC and simply fires from the hip, leaning into it exactly the way he had been taught in Basic Training back in Australia. Carter's Owen keeps chattering – as his driver keeps throwing up fresh magazines – wiping out most of the VC crew. There is at least one of them left though, who manages to pull the lanyard to fire the RCL's second shell.

Noooooo!

There is a flash, and the shell roars forth . . . to hit the branches of the fallen rubber tree, right next to Carter's APC. Carter is dazed by the explosion, but *still* manages to keep firing, killing three more VC. With discretion now the better part of valour, he quickly scrambles back into the protection offered by his APC, as the body of the beast is now sprayed with VC bullets from far and wide.

Push on?

Not yet.

Long training has taught Lieutenant Roberts that the way the VC work means that where there is one anti-tank weapon there is more than likely two. It is with that in mind that he pauses the advance, proceeding carefully, not prepared to place at risk the lives of an APC crew and the Alpha Company soldiers they carry.

The worst would be to bypass an anti-tank weapon and be attacked from their unprotected rear, and so now Roberts calls a halt, so that each APC commander can scan the area between themselves and their adjacent APC to ensure there is no sign of any light artillery.

In Roberts's own APC, Captain Mollison cannot *bear* the delay and says so, with some force. He *demands* they proceed at full pace.

'We are looking for a second anti-tank weapon,'[57] Lieutenant Roberts explains.

And what is more, you misunderstand, Captain Mollison. You are not in command either of this APC or this Troop. I am.

We will move when I say, and not before.

'I told Mollison what I was doing and that was that . . .' Roberts will recount.[58]

Lieutenant Adrian Roberts gives the order.

'Advance . . .'

As one, the seven APCs ease slightly forward.

'Hold the line steady . . .'

'Keep pushing on . . .'

'Bravo 30 hold back a bit . . .'

At this juncture, however, Roberts realises that the left-hand section has stone-cold stopped entirely . . .

Unbeknownst to Roberts, Sergeant Blue O'Reilly's left-hand section has suddenly been confronted by a VC machine-gun crew who have now opened fire on the only pod of APCs, which – oh, Christ! – have no metal shields.

Noooooo!

On the next carrier along, on the far left – 23 Bravo – Corporal Peter Clements is not so fortunate and several bullets hit him amidships. Clements is just 21 years old from the most unheard-of place in Western Australia that no-one's ever heard of: Cunderdin. As the bullets penetrate the American flak jacket he is wearing, Corporal Clements falls back down the hatch of his machine, and is immediately replaced by two soldiers of Alpha Company who, with extraordinary bravery, climb out of the same hatch to take his place . . . only to be immediately shot themselves, and fall back inside to now lie beside Clements, bleeding heavily.

23 Bravo's driver, with three heavily bleeding bodies beside him, and other soldiers rushing to try to stem the flow, guns his machine forward, straight at the machine-gun crew, who *keep* firing. The driver runs over them and, for the moment at least, that threat is nullified.

Roberts takes immediate action, calling for his 2IC, Sergeant Noel Lowes.

Do you think you can get to Clements' APC and take command? He has no sooner asked than Lowes is on his way, scrambling out of Roberts's APC and zig-zagging his way over, taking whatever cover he can and hoping against hope that any of the enemy who have lined him up and fire will miss him because of his sudden change of direction.

It has been the hairiest run of Sergeant Lowes' life, and he has nearly been killed half-a-dozen times – the bullets whining past his head like angry hornets – but now, just up ahead is the stricken carrier desperately in need of his command to replace the wounded Clements.

But now to the closest call of all.

When those soldiers on the APC look down to see an olive-skinned fellow in khakis running at them and attempting to board, their guns come up at once. It would only have taken one of them to shoot and it would have been all over. But Lowes is saved by his black beret, the signature headwear of 1 APC Squadron.

The point?

Charlie don't wear black berets!

They hold their fire and Lowes takes command, soon reporting to Lieutenant Roberts over the radio just how grim it is: Clements is dying and there are two other wounded soldiers on board.

Roberts doesn't hesitate and orders Lowes to take the APC straight back to base, in the hope of saving the lives of the three wounded soldiers on board.

Yes, it will leave them shy an APC and that *might* be crucial in saving the lives of all Delta Company, but this decision has come from his gut rather than his head.

Captain Mollison immediately protests – not prepared to lose the APC containing a platoon HQ, and a part of one of his platoons – and gives an order of his own. Clements' APC, he tells Roberts, is to stay with the squadron.

Over-ruled. Sergeant Lowes follows my orders, not yours, Captain Mollison, and that is the end of it.

Whatever the struggle between Roberts and Mollison, there is equally no doubt who Roberts's driver, Corporal Bill O'Rourke, must answer to. O'Rourke will do *exactly* what Lieutenant Roberts tells him to, as Roberts is his immediate superior.

Roberts now furiously tries to raise Sergeant O'Reilly on the radio, unaware that the commander of the left-hand section has lost consciousness. But now a reedy voice comes over the radio, a little disembodied.

It is O'Reilly. He has come to. The good news is that, though wounded, he feels capable of fighting on.

In the meantime, the APCs on the right-hand side of the advance, not knowing what had happened on the left, continue the pell-mell advance to the helter-skelter north towards the position of Delta! How do they know when they are getting close?

Alas, by the artillery shells that are landing all around! Lieutenant Roberts reaches down mechanically for his steel helmet and perches it atop his beret. Under the circumstances, it's a mere gesture arising from the sense of numbness now enveloping him, but it makes him feel safer.

Just before the last encounter Adrian Roberts had radioed to call for a pause in the barrage on their approaches to Delta, but clearly there has been an error in communication, because even as the APCs roar north through the rubber plantation there are explosions all around and the tell-tale sound of metal on metal, as they are hit by pieces of shrapnel.

It is nothing less than terrifying, and while their signallers roar back to Fire Control to *Cease artillery fire!*, all are excruciatingly aware that just one direct hit will take out an entire APC and all who are in it.

•

It is a strange thing indeed to walk through a rubber plantation in the deep twilight, not only hearing the battle ahead, but feeling it through their feet.

Such is the situation for Bravo Company as they head to the aid of Delta, towards the roar of the artillery, each shell sending out shock waves, making the ground tremble and the trees shake – or maybe it's their hearts trembling, and their knees shaking.

But they continue to push hard regardless, eager to help save Delta and . . .

And what now?

Suddenly, out to their south-east, they first hear the roar of their own APCs, and shortly thereafter see them.

Halt!

Major Noel Ford yells the order, as with this roar it is not only beside the point to whisper but an entirely useless exercise.

Bravo Company now watches, gobsmacked, as the APCs push through right ahead of them. Thank Christ they had not been *in front* of those APCs, as in this descending twilight they would have risked being mistaken for Charlie. And yet only now does Bravo Company realise what the APCs have been roaring *at* – a mass of enemy who are now splintering in the face of these mechanical monsters.

'To give them their due,' Lieutenant John O'Halloran will recall, 'the VC kept firing and I saw many of them crushed and disappear under the tracks of the heavy machines. You could barely hear the screaming from all the other noises.'[59]

And yet now one of the shards of the shattered VC is coming their way!

A firefight breaks out, Bravo Company firing on the VC who fire back in turn and, in all the confusion and spitting machine guns, the worst fears of Major Ford's men are realised, as one of the APCs mistakes them for enemy, and starts coming straight at them, with a trigger-happy Alpha Company machine-gunner firing at them.

Down!

Bravo Company machine-gunner Carey 'Bluey' Johnson – a dogged Digger from Newcastle – takes a bullet through each shoulder, and one along the crease of his jaw. Mercifully, the APC realises its mistake and turns and heads back south, to rejoin the main force fracas, but what of Bluey?

With the firefight against the VC ongoing, as bullets fly and with white sap bursting forth all around them, Bravo Company needs Bluey's machine gun. Lieutenant O'Halloran sends a soldier forth to get his gun as the top priority.

And so it is that Bravo is able to get the good news.

For no sooner has the soldier got his hands on Bluey's machine gun than the outraged Novocastrian leaps to his feet and says, 'I have carried the bloody thing this far I am not giving it away now!'[60]

Whereupon he runs forward once more, firing on the fleeing VC as he goes.

Badly bloodied, yes, but Bluey is going to be all right!

As it is, between the rampaging APCs and Bravo Company, the force that would have given Bravo the most trouble between themselves and Delta Company has been shattered, and as the sound of the APCs' motors recede, the way is clear for Bravo to push even harder to get through. Mercifully, there is no enemy resistance, though they continue to hear lots of gunfire, even as shells whistle overhead.

CHAPTER FOURTEEN

THERE GOES THE CAVALRY

The bullets whistled into space,
The pom-pom gun kept up its braying,
The four-point-seven supplied the bass –
You'd think the devil's band was playing.

A valiant comrade crawling near
Observed his most supine behaviour,
And crept towards him – 'Eh! what cheer?'
'Buck up,' says he, 'I've come to save yer.'

A. B. 'Banjo' Paterson, 'That V.C.'

1845 hours, 18 August 1966, Long Tan plantation, bugle boys for Company D

Is that what it was like for Custer's last stand?

A small posse of men, surrounded by such an overwhelming number of enemy that, no matter how many you bring down, there are always three more coming? Add the trumpets and the hell-fire of shell-fire and that is what it fucking feels like!

The problem now, for the soldiers of Delta Company, is that Charlie has wised up and is starting to come at them from many angles. After one attack comes in at five o'clock, they and the artillery have no sooner beaten it off than another comes in at two o'clock. In extremis, that one is beaten back and now waves of them are coming at them at four o'clock!

The most unnerving thing of the lot?

The bravery of these bastards.

No sooner has a bugle call warbled out than a line of enemy soldiers would come at them, quickly broken up by the shells and their own Delta fire. The survivors would sink to the earth and now when the next wave comes through, and the same thing happens, the survivors of the previous wave fill in the gaps and the wave keeps coming, before being broken up again . . . before it happens again, and they keep getting closer!

'And this was happening on all fronts,' Dave Sabben will recall, 'but at different times. But now we didn't have the time between assaults to load the magazines, so we were sort of getting four and five rounds in a magazine, face the enemy and then reload quickly and then be ready for the next lot.'

No-one has ever seen anything like it.

'It was like a self-replenishing wave. And you'd think, well, you know, bang, there's a dead VC. And then a minute, a few, 10 seconds later, another one would rise from the ground, you think the dead come to life.'[1]

The question now is whether darkness or Delta will fall first. If the former, the latter just might survive after all, meaning Charlie must even now be girding his loins and stiffening his sinew for his own all-or-nothing charge.

Geoff Kendall feels the same, ruminating darkly that back in Australia his darling wife is about to have a child in a week's time and that child will be very lucky to grow up with a father as his own life is very likely about to end. Their fate is near, all can feel it. And now a benediction to the battle from their commander: 'Shrink the perimeter,' Harry Smith cries out, 'and surround the wounded!'[2]

It is close to the most desperate card left in his deck, but as the enemy continues to press he has no choice but to play it. They shrink back until a wall is formed around the wounded. They wait for the next flood of enemy. They know they won't wait long.

1855 hours, 18 August 1966, Delta Company HQ, three cheers for Bravo!

Bravo, Bravo, Bravo.

There they are!

Just up ahead now in the gloom, Bravo Company can discern Delta Company's position, immediately prompting the new arrivals to shout.

'Don't shoot! Don't shoot! BRAVO COMPANY!'

They have finally made it. With no space this time for *hail fellow, well met*, Delta and Bravo Companies are reunited, about four hours and as many years – seemingly – since they had farewelled each other.

Relieved beyond measure to see them, Smith quickly orders Ford and his men to occupy the south-west section of the perimeter at seven to eight on the clock face, pausing only as Major Ford starts, uselessly, brandishing his Browning pistol.

'Sir,' one of the Delta Company soldiers says gently, 'you do not have a magazine in your Browning.'

'Oh,' Ford replies a little vaguely, 'my batman must have forgotten it.'[3]

Lieutenant John O'Halloran, meanwhile, is keeping an eye out for Gordon Sharp, and is a little worried about not spotting him yet, but in any case there is no time to dwell.

They must take up their position and defend against possible further attacks, while also being *very* careful not to shoot any of their own.

'Don't shoot,' Lieutenant O'Halloran tells his men, whereupon two of his corporals fire off two rounds.

'I thought I told you blokes not to open fire!' O'Halloran yells at them, outraged.

'Well,' says Corporal Spike Jones mildly, pointing where they had shot, 'there are two dead nogs over there who were crawling up the back of us.'[4]

Ah. As you were. Carry on.

In the meantime the rest of the survivors of Delta and the newly arrived of Bravo Company stand to, lying low with their weaponry trained, unsure what to expect. Is Charlie about to launch again *en masse*? Or could it really be all over?

•

Wait!

Listen!

Actually, such is the noise of the artillery still falling, it is more that you can *feel* the rumbling of heavy vehicles approaching, coming from the south.

Could it be . . . ?

Is it them?

It is!

Here comes the cavalry!

It is three APCs coming through the plantation, and their trajectory takes them just 50 metres south of where Geoff Kendall's 10 Platoon are defending the perimeter in the six o'clock position.

A ragged cheer goes up. The boys are here!

But what now?

To the astonishment of all, however, those same APCs have no sooner reached the edge of their perimeter than they turn to their right, proceed some 100 metres and now do a loop back whence they came?

What on *earth* is going on?

The answer is not clear. And yet there is no doubt that the APCs have put the wind up the VC as those who had been lying doggo outside the 10 Platoon section of the perimeter quickly slink away.

•

It is only now, for the first time – now that they are through the waves, which have mercifully finally ceased – that Sergeant Ron Richards in the APC on the far right-hand side realises that they are all alone. With no knowledge of what had befallen Corporal Clements and the left-hand section, he, together with the commanders of the two other APCs, Carter and Gross, now understand that Lieutenant Roberts and all the rest are still some 200 metres behind them, and so they now must return to the throng.

1900 hours, 18 August 1966, Long Tan plantation, loop-de-loop

Fix bayonets.

It is now obvious that the VC will soon be upon them. At least let us go down fighting.

On the south-western perimeter 10 Platoon's Sergeant Neil Rankin looks at Yank Akell beside him, who grimaces back. It really has come to this. They have fought with everything they have in them, but their fate is obvious. They are going down. But . . . hang on! What's that??

As before, it starts with a sound that none hear. It is barely a vibration, making little headway against the Armageddon of sound that fills Delta's ears. But now it grows, a rumbling grumbling that tumbles into a dull roar that cuts to the fray. The APCs! THE BLOODY APCS ARE COMING! And not just two or three like last time. All of them!

As the three errant APCs on the far right have returned to join the rest, just as the three APCs bearing Colonel Townsend and his HQ join them, it means that no fewer than nine APCs are on the charge!

Akell, Rankin and the rest of Delta Company first hear the APC machine guns start chattering, and now they see them, the blasting behemoths rolling right through the VC, crushing them and lifting every Delta man.

'They were a wonderful sight,' Akell will recall, 'pushing through us with their machine guns firing and so forth, straight towards the enemy, and at that particular stage, our internal feelings just completely changed. It went from . . . we were going to die in the next few minutes, to one of complete relief, excitement – it [now] looked that we just might get out of this.'[5]

With no more waves of VC coming at them, Morrie Stanley calls off the artillery at 1902 hours, which means all of Delta Company can hear the contact that the APCs are having with the retreating Charlie, and they can even see flashing silhouettes of the vehicles through the trees, together with the tracer rounds the retreating VC are firing at them.

For 2 and 3 Troop, this is as hairy as Great-Aunty Agatha's chin. They are under heavy fire from the enemy, who, nevertheless, are clearly scattering because they have no choice.

'The sound 2500 people shooting at you makes,' Adrian Roberts will recount, 'is quite incredible – the *crack, crack, crack* of the rounds – and the scary part is seeing the tracers. Tracers are one in every five rounds and the whole sky was lit up.'[6]

Their engines roaring, their tracks clanking, they push to the east, even as bullets clink against their sides and the darkness falls, all of them taking heavy fire from the machine-gun and small-arms fire. Adrian Roberts keeps firing himself, while making sure – as they all do – to keep his entire body down behind the gun-shield. It does not mean he is invulnerable, but as the bullets hit the shield *en masse*, he is certainly very glad he has it.

'What I remember,' Roberts will recount, 'were these . . . explosions, white explosions all around . . . in the trees, and if you looked left and right there was tracer fire. There was our tracer and their tracer fire. Their tracer fire is green . . . Ours is yellow.'[7]

But wait! While many of the VC continue to scatter, some brave souls ready themselves to provide serious resistance to the APCs. Positioned on the south-west corner of the perimeter, Private Len Vine can just see in the gloom three VC setting up a recoilless rifle and aiming it at the foremost APC. Bringing his own rifle to bear, feeling that the fate of the Australians in the APC depends on him, Vine aims, fires and has the satisfaction of seeing the one who is about to fire go down. With extraordinary bravery the next VC steps up, only for Vine to shoot him too, whereupon the third VC, with staggering bravery picks up the recoilless rifle and aims . . . whereupon Vine successfully brings him down, too.

On and on into the kaleidoscopic maelstrom the APCs push.

•

In the wake of such an extraordinary episode, other chopper pilots might be expected to make like the Pope, after surviving a trip through a storm with Dodgy Airways and kiss the ground.

Not Frank Riley though.

Barely acknowledging the horror of what they have just been through, let alone the triumph, he simply removes his headphones and says vaguely to the others, 'I think I'll head up to the Operations Centre and see what's happening. Maybe we can help.'[8]

The others look at each other. They know how to translate.

Frank means: 'That was really good. I wonder if there are any more jobs like that?'

Slowly, they follow him to the Operations Centre, where they find their Commanding Officer, Wing Commander Ray Scott, has arrived.

'He was pleased to see that we had returned safely,' Bob Grandin would recount. 'He was a little upset with our decision to go without his knowledge. We were congratulated for the safe and accurate delivery of the ammunition. We were then told to return to our helicopters and wait for further orders.'[9]

Quite.

The chopper pilots move away from the Operations Centre with no little reluctance as they now feel an enormous personal attachment to Delta Company and want to know how they are faring. (From what they have heard, the answer is 'Better than before,' as they now at least have ammo, but it is still going to be touch and go whether they survive or not. The atmosphere inside the Operations Centre is one of impending disaster.)

Ambling away, they strain to hear the last snatches of transmissions from Delta Company.

Arriving back at Kangaroo Pad, they find that the rest of RAAF No. 9 Squadron has joined them.

•

Wonderfully, this time as the APCs approach, they neither loop nor divert. Rather, they approach slowly, feeling their way through the rubber trees, knowing Delta Company is close. And now, as some of the soldiers on the eastern perimeter flick their torches on and off to let the APC commanders know where they are, the metallic beasts come to the edge of Delta's perimeter and a ragged cheer goes up, even as the rain stops.

They feel like heaven itself is smiling on their salvation.

The timing is unbelievable! Bob Buick and the survivors of 11 Platoon leap to their feet, yelling and jumping!

'WE'RE HERE! We're here!' The APCs are made well aware of which are the Australian positions in the enveloping darkness – the distant figures leaping for joy.

The cavalry *are* here! Bob Buick is not the only one who thinks he is in a Hollywood adventure tale for it really is 'just like in the movies. I felt like one of those Yankees saved from the Indians.'[10]

As disinclined as many of the Diggers are to show extreme emotions, the arrival of the APCs is such a special occasion that Bravo Company's Lieutenant John O'Halloran will observe 'some grateful D Company survivors going up to the machines and pressing their lips to the mud-caked metal'.[11]

Others content themselves with patting the metal, like they are good big dogs that have come to heel.

And D Company are not the only ones beside themselves with joy and relief. If not for the arrival of the APCs, O'Halloran notes, 'I have no doubt our small B Company contingent of reinforcements would have been wiped out along with the remainder of D Company.'[12]

As soon as the APCs come to a halt, Major Harry Smith moves towards them and is right there when Major Charles Mollison himself emerges.[13]

At this moment Colonel Townsend emerges from Ian Savage's APC, accompanied by his signallers, and formally takes charge.

His first orders are for Lieutenant Roberts to reposition the APCs on the eastern side of the perimeter, which is the direction that the enemy was last seen. Have them facing out and with even their pocket-lights turned off so as not to provide a target for whatever VC snipers and mortar teams might still be in the area. Captain Mollison, have your men unload the ammunition and *materiel*, and distribute them to Delta Company. And position your men between the APCs, to provide a screen for Delta, ready for any counter-attack.

Once in position, the engines are again cut and the Alpha Diggers quickly take up their positions, ready for anything. Yes, right now there is not a single enemy in sight, and no shots being fired, but that is no guarantee against a sudden counter-attack.

Things begin to settle, with Alpha Company medics now feverishly helping Phil Dobson care for the wounded, and there are already moves to get the first of them from the ditch and into the ambulance APC in preparation for their evacuation. One of the first to arrive is Delta Company Sergeant Major Jack Kirby, with a wounded man over each shoulder. Sergeant Jim Myles of Alpha Company is convinced they must be dead, but once Kirby lays them down he can see they simply have bad leg wounds which prevent them walking.

Now that the APC engines are turned off, and the enemy is no longer firing and there is no close artillery, all is suddenly quiet.

As complete darkness closes in the only thing that can be heard is the loud metallic clicking of the hot APC diesel engines cooling, and a lot of low moaning coming from their east. There are wounded men out there, likely from both sides.

Despite the relief that the APCs, Alpha and Bravo Companies have arrived, the mood is dark, as word spreads of the casualty rates. There are four dead Australian soldiers right here, and maybe a couple of dozen injured – some of them critically, others remaining on duty – while at least another dozen blokes are still missing, presumed dead.

God help us all.

Those figures are not yet confirmed, but it is already the most devastating loss of Australian life in wartime since the Korean War. All ears continue to strain for the tiniest sound of movement, perhaps of enemy soldiers crawling towards them? But beyond the odd shot coming from afar – likely VC commanders signalling their soldiers where to safely gather – there is nothing.

For 20 minutes everyone remains on high alert, until the order comes to stand down. Small patrols have gone out and determined that the enemy really has gone. And in the meantime, nearly everyone has been accounted for in each platoon in terms of the dead and wounded. By all accounts it is clear that 11 Platoon had been devastated, losing about 15 blokes, though it is not sure they are all dead, only missing.

And so to the business at hand.

Once the APCs and newly arrived troops are placed in defensive position, and the Delta Company wounded are being dealt with, Colonel Townsend convenes an O Group meeting in 2nd Lieutenant Ian Savage's APC, with Major Harry Smith, Alpha and Bravo Companies' Majors Mollison and Ford, and the Delta Company Sergeant Major Jack Kirby.

Colonel Townsend has a plan.

The dead and wounded will be evacuated aboard the APCs, together with the rest of Delta Company, to the edge of the plantation where choppers will fly the casualties back, while Alpha and Bravo Companies will walk out and . . .

And, sorry, what?

Lieutenant Dave Sabben – positioned no more than 20 metres away, his weapon cocked against a counter-attack – cocks his ear as a furious debate breaks out.

For Major Harry Smith can't contain himself.

'You want us to leave the battlefield?'

'Yes.'

'What about our missing men, still out there, some of them likely wounded, not dead? We don't want to leave. We want to stay right here, where it will be safer for everyone, send out a patrol to gather the wounded and in the meantime we can clear a Landing Zone by having the APCs knock over some trees first thing tomorrow morning. I *urge* you, Sir, to reconsider and allow us to stay here!'

(Beyond everything else, it seems against nature, against 2000 years of military tradition, to abandon ground that they have shed so much blood to hold.)

But Harry Smith can urge all he likes. Colonel Townsend outranks him and makes no bones about it.

'We won't be doing that. We have to get the wounded we do have out of here and back to medical care at Vung Tau, and not complicate things by staying here in force and needing to defend against a possible counter-attack.'[14]

With so many already dead, Colonel Townsend will not risk losing more in another battle tonight.

Outraged, but holding it together – just – Smith approaches both Majors Ford and Mollison, to get their support, and both agree. The trio of company commanders now approach Colonel Townsend once more, urging him to change his mind, but it makes no difference.

As Lieutenant Sabben continues to listen in, Colonel Townsend, in a very un-'mouse' like fashion, says 'No,' in a manner that will brook no arguing. Smith and his fellow company commanders might think this spot now secure, but Townsend does not and has no interest in stopping here in the darkness, with an unknown number of enemy nearby.

As to even the idea of landing choppers in the darkness in a small clearing in rubber trees, that is madness. This had not been Colonel Townsend's battle to fight, but having arrived at the death, he is determined to make his mark on the aftermath. They will *not* go after the wounded tonight. The first job is to consolidate their position, and it is with that in mind, Townsend orders Morrie Stanley to resume with the artillery and lob shells at Charlie's most likely pathways in the hope of knocking a few more over. Once all is stable, the real work of getting the dead and wounded out must begin.

On the key subject of where the choppers should land to get them out, Townsend orders that, once the most grievously wounded have been stabilised and can be transported, they return to the relatively open spot where Delta and Bravo Companies had had lunch . . . surely five years earlier? . . . which is some 750 metres to their west.

Meanwhile, in the darkness each company does its reaper's roll-call – a ghastly process, where some names are left hanging: Salveron . . . ? Grant . . . Jewry . . . Meller?

•

At Kangaroo Pad, back at 1ATF base at Nui Dat, Flight Lieutenants Riley, Grandin, Dohle and Lane continue to wait for further orders with the rest of their newly arrived comrades from RAAF No. 9 Squadron – their numbers including Squadron Leader Laddie Hindley, their Flight Commander. Most likely, they have been told, they will be required to fly in to do a dustoff to get out the wounded soldiers.

When?

They will be advised.

And so they sit, and talk. Among them is Col Joye, whose celebrity is rather beside the point right now, though talking to him at least helps pass the time. 'Naturally,' Hindley will recall, '[Col] was a very interesting person to converse with, but his main desire was to get my approval to travel in the helicopter to the evacuation area and back to Vung Tau, which I could not approve.'[15]

Although he gets no joy from Hindley, Col takes it well, his Brylcreem doesn't miss a beat and his famous long and lanky face creases into a grin as the questions continue. *So what is Chuck Berry really like?*

•

Colonel Townsend is speaking softly into the radio, giving the final Sitrep of casualties to 1ATF HQ. On the other end, an ashen-faced Brigadier Jackson says little, as he tries to grapple with just how catastrophic the battle has been. So far, Townsend advises, 6RAR Delta Company has suffered four confirmed dead, 16 wounded and 15 missing, presumed dead.

When it is at last mercifully over, without a word, Brigadier Jackson hands the receiver over to his signaller, before turning, walking away and slumping in a chair even as he buries his head in his hands. The responsibility of this job! The sheer crushing *weight* of it all. Could he have done things differently? Should he have shared the information he had about there being a large enemy unit in the very area Delta Company had moved out into?

The haunting questions rattle around his very soul. He has no answers.

•

A quick word, Mister Roberts?

Standing by his APC, Lieutenant Adrian Roberts looks up to see the rotund figure of CSM Jack Kirby hovering, and he has come on a delicate matter.

It's about my blokes of Delta Company. If it's all right with you, they'd rather not do the job of loading the four dead blokes into the lead APC, 30 Bravo.

Already shattered with exhaustion, this risks breaking them completely. Can you get your blokes to do it?

Of course, Sergeant Major. Understood.

Each of the four dead men are swathed either in their hoochies or in the same blankets that the cases of ammo had come wrapped in as they fell from the sky down on Delta. The men of Roberts's own 3 Troop move with enormous care, as they place them oh so gently into the back of Ian Savage's APC, all with overwhelming sadness. By now all the battle-lust is gone and the harsh reality of dead Diggers is hitting everyone hard. Paul Large, Jack Jewry, Max Wales and Rick Aldersea are all loaded not on top of each other, as logic would suggest, but side by side as dignity dictates, the whole operation being conducted in such silence it's as if it has come from the tomb.

Loading the wounded is far more problematic, as they have to be moved so carefully, and each man made comfortable on a stretcher and in a position where he can be still administered care, before the next wounded man is put in. And with so many it is well over three hours before they are all loaded.

In the meantime . . . quiet now!

Out to the eastern front of Delta Company – back where most of the battle had taken place – the Diggers not involved with loading the dead and wounded can distinctly hear the sounds of groans coming from the darkness.

Could it be the wounded members of Delta Company's 11 Platoon, the 15 blokes still missing?

When quiet coo-ees get no result, it is clear something will have to be done – even if Captain Mollison has forbidden all efforts at rescue tonight as too dangerous. Ignoring the order, two soldiers – Corporal Ross Gibson and Private Peter Bennett – take their lives in their hands and with their hearts in their mouths crawl forward, determined to get close enough to investigate the groans. They are armed with nothing more than an Owen sub-machine gun, a night compass and their wits, which are all about them and tingling like mad. It is an agonising task, caught between the need for speed and the care for caution, and they return an hour later reporting that, while they can hear sounds in the night, none responds to their hissed calls. Using the information garnered, Corporal Ross Smith gets the permission of Captain Mollison and goes out again, this time with Privates Peter Bennett and Ernie Dare.

They can hear moaning!

Ours or theirs?

Clearly they need to speak in code.

'Anyone from Sydney?' they hiss in the night.

Better still, the question that will sort out who are Aussies, and who might be Charlie just pretending to be a Digger.

'Who won the rugby league grand final?'[16]

A burbled 'Dragons' in the night will see them crawl forward at all speed.

If they say 'Rabbitohs' they deserve bullets anyway.

In fact, all they get is more moans and the sound of more men being dragged away. It is the VC coming for their wounded, not Australians.

It is hopeless, and they must return with nothing to show for their effort bar beating hearts that will take some time to calm. There must be some of their own wounded still out there. They just don't know where to find them.

•

No more than 100 yards from where he had first been hit out on the left of 11 Platoon, it has been a long haul for Barry Meller, and a difficult one, crawling through the darkness and trying to dodge the half-dozen VC soldiers he comes across. Meller keeps crawling for as long as he can, but in the end the amount of blood he has lost sees him nearly pass out and he knows he is not going to make it. Coming across a dead Viet Cong he grabs the man's pack, opens it, and helps himself to his ground sheet, which he wraps around himself. After finding a nearby spot behind a fallen tree, he sleeps or passes out, he will never be sure which.

2245 hours, 18 August 1966, Long Tan plantation, gentlemen, start your engines

At the conclusion of his own O Group, Lieutenant Adrian Roberts is satisfied that the other eight APC commanders understand his plan. Once underway they will go fast and furious, with Lieutenant Ian Savage's APC, loaded with the dead, in the lead. It will be the only one with headlights on, and it will be the job of all APCs behind to follow tightly, focus on the red tail-lights on the backs of the APCs in front.

They may, or may not be, attacked by the enemy. If they are attacked, they must instantly turn their headlights on before halting in 'herringbone formation'. This means every carrier swinging out at 45 degrees successively to the left and right – and opening fire. We will form a perimeter and the soldiers can add to the firepower of our defence from there.

Finally, all is ready. With Delta Company – surviving, wounded and dead – now in the APCs. Ian Savage knows that if he does not weave an accurate path through the plantations, there will be a pile-up that will beat any rush-hour smash.

Waiting for Roberts's call on the radio, Savage looks down into the darkness, and whispers to Trooper Geoff Newman, his driver: 'Boy, this will be the ride of your life.'[17] It is a warning and a command. Don't stuff this up, you won't live to regret it if you do. Ideally they will move so fast that Charlie, if he is out there, will not be able to draw a bead on them.

A single word comes through from Roberts: 'GO.'[18]

No sooner said than done, as the engines roar, the lights glare, and the APCs head off at full speed through the rubber trees, leaving the soldiers of Alpha and Bravo Companies in their wake.

Ian Savage's driver leads the way, flat strap, through the rain, racing through the gaps between the trees that always seem to be exactly a foot smaller than APC size, as they weave and cleave through the plantation, trees thrashing back against them as they pass until Savage's APC goes straight . . . straight into a bloody drainage ditch. The important thing is not to panic; some inspirational words are in order:

'For Christ's sake mate, get us out of this one, don't bog now!'[19]

Newman is thinking exactly the same thing and, in moves worthy of Jack Brabham, he slides the APC along, over and through; an inspired piece of driving that he wouldn't be able to repeat in a hundred attempts – and something he prays he will never attempt again. The wagon train of war rumbles on and the APCs speed towards a clearing where helicopters are due to land to take the wounded Delta men to medical care that amounts to more than a bandage and a reassuring word.

After arriving at the designated spot on the map – the clear space on the edge of the plantation – the next question is how to make it clear to the chopper pilots where they are. Colonel Townsend gives the orders: essentially, it is wagon-train formation, forming a circle in this time of danger, their machine guns pointing out, and the infantry ranged in the gaps between them. But leave the topside hatches of the APCs open with all internal lights on, so each vehicle shines a light into the sky. It ain't Mascot, but it'll do, forming a clear Landing Zone that the pilots will see from on high, while remaining relatively dark to any of the enemy in the area. Still, if Charlie wants to try again, Digger is ready.

Meanwhile, a directive has come through from 1ATF. While the day had started with Operation Vendetta, the night has become Operation Smithfield, named for Harry Smith, his men and the field of battle they've been operating in. ('Smith's having a field day out there!')

•

At long last, there is movement at the station, or at least at Kangaroo Pad, as an American dustoff helicopter lands. Wing Commander Ray Scott, having spoken to his men earlier as they cooled their heels awaiting US support, now calls his pilots to gather around.

'The troops have withdrawn to a cleared area on the western side of the rubber,' he advises. 'We don't know if the enemy are still in the area or planning a counter-attack. So that we don't give away their position, we won't use landing lights as we come into their position.'

'Do you want us to go in first?' asks the skipper of the US chopper.

'Yes. You have the specialist gear on board,' Raw replies. 'Take the most seriously injured.'

'Roger.'

'I'll go next,' he continues. 'Then I want each of you to take off as the preceding helicopter clears the area. Laddie, you can organise an order. Take your time and good luck.'

Not long after the Yank chopper has soared into the night sky, Flight Commander Laddie Hindley, once a World War II fighter pilot, approaches Frank Riley.

'I think you've done your bit, Frank,' he says softly. 'We'll only use you if necessary.'

Frank is pissed off at the very idea of it. He has led the whole show to this point, and now he has to wait at the back of the queue? It's not right!

'Shit, mate,' he replies. 'I want to go back in.'

'Let's see,'[20] Laddie replies, evenly.

•

Experienced hands can tell this first one must be a Yank chopper even before it lands. Just as Yanks swagger when they walk, they fly like they own the skies *and* the ground. To be a US dustoff pilot you need two tours of duty and they have a cool confidence born of brutal and bloody experience.

And yes, there had been strict orders issued by the Australian command *not* to use landing lights, but he is a Yank and doesn't care for strict orders from Australians. He comes down with all his landing lights glaring below and has no trouble finding the spot in the middle of the APCs, coming in for a smooth landing. The doors are opened and the three most seriously wounded Diggers are quickly stretchered on board before the chopper whisks away again.

Things are not so easy for the six Australian choppers which follow. They have taken off from Nui Dat with no lights on.

This is no easy task in what is still a dark and stormy night, and it is made worse for the lead Australian chopper pilot, Wing Commander Ray Scott, when the bright light at the Landing Zone he has spotted suddenly disappears.

(Unbeknownst to him, this had been the fully laden American chopper, whisking away and suddenly turning off its landing lights.)

'[The] only semblance of light now visible was a small, hazy red/purple glow,' he will recount, 'which frequently appeared to waver and disappear in the poor visibility.'[21]

Perhaps compensating for the blazing landing lights of the now departed American chopper, Colonel Townsend had decreed that the hatches must be closed with the only light now coming from four Diggers holding up torches to the night sky in each corner of the Landing Zone. The result is that, in contrast to the Yank, the Australian pilots must lower themselves cautiously – like an old blind man getting into a too-hot bath – aware of the peril they might be in and also creating; but better that than tipping into the earth and the blades slicing through their waiting countrymen.

But after waiting their turn, each pilot – after making sure there is no sign below of the red anti-collision light each chopper has on its top side – lands, before the wounded are assisted on board and they are away.

Private Ron Eglinton is carrying one of the stretchers to a chopper when his arm gives out and he drops the front of the stretcher. What's the problem?

Oh nothing, I was shot in the ribs a while ago but I'm fine.

Get in the chopper!

No, that's for the wounded blokes.

GET IN!

He gets in.

Meantime, Lance Corporal Dennis Spencer – swathed in bloody bandages to stem the wounds he'd suffered trying to take the radio forward to 10 Platoon – sits, dazed, in the second-last chopper evacuating them. His most profound sensation is wonder at the sudden quiet. No artillery. No shots being fired at you, or beside you. Just the beautiful thrum of blades as they head towards the lights of Vung Tau. It is like being plucked from your real world of hell and into a glorious dream; but it is the dream that seems real. Was everything that just happened before a nightmare, then? All that death and destruction? It scarcely seems fathomable.

And yet these bloody bandages and the wounded bloke beside him says it all happened. And now, here he is. Only six minutes after taking off, the chopper touches down at 36 Evac Hospital, an American unit, used to taking a mass of wounded in minutes and with no time for modesty or manners.

Only seconds after the chopper settles, there stands a huge Black American soldier, a medical orderly, who is all business and care, for care is his business.

'Where you hit?' he asks in a drawl that must be from somewhere south of Alabama, if there is such a place. Dennis Spencer has no sooner pointed to his bloody abdomen than the magnificent Yank gets down to business, and in a second he is out of his seat and in the arms of his saviour, being carried like a red rag doll towards a huge hangar! Inside the hangar are rows of beds, doctors and surgeons in white coats each looking cleaner than the last. The Yank slaps Dennis on a table and brings out a set of giant scissors. SNIP! SNIP! SNIP! Three cuts and Dennis has lost his boots, trousers and shirt and is lying stark naked!

These Yanks are not mucking around. The doctors and nurses talk to the wounded men quickly, their eyes already doing a triage and their words flow: who is a priority, who can wait and who will need a miracle to make it. In a flash, Dennis is done, dazed and with his wounds cleaned and freshly swathed being served a hot meal in a ward by a smiling nurse. What the hell was that? That was the fastest and best medical treatment in the world. It only adds to the unreal feeling of it all; shattered soldiers, wearing white robes, propped up in actual beds . . . is this still a dream? For many it is, morphine and anaesthetic wiping their minds of what occurred so their mates can see that terrible flash of consciousness when reality kicks through the drugs. What the hell just happened?

0020 hours, 19 August 1966, Long Tan plantation, conga line in the darkness

All right for some.

Both Bravo and Alpha Companies must get out of the plantation on 'Shanks's pony', which is easier said than done. It is Bravo Company who leads the way in single file, pushing towards the co-ordinates that they have been given, with Alpha Company falling in behind.

In the moonless pitch-blackness it is no easy thing, and they must simply follow the diktat of the luminescent compass bearings held by the lead man wherever it leads them, while each man has to hold on to the webbing of the man in front so as not to get lost in the dark. This also means they must constantly stop when the point man either runs into a tree or falls over a log – the cries are constant: 'Wait . . . ! Line broken! . . . Stop! Stop . . . !' followed eventually by 'Go . . . go . . .' – but an hour later they can tell by the sounds of the choppers landing and taking off in the near distance that they must be getting very close.

•

Frank Riley remains like a caged lion. The first of the choppers have gone now, and they are among the last few remaining at Kangaroo Pad, with still no word on whether or not they will be needed. Every chopper that takes off from the Landing Zone reports, 'Taking off, now,' to let the next chopper know the way is clear, before the departing chopper heads to Vung Tau with their wounded. But there is still no way of knowing if Frank and Bob's chopper will be needed.

To pass the time and settle Frank down, Bob Grandin turns the discussion to how they best do this if they do get the call. True, compared to their last assignment this is a lesser challenge, but to land a chopper on a small space in complete darkness is still no small thing and it will require all of them working as a team.

The crewmen will have to maintain watch on both sides for any obstacles they might hit, ready to shout out the instant they sense danger, while Grandin himself will keep his eyes on the dials and call rates of descent, while also looking through the windscreen under his feet. And Frank will fly her, taking in all the information, including watching his own dials to bring her down safely.

Listening to the radio, they can follow events and are aware of the angst that the American chopper used its landing lights – possibly signalling to every VC within 10 clicks precisely where the Australians could be found. It would only need one of those VC to come forward with a rifle and he would be able to bring further choppers down with impunity.

Other radio chatter has given fair warning of how difficult many of the succeeding choppers had found it to locate the right spot, while still others had had to make several aborted attempts before landing safely.

The radio crackles.

'Taking off now,' says the pilot of the eighth chopper to go in.

It is quickly followed[22] by the voice of their superior, Squadron Leader Laddie Hindley.

'Now, Frank,' he says simply.

Their time has come.

Frank brings the bird down expertly in the middle of the APCs. There are no wounded left! Will you take the bodies? 'Sure,' says Frank. The bodies of the first three dead Diggers – on stretchers, and wrapped in ponchos – are gently placed in the back of the chopper.

One body remains.

It is carried, solo, by a Digger, who, with tears in his eyes, hands it over to RAAF Leading Aircraftman, Bluey Collins.

'Look after him for me, mate,' the Digger says to Collins. 'He was my mate.'[23]

Riley pulls up, eases forward on the joy-stick and the chopper of the fallen flies to the heavens above, heading for Vung Tau.

Dustoff is now completed, and . . .

And just as they are airborne, the night sky to their front is filled with the light of a massive throbbing explosion, followed an instant later by what sounds like 10 claps of thunder at once.

The radio roars with the alarmed voice of Wing Commander Ray Scott: 'ARE YOU All RIGHT, FRANK?'

No they're *not* fucking well all right.

They are pissed off.

'STOP THE ARTILLERY!' Grandin roars back.

'There is no artillery.'

'Well, what the hell was that?'[24]

Turns out, it is the Americans, dropping bombs. They have been given a 'free' drop zone where they think the VC might have settled for the night, and it turns out to be on a hill 2000 metres to their north, Nui Dat 2.

In the distance there is now the occasional burst of artillery fire and US air-strikes as the fleeing VC are harassed for their trouble on the most likely escape routes they'd take.

Relieved, sort of, Frank Riley and his crew – together with their shocking cargo – continue back to Nui Dat, trying to keep their minds off the ghastliness of it all. Alas, the backwash from the rotors tugs the ponchos away.

'I spent the trip trying not to look at the bodies,' Flight Lieutenant Bob Grandin will recall. 'Their faces were young and innocent. No worry whatever showed on their beautiful faces.'[25]

It is 0050 hours, 19 August 1966.

With the departure of the last chopper, the artillery is recommenced, pounding likely areas of VC congregation, while avoiding the area where 11 Platoon had been ambushed, on the reckoning their own Diggers are still there, and hopefully some of them might be alive.

•

Wh . . . ?

What . . . ?

Where . . . ?

A stirring in the darkness, even beyond the explosions.

Out in Long Tan rubber plantation, it is Private Jim Richmond, coming to as the ground vibrates once more with shell-fire, the stench of cordite fills the air and blasts of thunder roll over him from close quarters.

To his amazement, he is still alive, though it feels like he is dying of thirst. Slipping in and out of consciousness, most of his stirring comes with renewed blasts. Jim feels crook all over, but particularly on his side where he is now aware that he has a deep wound from the shrapnel. He rolls over so the wound goes straight in the mud, in the hope that that will stem some of the blood flow.

Shells keep coming, and he listens to each one, thinking every time, 'This one's going over, and this one's falling short, and this one's for you, Jim.'

Miraculously though, for the moment, the one with his name on it hasn't fallen yet.

He is sick with worry. Not for himself, but for his widowed mother back in Brisbane, knowing that if he dies, 'she would be up shit creek'.[26]

All he wants to do now is *live*. For her. And yes, all right, for him.

With that in mind, he weakly calls out 'Medic!'[27] at one point, in the vain hope there is one of his own within coo-ee, but when his only reward is a couple of shots fired in his general direction he stops. Other moans in the night, and the sound of movement, indicate that he is not the only wounded in the area. But he is certainly the only to shout out in English.

Jesus. His poor mother.

Unaccustomed as he is, he begins to silently pray.

'Oh God, please just let me make it through the night alive, and if ever I get back to Australia, I promise I will go to church every Sunday for the rest of my life.'[28]

Unbeknownst to Richmond, no more than 100 metres away, Private Barry 'Custard' Meller is also still alive, wrapped in the ground sheet he has taken off a dead enemy soldier, and taking shelter under a rubber tree. He is unarmed, having abandoned his rifle when it had been apparent that he could either crawl or keep his rifle but not both. This tree had come at the limits of his energies and he knows he cannot go further. He may or may not survive till morning. If he does, his best hope is that his mates in 6RAR will get to him first, and not the VC. Either way, it is beyond his capacity to do anything more to save himself.

•

Out of the darkness and approaching the Landing Zone, still stumbling but infinitely relieved to be here, come the men of Alpha and Bravo Companies.

With the three companies now reunited once more, the dead and wounded evacuated, and the APCs still in position, all that remains is for them all to get through to the dawn intact so they can go once more to retrieve their own dead and wounded.

It is still unsure where the enemy is, and it is quite possible they will launch another massive attack.

Under the circumstances, it is decided that the shattered Diggers of Delta Company can sleep, while Alpha and Bravo Companies provide the firepower between the APCs to defend the perimeter, against the potential for enemy attack. It is Bravo Company that pulls the first stint and Lieutenant John O'Halloran's platoon in the front line – rifles loaded, machine guns primed – ready for whatever the night might throw at them.

In the meantime, now relieved of their defensive duties, the Delta Diggers sink gratefully to the ground, and many are something between asleep and comatose within seconds.

But not all.

Many lie there, whispering.

'Where's Shorty? Did he make it?'

'I haven't seen Largey? Is he with you?'

'Eggo! You're alive!'

Major Harry Smith, meanwhile, is caught between trauma at what has happened – 'Afterwards I thought, shit, why am I alive?'[29] – and the need to get organised for the morrow.

Where is Colonel Townsend? There are a few things he needs to be told.

•

Hush now.

All quiet on the Western Front.

Even the artillery has finally stopped for the night. And there are no more American planes dropping napalm on a whim, a wing and a prayer. Most of Delta Company, and a fair measure of Alpha and Bravo Companies, have fallen into a deep and exhausted slumber, while the latter two have still provided the firepower needed to guard the perimeter between the APCs.

Ah, but lean in. Within one of the APCs, Roberts and his crew are wide awake, unable to sleep and talking over the events of the afternoon and evening. All are in what Roberts will describe as a state of 'dazed shock'.

Two APCs along, Harry Smith is arguing as respectfully as he can with Colonel Townsend, among others, as they go over the plans for the morrow. The Colonel believes Delta should head straight back to Nui Dat and even take two days R & R in Vung Tau, but Smith simply will not hear of it, and is insistent – again to the point of insubordination, for Townsend is straining his own veneer – that when it comes to retrieving their own men, it is imperative that Delta be to the fore.

'I thought it was essential for our own morale and peace of mind,' Smith will note, 'that my courageous men be first back in to recover our missing soldiers and first to see what we had done to the enemy.'[30]

Brigadier Jackson has passed on his orders that they will have freedom of movement so long as they stay within artillery range, and it is his expectation that the operation will take two to three days.

Overhead artillery fire continues, targeting likely Viet Cong contingents to the east of the battlefield, as the US Air Force, in close support, delivers a total of 12 air-strikes to attendant locations.

•

Good God. Is she really a 17-year-old Sydney girl standing all alone in Vung Tau in the middle of the night?

She is. And all because of American propriety. Once arrived back in Vung Tau, the Americans had taken the view that it would be quite improper for Little Pattie to have shared accommodation with the Joy Boys, as on a US base men and women do *not* mix after dark, at least not officially. And so, shaking, she peers into the darkness, through the fencing, past the grass yard and sees sandbags by the front door. Lots and lots of sandbags.

What to do? The only thing she can, the thing her mother had always told her: Put your best foot forward, Pattie.

Walking towards the darkened building, there is the sudden creak of a door, followed by a cry: 'I was told a pretty girl was coming!'[31]

It proves to be a young Black US soldier who, wonderfully, is welcome itself.

Sensing her vulnerability, the young man takes her bag and bids her to follow him.

'I'm going to look after you, I'll take care of you,'[32] he says, taking her inside and showing her to a crisp clean room where she will be sleeping tonight. Except she won't be sleeping tonight, she can't. Sleep can't compete with adrenalin and Pattie gets up and walks out back to the lobby and sits with the soldier. 'What am I doing here?' she thinks. 'Where is my family?'

All she knows is that Col is still out there, somewhere, over there near Nui Dat, right in the middle of that murderous muddle of war she and the Joy Boys had flown over in silence, after which the Joy Boys had been hustled off to 'male accommodation' somewhere miles away on this endless base.

And here she is.

Vietnam.

'Overseas.'

Now, she is less scared than . . . bewildered at how quickly everything has happened. At least the kind American soldier keeps up a steady run of patter, which mostly helps.

But now his radio sparks and he holds it to his ear, murmuring:

'Yeah right . . . Oh . . . Another Ossie killed?'[33]

Yes, another Aussie killed. Pattie starts counting as each message breaks through their talk; each stuttering spark of static signalling another man, another Australian, dead. She stops counting at 12.

But nothing stops the body-bags. For as the evening stretches surreally on; trucks pull up and the friendly GI has to jump up and cheerfully help unload body-bags, which are brought into the lobby, to be moved somewhere in the morning? Australians? She doesn't know. Probably Americans.

It all just seems so . . . ghastly . . . so ghastly, it surely must be happening to someone else? It is so out of her realm that it seems unreal, and is less upsetting than she would have thought. Just two weeks ago, if she had been confronted by a pile of dead bodies in bags in the foyer of Sydney Girls High, she would have burst into tears. Now she looks upon them with a strange kind of benign horror. Little Pattie watches and thinks how strange it is that this isn't upsetting. Australians keep dying on the radio, dead Americans keep coming into the lobby. She keeps talking to the GI, he's lovely. *What's Sydney like?* Not like this. It will be dawn soon. The sun must come again.

•

In the ward of the American 36th Evacuation Hospital at Vung Tau, it is the most extraordinary thing. No fewer than 23 wounded Australians have been brought in from the Battle of Long Tan, and *all* of them are still alive. The medic, Phil Dobson, had done an amazing job in binding their wounds, stemming their blood flow and stabilising their conditions, just as the evacuations via APC and chopper had also been accomplished with a maximum of professionalism.

'As I looked along the rows of casualties in the unnatural quiet,' Red Cross Field Force Officer, Jean Debelle, will comment, 'the stunned and wounded eyes, as much as the damaged bodies, identified those in the ward who had survived the battle in the rubber plantation. I heard no moans or crying. I was mentally prepared for tears from the men. I saw none . . . The only sound in the ward was the clump of army boots on the concrete floor as the medical staff hurried about their work of healing.'[34]

•

In his own hospital bed in Malaysia, Captain Bob Keep wakes to devastating news. A major attack by an enormous force of the enemy has left many dead Australians at Long Tan, just next to Nui Dat.

'I just disintegrated totally . . .' he will recount. 'So in some way it was, you know, a personal tragedy that I wasn't able to get the message through. But then it was too late for me.'[35]

Would things have been different, if only he had been listened to? He is sure that is the case, and the certainty of it will haunt him for the rest of his days.

CHAPTER FIFTEEN

DAWN'S HARVEST

When the hurly-burly's done,
When the battle's lost and won.

William Shakespeare, *Macbeth*

Only the dead have seen the end of war.[1]

George Santayana

0530 hours, 19 August, dustoff site, western edge of Long Tan plantation

Those Diggers staring with glazed and blood-shot eyes to the small but telling glow in the east? That's 6RAR's Delta Company. They're aware they've made it through the night and will shortly see a sunrise which they had thought would never be theirs again.

In the first nudge of the dawn proper there is gloomy movement.

Many have slept badly, some have not slept at all, still others have slept but in all their maudlin lugubriousness over the shocking defeat yesterday, are even more desperate to get back into the plantation to search for their mates. Yesterday was the worst day for Australia since the war began, and not since the early stages of the Korean War had so many – likely – been killed in a single action. And it might not be over yet. If they can attack like that yesterday, they can attack today.

Time for another dingo's breakfast.

And can we get going? Go and get our blokes, and get out of here?

No. To the disbelief, deep frustration and rising rage of many – and no-one more than Major Smith – it is a good TWO HOURS before Colonel Townsend emerges from his APC, even as American choppers land. They are bringing fresh troops in the form of 5RAR's D Company, while 6RAR's Charlie Company has also been brought out in more APCs, meaning that, right now, there are no more than 200 soldiers defending the base at Nui Dat, and virtually no serviceable APCs.

At last the brass feel they have enough assembled strength to retrieve the dead and look for the wounded. They're hoping against hope there'll be some of the latter, but they won't know until they look.

Colonel Townsend gathers his officers – including Major Harry Smith who is still chafing at the bit to get going – and gives them their orders.

We will move out at 0845 hours. (*The man with the rising colour, biting his tongue is Harry Smith. STILL more than an hour before they set off!*)

Delta Company will return to the battlefield to recover their dead, with 5RAR moving in APCs to cover their eastern flank as they do so. Alpha Company is to return to where it and 2 and 3 Troop fought yesterday and search for the fallen, all to keep both eyes out for any VC survivors from D445 Battalion. Oh, and just so we are clear, Captain Mollison, all companies aboard the APCs are under the command of the APC commander, until such times as you disembark.

Colonel Townsend's words are briefly drowned out by the sound of a Sioux chopper landing in the same circle as the night before. It is Brigadier Jackson arriving to take charge of the whole operation.

The sun that was such a stranger yesterday beats brightly down upon the Australians as they set off with a dark purpose familiar to generations of warriors: to find their dead, honour them and bring them back on their shields. And yes, maybe find survivors, but everyone is realistic. There can be little hope of that. If not dead from wounds initially suffered, they surely would have been killed since by either the artillery that has pounded them or the attention of Charlie himself.

And so they go forward in bright sunshine, but with darkness in their hearts. In the lead are the men of 6RAR's Delta Company, aboard the APCs as a right forward company, while 5RAR's Delta Company are in their own APCs as a left forward company. 6RAR's Bravo and Charlie Companies and the other units are on foot, covering the flanks. The progress is slow, with scouts forward, all on the lookout for a possible ambush. In short order they arrive at the battlefield proper, marked by suddenly shattered trees shorn of leaves, enormous craters, shredded earth and, oh God . . . bits of bodies, followed by the torsos and men they were once attached to.

Jesus Christ, Mother Mary, have mercy on us all.

(A curiosity of war is that while hatred for the enemy is the fuel that drives much of the close-contact combat, that hatred instantly disappears once confronted with your handiwork, replaced by an empathetic humanity. There but for the Grace of God . . .)

The gore is indescribable as for the first time they see close up what the shells and their own bullets have wrought on those waves of soldiers.

Delta Company dismount.

Lieutenants Sabben and Kendall, with their men, get off the APCs as each platoon goes back to the point on the perimeter they had defended the afternoon and evening before. They begin to gather the enemy dead and retrieve what few weapons have been left behind – for it is clear that the surviving enemy had been here in the night or at first light to evacuate the conscious wounded and salvage the weapons.

To make it all even more grisly, most of the enemy who had been killed by Delta Company in front of the perimeter had subsequently been raked by artillery fire for the rest of the battle, meaning that right in front of the company defences, there is barely an intact body remaining. As much as possible they try to put body pieces back together on the same piece of canvas, and the USHQ required 'body count' really does become a head-count, as that is the only way to make sure you are accurate.

As shocking and distasteful as it is, the confirmed death toll of the enemy steadily rises – 20 . . . 30 . . . 40 . . . – and so, too, does the mood among the Australians lift. No, they still don't like body counts, but this really does change things. Yes, they had taken a pounding last night, and had many casualties, but it was nothing like this. Instead of suffering a terrible defeat the previous day, it is really starting to look like an amazing victory, at least if such things can be quantified by the relative depths of disaster on both sides.

'We could see that [we] had accounted for ourselves well,' Dave Sabben would recount. 'Yes, we had lost mates but it hadn't been in vain and we had made a big impact.'[2]

That impact is underscored by the swarms of flies already buzzing all around the bodies. As you approach you can see and hear them, gorging on the already rotting bodies.

Just within the bounds of security, trying not to expose themselves to the possibility of ambush, Harry Smith and Delta Company are soon moving on, eager to get to the point where 11 Platoon had been ambushed, their hearts in their mouths, not sure what they are about to find. Everything suddenly seems so . . . deathly silent . . . bar one thing. As they get closer, they realise it is the haunting sound of one of the platoon's radios, which had been abandoned in the scramble to get out, still crackling away in the forest. It has clearly been going since the battle.

Suddenly a cry up ahead.

The hands of the Diggers fly to triggers.

It is someone standing up, just, and leaning against a tree.

It is an Australian soldier, weakly waving!

Medic! We need a MEDIC on the double!

Who is it?

Why it is Private Barry 'Custard' Meller, leaning back on a rubber tree and holding his bloody side. He is weak, but he is alive!

Where is the MEDIC?

'Hey Custard, how are ya?' the first Digger to get near him calls out.

Custard looks him up and down and slowly replies, 'You bastards took your fucking time, didn't you?'[3]

Who can disagree?

Once Meller is taken in hand – with some water in him, he is soon groaning – the men of Delta keep moving, slowly, carefully. Just 10 minutes later, here they are.

Oh dear God, and there *they* are.

It is our men. The lost men of 11 Platoon.

We have come to the spot where they made their last stand, where no fewer than – count 'em – 13 Diggers lie dead. Most movingly, for the most part their heads are still over their rifles as if they are about to shoot, and those rifles are still pointed to where the enemy had been attacking them.

They are in sum, in this moment of discovery, the very apotheosis of Laurence Binyon's famous poem, 'For the Fallen' . . .

They went with songs to the battle, they were young,
Straight of limb, true of eye, steady and aglow.
They were staunch to the end against odds uncounted;
They fell with their faces to the foe.

They shall grow not old, as we that are left grow old:
Age shall not weary them, nor the years condemn . . .

The most extraordinary and moving thing is that all the rain has washed the blood off them and cleaned their wounds to the point that you could swear, I mean just swear, that they are still alive!

'They all had their rifles and they had all actually sort of died in the firing position,' Adrian Roberts will recall, 'or they seemed all to be dead in the firing position.'[4]

When they gently remove the rifle from one dead Digger, his finger had been so firmly on the trigger that a shot rings out! Mercifully, no-one is killed. It is one thing to die by 'friendly fire', but to die at the hand of a dead friend would be the ultimate in horror and . . .

And hang on, is one of the dead even *speaking*?

'Sergeant Buick, Sergeant Buick . . .'

Wait? What? *Where?*

Over there!

Some metres away from the 13 dead Diggers they have discovered they find Private Jim Richmond, still alive, and lying in the mud. When they turn him over, his wound is ghastly – Medic! – but probably manageable. Richmond will later note that he had been practically unconscious when his mates from Delta Company had arrived. It had been like a dream.

'Then I heard Sergeant Buick's voice,' Richmond will recount. 'So I put me hand up. He's not a good-looking bloke, Bob, but I nearly could have kissed him that day anyway.'[5]

Again, like Meller, Richmond is stabilised, and quickly taken back to the clearing on an APC where a chopper can whisk them to the American 36th Evacuation Hospital at Vung Tau.

Kev Branch of 10 Platoon is observing the APC's movements and moving himself into position to face off the next attack when he comes across an old friend. It is his fellow scout, Doug Salveron. He is lying on the ground with a hole through his head.

Branch bursts into tears. He keeps moving, but he will never forget that sight or that thought, so simple, so matter of fact, so bloody sad.

Lieutenant John O'Halloran will be equally haunted.

Where is Sharpie?

Over there.

It is Gordon, lying face-down beside the Chinese-made AK-47 he had picked up after the first contact the afternoon before. His head is a little turned, his face also washed clean by the rain, but his eyes are open. Gently, O'Halloran reaches down and closes the eyes of Gordon Sharp, his friend of most of the last two decades, from their days in primary school together. Inevitably, images flash forth: Gordon riding bikes through the streets of Tamworth, Gordon scoring a try, Gordon playing cards, Gordon and he fighting over women, Gordon breaking both wrists back at Scheyville, but insisting he would continue anyway . . .

And now he lies here, *dead*. O'Halloran feels numb, and moves on. Over his shoulder he can hear Harry Smith on the radio, asking for a small bulldozer to be brought forth, to help bury the enemy dead.[6]

Let them get on with it.

For the moment they will do it without 11 Platoon's John Heslewood who had been with them all the day before when they had been hit. Here now, with his mates lying dead before him, the enormity of it all hits him anew and he sinks to the ground and sits, unmoving, and with a thousand-yard stare.

Elsewhere, high emotions are more manifest.

Bob Buick bursts into tears at the first sight of his men and is just trying to compose himself some 10 minutes later when the first intruders happen to arrive. They are officers and others, some from the press, come from Nui Dat and as far away as Saigon, who have had nothing whatsoever to do with the battle, but have now come in the aftermath, eager to have some small part of it, many of them with cameras. And there is something about them – a joyousness maybe? – that is just so jarring.

They care *only* about the enemy body count. They care nothing for what truly counts – the number of Australian dead.

And Buick is not the only one who feels this way, CSM Jack Kirby grabs a newspaper bloke who is talking too loudly and getting too close, and smiling too much. Taking him by the collar of his shirt, he physically suspends him in a rubber tree and walks away.

Buick, emotionally shattered, takes it way too far when he actually punches an officer who 'makes an undignified and unwarranted remark about my dead soldiers'.[7]

Intervening, RSM George Chinn barks sharply and sends Buick off to count the dead, before he explains to the officer that he must excuse his men, for they are a bit raw after so many deaths – while still making it absolutely clear he is on Buick's side.

Others of Delta Company feel the same in the face of the arrival of various top brass including generals, accompanied by photographers.

'They were getting around in their nice, starched greens and pointing a rifle at a dead body and their mates were taking photos of them,' John Heslewood will recall. 'They would come up and talk to you and a few of the boys told them to get out. They didn't want to talk to them.

Didn't want to talk about what happened. That upset the blokes more than anything else . . . The brigadier came to have a look around to say he had been there.'[8]

All up, the emotions of Delta Company in the face of their own dead prove too strong, and they are ordered away, to other tasks, while other soldiers start to gently gather up the dead of 11 Platoon.

And yet even now there is no respite for Delta as they are confronted by the sheer pathos and tragedy of the enemy dead.

'One of the thoughts that will always remain with me,' Bill Akell will recall, 'is . . . a young kid, a dead Viet Cong [fighter], I reckon he was about 16 or 17 years old, and he was propped up against a rubber tree and it looked as though his eyes were looking at my eyes. The horrible thing about it was that there was no bottom half.'[9]

Major Harry Smith will be similarly affected, and for the rest of his days will remember the blood daubed on the trees right by the line of the enemy's retreat. Yes, there are body parts everywhere but it is the blood that haunts, 'the blood of all the others that were dragged away, wounded, suffering . . . That worries me more than a dead body.'[10]

The fact that much of the blood is daubed in long streaks across the ground convinces many that whatever the official death count, it is likely a lot higher.

In other parts, the blood runs down the trees side by side with the white latex coming from where the bullets have hit. The whole world seems to be either weeping or bleeding.

Making the task even more gut-wrenching is the need to follow orders to search each corpse for diaries, letters, maps, written commands and all the rest to give to Intelligence. Private Terry Burstall of 12 Platoon is going through the pockets of one dead enemy soldier when he comes across a waterproof photo album containing four photographs.

He looks closely, and will remember the images he sees for the rest of his days. Here is the dead man, back when he was probably at his happiest, smiling, with his arm around an equally smiling, beautiful young woman. And here are two kids, about eight or ten years old, and still another of the dead man and a male friend holding hands, in the manner that Asians often do, outside a house with a narrow front.

It is all so appalling.

Just last night, to Burstall, this bloke had been one of those flitting figures in the distance, a nameless enemy deserving to be killed, and so he was. But now Burstall sees him for what he truly was: a man just like him, with a wife and two kids who loved him, and friends, doing his duty for his country . . . just like him. And now here he lies.

Burstall is deeply moved.

'It was the first time that day,' he will recall, 'I had come close to seeing the bodies as anything but inanimate objects. It hadn't occurred to me that morning but all these bodies were human beings who had mothers and fathers and children and loved ones . . .'[11]

With the bulldozer still not arrived, Burstall does what they are all doing – takes his shovel and digs the poor bastard a shallow grave, before moving on. At least there are plenty of shell-holes about, which makes the task a whole lot easier.

Here and now, not all the enemy are dead. When John O'Halloran's platoon comes across a young, wounded Vietnamese soldier, O'Halloran gets their interpreter to ask him some questions. After only a short time the interpreter calls out, using his nickname for the Australian officer, 'Bwana, he just like you.'

'What in the bloody hell do you mean, he is like me?'

'He is like you because he is a conscript. Except he comes from North Vietnam!'[12]

•

Little Pattie is beside herself, and still knows nothing despite all the efforts being made on her behalf by her friendly GI from the early morning onwards. Everyone is busy, nobody knows about some missing singer called Col. Every hour without news is an hour where she keeps imagining the worst. *Col was left behind. Col was killed by a stray mortar. Col was captured.*

Pattie keeps checking her watch, thinking that something must break by noon. Sure enough, at 11 am a car pulls up outside the lobby where Little Pattie is waiting. It's an Australian car!

The back door opens.

And out gets . . . Col Joye. She runs towards him.

He doesn't say a word.

She doesn't say a word.

He looks like hell.

To him, she looks like heaven – she is *safe*!

They are both too emotional to say anything at all.

Finally, gathering himself, Col breaks the silence: 'Hurry up! We're getting in the car. We're gonna do a show at the 36 Evacuation Hospital in Vung Tau!'[13]

Pattie waves to the smiling GI as she runs to Col and the car. The show must go on. Rock'n'roll.

•

General Westmoreland has been given that rarest and most treasured of all things in Vietnam for an American officer: good news. Believe it or not, General, Sir, an ANZAC Company has routed a VC Regiment! Casualties: only 33 per cent! The US has gotten used to losing entire companies to VC ambushes and yet these ANZAC bushmen have beaten an ambush and defeated a battalion or more? Westy does not believe it, intel is requested once more from Nui Dat and, with confirmation of the extraordinary rout, Westy is in the air at once. He will visit this good news personally and be photographed while seeing this miracle himself.

All up, the discovery of the 13 dead Diggers and the two wounded men means that all of the 15 missing Australians are now accounted for. But the work on this day is far from done, as they continue to search for enemy bodies, while always being keenly aware that the enemy might launch a counter-attack at any moment.

And it is not as if there aren't a few more VC still left alive in the field.

At least three times in the morning, shots ring out.

The first time, it is Sergeant Bob Buick who comes across, by his account, a grievously wounded enemy soldier who clearly does not have long to live.

'The poor bastard was lying there with half a metre of his gut spread over the ground,' Buick will recount in his memoir. 'A closer look revealed that most of his head was blown off exposing brain tissue. I couldn't believe he was still alive . . . Maybe his nerves were causing the twitching, the poor fucking brave bastard, his heart was still working, a quarter of his brain was spilling out of his skull and most of his guts were lying over the ground.

'I couldn't handle this. It was too much pain for me knowing that he could not possibly survive. I aimed my rifle and shot him twice through the heart. I hope I gave him the peace he deserved. I have only on very rare occasions spoken about that tragic event and this is the first time

I have put it in writing. I have never considered what I did morally right or wrong – it was something I had to do.'[14]

It was an admission that would cause Buick no small of amount of grief with allegations that he had committed a war crime.

'My reason for [including it in my book],' he will tell the author, 'was to demonstrate warts and all of the war, and although I was a professional soldier one does not lose their moral character and empathy towards others who the previous day was hell-bent on killing me and my comrades. I've been haunted since by the death and destruction that happened that day, proud to have made a strong contribution to the victory by doing what I did in directing the artillery fire mission to protect 11 Platoon and preventing the enemy from over-running us that would have prevented the loss of the whole company of 105 Australians and three Kiwis. The next morning was horrifying as I tried to detail in my book, [but it is what happened.]'[15]

Harry Smith has no problem with the act, at the time, or later.

'Not an angry shot was fired . . . over the next three days . . .' he will carefully note, 'except for a couple of rounds to kill two mortally wounded enemy . . . poor bastards with their innards and brains spilling out of their ragged bodies – and barely alive in awful agony.'[16]

These were, Smith firmly claims, 'acts of compassion . . .'[17]

A little later, a wounded VC seemed determined to fight on and take an Australian with him if he could, and is shot. Another time, a similar situation to the one faced by Bob Buick emerges, with the same result.

Captain Alan Hutchinson, a Forward Observer with 5RAR, would later recount: 'I remember two shots. About 50 metres away, I couldn't see it. Somebody said, "What happened?" "We're just finishing off a couple of them, too badly wounded to survive." Very quickly orders arrived that there would be no more of that.'[18]

Three members of the VC who are found badly wounded, but who present no threat, are choppered to the hospital at Vung Tau where they are cared for.

By mid-afternoon, as the Australians continue to search, the number of enemy dead has risen to an extraordinary 170-odd when two extraordinarily well-appointed Hueys – with two large leather seats in the middle, instead of the usual tiny canvas seats with impossibly small metal frames – arrive at the edge of the plantation and disgorge the highest-ranking officer of the Free World Forces effort in Vietnam, General

William Westmoreland, accompanied by a gaggle of press. In a war that is not going well – with American casualties alone of up to 1000 a month – this is a rare bit of good news and the American commander is eager to get to the bottom of a seemingly unbelievable story of how Australians and New Zealanders had taken on a force 20 times their size and won!

'Aggressiveness, quick reaction, good use of firepower and old-fashioned Australian courage have produced outstanding results,'[19] he tells the press.

Squired around the battlefield by Brigadier Jackson, who looks tiny beside him, General Westmoreland and his entourage come across a graveyard group of D Company Diggers, with shovels in hand, digging a large pit into which they are about to bury the row of VC cadavers that have been collected beside it.

In a chatty mood in the wake of this rare triumph of arms alone by this impossibly small posse of Australians, the American General swaggers up to the nearest Digger, one 'Wild Bill' Doolan, and says in his thick South Carolina drawl, 'You've done a good job, fellows, but this is the dirty part.'

Doolan looks him up and down and casually replies, 'She'll be right, mate. We can handle it.'[20]

And yet?

It really is a stinking, horrible task as the Australians must not only carefully begin the process of getting their own dead back to Nui Dat – just as with the dead of last night, they are put in the back of Ian Savage's APC, which slowly heads back to the 1ATF base – but also gathering up the body parts of their blown apart enemy that have been left on the battlefield. It is grisly, awful work, to pick up an arm, a leg, a torso with entrails trailing behind and drag it towards the hastily dug communal ditch, a nice term for a mass grave. And yet, strangely, that is not the worst of it. No, that's still the photos they carry. They were told to gather them for Intelligence, but it is the heart not the head that registers each image.

It is a shocking thing to be looking down upon a dead face of a slain enemy while holding in your hand a family group shot, working out which one he is among many brothers and sisters, or with his children – and knowing that in short order they will hear of a battle, and the death of their loved one.

Christ.

All of the thrill of victory of the early morning – *we beat the bastards, and we smashed Charlie!* – is now gone, as they keep going through the afternoon, and the next day, still burying the dead, gathering their effects, and also making piles of all the weaponry, the carbines, machine guns, AK-47s, Claymore mines – *easy, eeeeeeasy* . . . – mortar bombs, recoilless rifles and so forth.

The bodies are taken to the pits and covered with earth, while the personal effects, and documents, and even such things as pressed flowers from home in the pages of a book, are placed in an ever-growing pile under one of the rubber trees that the Intelligence mob will soon painstakingly go through to see what unit they were from, what rank they held, where they come from and so forth.

It is, for most of the Australian soldiers, a devastating exercise.

'It was this letdown,' Dave Sabben would thoughtfully recount, 'this awful dread . . . Not that *we* had caused it because for most of them we weren't witnessing people that *we* had actually shot. We knew that artillery had fallen or someone else in the company had shot them or something; it wasn't a personal guilt but it was just an overwhelming dread of just loss. I mean, yes, they were enemy soldiers, but by that stage we knew that they . . . were like us. They were trained like us, they were serving their country like us . . .'[21]

Still, through it all, the pile of personal effects keeps growing, the detritus of so many lives lost, the embodiment of so many grieving families. Even decades later it will be this image that will most haunt Sabben, even more than the dead bodies and mangled faces of the departed.

'No-one will ever know how pathetic it was to see them sitting there just under a rubber tree; collected lives sitting there waiting to be disposed of. It's terrible.'[22]

Like vultures with view-finders the photographers gravitate around the corpses and the weapons beside them, while not one of them shows any interest in the growing pile of personal family memorabilia which, yesterday, had meant so much to so many.

By the next day the enemy death toll is up to 245, which is the figure settled on despite more cadavers being discovered over the next fortnight – and despite the fact that the Vietnamese, aware of how the key metric for the American military and American press was how many enemy KIA, always made an effort to remove as many of their dead as they could.

The body count stops just before noon on Friday. Why? Because that time in Long Tan is three bells in Canberra, and the Holt Government wants to announce the astonishing figure – a greater victory than even we thought! – in the House before Parliament rises for the weekend. The figure is radioed to Canberra, Parliament rises and the body count does not. There are areas still unexplored that will officially remain that way; the true death toll will never be known. It is not quite the Fog of War, more like the Foghorn of Politicians; truth is the first casualty of war and accuracy the last of Long Tan.

Once done, Brigadier Jackson, exhausted, shattered, retires to his tent and barely gets out of bed. His Aide-de-Camp will subsequently become so concerned he contacts the highest-ranking medical officer in Vung Tau, who comes up, examines Jackson and tells him that unless he goes on a week's break to Vung Tau he will sign an order sending him home as 'medically unfit'[23] to serve.

'He spent most of the time,' his Aide-de-Camp, Lieutenant David Harris, will recount, 'lying on his bed, in a villa overlooking Vung Tau.'[24]

As to Delta Company, they finally make it back to Nui Dat three days after the battle, getting in at 1940 hours on 21 August. The mood is subdued. In Dave Sabben's tent, which he had shared with Gordon Sharp, half the tent is now just an empty bed. Sabben just sits and stares at it for a while, trying to come to grips with the implications of what they'd been through.

Like all of the Diggers, his thoughts turn to the families of the dead and how it must feel for them to find out their son won't be coming home.

•

It is Mrs Roma Sharp who sees them first.

She and her husband, Eric, are just returning from Saturday evening Mass in the Saint Nicholas Church when, as they pull into the driveway of their home at 70 White Street, East Tamworth, she sees a trio of men hovering nervously at their front gate.

Oh, God. No. Please no.

It is a priest, an Army officer and a policeman.

No!

And yet, as much as she wishes to deny it, she truly knows the shocking truth from the moment she sees them.

Gordon, dear Gordon, must have been killed.

The Army man, Warrant Officer John Cosgrove – who has left his worried wife and anxious home (they have their own boy, Peter, in the Army) to do this miserable task – regrets to inform them that Lieutenant Gordon Cameron Sharp, Second Lieutenant, 6th Battalion, the Royal Australian Regiment, had been killed on the evening of 18 August in a battle near the Vietnamese village of Long Tan.

The priest assures them that dear Gordon is now in a better place, in the arms of our Lord and Saviour Jesus Christ.

And the policeman is just there, affirming that . . . that he is so very, very sorry.

Roma Sharp collapses and has to be put to bed.

And where is their dear son?

The answer comes back: at the morgue in Vung Tau, and he will shortly be buried at a nearby cemetery – unless the Sharps pay the Federal Government $1000 to repatriate him. Furious phone calls ensue, with both the local Catholic priest and local Federal member becoming involved, before the Holt Government agrees that not only the body of Lieutenant Gordon Sharp, but the bodies of all those killed at Long Tan will be flown back to Australia.

In the case of Gordon Sharp he is accorded a large military funeral, with his flag-draped coffin pulled on a gun carriage through the Tamworth CBD as the people weep.

Similar tragic scenes, of course, take place all over the country.

In Coolah, the Large family get a knock on the door on the morning of 21 August, to find their close neighbours the Botfields there.

Have you heard the news?

No, what?

There has been a huge battle in Vietnam. Eighteen Australians have been killed. They said it was 6RAR, Delta Company. Isn't that Paul's company?

Yes.

For the next few hours, Paul's sister, Sandra silently prays, 'Please, God, don't let it be Paul. Please, God, don't let it be Paul. Please, God, don't let it be Paul . . .' and she keeps it up until in the late morning there is a knock on the door. It is the local policeman, bearing a cable. He is ashen-faced.

'Is your mother home?'

'She's in the kitchen.'

Silently, the constable hands her the cable and she opens it.

TELEGRAM

MELBOURNE TLX VIC 84/83 2.50P 21ST (PHONED FROM SYDNEY 3.25 PM)

AHFPD15C

ACKNOWLEDGEMENT DELIVERY MRS O D LARGE

8 HOSPITAL ST COOLAH NSW

IT IS WITH DEEP REGRET THAT I HAVE LEARNED THAT YOUR SON 2781704 PRIVATE PAUL ANDREW LARGE HAS BEEN KILLED IN ACTION ON 18TH AUGUST 1966 IN THE PHUOC TUY PROVINCE VIETNAM STOP I DESIRE TO CONVEY TO YOU IN YOUR SAD BEREAVEMENT MY SINCERE PERSONAL SYMPATHY AS WELL AS THAT OF THE GOVERNMENT OF THE COMMONWEALTH OF AUSTRALIA AND OF THE MILITARY BOARD STOP

. . . MALCOLM FRASER MINISTER FOR THE ARMY

(8 2781704 18TH 1966) 13[25]

Mrs Olga Large dissolves into tears of grief, only to rise again with tears of *rage*.

'Why did the Government do this?

'How can they send young men to war after training them for just a year?

'Why are they sending conscripts when there are Regular Army soldiers still back here?'[26]

In Brisbane, Beryl Gant is in her own kitchen, listening to *Somewhere My Love* on the trannie, and trying to read a book at the same time when she sees a green Army car pull up outside, and the next thing there is a knock on the door. It proves to be an Army officer, accompanied by an Army chaplain, who breaks the news.

There'd been a big battle in Vietnam. Kenny had been killed.

'No,' Beryl Gant is insistent. 'It can't be him.'[27]

There must be some mistake. There will be some name mix-up, she is sure of it. Her Kenny can't *possibly* be dead.

For the rest of her life, she will set a place at the table for Kenny, God rest his soul.

Down Bendigo way, Shorty Thomas's brother Pat had just returned home from a night out when he sees an unfamiliar car in the driveway.

'As soon as I stepped in the door they said, "David's been killed,"' he will recount. The shocking news has been brought to the family by a local Salvo, assisted by an Army officer.

'My mother really struggled,' Pat will remember. 'She learnt to cope with it but never got over it.'[28]

In Western Australia, Jim Aldersea is at home when he picks up the phone to find it is a military officer from Canberra, who, with little preliminaries, simply says: 'Do you know Private Richard Aldersea?' before making some reference to Jim's brother being '... wounded'.

Alarmed, not sure he has heard correctly – *wounded?* – Jim asks, 'How bad is he?'

'He's dead. He was *fatally* wounded.'[29]

Aghast, the eldest Aldersea son has to head out in search of his parents, finally flagging them down on the road between Pemberton and Northcliffe, to give them the devastating news.

It's Rick. He's dead.

All parents of the fallen are, of course, devastated. Some never lose their rage, with people like the Sharps and Thomases declining thereafter to answer the Army's letters, attend any commemorations or pretend that they are anything other than devastated and embittered to have lost their sons in a war that they were compelled to fight in.

Inevitably, Australia's Communist newspaper, *Tribune*, is savage in its coverage.

> **'Victory' rings hollow to the bereaved**
>
> **SENSELESS KILLINGS IN VIETNAM: BRING LADS HOME NOW**
>
> National Service conscript boys of 20 and 21 were the main Australian victims of the tragedy at [Long Tan] South Vietnam, last Thursday . . .
>
> As Labor Opposition spokesman Allan Fraser MHR said in Parliament last week, it is becoming 'a war of endless killing and pointless extermination.'[30]

That part of the press, however, remains in a tiny minority and for most of the rest Long Tan becomes an instant exemplar of Australian bravery, a legend born overnight: as exemplified by a story that appears in the *Sydney Morning Herald* three days after the battle.

Australians 10ft Tall In American Eyes

NEW YORK, Sat. — To be an Australian in America today is to feel 10 feet tall. The epic, and tragic, story of the four-hour battle waged by the Australian soldiers against the Vietcong was headlined across the United States. It was a bulletin on all radio stations. President Johnson was told of the battle while touring the country areas of New York State. Americans have conflicting views about the rights and wrongs of the Vietnam war, but all place a high premium on courage. The valiant fight put up by the heavily outnumbered Australians on that Vietnam rubber plantation brought high praise—praise that reflected on every Aussie.

For many Americans it brought back the legend of Digger valour in the South-West Pacific during World War II. In New York, the top-rated television program, 'The Today Show,' watched by 10 million Americans, made a special feature of the battle. Ace TV news commentator Dean Brelis spoke with emotion when he praised the Australian bravery and said, 'The United States is lucky to have them on our side.'[31]

AAP, meanwhile, has no doubt what the battle was all about.

SAIGON, Sunday (AAP). — The big Communist force which clashed in a bloody battle north of Baria last week with the Australian Sixth Battalion was on its way to attack the Australian Task Force headquarters. The Communists planned to strike between the Australian artillery battery and the adjoining New Zealand battery.

One of three North Vietnamese soldiers captured in the battle revealed this to interrogating Australian officers. The Communist force had a detailed plan of the task force area, and, according to the prisoner, knew of weak spots in the barbed wire entanglements through which elements of the force could infiltrate in strength.

Since the task force arrived in central Phuoc Tuy province three months ago, local guerrillas have made almost nightly probes of the outer perimeter of the camp, building up a picture of the defences. The big attack, with mortars, grenade launchers, .50 calibre machine-guns

> and automatic rifles, was to have been launched about three o'clock yesterday morning.
>
> If the enemy force had broken through the camp perimeter wires, they would have tried to over-run both the Australian and New Zealand batteries. This would have severely limited the firepower of the task force.
>
> Instead, while moving towards the task force area, the Communists ran into Delta Company of the Sixth Battalion.[32]

At least by that account, Long Tan – that accidental battle – could have saved Australia from no less that its own Dien Bien Phu, a calculated devastation designed to humiliate a nation and so shock its people that it would release its grip on Vietnam.

Instead the survival and final triumph of Delta Company against all odds becomes a source of inspiration.

In that battle, no-one had beaten the odds more than Sergeant Major Jack Kirby, who so often risked his life to save Delta that mathematics itself was humiliated. Or was it?

For, less than six months later, while Delta Company is on patrol on 6 February 1967, near the village of Dat Do, south-east of Nui Dat, a single shot is heard just south of Delta's position. A VC sniper? A VC patrol? No-one is sure – just that there are no Australians or Kiwis or Americans in that direction – which most likely means Charlie.

Better play it safe and let the artillery sort it out, dropping a few shells in to maybe catch him on the fly. The co-ordinates are called in, and a New Zealand battery of six howitzers oblige, only for their shells to land too far off. Delta calls in corrected co-ordinates. Only a minute later the men of Delta are shocked when the first shell lands among them! Followed by five more! Every man-jack of them leaps for whatever cover they can find. Alas, *alas*, some never get up again. One of them is Jack Kirby. His bleeding body is dragged on a groundsheet to marshland nearby as the medevac chopper is called in. Lilies surround his body as the chopper lands; but it is too late. Sergeant Major Kirby is dead, as are three other Australian soldiers, with 13 wounded.

•

Nearly three years have passed since 18 August 1966. Just before the third anniversary, Sergeant Neil Rankin, who had been in the thick of the Battle of Long Tan, and is now back on his second tour, is given a sacred mission by his 6RAR commanders.

Sergeant Rankin, go out into the Long Tan plantation in an APC and find the right place for a memorial. We have prepared a massive concrete cross 10 foot high, with a plaque of commemoration at its centre.

As Rankin alights from the APC and walks into the empty plantation all is quiet and he quickly notes the rubber trees still bearing 'the scars of small arms and heavy machine-gun fire', much as his mind still carries the scars of that day, with the pain of the memory of his lost friends never fading. He had been with 11 Platoon until just before the battle itself, swapping with Sergeant Bob Buick, and had often wondered if that had saved his life.

So, now, just where did his mates die?

Rankin sees it in a second. It is that spot right there, where 11 Platoon was first attacked *en masse*, and in fact the very spot where Lieutenant Gordon Sharp died. It is all round here that the .50 calibre machine guns of the VC killed 13 men of 11 Platoon, and wounded eight more.

'With the heel of my boot,' Rankin will recount, 'I marked the site where the cross was to be erected. The cross was flown in, slung underneath a helicopter and positioned on the battlefield where three years earlier the bloodiest battle involving Australian troops took place.'[33]

The actual ceremony to dedicate the cross is attended by all of 6RAR and includes the 10 current soldiers who, like Rankin, had fought in the battle themselves.

On the occasion of the original battle, Long Tan had resounded to many shattering bugle calls of the VC bugle. But on this day a sole bugle plays the oh so haunting 'Last Post' . . . before two bagpipers stand either side of the cross and play the 'Piper's Lament'. Tears begin to flow as they silently sing the haunting words:

I've seen the smiling
Of fortune beguiling,
I've tasted her pleasures
And felt her decay;
Sweet is her blessing,
And kind her caressing,
But now they are fled
And fled far away.

Standing at rigid attention, trying not to howl outright, a thought crosses Rankin's mind.

'Where I put that cross – in 11 Platoon's position – I knew it was in the blood of that platoon. It was important to me that that was where that cross stood.'[34]

Will this land be held? Will this cross stand? No-one knows at the time. But none there will ever forget this consecration or those who fell.

Vale.

EPILOGUE

Hearty congratulations to the 6th Battalion Royal Australian Regiment and a company of the 5th Battalion RAR for their fine show in Operation SMITHFIELD . . . our troops have won a most significant victory over the enemy and one of the most spectacular in Vietnam to date.

SIGNED W. C. WESTMORELAND, General, Commander USMACV[1]

A few days later when D Coy 6RAR returned to Nui Dat, Bob Buick, the Platoon Sergeant for 11 Platoon came over to our gun position and put his hand out to shake mine and said, 'Thanks, mate.' That said it all. I was proud to be a gunner.[2]

Jim King, 105th Field Battery

Yet we were wrong, terribly wrong. We owe it to future generations to explain why.[3]

Former US Secretary of Defense Robert McNamara in his 1995 memoir, *In Retrospect*, on the US involvement and management of the Vietnam War, which saw 58,000 American fatalities

For the survivors, the Battle of Long Tan would be a constant shadow, a wound on their soul, for the remainder of their time in Vietnam and beyond.

'The sense that we had gone through something that was so terrible that a third of us had either died or was wounded,' Dave Sabben would gravely recount, 'never left the company. It was like the ghosts were still in the company area. We were always aware that we weren't the company that we were . . .'[4]

One salve to their soul was that, in terms of the Australian war effort, at least their 18 comrades had not died in vain, and there would be many signs in the months – and years – to come that the VC were shocked by their defeat and determined to steer clear of the Australians thereafter.

Long Tan veterans report that after the battle they had to go 'looking for a fight', as the enemy seemed to recede before them, whichever direction they headed.

The following year, 7RAR would intercept a VC courier and find a message on him from command that intrigued and flattered in equal measure. The translated gist of it: 'If you come into contact with Australian soldiers, stop. Don't persist because that's not your job, you are not here to fight the Australians, you are here to convert the civilians so stop contacting the Australians.'[5] The message went on: 'If you see Australians go the other way or hide.'[6]

And yet, if the Australians indeed won the battle, no-one could claim they would go on to win the war, any more than the Americans did. The predictions of Ho Chi Minh – that he could lose 10 men for every enemy soldier, and he would still win – were proved absolutely correct.

On 30 January 1968, the 'Tet Offensive' began, which saw tens of thousands of Communist troops launching simultaneous attacks on 100 sites across South Vietnam. On the television screens of America it was the Government of Lyndon Baines Johnson who lost as the public could see for themselves that no quick victory was at hand, as promised. In the words of General Vo Nguyen Giap: 'After the Tet Offensive, the Americans moved from the attack to the defence. And defence is always the beginning of defeat.'[7]

The warnings of the Generals MacArthur and de Gaulle to President John F. Kennedy that if America went into Vietnam they would be handed their helmets also proved prescient.

As North Vietnam kept flooding ever more of their cadres to the South, America and her allies lost the stomach for the fight. Nui Dat was handed over to the South Vietnamese Army by November 1971 and the last Australian infantry battalion left Vietnam the following month. At the time of departure, Australian forces had suffered a total of 423 fatalities during their time in Vietnam, with 2398 wounded. Not surprisingly, the ARVN proved incapable of filling the vacuum left by the Australians and the VC soon ruled unchallenged once more.

The last American troops left Vietnam in 1973. After the South Vietnamese Army collapsed in 1975, the North Vietnamese Army moved in, and Saigon fell on 30 April 1975.

The last American citizens left on that day – as the iconic images would show – holding onto helicopter skids on the roof of the American Embassy.

Even by that time the very premises on which the Vietnam War had been based had been completely discredited, generating great bitterness, which exists to this day, over the USA – and Australia – being there in the first place.

Though denied at the time, the role of the Americans in the assassination of South Vietnam's President Diem would become beyond dispute when the 'Pentagon Papers' were published in 1971. They documented how US Ambassador Cabot Lodge not only gave the okay for the CIA to help with tactical planning of the coup, but offered US embassy protection for South Vietnamese Generals and their families if the coup went wrong and Diem remained in power!

As to the Gulf of Tonkin incident, upon which the authorisation for the whole Vietnam War rested, the years would also provide ample proof that the North Vietnamese never did launch those decisive 20 torpedoes at American destroyers and they were, in fact, either dolphins or weather effects on the radar misinterpreted by sonarmen.

Long after the war was over, and North and South Vietnam had reunified as the Socialist Republic of Vietnam – as happened in 1975 – the former principal architect of the whole Vietnam War, the former United States Secretary of Defense Robert S. McNamara visited Hanoi, and met with none other than his old adversary, General Vo Nguyen Giap.

What happened on 4 August 1964?'

'Absolutely nothing,'[8] Giap replied.

Which settled it.

In McNamara's words, 'It's a pretty damned good source.'[9]

In his memoirs, released in 1995, McNamara was remarkably candid in acknowledging that the whole Vietnam War had been wrong-headed from the first, that it was never a war that could be won, that US troops should have been pulled out of the country as soon as that had become clear. He had even gone on to say that was as early as 1963. McNamara admitted that the Presidents he served had made the wrong call: 'People are human; they are fallible. I concede with painful candour and a heavy heart that the adage applies to me and to my generation of American leadership regarding Vietnam. Although we sought to do the right thing – and believed we were doing the right thing – in my judgement, hindsight proved us wrong.'[10]

As for those who died for this error?

'That our effort in Vietnam proved unwise does not make their sacrifice less noble. It endures for us all to see. Let us learn from that sacrifice and, by doing so, validate and honour it.'[11]

As to Australia, documentation emerged proving it never actually had been invited by the South Vietnamese Government to send troops to the war. The Pentagon Papers proved that the said invitations actually came from the Australian Embassy in Saigon.

With the benefit of some 75 years after it was first proposed, we can now also say that President Eisenhower's 'Domino' theory has been proved false. Despite the fact that the West lost the Vietnam War and North Vietnam and South Vietnam did indeed unite to become fully Communist, the dominos did not continue to fall all the way to Australia or even remotely close to it. The riddle remains this: did the dominos stop because of Vietnam or despite of it? It is a Rorschach riddle, answered in the eye of the beholder, but the domino theory is a *raison d'être* which seems to recede in reason the further we get from the Cold War.

When it comes to the lasting memory of the Vietnam War in Australia, despite the fact that the Diggers would participate in many other famous Australian battles in their time there – Ap My An, Ba Ria, Binh Ba, Coral, to name a few – none would come close to the renown of Long Tan.

Not only is 18 August now recognised as Long Tan Day but it has also become the official day of commemoration for the Vietnam War, and is also tagged as Vietnam Veterans' Remembrance Day.

•

Ho Chi Minh remained in Hanoi during his final years. His health began to falter by 1969, precluding his active participation in politics. He continued his call for a united Vietnam, demanding the withdrawal of all non-Vietnamese forces in South Vietnam. It was a dream and a destiny he would not live to witness. Ho Chi Minh died on 2 September 1969. He was 79 years old. In the capital, Hanoi, you can still see his body displayed in a glass coffin, inside a large mausoleum.

•

Arthur Calwell might never have become Australian Prime Minister, but his views that Australia had no place getting involved in a Vietnamese civil war were vindicated – even though in the November 1966 election, the Vietnam War was so popular in Australia that **Prime Minister Harold Holt** increased his majority by nine seats to record the biggest Parliamentary majority in Australian history. Gough Whitlam took over as Labor leader on the strength of it.

As to **Peter Kocan**, who had shot Calwell in 1966, he was convicted of attempted murder and sentenced to life imprisonment starting out at Long Bay prison and winding up in Morisset Psychiatric Hospital, where Calwell visited him. Calwell lived to see Whitlam elected in 1972 – before dying the following year. Peter Kocan was released in 1976 and went on to re-establish a stable life, becoming such a successful writer that in 2010 the Australia Council Literature Board presented him the $50,000 Emeritus Award for his exceptional contribution to Australian writing.

Wayne Haylen, the conscientious objector who had collared Kocan on the night, went on to a distinguished legal career, becoming a QC and then Judge of the NSW Industrial Court.

•

After two years in Vietnam, **Brigadier Oliver Jackson** returned to Australia in 1967, joining the staff of Australian Headquarters, before becoming Chief of Staff of the 1st Australian Division. After retiring from the army in 1974, following no less than 37 years of service, he devoted himself to sailing and gardening. Jackson settled in Sydney and later in Burradoo, New South Wales, where he died on 7 May 2004, aged 84.

•

After his time in Vietnam was over **Colonel Colin Townsend** became Commanding Officer, Corps of Staff Cadets, at Duntroon and Commander, First Military District, at Brisbane before retiring in 1980 to raise beef cattle. Thereafter, he moved to Gympie in 1993 contributing to the local RSL, Legacy and the Vietnam Veterans Association. He died in Gympie on 10 June 2006, aged 79. At his funeral serving members of the battalion he founded, 6th Battalion Royal Australian Regiment, carried the coffin to the hearse while pipers played 'Amazing Grace'.

•

Major Harry Smith stayed with the Australian Army for a further 10 years after Long Tan, rising to the rank of Colonel.

'I went to One Commando in Sydney,' he would recount in discussing his book, *The Battle of Long Tan: The Company Commander's Story*, 'jumping out of aeroplanes, amphibious exercises, boats, all sorts of things like that. Not getting shot at.'[12]

Part of his remaining time in the Army was spent as senior administrative staff officer at HQ Western Command in Perth, where he conceived such a passion for sailing he founded the Western Command Army Sailing Club. Back on the east coast in 1972, Smith became Chief Instructor to the Army Parachute Training School at Williamtown RAAF where, some years later, he was injured in a parachuting mishap that damaged his spine and neck to such an extent he was medically downgraded as unfit for infantry field service. He left the service in 1976, taking a job with a Sydney firm marketing sea safety equipment. Sailing became his main interest and recreation. He and his wife settled in Hervey Bay in 2003, from where he would frequently head off sailing his yacht.

He admits he was 'a changed man' after Vietnam, 'and blotted it out', but was eventually diagnosed with PTSD.

'I keep it under control. I have been lucky that I have been sailing over the last 25 years, sailing to Cape York for six months of the year. That was my outlet. That keeps me involved in other things. I am sure if I dwelled on what happened in Vietnam I would probably go gaga but I am not prepared to do that. When you have more time on your hands your mind dwells on nasty thoughts and pieces of bodies.'[13]

He holds no ill-will towards his former enemy.

'In 2016 I had an evening with former enemy at a restaurant in Vietnam, we got on very well. They were very friendly, as we were, and we talked about the battle. Their biggest problem was that they didn't know where we were and they didn't know how many of us there were. They couldn't understand why we were able to withstand their assaults. They had bad weather, they couldn't see very well through the monsoon rain, [but] we could see them.'[14]

Beyond that, much of his energies would be devoted to seeing his men receive proper recognition for their derring-do at Long Tan, as he remained a trenchant critic of the way the medals had been allocated.

In the book he published in 2015, *Long Tan: The Start of a Lifelong Battle*, he was outspoken in his disdain for his former superior officers and even went so far as to accuse Jackson and Townsend of fabricating claims.

But we'll get to that.

•

Major Noel Ford, Officer Commanding Bravo Company, 6RAR, came to a tragically sad, if mysterious end. After returning from his tour of Vietnam, one day in 1968 – on his way from his home in Victoria to rejoin 6RAR at Townsville – he parked his car by Bondi Beach, went for a swim, and was never seen again.

•

Captain Charles Mollison stayed with the Army for another two decades, retiring as a Lieutenant Colonel in 1984. In 2005, he self-published a book called *Long Tan and Beyond* with his own account of what occurred. In this book Mollison still holds firm to his belief that orders were disobeyed.

•

After returning to a career in graphic art, **Lieutenant David Sabben** retired from the IT industry in 2004, and now lives quietly on the Mornington Peninsula with his wife, Di. He has participated in many podcasts about the battle, and done the graphic design for an animated film describing events in minute detail. Sabben also provides an interactive PowerPoint presentation of the battle. I regard him as the greatest expert I have come across of what actually happened at Long Tan.

•

Lieutenant Geoff Kendall regarded the rest of the Vietnam War, not surprisingly, as something of an anti-climax. After the war, he learnt Chinese at the RAAF School of Languages and the British Ministry of Defence language school in Hong Kong. Kendall eventually became a military training instructor at Canungra. After 24 years in the Army, he bought a hardware store, ran it for 11 years and then retired to Bribie Island, up from Brisbane. He is currently working on his golf handicap.

•

It is remarkable that so many of the men of Long Tan survived and I was lucky enough to have the chance in 2022 to listen to their accounts of this battle; but the voice I missed most was that of **Jack Kirby** who was repatriated and buried at Mount Thompson Memorial Gardens in Brisbane. He first glimmered in the accounts of his comrades of their early months together, a constant source of care and wisdom in confusing times. But in battle itself he positively gleamed; his bravery and inspiration for them shining through each tale. He seemed to be everywhere and was admired by everyone. It's extraordinary to me that he did not receive the Victoria Cross – as Harry Smith had initially recommended – for his simply inspirational actions. I really hope that, whatever else, this book will do something to gain him wider recognition.

Vale, Jack Kirby DCM. You were a fine man, and a great Australian soldier. If not for you, many more of your countrymen would have died and been wounded at Long Tan.

•

Sergeant Bob Buick returned from Vietnam in 1967. Remaining with 6RAR, he moved to Townsville. In late 1968 he was posted to the School of Infantry, and held a variety of training posts across Australia before retiring from the army in 1980. Over the next 15 years, he sold real estate and managed a wholesale liquor outlet. In 1999, he and his wife, Beverley, settled on the Sunshine Coast near Mooloolaba, where he still lives.

There would be an ongoing controversy over Buick's shooting of the wounded VC soldier, the day after the battle, with added claims on it. In 1986, an article appeared in *The Age,* by Stuart Rintoul, quoting Terry Burstall of 12 Platoon.

'There must have been 20 blokes alive there when we went through them in the morning. I'd say we killed about 17, murdered them. We murdered those poor bastards.'[15]

There is no evidence to support the claim – no-one else affirming the same thing happened and so many actively denying it that, personally, I give it no credence. The most likely explanation I can find is from Geoff Kendall who recalls that troops were given orders to shoot at any enemy they saw who appeared to be armed and in 'kill position'. This led to quite a few armed VC corpses facing towards them being shot, and a few dying armed men as well. These killings were not reprisal in his view, and certainly not the intent of the order given, but self-defence.

Despite bitter criticism of Buick, Harry Smith remained unwavering in his support.

'I believe Bob's decision was correct borne of sympathy, not hate, despite the 13 dead soldiers he lost from 11 Platoon the day before. I would have done the same to put the poor bastard out of his misery.'[16]

•

Once returned from his tour of duty in Vietnam, **Lieutenant John O'Halloran** returned to Tamworth, and quickly caught up with old friends. There was one family he particularly wanted to see, however, and did not tarry long before heading off to see the grieving parents of Gordon Sharp, in their home near the lookout at the east end of town.

Walking to the rear to knock on the door, just as he had always done in days of yore, he was suddenly confronted in a manner that would stay with him for the rest of his days.

For it is Gordon's mother who opens the door and, instead of greeting him in the sad but friendly manner he had been expecting, launches into a tirade of abuse that directly blames him for her son's death.

'Gordon didn't want to go to Vietnam but you did,' O'Halloran will quote her shouting, in his book *Platoon Commander*. 'You are the one who should be dead, not him.'[17]

Profoundly shocked but understanding there was no point in arguing, O'Halloran left.

Thinking back on the priest who had visited Nui Dat just before the Battle of Long Tan and promised the Lord's protection for Gordon and all of them, O'Halloran will never attend church again for the rest of his life.

In civilian life, he pursued a long career in the insurance field. Meeting his wife, Lesley, in Perth, they travelled extensively before settling in Darwin. O'Halloran was on the ground in that city processing insurance claims in the wake of Cyclone Tracy in 1974. Several changes of profession later, they relocated to Perth, eventually buying into an insurance company.

John retired at 65 and still resides in Perth with his wife.

As to **Mrs Roma Sharp**, she lived for another three decades, in fact passing away 30 years to the day after her son, much of that time filled with reminiscing about him.

'No matter what the conversation,' a friend would recall, '"my dear Gordon" would always be spoken of by her.'[18]

She would be buried beside her husband, Eric, right next to Gordon Sharp's final resting place, at Lincoln Grove cemetery on the edge of Tamworth.

•

Other families, of course, would equally never recover from the loss of their loved ones at Long Tan, placing some of the survivors in a delicate position as they tried to get on with their own lives back in Australia.

'**Frank Topp**'s parents came down regularly to see me and they struck up a friendship with my parents . . .' John Robbins would recount. 'They wanted to talk about it all of the time, but I didn't want to. I can understand it now as a father, I can understand where they came from, but they would want to know if there was just one little thing, probably because I talked to him last, but they wanted to get some comfort from that or whatever. I apologise if Mrs Topp ever sees this tape, but I have got to say that I was pleased when they stopped asking me questions about it. There wasn't that much I could tell them about it, I wasn't beside him when he was killed or anything. I was pleased I had that lunch time chat with him but there wasn't much more I could say, I didn't really know him.'[19]

Another who would be troubled for a long time to come was **Jim Richmond**, who had survived against all odds, only to be haunted by the memory of those who didn't.

'The dream I have all the time is all the young blokes that were killed on the day. I still see their faces. Like Doug, Shorty, Mitch, Glenn Drabble . . . you still tell them that when I wake up in that morning you know, that next morning that they'd all wake up with me, but they never do.'[20]

And **Private Harley Webb**, the reo who joined 12 Platoon on the day of the battle only to be wounded so badly that even 'Doc' Dobson was convinced, 'This poor bastard's not going to make it'[21]?

He made it.

Just three weeks after being airlifted to Vung Tau and operated on, he was back in Perth at Hollywood Hospital to begin a long convalescence. Once released, he returned to a successful life as a farmer in Albany, dining with old mates at the 50th anniversary of Long Tan at Brisbane's Enoggera Barracks, accompanied by his son Craig, who had served in Afghanistan, Iraq and East Timor.

He passed away in July 2021, at the age of 76. In the obituary carried in the *Albany Advertiser*, his wife of 51 years, Jean, talked of what a fine husband and father he had been, all while suffering from post-traumatic stress disorder.

'He always was most anxious around Anzac Day and Vietnam Veterans Day,' she said. 'Harley sought treatment. He attended the welcome home parade in Sydney, meeting up with fellow Vietnam veterans, which led to more reunions, which helped immensely with the healing process.'[22]

•

In 2006, Defence Minister Dr Brendan Nelson is walking through a crowded shopping centre in Mount Gravatt, Brisbane, when suddenly he feels a hand clasping his elbow. He turns to see a gaunt, dishevelled man in his sixties looking at him intently. Steeling himself for an harangue from an aggrieved elector over some issue or another, the politician is surprised.

'Dr Nelson,' the man says, 'Kenny Gant was my best mate. He was killed at Long Tan. Do what you can to remember him.'

Before the Minister can speak, the man speaks once more, in quick explanation of his own bent body.

'I was run over by a tank,' he says and then turns and walks away into the crowd. He's gone but his words remain as does that name: **Kenny Gant**.

Ten years later Nelson is the Director of the Australian War Memorial, and that name comes to him again. The 50th Anniversary of Long Tan is approaching. There will be a special 'Last Post' ceremony at the War Memorial to honour one fallen on that day. It will be Kenny Gant. A couple of weeks before the ceremony, one of Kenny's other mates gets in touch. Did Dr Nelson know that Kenny was a singer? In fact, don't know if anyone knows this, he recorded four songs as a present for his mother, at a professional recording studio, just before he left for Vietnam. A few days later, Brendan Nelson sits in his office and puts a CD in his computer; through the speakers comes the voice of Kenny Gant singing 'Danny Boy'. He weeps.

And on the anniversary eve of the battle, the voice rings out after the wreaths are laid for Long Tan; as veterans old and young stand and try to hold back a tear as Ken's voice crosses 50 years:

O Danny boy, the pipes, the pipes are calling
From glen to glen and down the mountainside
The summer's gone and all the roses falling
'Tis you, 'tis you must go and I must bide . . .

But come ye back when summer's in the meadow
Or all the valley's hushed and white with snow
'Tis I'll be here in sunshine or in shadow
O Danny boy, O Danny boy, I love you so

•

In May 2010, the word comes through to many of **Major Morrie Stanley**'s old colleagues that the Kiwi has been diagnosed with terminal cancer. Moving quickly, Harry Smith, Dave Sabben and Bob Buick – who all these years on form a tight trio among Long Tan veterans – arrange to fly over on a surprise visit. They talk, they reconnect, they reminisce, they mourn those who were lost at Long Tan and those who have been lost since. When Morrie Stanley passes away four months later, Smith, Sabben and Buick are among the first informed and they subsequently help the family organise a 'fitting military funeral for Morrie which included a Haka send off'.[23]

•

Lieutenant Adrian Roberts returned to Vietnam in 1971 with the AATTV, before joining the US Special Forces in training Cambodian troops. After the Vietnam War had concluded, he returned to Portsea Officer Cadet School where he worked as a trainer, passing on all the military knowledge he had gleaned from his vast experience. He served for another decade and a half in various military posts, including lecturing at the Staff College in England, and an extended period in the Office of the Chief of General Staff, before becoming Lieutenant Colonel commanding the Army's Armour Centre. In 1984, he was promoted to Colonel before retiring in 1988, and settling in Canberra. Dr Peter Williams, one of my researchers, interviewed him for this book just a few weeks before he died in late 2021. The Defence Honours and Awards Appeals Tribunal in 2016 found that Colonel Roberts displayed sound judgement and decisive leadership in engaging his troop against the enemy, and his gallantry and determination in the words of CO 6RAR 'saved the day'. The Tribunal was of the view that many of his actions and decisions were 'courageous'.[24]

One of Roberts's regrets – which, for what it's worth, I concur – is that the heroism of Sergeant Noel Lowes in getting to Clements' APC and taking charge under fire during the battle was not acknowledged with an award for valour.

'Lowes did an exceptionally brave thing that day,' he commented in 1986, 'and I really feel sorry that, in my inexperience, he was never cited for an award.'[25]

•

Flight Lieutenant Frank Riley continued his RAAF career, completing another tour of Vietnam in 1970. After being posted to the RAAF Butterworth Malaya base in 1972, he took part in another stunning act of derring-do with his chopper when he was able to pluck the pilot of a Royal Malaysian Air Force Sabre jet from the sea less than 90 seconds after he ditched.

Squadron Leader Riley was awarded the Distinguished Flying Cross for his bravery during the Battle of Long Tan.

After no less than 21 years of service, in 1974 Riley was discharged early from the RAAF on medical grounds and spent the last seven years of his life as a Totally Permanently Incapacitated veteran. He died in late 1981, aged just 52. The cause of death was not certain, though as he had been advised by his doctor to stop drinking, and whenever Bob Grandin ran in to him in their years after Long Tan it would be in a bar where Riley was raising hell, alcohol would not have helped. Whatever it was, *bravissimo*, Flight Lieutenant Frank Riley. Of all of the heroes of Long Tan, of all the key players on which the fate of the entire battle turned, you were foremost.

•

Flight Lieutenant Bob Grandin returned to Australia following his 12 months in Vietnam. He was subsequently posted to The Transport Support Flight, flying DC3s from Butterworth in Malaysia to locations throughout South-East Asia. From there he progressed to the RAAF

Academy at Point Cook where he served as Flight Commander. During this time, he completed a Bachelor of Science before resigning his commission to pursue a career in teaching – becoming a principal at two Anglican schools in Queensland. He subsequently received a PhD for Education in Alternative Schooling. His research examined the mental health of school children and education for disengaged youth.

This background saw Grandin become one of the key driving forces for the writing and formation of a book *The Battle of Long Tan: As Told by the Commanders*. Others involved were Harry Smith, Bob Buick, Dave Sabben, Geoff Kendall, Morrie Stanley and Adrian Roberts.

As you will gather, I am deeply indebted to many of these men myself, and others, for helping me build this account on a solid base with intimate knowledge thrown in. I offer my particular thanks to Dave Sabben, who allowed me to interview him extensively, constantly call on his expertise and attention, and then vetted the text from first to last! Bob Grandin was similarly generous when it came to the action of the choppers, and also vetted the book, drawing on his extensive knowledge of the whole action. I don't say they agreed on every tiny point – but they did allow me to eliminate a lot of needless error, and beyond that gave me great insights and were able to add what I treasure most, accurate FD, Fine Detail! I also thank for their input, fellow veterans, Dave 'Bluey' Collins, Adrian Roberts just before he passed away, Peter Tedder, Frank Alcorta, Alan Hutchinson, Ernie Chamberlain, Eddie Tricker, Doug Child, Norm Austin, Ian Savage, Bruce Lane, David Harris and Mike Shevak. I particularly thank John O'Halloran, who was so generous in sending me the original manuscript of *The Platoon Commander*, so I could parse for nuggets in his raw copy and it was tremendously useful, helping to fill in gaps in my knowledge. My warm thanks to Cate McGregor, too, for her kindness in sharing the work she has done on bringing the story of Phil Norris to life, published in *The Australian*. I was pleased to be able to talk to Col Joye and Little Pattie, as well as the sister of Paul Large. And I was deeply privileged to spend the better part of an afternoon with Harry Smith himself, discussing some of the finer points. In person, even at the age of 86, I was reminded of the famous remark of the Duke of Wellington in 1809, 'I don't know what effect these men will have on the enemy, but by God, they terrify me.' Meeting him, talking to him, I really got a sense of just why his men were so highly trained, so superbly prepared for the calamity that befell them, and triumphed anyway. With Smith as your Commanding Officer, there would have been no alternative. Bravo.

•

One of the choppers flown for the ammo drop over Long Tan, the Iroquois A2-1022, met a curious fate. For in the Nyngan floods of 1990, a chopper was needed to evacuate local citizens in peril and an old Iroquois was provided by the RAAF. Afterwards, given that it was due to be retired in any event – 'clapped out' wouldn't come close to describing it – the old girl was given to the town of Nyngan as a memento of the dramatic rescues. In short order it was installed on the ground next to the Nyngan railway station until one day a former member of the RAAF No. 9 Squadron was heading for the train at Nyngan and . . . bloody hell! That chopper is *the* chopper! Frank Riley's Long Tan chopper! If a mechanical VC could be awarded, this whirlybird would get it! What were the odds? That helicopter, which should have been in a museum, was already a monument but to flood relief!

Members of the Caloundra Sub Branch of the RSL ask if they can purchase it for more appropriate display, replace the train station Huey with another, and restore Riley's piece of history to its former glory? Permission is granted and the restoration is painstakingly done. But that is not journey's end. When the producers of the movie *Danger Close* found out about it, they convinced the Caloundra RSL to allow them to transport the mighty mechanical warrior to the Gold Coast, where the movie version of Long Tan was being shot. And so Riley's Huey flies once more, on film, starring as itself! The chopper remains proudly on display today at Caloundra, in the air once more outside the RSL, mounted on a pole 30 feet up into the sky and suitable for selfies at an appropriate angle.

•

Exactly what **Captain Bob Keep** did after his traumatic Vietnam experience is not immediately apparent – and with my researchers, we have trawled for trace of him, extensively. He died in 2004 at the age of 64.

•

Sadly, the APC commander, **Corporal Peter Clements**, died of his wounds just nine days after the battle. He was 21 years old. His body was transported back to Australia and he is buried in the Moora Cemetery, Western Australia.

•

Now when it comes to **Gunner Phil Norris**, who took shrapnel in the head on the night of the original VC mortar attack, therein lies a strange tale.[26]

In August 2016 the one-time Warrant Officer Paddy Durnford, who had become mates with Norris in Vietnam and had been devastated by the news of his death, was at the Australian War Memorial with many other Vietnam veterans for the opening of the Australian Vietnam Forces National Memorial, and took the time to pay his respects to his fallen comrade, hoping to bow his head before his name on the Honour Roll, and remember the good times.

But hang on?

Phil's name is not there!

What the hell is going on? Phil had given his life for his country, made the supreme sacrifice, and through some shocking stuff-up his name is not even on the wall at the War Memorial! Phil's name was certainly up on the wall at 6RAR's barracks in Wacol, Brisbane, but not here.

Furious, Durnford writes an outraged letter to the Department of Veterans' Affairs, excoriating them for the omission, only to receive a reply that not only spikes his guns, but completely stuns him.

There is indeed a very good reason Phil Norris is not on the wall.

He's *alive*!

But no, for privacy reasons, the DVA cannot simply hand over details of where he is.

Undeterred – and as later revealed by the writer Catherine McGregor in a superb piece in *The Australian Magazine*, which my account has relied on – the redoubtable Durnford pursues other avenues of inquiry and finally gets his man. Phil Norris is in the psychiatric hospital in Sydney's Rozelle. After being repatriated from Vietnam with brain damage, Phil had first been moved there in 1970, and his wife Maryanne had regularly visited him with their daughter, Mary.

It must have been extraordinarily hard for Maryanne. They had known each other for less than a year before their wedding, and been married for just a couple of weeks when he had gone to Vietnam, to now return like this? He was, one way or another, not the man she married.

And, one way or another, Maryanne's visits had petered down to nothing in just two or three years, leaving Norris to be visited now only by his mother and brother. When they had died too, there was nothing. All his mates from Vietnam thought he was dead, after all. And so he stayed at Rozelle, not quite forgotten by the world, for by some he was fondly remembered. They just didn't know that his heart was still beating, that the man was still there, albeit brain-damaged.

At least Norris's welfare was overseen by caring staff at the hospital and one Sister in particular, Elizabeth Miles.

Due to the unstinting efforts of Paddy Durnford and Sister Miles, Phil Norris was finally reunited with his daughter, now Mary Howell of Maitland, who had by this time formed a family of her own.

Dad, you not only have a daughter and son-in-law who love you, you have three grandsons who feel the same!

Altogether they are able to form a loving bond and many visits ensue.

'And he even asked me about Mum,' Mary Howell would tell McGregor. 'He wanted to know where she was now. I paused and thought, "How am I going to deal with this?" I told him, "She got sick and died, Dad." He went quiet and just nodded. Then he asked me what day of the week it was and I told him it was Friday. Then he asked which year. I told him it was 2010. Again, he nodded quietly and asked, "What happened to the rest of the years?"'

Phil Norris died later that year, some 44 years after previously thought. With apologies to Mark Twain, news of his death had been greatly exaggerated.

He was buried at Pinegrove Cemetery in Minchinbury near his mother Olive's grave, just as had been his mother's dying wish. Over the grave, his daughter Mary, flanked by a few Vietnam vets, gave a brief eulogy.

'Real super-heroes don't wear capes,' she said. 'They wear slouch hats.'[27]

•

Sergeant Frank Alcorta remained with the Australian Army until June 1967. After the Army he served as a patrol officer in New Guinea and would claim that in 1973–74 he was the first man to cross New Guinea from north to south. After the efforts of Major Harry Smith, Alcorta – after initially being recommended by Smith for the Military Medal, knocked down by Colonel Townsend to Mentioned in Dispatches – was one of those awarded the Medal of Gallantry for his acts of bravery at Long Tan.

•

Private Paul Large was laid to rest with a military funeral in his hometown of Coolah. In memory of Paul and his fellow soldiers, the newly named Vietnam War Memorial Avenue, near the town's hospital, was planted with native flowering ironbark trees on the very evening after Paul Large's funeral, by members of the Coolah Sub Branch of the RSL. Paul Large and each of his fellow fallen soldiers from the battle had a tree devoted to their memory.

•

Private Terry Burstall, to whom this book owes so much in terms of bringing to life the experience and dialogue of the Diggers, reports in an addendum to his own book that he left the Army in 1968 before going to New Guinea 'and for three years lived as a semi-recluse managing a copra and cocoa plantation'.[28] He now lives in Brisbane.

•

Signaller Bill 'Yank' Akell, the hero who ran the spare radio through heavy fire to get to 10 Platoon, remained in the Army, rising to Warrant Officer. He has been back to Long Tan a couple of times. Like many of those who fought in the battle, the experience marked him, traumatised him in a manner even deeper than the welts he still bears on his arms and torso, which he believes are from exposure to Agent Orange.

'I just wanted to wander into the rubber [tree] plantation by myself and have a couple of minutes with my own thoughts,' he told the ABC's Margaret Burin. 'It was like there was a glass wall in front of me. My body wouldn't let me. I started to shake and tears were just running down my face. I nearly collapsed. Long Tan lives with you for the rest of your life.'[29]

•

Col Joye and **Little Pattie** are still great friends and both going strong, in their mid eighties and early seventies respectively. In late April of 2022, I had the pleasure of interviewing them together in the kitchen of Col's beautiful house in Sydney, and it was a joy to see just how much they still enjoy each other's company. Sure, it's nigh on 60 years from that Vietnam Tour, but Big Col is still like Little Pattie's big brother and they delight in finishing each other's sentences and prompting the other to tell particular stories of those days they can never forget. Their love for each other, reverence for the fallen and eagerness to honour Long Tan for the rest of their lives was truly touching. Both have had very successful and fulfilling lives since. (And to see Col with his lovely wife of 46 years, Dalys, was also a great pleasure, although Dalys did mention several times it took Col eight years to propose.) Little Pattie still performs regularly at Vietnam Veteran reunions as did Col until his retirement a few years ago. Bravo, the two of them.

•

Though the original cross put up at Long Tan in 1969 was taken by a local Catholic farmer to mark his own father's grave, in 1987 that cross was located by Terry Burstall, and for the next 30 years was housed in the Dong Nai Museum in Bien Hoa. In an act of great graciousness, in 2017 the Vietnamese Government made a gift of the Long Tan Cross to the people of Australia and it is now on display at the Australian War Memorial. In 1989, a replica cross was respectfully placed at the site itself by the Long Dat District People's Committee. The cross still stands – one of just two monuments to fallen soldiers of foreign armies permitted to stand on Vietnamese soil. The other one – I note with some surprise – is an obelisk standing in Dien Bien Phu in memory of the French forces involved in that battle.

In Australia the cross at the War Memorial is but one of many public commemorations to Long Tan, which remains high in the public consciousness as the most iconic battle of the Vietnam War. It is commemorated with a Long Tan Street in the Sydney suburb of Bardia, a Long Tan Bridge in New South Wales at Springwood and a Long Tan Road which runs through central Canberra, and another in Townsville.

In 1987, Prime Minister Bob Hawke designated the anniversary day of the battle, 18 August, as 'Vietnam Veterans' Day' a commemoration distinct from Anzac Day.

In popular culture there have been many books, dozens of podcasts, a notable documentary in 2006, narrated by Sam Worthington, and a popular film in 2019, called *Danger Close: The Battle of Long Tan* directed by Kriv Stenders and starring Travis Fimmel. There is even – and this is perhaps the ultimate arbiter of the battle's enduring appeal – a video game *Rising Storm 2: Vietnam* where Long Tan is one of the options, and you can either play as the Australian or Viet side.

•

As you can see, many of the main players of Long Tan are gone, but the debate over what happened there that day, what it meant, who is to blame, to whom is owed most credit and so forth goes on. And on. And on.

One of the key points of contention is whether or not Delta Company had been the victim of a planned ambush.

One thing, at least, would always be clear to Bob Buick – and I might note, at the conclusion of this book, is also clear to me.

'The Viet Cong,' he will say, 'have always stated that they ambushed the Australian force, but if you know anything about ambushes, you would know that this battle was no ambush. For many years this one word "ambush" has continually been bandied about by historians as part and parcel of the battle. The great majority of those who were there, including myself, have always denied that 11 Platoon and Delta Company was ambushed and believe that those who promote the ambush theory are wrong . . . We were the point platoon that met a very large enemy force. In my opinion, neither group knew the other was there. The lack of field preparations by an ambushing force such as mines or dug in weapons pits to protect an ambushing force indicates quite clearly to me that we had what is called an "encounter battle".'[30]

Can anyone, seriously, disagree?

In my view there is no chance it was a deliberately executed ambush of a patrol lured to the spot. If the whole thing was well thought out by the NVA and VC, why on earth would they not have hit Delta at their most vulnerable, crossing the Suoi Da Bang, with their rifles held high above their shoulders. And even allowing them to get into Long Tan plantation, why not hit them when they are halfway across the clearing, and fully exposed, rather than on the edge of the clearing where they could crawl to cover?

And when the APCs came, why wouldn't they have been hit while crossing the Suoi Da Bang in turn? If not quite sitting ducks, the APCs were at least barely floating ducks, and had the initial mortar attack been part of a process by the VC to 'lure the tiger from the mountain', as the

VC themselves claimed, surely they would have been better prepared to unleash those very ambushes.

None of it makes any sense.

The other question is, was there really an attack on the 1ATF planned, which the Battle of Long Tan thwarted?

For me it seems obvious that an attack was planned, and that the Battle of Long Tan thwarted it.

Otherwise, as Dave Sabben has noted to me several times: why the hell was there at least 2000 armed soldiers secreted so close to the 1ATF base?

And the fact that the major attack on the base never materialised is fair evidence that the NVA and VC called off the attack after suffering so many casualties and being thrown into such disarray.

Either way, the military significance of the Battle of Long Tan was that it was the last time the enemy issued any major challenge to the Australian presence in the province.

•

On the 50th anniversary of the Battle of Long Tan, on 18 August 2016, **Lieutenant Gordon Sharp** was remembered at the Australian War Memorial, with a moving 'Last Post' ceremony which included an account of Sharp's life by Trooper Mark Donaldson VC. A large crowd of family, old schoolmates, friends and 6RAR veterans were present, many of them organised by Gordon's old friend John O'Halloran, before they retired to a nearby hotel for a dinner to toast his memory.

On the same day, at Long Tan itself, a 50-year commemoration service was planned and it was to include a small concert by Little Pattie herself! Alas, when no fewer than 3500 Australians sought visas to attend, the Vietnamese Government – perhaps fearing a triumphalist display, boasting a 'Victory Concert' on ground that had been a rare, bitter defeat for them – cancelled it with just one day's notice.

As reported: 'A Vietnamese Government source told the ABC the Australian Consulate promised to hold a "low key" event. However, the gala dinner, concert and the expectation of more than 1000 Australians at the Long Tan memorial cross was seen as an insensitive celebration.'[31]

In the end, after personal intervention by Australian Prime Minister Malcolm Turnbull with his Vietnamese counterpart, a small ceremony was conducted with a gathering of about 1000 Australians, mostly veterans and their families.

•

Sadly, the tight camaraderie and unity that had so helped both Delta Company and 6RAR triumph at Long Tan would not endure long as, both for the rest of the war and more particularly after it, there would be oft bitter dissension over who did what and who was most deserving of the laurels of victory.

A fair measure of the bitterness towards the top brass flows from the fact many felt that Delta Company should never have been sent into Long Tan plantation in the first place, given what was known.

'There is no way in the world,' Smith would say, 'I would have sallied forth into the rubber plantation with 100 men to face an enemy regiment with 2000 or more soldiers.'[32]

That, however, was just a beginning.

Much of the bitterness came over the awarding of medals.

Just three days after the battle, Colonel Townsend called Major Smith on his field telephone while he was still out at Long Tan involved in the clean-up, and asked him to prepare citations for gallantry awards to be ready for his signature. This was no small task given the careful deliberations that would need to be made, which included consulting his fellow officers, and the enormous number of forms that would have to be filled in, complete with complete personal details of the individuals involved.

'I did wonder at the lack of understanding,'[33] Smith would comment.

Nevertheless, he did his best. Among other things, as noted, Smith sought a Victoria Cross for Jack Kirby, only to be told by Colonel Townsend that he would only sign for a Distinguished Conduct Medal. Other recommendations were also nixed, with Townsend ordering Smith to remove several names, including those of the dead. Smith had no choice but to comply.

In the end, Smith left 16 citations with Townsend.

To his shock, when the awards were announced, four months to the day after they were submitted by Smith, no fewer than half of the Delta Company men he had recommended received nothing while others were downgraded.

Many explanations were proffered but at least part of the problem was that the British Imperial awards system had a quota whereby only a certain number of awards could be given – no more than one medal for every 250 men, every six months – even if many members of a Company displayed great bravery in the one action.

Personally Smith was awarded the Military Cross, Jack Kirby a Distinguished Conduct Medal and Bob Buick a Military Medal, while Dave Sabben and Geoff Kendall were Mentioned in Dispatches.

Most galling for Smith, though, was not merely that his recommendations for bravery awards had been substantially ignored by Colonel Townsend and Brigadier Jackson. It was that the two highest awards for bravery for the Battle of Long Tan – Distinguished Service Orders, just one down from the Victoria Cross – went to . . . Brigadier Jackson and Colonel Townsend!

Defenders of the awards to these two senior military officers would insist that, rather than being just for the Battle of Long Tan itself, they were apt recognition for the entirety of their careers.

In defence of the awards Major General Peter Abigail, Major General Steve Gower and Brigadier Gerry Warner, would insist in a piece written in the 2008 *Long Tan Recognition Review*, that the DSOs awarded to Jackson and Townsend 'relate to their entire periods of command'.[34]

And yet, their citations, published in the *London Gazette* are unequivocal, with Brigadier Jackson's reading: 'in one action (Long Tan) on August 18, 1966, he personally directed the engagement which accounted for 254 enemy dead by body count with very light comparative losses to his own troops. His able personal direction was a decisive factor.'

Similarly, the citation for Townsend's DSO states: 'As soon as the initial heavy contact with the enemy was made by his company (Delta) on patrol he moved immediately with a relief company in armoured personnel carriers to join his company and took firm and effective control of the battle.'[35]

Both Harry Smith and Adrian Roberts took strong exception to both citations, making the point that not only were they demonstrably not accurate – neither Jackson nor Townsend had much to do with the battle itself – but by awarding them such high battle honours, under the quota system it denied medals to others who had actually been in the thick of it and, after covering themselves with glory, deserved to be covered in the metallic manifestation of the same.

Smith was particularly scathing, saying 'these citations, written by his seniors, could be considered as tantamount to perjury'. After all, as he reasonably points out, the idea that Brigadier Jackson 'personally directed' the battle is demonstrable nonsense when, during the course of the entire action, the Brigadier 'certainly didn't give any orders to me'.

Smith goes further still.

'He was decorated for personal leadership but he should have faced a military inquiry into why he didn't assess the intelligence he was getting. A junior signals officer had told him there was a large VC [Viet Cong] force in the area, but Jackson didn't tell anybody else.'[36]

As he also points out, their gain was the loss of recognition to others more deserving.

'The ugly truth about Long Tan, and in fact the entire Vietnam War over a decade, is that senior officers took most of the awards at the expense of soldiers who fought in action. There were 726 awards given out in those 10 years, and of those Private soldiers received only 61 awards, of which just 22 were medals. Many more went to major-generals, brigadiers, colonels and lieutenant colonels far from the action.'[37]

I know. Staggering, yes? And the numbers are worth repeating: 726 awards given in 10 years of the Vietnam War, and just three per cent of them are medals for Privates.

Without wishing to insert myself in a minefield not of my making, I do believe Harry Smith has had a point all along. Both Jackson and Townsend were distinguished officers who no doubt did deserve recognition. But to tie that recognition to their service at Long Tan – thus denying it to others – seems ludicrous to me. By any measure the Battle of Long Tan was not the finest moment for either fine officer, and to say that Townsend 'took firm and effective control of the battle', is simply well outside the historical record when there was barely a shot fired in anger after his arrival.

And so began a long and relentless campaign by Smith, energetically assisted by Sabben and Buick, to get appropriate recognition for those of his men who had missed out entirely.

True, there was something of a problem in that his original recommendations were filed and sealed for 30 years. But that's all right, Your Honour. He'll wait. When finally he gained access in 1996, it was to find that the paperwork for some had disappeared, while for others notations had been added to downgrade them.

It would take a day under 40 years of disappointment and rote rejection by review boards, before in the final days of the Howard Government, on 12 October 2007, an independent panel was at last appointed to review this damning delay and incredible omission.

In 2007, Smith was upgraded to the Star of Gallantry while Sabben and Kendall were awarded the Medal for Gallantry. In 2009, Flight Lieutenant Cliff Dohle was awarded the Distinguished Service Medal and Delta Company the Citation for Gallantry.

Still Harry Smith was not satisfied and in 2016, all of Adrian Roberts, Frank Alcorta and Barry Magnussen were also awarded the Medal for Gallantry, while Gordon Sharp and six others were recognised with a Commendation for Gallantry.

It was neither a beginning nor an ending, as other pushes for recognition go on.

Back on 2 September 1966 those in the RAAF chopper crews were among those waiting on Kangaroo Pad – now turned into a parade ground – ready to receive South Vietnamese medals from an ARVN General, even as furious messages were going back and forth between Brigadier Jackson and Canberra. Finally, the Brigadier, with acute embarrassment, had to tell the General the Australians could not accept the medals as under British regulations they could not wear foreign awards. After a jeep was dispatched to Baria and returned, the chopper crews and those of 6RAR present were eventually given Vietnamese dolls and wallets instead that Jackson then handed out. Harry Smith got a wallet; Flight Lieutenants Frank Riley and Bob Grandin were among those who got a doll.

Eventually Delta Company would indeed get an Australian unit citation as well as the South Vietnamese citation, though it was not approved until 2009, but is now proudly worn by participants in the battle. Alas, despite representations by Harry Smith that the Australian unit citation should be awarded to those manning the artillery, the APCs and the helicopters, the government would never agree.

'So,' Bob Grandin recounts, 'members of Delta have three ribbons that they wear on their right breast, which identify to those observing that this person was a part of this historic battle. I wear only the one from the South Vietnamese Government to identify that I participated in this battle. I believe it would be appropriate recognition and an issue of great pride for people like me to be able to wear both the Australian and South Vietnamese ribbons. I believe it casts a shadow over our government's understanding of the battle . . . [and] the parts played by ALL the units, and the lack of recognition for all units is unjust.'[38]

Again, this is not a battle of my making, but I agree.

I note also that the Americans were faster to honour the men of Delta Company than the Australian Government; by about four decades. General Westmoreland was so enamoured by the effort of the 'Ossies' that he arranged a Presidential Citation for Delta Company; a rare and deserved honour, bestowed on 18 August 1968.

And I also note the injustice of no medals being awarded to the artillery. All veterans I spoke to au fait with the situation agree that Captain Morrie Stanley should at least have been awarded the Military Cross, but ended up only with being Mentioned in Dispatches.

The whole medal miasma – drawn out, dragged out, dragged down, put-up, put-down, procrastinating process of recognition and robbed reward – has been a sad and haunting echo of the way Vietnam has been viewed for way too long in this country: as a war best forgotten.

I disagree. There are enormous lessons to be learnt from it, starting with the need to only go into wars with a clear and realisable objective, and with a real exit strategy. I believe that Arthur Calwell was proven right with his warnings that Australia never should have gone into a civil war in Asia.

But whether you agree or disagree with Australia going into the Vietnam War it changes naught the need to honour the commitment and sacrifice of the Australian soldiers who served there.

Since the Vietnam War started, when we gravely intoned 'Lest We Forget', the men who fought and died in Vietnam were least thought of. Far easier to focus on the perpetual past of Gallipoli and the Western Front of World War I, or on the Diggers of World War II who, until a decade or so ago, still walked proudly in their thousands every Anzac Day. When they returned from Vietnam, the RSL did not offer a warm welcome to the most recent veterans to join, as, broadly, the view was that they had not fought in 'a real war'.

For much of Australia, Vietnam was not just a murky shadow but a *loss*, and it has taken many decades to realise the injustice of not properly honouring those who gave their lives, those who served and – in too many cases – sacrificed their psyches in the jungle.

Things have changed across the board. Not least of it is the fact that the Vietnamese people themselves are now widely regarded in Australia as what they are: warm, friendly and remarkably generous-hearted towards us, a people who invaded their land, just as so many peoples had before.

We now understand much better than we ever did that the primary motivation of the VC and the NVA soldiers – whatever the grand Communist visions of Ho Chi Minh – was simply to rid their land of invaders.

The Vietnamese themselves seem to understand better than they ever did that however wrong-headed the war, the motivation of most of the Australian soldiers who fought there was not evil but to do their duty as they saw it at the time. The stories of the former enemy combatants of Long Tan, like Harry Smith himself, now meeting around the dinner table and – through translators – talking in rueful if friendly manner of those terrible few hours are legion.

Australia and Vietnam now enjoy warm relations.

In Australia itself, the esteem in which Vietnam veterans are held has risen. Now it is they who are loudly applauded every Anzac Day as they shuffle-march past. They do grow old, these remarkable men – many of them now in their late seventies and eighties – and we should honour them while we can, the way veterans of our other wars have been honoured.

Those who are gone will never know of the medals they got at last; but they earnt them over 50 years ago and their story, their glory and their loss shall be remembered. At the going down of the sun, and in the morning, we really should remember and honour both those sons who never returned, and those who returned but were forever damaged by their experience. It has been an honour and a privilege to attempt to bring to life this iconic battle, to talk to so many of the veterans of it, and my key hope is that I have done their extraordinary story justice.

Vale.

APPENDIX

LEST WE FORGET

Pte Aldersea, Richard A	Unit: 6RAR; Age: 20; Regular Army enlistee Born: Perth, WA Civ: Mechanic; Married KIA – Chest wounds Commem: Karrakatta Cemetery, WA
Cpl Clements, Peter E	Unit: 1 APC Sqn; Age: 21; Regular Army enlistee Born: Cunderdin, WA Single WIA – Died at hospital Commem: Moora Cemetery, WA
Pte Drabble, Glenn A	Unit: 6RAR; Age: 21; National Serviceman Born: Brisbane, Queensland. Civ: Blinds installer; Single KIA – Gunshot wound to head Commem: Garden of Remembrance, Queensland Buried at: Pinnaroo Cemetery, Queensland
Pte Gant, Kenneth H	Unit: 6RAR; Age: 21; National Serviceman Born: Brisbane, Queensland Civ: Butcher; Single KIA – Gunshot wounds Commem: Garden of Remembrance, Queensland Buried at: Mt Gravatt Cemetery, Queensland
Pte Grant, Ernest F	Unit: 6RAR; Age: 20; Regular Army enlistee Born: Thurgoona, NSW Civ: Farm hand; Single KIA – Gunshot wounds Commem: Albury Cemetery, NSW

Pte Grice, Victor R	Unit: 6RAR; Age: 21; National Serviceman Born: Ballarat, Victoria Civ: Storeman; Single KIA Commem: Garden of Remembrance, Queensland Buried at: Pinnaroo Lawn Cemetery, Queensland
Pte Houston, James M	Unit: 6RAR; Age: 22; Regular Army enlistee Born: Wallsend, NSW Civ: Station hand; Married KIA – Gunshot wounds Commem: Garden of Remembrance, Queensland Buried at: Mt Thompson Crematorium, Queensland
L/Cpl Jewry, Jack	Unit: 6RAR; Age: 21; National Serviceman Born: St Mary's, NSW Civ: Apprentice electrician; Married KIA – Gunshot wounds Commem: Garden of Remembrance, NSW Buried at: Pine Grove Memorial Park, NSW
Pte Large, Paul A	Unit: 6RAR; Age: 21; National Serviceman Born: Wellington, NSW Civ: Manager; Single KIA – Gunshot wounds Commem: Garden of Remembrance, NSW Buried at: Coolah Cemetery, NSW
Pte McCormack, Albert F	Unit: 6RAR; Age: 21; National Serviceman Born: Launceston, Tasmania Civ: Clerk; Single KIA Commem: Carr Villa Memorial Park, Tasmania
Pte McCormack, Dennis J	Unit: 6RAR; Age: 21; National Serviceman Born: Adelaide, SA Civ: Labourer; Single KIA – Gunshot wounds Commem: Garden of Remembrance, Queensland Buried at: Pinnaroo Cemetery, Queensland
Pte Mitchell, Warren D	Unit: 6RAR; Age: 21; National Serviceman Born: Dalby, Queensland Civ: Clerk; Single KIA – Gunshot wounds Commem: Garden of Remembrance, Queensland Buried at: Mt Gravatt Cemetery, Queensland

Pte Salveron, Douglas J	Unit: 6RAR; Age: 21; National Serviceman Born: Brisbane, Queensland Civ: Student; Single KIA – Gunshot wounds Commem: Garden of Remembrance, Queensland Buried at: Mt Gravatt Cemetery, Queensland
2Lt Sharp, Gordon C	Unit: 6RAR; Age: 21; National Serviceman Born: Tamworth, NSW Civ: Television cameraman; Single KIA – Gunshot wounds Commem: Garden of Remembrance, NSW Buried at: Tamworth Memorial Park, NSW
Pte Thomas, David J	Unit: 6RAR; Age: 21; Regular Army enlistee Born: Bendigo, Victoria Civ: Skilled labourer; Single KIA – Chest wounds Commem: Kangaroo Flat Cemetery, Victoria
Pte Topp, Francis B	Unit: 6RAR; Age: 19; Regular Army enlistee Born: Toowoomba, Queensland Single KIA Commem: Helidon Cemetery, Queensland
Pte Wales, Maxwell R	Unit: 6RAR; Age: 22; Regular Army enlistee Born: Goondiwindi, Queensland Single KIA Commem: Moree Cemetery, NSW
Pte Whiston, Colin J	Unit: 6RAR; Age: 21; National Serviceman Born: Sydney, NSW Civ: Postman; Single KIA – Gunshot wounds Commem: Garden of Remembrance, Victoria Buried at: Crib Point Cemetery, Victoria

ENDNOTES

1 Calwell, Speech to the House of Representatives, 4 May 1965.

Prologue

1 Karnow, 'A Verdict on Vietnam', *The Washington Post*, 28 October 1984.
2 Templer, 'General Vo Nguyen Giap obituary', *The Guardian*, 5 October 2013.
3 Karnow, *Vietnam: A History*, Penguin, Victoria, 1984, p. 126.
4 Karnow, *Vietnam*, p. 126.
5 Ho Chi Minh, *Selected Works*, Vol. 3, Foreign Languages Publishing House, Hanoi, 1960–62, pp. 17–21.
6 Donaldson, *America at War Since 1945: Politics and Diplomacy in Korea, Vietnam, and the Gulf War*, e-book edition, Greenwood Publishing Group, US, 1996, p. 76.
7 Karnow, *Vietnam*, p. 216.
8 Karnow, *Vietnam*, p. 216.
9 Karnow, *Vietnam*, p. 216.
10 Karnow, *Vietnam*, p. 216.
11 Karnow, *Vietnam*, p. 216.
12 Karnow, *Vietnam*, p. 216.
13 Karnow, *Vietnam*, p. 216.
14 Karnow, *Vietnam*, p. 217.
15 Windrow, *The Last Valley: Dien Bien Phu and the French Defeat in Vietnam*, e-book edition, Hachette, UK, 2011, p. 241.
16 Karnow, *Vietnam*, p. 191.
17 *Maryborough Chronicle*, 9 April 1954, p. 1.
18 *Tampa Bay Times*, 4 April 2004.
19 Royal United Services Institute for Defence and Security Services, 'Three Vietnam Wars', Paper based on presentation by Colonel David S. Wilkins, March 2020.
20 Karnow, *Vietnam*, p. 224.
21 Karnow, *Vietnam*, p. 227.
22 Karnow, *Vietnam*, p. 230.
23 *The Age*, 13 May 1954, p. 4.
24 *Daily Mercury*, 11 May 1954, p. 2.
25 John F. Kennedy Library, News Conference 12, President John F. Kennedy, Palais Chaillot, Paris, 2 June 1961.
26 Sexton, *War for the Asking*, Penguin, Ringwood, 1981, p. 30.
27 *New York Times*, 8 October 1970, p. 3.
28 O'Donnell, Powers and McCarthy, *Johnny, We Hardly Knew Ye*, Little, Brown & Co., Boston, 1970, p. 14.
29 Curran, 'Curtain, Champion of Empire', United States Study Centre, March 2011.
30 Ham, *Vietnam: The Australian War*, HarperCollins, Sydney, 2007, p. 6.
31 *Time*, 'Saigon: Memories of a Fallen City', 12 May 1975.
32 Mackay, *Australians in Vietnam*, Rigby, Adelaide, 1968, p. 14.
33 *The Independent*, 20 December 2013.
34 Halberstam, *The Making of a Quagmire*, Rowman and Littlefield, New York, 2008, pp. 128–29.

35 Halberstam, *The Making of a Quagmire*, p. 128.
36 O'Donnell, Powers and McCarthy, *Johnny, We Hardly Knew Ye*, p. 18.
37 *Canberra Times*, 4 November 1963, p. 1.
38 Collins, Patsy, Affidavit In Any Fact by Mrs. R. A. Reid #1, legal document, 22 November 1963, University of North Texas Libraries, The Portal to Texas History, Dallas Municipal Archives.
39 Geoffrey Kendall interview, Australians at War Film Archive, 16 July 2004.
40 Grandin, *The Battle of Long Tan: As Told by the Commanders to Bob Grandin*, Allen & Unwin, Crows Nest, 2004, p. 11.
41 Grandin, *The Battle of Long Tan*, p. 11.
42 Beschloss, *Taking Charge: The Johnson White House Tapes, 1963–1964*, Simon & Schuster, New York, 1997, pp. 262–63.
43 *New York Times*, 13 June 1964, p. 10.

Chapter one: The apocalypse beckons

1 Beschloss, *Taking Charge*, p. 498.
2 Beschloss, *Taking Charge*, p. 498.
3 McNamara, *In Retrospect: The Tragedy and Lessons of Vietnam*, Random House, New York, 1995, p. 134.
4 McNamara, *In Retrospect*, p. 134.
5 McNamara, *In Retrospect*, p. 134.
6 McNamara, *In Retrospect*, p. 134.
7 McNamara, *In Retrospect*, p. 134.
8 McNamara, *In Retrospect*, p. 134.
9 Tonkin Gulf Resolution; Public Law 88-408, 88th Congress, 7 August 1964; General Records of the United States Government; Record Group 11; National Archives.
10 *Canberra Times*, 11 August 1964, p. 2.
11 *Canberra Times*, 11 November 1964, p. 4.
12 Burstall, *The Soldiers' Story*, University of Queensland Press, St Lucia, 1986, p. 5.
13 Hansard, House of Representatives, Sir Robert Menzies, 10 November 1964.
14 Hansard, House of Representatives, Sir Robert Menzies, 10 November 1964.
15 Burstall, *The Soldiers' Story*, p. 5.
16 Burstall, *The Soldiers' Story*, p. 5.
17 Cameron, *The Battle of Long Tan*, Penguin Random House, Australia, 2016, p. 86.
18 *Canberra Times*, 11 March 1965, p. 1.
19 *Canberra Times*, 11 March 1965, p. 1.
20 *Tribune*, 12 May 1965, p. 1.
21 Australian Politics.com, 'Sir Robert Menzies Announces Military Commitment To South Vietnam'.
22 *Australian*, 30 April 1965 (from Burstall, *The Soldiers' Story*, p. 6).
23 *Sydney Morning Herald*, 3 May 1965, p. 6.
24 *Sydney Morning Herald*, 3 May 1965, p. 6.
25 *Sydney Morning Herald*, 3 May 1965, p. 6.
26 *Sydney Morning Herald*, 3 May 1965, p. 6.
27 Calwell, Leader of the Opposition speech to the House of Representatives, 4 May 1965.
28 Burstall, *The Soldiers' Story*, pp. 5–6.
29 O'Halloran and Teague, *The Platoon Commander*, e-book edition, Hachette, Australia, 2021, p. 38.
30 Beryl Gant interview, Australians at War Archive Transcript, 22 May 2000.
31 Australian War Memorial, Private Errol Noack case study.
32 *Sydney Morning Herald*, June 2016.
33 *Sydney Morning Herald*, June 2016 [reported speech].
34 *Canberra Times*, 2 July 1965, p. 3.
35 *Canberra Times*, 2 July 1965, p. 3.
36 *Canberra Times*, 2 July 1965, p. 3.
37 Grandin, *The Battle of Long Tan*, p. 20.
38 *Canberra Times*, 1 July 1965, p. 4.
39 *Canberra Times*, 1 July 1965, p. 4.

Chapter two: Home on the rifle range

1 O'Halloran and Teague, *The Platoon Commander*, p. 49.
2 Heard, *Well Done Those Men*, Scribe, Melbourne, 2005; Ham, *Vietnam*, p. 173.
3 Ham, *Vietnam*, p. 173.
4 Cameron, *The Battle of Long Tan*, p. 26.
5 Ham, *Vietnam*, p. 173.
6 Ham, *Vietnam*, p. 173.
7 Ham, *Vietnam*, p. 173.
8 Cameron, *The Battle of Long Tan*, p. 26.
9 John Robbins, Australians at War Film Archive, UNSW, 28 April 2004.
10 Caulfield, *The Vietnam Years*, p. 82.
11 Caulfield, *The Vietnam Years*, p. 89.
12 Robert Buick, Australians at War Film Archive, 23 July 2004.
13 O'Halloran and Teague, *The Platoon Commander*, p. 41.
14 Sabben, 'Long Tan: The Principles of War Podcast'.
15 Grandin, *The Battle of Long Tan*, pp. 21–22.
16 Grandin, *The Battle of Long Tan*, p. 23.
17 Sabben, speech, 'From Scheyville to Vietnam: My Conscription Experience', 30 May 2015.
18 Grandin, *The Battle of Long Tan*, p. 22.
19 *Hawkesbury Gazette*, 8 July 2016.
20 O'Halloran and Teague, *The Platoon Commander*, p. 71.
21 'Principles and Techniques of Leadership', Department of Tactics, West Point, New York, 1953.
22 *Canberra Times*, 12 August 1965, p. 20.
23 Author interview with Dave Sabben, 17 February 2022.
24 Australian Army, 'Manual of Land Warfare, Part Two: Infantry Training', Volume 1, Pamphlet 2, The Rifle Platoon, 1986.
25 O'Halloran and Teague, *The Platoon Commander*, p. 63.
26 O'Halloran and Teague, *The Platoon Commander*, p. 63.
27 O'Halloran and Teague, *The Platoon Commander*, p. 46.
28 Cameron, *The Battle of Long Tan*, p. 88.
29 *Canberra Times*, 16 December 1965, p. 4.
30 *Canberra Times*, 17 December 1965, p. 3.
31 *Canberra Times*, 17 December 1965, p. 3.
32 *Canberra Times*, 17 December 1965, p. 3.

Chapter three: 6RAR complete

1 White House Tape, 1 February 1966, Conversation Number: WH6602.01, University of Virginia.
2 McAulay, *The Battle of Long Tan*, Random House, Sydney, 1987, p. 34.
3 Grandin, *The Battle of Long Tan*, p. 25.
4 Grandin, *The Battle of Long Tan*, p. 25.
5 Author interview with Dave Sabben, Mornington Peninsula, 16 February 2022.
6 Author interview with Dave Sabben, 16 February 2022.
7 Author interview over phone with Dave Sabben, 24 April 2022.
8 This quote is popularly attributed to Orwell, but it is likely a paraphrase by Richard Grenier, *The Washington Times*, 6 April 1993, p. F3.
9 Author interview with Dave Sabben, 16 February 2022.
10 McLachlan, Living History, *War Stories: Long Tan Veteran Dave Sabben*, YouTube video, 12 August 2019.
11 Cameron, *The Battle of Long Tan*, p. 105.
12 *Canberra Times*, 23 April 1966, p. 1.
13 Australian Government, Department of Prime Minister and Cabinet, PM Transcripts, Harold Holt Parliamentary Statement, 2 November 1967.
14 Grandin, *The Battle of Long Tan*, p. 8.
15 The Battle of Long Tan website, 'Biography: Lieutenant Colonel Harry Smith'.
16 White House Tapes, 1 February 1966, Conversation WH6602.01, University of Virginia.
17 Author interview with Dave Sabben, 16 February 2022.

18 Mollison, *Long Tan and Beyond*, Cobb's Crossing, Woombye, 2004, p. 46.
19 Author interview with Dave Sabben, 16 February 2022.
20 Author interview over phone with Dave Sabben, 24 April 2022.
21 Author interview over phone with Dave Sabben, 24 April 2022.
22 Ham, *Vietnam*, p. 178.
23 Ham, *Vietnam*, pp. 178–79.
24 Ham, *Vietnam*, p. 179.
25 Australian Government, Department of Prime Minister and Cabinet, PM Transcripts, Harold Holt Parliamentary Statement, 8 March 1966.
26 *Canberra Times*, 9 March 1966, p. 2.

Chapter four: Delta dawn

1 Karnow, *Vietnam*, p. 87.
2 Robert Buick interview, Australians at War Film Archive, 23 July 2004.
3 Author interview with Dave Sabben, 17 February 2022.
4 Burstall, *The Soldiers' Story*, p. 28.
5 Author interview over phone with Dave Sabben, 24 April 2022.
6 Author interview with Dave Sabben, 16 February 2022.
7 Author interview with Little Pattie and Col Joye, 28 April 2022.
8 Buick, *All Guts and No Glory: the story of a Long Tan warrior*, e-book edition, Allen & Unwin, Sydney, 2000, p. 44.
9 Author interview over phone with Dave Sabben, 24 April 2022.
10 Author interview with Dave Sabben, 16 February 2022.
11 Author interview with Dave Sabben, 16 February 2022.
12 O'Halloran and Teague, *The Platoon Commander*, p. 72.
13 Horner, 'Why Was 5 RAR Stationed At Nui Dat?' in *Vietnam Vanguard: The 5th Battalion's Approach to Counter-Insurgency, 1966*, edited by Ron Boxall and Robert O'Neill, ANU Press, Acton, 2020, pp. 21–44.
14 Horner, 'Why Was 5 RAR Stationed At Nui Dat?', *Vietnam Vanguard*, pp. 21–44.
15 Horner, 'Why Was 5 RAR Stationed At Nui Dat?', *Vietnam Vanguard*, pp. 21–44.
16 Dave Sabben interview, Australians at War Film Archive, 25 May 2000.
17 *Northern Daily Leader*, 12 August 2016.
18 *Northern Daily Leader*, 12 August 2016.
19 Paul Large, Letter, 3 April 1966, from Australian War Memorial, Last Post Ceremony commemorating the service of (2781704) Private Paul Large.
20 Tucker, 'Ho Chi Minh: Replies to an Interview with Japanese NDN TV, April 1966', *Encyclopedia of the Vietnam War: A Political, Social, and Military History*, ABC-CLIO, Santa Barbara, 1998, pp. 1573–74.
21 Tucker, 'Ho Chi Minh', *Encyclopedia of the Vietnam War*, 1998.
22 Tucker, 'Ho Chi Minh', *Encyclopedia of the Vietnam War*, 1998.
23 Beryl Gant interview, Australians at War Film Archive, 22 May 2000.
24 Beryl Gant interview, Australians at War Film Archive, 22 May 2000.
25 The Battle of Long Tan website, 'Remembering 21 year old Private Paul Large'.
26 The Battle of Long Tan website, 'Remembering 21 year old Private Paul Large'.
27 Mollison, *Long Tan and Beyond*, p. 56.
28 Grandin, *The Battle of Long Tan*, p. 14.
29 Grandin, *The Battle of Long Tan*, p. 18.
30 Author interview with Dave Sabben, 16 February 2022.
31 The Battle of Long Tan website, 'Remembering 21 year old Private Paul Large'.
32 O'Halloran and Teague, *The Platoon Commander*, p. 56.
33 Australian War Memorial, Private Errol Noack case study.
34 Australian War Memorial, Private Errol Noack case study.

Chapter five: Good morning, Vietnam!

1 Robert Hagerty interview, Australians at War Film Archive, 26 March 2004.
2 Beryl Gant interview, Australians at War Film Archive, 22 May 2000.

3 O'Halloran and Teague, *The Platoon Commander*, p. 64.
4 Grandin, *The Battle of Long Tan*, p. 12.
5 Caulfield, *The Vietnam Years*, pp. 137–38.
6 Robert Buick interview, Australians at War Film Archive, 23 July 2004.
7 McAulay, *The Battle of Long Tan*, p. 8.
8 Caulfield, *The Vietnam Years*, p. 152.
9 O'Farrell, *Behind Enemy Lines*, Allen & Unwin, Sydney, 2001, pp. 141 and 192.
10 Author interview with Bob Grandin, Buderim, 19 February 2022.
11 Burstall, *The Soldiers' Story*, p. 11.
12 Skitch, 'War in Vietnam – A Surveyor's Story', p. 28.
13 Robert Buick interview, Australians at War Film Archive, 23 July 2004.
14 Sunshine Coast Council, Heritage, Lawrence Drinkwater interview, 1 June 2001.
15 Noel Grimes interview, Australians at War Film Archive, 4 May 2004.
16 McNeill, *To Long Tan: The Australian Army and the Vietnam War 1950–1966, The Official History of Australia's Involvement in Southeast Asian Conflicts 1948–1975, Vol. II.* Allen & Unwin, Sydney, 1993, p. 249.
17 Burstall, *The Soldiers' Story*, p. 13.
18 Walsh, '50 Years Ago Australian Forces Arrive in Vietnam', Battle of Long Tan blog, 8 June 2015.
19 Burstall, *The Soldiers' Story*, p. 14.
20 Smith, *The Battle of Long Tan: The Company Commanders Story*, e-book edition, Big Sky Publishing, 2019, p. 131.
21 McNeill, *To Long Tan*, pp. 281–82.

Chapter six: Fire, fire, burning bright

1 *Canberra Times*, 13 June 1966, p. 3.
2 Author interview with Bob Grandin, 19 February 2022.
3 Chamberlain, 'Appendix D: The Enemy: Uncontested Tenancy Prior to the Arrival of 1 ATF', in *Vietnam Vanguard*, edited by Ron Boxall and Robert O'Neill, ANU Press, Acton, 2020.
4 Burgess, Pat, 'The village of hidden hate', *The Bulletin*, Vol. 98, No. 5020, 21 August 1976.
5 Grandin, *The Battle of Long Tan*, p. 11.
6 Ham, *Vietnam*, p. 196.
7 O'Halloran and Teague, *The Platoon Commander*, p. 74.
8 Buick, *All Guts and No Glory*, p. 66.
9 Burstall, *The Soldiers' Story*, p. 14.
10 Author interview with Bob Grandin, 19 February 2022.
11 Burstall, *A Soldier Returns: A Long Tan Veteran Discovers the Other Side of Vietnam*, University of Queensland Press, St Lucia, 1990, p. 5.
12 Walsh, '50 Years Ago Australian Forces Arrive in Vietnam', Battle of Long Tan blog, 8 June 2015.
13 McLachlan, Living History, *War Stories: Long Tan Veteran Dave Sabben*, YouTube video, 12 August 2019.
14 Burstall, *The Soldiers' Story*, p. 17.
15 O'Halloran and Teague, *The Platoon Commander*, p. 77.
16 Mollison, *Long Tan and Beyond*, p. 90.
17 O'Halloran and Teague, *The Platoon Commander*, p. 81.
18 Terry Burstall, *The Soldiers' Story*, p. 30.
19 Geoffrey Kendall interview, Australians at War Film Archive, 16 July 2004.
20 Buick, *All Guts and No Glory*, pp. 71–72.
21 Smith, *The Battle of Long Tan*, p. 101.
22 Buick, *All Guts and No Glory*, p. 71.
23 O'Halloran and Teague, *The Platoon Commander*, p. 84.
24 Author interview with Dave Sabben, 16 February 2022.
25 Burstall, *The Soldiers' Story*, p. 33.
26 Burstall, *The Soldiers' Story*, p. 33.
27 McNeill, *To Long Tan*, pp. 283–84.

Chapter seven: Trouble in the wind

1 von Clausewitz, *On War*, edited and translated by Michael Howard and Peter Paret, Princeton University Press, Princeton, 1976, p. 101.
2 Joseph Heller, *Catch-22*, Simon & Schuster, New York, 1961.
3 Ham, *Vietnam*, p. 215.
4 Author interview with David Harris, 29 May 2022.
5 Doug Child interview with Dr Peter Williams, 3 May 2022.
6 Author interview with David Harris, 29 May 2022.
7 Beryl Gant interview, Australians at War Film Archive, 22 May 2000.
8 Cameron, *The Battle of Long Tan*, p. 99.
9 Cameron, *The Battle of Long Tan*, p. 99.
10 O'Neill, 'Operation Holsworthy', 5th Battalion The Royal Australian Regiment Association Website.
11 O'Neill, 'Operation Holsworthy', 5th Battalion The Royal Australian Regiment Association Website.
12 O'Neill, 'Operation Holsworthy', 5th Battalion The Royal Australian Regiment Association Website.
13 O'Neill, 'Operation Holsworthy', 5th Battalion The Royal Australian Regiment Association Website.
14 Ham, *Vietnam*, p. 215.
15 Ham, *Vietnam*, p. 215.
16 John O'Brien, 'Said Hanrahan', 1919.
17 Ham, *Vietnam*, p. 215.
18 Ham, *Vietnam*, p. 215.
19 Mollison, *Long Tan and Beyond*, p. 110.
20 Mollison, *Long Tan and Beyond*, p. 110.
21 Mollison, *Long Tan and Beyond*, p. 111.
22 Mollison, *Long Tan and Beyond*, p. 111.
23 Mollison, *Long Tan and Beyond*, p. 111.
24 *Danger Close: The Battle of Long Tan*, Facebook post, 7 June 2019.
25 Australian War Memorial, Army Commanders' Diary, Vietnam, Infantry Units, 6 Battalion Royal Australian Regiment, Series: AWM95, Item No. 7/6/5, 1–31 August 1966.
26 Dapin, *The Nashos' War: Australia's National Servicemen and Vietnam*, Viking, Australia, 2014, p. 123.
27 Brian Mortimer interview, Australians at War Film Archive, 26 March 2004.
28 Buick, *All Guts and No Glory*, p. 78.
29 Burstall, *The Soldiers' Story*, p. 42.
30 Buick, *All Guts and No Glory*, p. 78.
31 Buick, *All Guts and No Glory*, p. 78 [reported speech].
32 Buick, *All Guts and No Glory*, p. 78.
33 O'Halloran and Teague, *The Platoon Commander*, p. 125.
34 Buick, *All Guts and No Glory*, p. 78.
35 O'Halloran and Teague, *The Platoon Commander*, p. 125.
36 Mollison, *Long Tan and Beyond*, p. 113.
37 Burstall, *The Soldiers' Story*, p. 42.
38 Contemporaneous notes provided by David Harris to the author, 30 May 2022.
39 Contemporaneous notes provided by David Harris to the author, 30 May 2022.
40 Contemporaneous notes provided by David Harris to the author, 30 May 2022.
41 Mollison, *Long Tan and Beyond*, p. 118 [reported speech].

Chapter eight: Cometh the hour

1 Caulfield, *The Vietnam Years*, p. 100.
2 Burstall, *The Soldiers' Story*, pp. 44–45 [reported speech].
3 Burstall, *The Soldiers' Story*, pp. 44–45 [reported speech].
4 Burstall, *The Soldiers' Story*, pp. 44–45.

5 Grandin, *Answering the Call: Life of a Helicopter Pilot in Vietnam and Beyond*, e-book edition, Big Sky Publishing, Australia, 2019, p. 85.
6 Author interview with Little Pattie and Col Joye, 28 April 2022.
7 Grandin, *Answering the Call*, p. 86.
8 Grandin, *The Battle of Long Tan*, p. 105.
9 O'Halloran and Teague, *The Platoon Commander*, p. 91.
10 O'Halloran and Teague, *The Platoon Commander*, p. 92.
11 O'Halloran and Teague, *The Platoon Commander*, p. 92.
12 Burstall, *The Soldiers' Story*, p. 47.
13 O'Halloran and Teague, *The Platoon Commander*, p. 92.
14 Smith, *The Battle of Long Tan*, p. 165.
15 O'Halloran and Teague, *The Platoon Commander*, p. 92.
16 O'Halloran and Teague, *The Platoon Commander*, p. 91.
17 Cameron, *The Battle of Long Tan*, p. 122.
18 O'Halloran and Teague, *The Platoon Commander*, p. 93.
19 Stanley, 'Gunfire at Long Tan: the FO's story', 6RAR website.
20 Australian War Memorial, Last Post Ceremony commemorating the service of (1200265) Private Francis Brett Topp.
21 Smith, *The Battle of Long Tan*, pp. 140–41.
22 O'Halloran and Teague, *The Platoon Commander*, p. 93.
23 Burstall, *The Soldiers' Story*, pp. 50–51.
24 Walsh, 'Little Pattie and Col Joye Concert at Nui Dat', Battle of Long Tan blog, 14 April 2016.
25 Author telephone interview with Dave Sabben, 12 March 2022.
26 Smith, *The Battle of Long Tan*, p. 143.
27 Author telephone interview with Dave Sabben, 12 March 2022.
28 Grandin, *The Battle of Long Tan*, p. 119.
29 *The Battle of Long Tan Documentary*, Red Dune Films, 2006.
30 *The Battle of Long Tan Documentary*, Red Dune Films, 2006.
31 Geoffrey Kendall interview, Australians at War Film Archive, 16 July 2004.
32 Dave Sabben interview, Australians at War Film Archive, 25 May 2000.
33 Burstall, *The Soldiers' Story*, p. 57.
34 Australian War Memorial, Army Commanders' Diary, 1–31 August 1966.
35 Author interview over phone with Dave Sabben, 24 April 2022.

Chapter nine: Rocked

1 Author interview with Little Pattie and Col Joye, 28 April 2022.
2 Australian War Memorial, Army Commanders' Diary, 1–31 August 1966.
3 Australian War Memorial, Army Commanders' Diary, 1–31 August 1966.
4 Robert Buick interview, Australians at War Film Archive, 23 July 2004.
5 Burstall, *The Soldiers' Story*, p. 53 [reported speech].
6 Burstall, *The Soldiers' Story*, p. 53.
7 John Robbins interview, Australians at War Film Archive, 28 April 2004.
8 John Robbins interview, Australians at War Film Archive, 28 April 2004.
9 Author's note: with a nod to the famous Redgum song, 'Only 19', by John Schumann. The lyrics are: 'God help me/I was only 19' and, in verse 4, 'God help me/He was going home in June'.
10 Burstall, *The Soldiers' Story*, p. 54.
11 Burstall, *The Soldiers' Story*, p. 54 [reported speech].
12 Burstall, *The Soldiers' Story*, p. 54 [reported speech].
13 Australian War Memorial, Army Commanders' Diary, 1–31 August 1966.
14 *The Battle of Long Tan Documentary*, Red Dune Films, 2006.
15 Cameron, *The Battle of Long Tan*, p. 123.
16 Australian Government, Defence Honours and Awards Tribunal, 1 August 2016.
17 *The Battle of Long Tan Documentary*, Red Dune Films, 2006.
18 *The Battle of Long Tan Documentary*, Red Dune Films, 2006.
19 McAulay, *The Battle of Long Tan*, p. 10.
20 John Robbins interview, Australians at War Film Archive, 28 April 2004.
21 Burstall, *The Soldiers' Story*, p. 57.

22 John Robbins interview, Australians at War Film Archive, 28 April 2004.
23 Buick, *All Guts and No Glory*, p. 83.
24 Author interview with David Collins, Buderim, 19 February 2022.
25 Robert Buick interview, Australians at War Film Archive, 23 July 2004.
26 Author interview with David Harris, 29 May 2022.
27 Burstall, *The Soldiers' Story*, p. 53.
28 Dave Sabben interview, Australians at War Film Archive, 25 May 2000.
29 Dave Sabben interview, Australians at War Film Archive, 25 May 2000.
30 *The Battle of Long Tan Documentary*, Red Dune Films, 2006.
31 *The Battle of Long Tan Documentary*, Red Dune Films, 2006.
32 *The Battle of Long Tan Documentary*, Red Dune Films, 2006.
33 Hunter, 'It's an Honour and a Privilege', Australian War Memorial, blogpost, 1 June 2021.
34 Author interview with Little Pattie and Col Joye, 28 April 2022.
35 ABC PM, 'Little Pattie's encore in Vietnam', 17 August 2009.

Chapter ten: Fight and flight

1 Burstall, *The Soldiers' Story*, p. 77 [reported speech].
2 Burstall, *The Soldiers' Story*, p. 77 [reported speech].
3 Robert Buick interview, Australians at War Film Archive, 23 July 2004.
4 Robert Buick interview, Australians at War Film Archive, 23 July 2004.
5 Robert Buick interview, Australians at War Film Archive, 23 July 2004.
6 Burstall, *The Soldiers' Story*, p. 76.
7 Frank Alcorta interview with Dr Peter Williams, 9 January 2022.
8 Cameron, *The Battle of Long Tan*, p. 177.
9 Cameron, *The Battle of Long Tan*, p. 177.
10 Burstall, *The Soldiers' Story*, p. 60.
11 Dapin, *The Nashos' War*, p. 135.
12 Dapin, *The Nashos' War*, p. 135.
13 Dapin, *The Nashos' War*, p. 135.
14 Burstall, *The Soldiers' Story*, p. 61.
15 Conversation with Army veteran, who recalled these exact words from a Long Tan veteran.
16 Burstall, *The Soldiers' Story*, p. 61.
17 Burstall, *The Soldiers' Story*, p. 74 [reported speech].
18 Burstall, *The Soldiers' Story*, p. 73.
19 Burstall, *The Soldiers' Story*, p. 73.
20 Author interview with David Harris, 29 May 2022.
21 Burstall, *The Soldiers' Story*, p. 74.
22 McAulay, *The Battle of Long Tan*, p. 69.
23 Burstall, *The Soldiers' Story*, p. 74.
24 *The Battle of Long Tan Documentary*, Red Dune Films, 2006.
25 *The Battle of Long Tan Documentary*, Red Dune Films, 2006.
26 Smith, *The Battle of Long Tan*, p. 153.
27 *The Battle of Long Tan Documentary*, Red Dune Films, 2006.
28 Smith, *The Battle of Long Tan*, p. 155.
29 Smith, *The Battle of Long Tan*, p. 155.
30 *The Battle of Long Tan Documentary*, Red Dune Films, 2006.
31 Adrian Roberts interview, Australians at War Film Archive, 15 May 2000 [reported speech].
32 Grandin, *The Battle of Long Tan*, p. 66.
33 Author interview with Bob Grandin, 19 February 2022.
34 Australian War Memorial, Army Commanders' Diary, 1–31 August 1966.
35 Author interview with Bob Grandin, 19 February 2022.
36 Ham, *Vietnam*, p. 236.
37 Austin, My Vietnam War, unpublished manuscript.
38 Cameron, *The Battle of Long Tan*, p. 177.
39 Bob Grandin interview, Australians at War Film Archive, 1 May 2000.
40 Bob Grandin interview, Australians at War Film Archive, 1 May 2000.
41 Bob Grandin interview, Australians at War Film Archive, 1 May 2000.

42 Grandin, *The Battle of Long Tan*, pp. 145–46 [reported speech].
43 Grandin, *The Battle of Long Tan*, pp. 145–46 [reported speech].
44 Bob Grandin interview, Australians at War Film Archive, 1 May 2000.
45 Grandin, *Answering the Call*, p. 90.
46 Grandin, *The Battle of Long Tan*, pp. 145–46 [reported speech].
47 McAulay, *The Battle of Long Tan*, p. 68.
48 Richter, 'The Story of a Chopper Pilot, Two Rock Stars and the Vietnam War', Ipswich City Council, Ipswich First, August 2019.
49 Ham, *Vietnam*, p. 236.
50 Ham, *Vietnam*, p. 236.
51 Bruce Lane interview with author, 23 February 2022.
52 Author interview with Bob Grandin, 19 February 2022.
53 Author interview with Bob Grandin, 19 February 2022.
54 Grandin, *Answering the Call*, p. 90.

Chapter eleven: Shells in hell

1 *The Islander*, 'Remembering Long Tan 51 Years Ago', 16 August 2017.
2 Australian War Memorial, Army Commanders' Diary, 1–31 August 1966.
3 Author interview over phone with Dave Sabben, 20 May 2022.
4 Dave Sabben interview, Australians at War Film Archive, 25 May 2000.
5 Radschool Association Magazine, 'Gunfire at Long Tan: The Kiwi O's Story', Vol. 28.
6 Bedford, 'Vietnam veteran David Beahan tells the story…', *The Armidale Express*, 1 August 2016.
7 McLachlan, Living History, *War Stories: Long Tan Veteran Dave Sabben*, YouTube video, 12 August 2019.
8 Burstall, *The Soldiers' Story*, p. 82 [reported speech].
9 McLachlan, Living History, *War Stories: Long Tan Veteran Dave Sabben*, YouTube video, 12 August 2019.
10 McLachlan, Living History, *War Stories: Long Tan Veteran Dave Sabben*, YouTube video, 12 August 2019.
11 Dapin, *The Nashos' War*, p. 136.
12 Dapin, *The Nashos' War*, p. 137.
13 Burstall, *The Soldiers' Story*, p. 81.
14 Grandin, *The Battle of Long Tan*, p. 156.
15 John Heslewood interview, Australians at War Film Archive, 16 April 2004.
16 Burstall, *The Soldiers' Story*, p. 62.
17 Burstall, *The Soldiers' Story*, p. 62.
18 Burstall, *The Soldiers' Story*, p. 62 [reported speech].
19 Burstall, *The Soldiers' Story*, p. 62.
20 Burstall, *The Soldiers' Story*, p. 62.
21 Burstall, *The Soldiers' Story*, p. 62.
22 Cameron, *The Battle of Long Tan*, p. 192.
23 Cameron, *The Battle of Long Tan*, p. 192.
24 Cameron, *The Battle of Long Tan*, p. 192.
25 Cameron, *The Battle of Long Tan*, p. 196.
26 Cameron, *The Battle of Long Tan*, p. 196.
27 Grandin, *The Battle of Long Tan*, p. 154.
28 Grandin, *The Battle of Long Tan*, p. 154.
29 Buick, *All Guts and No Glory*, p. 87.
30 Grandin, *The Battle of Long Tan*, p. 156.
31 Grandin, *The Battle of Long Tan*, p. 156.
32 Robert Buick interview, Australians at War Film Archive, 23 July 2004.
33 *The Battle of Long Tan Documentary*, Red Dune Films, 2006.
34 Grandin, *The Battle of Long Tan*, p. 156.
35 John Burns interview with Dr Peter Williams, 26 October 2021.
36 John Burns interview with Dr Peter Williams, 26 October 2021.
37 Sabben, 'The Battle of Long Tan', Powerpoint presentation.
38 Mollison, *Long Tan and Beyond*, p. 146 [reported speech].

39 Mollison, *Long Tan and Beyond*, p. 146 [reported speech].
40 Mollison, *Long Tan and Beyond*, p. 157.
41 Mollison, *Long Tan and Beyond*, p. 157.
42 Mollison, *Long Tan and Beyond*, p. 157.
43 Australian War Memorial, *Battle of Long Tan: edited version*, Australian War Memorial Film Archive, F03370, 1986.
44 Frank Alcorta interview with Dr Peter Williams, 9 January 2022.
45 Buick, *All Guts and No Glory*, p. 183.
46 Burstall, *The Soldiers' Story*, p. 76 [reported speech].
47 Author's note: Many accounts of this moment have Buick shouting: 'Every man for himself!' If he did say that it would only seem reasonable under the circumstances. It was not a moment for anything other than a mad scramble, as they were about to be overwhelmed. But, for the record, given Buick's vociferous insistence that he said no such thing, it is worth noting that his central point is correct. Not one of those who claim he said it were within a bull's roar at the time, and the whole thing was said in the middle of a heavy battle. How could they have heard it?
48 Burstall, *The Soldiers' Story*, p. 85 [reported speech].
49 Burstall, *The Soldiers' Story*, p. 85 [reported speech].
50 Burstall, *The Soldiers' Story*, p. 77.
51 Burstall, *The Soldiers' Story*, p. 77.
52 Burstall, *The Soldiers' Story*, p. 85.
53 Burstall, *The Soldiers' Story*, p. 87 [reported speech].
54 Burstall, *The Soldiers' Story*, p. 87.
55 Burstall, *The Soldiers' Story*, p. 86.
56 Burstall, *The Soldiers' Story*, p. 85.
57 Burstall, *The Soldiers' Story*, p. 86 [reported speech].
58 Burstall, *The Soldiers' Story*, p. 86.
59 Burstall, *The Soldiers' Story*, p. 87.
60 Author interview with Dave Sabben, 16 February 2022.
61 Author interview with Dave Sabben, 16 February 2022.
62 Author interview over phone with Dave Sabben, 20 May 2022.
63 Burstall, *The Soldiers' Story*, p. 90 [reported speech].
64 Burstall, *The Soldiers' Story*, p. 90.
65 Dapin, *The Nashos' War*, pp. 132–33.

Chapter twelve: Floating targets

1 Author interview with David Campbell, Buderim, 20 February 2022.
2 Author interview with Bob Grandin, 19 February 2022.
3 Ham, *Vietnam*, p. 237.
4 Ham, *Vietnam*, p. 237.
5 Ham, *Vietnam*, p. 237.
6 Author interview with Bob Grandin, 19 February 2022.
7 Author interview with Bob Grandin, 19 February 2022.
8 Grandin, *The Battle of Long Tan*, p. 170.
9 Grandin, *The Battle of Long Tan*, p. 170.
10 Grandin, *The Battle of Long Tan*, p. 170.
11 Grandin, *The Battle of Long Tan*, p. 170.
12 Author interview with Dave Sabben, 16 February 2022.
13 Hazard Ground Podcast, Episode 144: Dave Sabben (Battle of Long Tan), 28 November 2019.
14 Author interview with Dave Sabben, 21 May 2022.
15 Author interview with Dave Sabben, 16 February 2022.
16 Mollison, *Long Tan and Beyond*, p. 160.
17 Mollison, *Long Tan and Beyond*, p. 160.
18 Mollison, *Long Tan and Beyond*, p. 160.
19 Mollison, *Long Tan and Beyond*, p. 160.
20 Author interview over phone with Dave Sabben, 25 May 2022.
21 Author interview over phone with Dave Sabben, 25 May 2022.
22 Burstall, *The Soldiers' Story*, p. 83.

23 Dave Sabben interview, Australians at War Film Archive, 25 May 2000.
24 Dave Sabben interview, Australians at War Film Archive, 25 May 2000.
25 Burstall, *The Soldiers' Story*, p. 94.
26 Burstall, *The Soldiers' Story*, p. 94.
27 Burstall, *The Soldiers' Story*, p. 105.
28 Burstall, *The Soldiers' Story*, p. 105.
29 Dave Sabben, 'Long Tan: The Principles of War Podcast' [reported speech].
30 Hazard Ground Podcast, Episode 144: Dave Sabben (Battle of Long Tan), 28 November 2019.
31 Author interview with Dave Sabben.
32 Burstall, *The Soldiers' Story*, p. 103 [reported speech].
33 Burstall, *The Soldiers' Story*, p. 103.
34 Burstall, *The Soldiers' Story*, p. 107.
35 Burstall, *The Soldiers' Story*, p. 104.
36 Burstall, *The Soldiers' Story*, p. 104 [reported speech].
37 Burstall, *The Soldiers' Story*, p. 104 [reported speech].
38 Lucas, 'Long Tan Survivor Remembers the Day All Hell Broke Loose', *The West Australian*, 16 August 2016.
39 Adrian Roberts interview with Dr Peter Williams, 1 November 2021.
40 Adrian Roberts interview with Dr Peter Williams, 1 November 2021.

Chapter thirteen: Delta Company's last stand

1 Sunshine Coast Council, Heritage, Lawrence Drinkwater interview, 1 June 2001.
2 Australian War Memorial, Army Commanders' Diary, 1–31 August 1966.
3 Grandin, *The Battle of Long Tan*, pp. 195–96.
4 Dave Sabben interview, Australians at War Film Archive, 25 May 2000.
5 Burstall, *The Soldiers' Story*, p. 101.
6 Geoffrey Kendall interview, Australians at War Film Archive, 16 July 2004.
7 Burstall, *The Soldiers' Story*, p. 102.
8 Author interview over phone with Dave Sabben, 25 May 2022.
9 Adrian Roberts interview with Dr Peter Williams, 1 November 2021.
10 Australian Government, Department of Veterans' Affairs, Anzac Portal, 'Francis Adrian Roberts, Long Tan – Part 3'.
11 Frank Alcorta interview with Dr Peter Williams, 9 January 2022.
12 Frank Alcorta interview with Dr Peter Williams, 9 January 2022.
13 Parer, 'The Many Splendid Lives of the Legendary Frank Alcorta', PNG Attitude website, January 2013.
14 Australian Government, Defence Honours and Awards Tribunal, 1 August 2016.
15 Australian Government, Defence Honours and Awards Tribunal, 1 August 2016.
16 Adrian Roberts interview with Dr Peter Williams, 1 November 2021.
17 Australian War Memorial, *Battle of Long Tan: edited version*, F03370, 1986.
18 Adrian Roberts interview with Dr Peter Williams, 1 November 2021.
19 Adrian Roberts interview with Dr Peter Williams, 1 November 2021.
20 Adrian Roberts interview with Dr Peter Williams, 1 November 2021.
21 Burstall, *The Soldiers' Story*, p. 115.
22 Australian War Memorial Media Collection, Oral History Transcript, Adrian Roberts interviewed by Ian McNeill, recorded February 1978.
23 Burstall, *The Soldiers' Story*, p. 93 [reported speech].
24 Ham, *Vietnam*, p. 231.
25 Burstall, *The Soldiers' Story*, p. 93.
26 Burstall, *The Soldiers' Story*, p. 93.
27 Burstall, *The Soldiers' Story*, p. 104.
28 O'Halloran and Teague, *The Platoon Commander*, p. 102.
29 Smith, *The Battle of Long Tan*, p. 149.
30 Burstall, *The Soldiers' Story*, p. 106.
31 Burstall, *The Soldiers' Story*, p. 106.
32 Burstall, *The Soldiers' Story*, p. 106.
33 *The Battle of Long Tan Documentary*, Red Dune Films, 2006.

34 Peter Tedder and Alan Hutchinson interview with Dr Peter Williams, 9 November 2021.
35 *The Battle of Long Tan Documentary*, Red Dune Films, 2006.
36 Cameron, *The Battle of Long Tan*, p. 261.
37 *The Battle of Long Tan Documentary*, Red Dune Films, 2006.
38 Grandin, *The Battle of Long Tan*, p. 194.
39 Smith, *The Battle of Long Tan*, p. 154.
40 McAulay, *The Battle of Long Tan*, p. 109.
41 Burstall, *The Soldiers' Story*, p. 105.
42 Chenery, 'Recalling the Horror of Long Tan: "I was Too Bloody Busy to be Frightened"', *The Guardian*, August 2009.
43 The Battle of Long Tan website, 'Battle Timeline'.
44 Burstall, *The Soldiers' Story*, p. 102.
45 Burstall, *The Soldiers' Story*, p. 102.
46 Burstall, *The Soldiers' Story*, p. 102.
47 Burstall, *The Soldiers' Story*, p. 102.
48 *The Age*, 18 August 1986, p. 11.
49 Noel Grimes interview, Australians at War Film Archive, 4 May 2004.
50 Burstall, *The Soldiers' Story*, p. 102.
51 Dave Sabben interview, Australians at War Film Archive, 25 May 2000.
52 Burstall, *The Soldiers' Story*, p. 102.
53 Burstall, *The Soldiers' Story*, p. 102.
54 *The Age*, 18 August 1986, p. 11.
55 *The Age*, 18 August 1986, p. 11.
56 *The Age*, 18 August 1986, p. 11.
57 Australian War Memorial, *Battle of Long Tan: edited version*, F03370, 1986 [reported speech].
58 Adrian Roberts interview with Dr Peter Williams, 1 November 2021.
59 O'Halloran and Teague, *The Platoon Commander*, p. 104.
60 O'Halloran and Teague, *The Platoon Commander*, p. 104.

Chapter fourteen: There goes the cavalry

1 McLachlan, Living History, *War Stories: Long Tan Veteran Dave Sabben*, YouTube video, 12 August 2019.
2 Cameron, *The Battle of Long Tan*, p. 279.
3 Smith, *The Battle of Long Tan*, p. 173.
4 O'Halloran and Teague, *The Platoon Commander*, p. 105.
5 Cameron, *The Battle of Long Tan*, p. 262.
6 Adrian Roberts interview, Australians at War Film Archive, 15 May 2000.
7 Adrian Roberts interview, Australians at War Film Archive, 15 May 2000.
8 Author interview with Bob Grandin, 19 February 2022.
9 Grandin, *Answering the Call*, p. 94.
10 McAulay, *The Battle of Long Tan*, p. 109.
11 O'Halloran and Teague, *The Platoon Commander*, p. 120.
12 O'Halloran and Teague, *The Platoon Commander*, p. 120.
13 Smith, *The Battle of Long Tan*, p. 184.
14 Author interview over phone with Dave Sabben, 24 April 2022.
15 Hindley, *The Joys and Dangers of an Aviation Pilot*, The Air Power Development Centre, Canberra, 2013.
16 Mollison, *Long Tan and Beyond*, p. 183.
17 McAulay, *The Battle of Long Tan*, p. 121.
18 McAulay, *The Battle of Long Tan*, p. 121.
19 McAulay, *The Battle of Long Tan*, p. 122.
20 Grandin, *Answering the Call*, p. 95.
21 Clark, *The RAAF at Long Tan*, The Air Power Development Centre, Canberra, 20 July 2010.
22 Author interview over phone with Bob Grandin, 21 March 2022.
23 Author interview with David Collins, 20 February 2022.
24 Author interview with Bob Grandin, 19 February 2022.
25 Author interview with Bob Grandin, 19 February 2022.

26 Burstall, *The Soldiers' Story*, p. 129.
27 Burstall, *The Soldiers' Story*, p. 129 [reported speech].
28 Burstall, *The Soldiers' Story*, p. 129 [reported speech].
29 Chenery, 'Recalling the Horror of Long Tan', *The Guardian*, August 2009.
30 Smith, *The Battle of Long Tan*, p. 187.
31 Author interview with Little Pattie and Col Joye, 28 April 2022.
32 Author interview with Little Pattie and Col Joye, 28 April 2022.
33 Author interview with Little Pattie and Col Joye, 28 April 2022.
34 Lamensdorf, *Write Home for Me: A Red Cross Woman in Vietnam*, Random House, Milsons Point, 2006, p. xx.
35 Ham, *Vietnam*, p. 217.

Chapter fifteen: Dawn's harvest

1 Santayana, 'Tipperary', from *Soliloquies in England and Later Soliloquies*, Charles Scribner and Sons, New York, 1922.
2 Hazard Ground Podcast, Episode 144: Dave Sabben (Battle of Long Tan), 28 November 2019, YouTube video, https://www.youtube.com/watch?v=UzSIZpYkmtQ
3 Peter Tedder and Alan Hutchinson interview with Dr Peter Williams, 9 November 2021.
4 Australian War Memorial Media Collection, Oral History Transcript, Adrian Roberts interviewed by Ian McNeill, recorded February 1978.
5 Jim Richmond interview, Australians at War Film Archive, 21 May 2000.
6 O'Halloran and Teague, *The Platoon Commander*, pp. 151–52.
7 Buick, *All Guts and No Glory*, p. 103.
8 Caulfield, *The Vietnam Years*, 2011.
9 Burin, 'Vietnam War: Veterans hope for answers from former enemy in return to Long Tan', ABC News, 17 August 2016.
10 Chenery, 'Recalling the Horror of Long Tan', *The Guardian*, August 2009.
11 Burstall, *The Soldiers' Story*, p. 139.
12 O'Halloran and Teague, *The Platoon Commander*, p. 110.
13 Author interview with Little Pattie and Col Joye, 28 April 2022.
14 Buick, *All Guts and No Glory*, pp. 100–101.
15 Buick email to author, via researcher Barb Kelly, 27 May 2022.
16 Buick, *All Guts and No Glory*, p. 101.
17 Smith, *The Battle of Long Tan*, p. 184.
18 Peter Tedder and Alan Hutchinson interview with Dr Peter Williams, 9 November 2021.
19 Australian Army, Headquarters 1 Australian Task Force, Commanding Officer After Action Report, Operation Smithfield, Item No. 1/4/26, Series: AWM95.
20 McAulay, *The Battle of Long Tan*, p. 134.
21 David Sabben interview 2, Australians at War Film Archive, Anzac Portal.
22 David Sabben interview 2, Australians at War Film Archive, Anzac Portal.
23 Author interview with David Harris, 29 May 2022.
24 Author interview with David Harris, 29 May 2022.
25 Telegram sent to the family of Paul Large advising of his death in Vietnam, Virtual Australian War Memorial, https:vwma.org.au/explore/people/654426.
26 Author interview with Paul Large's sister, Sandra Fleming, 10 May 2022.
27 Beryl Gant interview, Australians at War Film Archive, 22 May 2000.
28 Romensky, 'Long Tan: Keeping a brother's memory alive after Vietnam War', ABC News, 18 August 2016.
29 The Battle of Long Tan website, 'Remembering Private Dick Aldersea killed in the Battle of Long Tan'.
30 *Tribune*, 24 August 1966, p. 1.
31 *Sydney Morning Herald*, 21 August 1966, p. 2.
32 *Canberra Times*, 22 August 1966, p. 5.
33 Campbell, '"With the Heel of my Boot I Marked the Site": the story of the Long Tan Cross', Australian War Memorial, September 2012.
34 Campbell, '"With the Heel of my Boot I Marked the Site"', Australian War Memorial, September 2012.

Epilogue

1 Australian Army, Headquarters 1 Australian Task Force, Commanding Officer After Action Report, Operation Smithfield, Item No. 1/4/26, Series: AWM95.
2 King, *A Gun Sergeant's Recollections of Long Tan – From the Gun End*, 6RAR Association website.
3 McNamara, *In Retrospect*, p. xvi.
4 Caulfield, *The Vietnam Years*, p. 215.
5 Martin Walsh, Red Dune Films, *Danger Close: The Battle of Long Tan Battle – Battle Animation*, August 2020.
6 Author interview with Dave Sabben, 16 February 2022.
7 Templer, 'General Vo Nguyen Giap obituary', *The Guardian*, 5 October 2013.
8 *The Seattle Times*, 9 November 1995.
9 *The Seattle Times*, 9 November 1995.
10 McNamara, *In Retrospect*, p. 333.
11 McNamara, *In Retrospect*, p. 333.
12 *The Guardian*, 12 August 2019.
13 Chenery, 'Recalling the Horror of Long Tan', *The Guardian*, August 2009.
14 Chenery, 'Recalling the Horror of Long Tan', *The Guardian*, August 2009.
15 *The Age*, 18 August 1986, p. 11.
16 Smith, *The Battle of Long Tan*, p. 184.
17 O'Halloran and Teague, *The Platoon Commander*, p. 129.
18 'Sharp victory for fallen Long Tan soldier', *Northern Daily Leader*, 12 August 2016.
19 John Robbins interview, Australians at War Film Archive, 28 April 2004.
20 Jim Richmond, interview, Australians at War Film Archive, 21 May 2000.
21 Lucas, 'Long Tan Survivor Remembers the Day All Hell Broke Loose', *The West Australian*, 16 August 2016.
22 Makse, 'Family pays tribute to Vietnam veteran Harley Webb', *Albany Advertiser*, 15 July 2021.
23 The Battle of Long Tan website, 'Morrie Stanley – 161 Battery Royal New Zealand Artillery'.
24 Australian Government, Defence Honours and Awards Tribunal, 1 August 2016.
25 Australian War Memorial, *Battle of Long Tan: edited version*, F03370, 1986.
26 MacGregor, 'Finding Gunner Norris', *The Australian*.
27 MacGregor, 'Finding Gunner Norris', *The Australian*.
28 Burstall, *The Soldiers' Story*, p. 171.
29 Burin, 'Vietnam War', ABC News, 17 August 2016.
30 Buick, *All Guts and No Glory*, p. 97.
31 ABC News, 'Long Tan: Vietnamese authorities cancel 50th anniversary commemoration event', 18 August 2016.
32 Chenery, 'Recalling the Horror of Long Tan', *The Guardian*, August 2009.
33 Smith, *The Battle of Long Tan*, p. 277.
34 Walsh, 'Long Tan – A quest for Honour and Integrity', Battle of Long Tan website, 18 January 2011.
35 *Canberra Times*, 15 January 2011.
36 *Sydney Morning Herald*, 12 August 2006.
37 Hansard, House of Representatives, 24 May 2010, p. 3882 and *Sydney Morning Herald*, 30 December 2010.
38 Author interview over phone with Bob Grandin, 28 May 2022.

BIBLIOGRAPHY

Books

Beschloss, Michael R., *Taking Charge: The Johnson White House Tapes, 1963–1964*, Simon & Schuster, New York, 1997

Boxall, Ron and O'Neill, Robert (editors), *Vietnam Vanguard: The 5th Battalion's Approach to Counter-Insurgency, 1966*, ANU Press, Acton, 2020

Buick, Bob, with McKay, Gary, *All Guts and No Glory: the story of a Long Tan warrior*, e-book edition, Allen & Unwin, Sydney, 2000

Burstall, Terry, *A Soldier Returns: A Long Tan Veteran Discovers the Other Side of Vietnam*, University of Queensland Press, St Lucia, 1990

Burstall, Terry, *The Soldiers' Story*, University of Queensland Press, St Lucia, 1986

Cameron, David W., *The Battle of Long Tan*, Penguin Random House, Australia, 2016

Caulfield, Michael, *The Vietnam Years: From the Jungle to the Australian Suburbs*, e-book edition, Hachette, Australia, 2007

Chamberlain, Ernest, *The Viet Cong D445 Battalion: Their Story*, Ernest Chamberlain, Pt Lonsdale, 2011

von Clausewitz, Carl, *On War*, edited and translated by Michael Howard and Peter Paret, Princeton University Press, Princeton, 1976

Dapin, Mark, *The Nashos' War: Australia's National Servicemen and Vietnam*, Viking, Australia, 2014

Donaldson, Gary, *America at War Since 1945: Politics and Diplomacy in Korea, Vietnam, and the Gulf War*, e-book edition, Greenwood Publishing Group, US, 1996

Fairhead, Fred, *The Battle of Long Tan: A Reappraisal*, Avonmore Books, Kent Town, 2019

Grandin, Bob, *Answering the Call: Life of a Helicopter Pilot in Vietnam and Beyond*, e-book edition, Big Sky Publishing, Australia, 2019

Grandin, Bob, *The Battle of Long Tan: As Told by the Commanders to Bob Grandin*, Allen & Unwin, Crows Nest, 2004

Karnow, Stanley, *Vietnam: A History*, Penguin, Victoria, 1984

Halberstam, David, *The Making of a Quagmire*, Rowman and Littlefield, New York, 2008

Ham, Paul, *Vietnam: The Australian War*, HarperCollins, Sydney, 2007

Heard, Barry, *Well Done Those Men*, Scribe, Melbourne, 2005

Heller, Joseph, *Catch-22*, Simon & Schuster, New York, 1961

Hindley, Leigh 'Laddie', *The Joys and Dangers of an Aviation Pilot*, The Air Power Development Centre, Canberra, 2013

Ho Chi Minh, *Selected Works*, Vol. 3, Foreign Languages Publishing House, Hanoi, 1960–62

Lamensdorf, Jean Debelle, *Write Home for Me: A Red Cross Woman in Vietnam*, Random House, Milsons Point, 2006

Mackay, Ian, *Australians in Vietnam*, Rigby, Adelaide, 1968

McAulay, Lex, *The Battle of Long Tan: The Legend of Anzac Upheld*, Random House, Sydney, 1987

McNamara, Robert S., *In Retrospect: The Tragedy and Lessons of Vietnam*, Random House, New York, 1995

McNeill, Ian, *To Long Tan: The Australian Army and the Vietnam War 1950–1966, The Official History of Australia's Involvement in Southeast Asian Conflicts 1948–1975, Vol. II*, Allen & Unwin, St Leonards, 1993

Mollison, Charles S., *Long Tan and Beyond*, Cobb's Crossing, Woombye, 2004

O'Donnell, Kenneth, Powers, David and McCarthy, Joe, *Johnny, We Hardly Knew Ye*, Little, Brown & Co., Boston, 1970

O'Farrell, Terry, *Behind Enemy Lines*, Allen & Unwin, Sydney, 2001

O'Halloran, John and Teague, Ric, *The Platoon Commander*, e-book edition, Hachette, Australia, 2021

Sabben, Dave, *Through Enemy Eyes*, Allen & Unwin, Sydney, 2005

Santayana, George, *Soliloquies in England and Later Soliloquies*, Charles Scribner and Sons, New York, 1922

Sexton, Michael, *War for the Asking*, Penguin, Ringwood, 1981

Smith, Harry, *Long Tan, The Start of a Lifelong Battle*, Big Sky Publishing, Newport, 2015

Smith, Harry, *The Battle of Long Tan: The Company Commanders Story*, e-book edition, Big Sky Publishing, Australia, 2019

Windrow, Martin, *The Last Valley: Dien Bien Phu and the French Defeat in Vietnam*, e-book edition, Hachette, UK, 2011

Articles

ABC News, 'Long Tan: Vietnamese authorities cancel 50th anniversary commemoration event', 18 August 2016, https://www.abc.net.au/news/2016-08-17/vietnam-police-block-access-to-long-tan-site/7756984

Austin, Sergeant Norm, My Vietnam War, unpublished manuscript

Bedford, Matt, 'Vietnam veteran David Beahan tells the story . . .', *The Armidale Express*, 1 August 2016, https://www.armidaleexpress.com.au/story/4067251/there-were-many-battles-but-there-was-only-one-long-tan-david-beahan/

Burgess, Pat, 'The village of hidden hate', *The Bulletin*, Vol. 98, No. 5020, 21 August 1976, https://nla.gov.au/nla.obj-1430458182/view?sectionId=nla.obj-1645446592&partId=nla.obj-1430683824#page/n15/mode/1up

Burin, Margaret, 'Vietnam War: Veterans hope for answers from former enemy in return to Long Tan', ABC News, 17 August 2016, https://www.abc.net.au/news/2016-08-17/vietnam-veterans-hope-for-answers-upon-return-to-long-tan/7749238?nw=0&r=HtmlFragment

Campbell, Emma, '"With the Heel of my Boot I Marked the Site": the story of the Long Tan Cross', Australian War Memorial, September 2012 https://www.awm.gov.au/articles/blog/with-the-heel-of-my-boot-i-marked-the-site-the-story-of-the-long-tan-cross

Chenery, Susan, 'Recalling the Horror of Long Tan: "I was Too Bloody Busy to be Frightened"', *The Guardian*, August 2009, https://www.theguardian.com/australia-news/2019/aug/11/recalling-the-horror-of-long-tan-i-was-too-bloody-busy-to-be-frightened

Curran, James, 'Curtain, Champion of Empire', United States Study Centre, March 2011, https://www.ussc.edu.au/analysis/curtin-champion-of-the-empire

The Islander, 'Remembering Long Tan 51 Years Ago', 16 August 2017, https://www.theislanderonline.com.au/story/4858895/remembering-long-tan-51-years-ago/

Karnow, Stanley, 'A Verdict on Vietnam', *The Washington Post*, 28 October 1984, https://www.washingtonpost.com/archive/entertainment/books/1984/10/28/a-verdict-on-vietnam/ca05dbd0-1838-4998-8be0-42c14b5ad1e5/

Lucas, Jarrod, 'Long Tan Survivor Remembers the Day All Hell Broke Loose', *The West Australian*, 16 August 2016, https://thewest.com.au/news/wa/long-tan-survivor-remembers-the-day-all-hell-broke-loose-ng-ya-115579

MacGregor, Catherine, 'Finding Gunner Norris', *The Australian*, 16 August 2016 https://www.theaustralian.com.au/news/inquirer/battle-of-long-tan-50-years-on-finding-gunner-norris/news-story/5f4d0f678f55d9b01991ae2f0b98067b

Makse, Sarah, 'Family pays tribute to Vietnam veteran Harley Webb', *Albany Advertiser*, 15 July 2021, https://www.albanyadvertiser.com.au/news/albany-advertiser/family-pays-tribute-to-vietnam-war-veteran-harley-webb-a-man-with-a-sharp-dress-sense-and-even-sharper-wit-ng-b881929986z

Northern Daily Leader, 'Sharp victory for fallen Long Tan soldier', 12 August 2016, https://www.northerndailyleader.com.au/story/4093485/sharp-victory-for-fallen-long-tan-soldier/

Romensky, Larissa, 'Long Tan: Keeping a brother's memory alive after Vietnam War', ABC News, 18 August 2016, https://www.abc.net.au/news/2016-08-18/long-tan-keeping-brothers-memory-alive/7761746

Tampa Bay Times, 4 April 2004, https://www.tampabay.com/archive/2004/04/04/au-revoir-dien-bien-phu

Templer, Robert, 'General Vo Nguyen Giap obituary', *The Guardian*, 5 October 2013, https://www.theguardian.com/world/2013/oct/04/general-vo-nguyen-giap

Tucker, Spencer, 'Ho Chi Minh: Replies to an Interview with Japanese NDN TV, April 1966', *Encyclopedia of the Vietnam War: A Political, Social, and Military History*, ABC-CLIO, Santa Barbara, 1998

Newspapers and magazines

The Age
Albany Advertiser
The Armidale Express
The Australian
Canberra Times
Daily Mercury
The Guardian
Hawkesbury Gazette
The Independent
The Islander
Maryborough Chronicle
New York Times
Northern Daily Leader
Time
Tribune
The Seattle Times
Sydney Morning Herald
The Washington Post
The West Australian

Online Sources

ABC PM, 'Little Pattie's encore in Vietnam', 17 August 2009, https://www.abc.net.au/radio/programs/pm/little-patties-encore-in-vietnam/1392206

Army Commanders' Diary, Vietnam, Infantry Units, 6 Battalion Royal Australian Regiment, Series: AWM95, Item No. 7/6/5, 1–31 August 1966, https://battleoflongtan.com/wp-content/uploads/2016/04/AWM95-7-6-5_6RAR-Diary.pdf

Australian Army, Headquarters 1 Australian Task Force, Commanding Officer After Action Report, Operation Smithfield, Item No. 1/4/26, Series: AWM95, https://battleoflongtan.com/wp-content/uploads/2016/04/Long-Tan-After-Action-Reports.pdf

Australian Army, 'Manual of Land Warfare, Part Two: Infantry Training', Volume 1, Pamphlet 2, The Rifle Platoon, 1986, https://www.army.gov.au/sites/default/files/2019-11/mlw_2-1-2_the_rifle_platoon_1986_full_obsolete_0.pdf

Australian Government, Defence Honours and Awards Tribunal, 1 August 2016, https://defence-honours-tribunal.gov.au/wp-content/uploads/2016/08/2016_DHAAT_27_Smith-Sharp-Decision-Report.pdf

Australian Government, Department of Prime Minister and Cabinet, PM Transcripts, Harold Holt Parliamentary Statement, 8 March 1966, https://pmtranscripts.pmc.gov.au/release/transcript-1266

Australian Government, Department of Prime Minister and Cabinet, PM Transcripts, Harold Holt Parliamentary Statement, 2 November 1967, https://pmtranscripts.pmc.gov.au/release/transcript-1711

Australian Government, Department of Veterans' Affairs, Anzac Portal, 'Francis Adrian Roberts, Long Tan – Part 3', https://anzacportal.dva.gov.au/resources/francis-adrian-roberts-long-tan-part-3

Australian Politics.com, 'Sir Robert Menzies Announces Military Commitment To South Vietnam', https://australianpolitics.com/1965/04/29/menzies-vietnam-commitment-announcement.html

Australian War Memorial, *Battle of Long Tan: edited version*, Australian War Memorial Film Archive, F03370, https://www.awm.gov.au/collection/F03370

Australian War Memorial, Last Post Ceremony commemorating the service of (1200265) Private Francis Brett Topp, https://www.awm.gov.au/collection/C2647810

Australian War Memorial, Last Post Ceremony commemorating the service of (2781704) Private Paul Large, Letter, 3 April 1966, https://www.awm.gov.au/collection/C1423279

Australian War Memorial, Private Errol Noack case study, https://www.awm.gov.au/learn/memorial-boxes/2/case-studies/errol-noack

Australian War Memorial Media Collection, Oral History Transcript, Adrian Roberts interviewed by Ian McNeill, recorded February 1978, https://s3-ap-southeast-2.amazonaws.com/awm-media/collection/S01475/document/1865942.PDF

The Battle of Long Tan website, 'Battle Timeline', https://battleoflongtan.com/timeline/

The Battle of Long Tan website, 'Biography: Lieutenant Colonel Harry Smith', https://battleoflongtan.com/wp-content/uploads/2016/04/Long-Tan-Harry-Smith-Biography.pdf

The Battle of Long Tan website, 'Morrie Stanley – 161 Battery Royal New Zealand Artillery', https://battleoflongtan.com/morrie-stanley-161-battery-royal-new-zealand-artillery/

The Battle of Long Tan website, 'Remembering 21 year old Private Paul Large', https://battleoflongtan.com/remembering-21-year-old-private-paul-large/

The Battle of Long Tan website, 'Remembering Private Dick Aldersea killed in the Battle of Long Tan', https://battleoflongtan.com/remembering-private-dick-aldersea-killed-battle-long-tan/

Calwell, Arthur, Speech to the House of Representatives, 4 May 1965, https://australianpolitics.com/1965/05/04/calwell-response-to-vietnam-commitment.html

Clark, Dr Chris, *The RAAF at Long Tan*, The Air Power Development Centre, Canberra, edited transcript of seminar presented on 20 July 2010, https://www.radschool.org.au/Books/The%20RAAF%20at%20Long-Tan.pdf

Collins, Patsy, Affidavit In Any Fact by Mrs. R. A. Reid #1, legal document, 22 November 1963, https://texashistory.unt.edu/ark:/67531/metapth339905/, University of North Texas Libraries, The Portal to Texas History, https://texashistory.unt.edu, Dallas Municipal Archives

Danger Close: The Battle of Long Tan, Facebook post, 7 June 2019, https://www.facebook.com/battleoflongtan/posts/born-8-june-1945-21-year-old-private-paul-large-a-conscript-from-coolah-in-new-s/10156734809803375/

Hansard, House of Representatives, Sir Robert Menzies, 10 November 1964, https://parlinfo.aph.gov.au/parlInfo/search/display/display.w3p;query=Id%3A%22hansard80%2Fhansardr80%2F1964-11-10%2F0082%22;src1=sm1

Hazard Ground Podcast, Episode 144: Dave Sabben (Battle of Long Tan), 28 November 2019, YouTube video, https://www.youtube.com/watch?v=UzSIZpYkmtQ

Hunter, Claire, 'It's an Honour and a Privilege', Australian War Memorial, blog-post, 1 June 2021, https://www.awm.gov.au/articles/blog/patricia-amphlett

John F. Kennedy Library, News Conference 12, President John F. Kennedy, Palais Chaillot, Paris, 2 June 1961, https://www.jfklibrary.org/archives/other-resources/john-f-kennedy-press-conferences/news-conference-12

King, Jim, *A Gun Sergeant's Recollections of Long Tan – From the Gun End*, 6RAR Association website, http://6rarassociation.com/docs/Jim%20King%20Story.pdf

McLachlan, Mat, Living History, *War Stories: Long Tan Veteran Dave Sabben*, YouTube video, 12 August 2019, https://www.youtube.com/watch?v=q4osOEHwdmA

O'Neill, Robert J. 'Operation Holsworthy', 5th Battalion The Royal Australian Regiment Association Website, https://www.5rar.asn.au/ops/hlswthy2.htm

Parer, Rob, 'The Many Splendid Lives of the Legendary Frank Alcorta', PNG Attitude website, January 2013, https://www.pngattitude.com/2013/01/the-many-lives-of-the-legendary-frank-alcorta-at-last-recognition-of-australia-png-hero-.html

Radschool Association Magazine, 'Gunfire at Long Tan: The Kiwi O's Story', Vol. 28, http://austradesecure.com/radschool/Vol28/Page12.htm

Richter, Jodie, 'The Story of a Chopper Pilot, Two Rock Stars and the Vietnam War', Ipswich City Council, Ipswich First, August 2019, https://www.ipswichfirst.com.au/the-story-of-a-chopper-pilot-two-rock-stars-and-the-vietnam-war/

Royal United Services Institute for Defence and Security Services, 'Three Vietnam Wars', paper based on presentation by Colonel David S. Wilkins, March 2020, https://www.rusinsw.org.au/Papers/20200128.pdf

Sabben, Dave, 'Long Tan: The Principles of War Podcast', https://theprinciplesofwar.com/podcast/25-long-tan-3-to-vung-tau/

Sabben, Dave, speech, 'From Scheyville to Vietnam: My Conscription Experience', 30 May 2015, http://www.mhhv.org.au/wp-content/uploads/From-Scheyville-to-Vietnam-my-conscript-experience-Dave-Sabben-MG.pdf

Sabben, Dave, The Battle of Long Tan, Powerpoint presentation, https://battleoflongtan.com/animated-long-tan-presentation/

Skitch, Bob, 'War in Vietnam – A Surveyor's Story', p. 28, http://rasurvey.org/Viet/Part%201.pdf

Stanley, Morrie, 'Gunfire at Long Tan: the FO's story', 6RAR website, http://6rarassociation.com/docs/FOs%20Story%20Long%20Tan.pdf

Sunshine Coast Council, Heritage, Lawrence Drinkwater interview, 1 June 2001, https://heritage.sunshinecoast.qld.gov.au/Stories/War/Veterans-Voices/Lawrence-Drinkwater

Tonkin Gulf Resolution; Public Law 88-408, 88th Congress, 7 August 1964; General Records of the United States Government; Record Group 11; National Archives, https://www.archives.gov/milestone-documents/tonkin-gulf-resolution

Walsh, Martin, '50 Years Ago Australian Forces Arrive in Vietnam', Battle of Long Tan blog, 8 June 2015, https://battleoflongtan.reddunefilms.com/2015/06/50-years-ago-australian-task-force-arrives-in-vietnam/

Walsh, Martin, 'Little Pattie and Col Joye Concert at Nui Dat', Battle of Long Tan blog, 14 April 2016, https://battleoflongtan.reddunefilms.com/2016/04/little-pattie-and-col-joye-concert-at-nui-dat-vietnam-war-18-aug-1966/

Walsh, Martin, 'Long Tan – A quest for Honour and Integrity', Battle of Long Tan website, 18 January 2011, https://battleoflongtan.reddunefilms.com/2011/01/long-tan-a-quest-for-honour-and-integrity/

White House Tape, 1 February 1966, Conversation Number: WH6602.01, University of Virginia, https://millercenter.org/the-presidency/educational-resources/lbj-and-eugene-mccarthy-on-the-assassination-of-dgo-dinh-diem

Interviews

Australians at War Film Archive interviews

Adrian Roberts interview, Australians at War Film Archive, 15 May 2000, https://australiansatwarfilmarchive.unsw.edu.au/archive/htmlTranscript/2558

Beryl Gant interview, Australians at War Film Archive, 22 May 2000, https://australiansatwarfilmarchive.unsw.edu.au/archive/htmlTranscript/2578

Bob Grandin, interveiw, Australians at War Film Archive, 1 May 2000, https://australiansatwarfilmarchive.unsw.edu.au/archive/2572

Brian Mortimer interview, Australians at War Film Archive, 26 March 2004, https://australiansatwarfilmarchive.unsw.edu.au/archive/htmlTranscript/644

Dave Sabben interview, Australians at War Film Archive, 25 May 2000, https://australiansatwarfilmarchive.unsw.edu.au/archive/htmlTranscript/2585

David Sabben interview 2, Australians at War Film Archive, Anzac Portal, https://anzacportal.dva.gov.au/resources/media/video/interview-2-second-lieutenant-david-sabben

Geoffrey Kendall interview, Australians at War Film Archive, 16 July 2004, https://australiansatwarfilmarchive.unsw.edu.au/archive/htmlTranscript/2139?asPdf=y

Jim Richmond interview, Australians at War Film Archive, 21 May 2000, https://australiansatwarfilmarchive.unsw.edu.au/archive/htmlTranscript/2576?asPdf=y

John Heslewood interview, Australians at War Film Archive, 16 April 2004, https://australiansatwarfilmarchive.unsw.edu.au/archive/htmlTranscript/1749?asPdf=y

John Robbins, Australians at War Film Archive, NSW, 28 April 2004, https://australiansatwarfilmarchive.unsw.edu.au/archive/htmlTranscript/1905?asPdf=y

Noel Grimes interview, Australians at War Film Archive, 4 May 2004, https://australiansatwarfilmarchive.unsw.edu.au/archive/htmlTranscript/1939?asPdf=y

Robert Buick, Australians at War Film Archive, 23 July 2004, https://australiansatwarfilmarchive.unsw.edu.au/archive/htmlTranscript/2181?asPdf=y

Robert Hagerty interview, Australians at War Film Archive, 26 March 2004, https://australiansatwarfilmarchive.unsw.edu.au/archive/1732

Author interviews

Author interview with Bob Grandin, Buderim, 19 February 2022
Author interview over phone with Bob Grandin, 21 March 2022
Author interview with Bruce Lane, 23 February 2022
Author interview with Dave Sabben, 16 February 2022
Author interview with Dave Sabben, 17 February 2022
Author interview over phone with Dave Sabben, 12 March 2022
Author interview over phone with Dave Sabben, 24 April 2022

Author interview over phone with Dave Sabben, 20 May 2022
Author interview with Dave Sabben, 21 May 2022
Author interview over phone with Dave Sabben, 25 May 2022
Author interview with David Campbell, Buderim, 20 February 2022
Author interview with David Collins, Buderim, 19 February 2022
Author interview with David Harris, 29 May 2022
Author interview with Little Pattie and Col Joye, 28 April 2022
Author interview with Paul Large's sister, Sandra Fleming, 10 May 2022

Other interviews

Adrian Roberts interview with Dr Peter Williams, 1 November 2021
Doug Child interview with Dr Peter Williams, 3 May 2022
Frank Alcorta interview with Dr Peter Williams, 9 January 2022
John Burns interview with Dr Peter Williams, 26 October 2021
Peter Tedder and Alan Hutchinson interview with Dr Peter Williams, 9 November 2021

TV, Film and Video

Martin Walsh, Red Dune Films, *Danger Close: The Battle of Long Tan Battle – Battle Animation*, 11 August 2020, YouTube video, https://www.youtube.com/watch?v=xT6Dzd0_Xfg
The Battle of Long Tan Documentary, Red Dune Films, 2006, https://battleoflongtan.com/film-detail/battle-long-tan-documentary/

Other Sources

Buick email to author, via researcher Barb Kelly, 27 May 2022
Contemporaneous notes provided by David Harris to the author, 30 May 2022

INDEX

5th Battalion Royal Australian Regiment (5RAR), 37; 1RAR replacement, 104; 1st Australian Task Force, 73, 75; Charlie Company 161; D Company, 381; departure for Vietnam, 58–9; farewell parade, 98; Nui Dat base construction, 99, 115–16, 124, 140–1; Operation Holsworthy, 159–62; praise from Westmoreland, 401; support of 6RAR, 250, 382

6th Battalion Royal Australian Regiment (6RAR), 37; 1RAR replacement, 104; 1st Australian Task Force, 73, 75; acclimatisation, 110; address from Chinn, 77–8; Alpha Company *see* Alpha Company (6RAR); arrival in Vietnam, 105–8; attack on, 251; 'Baby Battalion', 48; 'birthday', 107; Bravo Company *see* Bravo Company (6RAR); 'Brisbane's own', 98; Charlie Company, 12, 41, 50, 60, 143, 185, 187, 190, 195, 250, 381; departure for Vietnam, 59, 76–7, 95, 99, 102–4; farewell parade, 98–9; first aerial convoy, 116; impression of Delta Company, 67; jungle warfare training, 83–5; memorial, 399–400; nucleus, 12; Nui Dat base construction, 124, 140–1; Nui Dat 2 patrol, 165–7; Operation Enoggera, 133, 134–5; Operation Foxhole training, 94–5; praise from Westmoreland, 401; Rockhampton exercises, 63–5; semi-war footing, 58; size, 39; Snap Shooting Range practice, 80–1; troop numbers, 117

Abigail, Major General Peter, 423
Agent Orange, 99, 418
Ainslie, Private Peter, 222
Akell, Private Bill; nickname, 248; post-war life, 418; recollection of dead VC, 387; relief at APC arrival, 359–60; shooting VC, 329; spare radio mission, 248–51
Alcorta, Sergeant Frank; 6RAR posting, 37–8; APC contact, 240, 292–3, 325; bravery, 334; contact with VC, 333–4; Medal of Gallantry award, 418, 425; post-war life, 414, 417–18
Aldersea, Jim, 396
Aldersea, Private Rick, 328–9, 366, 396
Alpha Company (6RAR); 2 Platoon, 333; 3 Platoon, 166; APC transport, 292–3, 351; contact with VC, 144–5, 180; Delta Company support, 240, 245, 251–2, 257, 289; departure from Long Tan, 372–3; medics, 363; patrols, 99, 143, 164–70, 180, 185, 190, 195; reunion with Bravo and Delta Companies, 376
Alsop, Joe, li
Amphlett, Joe, 82–3
Amphlett, Patricia *see* Little Pattie
Anne-Marie outpost, xxx
Ap Bac, xliii
Ap Tan Thoi, xliii
Armed Propaganda Brigade for the Liberation of Vietnam, xxii
Armoured Personnel Carriers (APCs), 94–5, 116, 130, 176, 231, 250, 351, 377; 1 APC Squadron beret, 352; 2 Troop, 107, 243, 256, 330, 360; 3 Troop, 133, 256, 313, 324, 330, 360, 366; 23 Bravo, 352; 30 Bravo, 366; Alpha Company mistaken fire, 354–5; arrival, 358–62; attack on VC, 333, 335–6; 'battle taxis', 133; Delta Company assistance, 281, 287, 288–92, 311, 324, 325, 354; 'floating' capacity, 313, 314; M113, 107–8; 'pivot steering', 292; retrieval of deceased mission, 381–2; Roberts' plan, 368–9; 'sitting duck' analogy, 420; supply, 243; Townsend's orders, 362; VC machine-gun attack, 351–2; VC resistance, 360–1
Army of the Republic of Vietnam (ARVN), xliii; appearance, 115; arrival in Long Tan, 91; awards to Australian soldiers, 425; job, 115; US nickname, 115
Artillery School, 42
Austin, Sergeant Norm, 259, 414
Australia; alliance with America, xxxix; anti-war protests, 9–10, 73–4; Communism as threat, and, xxxix, 4, 74; declaration of war, 75; media response to Vietnam War, 9, 11, 396–8; memory of Vietnam War, 404; 'Military Working Agreement', 73; Nashos

Australia *continued*
see National Service (Nashos); recognition of Vietnam veterans, 426; reporting of Diem assassination, xlviii; response to Dien Bien Phu, xxxv–xxxvi

Australian Army, 16; 1st Armoured Personnel Carrier Squadron, 73, 125; 1st Australian Task Force, 73, 87; 1st Battalion Royal Australian Regiment (1RAR), 9, 44, 68, 74, 104, 124; 1st Field Regiment of the Royal Australian Artillery, 171, 344; 1st Recruit Training Battalion (1RTB), 17; 2nd Battalion Royal Australian Regiment (2RAR); 4th/19th Prince of Wales's Light Horse, 117, 133; 5RAR *see* 5th Battalion Royal Australian Regiment (5RAR); 547 Signal Troop, 151, 204; 6RAR *see* 6th Battalion Royal Australian Regiment (6RAR); 7RAR, 402; 101 Battery, 95; 103rd Field Battery, 42–3, 124–5, 176, 178, 253; 103rd Signals Squadron, 125; 105th Field Battery, 124, 253; 131 Divisional Locating Battery, 178; 547 Signal Troop, 121; 'Baby Battalion', 48; battalion structure, 23; casualties, 100, 143, 144, 218, 219–20, 224, 239, 294, 296, 329, 337, 347–8, 363, 366–7, 379, 384–5, 387, 390, 394–6, 398, 402; combat rations, 145; company structure, 23; Delta Company *see* Delta Company (6RAR); hierarchy, 20; intelligence operations, 130; Logistics Support Group (1ALSG), 75; mail from home, 157–8; nicknames, 125; objective, 71, 85; platoon structure, 22; relationship with RAAF, 137–9, 258–9; retrieval of deceased soldiers, 381–93; rotations, three-day, 125–6; section structure, 22, 24–5, 89; selective compulsory national service, 5, 6–7; Special Air Service Regiment SAS unit, 125, 140; US Army, and, 44, 70–71, 112–13

Australian Army Force Vietnam (AAFV), 73

Australian Army Training Team Vietnam (AATTV); Commanding Officer, xxxix, 77; South Vietnam deployment, xli, xlii

Australian Force Vietnam (AFV), 73

Australian Task Force Headquarters, 101

Australian War Memorial, 411, 416, 419, 421

Back Beach camp, 110, 111, 115

Bao Dai, Emperor, xxii, xxvii, xxxiii, xxxiv

Baria province *see* Phuoc Tuy province

Barker, Greg, 73

Bartsch, Private 'Bluey', 144

The Battle of Long Tan: As Told by the Commanders, 414

The Battle of Long Tan: The Company Commander's Story, 406

Beahan, Private Dave; 6RAR posting, 37; best man offer, 158–9; contact with VC, 268; friendship with Large, 37, 41, 99; section training, 39–40

Béatrice outpost, xxix

Bennett, Private Peter, 367

Bextrum, Private Neil, 269, 347

'beyond the wire', 191

Bien Hoa, 44, 104, 124, 244; Dong Nai Museum, 419

Bigglesworth, Major James, 263

Binh Ba, 159–60; 5RAR patrol, 160–2, 182, 250

'blocking position', 186

'body count', 102, 383, 393

booby traps, 78, 128

Boom-Boom girls, 111, 127

Borger, Private Kevin, 100

Branch, Private Kev, 241, 385

Bravo Company (6RAR), 12, 41, 50, 60, 364, 372–3, 376; casualties, 144; contact with VC, 220–1, 354–5; D445 mortar launch base discovery, 189, 195; Delta Company, and, 65, 233, 243, 274, 291, 339, 354, 357–8; Long Tan patrol, 182, 183, 185–7, 191, 192, 195–202, 220–1; position, 142, 143; retrieval of deceased after Long Tan, 382

Brett, Private Ronnie, 38, 292, 325, 333–4

Brown, Shorty, 174, 176, 273, 320, 321, 377

Browne, Malcolm, xlv

Buddhists; Diem regime treatment, xliv; protests, xliv–xlv; Thich Quang Duc, xlv–xlvi

Buick, Beverley, 97

Buick, Sergeant Bob, xvi; arrival of APCs, 362; artillery instructions, 254, 272, 282–3; assessment of Nui Dat defences, 122; battlefield roll call, 281; clearing Large's rifle, 301; combat with VC, 253–4, 281–2; discipline at Nui Dat, 149; emotional turmoil, 390; 'encounter battle' theory, 420; feeling of futility, 240; Kendall, and, 147; King's recollection, 401; Long Tan orders, 237; Long Tan patrol, 207–8, 210, 214, 216; Long Tan VC contact, 218, 222, 223, 225; military experience pre-Vietnam, xvi, 24; Military Medal, 423; Operation Enoggera, 136; placement, xvi, 56; post-war life, 408, 412, 414; pre-deployment home visit, 97; promotion to Acting Platoon Sergeant, 313; radio supply, 256; reaction to deceased, 386; retreat order, 294, 296; return to the battlefield, 389–90, 408; Sharp, and, 175–6, 187, 239, 318; swap with Rankin, 399; Todd, and, 311–12; warning of shell attack, 173; weapon pit slip, 174–5

Buick, Tracey, 97

Bundy, McGeorge, li

Burns, Bombardier John, 178, 286

Burstall, Private Terry; conversation with Webb, 209; description of weather, 124; encounter with Hornung, 273; location of memorial cross, 419; Operation Enoggera, 138; patrol positions, 174, 176, 320–1; posting, 104; post-battle observations, 408; post-war life, 418; reaction to death of VC soldier, 387–8; sleeping on duty, 145–6; use of live ammunition, 114

Calwell, Arthur; attempted assassination, 132–3, 158, 405; death, 405; response from Menzies, 49; stance on Vietnam War, 10–11, 18, 48, 74–5, 131, 405, 425
Cameron, Clyde, 5
Campbell, Tubby, 108
Canungra Jungle Training Centre, 83, 109
Cao Xuan Nghia, xxix
Carter, Corporal John, 350–1, 359
Casey, Richard, xxxv–xxxvi
Chamberlain, Ernie, 414
Child, Doug, 414
China; Ho Chi Minh's attitude towards, xxiii–xxiv; occupation of Vietnam, xxi
Chinn, Regimental Sergeant Major, 12; assessment of VC, 77–8, 148; beer supply, 107; character, 77, 145–6; Delta assistance mission, 279, 308; military career, 77; support for Buick, 386
Clements, Corporal Peter, 352, 353, 359, 415–16, 428
Cogny, General René, xxx, xxxii–xxxiii
Col Joye and the Joy Boys; accommodation, 378; concern for safety, 229–30, 365–6, 388–9; friendship with Little Pattie, 418–19; helicopter transport, 234; troop entertainment, 82, 189, 193, 194–6, 203, 206, 213
Cold War, xxvii, 404
Collins, Leading Aircraftman 'Bluey', 414; ammunition drop mission, 302, 304, 308; concern for Delta Company, 227; meeting Col Joye, 193; retrieval of deceased, 374
Communism, xx, xxiii, xxxvi; alarm over, xxxix; Diem attack, xxxiv–xxxv; threat of, 74–5
'Contact Fire Mission', 43
'cordon and search', 182
Cosgrove, Warrant Officer John, 394
counter-insurgency doctrine, 85
Cubis, Lieutenant Colonel Richmond, 184, 250
Curtin, John, xxxix

Danger Close: The Battle of Long Tan, 43, 419–20
Dare, Private Ernie, 367
Dat Do, 92, 134, 398
Davis, Private Graeme 'Doc', 269, 300, 312, 313, 338
de Castries, Brigadier General Christian, xxx, xxxii
de Gaulle, General Charles, xxiii, xxxviii–xxxix, xlii, li, 5, 402
De Puy, General William, 71
Debelle, Jean, 379–80
Defensive Fire (DF), 213
Delta Company (6RAR), 12, 41, 50; 4 Section/11 Platoon, 298; 10 Platoon, 52, 90, 146, 198, 203–5, 209, 212, 214, 232–3, 241–2, 247, 265–6, 273, 317, 320, 343, 358; 11 Platoon, 48, 90, 146, 173, 187, 190, 198, 203, 206–16, 219, 221, 228–9, 231, 233, 237, 241–2, 244–7, 253–6, 265–6, 271–2, 283, 294–5, 300, 304–5, 317–18, 320, 367, 400; 12 Platoon, 37, 48, 69, 90–1, 190, 198–9, 203, 209–10, 212, 214, 233, 265–8, 284–5, 293, 300, 317, 343; ambush, contention as to, 420; artillery call-in, 145; attack on perimeter, 338–9; attire, 68–9; award citations, 422–3, 425; casualties, 366–7; Citation for Gallantry, 425; command, 48; completion, 41; contact with VC, 143–4, 146, 209, 241; criss-crossing with VC, 154; ethos, 67–8; HQ, 275; inspiration derived from, 398; logo, 66; Long Tan aim, 335; Long Tan deployment, 422; manpower shortage, 243–4; Operation Hobart, 142–8, 150; parade, 53; patrols, 142, 159, 190–3, 195, 198, 200, 203–9; Presidential Citation, 426; reunion with Bravo Company, 357–8; shorthand-speak, 66–7; training, 54, 59–61, 63–5, 69–70, 88–91, 114; trouble, 240, 257; Westmoreland's praise, 426
Dien Bien Phu, xxvii–xxxv, 249, 398, 419
Dinham, Lieutenant Peter, 333, 334
Dobson, Corporal Phil; Alpha Company assistance, 363; assistance to Webb, 322–3, 410; medic role, 255–6, 338, 340, 379
Dohle, Flight Lieutenant Cliff; ammunition drop mission, 261, 263, 278, 303, 307–8, 324; Distinguished Service Medal, 425
Doolan, Private Bill 'Wild Bill', 345–6, 391
Dowling, Air Commodore John, 259
Doyle, Private Peter, 242
Drabble, Private Glenn, 318–19, 410, 428
Drinkwater, Corporal Laurie, 122, 137, 293, 326, 347, 348
Duncan, Phil, 57
Durnford, Warrant Officer Paddy, 416, 417

Eglinton, Private Ronnie, 224, 318, 319, 338, 346–7, 349, 371
Eisenhower, President Dwight D.; 'Domino' theory, xxxi–xxxii, 404; praise of Diem, xxxv

Enoggera Barracks, 12, 37, 39–44, 50–61, 90–1, 99, 220, 267, 281, 411
Esler, Harry, 242

Fabian, Doug, 297, 299–300
Fairhall, Allen, 71, 73
fan patrols, 196
fighting patrol, 182
fire control, 68–9, 253
fire support, 95
Forces Terrestres du Nord, xxx
Ford, Major Noel; assessment of VC, 148; Bravo Company command, 142; disappearance, post-war, 407; Long Tan patrol, 183, 185, 186, 189, 196–202, 221; O Group meeting, 364; orders, 354; securing perimeter, 357–8; support of Delta Company, 244, 274
Foreign Legion Army, xxix
Forsyth, 'Bushy', 317
France; Binh Ba occupation, 160; defeat at Dien Bien Phu, xxxii–xxxiii; Democratic Republic of Vietnam, attack on, xxiii; Ho Chi Minh's attitude towards, xxiii–xxiv; Kennedy visit, xxxvii–xxxvix; occupation of Vietnam, xix–xxi, xxviii

Gabrielle outpost, xxx
Gant, Beryl, 96, 102, 137, 395
Gant, Private Kenny; death, 224, 318, 395, 428; departure from Australia, 102; friendship with Richmond, 41; nickname, 14; Operation Enoggera, 137; pre-deployment home visit, 96; remembrance, 411; singing, 14, 34–5, 411–12; St Christopher medal, 158
Gardiner, Lieutenant Trevor, 167
Gerron, Major Dick, 258–9
Gibson, Corporal Ross, 367
Gower, Major General Steve, 423
Graham, Private Ken, 269
Grandin, Flight Lieutenant Bob; ammunition drop mission, 303–8, 361; daily routine, 193; Delta Company assistance, 227, 257, 260, 264, 277–8; dustoff mission, 365; evacuation mission, 373–5; military experience and placement, xvi; post-war career, 413–14; reunion with Riley, 413; South Vietnamese award, 425; transporting entertainers, 193, 195–6
Grant, Private Ernie, 296, 365, 428
Grice, Signaller Vic, 207, 208, 209, 239, 240, 254, 294, 428
Grimes, Private Noel, 123, 347, 348
Gross, Corporal Richard, 333, 334, 359
guerrilla warfare, xli
Gulf of Tonkin Resolution, 2–3, 4, 403

Hagerty, Major Bob, 102, 230, 243
Halberstam, David, xlv, xlvi
Halls, Private Brian, 275
Hang Pac Bo, xvii–xx
'Harassment and Interdiction' (HI) fire, 171, 213
Harkins, General Paul D., xl, lii
Harrington, Corporal, 278
Harris, Lieutenant David; concern for Delta Company, 230–1, 258; impression of Jackson, 250, 393; interest in Keep's predictions, 154–6; observations on shelling, 184
Hayes, Flight Lieutenant Max, 193–4
Haylen, Wayne, 73–4, 131, 132, 405
heavy machine gun (HMG), 128, 231, 238, 247, 271, 316, 319, 399
Heslewood, Private John, 340; ammunition shortage, 298; anger towards senior officers, 386–7; attack on 11 Platoon, 244; decisions regarding position, 297–9; Kirby's support, 340; observations of VC, 272; Robbins, and, 38, 318
Hill, Leading Aircraftman, 278
Hindley, Squadron Leader Laddie, 365, 370, 374
HMAS *Sydney*, 11, 99, 107
Ho Chi Minh; aliases, xix, l; army *see* Viet Cong (VC); characterisation of war with US, 93–4, 402; Chinese versus French occupation, attitude towards, xxiii–xxiv; death, 404; declaration of independence speech, xxii–xxiii; destiny, xix, 404; education, xix; French defeat, recording of, xxxiii; Hanoi mausoleum, 404; land redistribution program, xxxv; mass assassination of Diem sympathisers, xxxvi–xxxvii; meeting with Ngo Dinh Diem, xxv–xxvi; North Vietnam leadership, xxxiii; predictions, 402; 'Uncle' title, xix; VC efforts, 229; Vietnamese independence, plan for, xix–xx, xxiii
'Ho Chi Minh sandals', 125–6, 196, 200, 205
Hoa Long, 92, 134
Holsworthy Barracks, 37, 42
Holt, Harold, 57; address to Parliament, 74–5, 393; majority government, 405; reaction to first Nasho death, 100; repatriation of deceased, 394
Honnor, Major Harry, 223, 256, 327, 345
'hoochies', 67, 85
Hornung, Private Brian, 246–7, 248, 273
Houston, Private James, 429
Howell, Mary, 417
Hutchinson, Captain Alan, 390, 414

Iroquois helicopters, *see* Royal Australian Air Force (RAAF)

Jackson, Brigadier Oliver, 179, 288; 1st Australian Task Force location selection, 87; alert from Harris, 230; character, 117;

clearance, 257, 276, 278, 279; confrontation with Raw, 259, 260; death, 405; Distinguished Service Order, 423; emotional turmoil, 366, 393; Harris's impression, 154; impression of war, 6, 73; inspection of Nui Dat shelling, 184; Iroquois request, 258; Keep, and, 126–7, 153, 156, 163, 245; military experience, xv; Operation Enoggera, 137, 138–9; Operation Hobart, 150; orders, 377; patrol for VC, 150; placement, 73, 117; post-war life, 405; reaction to Noack's death, 100; request for helicopter support, 259–62; retirement, 405; retrieval of deceased mission, 382, 391; unease about Delta Company, 249–50
Jewry, Lance Corporal Jack, 14, 158, 337, 365, 366, 429
Johnson, Carey 'Bluey', 355
Johnson, President Lyndon Baines, xlviii; assent to office, xlix; attitude towards Vietnam involvement, li–lii, 4, 50, 62; conundrum, 98; 'credibility gap', 97–8; Gulf of Tonkin Resolution powers, 2–3; Ho Chi Minh's address, 94; political impact of Tet Offensive, 402; promotion of Westmoreland, lii
Jones, Corporal Robin 'Spike', 197, 358

Kapooka Army Recruit Training Centre, 7, 13, 14, 16, 19–39, 149
Karnow, Stanley, xxxiv, xxxv
Keen, Sergeant Harry, 196–7
Keep, Captain Bob, xvi, 126–7; allegation of homosexual advances, 163; character, 126, 127, 155, 162; death, 415; emotional turmoil, 380; evacuation to Vung Tau, 163; non-Army attire, 155; predictions about VC, 126–7, 128, 152–5, 162, 230, 245, 380; US response to intelligence, 154
Kendall, Lieutenant Geoff, xv–xvi, 57; assistance to Hornung, 246–7; character, 52; commendation of Akell, 251; concern about 10 Platoon, 245–6; description of VC casualties, 327–8; enlistment in Australian Army, l–li; Long Tan patrol, 146, 147, 205, 208, 241; Medal for Gallantry, 425; Mentioned in Dispatches, 423; NCO, 56; O Group role, 90, 192; orders, 241, 267, 317; post-war life, 407, 414; pre-deployment home visit, 97; recollection of order to shoot enemy, 408–9; retrieval of deceased mission, 383; rumination about death, 357; salute warning, 56; Sharp, and, 232, 318; Smith, and, 86, 273; spotting Todd, 336
Kennedy, President John F., xxxvii, 74, 402; assassination, xlviii–xlix; meeting with de Gaulle, xxxvii–xxxix, xlii; military 'advisers' to Vietnam, xxxviii–xxxix, xli, xlviii; reaction to Diem assassination, xlvii; recording of conversations, li; withdrawal of US, xlvi–xlvii
'killer patrols', 130
King, Jim, 401
Kirby, Warrant Officer Jack, Company Sergeant Major; admiration, 408; ammunition box near-miss, 309 ; ammunition request, 266–7; assistance to wounded, 321–2, 363; award, 422; character, 55, 267; Company Aid Post role, 322; death, 398; encounter with Burstall, 273–4; Distinguished Conduct Medal, 423; distribution of ammunition, 310; encouragement to troops, 310, 346; Heslewood assistance, 340; instruction to Akell re radio, 248; military experience, xvi; O Group, 54, 192; orders, 53, 274, 320, 329, 348; organisation of ammunition, 338; physical aptitude, 60; protection of Robbins, 340; reaction to media, 386; repatriation and burial, 408; request to Roberts re deceased, 366
Kocan, Peter, xlix, 131–2, 405

Laird, Melvyn, 97–8
Lane, Flight Lieutenant Bruce, 137–9, 261, 263, 278, 307, 365, 414
Large, Dulce, 96
Large, Olga, 395
Large, Private Paul 'Largey', xvi, 13–14, 377; accidental discharge of Armalite, 148–9; character, 26, 123, 139; death, 347, 366, 394–5, 418; engagement to Noeline, 158–9; firing prowess, 25; friendships, 37, 41; legal victory against Corporal, 169; letter regarding Delta Company prowess, 90–1; patrol position, 123; pre-deployment home visit, 96–7; pride as 'Digger', 99; scorpion sting, 139; section training, 39–40; wet cigarettes, 301
Large, Sandra, 394–5, 414
Large, Vic, 96
Levers Plateau, 58
Little Pattie; accommodation, 278; 'Dance Puppet Dance' hit, 213; helicopter ride, 234, 235, 243; impression of Vietnam, 194; Joye, and, 378, 388–9, 419; outfit, 196; post-Vietnam life, 418–19, 421; reaction to casualty report, 379; troop entertainment, 81–3, 189, 193, 195, 203, 206, 213–14, 229–30
Lodge, Cabot, 403
Long Dat District People's Committee, 419
Long Dien, 92, 134
Long Phuoc; anger of civilians, 138; approaches, treacherous, 133; brass statue, 135; captured VC inventory, 137; civilian casualty, 136–7; evacuation of civilians, 134;

Long Phuoc *continued*
razing, 136–8; road junction with Long Tan, 330; 'souvenir' hunting, 135–6; tunnels, 134, 135; VC fortification, 134
Long Tan; 50th anniversary ceremony, 411, 421; 'ambush' debate, 420–1; ARVN approach, 91; contact with VC, 216–21; evacuation of civilians, 92, 119; foreign occupation, xxi–xxii; location, xx–xxi; memorial cross, 419; military significance of battle, 421; officer experience, 257–8; popular culture references, 419–20; public commemorations, 419; RAAF leaflet drop, 193–4; rubber plantation patrol, 192, 195–7, 203–11
Long Tan and Beyond, 407
Long Tan Bridge, 419
Long Tan Cross, 419
Long Tan Recognition Review, 423
Long Tan Day, 404
Long Tan Road, 419
Long Tan Street, 419
Long Tan: The Start of a Lifelong Battle, 407
Lovegrove, Lawrie, 96
Lowes, Sergeant Noel, 332, 352–3, 413

MacArthur, General Douglas, xxxviii, xlvi, 5, 402
McCarthy, Eugene, 62
McCarty, Major General Chester, xxxii
McCormack, Private Albert, 429
McCormack, Private Dennis, 429
McFarlane, Major Brian, 143
Mackay, Brigadier Ken, 70–1, 73
Mackinnon, Dan, 6–7
McNamara, Trooper Paul, 350
McNamara, Robert, 1–2, 401, 403
Magnussen, Private Barry, 149, 295, 318, 425
Mao Tse-Tung, xix, xx, xxvii
Marchant, Corporal Cliff, 302
Martin, Corporal Mike, 136
May, Private Allen; assistance to Fabian, 297, 299–300; shooting VC, 224–5, 348–9
Mekong Delta, xxxvi
Meller, Private Barry 'Custard', 207–8, 365, 376; confrontation with VC, 297–8; injuries, 223, 254, 295, 297; inquiry about Grice, 294; rescue, 384; spotting and shooting duty, 239, 253–4; use of ground sheet, 368
Menzies, Sir Robert, xxxix; announcement of entry into war, 8, 18, 74–5; co-operation with Johnson, 8; resignation, 57; response to Calwell, 49; support of South Vietnam, 4–5, 48–9
Miles, Elizabeth, 417
Miller, Chico, 315–16
Mitchell, Private Warren, 224, 410, 429
Mollison, Captain Charles, xv, 97, 332, 362, 382; Alpha Company command, 67–8, 145, 159, 165, 180; book, 407; Nui Dat 2 patrol, 167–8, 170, 186; orders, 240, 314, 334; post-war career, 407; protest about APCs, 353; reaction to APC assistance, 288–9, 283; rescue efforts, 367
Moore, Bluey, 224
Morrison, Captain, 1, 2
Morse, Senator Wayne, 2–3
Mortimer, Corporal Brian 'Doc'; assistance to Norris, 179–80; sentry duty, 170, 171–2
Muller, Laurie, 45
Murphy, Captain Pat, 201–2
Myles, Sergeant Jim, 363

napalm, 44, 110, 244, 249, 258, 265, 277, 280, 285, 287
National Liberation Front (NLF), xlii–xliii; Australian recognition, 18; co-ordination role, 127; headquarters, 133
National Service (Nashos), 5; 'appreciations', 38–9, 88; Basic Fitness Assessment, 23; Basic Training, 22, 31, 37, 350; 'birthday ballot', 6–7; casualties, 100; civilian treatment, 45; coded language, 30; collective reaction, refining, 36; conscientious objectors, 7; contract drills, 40; Corps Training, 37; daily routine, 23; duration, 30; endurance training, 47; firing drills, 25; friendships, 41; graduation, 47; Gunners Course, 42; hand signals, 24, 40, 58; instructors, 33, 41; Long Tan patrol, 198; map-reading, 32, 40; Officer Training Course, 25–34; patrolling and tracking practice, 40; recruit reception, 19–22; Regular Army's perceptions, 50–1, 57, 58; rifle drills, 36; Scheyville Officer Training Unit, 30, 38–9, 44–6; section training, 39–40; specialisation, 37; values, 33; weapon-handling, 24, 31, 40, 42
Needs, Private Johnny, 166
Nelson, Dr Brendan, 411
Newman, Trooper Geoff, 368–9
New Zealand 161st Battery *see* Royal New Zealand Artillery
Nghia, Major, xlvii
Ngo Dinh Diem, xxiv; arrest, xxv; Asia's 'miracle man', xxxv; assassination, xlvii–xlviii, 62, 403; career, xxv; Communist agents, attack on, xxxiv; education, xxv; flight from coup, xlvii; Johnson's hindsight, 62; Korea as model, xxxv; meeting with Ho Chi Minh, xxv–xxvi; release, xxvii; South Vietnam leadership, xxxiii, xxxiv; treatment of Buddhists, xliv; VC prisoner interrogation, xxxiv
Nguyen Dynasty, xxi

Nguyen van Nhung, Captain, xlvii
Nhu Diem, xlvii, xlviii
Noack, Private Errol 'Flex', 14–15, 100
Norris, Maryanne, 97, 182, 183, 253, 416, 417
Norris, Phil, 15, 20, 37; Artillery School training, 42–3; death, 253, 417; marriage, 97; mortar shelling, 179–80, 182–3, 416; patrol swap with Mortimer, 170, 179; repatriation, 416–17
North Vietnam; creation, xxxiii; guerrilla warfare training, xxxv; Gulf of Tonkin attack, 3, 403; Ho Chi Minh leadership, xxxiii; land redistribution program, xxxv; reunification with South Vietnam, 403
North Vietnamese Army (NVA); entry to South Vietnam, xxxvii, 211; Operation Rolling Thunder aim, 6; Phuoc Tuy presence, 130, 166; primary motivation, 427; uniform, 128, 211; VC battalion, 316
Nui Dat base, 87–90; 1ATF Australian base, 92, 109, 113, 115, 116, 124, 153, 290–2, 421; Alpha Line, 92, 120, 122, 134; artillery compound, 290; construction and layout, 119–21, 124–5, 126, 140; defences, 122; Eagle Farm, 125, 262, 278; Fire Support Control Centre, 181, 234, 244; Jackson's concerns, 249–50; Kangaroo Pad, 116, 125, 196, 227, 263, 278, 324, 365; map, 120; mortar shelling, 174–82, 184; patrols, 164; securing, 101, 134; 'Set Room', 151; Task Force Operations Centre, 257–64; Tiger 5, 125; transfer to South Vietnamese Army, 402; troop population, 125, 140; VC and, 152–6, 159, 196–8, 421
Nui Dat 2, 119, 141, 154, 156, 159, 163, 165–9, 182, 205, 216, 223, 228, 232, 280

O'Brien, Major Owen, 12, 77, 279, 308
O'Callaghan, John, 100
O'Donnell, Sergeant Bill, 181
O'Halloran, Dick, 164
O'Halloran, 'Digger', 47
O'Halloran, Grace, 47
O'Halloran, Lieutenant John, 142, 178, 339, 354, 355, 358, 385, 414; arrival of APCs, 362; Basic Training, 13; book, 409, 414; farewell parade, 99; first test in combat, 142; friendship with Sharp, 13, 31, 90, 176, 385–6, 409, 421; graduation, 47; introduction to platoon, 54; Long Tan patrol, 196–8, 200, 201, 202; officer training, 26, 31, 45, 47; Operation Enoggera, 136; opinion on Nashos and Regular Army, 19; placement, 48, 52; post-war life, 409–10; pre-deployment home visit, 96; protection, 87; reaction to Sharp's death, 385; religious faith, 164; response to Vietnamese conscript, 388
O'Neill, Captain Robert J., 160–1
Operation Enoggera, 133–39
Operation Foxhole, 94–5
Operation Hobart, 142–8, 150
Operation Holsworthy, 159–60
Operation Rolling Thunder, 6
Operation Smithfield, 369, 401
Operation Vendetta, 192, 369
O'Reilly, Sergeant Blue, 330, 336, 351–2
O'Rourke, Corporal Bill, 353
Oswald, Lee Harvey, xlviii–xlix

Parr, Private Alan 'Blue', 310
Passey, Major Brian, 243, 256–7, 274
People's Army of Viet Nam, xxviii
Peters, Captain Les, 180
Pham Van Dong, xvii, xix
Phuoc Tuy province, xxi; Australian objective, 71, 153, 157; map, 72; Route 2, 129
The Platoon Commander, 409, 414
'Pogos', 67, 125, 290, 326, 345
The Principles of Leadership, 33–4
Prowse, Sapper Leslie, 143
Puckapunyal training camp, 7, 13, 15, 16, 29

'Queensland Cong', 94–5
Rankin, Sergeant Neil, 70, 321, 359; 6RAR memorial mission, 398–400; mortar shelling, 247–8
Raw, Group Captain Peter, 139. 163, 258–9, 260–2, 370
'Red menace', xxxix, 265
'Regimental Fire Mission', 43
Reilly, Corporal Brian, 273, 343
Rencher, 'Pom', 108
Richards, Sergeant Ron, 330, 359
Richards, Captain Trevor, 151, 152, 153, 159
Richmond, Private Jim, 41, 218–19, 283–4, 375–6, 385, 410
Riley, Flight Lieutenant Frank, 61, 365; ammunition drop mission, 303–8, 324; character, 112; daily routine, 193; death, 413; Delta Company assistance, 227, 257, 260–4, 277–8; Distinguished Flying Cross award, 413; evacuation mission, 370, 373–5; military experience, xvi; post-war life, 413; restoration of chopper, 415; South Vietnamese award, 425; transporting entertainers, 193, 195–6
Rising Storm 2: Vietnam, 420
Robbins, Lance Corporal John, 217–18, 226, 231–2, 237, 295–7, 318; boot incident, 21–2; conversations with Topp, 202, 214; friendship with Heslewood, 38; mindset, 119–20; Nasho, 21; post-war life, 410; praise for Dobson, 340; prayer, 223–4; response to 'Doc' Davis, 300

Roberts, 2nd Lieutenant Adrian, 134, 242–3, 256–7, 330; annoyance at Alpha Company, 276; anti-tank weapon search, 351; APC instructions, 288, 352–3, 368–9; casualties, and, 102, 335, 366, 385; character, 133, 243; 'check fire' command, 336; concern for Delta Company, 290–3, 324–5, 330; 'dazed shock' state, 377; death, 413; description of battle sights and sounds, 360; exception to DSO citations, 423; identification of VC, 332, 350; Medal for Gallantry, 425; military experience, xvi; order to advance, 332, 334, 351; placement, 133; post-war life, 412–13, 414; promotion, 412; regrets, 413; Suoi Da Bang crossing, 313; understanding of VC anti-tank weapons, 351
Robinson, Barry, 73, 131, 132
Rowe, Major John, 152, 153, 162, 163, 170
Royal Australian Air Force (RAAF); No. 9 Squadron, 108, 112, 130, 137, 141, 244, 324, 361, 365, 415; No. 35 Squadron, 106, 108; 161 Recce Flight 'Possum' helicopter, 164; authority of aircraft captain, 260–1; 'Brylcreem boys', 125; Caribou planes, 117; commanding officer, 73; Iroquois A2-1022, 415; Iroquois (Huey) UH-1B, 73, 110, 137, 193, 258–9, 292, 305, 390; relationship with Australian Army, 137–9, 258–9; Vung Tau Air Base, 108, 117, 125; 'Wallaby Airlines', 106
Royal Australian Navy, 73
Royal New Zealand Artillery, 118, 125, 192, 198, 212, 213, 223, 227–8, 251–3, 256, 285–7, 397, 398
Ryan, Private Terry, 270–1

Sabben, Lieutenant David, 176, 357, 364, 365; 1ATF Base attack theory, 421; 11 Platoon support, 267–71, 300, 310; academic achievement, 32; 'appreciations', 39, 301, 311, 313; artillery fire call-in, 284; assessment of Chinn, 77; character, 25, 55–6, 69; concern about manpower, 266; Delta Company logo design, 66; description of artillery fire, 328; dustoff call, 139; 'endless loop' thought process, 268–9; finding VC rope measuring device, 156; graduation, 47; introduction to platoon, 54; Kirby, and, 55, 266–7; Long Tan patrol, 199, 209, 212; Medal for Gallantry, 425; Mentioned in Dispatches, 423; notes discipline and courage of VC, 342–3; Nui Dat base construction, 140; Nui Dat night patrol, 172; O Group role, 90, 191; officer training, 26, 29, 31–3, 44–5, 47, 268–9; Operation Enoggera, 136; orders to shoot VC, 315–16; organisation of 11 Platoon, 312–13; placement, xv, 48, 50, 69; post-war life, 407, 412, 414; praise for Delta Company training, 89; pre-war career, xv; reaction to Large's death, 348; recount of battle, 401; religious faith, 97; retrieval of deceased mission, 383, 392; Rockhampton exercises, 63–6; Sharp, and, 209; shooting of enemy soldiers, 270; Smith, and, 51, 86, 265–6, 320; Todd, and, 70, 338; volunteer for National Service, 16–17
Sai Gon River, 71
Saigon, 71, 402
Salveron, Private Doug, 14, 41, 219–20, 224, 365, 385, 410, 430
Savage, Second Lieutenant Ian, 256, 368–9, 414; driver for entertainers, 234–5, 243
Scott, Wing Commander Ray, 261, 361, 370, 371
'Search and Destroy' command, 79, 91
Serong, Colonel Ted; approach to warfare, xli–xlii; duty, xl–xli; military credentials, xxxix–xl
Sharp, Eric, 13, 47, 393, 410
Sharp, Lieutenant Gordon Cameron, 358, 393, 430; artillery call-in, 237–8; Buick, and, 175–6, 187, 239; burial site, 410; card games, 170, 171, 173, 175; character, 90, 147, 176; Commendation for Gallantry, 425; contact with VC, 209–10, 215, 221–2, 225, 229; death, 239, 267, 318, 393–4, 399; graduation, 47; introduction to platoon, 54; Long Tan patrol, 200, 202, 207, 208, 209, 212, 215–16; military funeral, 394; National Service enlistment, 12; O Group meetings, 90, 192, 210; O'Halloran, and, 13, 31, 176, 358, 385–6, 409, 421; officer training, 29, 45, 46, 47; placement, 48, 50, 52, 394; pre-deployment home visit, 96–7; pre-war career, xv; Rankin, and, 70; regard for military protocols, 170–1; religious faith, 164; remembrance, 421; shell 'walk in', 229; Smith's criticism, 86; stance on conscription, 13, 47, 147; wrist injury, 46, 386
Sharp, Admiral Grant, 1, 2
Sharp, Roma, 13, 47, 393, 409–10
'shell dressings', 289
Shevak, Mike, 414
Shoalwater Bay, 94, 109
Smeaton, Major, 144–5
Smith, Lance Corporal Graham, 188, 282, 306
Smith, Major Harry, 39, 53, 97, 176, 314, 343, 362, 381, 382, 414–15; 'acts of compassion', 390; admiration for Buick, 187; 'appreciation', 339; award citations, 422–4; beret, 52; books, 406, 407; character, 41, 50–2, 54, 58, 59, 86, 215; communication with Huey pilots, 292; concerns, 276,

287–8; criticism of Delta Company officers, 86; Delta Company patrols, 188, 190; expectations and training of Delta Company, 54, 59–60, 63–70, 85–6, 88–90, 92–3, 114, 210; first contact with VC, 146; flow of battle, emphasis on, 88; helicopter request, 251–2; impact of war, 406; impression of Nashos, 50, 51; impression of US Army, 68–9; Jackson, and, 407; Kendall, instruction to, 273; Long Tan patrol, 200, 201, 202, 203, 210; military career, xv, 59, 406; Military Cross, 423; mindset during battle, 344; nickname, 50; Nui Dat night patrol, 172; O Group meetings, 89–90, 192, 203; Operation Enoggera, 135; Operation Smithfield, 369; orders, 221, 234, 248, 255, 265–6, 320, 327, 340–2, 357–8; placement, 12, 37; post-war life, 406–7, 412, 414; promotion, 406; recollection of deceased, 387; red smoke grenade throwing, 306; report of attack on 6RAR HQ, 251; request for support, 232–3, 243–4, 258, 275, 311, 324; sections as key, 89; South Vietnamese award, 425; Star of Gallantry award, 425; support for Buick, 409; Townsend, and, 60, 61, 63–5, 189, 192, 364, 377, 407; unit building philosophy, 93; Vickers machine gun comment, 329
snake pits, 79
Socialist Republic of Vietnam, 403
South Vietnam; Australian involvement, 5, 8, 71, 74–5, 85; Buddhist protests and monk immolation, xliv–xlvi; Catholicism, xliv; civilian anger, 138; collapse of army, 402; creation, xxxiii; Diem puppet government, xxxvi; leadership, xxxiii; paid operative intelligence, 127; reunification with North Vietnam, 403; US Army arrival, 6; US military 'advisers', 3; VC presence, 71; Western powers, support from, xxxvi
Spencer, Lance Corporal Dennis, 248, 318, 319, 371–2
Stanley, Captain Maurice 'Morrie', 119, 254, 412, 414; artillery instructions, 327, 349, 365; Buick's appeal to, 282–3; character, 118; Long Tan patrol, 201–2, 211–12; Long Tan VC contact, 222–3; Mentioned in Dispatches, 426; military experience, xvi; orders, 246, 342, 345, 360; response to Smith's gun drop order, 340–1; role, 118, 192; 'Shelldrake' code name, 222; support for 11 Platoon, 233–4, 311
Stirling, Leading Aircraftman George, 304, 308
Suoi Da Bang stream, 183, 185, 186, 190, 199, 291, 304, 313–14

Tactical Area of Responsibility (TAOR), 125–6
Tan Son Nhut International Airport, 105
Taske, Captain John, 181, 182
Tedder, Major Peter, 341, 414
'Tet Offensive', 402
Thanh My Tay, xxxvi
Thich Quang Duc, xliv, xlv–xlvi
Thomas, Private David, 191, 196–7, 202, 274, 430
Thomas, Pat, 396
Thomas, Shorty, 41, 219–20, 224, 396, 410
Tin Can Bay, 83
Todd, Sergeant Paddy; Buick, and, 311–12; character, 56, 70, 148; consolation of Large, 149; crawl to Delta Company HQ, 312, 315, 316–17, 323, 336–7; missing, 318; mortar injury, 312; night patrol, 173; placement, 56; Sabben, and, 70
Topp, Private Frank, 172–3, 190, 191, 202, 214, 218, 410, 430
Townley, Artillery Intelligence Officer Captain Jim, 184
Townsend, Lieutenant Colonel Colin, 92, 107, 157, 185, 203, 256, 290–1, 381; 6RAR expectations, 58, 60, 63–4; address to 6RAR, 76; aircraft light decree, 370, 371; casualty Sitrep, 366; character, 288; death, 405; Distinguished Service Order, 423; evacuation plan, 364–5; Long Tan mission, 142; military experience, xv, 12; nickname, 12, 52, 76, 189; orders, 185, 188, 332, 339, 362, 365, 369, 382; post-Vietnam War career, 405; response to Mollison's warning, 186; Smith, and, 60, 61, 63–5, 189, 192, 233, 244, 245, 251–2, 377
Tricker, Eddie, 414
tripwires, 79
Tronc, Private Ken, 173

United States Air Force; 8th Tactical Fighter Wing, 277; 173rd Airborne Division, 44, 113, 127, 133–4; air-strikes, 374, 378; assistance to Australians, 260–4, 370–1; C-47 planes, 151; 'Chinooks', 116, 244, 344–5; dustoff mission, 370, 374; F-100 Super Sabre jets, 105; Phantom F4-II jets, 105, 244, 258, 275, 276–7, 280, 287; Weapons Systems Operators 'Wizzos', 277, 280
United States Army (US Army); 2/16th Infantry US 1st Division, 113; 2/35th Artillery Battalion, 123–4, 253, 275; 9th Marine Expeditionary Brigade, 5–6; 315th Air Division, xxxii; AP Bac ambush of helicopters, xliii; appearance and manner, 112–13; Australian Army, and, 44, 71, 112–13; C rations, 114; casualties, 44, 92, 113, 134, 391; gunner support, 253; 'psychological warfare', 44; reaction to Keep's intelligence, 154; Smith's impression,

United States Army (US Army) *continued* 68–9; 'support staff' numbers, 98; troop numbers, 62, 98, 112
United States of America; alliance with Australia, xxxix; Diem visit, xxxv; Ho Chi Minh's characterisation of war, 93–4; humiliation, 11; 'Military Working Agreement', 73; peace offensive, failure of, 94; 'Pentagon Papers', 403, 404; revision of Vietnam War involvement, 403–4; role in Diem assassination, 403; South Vietnam leader preference, xxxiv; warnings re Vietnam involvement, xxxvii–xxxix, xxlii, xlvi, li, 402; withdrawal from Vietnam, 402–3
USS *Turner Joy*, 1

Vernon Sturdee, 107–8
Viet Cong (VC); 21 Company Chau Duc District, 134; 274th Regiment, 127, 151, 245; 275th Regiment, 127, 151, 152, 153, 159, 163, 245, 250; admiration for Australians, 402; 'ambush' debate, 420; anti-tank weapons, 351–2; attack on 11 Platoon, 244; Ap Bac helicopter ambush, xliii, 258; Binh Ba occupation, 160–2; casualties, 144, 148, 348, 351, 387–8, 392–3; 'Charlie' nickname, 78; Chinn's assessment, 77–8, 148; combat with 10 Platoon, 241–3, 246–7; contact with Delta Company, 216–21; D445 Battalion, 92, 122, 128, 134, 142, 148, 152, 167, 184, 209, 333, 382; D445 Provincial Mobile Battalion, 127–8; defeat at Long Tan, 401–2; fighting prowess, 78, 335–6; fortification of Long Phuoc, 134; growth, xli; intelligence reports, 116, 127–9, 141–2, 151, 154, 169; HQ 5th Viet Cong Division, 151; interrogation by Diem regime, xxxiv; Jackson's impression, 6; Keep's predictions, 126–7, 128, 152–5, 162, 230, 245; Long Tan presence, 150, 195–8, 205, 208; Nui Dat proximity, 122, 152–4, 159, 421; patrols, 141; presence in South Vietnam, 71, 88; primary motivation, 427; RAAF leaflet drop, 193–4; radio signal tracking, 151–2, 170; reception in South Vietnam, xliii; 're-education camps', 128; resistance to APC, 360–2; Sharp's contact, 209–10; 'shoot and scoot' attack method, 86, 148, 174, 202, 225–6; shooting of wounded soldiers, 389–90; size, 3, 127–8; tactics, 78–80, 86, 272, 281; track marks, 125–6; uniform, 107, 126, 128, 332, 347
Viet Nam Doc Lap Dong Minh (Viet Minh), xxiii, xxvii–xxxvi, xxxix, 88
Vietnam; 17th Parallel division, xxxiii; bitterness over war, 403; Chinese occupation, xxi; climate, 108, 109, 110, 124, 313; Cold War, testing ground for, xxvii; Declaration of Independence, xxii–xxiii; empire, xxii; French occupation, xx, xxi–xxii, xxviii, xxxiii; landscape, 109; Long Tan *see* Long Tan; North *see* North Vietnam; post-war relations with Australia, 427; reunification, 403; South *see* South Vietnam; US military 'advisers', xxxviii–xxxix, xli, xlviii, 3
Vietnam Veterans' Day, 404, 419
Vine, Private Len, 360–1
Vo Nguyen Giap, xvii, xix, xxii; American defeat, 402; leadership of Viet Minh, xxvii; meeting with McNamara, 403; 'Red Napoleon' title, xxviii; strategy for French defeat, xxviii, xxx, xxxxii
Vung Tau, 71, 75, 100, 103, 106, 107–12, 109, 116, 117, 125; 36th Evacuation Hospital, 372, 379, 385, 389; Keep's evacuation to, 163; military hospital, 181, 183, 364; R & R, 110–11, 123–4, 157, 187, 377

Wales, Private Max, 329, 366, 430
'walk in the weeds', 121
Walker, Lance Bombardier Willie, 341
Warner, Brigadier Gerry, 423
Warr, Lieutenant Colonel John, 157
Wass, Sergeant Tassie, 235
weaponry; AK-47s, 208, 211, 337; Armalite rifle, 15, 46–7, 148, 193; bayonets, 349; Claymore mines, 79, 122, 166; M47 bombs, 277; M60 machine gun, 60, 114, 121, 190, 193, 329, 334; Owen guns, 193, 249, 329; self propelled guns, 253; SLR, 46, 193, 309; tracer bullets, 47; VC tactics, 79–80; Vickers machine gun, 329
Webb, Private Harley, 322, 323; attitude, 321; conversation with Burstall, 209–10; Delta Company 'reo', 172, 321; injury, 322, 410; introduction to Smith, 190; medical attention, 323; post-war life, 410–11
Westmoreland, Lieutenant General William C, lii, 70–1, 73, 389, 391, 401, 426
Whiston, Private Colin, 172–3, 190, 281, 430
Whitlam, Gough, 405
Wilson, Prime Minister Harold, xlii
Wilton, General, 71, 87–8, 130; 'Military Working Agreement' signing, 73
Winterford, Bill, 143
Wright, Mr T, 9–10

Xa Cam My, Battle of, 113

Youth Campaign Against Conscription (YCAC), 73